Journey ^{to the} United States of North America

***

Viaje ^{a los} Estados Unidos del Norte de América

Journey ^{to the} United States of North America

* * *

Viaje ^{a los} Estados Unidos del Norte de América

Lorenzo de Zavala

English translation by Wallace Woolsey
Edited, with an Introduction, by John-Michael Rivera

Arte Público Press
Houston, Texas

This volume is made possible through grants from the City of Houston through The Cultural Arts Council of Houston, Harris County. Special thanks to Special Collections and Archives of the University of Houston Libraries for permission to reproduce pages of the original text.

SPECIAL THANKS FOR MAKING THIS BOOK POSSIBLE
THE SUMMERLEE FOUNDATION

Recovering the past, creating the future

Arte Público Press
University of Houston
452 Cullen Performance Hall
Houston, Texas 77204-2004

Cover design by Adelaida Mendoza
Cover photo courtesy of The San Jacinto Museum of History, Houston

Zavala, Lorenzo de, 1788–1836.
    [Viaje a los Estados Unidos del Norte de America. English]
    Journey to the United States of America = Viaje a los Estados Unidos del Norte de América / by Lorenzo de Zavala ; English translation by Wallace Woolsey ; introduction by John-Michael Rivera.
      p.   cm.
    ISBN-10: 1-55885-453-3 (trade pbk. : alk. paper)
    ISBN-13: 978-1-55885-453-6 (trade pbk. : alk. paper)
    1. United States—Description and travel. 2. United States—Politics and government—1815–1861. 3. Political culture—United States—History—19th century. 4. Zavala, Lorenzo de, 1788–1836—Travel—United States. 5. Mexicans—United States—Biography. 6. United States—Foreign public opinion, Mexican. 7. Public opinion—Mexico. 8. United States—Relations—Mexico. 9. Mexico—Relations—United States.   I. Woolsey, Wallace. II. Title.
    E165.Z3913   2005
    973.5'6—dc22
                                                    2004055419
                                                      CIP

5 6 7 8 9 0 1 2 3 4   10 9 8 7 6 5 4 3 2 1

Contents

INTRODUCTION

Lorenzo de Zavala's Journey to the United States

> Two things have caused me to write of this journey. The first is that I have believed that nothing can give more useful lessons in politics to my fellow citizens than the knowledge of the manners, customs, habits, and government of the United States, whose institutions they have so servilely copied. Secondly, because since I offered in my Historical Essay to publish my memoirs, it is now time that I begin, although it may be in incoherent bits and pieces as circumstances permit. (Prologue 1)

In 1830, the Mexican exile Lorenzo de Zavala made an historic journey to the United States. A product of this journey is an incredibly important, although little known, travel narrative, *Viaje a los Estados Unidos del Norte América* (Journey to the United States), a meticulously written narrative about the democratic culture and institutions of the United Sates. Zavala's narrative not only stands as a major document of early Mexican-American letters, but also as one of the first theoretical and ethnographic examinations of democracy as a political and cultural institution. Thus, Zavala's book challenges the widespread acceptance by American scholars that Alexis de Tocqueville's *Democracy in America* (1835) is the first book to take United States democracy as a focus of political and cultural study.[1] With the inclusion of Zavala's narrative into the Recovering the U.S. Hispanic Literary Heritage Project series, Zavala's story of democratic peoplehood will no doubt, in time, be read as one of the founding political texts of U.S. and Mexican democratic culture. As such, he should be placed alongside such political thinkers as Jefferson, Prieto, Hidalgo, Madison, Mill, and Tocqueville.

Equally important is that Zavala wrote his narrative in order to represent

and participate in a story of peoplehood that he hoped would help in the creation of a liberal national identity for the Mexican people. Published in limited numbers in Paris in 1834 and posthumously for the first time in Mexico on the eve of the US-Mexico War in 1846, Zavala's book stands as one
of the first texts to investigate the early relationship between not only the
constitutions of Mexico and the United States, but also of the two peoples
themselves.[2] Standing as a cultural mediator between the two, Zavala was
fostering comprehension of the foundations of Mexican and American democratic peoplehood during the years that led up to the US-Mexico War of
1846–1848. Indeed, Zavala's text renders a complicated portrait of US/Mex-
ico relations and the colonial contact between the two states that began in
1821–1824—the monumental period when the colonized people of Mexico
broke away from Spanish despotism and created a national, democratic constitution under the United States' imperial gaze at Mexican lands to the west.

Zavala's narrative, therefore, extends our modern understanding that
narratives of Chicano peoplehood begin with the conquest of 1846 and the
US-Mexico War.[3] As Carl Gutiérrez Jones argues, Chicano historians assert
that Mexican American communities grew out of the signing of the Treaty
of Guadalupe Hidalgo in 1848, which ended President Polk's aggressive
expansion into Mexico.[4] Juan Gómez-Quiñones argues that this document
and this year would mark the liminal moment when the racialization of
Mexicans that occurred in the language of the treaty would lead to a distinct
minority collective consciousness.[5] Gómez-Quiñones' argument leads me
to explore the cultural forms in the public sphere that led to the racialization of the Mexican people. However, I think we need to also consider the
seeds of imperialism that led to the war, the treaty, and the collective self-
understanding of Mexicans as a racialized and bifurcated minority people
in the United States. According to historian Emma Pérez, although the
Treaty of Guadalupe Hidalgo in 1848 is an extremely important marker for
understanding the racial and political constitution of Mexican-American
peoplehood, the reliance on 1848 as a liminal marker for the sole emergence of Chicano identity inevitably conflates the Mexican and U.S. period between the years 1821–1836 and does not consider the historical significance of this period and how these fifteen years set the stage for the
U.S.-Mexico War, the Treaty of Guadalupe Hidalgo and Mexican-American political subjectivity.[6] It was during these years that Mexico emerged
as a nation by breaking away from more than 300 years of Spanish Colonial rule, wrote a democratic constitution modeled upon the liberal and federalist traditions of the Enlightenment, and began to feel the effects of the
expansionist U.S. policies of the Monroe Doctrine that the United States
guised as democratic protectionism. This colonial and imperialist back-

ground in US-Mexico relations was the foundation for the politically constituted Mexican-Americans who, Gómez-Quiñones argues, emerged in 1848. Gilbert González and Raúl Fernández point out that we need to historicize the period prior to 1848 in order to account for the complicated and contradictory manner in which Mexicans in the United States imagined their political, racial and economic identity (González and Fernández 1–23).[7] The Monroe Doctrine's neocolonial rhetoric and the contemporaneous constitution of the nation of Mexico, written in 1824, had great impact on how Mexican-Americans and Chicanos would later imagine their social imaginary and democratic collectivity, as well as on how Anglo-Americans would racialize Mexicans and Mexican Americans.[8]

Zavala's *Journey* stands as a representative cultural text of this early and dynamic period in American and Mexican histories and renders a more complete and complicated portrait of the contradictory but interconnected making of the Mexican national, the United States-Anglo, and the bifurcated people who are now defined as Mexican-Americans.

As one of the principal architects of the Mexican Constitution of 1824, Zavala argued that the U.S. Constitution and its liberal principles could be translated to the people of Mexico, who had just emerged from Spanish colonialism. In part, then, Zavala's *Journey* is a panegyric look at U.S. democracy, a utopian primer of liberal democratic mores. Indeed, as the above epigraph indicates, Zavala's interest is in both the government and manners of the United States precisely because he feels they serve as representative examples of democracy. Through a travel narrative that reads like an ethnography of democratic mores and governance, he attempts to render a detailed portrait of the United States for a newly constituted Mexican people, whom he feels have not yet fully fostered the manners, norms and ideals to sustain a democratic political systems. For the liberal Zavala, U.S. democracy and its norms and ideals are the cornerstone of individual Enlightenment, political autonomy and cultural organization.

And yet, there is an adverb in this opening paragraph of the *Journey* that deeply contradicts the panegyric aspects of his travels, for he emphatically writes in a qualifying end clause that the Mexican people have "servilely" copied the democratic institutions of the United States. That Zavala conjures a word that connotes the "spirit of slavery" to describe the relationship that the newly formed democratic nation has with the United States undoubtedly reveals Zavala's own complicated understanding of US-Mexican political and cultural relations in the early nineteenth century. As we know, slavery was a system of extreme personal and collective domination in which a slave had no relationship that achieved legal or political rights or recognition other than with the master (Hahn 16).[9] In other words, slavery was an institution that prevented the emergence of autonomous and liberal political peoplehood precisely because the representation of the people, the demos, was the normalized white colonial master. As I will discuss in the following pages, Zavala's reference to "the sprit of slavery" to describe US-Mexico relations serves as the narrative's political leitmotif and speaks to the contradictory rhetoric that emerged in the wake of the Monroe Doctrine of 1823, a document that awakened the United States' own "spirit of slavery" towards Mexico.

From the above quote we can infer two interrelated yet contradictory logics that inform his travel narrative: on the one hand, it is a call for the making and establishing of a collective Mexican peoplehood that develops from his utopian representations of the mores and liberal governance of U.S. democracy; on the other hand, he qualifies his story by insinuating that Mexicans should not form their peoplehood with the "spirit of slaves," as imitative subjects who have become dependent upon U.S. institutions. In this, Zavala's *Journey* reveals a contradiction that develops from both a desire to erase the legacy of Spanish colonialism and the desire to build a liberal Mexican state ironically based on an emerging American empire that had its gaze upon Mexico's lands.

Zavala's journey to translate the manners, norms and ideas of U.S. democracy for Mexican enlightenment presents us with an interesting way to reexamine what Pratt refers to as the "transcultural" logic of travel narratives. For Pratt, travel narratives enact an ethnographic function of *transculturalization,* which is the process whereby subordinate or marginal groups select and invent materials transmitted to them by a dominant or metropolitan culture (Pratt 1–11).[10] Transcultualization occurs within the narrative and historical space of colonial encounters, a public space in which peoples geographically and politically separate come into contact with each other and establish ongoing relations, usually involving conditions of coercion, racialization, radical inequality, and intractable conflict. Transculturalization is what occurs in the contact zone, or "colonial frontier of the Southwest," for it is in this space where political peoples constitute one another, although this subjectification is usually asymmetrical (Pratt 6). My contention is that we need to look at the narrative act of transculturalization as not simply a byproduct of nationalism, but rather as the core cultural logic of democracy. For it is through acts of transculturalization that democratic knowledge and peoplehood emerge. However, because this occurs through asymmetrical and colonial relations, the emergence creates a democratic ideal of peoplehood that is based on colonial presuppositions and racial inequality. Understanding democracy as a political system that emerges from colonial relations, as well as from legislative and political doctrines, lets us understand that the democratization of people develops through a process where the metropolitical center of colonial power bestows "enlightenment" and political norms upon another colonized country.

This idea of transculturalization renders for us a very complicated and succinct portrait of the cultural and political function of Zavala's travel narrative in his attempts to forge a Mexican nation. According to political philosopher Roger Smith's recent look at the foundational role that narrative plays in the emergence of a political collectivity, "stories of peoplehood" are narratives that constitute a given group as a political and organized body, an autonomous collective democratic people (*Stories of Peoplehood* 8–9). In effect, Smith is trying to locate the embedded constitutive stories (cultural forms) that enable the social imaginary, which are cultural ways of creating and understanding peoplehood, to become collective entities themselves, mediating collective life. What is important to point out when reading Zavala's story of peoplehood is that the idea of a "national people" is a paradigm of the modern social imaginary. As Dilip Parameshwar Goankar argues, a nation's distinctive features include its representation as "we"; its transparency between individual and collectivity; its agential subjectivity, in which a people acts in time; its unfolding in progressive history; and its posited environment of mutuality with other national peoples (5).

Zavala's story of peoplehood is complicated in that it presupposes a complex transnational matrix of democracy and colonialism—informed by the legacy of imperial Spain, the emerging nation of Mexico, and, most immediately, the United States' expansionist gaze towards Mexico. What further complicates Zavala's narrative is that it is written in a complex period of Mexican and American nation building, a period when the emergence of both nations is interrelated. In the 1830s, Mexico and the United States were both in the early foundations of their respective nations and both were struggling to find a collective political identity. Mexico was a newly formed nation that within a decade had gained its independence from Spain and created a democratic constitution. The United States in 1834 had been a democratic nation in the strict sense of the term for only 46 years, after the states had ratified the Constitution in 1788. However, the process of nation building for the United States was by no means complete. In fact, it was only in the 1830s that the United States would begin to promote its "Manifest Destiny" as a nation with stories of peoplehood that would help (re)define its national borders; its expansionist rhetoric, in fact, justified and motivated the conquest and colonization of Mexican and Native American lands.

Within this complex matrix of nation building, Zavala first attempts to create a national "we" in "We the people of Mexico," only to find himself thereafter living in exile in Paris and then Texas, trying to come to terms with his own transnational search for peoplehood. Zavala's *Journey* is a story of peoplehood that attempts to resolve the contradictions of creating a national people that emerged from Spanish colonialism only to find Mexico in an asymmetric relationship with a Jacksonian America forging its own story of peoplehood by expanding into Mexico's borders and Texas. Zavala's *Journey* illustrates his contradictory desire for the creation of Mexican and then Texan peoplehood in the wake of both an external and his own colonial social imaginary.

The Spectacle of Lorenzo De Zavala

> I was leaving the anarchy of Mexico where I had seen myself so often exposed to being the victim of parties. . . . Oh Niagara! With my eyes fixed upon your swift currents, they seemed to indicate that I was completely engrossed in the grandiose spectacle, I was seeing in you the most melancholy representation of our disastrous revolutions. I was reading in the succession of your waves the generations that hasten on to eternity, and in the cataracts that proceed to your abyss the strength of some men that impels others to succeed them in their places. (*Journey* 69)

The above epigraph is one of the most revealing instances of Zavala's own social imaginary and his motivations to look at the spectacle of U.S. democracy. Leaving the unrest of a newly formed Mexican nation, Zavala looks at the spectacle of Niagara Falls and sees Mexico's "disastrous revolution" and his own inability to succeed as a liberal statesman in the country he ironically helped to free from the despotism of imperial Spain. Zavala's personal reminiscence of Mexico while looking at the natural spectacle of the United States is paradigmatic of his own journey toward Mexican selfhood in his travels. Indeed, as he notes in the first epigraph quoted above, Lorenzo de Zavala wrote his travel narrative, in part, as a personal memoir, an autobiographical self-fashioning of a Mexican political statesman. It is worth detailing the autobiographical self he creates in this collective story of Mexican peoplehood, for both are constructed through the journey and descriptions of the mores and governance of the United States.

Zavala's travel narrative presents us with a bifurcated spectator whose experiences in the United States are "transferred" to the newly constituted Mexican self that has emerged from Imperial Spain, thus converting the journey to a mode of individual as well as collective introspection. Here, we have, in part, a narrative where the inner and outer historical worlds collide from the legacy of Spanish colonialism. This collision is complicated by his national and cultural subjectivity as part of the still unsolidified collectivity of Mexico and the outer United States world he observes in his travels. Zavala's complicated introspection finds its impetus through what Pratt refers to as the intersubjective logic of travel narratives, which are mediated through the colonial worlds the subject is viewing. For Pratt these "autoethnograhic expressions" are instances in which colonized subjects undertake to represent themselves in ways that engage with the colonizer's own terms ((7,9,102). In the case of Zavala, his *Journey* can be read as an autoethnographic story of peoplehood that responds to or engages in dialogue with the U.S. metropolitan political institution of democracy.

Nevertheless, Pratt's notion of autoethnography does not neatly fit the political and cultural figure of Lorenzo de Zavala. Although I began this introduction by pointing out that Zavala is trying to come to terms with the "spirit of slavery" that underpins Mexico's relations with the United States, I am not willing to label Zavala a colonial subject *of* the United States, at least not in his own eyes or in a strict post-colonial sense. It is important to note that before he began to self-fashion himself as a Mexican politico in the United States, under Spanish colonial rule, he was a Creole. As Ralph Bauer argues in *The Cultural Geography of Colonial American Literatures*, creoles occupied an "ambiguous" political space, neither colonized nor colonizers, but rather colonials who often stood apart from the geo-political interests of the Spanish imperial metropolis (5–23). What the complicated figure of Zavala represents, as I will show in the sections that follow, is an ambivalent Mexican self-fashioning that develops first under the rule of imperial Spain as a Creole, a subjectivity that would affect the writing of *Journey*.

When Zavala was born in Yucatán in 1788, Mexico (New Spain) was under Spanish rule, and the *Gachupines*—the immigrant Spaniards, who were the representatives of the crown in New Spain, were in political control. Under Spanish rule, only the elite Spanish-born immigrants were able to hold any significant political office. The remainder of the population of New Spain was composed of Creoles like Zavala, who was a third generation Yucatecan. Under Spanish colonial rule, the Gachupines controlled the economy, education and the Church. Although Zavala attended school, the ideologies of the Spanish crown discriminated against Creoles, and inequality affected their ascendance in the political and religious hierarchy.[11] Creoles like Zavala, however, desired to improve their conditions. Having no political ties to Spain, the Creoles looked upon New Spain as their homeland and looked upon the people inhabiting the provinces as their compatriots. The Spanish monarchy and the Gachupines considered Creoles subjects of the crown whom they exploited and racialized for political control and for the Crown's economic gain. Moreover, Creoles like Zavala did not believe in the conviction that the Gachupines should remain as the sole representatives of a Mexican people who were struggling for their own autonomy from Spain; they were people who found themselves creating a social imaginary tied to Mexican lands rather than Spain. In this way, the Creole social imaginary that emerged in New Spain threatened the Crown's dominance in the Americas.

The Spaniards viewed the Creoles, who had lived in New Spain for generations, in thoroughly negative terms. Indeed, a number of Spanish natural historians and ethnographers argued that the savagery of the lands affected the character and disposition of the Creoles in the New World. In other words, the Spanish were creating their own imperial stories of peoplehood that imagined the savage environment and the Indians who inhabited the lands as markers for collective Creole racialization (creolization). Creoles were collectively seen as a distinct racial type separate from the people who made up and represented the body of the Spanish King, Ferdinand VII (Bauer 129).

Growing up under the powerful racial ideologies of creolization, Zavala searched for a political philosophy that would help liberate the Creoles and facilitate the transfer of power from the Metropolis to colonial New Spain. Spain, for Zavala, was a despotic imperial power, and he often speaks of Spain in the *Journey* as holding a tyrannical yoke over the people and inspiring terror. Zavala thought that only by separating from Spain and placing the control of the government in the hands of the people could the privilege of the clergy and the Gachupines be broken and the conditions of the natives be improved. Zavala would find the impetus for his anti-colonial stance at an early age at the seminary in Mérida, where he would teach himself French and English and read the important thinkers of the European and American Enlightenment. There, he would begin his life-long studies of liberalism and democracy through the writings of Locke, Abbe Reynal, Rousseau, and later Jefferson. Although critical of Rousseau's failed influence on France's government and revolution, Zavala found in Rousseau the worth of the liberal self and the idea that government should be based on the democratic consent of the people and should guarantee the rights of the citizen, not hinder them. At the onset of the Mexican independence movement in 1810, Zavala and other liberal thinkers in the Yucatán would meet weekly to debate the writings of Locke, Voltaire, and Rousseau.[12] The Enlightenment and its political ethos, democracy, would fuel the young Zavala's political and self-understanding, and serve as the basis for his political thought throughout his life. Most importantly, the Enlightenment would serve as the basis for Zavala's belief in the universal norms and ideals that underwrote the egalitarian formation of a liberal people and their pivotal role in the creation and maintenance of sovereign nations. Zavala felt that the idea of a free and autonomous people, with individual and collective rights, who were subject to each other, was fundamental to the emergence of a new Mexican state. He would spend his life trying to create a state that guaranteed the rights of the people. Zavala's belief in a liberal state was antithetical to the Spanish monarchy and the colonialism that created people as subjects and objects of the crown, rather than Enlightened free thinkers with individual rights and autonomy.

Zavala defined himself as a liberal thinker, circulated his ideas about democratic governance, and critiqued Spanish colonialism through the creation of one of the most powerful democratic institutions, the newspaper. In 1813, he would serve as a principal editor for *El Aristarco,* which he felt would "for the first time [bring] liberty and equality" to Mexico (Zavala *Ensayo* 1830) 123). He also founded and edited *El Redacter Meridiano* (The Mérida Compiler) and *EL Filósofo Meridiano* (The Mérida Philosopher). Zavala believed that newspapers were central to the dissemination of liberal democratic ideals and the perfect discursive medium in which to critique the Spanish crown. For Zavala, newspapers were the cornerstones of democracy. In this way, Zavala was one of the first Mexican cultural workers to create and maintain the public spheres within the Yucatán Spanish colony and Mexico City, for his newspapers were extremely important in influencing and disseminating democratic knowledge and Creole collectivity in various parts of Mexico (Cleaves 5–12). Indeed, Zavala points out on numerous occasions in the *Journey* that there is a direct correlation between newspapers and the "emancipation" of Mexicans from servitude under Spanish colonialism. For Zavala, popular sovereignty, liberalism, and freedom are directly related to the public circulation of thought and criticism. And the newspaper was the form of publicity that could help promote and maintain citizenship (88). It is worth noting that Zavala's creation of newspapers and their facilitation of critical public spheres in Colonial Mexico reveal that the emergence of "the public sphere" was not isolated to Europe, as Jürgen Habermas has argued in his influential book, *The Structural Transformation of the Public Sphere* (24–41). Moreover, it further reveals that public spheres and stories of peoplehood can emerge within the ideological constrictions of colonialism. What is important to point out, however, is that despite the colonial power of Spain, from his beginning, Zavala was actively writing stories of peoplehood on behalf of the creation and maintenance of Mexican democracy.

Because of his political treatises and indictments of the Spanish crown in his newspapers, Zavala was imprisoned in 1814. He would spend three years in the dismal and partly submarine vaults of the old fort San Juan de Ulúa. Despite his incarceration, he was able to smuggle books in, and he continued his work on political philosophy, natural science, history, and geography and trained himself as a medical doctor. It was also here that he began forming a secret Masonic lodge through which to form political alliances. Zavala was released in 1817, and his time in jail did not cause him to change his political beliefs. Zavala continued to publicly criticize the Spanish crown and fight for the independence of Mexico. He joined and took a leading role in numerous political organizations and societies to forge the Mexican independence movement from 1810 to 1821. During these years, Zavala would become a principle thinker and revolutionary and was chosen as one of the principle delegates to draft a statement of demands of the colonies on the Spanish crown. Once Mexican independence was achieved under the Plan de Iguala, in 1821, Zavala was elected to the first Mexican Congress as one of its "founding fathers."

As a principal signer and designer of the Mexican constitution, Zavala fought vehemently against a monarchical and centralized government. He felt that a liberal and federalist state would best serve the Mexican people and would allow for equality among all of its inhabitants. Indeed, he was one of the few Creoles who fought for the property rights of the indigenous peoples of Mexico and was one of the first champions of mestizo rights. He was also one of the chief proponents against slavery and fought vehemently to exclude slavery from the new nation and its constitution (Cleaves 32–69).

After participating successfully in the creation of a national constitution, Zavala was made a state representative and later the governor of the state of Mexico. He was also involved in creating the first public libraries in Mexico, in reforming public education for all of Mexico's citizens, and in founding the national bank and struggling to alleviate the national debt.

Despite his foundational work on the Mexican constitution, public education and the sovereignty of the Mexican people, in the end, Zavala would never live in a Mexican democratic republic. Because of the strong centralized factions in Mexico City, who were still influenced by the Spanish Crown, the Church and the Gachupines, Zavala was labeled a liberal reformer and exiled, in 1833, when Santa Anna assumed the presidency through a coup d'etat (Cleaves 74). Because of his belief in the Enlightenment and liberalism, Zavala specifically rejected the legacy of Spanish colonialism that the centralists maintained. The centralists praised the reform-minded Bourbon administration of the Spanish colonies before independence and emphasized a strong central government (Camp 23–50). They were also not fully behind liberal reforms and Zavala's idea of the state, for his ideals were against the postcolonial absolutist government.

The centralists favored a strong executive because, they argued, it would follow naturally after centuries of authoritarian colonial rule. They also felt that the Catholic Church should play a major part in government.[13]

Zavala and the liberals, on the other hand, wanted a much more definitive separation of Church and State. Indeed, Zavala often argues in *Journey* that religion is detrimental to true democratic peoplehood and that Catholicism, in particular, was the primary obstacle of true democratic reform in Mexico following its independence. In many ways, Zavala's political philosophy was ironically not much different from Andrew Jackson's, whom he admired and would meet while in the United States. Like Jackson, Zavala found the operations of authority crippling, not enlivening, the talents of the people. As a critic of a colonial system that stifled the potential of the people, Zavala followed Jackson's Republican belief in a diffused government, where the nation emerged and maintained its collectivity through the people themselves.

Zavala's beliefs in a strong and secular democratic state of a people bestowed with natural rights under a Republican-inspired, federalist government clashed bitterly with the centralist's absolutist's ideals of political governance. When General Anastasio Bustamante gained power in late 1829, Zavala's political career as a Mexican liberal leader would change drastically. Zavala begins his *Journey* by writing that the Bustamante regime and a centralist-controlled newspaper had labeled him a traitor, declaring that his liberal ideals had led the "nation to the brink" of self-destruction. Moreover, because of his leadership in a liberal revolt in 1828 against the centralists, started at the Acordada prison and followed by days of riots and looting of Gachupín businesses, as well as by President Manuel Gómez Pedraza going off in exile, Zavala became the object of hatred among the conservatives, who would later have the last word on his political leadership (Cleaves 86–87). When in 1830 Zavala's liberal associate, President Vicente Guerrero, was deposed, Zavala was under severe pressure from conservatives and, fearing for life and limb, went into exile, a bitterly defeated Mexican liberal who had lost the country that he felt he had built (Sierra 222-25).

Zavala's Utopian America

In 1830, Zavala left Vera Cruz, Mexico, for the United States in the schooner "The United States." Although he would leave his homeland as a political refugee, Zavala traveled to the United States in hopes that his journey would help to forge a democratic Mexico. He wished to create a distinct democratic Mexican peoplehood, one that could emerge from the despotic legacy of colonial Spain and the centralists who had led the nation back to political despotism. By representing the mores and governance of the American people, he believed he could establish a transcendent national model of state and peoplehood through narrative representation of the United States. In doing so, Zavala's travel narrative employs a classical ethnographic element of the objective observer. But Zavala also remains the romantic political historian trying to relate a Mexican story that, to Zavala, had not as yet been fully realized. He does this by employing and representing traditional concepts of the travel narrative itself, one that attempts to create an all-seeing and all-knowing spectator who is guided by the very Mexican people he is trying to serve. As he states in the prologue, the Mexican people are his "Maecenas, and they guide my steps through the United States." Nevertheless, as much as Zavala's "Maecenas" guides his travels, the reader is always aware that Zavala's journey is meant to be instructive, "and that the book be read with attention . . . that when you have finished it, you will have changed many of your ideas—not in prejudice to reason, nor even less to morality, nor to religion, whatever it may be, but in favor of them"(5). Addressing his implied Mexican audience throughout his narrative, Zavala entices a public to repeat his experiences. What Zavala sees, the Mexican reader will see; what Zavala feels, the Mexican reader will feel and, in doing so, will become part of the very people he imagines in the narrative.

This act of bringing the public into his travels is unique, although contradictory because Zavala envisions Mexican peoplehood by gazing upon an imperialist country that had already begun to declare its Manifest Destiny in the Americas at the expense of lands and peoples that had once been part of New Spain, including Las Floridas and Louisiana—the American Republic was at the very doorstep of Mexico in its advance westward. As the first Mexican travel narrative to explore the United States,[14] Zavala's is in some ways antithetical to traditional European and American travel narratives. Travel writing from its generic inception had historically been used to undertake a nationalistic civilizing project and to project racial otherness. In the traditional narratives, the traveler "represents" terra incognita and the colonized subjects in the land visited to his White European audience in order to create and maintain difference and strangeness between the colonizer and colonized. By depicting and defining the primitive other and his environment, travel writers were able to (re)define their world as politically or culturally civilized by creating otherness. These stories of peoplehood would also underwrite the political and cultural justification for expansion into a given region or country that the traveler defined as uncivilized and primitive. As such, travel writing, which was, in some cases, funded by metropolitan governments, was one of the first discursive institutions of empire building and served to introduce and reinforce racial and colonial relations between two distinct geopolitical spaces.[15]

What makes Zavala's narrative so interesting is that his journey to the United States is in stark contrast to the imperialist mission that has been traditionally associated with the white European and the American travel narratives to Mexico that were published after his work.[16] Zavala did not make his U.S. journey to implement an imperialist expansion into the United States. As stated above, Zavala looked to the United States in order to compare and contrast his own government and nation with the "modern" and still emerging nation to the north. Zavala's comparative project of peoplehood hinges upon his consideration of the United States as a theoretical space, where he can question and explore the very logic of democracy itself. In this way, Zavala's journey is rooted in the Greek notion of *theoria*, which in classical political philosophy is associated with modes of seeing, such as journey, travel, spectacle and observation.[17] Emerging as both political epistemology and cultural ontology, *theoria* is what enabled the production of individual and collective political knowledge through the cultural act of travel. A traveler's imagined journey to another cultural space and the political theory that develops from travel are interrelated. As political philosopher Sheldon Wollin argues, "*theorias* took the form of a story told by a traveler who has recently returned from a voyage." In these travels, he—the traveler is usually a "he" because he renders himself as a masculine vessel of the nation—journeys in order to represent the "foreign" space solely for the benefit of his given country of origin. What is crucial about the Greek *theorias* is that many of these travel writings emplot a story of political utopia. The traveler represents the foreign space as an ideal political community, and, in doing so, the writer attempts to identify the "foreign" people and environment as ideal. This is to an important degree different from the colonial presuppositions of later European travel narratives that represent the space of destination as uncivilized. Inevitably, these travel narratives construct the spaces as inferior in order to promulgate their own worldview of civility.

Employing early natural science and ethnographic devices of description, the largely embellished Greek narrative of a foreign space is both fiction and nonfiction, straddling both genres in order to create the perfect political state. As both an ethnographer and political philosopher, the logical function of the narrator is to describe the conditions that make the given utopia possible. This enables the traveler to disseminate knowledge of the foreign space solely for the task of creating a collective peoplehood in the country of the traveler's origin.

An ardent student of the Greek travelers and political philosopher's, Zavala imitated and enacted a *theoria* through his *Journey* to the United States, a space where Zavala could represent democracy as a utopian spectacle, one that could serve as a prescription for Mexico's post-independence troubles. It is important to note that Zavala's travel narrative reflects what the Mexican public sphere at the time was displaying about the American republic. Many of the newspapers were looking to the United States as a political model and felt that Mexicans should look to their neighbors to the north for guidance.[18] An anonymous letter to *El Sol*, for example, wrote that the United States was a stable system of government and harbored "virtuous" people. The letter concludes by noting that the Mexican view of the world had been obscured by Spanish colonialism and that an understanding of the United States would lead Mexicans out of political ignorance (Brack 18). In addition to published letters, the popular newspaper, the *Gaceta de México* published hundreds of panegyric articles and editorials on the United States and even published the nationalistic works of Benjamin Franklin. The *Diario de México* went as far as serializing the U.S. Constitution, framing it as a model for Mexico's own democratic peoplehood (Brack 18, Hale 190–195).

Reflecting Mexico's fascination with the United States, Zavala enters the United States to do three things in his *Journey*: to explain the political system and its people, to criticize the political system that he has left behind, and to posit a prescription that can lead Mexicans to a fully realized democratic peoplehood. Zavala undertakes this task by emploting a Jacksonian America that is, for the most part, full of democratic possibility. From New Orleans to Washington, DC, Zavala meticulously describes the United States as a nation whose political institutions have evolved to a model state of progress:

> If I were trying to produce a work that was a luxury item with engravings, I would have prepared immediately beautiful plates on which would be pictured steamboats, workmen leveling the land and laying planks of wood and iron to form roads, meadows bathed by streams, cities divided by navigable rivers, cities being born of the earth and dedicating themselves to improving it immediately, rooms filled with children of both sexes learning to read and write, workers and craftsman with plow or instrument in one hand and the newspaper in the other, six thousand temples of diverse cults in which man raises his vows to the creator in accordance with the dictates of his heart, in short tranquility and abundance bringing happiness to fifteen million people. Such is the idea that I have of the United States of the North and the impressions that I received from New Orleans to Cincinnati (50).

The above quote is not isolated. In each chapter, Zavala sets out to meticulously describe each U.S. city's history, geography, culture, and political institutions in such a way as to construct an ideal political community. The people of the United States, he finds, have no social or class distinctions, and the laws have been set up, for the most part, under the auspices of equality. He writes, "No law, no custom, no historical record exists in that country whose tendency would be to form an aristocratic class" (92). This was to contrast with the Spanish colonial system that still had its hold on Mexico. Under Spanish colonialism, he argues, "There was an absolute separation between the conquerors and the conquered. The former had the wealth, privileges and the pleasure that provided the inclination and the tastes that they engendered"(71). Zavala argues that because of this Spanish colonial legacy, Mexico has legislated "exceptional laws: to perpetuate a privileged aristocracy that is antithetical to Republican ideals" (71).

In the United States, however, the stability of the American people and their institutions are the direct result of the dispersion of material prosperity and the ability for most Americans to hold private property. This, Zavala writes, allows for a democracy in which citizens participate in all matters of state formation. This democratic participation is based on a deliberative model where citizens are able to foster bourgeois identities and form public spheres through debate. Indeed, in the United States Zavala finds the formation of reasoned political spheres in every city, cultivated through the public circulation of legislation and political resolutions found in newspapers and posters. Moreover, reasoned discourse among the American people and their representatives has created a utopian political system, where discourse and not wars and revolution constitute the people of the nation.

Zavala's panegyric, of course, was not unprecedented at the time. He was in many ways merely capturing the feeling that Americans themselves proclaimed in the 1830s. Indeed, Americans in the age of Jackson were defining their country and its government as utopian, unique among the nations of the world. Ralph Waldo Emerson represented this well when he wrote that the perpetuation of American government, "will be a matter of deep congratulation to the human race; for the Utopian dreams which visionaries have pursued and sages exploded, will find their God to bestow upon United America."[19] As historian Daniel Feller argues, Americans in 1830 placed their faith in the beneficent workings of national self-interest. "In their thinking," he states, "liberty became the key to individual achievement and social advance. In the expansive space of the United States, people might at last reach their true potential."[20] The United States's utopian mission was declared by all in the Age of Jackson. Indeed, Daniel Webster prophetically stated to a large audience at Bunker Hill, "Let our age be the age of improvement. . . . Let us develop the resources of our land, call forth its powers, build up its institutions, promote all its great interests, and see whether we also in our day and generation, may not perform something to be remembered."[21] The United States's nationalist rhetoric appealed to Zavala's own nationalist desires for Mexico. Moreover, as someone who was still fighting the political legacy of colonial Spain, what Zavala found so appealing was that Americans fashioned themselves a people who had released themselves from the shackles of old-world tyranny and oppression and were free to pursue their own happiness.

Emerson anticipated that travelers like Zavala would come to the United States and find that "the free institutions which prevail here and here alone have attracted to the country the eyes of the world."[22] Politician and writer Hugh Swinton Legre echoed Emerson when he wrote that in the subject of America there is no "nobler and more interesting of contemplation and discourse, than the causes which lead to the foundation of this mighty empire—than the wonderful and almost incredible history of what it has since done and is already grown to—than the scene of unmingled prosperity and happiness that is opening and spreading all around us—than the prospect as dazzling as it is vast, that lies before us" (6). Indeed, Zavala is in some ways representative of a number of travelers who came to the United States in the 1820s and 1830s to represent its political utopia for their own countries, journeyers who were trying to see America as a unique place in world history. Much like Zavala, the Marquis de Lafayette, John Hector Crèvecoeur and Alexis de Tocqueville were all panegyric in their travel narratives of the United States and representative, for the most part, of the utopian rhetoric that flourished in the Age of Jackson. For Crèvecoeur, America was the birthplace of the new American man; in Lafayette's semificttional travel narrative *Notions of the Americans*, he noted that Americans are the freest and the happiest in the world. In Tocqueville's *Democracy in America*, he would find an absolute democracy. Zavala was not alone is his *theoria* and, like the above-mentioned French travelers, he came to prescribe and represent the political culture that emerged in the 1830s.[23]

Like the above-mentioned works, Zavala's also found cultural mores central to the political project that emerged in the United States. Indeed, each of Zavala's chapter frames its discussion with the manners of the Americans. Although geography and history are important to his comprehension of the American people, cultural manners are central to his representation of the utopian political system he identifies as having emerged in the United States. In fact, not one chapter nor more than two pages pass without Zavala discussing the manners of the Americans. He even addresses the most famous of all travel narratives to examine American manners,

Fanny Trollope's extremely popular *The Americans and their Manners.*[24] Unlike the acerbic wit of Trollope, however, Zavala's examination of American manners is much more guarded and inevitably reinforces his panegyric look at America. In *Journey*, Zavala goes as far as critiquing Trollope, taking exception with the "excessive" sarcasm of her look at American manners and noting that she did not fully understand the Americans (34–35).

For Zavala, manners are the cornerstone of the democratic progress of a nation, and they lead to the emergence of nationhood. Zavala's focus on manners as integral to the constitution of peoplehood anticipates Pierre Bourdieu's own understanding of the political significance of manners (96-99).[25] To Bourdieu, manners define a given individual's political world-view and help bring that subject to an understanding of his social imaginary, what Bourdieu calls the habitus. In other words, an individual's body actions initiate him/her into a particular political and classed collective. For Zavala, manners are the cornerstone of the democratic self and the people he is trying to foster; they are, in Zavala's narrative, the "origins" of the political (*Journey* 164). American manners are central to the logic of his *theoria* because he is trying to represent for Mexicans the gestures that constitute the body politic. Through certain embodied actions, he is trying to render a portrait of the universal democratic body, one that Mexicans should imitate.

Mexico and the Contradictions of Imitation

Zavala's emplotment of the Greek *theoria* to undergird his story of peoplehood, however, sets up many contradictions that neither the narrative nor Zavala himself ever truly resolved in his own lifetime. This, in part, is due to the fact that on the one hand he represents the United States as a liberal utopia so that, as he states in the introduction, Mexicans can emulate and create a liberal state. Yet, on the other hand, when he follows the *theoria*'s logic of locating the faults of his own country of origin and its inability to foster liberal ideals, he tends to re-inscribe the racial stereotypes of Mexico and Mexicans that fueled the expansionist rhetoric of 1830s. Ironically, at the very moment that he was setting up the United States as a model of democratic mores and governance, the United States was solidifying its expansionist policies towards Mexico. As Reginald Horsman argues, it was in the 1830s that American expansion took hold of the national imaginary, when Americans felt they should conquer and control the continent (187).[26] Written during this expansionist fervor, Zavala's *theoria* ironically sets up some rather striking contrasts between the two countries that at times repeats the expansionist discourse of the 1830s. For example, Zavala relates in his narrative that Mexican people have not cultivated the individual nor the collective democratic body (1-4). Zavala goes as far as castigating and racializing the Mexican body when he states in his journey,

> The Mexican is easy going, lazy, intolerant, generous almost to prodigality, vain, belligerent, superstitious, ignorant, and an enemy of all restraint. The North American works, the Mexican has a good time; the first spends less than he has, the second even that which he does not have; the former carries out the most arduous enterprises to their conclusion, the latter abandons them in the early stages; the one lives in the house, decorates it, preserves it against the inclement weather; the other spends his time in the street, flees from his home, and in a land where there are no seasons he worries little about a place to rest. (2)

In many ways this quote, which begins Zavala's narrative, falls prey to the stereotyping that has mediated the modern relations between the United States and Mexico. At the very time that Zavala was castigating the manners of Mexicans in his narrative, Americans were already gazing upon Mexico as politically and racially inferior. In the U.S. public sphere Mexicans were viewed "as little children who need to be educated in proper and economic behavior" (Wairda vi).[27] Mexico was seen as "developing" toward the United States model, presumably liberal, democratic, pluralist and oriented to free enterprise. Indeed, one of the first English-language public treatises in the United States to examine Mexican politics and to perpetuate this attitude was found in an a very long article, anonymously published in the *Democratic Review* in 1830, entitled "Politics in Mexico," which discussed Zavala's role in Mexican politics at length; the writer further gazes upon Mexico's political history only to conclude that the country must emulate the United States in order to catch up with America's level of development as a political, cultural and economic power.

The question arises if Zavala was consciously re-inscribing U.S. expansionist discourse in his *theoria*. Indeed, Zavala spends much of the book trying to address his critics and anticipating that his countrymen would yell: "How awful! See how that unworthy Mexican belittles and exposes us to the view of civilized peoples" (3). Zavala asks the reader not to take his critiques in a negative manner, for the Mexican people guide his pen, and he travels for the betterment of Mexico. One could argue, therefore, that he is merely imitating the logic of Greek *theorias*, which often spent time critiquing their country of origin. The critique, as mentioned above, was meant to help their country and lead it to political collectivity. Moreover, unlike nineteenth-century biological and ethnographic determinism that underpinned the racial characterization of Mexican people and their democratic potential, Zavala locates the reason for Mexico's political chaos in the legacy of Spanish colonialism (*Journey* 45). Throughout the journey, he goes to great lengths to point out the affects that Spanish colonialism has had upon Mexico's dispositions and its emergence as a democratic nation (*Journey* 164). Zavala's focus on the affects of Spanish colonialism as the root cause of Mexico's national character is in stark contrast to white America's racial stereotyping of Mexicans that had much deeper roots, not only in the doctrine of Manifest Destiny but also in the Spanish Black Legend (Horsman 34; Bauer 131).

Despite Zavala's structuring his narrative as a utopian *theoria,* he nevertheless offers stark contrasts between the United States and Mexico, contrasts that inevitably render Mexico as the more enlightened country. Zavala, for example, is extremely critical of the hypocrisy of the United States in professing enlightened ideals while maintaining a slavocracy. As a statesman who fought for the abolition of slavery in an independent Mexico, Zavala finds that when he travels from Mexico,

> . . . to the states which permit slavery in our sister republic, the philosopher cannot fail to feel the contrast that is noted between the two countries, nor fail to experience a pleasant memory for those who have abolished this degrading traffic and caused to disappear among us the vestiges of so humiliating a condition to the human race. (20)

He further states in his narrative that slavery "is not very natural in a country where they profess the principles of the widest liberty. Nothing, however, can overcome the concern that exists with respect to this particular subject"(90). More critical of U.S. slavery than any other author of a travel narrative at this time, Zavala goes on to ask questions that would haunt the United States for centuries: "How does one remedy that embarrassing situation of free colored people in the center of society?" "Will the day come when they [slaves] will be incorporated into the state and form an integral part of the community?" (91). In the end, slavery to Zavala is "degrading" (26) and "antiliberal"(28) precisely because it does not respect the individual liberties of all the subjects of the state. In other words, slavery is antiliberal precisely because the master/slave dialectic is antithetical to the logic of the liberal state. The government, which should be unobtrusive, should ensure freedoms of the people, not restrict them.

Zavala's opening point, that Mexicans imitate the United States servilely, or with the spirit of slavery, becomes clearer now that he has expressed his exact sentiments about slavery. If, according to Zavala, slavery is the ultimate anti-liberal act, then Mexico's "blind" imitation of the United States

xxvi   John-Michael Rivera

cannot foster a Mexican liberal state; it would merely replicate the mas-
ter/slave dialectic. If Mexico were to imitate the United States completely,
then it would in effect become a restricted liberal state that never fully
achieved its autonomy and liberty. This anti-liberal logic of imitating the
United States is fundamental to Zavala's story of peoplehood. And Zavala
returns to this point of imitation and the emergence of an autonomous liberal state in his conclusion. In many respects, the conclusion is the most
theoretical of all his chapters; it is here that he delves deeply into the logic
of democracy and what this form of political organization means for Mexico and its future.

In the coda to his treatise, Zavala instructs the Mexican people to avoid
reproducing a strict copy of U.S. democracy, but rather to become inspired
by the United States in order to create its own representative version, one
rendered with Mexico's own aesthetics of democratic peoplehood. Referring
to painting and the language of aesthetics to define the political relationship
between Mexico and the United States, Zavala theorizes that Mexicans must
become their own autonomous political artists. In the last sentences, he
wants the Mexican people to locate the theoretical space of what he has
described in his travels: the *ideal* of democracy and a liberal state:

> The model is sublime, but not to be imitated. Those who set
> themselves to copy a painting of Raphael or of Michael Angelo at
> times succeed in imitating some of the shadows, some of the char-
> acteristics that bring them somewhere within range of the original.
> However, they never manage to equal those sublime concepts.
> Original artists do not copy or imitate others, they invent, they cre-
> ate upon the models of nature, and they study her secrets and
> divine mysteries (182).

Zavala's comparison of the aesthetic and the political is similar to
political philosopher F.R. Ankersmit's idea that aesthetic representation is
the cornerstone of the "political reality" (121).[28] For Ankersmit, it is
through aesthetics that we come to understand the representational logic of
the body politic, and it is through aesthetic representation that the people
realize their collectivity as a nation. What makes Zavala so much more
nuanced than Ankersmit, however, is that Zavala himself creates an aesthetic story of representation, the travel narrative, as a model for the creation of peoplehood. Yet within this narrative, Zavala calls attention to the
mimetic fallacies of peoplehood as a strategy to reveal to Mexican "Maecenas" the fact that "stories of peoplehood" are presentational tools that
guide but do not define a people. In the end, it is not that Zavala wants Mexicans to mimic the United States and to become Americans; rather, his nar-

rative is an aesthetic representation that renders for them a portrait of becoming an autonomous national people who can emerge from the legacy of Spanish colonialism.

Epilogue
Texas Colonization: The Seed of Manifest Destiny

Once the way was opened to [Texas] colonization, as it should have been, under a system of free government, it was necessary that a new generation should appear within a few years and populate a part of the Mexican republic, and consequently that this new generation should be entirely heterogeneous with respect to the other provinces or states of the country. Fifteen or twenty thousand foreigners distributed over the vast area of Mexico, Oaxaca, Vera Cruz, etc., scattered among the former inhabitants cannot cause any sudden change in their ways, manners and customs. Rather they adopt the tendencies, manners, language religion, politics, and even the vices of the multitude that surrounds them. An Englishmen will be a Mexican in Mexico City, and a Mexican an Englishman in London.

While still in Paris, Zavala turned his eyes to Texas, where he hoped a liberal utopia could be constructed based upon enlightened ideas. Texas would serve as an alternative geopolitical space, located culturally and politically between Mexico and the United States. Zavala believed that liberalism would stand as the mediating form of political and cultural organization in such a way that a liberal Texas state could usher the heterogeneity of different individuals into a collective people. He further believed that Texas would be the space and the Texans the people to mediate the culture and politics between Mexico and the United States. It would become a geopolitical space forged through universal individual rights that would inevitably support a democratic collectivity. In other words, the diverse peoples who colonized Texas would come together and form a heterogeneous people, the Texans, through a collective belief in a democratic state that ensured individual rights. However, in the end, I want to suggest, his faith in liberalism led to a miscalculation of the anti-liberal expansionist policies of the United States.

Zavala had first supported the colonization of Texas in the 1820s while he was writing the Mexican constitution. Zavala believed that rapid population growth in Texas was vital to Mexico's survival as a newly formed nation. In many ways, he followed the liberal Argentine thinker, Juan Bautista Alberdi, who argued, "To govern is to populate" (Weber 158–209).[29] In 1824, Zavala was one of the framers of the Texas Colonization Law that authorized the Mexican congress to devise programs to populate Texas with "foreign inhabitants." The law guaranteed land, security, and exemption from taxes for four years to foreign settlers and imposed few restrictions. However, in order for Americans to own land they had to become Mexican citizens. They also would own their land under the auspice of an *empresario*, an immigrant agent of Mexico. Zavala also owned a large tract of land that he had inherited for his service in the Mexican government in the 1820s. By 1830, however, more than 7000 Americans had settled in Texas, outnumbering Mexicans in the region by more than 4000 (Weber 166). In 1830, three days before Zavala went into exile, Mexico ended settlement in Texas by foreigners, fearing that Texas was becoming far too populated with Americans. Pablo Obregón, Mexico's minister to Washington, had argued earlier that Americans would only become Mexicans citizens in name and their loyalty was still with the United States (Weber 158–169). One of the strongest opponents of Texas colonization, Lucas Alamán, prophetically declared that "Where others send invading armies. [North Americans] send their colonists" (Weber 168).

Since the presidency of John Quincy Adams in the 1820s, the United States had looked to Texas as an important target for eventual expansion westward. As a principal author of the Monroe Doctrine, Adams believed "that the whole continent of North America appears to be destined by Devine Providence to be peopled by one nation, speaking one language, professing one general system of religious and political principles, and accustomed to one general tenor of social usages and customs" (Stephanson 59).[30] Andrew Jackson would echo this sentiment as he hoped to annex Texas and "secure the U.S. borders and add to the nations riches." Numerous other statesmen and politicians had expressed interest in the annexation of Texas prior to the founding of the Republic of Texas (Stephanson 42–49). Even de Tocqueville observed "that the vast provinces extending beyond the frontiers of the Union towards Mexico are still destitute of inhabitants." White Americans, he continued, "will take possession of the soil and establish social institutions, so that when the legal wonder at length arrives, he will find the wilderness under cultivation, and strangers quietly settled in the midst of inheritance" (Tocqueville 156,160).

If Zavala did know about the United States's intentions for Texas, he did not write about it in his works. He did, however, refer to its fate at the end of *Journey* with a rather prophetic observation about United States expansion into the Mexican territories: "The American system will obtain a complete bloody victory"(213). One year after he would write this sentence, Zavala arrived in Texas in hopes of establishing a liberal republic. Texas at that time was primarily under the leadership of the American Stephen F. Austin, who was already organizing an Anglo-American independence movement from Mexico. Dismayed at the political situation in Mexico,

Zavala quickly supported the Texans' pursuit of autonomy from Mexico. He subsequently participated in writing another constitution, this time for Texas. Soon, thereafter, he served as a Texas governor and later the republic's first vice president. Once again, Zavala was involved in shaping a people. This time, however, he would do so as a Texan. Despite Zavala's work for Texas, however, some scholars argue that his personal letters reveal that he hoped Mexico would remain involved in Texas' political and cultural emergence (Cleaves 145). Indeed, Zavala argued that Spanish should be the official language of Texas and, in fact, he translated the constitution and saw that it was issued in both English and Spanish. For his commitment to a prosperous and liberal Mexico, however, many Texas politicians did not trust Zavala, fearing that he was simply using his position in Texas in order to return to Mexico with power. Zavala also grew tired of Anglo Texans' political pursuits and he resigned as vice president of Texas only one month after he took office. Nevertheless, there are no indications that Zavala ever intended to return to Mexico; in fact, he died on Texas soil in 1836.

Zavala did not live long enough to see the US-Mexico War or feel the racialization and later proletaritization of the Mexicans who lived in the United States. His colleague Juan Seguín summed it up well two years after Zavala had died, when he wrote that he and the other Texas-Mexican people had become "foreigners in their native land"(Seguín Personal Memoirs 98). This would have applied to Zavala also, but in many ways he was never fully a native of any land. Born under the Spanish crown in New Spain, briefly a citizen of an independent Mexico, later a political refugee in Europe and the United Sates, and again briefly a citizen of the Republic of Texas, Zavala was ironically a man without a people. Perhaps this explains his desperate, insistent intent on creating a peoplehood, first for Mexico and then for Texas.

Zavala's *Journey* was finally re-printed posthumously in Mexico on the eve of the US-Mexico war in 1846. By the time of its 1846 publication, Mexico had branded Zavala a traitor to the Mexican people for his role in establishing the Texas Republic (Cleaves 139–146). In the end, Zavala's participation in the founding of the Texas Republic would paradoxically help to facilitate the US-Mexico War and the "bloody victory." Zavala, however, was hardly a traitor of the Mexican people nor a blind devotee of U.S. liberalism. Rather, the complexity of Zavala and his *Journey* lies in the contradictions resulting from the dual legacy of Spanish colonialism and American imperialism, a legacy that continues to influence the development of Mexican-American peoplehood in the United States.

John-Michael Rivera
University of Colorado-Boulder

Acknowledgments

Many people have helped me recover Lorenzo de Zavala's *Journey to the United States of North America* from literary obscurity. First, I would like to thank Nicolás Kanellos for supporting me on this and so many other projects over the last two decades. My colleagues at the University of Colorado at Boulder have been very supportive, and I thank the English department, especially John Stevenson, for giving me the support and valuable time off to complete this work. I would especially like to thank Anna Brickhouse for both her friendship and brilliant editing. My colleagues and friends Vince Woodard and Frederick Aldama read early stages of my introduction, and I thank them for their support and honesty. I would also like to thank Dawn Letson at Texas Women's University for her guidance and advice during the early stages of this project. A special thanks to the distinguished Wallace Woolsey and his family. Lastly, I would like to thank Rhonda and Elyse for making my journey through life such a wonderful experience.

Notes

[1] See Sheldon Wolin's *Tocqueville Between Two Worlds: The Making of a Political and Theoretical Life*. New Jersey: Princeton University Press, 2001, pp. 4–9.

[2] The two versions are *Viaje de los Estados Unidos del Norte America*. Paris: Imprenta de Decourchant, Calle D'Erfurtm, Nº 1, Junto A La Abadía, 1834, and *Viaje de Los Estados-Unidos del Norte America*. Mérida de Yucatán: Impr. de Castillo y Compañía, 1846.

[3] Ramón Gutiérrez's *Corn Mothers* is an excellent exception to this trend.

[4] See Carl Gutiérrez Jones' *Rethinking the Borderlands: Between Chicano Culture and Legal Discourse*. Berkeley: University of California Press, 1995.

[5] See Juan Gómez-Quiñones, "On Culture." *Chicano-Riqueña* 5/2 (Primavera 1977): 29–47.

[6] See Emma Pérez's *The Decolonial Imaginary: Writing Chicanas into History*. Bloomington: Indiana University Press, 1999.

[7] See Gilbert González and Raúl A. Fernández, *A Century of Chicano History: Empire, Nations, and Migration*. New York: Routledge, 2003, pp. 1–29.

[8] In this way, I follow Kirsten Gruesz Silva's argument that the Monroe doctrine is essential for understanding early literary production of Latino authors. See *Ambassadors of Culture: The Transamerican Origins of Latino Writing*. New Jersey: Princeton University Press, 2002.

[9] See Steven Hahn's *A Nation Under our Feet: Black Political Struggles in the Rural South from Slavery to the Great Migration*. Cambridge: Harvard University Press, 2003, p. 16.

[10] See Mary Louis Pratt's *Imperial Eyes: Travel Writing and Transculturation*. New York: Routledge, 1992.

[11]For important examinations of Spanish Colonial and early Mexican political culture, see *The Soul of Latin America: The Cultural and Political Tradition.* New Haven; Yale University Press, 2003; Charles Hale's *Mexican Liberalism in the Age of Mora, 1821–1858.* New Haven: Yale University Press, 1968; Roderic Al Camp's *Politics in Mexico: The Democratic Transformation.* New York; Oxford University Press, 2003; and David Weber's *The Mexican Frontier, 1821–1846: The American Southwest under Mexico.* Albuquerque: University of New Mexico Press, 1982.

[12]An excellent study of Zavala that helped me synthesize his autobiographical self is W.S. Cleaves's The *Political Career of Lorenzo Zavala.* University of Texas Master's Thesis, 1931.

[13]For the role of religion in Mexican democracy, see Roderic L Camp's *Politics in Mexico: The Democratic Transformation* and Charles Hale's *Mexican Liberalism in the Age of Mora 1821–1853.*

[14]Another important narrative about U.S. democracy is Ramón de la Sagra's travel narrative, *Cinco meses en los Estados-Unidos de la América del Norte desde el 20 de abril al 23 de setiembre de 1835,* published one year after Zavala's *Journey.*

[15]There were hundreds of travel narratives and magazine articles about Mexico and its lands in the nineteenth century. With the exception of Philip Freneau's poetry and travel essays, most Anglo-American travel narratives to Mexico were published after 1834. See Eric Wertheimer's *Imagined Empires: Incas, Aztecs and the New World of American Literature, 1771–1876.* Cambridge: Cambridge University Press, 1999. There were, however, hundreds of travel narratives published in the years after the US-Mexico war.

[16]For a discussion of American and European travel narratives to Mexico see *A Century of Chicano History: Empire, Nations, and Migration.* Gilbert González, and Raúl A. Fernandez. New York: Routledge, 2003, pp. 72–83.

[17]For a discussion of *theoria*'s relationship to political culture, see Sheldon Wolin's *Tocqueville between Two Worlds: The Making of a Political and Theoretical Life.* New Jersey: Princeton University Press, 2001, pp. 113–127.

[18]See Gener M. Brack's *Mexico Views Manifest Destiny, 1821–1846: An Essay on the Origins of the Mexican War.* Albuquerque: University of New Mexico Press, 1975, pp. 20–22

[19]Quoted in Feller 116.

[20]See Daniel Feller's *The Jacksonian Promise: America, 1815–1840,* pp. 2–43.

[21]Quoted in Daniel Feller's *The Jacksonian Promise: America, 1815–1840* Baltimore: Johns Hopkins University Press, 1995, p. 8.

[22]Quoted in Feller *The Jacksonian Promise,* p. 7.

[23]St. John de Crèvecoeur, J. Hector, *Letters from an American Farmer and, Sketches of Eighteenth-Century America.* Edited, with an introduction by Albert E. Stone. Harmondsworth, Middlesex, England, New York: Penguin Books, 1981; *Lafayette in America: A Selective List of Reading Materials in English.* Edited by Janina W. Hoskins. Washington: Library of Congress, 1983. Alexis de Tocqueville, *Democracy in America.* New York: Vintage Books, 1961.

[24]See Frances Milton Trollope's *Domestic Manners of the Americans.* London: Whittaker, Treacher, & Co., 1832.

[25]See Pierre Bourdieu, *Outline of a Theory of Practice*. London: Cambridge University Press, 1977, pp. 96–99.
[26]*Race and Manifest Destiny: The Origins of American Racial Anglo-Saxonism* by Reginald Horsman. Cambridge: Harvard University Press, 1981, p. 187.
[27]See the *Souls of Latin America The Cultural and Political Tradition* for a discussion of the relationship between racialization of Mexicans and democracy (3–23).
[28]See F.R. Ankersmit's *Aesthetic Politics: Political Philosophy Beyond Fact and Value*. Palo Alto: Stanford University Press, 1996.
[29]See David Weber's *The Mexican Frontier, 1821–1846: The American Southwest under Mexico*. Albuquerque: University of New Mexico Press, 1982, pp. 158–209
[30]See Anders Stephanson, *Manifest Destiny: American Expansion and the Empire of Right*. New York: Hill and Wang, 1995, p. 59.

Works Cited

Ankersmit, F.R. *Aesthetic Politics: Political Philosophy Beyond Fact and Value*. Palo Alto: Stanford University Press, 1996.

Bauer, Ralph. *The Cultural Geography of Colonial American Literatures: Empire, Travel, Modernity*. Cambridge: Cambridge University Press, 2003

Bourdieu, Pierre. *Outline of a Theory of Practice*. London: Cambridge University Press, 1977.

Brack, Genero M. *Mexico Views Manifest Destiny, 1821–1846: An Essay on the Origins of the Mexican War*. Albuquerque: University of New Mexico Press, 1975.

Camp, Roderic. *Politics in Mexico: The Democratic Transformation*. New York: Oxford University Press, 2003.

Cleaves, W.S. "The Political Life of Lorenzo de Zavala." Thesis. University of Texas, 1931.

Crèvecoeur, J. Hector. *Letters from an American Farmer and, Sketches of Eighteenth-Century America*. Edited, with an Introduction, by Albert E. Stone. New York: Penguin Books, 1981.

De León, Arnoldo. *They Call Them Greasers: Anglo Attitudes Toward Mexicans in Texas, 1821–1900*. Austin: University of Texas Press, 1983.

Emerson, Edward Waldo and Waldo Emerson Forbes Emerson., ed. *The Journals of Ralph Waldo Emerson*. 10 vols. By Ralph Waldo Emerson. Boston: Houghton Mifflin, 1909–14.

Feller, Daniel. *The Jacksonian Promise: America, 1815–1840*. Baltimore: Johns Hopkins University Press, 1995.

Gilbert González and Raúl A. Fernández. *A Century of Chicano History: Empire, Nations, and Migration*. New York: Routledge, 2003.

Gómez-Quiñones, Juan. "On Culture." *Chicano-Riqueña* 5/2 (Primavera 1977): 29–47.

_____. *Roots of Chicano Politics, 1600–1940*. Albuquerque: University of New Mexico Press, 1994

Gruesz Silva, Kirsten. *Ambassadors of Culture: The Trans American Origins of*

Latino Writing. New Jersey: Princeton University Press, 2002.

Gutiérrez-Jones, Carl. *Rethinking the Borderlands: Between Chicano Culture and Legal Discourse.* Berkeley: University of California Press, 1995.

Habermas, Jürgen. *The Structural Transformation of the Public Sphere: An Inquiry into a Category of Bourgeois Society.* Massachusetts: MIT University Press, 1991

Hale, Charles. *Mexican Liberalism in the Age of Mora, 1821–1858.* New Haven: Yale University Press, 1968.

Horsman, Reginald. *Race and Manifest Destiny: The Origins of American Racial Anglo-Saxonism.* Cambridge: Harvard University Press, 1981.

Hoskins, Janina W. Ed. *Lafayette in America : A Selective List of Reading Materials in English.* Washington: Library of Congress, 1983.

Patterson, Anita Haya. *Democracy, Race and the Politics of Protest.* New York: Oxford University Press, 1997

Pérez, Emma. *The Decolonial Imaginary: Writing Chicanas into History.* Bloomington: Indiana University Press, 1999.

Pratt, Mary Louis *Imperial Eyes: Travel Writing and Transculturation.* New York: Routledge, 1992.

Seguín, Juan. *Personal Memoirs.* San Antonio, 1858.

Sierra, Justo. "Noticia Su Vida y Escritos," in Lorenzo de Zavala, *Viaje a los Estados Unidos del Norte de América* (Mérida: Imprenta de Castillo y Compañía, 1846), in Lorenzo de Zavala. *Obras.* México: Editorial Porrúa, 1976. 189–232.

Smith, Roger. *Stories of Peoplehood: The Morals and Politics of Political Membership.* Cambridge: Cambridge University Press, 2003.

Stephanson, Anders. *Manifest Destiny: American Expansion and the Empire of Right.* New York: Hill and Wang, 1995.

Tocqueville, Alexis de. *Democracy in America.* New York: Vintage Books, 1961.

Trollope, Frances Milton. *Domestic Manners of the Americans.* London: 1832.

Wairda, Howard J. *The Soul of Latin America: The Cultural and Political Tradition.* New Haven; Yale University Press, 2003.

Weber, David. *The Mexican Frontier, 1821–1846: The American Southwest Under Mexico.* Albuquerque: University of New Mexico Press, 1982.

Webster, Daniel. *The Writings and Speeches of Daniel Webster.* National ed. 18 vols. Boston: Little, Brown & company, 1903.

Wertheimer, Eric. *Imagined Empires: Incas, Aztecs and the New World of American Literature, 1771–1876.* Cambridge: Cambridge University Press, 1999.

Wolin, Sheldon. *Tocqueville between Two Worlds: The Making of a Political and Theoretical Life.* New Jersey: Princeton University Press, 2001.

Zavala, Lorenzo de. *Viage de los Estados Unidos del Norte America.* Paris: Imprenta de Decourchant, Calle D'Erfurtm, N° 1, Junto A La Abadía, 1834.

_____. *Viaje de Los Estados-Unidos del Norte America.* Mérida de Yucatán: Impr. de Castillo y Compañía, 1846.

VIAGE

A LOS

ESTADOS-UNIDOS

DEL NORTE DE AMERICA,

Por D. Lorenzo de Zavala.

PARIS,

IMPRENTA DE DECOURCHANT,

CALLE D'ERFURTH, N° 1, JUNTO Á LA ABADIA.

1834

VIAGE

A LOS

ESTADOS-UNIDOS.

DEL NORTE DE AMERICA.

~~~~~~

CAPITULO I.

Salida del autor de la capital de Méjico y los motivos. — Llegada á
Puebla, é indicaciones sobre el estado de los caminos. — Golpe
de vista rápido acerca de las diferentes temperaturas.—Llegada
á Vera-Cruz. — Salida precipitada de este puerto y los motivos.
—Breves reflecsiones acerca de los sucesos de Méjico. — Llegada
á la Baliza. — Descripcion de esta.—Continuacion en buque de
vapor hasta Nueva-Orleans. — Periódico realista que publicaban
unos Españoles. — Su objeto. — Clases de poblacion de Nueva-
Orleans y descripcion rápida de la ciudad. — Su comercio.—Su
rápido incremento.—Pintura hecha por M. Flint de esta ciudad.
—Los lagos.—Mercado.

———

Despues de la caida del general Guerrero, en
diciembre de 1829, arrojado de la silla presidencial
por el general D. Anastasio Bustamante, yo habia
permanecido en Méjico espuesto á todos los furores
del partido dominante. Esta posicion era tanto mas
peligrosa para mí, cuanto que uno de los pretestos

1

CAPITULO XII.

—

Washington es una ciudad nueva en el distrito de
Columbia cedido al gobierno general por el Estado
de Mariland. Su círculo es de dos leguas cuadradas
como el de Méjico. La ciudad es de aspecto triste,
aunque tiene vistas muy agradables. Pero las calles
son demasiado anchas y hay una gran distancia de
unas casas á otras. Se ha formado una poblacion por
grupos aislados de edificios, de manera que aun no
presenta aquel conjunto de casas y poblacion que
hace dar un golpe de vista de una ciudad. Hay un
pequeño teatro en Washington y varias posadas. La
de Gadsby, que es en la que yo estuve y seguramente
se reputa la mejor, es bastante cara y no ofrece las
comodidades que las de Baltimore, Filadelfia y Boston.

La principal calle es la que llaman *Pennsylvania*

avenue, se estiende por el centro de la ciudad desde
la casa del presidente al capitolio. Tiene mas de milla
y media. El presidente, como he dicho, no tiene guardias, ni alabarderos ni otro aparato. Va á su iglesia
presbiteriana los domingos como cualquiera ciudadano, y toma su asiento entre los demas sin ninguna
distincion. Cuando en los primeros meses del año
de 1833, vimos en Méjico al señor Pedraza, y despues al señor Farias funcionando de presidentes,
presentarse con la misma sencillez en los lugares públicos, y vivir en lo privado del mismo modo, crei-
mos que ya en la república mejicana se introducia
la simplicidad de nuestros vecinos en sus primeros
magistrados, y que jamas veriamos otra vez el aspecto y fausto vireinal, ¡dulce pero vana ilusion!!!
    A una milla de Washington, está un pueblo lla-
mado Georgetown, en donde está un convento de
monjas bajo el nombre de hermanas de la visitacion.
Habrá como sesenta cuyas principales ocupaciones
son dar educacion gratuita á las jóvenes que se confia
á su cuidado. La escuela gratuita está bajo la enseñanza de las mas jóvenes, que tienen mas de cuatrocientas niñas aprendices. El mas importante establecimiento consiste en una pension que se encuentra
en un estado bastante floreciente. Estos conventos
no son como los de España, en donde son encerradas las víctimas de un voto inconsiderado y prematuro para toda su vida. Cuando sus inclinaciones han
variado, ó sus intereses lo ecsigen, la ley no las fuerza
á permanecer encerradas, viviendo en un perpetuo

CONCLUSION.

Los Estados-Unidos, dice muy bien M. Hamilton,
son el pueblo quizá menos espuesto á revoluciones
en el dia. Pero su estabilidad consiste, añade, en la
única circunstancia de que la *gran mayoría de los
habitantes son propietarios*. No hay duda en que
esta es una, pero no la única causa de la tranquilidad inalterable de aquel dichoso pueblo. En los sistemas sociales no puede resolverse una cuestion por
la esplicacion de una sola circunstancia. La España,
por ejemplo, se mantuvo tranquila hasta el año
de 1808, bajo el yugo tiránico de la monarquía, inquisicion y gobierno militar; y esta paz sepulcral
no podia esplicarse solamente por una sola causa, á
saber, el *terror que inspiraba* la forma establecida.
Habia ademas la ignorancia, la supersticion, el inmenso influjo de los frailes y clérigos, apoyo de los
grandes, en suma, un órden de cosas establecido, y
coordinado de modo que unas sostenian á las otras.
Estableced en esa misma España ó en Méjico la *ley*

23

PROLOGUE

Two things have caused me to write of this journey. The first is that I have believed that nothing can give more useful lessons in politics to my fellow citizens than the knowledge of the manners, customs, habits and government of the United States, whose institutions they have copied so servilely. Secondly, because since I offered in my *Historical Essay* to publish my memoirs, it is now time that I begin, although it may be in incoherent bits and pieces as circumstances permit.

Because a hook written by me in which I criticized more or less severely the conduct of the rulers of the Republic in accordance with my conscience, in my capacity as minister of the Mexican Government in France, would not be in keeping with public policy, I have not been able to continue the *History of Mexico* beyond the year 1830, nor to publish the part of my memoirs prior to that period. On the other hand, I was not going to publish a partisan work, much less a collection of panegyrics. The historical truth must come out of the official documents, the press of the period, and the conscientious publications of the few men who divest themselves of personal and party feelings to transmit to posterity events as they are revealed to their understanding by a critical examination. Now that we have committed so many errors that have been so fatal to our fellow citizens, let us at least do the service of confessing them and of presenting ourselves as we have been. Coming generations will profit by these terrible lessons.

This book has no merit as far as originality is concerned. I can say that it has been no great mental effort for me because most of the descriptions, documents, and even many of the reflections, I have taken from others or from my own notes made concerning the places. I have added at the time of coordinating it some considerations that grew out

Vera Cruz to New Orleans by steamship.

New Orleans to Pittsburg by steamboat on the Mississippi and Ohio Rivers. Stops at Baton Rouge, Memphis, Louisville, Cincinnati, and Wheeling.

1

Pittsburgh to Erie by stagecoach.

Erie to Buffalo by steamer on Lake Erie.

Buffalo to Niagara by stagecoach.

Niagara to Quebec and back to Montreal by steamer on Lake Ontario arid the St. Lawrence River.

Montreal to St. Jean (Canada) by stagecoach.

St. Jean to Albany by steamboat on Lakes Champlain and George. Stops at Black Island (New York), Plattsburg, Ticonderoga, White-hall, Glens Falls, and Saratoga.

Albany to New York City by steamboat on the Hudson River.

New York to Philadelphia by steamboat on the Raritan Bay and Raritan River. Stop at Trenton (New Jersey).

Philadelphia to Baltimore by steamboat on the Delaware River and Chesapeake Bay.

Baltimore to Washington, D.C. and Mount Vernon and back to Washington, D.C. by stagecoach.

Return trip from Washington, D.C. to New York City by stagecoach and steamboat.

New York City to Albany by steamboat on the Hudson River.

Albany to Boston by stagecoach, Stops in New Lebanon (New York), Northampton (Massachusetts), Mount Holyoke (Massachusetts), and Lowell,

Boston to New York by stagecoach. Stops in Providence, Hartford, and New Haven.

New York City to West Point and return by steamboat on the Hudson River.

of the circumstances or events that I was relating. However, it should be very useful to Mexicans, for it is to them that I dedicate it. In it they will find a true description of the people whom their legislators have tried to imitate—a people that is hard working, active, reflective, circumspect, religious in the midst of a multiplicity of sects, tolerant, thrifty, free, proud and perservering,

The Mexican is easy going, lazy, intolerant, generous almost to prodigality, vain, belligerent, superstitious, ignorant and an enemy of all restraint. The North American works, the Mexican has a good time; the first

spends less than he has, the second even that which he does not have; the former carries out the most arduous enterprises to their conclusion, the latter abandons them in the early stages; the one lives in his house, decorates it, furnishes it, preserves it against the inclement weather; the other spends his time in the street, flees from his home, and in a land where there are no seasons he worries little about a place to rest. In the United States all men are property owners and tend to increase their fortune: in Mexico the few who have anything are careless with it and fritter it away.

As I say these things it must be understood that there are honorable exceptions, and that especially among educated people are to be found very commendable social and domestic virtues. There are also in the United States people who are prodigal, lazy, and despicable. But that is not the general rule.

I seem to hear some of my fellow countrymen yelling: "How awful! See how that unworthy Mexican belittles and exposes us to the view of civilized peoples." Just calm clown, gentlemen, for others have already said that and much more about us and about our forefathers, the Spaniards. Do you not want it said? Then mend your ways. Get rid of those eighty-seven holidays during the year that you dedicate to play, drunkenness and pleasure. Save up capital for the decent support of yourselves and your families in order try give guarantees of your concern for the preservation of the social order. Tolerate the opinions of other people; be indulgent with those who do not think as you do; allow the people of your country to exercise freely their trade, whatever it may be, and to worship the supreme Author of the Universe in accordance with their own consciences. Repair your roads; raise up houses in order to live like rational beings; dress your children and your wives with decency; don't incite riots in order to take what belongs to somebody else. And finally, live on the fruit of your labors, and then you will be worthy of liberty and of the praises of sensible and impartial men.

The people of Mexico are my Maecenas, but I do not follow in the way of others who fill a page with the praises of those persons whose patronage they solicit. The advantage of those who write without expecting a reward is that they say what they feel, and they are believed and respected.

In my writings I have never sought anything other than the truth. Whoever reads what I write, unless he has been badly advised, will find naturalness, frankness, good faith, an unquenchable desire for the public good and an insatiable love of liberty. If passion or affection be mixed in once in a while, surely it has been without my noticing or suspecting it.

You, my dear reader, try to read this book with attention, and I hope that when you have finished it you will have changed many of your ideas— not in prejudice to reason, nor even less to morality, nor to your religion, whatever it may be, but in favor of them.

CHAPTER I

The author's departure from the capital of Mexico and his reasons therefore.—Arrival at Puebla and comments on the state of the roads.—Rapid glance at different temperatures.—Arrival at Veracruz.—Hasty departure from that port and the reasons. —Brief reflections on events in Mexico.—Arrival at the Balize.—Description of this. —Continuation on a steamboat to New Orleans.—Royalist newspaper published by some Spaniards—Classes of the population of New Orleans and a quick description of the city.—Its commerce.—Its rapid growth.—Word picture of this city by Mr. Flint. —The lakes.—Market.

After the fall in December of 1829 of General Guerrero, who was ousted from the presidential chair by General Don Anastasio Bustamante, I had remained in Mexico exposed to all the fury of the dominant party. This position was all the more dangerous for me because one of the pretexts that they had alleged against Guerrero's administration was that I was one of the secretaries, and that my abuses and pilferings were carrying the nation to the brink. Neither could they forget that I had had a large part in the popular revolution of Acordada—a revolution covered with ignominy because of the looting that accompanied it and the illegality of its beginning, since it had as its purpose to substitute for the legally elected Don Manuel G. Pedraza another individual who had a smaller number of votes. However, he was more popular, and if the election had been carried out by direct vote, he would have garnered an immense majority in his favor. This is one of the great defects of the present constitution of the United Mexican States.

I was the object then of the hatred of the victorious party, and Don Lucas Alaman kept repeating this to me every day on the visits that he made to observe me. There was no daily paper of the Government or of the party that did not contain some diatribe, some slander, some incitement against me; and I, confined to my house, given over entirely to reading and private work, saw my existence threatened, following several assassinations carried out and the persecution loosed against the partisans of the previous administration. Finally, Minister Alaman made it clear to me that I should leave the country, and that this would be the only means of assuring my safety.

May 25, 1830, four years before the date on which I am beginning to write this book, I left Mexico City in the company of General Don Joss Antonio Mejia, then colonel and secretary of the Mexican legation to Washington. We had no escort because several friends had told me that I would not be very safe in the hands of people that could get rid of me with very little effort, and we preferred being exposed to attack by bandits, who after all would be satisfied with taking from us what we had, and at the most would give us a beating.

We arrived in Puebla de los Angeles and stopped at the house of Don Domingo Couto, a wealthy man of the city, whose family with every courtesy consoled us somewhat for our suffering in the past. At that time without the line of coaches that exists today linking Mexico City, Puebla, Jalapa and Veracruz, the trip was made in ten or twelve days with the greatest of inconvenience. There was no inn where the traveler could rest—I do not say with decency, but not even with the most common conveniences, such as bed, chairs, tables, glasses, plates, etc. Things have changed a great deal since that time, and it is to be hoped that they will continue to improve from day to day. In Jalapa there was already a French inn with good service, and it is certainly a comfort, after a hard trip, to find a well kept lodging in which are to be found the advantages of civilization.

As he descends to the beaches of Veracruz one begins to feel the blistering air of the low country of the tropics. The broad and vast plains of the plateau do not present, it is true, that vigorous vegetation, that perfumed air, that variety of flowers, fruits, birds and waters that arouse such great emotions in the traveler to the hot country. But a burning atmosphere, clouds of mosquitoes and other flying insects, poisonous reptiles, and the death—dealing yellow fever that threatens those born in cold or temperate climates, are terrible plagues that cause more of an unfavorable impression than they do of the gentler feelings of its advantages. But those who have enjoyed the wonderful evenness of the delightful climate of the Valley of Puebla, the constant salubriousness and uniform freshness of that of Toluca, the gentle and almost divine climate of Queretaro, what strong feelings must they not experience as they come into the hot country which Agustin believed to be uninhabitable, no doubt because he felt the coming of the south winds from the sands of Africa where his bishopric was? I, since I was born in Yucatan, had no reason to fear yellow fever. We arrived in Veracruz May 30.

As I was dining at the home of Mr. Stone, the American viceconsul at that time, on the day after my arrival, I received letters and public papers from Mexico City, in which it was announced that in that city Captain Don Mariano Zercero was to be executed, standing accused a few days earlier of having been implicated in a conspiracy. Such was the terror that this news caused us that Señor Mejía and I resolved to give the captain of the schooner United States five hundred dollars provided he would leave with us the next day for New Orleans where we had decided to go in order to travel up the Mississippi.

Since a north wind had blown up, the departure of the schooner was delayed until June 2 when we set sail in a boat that offered no type of conveniences, but which was taking me out of a country where at that time there were no guarantees, and even less for me who had been through so many risks and hazards in the bitter days when military power was governing that unfortunate nation.

The sight of the ocean, whose imposing majesty always produces a strong feeling in those who have not seen it, or have not seen it for some time, or contemplate it with the eyes of a philosopher, that grandiose spectacle produced in me profound meditations concerning the events to which I had been witness, and in many of them a participant, since my entrance into Mexico City in April of 1822, when I went there for the first time to discharge my duties as the deputy from the State of Yucatan, my native land, after having fulfilled that same mission in Spain the previous year. Eight years had passed, and I had seen the enactment of the most important historical dramas—a great nation lift itself up from a colonial nonentity, an empire formed, a national assembly convened, a Mexican general crowned, the throne in eclipse and the empire dissolved, the elevation from the embers of the monarchy of a federated republic, this people given a constitution and its states organized sovereign and independent, diplomatic relations established with the leading powers, with this republic taking its place among the nations of the earth. But, ah! What germs of civil dissention!

After six days of sailing—June 7—the captain announced to us that we were approaching the Balize, the New Orleans lighthouse. The first impression that one gets is the remarkable change in the color of the waters of the Gulf of Mexico some leagues before entering the mouth of the mighty Mississippi. This immense river battles against the waters of the ocean and causes them to back up in such a manner that for more than six leagues that water does not have the same taste as the sea water. The beaches are so low that they are seen, even when passing the Balize, as nothing more than mounds of earth at the level of the water, upon which there are a few miserable huts where it is scarcely conceivable that rational beings live. Floating on the current can be seen great pieces of wood, entire trees, that the force of hurricanes pulled loose two or three thousand miles away and which have been dragged along by the roaring currents of the tributaries of the Mississippi. The view of this entrance and even the course of the river as far as Fort Placquemines is unpleasant, for the only thing to be seen are reeds and wretched shrubs, the sight of which appears all the more distasteful because there are only mountains of mud and an endless number of lizards that look like pieces of dried wood.

We were forced to anchor twelve miles from the Balize up the river to await a favorable wind or the passing of some steamer of the type that are used to tow ships that arrive at the port and are willing to pay at the rate of twenty-five cents a ton. During the night the moon rose clear and beautiful, and its light, gently reflected in the turbid waters of the river, made pleasant the night whose silence was interrupted by the buzzing of an infinite number of mosquitoes that sucked our blood. The following day, June 9, we continued as far as Fort Placquemines, where we transferred to the steamboat that was going up to New Orleans towing two brigantines and a schooner. I arrived in New Orleans at seven o'clock in the evening on Thursday, June 10.

In that city a few Spaniards were publishing a newspaper entitled El Español, paid for by the government of Ferdinand VII. It was established with the purpose of serving as vanguard to the Barradas expedition, whose success was, as is well known, in accordance with the far-fetched ideas of the project. My arrival in New Orleans was announced by them with gross insults while *La Abeja (The Bee)* and the *Louisiana Advertiser* spoke of me with the praise and respect always due the unfortunate ones. I took lodging in the French inn of Madame Herries, one of the best in the city—good rooms, decent beds, plenty of well-seasoned food, although somewhat expensive, since it was no less than three dollars per day.

New Orleans is a city inhabited by small remnants of old Spanish families, a considerable proportion of French families, one half of the population made up of blacks and those of mixed blood, and the rest of North Americans who are, as is well known, a composite of the sons and descendants of the English, German, Irish and other peoples of Europe. In the city very little Spanish is spoken, much more French, and generally English, in which language are written the public registers of the authorities.

The overall view of the city offers nothing that can please the eyes of the traveler; there are no cupolas, nor towers, nor columns, nor buildings of handsome appearance and exquisite architecture. Its location, lower than the surface of the river and surrounded by lagoons and swamps, makes it gloomy and unhealthful. The character of the people is completely unlike that of the other cities of the United States. The river is at that point nearly a mile wide, and a wall of sand forms a powerful dike that extends for many leagues and is called the Levee; it keeps the waters of the great river from flooding the city and surrounding areas. In New Orleans the tide is hardly perceptible.

The location of New Orleans is ideal for a commercial city. A forest of masts comes into view as one approaches the Levee; and since the river is deep at this point, the ships have ready access to the bank where they can unload easily by means of wooden planks laid to the boats. There is not a city in the world that has the advantage of such extensive internal navigation. There are more than twenty thousand miles of navigable waters not only along the Mississippi, the Missouri, the Ohio and other great tributaries of the Mississippi, but along and through lakes and bays that put it in communication with Florida and other points.

When I arrived, there were more than a thousand boats, large and small, and at least five thousand sailors. When I was in the city in December of 1821, there were at the most forty thousand inhabitants, and today it is estimated that there are at least seventy thousand. Commerce has increased considerably, and the customs duties today amount to more than two million dollars. If yellow fever, intermittent fever, mosquitoes and the unbearable heat of summer did not offer such serious drawbacks to the growth of population, certainly New Orleans would become under the free and popular government that it has today one of the richest and most distinguished cities in the world. In spite of the plagues referred to, it is progressing rapidly and will become one of the leading cities of the New World.

The reader will not find displeasing the description which Mr. Flint gives of the city:

A thousand miles distance from the sources of the Mississippi River, and more than a thousand from those of the Ohio, in a sharp bend upon the east bank of the river is located New Orleans, the great commercial capital *of* the Mississippi Valley. Its position as a commercial city has no equal in the world, in my opinion. A short distance from the Gulf of Mexico, upon the banks of a river which it might be said waters the universe, six miles from Lake Pontchartrain arid connected to it by a navigable canal; with the immense flood of waters that descend from all directions and form pools connected easily by means of natural canals; with hundreds of steamers that frequent the port from fifty different points; with agricultural products from its owns state and from others that can compete with the richest of any country in the world. Its location is superior to that of New York. It has, however, one terrible disadvantage—the unhealthfulness of its location. If they could drain the immense swamps that lie between the city and the eternal forests, complete the improvements that the city has undertaken—in short, if they could bring it about so that the climate was not so humid, New Orleans would no doubt become the leading city of the Union.

Many efforts are being made to accomplish these great results. Unfortunately when the constellation of the Dog Star is at its zenith, yellow fever begins to appear in the east. But in spite of the fact that annually, or at least biennially, this pestilential plague visits the city; in spite of the fact that its mortal scythe destroys a multitude of unfortunate beings that are not acclimated and obliges the rich to seek out healthier places at considerable distances; and, finally, in spite of the terror that everywhere accompanies these plagues and to a certain degree is associated with the name of the city, its population is growing considerably.

Everywhere can be seen new buildings that are going up rapidly, and the appearance of the city is improving month by month. Americans come here from all of the states; their purpose is to accumulate wealth and go somewhere else to enjoy it. But death, which they are not disposed to take into account, obliges them to abandon the place before fulfilling their desires.

New Orleans is on an island formed on one side by the Mississippi, and on the others by Lakes Borgne, Pontchartrain and Maurepas, and the Iberville River, which separates from the Mississippi 120 miles above the city and flows into Lake Maurepas.

The market place is well supplied, and things are cheap. During the month that I was there there was a scarcity of vegetables which are abundant in March, April and May. The market is the Tower of Babel, for there one can hear blacks, mulattoes, Frenchmen, Spaniards, Germans, and Americans crying their wares in different languages. The *quadroon* women dress tastefully and neatly, and as they generally have very good figures and are beautiful, they present a striking contrast to the blacks from whom they are descended, and the philosopher cannot help noticing this variety of castes that forms surprising shades.

There are two distinct cities divided not by some river, or district, or other similar object, but by the type of buildings, customs, language and class of society. The fact is that this was a French colony in its beginnings, and it passed for some time into the hands of the Spanish; in the time of Charles IV, the Spanish government ceded it to France in an agreement on the settlement of certain debts and the occupation of the Florida territory. Napoleon sold it to the United States for ten million dollars, and from that time dates the rapid progress of Louisiana. Hence the diversity of customs and manner of living that in that city is one of the peculiar characteristics of its population.

CHAPTER II

French expedition and founding of the colony.—Occupation of Canada by the English.—It passes to the hands of the Spaniards.—Returned to the French in the time of the Republic.—North American marine trade.—Negotiations started with this in mind.—Mr. Livingston and Mr. Monroe, ministers for the republic.—Mm. Barbé.—Marbios on the part of the French.—Conclusion of the treaty.—Rapid progress of Louisiana after this agreement.—Arable lands under the control of the United States.—Difficulties in marking the boundaries of that immense territory.—Reflections of M. Barbé.—Marbois.—Products and trade of Louisiana.—Its government.—Theater.—The fair sex.—Holidays.—Catholics and Protestants.—Catholic slaves.—Religious consolation.—Father Cedella.—Cemeteries.—Battlefield in 1815.—Strategy of General Jackson.—Attack of English General Pakenham.—Defeat of the English. —Glorious triumph of the Americans.—Confidence and measures of the American general.—Regular troops of this country.—Opinion of the Princes Saxony-Weimar and Wurtemberg concerning these troops.—Method of replacements.—Brief thoughts on slavery.—General Guerrero's decree that abolished it in Mexico.—Harsh treatment that the slaves in Louisiana experience.—Antiphilosophical laws in the same state concerning this unfortunate class.—Reflections.—Influence of slavery on the progress of civilization.—Brief memoir on the haciendas of the hot lands of the Mexican republic.—An unpleasant happening before my departure from New Orleans.

In 1672 the French, who owned Canada, made an expedition along the Mississippi and descended it as far as the Arkansas River, about latitude 33° north. In 1682 the governor of Canada descended as far as the Gulf of Mexico, and gave the name of Louisiana to the lands through which the river ran in honor of Louis XIV. The French took possession of those areas from the mouth of the Mobile River as far as San Bernardo Bay, a distance of about 120 leagues beyond the mouths of the Mississippi. Louis XIV granted to Crozat, a rich financier, the exclusive trade in these colonies for twelve years. The grant came to an end in 1719, and when the colony was transferred to the West Indies Company, the latter sent a considerable number of colonists.

Father Charlevoix, a well-educated Jesuit who traveled through Louisiana in 1722, made fun of the writers who had praised so highly the mineral wealth of this province, and at the same time he prophesied its future prosperity because of the fertility of its lands and the abundance of waters and rivers. The colony was poorly governed; the company made war on the Indians, and in 1731 trade was declared free. A short time after this period the French government tried to realize the project of uniting Canada and Louisiana, with the purpose of closing off all communication by the English colonists with the western parts of the continent. In that period the English had not yet penetrated to the west of the Allegheny Mountains. Many Frenchmen had moved their families and their fortunes to Illinois, a country of unlimited fertility, watered by several navigable rivers, endowed with one of the mildest climates in the world. The colonists, instead of selecting points that they were able to occupy as their own property, fencing and clearing them to make them secure as they should, scattered themselves indiscriminately without any boundaries or limits.

In the war between France and England in 1754 the latter conquered, and the former agreed to cede all the territory existing on the east bank of the Mississippi, with the sole exception of Louisiana. A line drawn in the middle of the Mississippi separated the English possessions from the French. In 1764 Louisiana passed into the hands of the Spanish government by a secret treaty, but the administration remained in the hands of the French until 1768. After that, the two great revolutions of America and France occurred, and Napoleon, elevated to power and looking out over all points of the globe, had the idea of occupying Louisiana, in order to have a powerful influence in the great transactions of America which was beginning to attract the attention of Europe. By a secret treaty in 1800 he managed to bring about Charles IV's restoration of Louisiana to the French Republic. This agreement was not made public until the peace between Great Britain and France was signed, and it was fully revealed at the time of the Peace of Amiens, March 29, 1802. But when it was announced in England, from all sides came loud outbursts against the cession of Louisiana to France. Lord Hawkesbury said in the House of Commons that France had held Louisiana long enough without having reaped any benefit. On this occasion he came forth with the bold and unwise phrase: "We only wish to make an experimental peace."

General Bernadote, today King of Sweden, was named the first governor of the colony, but he refused the appointment, and in his place General Victor was named; he was on the point of departure to his new post when hostilities began anew between England and France.

During this interval when the Congress of the United States was informed of the cession of Louisiana to France, and the preparations of the latter to take possession, that body did not think it should remain indifferent to seeing established on its borders and in such important places a warlike nation that would not remain as inactive as the Spanish, and that soon would begin to raise questions about navigation on the Mississippi. Alarm was so great in the western part of the United States that President Jefferson had great difficulty in pacifying the inhabitants there, who were ready to resort to force. This would have put obstacles in the way of negotiations that the American government was trying to initiate with France, first for maintaining free navigation on the Mississippi, second that New Orleans would remain a free port for the products of the states of the interior, and finally to conduct matters to the point where they would bring about the transfer of power.

During this time Mr. Livingston, brother of the present minister of the United States in France, and well known as the cooperator with Fulton in the establishment of steamships, exercised the same charge that is today filled by the honorable Edward Livingston. He had made representations to President Jefferson concerning the crisis that would threaten the United States if the French Republic occupied Louisiana, and Jefferson could not deny the consequences of such an occupation. To treat with Napoleon he then gave the mission of envoy extraordinary to Mr. Monroe, instructing him that in case he did not obtain a satisfactory agreement conforming with the interests of the United States, he should communicate with the cabinets of Saint James and Madrid. Mr. Monroe, who was later president of the United States, had been an envoy during the time of the Directory, and his conduct had established for him a considerable reputation in France.

The mission committed to Mr. Monroe and Mr. Livingston was that of obtaining from the French government, by means of the proper indemnification, the cession of New Orleans and all the territory belonging to France on the east bank of the Mississippi, the middle of which was considered to be the dividing line between American and French territories. They had instructions that in the event that they were not able to obtain this, or as a last resort the free navigation of the Mississippi, and the circumstance of New Orleans remaining a free port, they should enter into negotiations with England with the purpose of making common cause with her against France. In the letter written to Mr. Livingston by President Jefferson are found these remarkable words: "The day that France takes possession of New Orleans she pronounces the sentence of lowered esteem for herself on the part of the United States, and she seals the alliance between two nations that together can maintain the exclusive possession of the ocean. From that moment on we shall link ourselves closely with the English nation, her navy, etc."

Mr. Monroe left New York March 8, 1803, the same day that there was delivered to the British Parliament the message from the crown that announced the approaching break with France, so that on his arrival Mr. Monroe found the French government well disposed to treat with the United States. Napoleon recognized that since he was at war with England he must change his outlook and his policy with respect to the control of

Louisiana. He could not fail to see that since the English were so powerful on the seas they would cut all his trade relations with the colony, and that they would occupy it at the first opportunity in order to sell it to the North Americans. By one of those masterstrokes that were so much a part of his nature he made up his mind to sell the colony to the United States. In this manner not only did he prevent the conquest that the English could make of that region, he also received a considerable amount of money in payment for it, which sum would be of great use to France in the circumstances in which she found herself with her resources exhausted and on the eve of a continental war.

There were two opinions in the cabinet of the first consul. M. Marbois was in favor of the measure for the reasons, set forth, and M. Talleyrand felt that the possession of Louisiana should in time indemnify France for her great losses because of the richness and fertility of the soil, its dominant position on the Mississippi and its trade; in case the English should occupy it, the French could do likewise with Hanover, which would be a pawn against its restitution.

The first consul did not change his decision, and the next day he called M. Barbé—Marbois and said to him,

> Mr. Minister, I renounce Louisiana. Not only do I want France to get rid of New Orleans, but of the entire colony without reserve. I commission you to handle this delicate subject with the agents of the United States. I need a great deal of money for this war, and I do not wish to begin it with fresh levies. If one were to arrange the terms of the price in view of the advantages that would accrue to the United States from this cession, certainly there would be no sum sufficiently large to cover it. I will lie moderate out of the need in which I find myself to make this sale—I want fifty million francs (a little less than nine million dollars), making it clear that I will not enter into any sort of treaty for less. Mr. Monroe will be here soon; begin by making him the proposal without any further preliminaries. You will keep me informed day by day and hour by hour of the progress of the negotiations. The cabinet in London will know the decisions of Washington, but they will not know mine. Maintain the greatest secrecy, and demand it of the American ministers.

The conferences began the following day, and the ministers of both countries, who had an equal interest in a prompt conclusion, carried the negotiations as far as they could in accordance with the instructions and powers of the Americans. But as I have said, they had them only for dealing with the left bank of the river including New Orleans, and not concerning the west side.

It was impossible to confer with their government over so great a distance on a matter that was so delicate when hostilities had already begun or were about to begin between England and France. Consequently the American ministers did not hesitate to take upon themselves the responsibility of dealing with that vast portion of North America belonging to France that extends along the banks of the greatest rivers of the universe. On this basis they signed the treaty. In a letter written by Mr. Jefferson to Mr. Monroe he said to him:

> Our project of acquiring by purchase New Orleans and the Florida territory is subject to so many combinations and diverse efforts that we cannot give definite instruction; it was necessary to send a minister extraordinary so that he and the regular minister might work with discretionary powers.

This clause indicates that the American envoys were confident that their conduct would be approved, and indeed it was. The negotiations were concluded on eighty million francs, with twenty million remaining on deposit to cover the claims of the United States against France. The treaty was ratified in "Washington, and Louisiana became a province of the United States.

From that time on states have been formed from that territory. The first was Louisiana, which takes in New Orleans and contains forty-eight thousand square miles, and then Missouri, a part of the extensive territory of the Missouri River, on the west side of the Mississippi, the extent of which is sixty-three thousand square miles. A state has not yet been formed from the Arkansas Territory, also a part of what was formerly the French province. It is about 550 miles long and 220 miles wide. The Northwest portion of the Missouri River to the shores of the Pacific is of enormous extension. The river runs for more than two thousand miles.

As one surveys the prodigious extent of these parts and the other possessions of the United States in the Northwest, as well as in Florida and Michigan, which are as yet sparsely populated, the calculation of Mr. Chateaubriand is not out of line when he says that the population of the United States *as of now occupies an eighteenth part of its territory.* M. de Marbois, employed for a long time in the United States, wrote:

> In these boundless regions the human race can multiply with complete freedom. There *for many centuries* there will be no obstacle to marriages, and parents will not fear that their descendants will lack for lands to feed the fruits of their gentle and honest conjugal union.

This calculation and these reflections are equally applicable to our United Mexican States, where unquestionably nature has been most provident with regard to the fertility of the land and the ease of subsistence.

In the United States there are in effect three hundred million acres of arable lands, not counting the vast stretches of the West and the Northwest. A great portion of these lands remain in the hands of the Government of the Union, and in the course of a few years they will produce for their territory many millions of dollars. There is no way of calculating their value.

All the unoccupied territories became, as a consequence of the treaties made with France and Spain, the property of the United States. The government in Washington had a great deal of difficulty in marking the limits of the territories that they were to occupy in accordance with the treaty made with France, since they are classified in geography only under the designation of unknown lands. The one commissioned to do so was Mr. Jacob Astor of New York, who founded a town on the banks of the Columbia named Astoria after him.

Says M. Marbois:

> Conquerors extend their states by force of arms; they become known for the blood that they spill and the desolation that they inflict in the countries that they occupy. The republic of the United States has extended itself by sending surveyors and wise men up to distances of five hundred leagues. Without force they establish the boundaries of their peaceful conquests, and with good laws they assure the lasting prosperity of the communities for which they were acquired.

When people speak of the city of New Orleans they seem to be filled with pride because of its rapid progress; it had a population in 1803 of only eight thousand persons.

> New Orleans, founded in 1707, which has remained unchanged for a century, has become in the short span of twenty-five years one of the most flourishing of cities—as soon as it became a part of the great community of the United States. A few years of good government have produced what many generations could not bring about under the dominion of *prohibitive laws and petty restrictions*. The town, which in the time of those laws stood still, has multiplied five times; its lands produce everything from the most necessary to the most delicate articles of luxury and comfort.

In the states of Louisiana and Mississippi sufficient sugar is manufactured to provide half the consumption of the United States. The other products of those lands are increasing proportionally. There are warehouses of pelts of beaver, ermine, martins, seals and other animals. Lands sold in the time of the French and Spanish governments have risen to an extraordinary price. I knew a former Spanish colonist, Don José Vidal, who made a considerable fortune with the lands that he acquired in Natchez at the time that it was a Spanish colony.

In the state of Louisiana there are two legislative chambers. It is the only state where I have seen the discussions carried on in two languages; the result is that often the Creole representative who speaks French is not understood by the American representative who speaks English. However, in the end the discussions are printed in both languages. Many newspapers are published half in French and the other half in English. There is also an interpreter who translates the speeches into the respective languages to be understood by everyone. Although this has the drawback that it can never be translated exactly as it was said, and much time is lost, there is an advantage, however, in that the interpreter may tone down some personal remarks in the discussion.

In New Orleans there is a French theater and an English one. The first is rather good, and I have seen some *vaudevilles* that were well sung and acted. The English travelers speak very disparagingly of the English theater. I believe indeed that it must not be very good because, generally speaking, the North Americans do not care for this type of entertainment, and as Mrs. Trollope says, they will think a long time before shelling out shillings to pay the price of admission.

The Creole women are pretty and charming. Although they are not as white as the North American women, they have better figures, dress with more charm, carry themselves better, and their manner is more open and pleasant.

As in all Catholic countries, Sunday is a day of fun in New Orleans. Stores of Catholics are open; there are dances, music and parties. During the morning they run to the cathedral to hear mass where people of all colors are gathered. The cathedral is a small temple that has no regular order of architecture and in no way resembles the churches of Mexico. The altars are like those of our small towns, except that the images are much better.

Although Catholics and Protestants agree that all men are children of God, brothers one to another and joint heirs to glory, only the former give practical examples of this profession of faith. In a Catholic church the black and the white, the slave and his master, the noble and the common man kneel before the same altar, and there is a temporary unawareness of all human distinctions; all come in the character of sinners, and there is no rank other than that of the ecclesiastical hierarchy. In this sacred precinct the rich man does not receive incense, no one's pride is flattered, nor does the poor man feel himself put down. The mark of degradation disappears from the brow of the slave as he sees himself admitted together with the free and the rich to lift his songs and prayers to the author of nature. In the Protestant churches such is not the case. All people of color are excluded or separated in one corner by bars or railings, so that even in that moment they have to feel their degraded condition.

The most wretched slave receives from the hands of the Catholic priest all the consolations of religion. He is visited in his sickness, comforted in his afflictions; his dying lips receive the sacred host, and in the final moments of his death agony the last voice that he hears is the sublime apostrophe that the Catholic addresses to the dying person: *Profiscere, anima christiana.* ("Depart in peace, oh Christian soul"). Why shouldn't all the slaves and blacks of Louisiana be Catholics? The congregation of the Protestant church consists of a few well-dressed ladies in the decorated pews, while all the paving stones of the cathedral are filled with people of all colors. I recall as an example that Father Antonio de Cedella. a Capuchin religious, with whom I made friends in 1822, but who is dead now was the oracle of the colored people and respected by all classes of the city. This Spanish ecclesiastic by his friendliness, his tolerance and other virtues had made himself honored and loved.

In New Orleans, as in Mexico, deep graves cannot be dug without striking water. The cemetery, on a parcel of land not more than half a mile from the city, surrounded by swamps, although of great extent, is scarcely sufficient for the necessities of the population.

A curious traveler interested in the glories of America cannot visit New Orleans without spending some time seeing the field of the famous action of General Andrew Jackson against the English troops who were under the command of General Edward Pakenham, in January of 1816. The plain on which the action took place is about four, miles from the city; it extends for about a mile, and at the time of the landing of the English it was covered with sugarcane.

Today it is used for pasture land. The Mississippi borders it on the west; on the east there is a thick woods of cypress and pine trees. There still remain the traces of the ditches that the American general ordered to be dug between the river and the swamp. The excavation could not have been deep because in a short time it caved in and filled with water. The trenches that were made were formed from sacks of cotton that were certainly very appropriate for the purpose because of the softness of the cotton which deadened the effect of the bullets. Behind these trenches General Jackson placed his riflemen, putting at the back of each one another to load in a moment so as not to lose time.

A week or two was spent in skirmishes until January 8 when Sir Edward Pakenham began to attack the line. The field in between up to the point of defense was completely open, and thus the English general left his troops unprotected to receive all of the enemy fire without any defense. Exposed to the terrible artillery fire, even at half a cannon shot distance, and then to the sure fire of the rifles, the invaders could not maintain the order of attack and broke ranks. The defenders at some points were six deep and inflicted horrible casualties. The daring Pakenham led the attack in person, struggling to reestablish order, but he was wounded by flack from the artillery that took both his legs, and was then killed by rifle fire. Generals Gibbs and Dean who followed him with the same courage suffered the same fate, and General Lambert, who finally saw the impossibility of gaining any advantage, ordered the retreat and the reembarkation of the troops.

The number of invaders was about 10,000 men, and that of the Americans 3,400. General Jackson reporting on his triumph informed his government: "There is no case in history of a more complete victory, nor one that cost less blood to the victors. Our losses were *six dead and nine wounded;* those of the enemy were more than 3,000 dead and as many more wounded." The defense was made by the brave American general with *volunteers from Tennessee and national militia from Kentucky with a* few *others from New Orleans* and a very small number of regular troops.

The great merit of General Jackson in these critical circumstances, in addition to his valor which no one disputes, was in having been able to inspire confidence in the inhabitants of New Orleans by the forcefulness of his character. The legislature of Louisiana had been hesitant, the people of the city came to the point of showing signs of wishing to enter into negotiations with the English. From the moment that he arrived in the city he put an end to all uncertainty. In a message addressed to the governor he said: "He that is not with us is against us. Those who have been drawn by lot must be obliged with severe penalties to join the line. We should fear more the hidden enemy than those whom we can see. The fatherland must be defended, and it will be."

In these trying circumstances the general had no troops, and it is easy to imagine the difficulties in which he must have found himself, with the terror that a numerous and well-disciplined army at the gates of the city inspired in the mothers, wives and daughters of those who were called to a combat against what appeared to be such great odds.

When he left the city for the battlefield with a few hundred men, he wrote to Mr. Edward Livingston, author of the law codes of Louisiana, and today minister plenipotentiary to France, saying to him: "Assure the inhabitants that the enemy will not get as far as the city and try to calm them."

But in the difficult situation in which he found himself he took on the powers of a dictator and declared martial law. He punished several deserters with death; he interned to the interior at a distance of 120 miles many Frenchmen who refused to take up arms; he arrested the French consul who tried to resist the carrying out of martial law; he banished a judge who provided an act of *habeas corpus* to free the French consul; in short he acted in accordance with what the unusual circumstances demanded of a man capable of such an undertaking. The people of New Orleans, convinced that the forcefulness of his character and the opportuneness of his provisions had saved the city, received him after the victory in triumph and as the liberator of the whole country.

I must not end this chapter without some mention of the regular troops of the United States and citing the testimony of respectable travelers in that area. The army of the American Union is composed of only six thousand men, but the order, the discipline, the spit and polish, the good manners are as though born in those soldiers. There is no officer who is not aware of his duties as a military man and as a citizen. His education is worthy of respect, and on this point I wish to cite the respectable testimony of the Duke of Saxony—Weimar who writes about some officers that he met in Washington in these terms:

> Most of the men with whom I have dealt are officers in the army. It would be difficult to find in Europe a corps of officers of better condition than that of this small American army. No one can be an officer if he has not had an outstanding education. Almost all are taken from the military academy at West Point; there are not those hasty promotions as in Europe. When you meet an American officer, you can be sure that he has all the qualities that will bring him esteem in the most select society.

The prince who writes this is the brother-in-law of the present King of England.

The Prince of Wurtemberg, who traveled in the United States in the year 1828, wrote on the same subject: "There is no country in the world," he said,

> where the soldiers are put to work more usefully. In Europe the soldier puts in the whole day in exercises, parades, cleaning his clothes and his arms, or in idleness. The American soldier is constantly occupied in some work. The rigorous discipline to which he is subjected keeps him *up* to a level of preparedness that is maintained in other countries with considerable effort. *No soldier in the world is better fed, better clothed and better paid than those of the*

United States. The government of this country has grafted its military institution on to the civil administration, and the result has been not only the improvement of the army, *but a* masterpiece of military order.

The manner of enlisting recruits is shown by the following advertisement that is seen in public newspapers: "Needed for the service of the country of the United States so many hundred men between the ages of eighteen and thirty-five years, healthy, and five feet six inches tall. A bonus of $5.00, plenty of food and clothing, with $5.00 salary per month. Those who wish may apply at such and such a place."

The lottery system, or draft, which up to the time of my departure was in force in our republic, is especially odious, and when I was governor of the State of Mexico, I confess that many times I winked at the fact that it was not carried out, in view of the repeated and painful petitions from laborers and workers. Only in the direst circumstances, such as those in which General Jackson found himself as we have seen, is everyone obliged to serve in the armed forces. The method of conscription in France alienated many people from the cause of Napoleon.

As he goes from the Mexican Republic to the states which permit slavery in our sister republic, the philosopher cannot fail to feel the contrast that is noted between the two countries, nor fail to experience a pleasant memory for those who have abolished this degrading traffic and caused to disappear among us the vestiges of so humiliating a condition of the human race. General Guerrero issued the decree December 16, 1829, by virtue of extraordinary powers, through the generous inspiration of Don José Maria Tornel. When I passed through New Orleans, there were more than one thousand slaves up for sale. These poor people are treated with great severity in Louisiana. They serve in homes and in inns and generally sleep on the ground.

When a master wishes to punish a slave, male or female, he will send that person to the jail with a note that contains the order for the number of lashes that the jailer is to administer. The poor man or woman returns home with the note that shows that the indicated punishment has been carried out. When the master deems it fitting, he orders that they tie the slave's hands, throw him face down upon the floor, and administer the beating in this manner. Often as one passes by the jail in the morning the cries and laments of those unfortunate people can be heard.

I am going to describe an event related by the Duke of Weimar, concerning whom I have already spoken, and who stopped at the same house where I was in New Orleans, with the difference that he traveled in 1826. "I cannot pass over in silence," says the prince, a scene that I witnessed on March 22—one which excited my profound indignation. There was at the inn a young female slave from[Virginia employed as chambermaid whose cleanliness and care in the service made everyone love her. A Frenchman who was staying at the inn asked for water early in the morning. The girl could not serve him with the speed that he wished since she was busy with other duties. He went downstairs, and when he found her in the patio busy with other chores, he struck her fiercely until he made her mouth and nose bleed. The poor creature, trying to defend herself, put her hand up to the attacker's throat, and he began to yell loudly. He escaped from the hands of the girl, went to his room, got together his clothing and trunks, and was getting ready to leave when the landlady, Madame Herries, trying to satisfy the cruel guest, ordered that they give the slave twenty-five lashes with a leather whip, and to double the pain of the victim this punishment was inflicted by her lover, who was a slave in the same house.

The Frenchman, not satisfied with this penalty, went to the police where when the unfortunate slave girl was brought in by two constables she was beaten again in the presence of the accuser. I am very sorry [adds the famous traveler] that I did not take the name of this evil Christian in order to publish it and denounce him to public scorn.

A few months before my arrival on March 7, 1830, the Louisiana legislature had passed two laws that contained extremely antiliberal provisions; they are as follows:

I. Whoever writes, publishes or distributes any writing that *has a tendency* to create discontent among the free colored population in this state or to introduce rebellion among the slaves, shall suffer, according to the gravity of the deed in the judgment of the court of justice, capital punishment, life imprisonment, or public works for life.

II. Whoever in public speeches, on the platform, in open meetings, in the pulpit, or anywhere else, whether it be in private conversations or by signs or actions, shall do or say anything that may *have a tendency to produce discontent* among the free colored people of the population of this State, or to incite rebellion among its slaves, or any one who shall knowingly have brought into it papers, pamphlets or books that may have the same tendency, shall suffer, according to the court's judgment the penalty of public works for not less than three years, nor more than twenty, or death.

III. Any person who shall teach, or shall cause to be taught any slave to read or write, shall suffer the penalty of from one to twelve months in prison.

The other law is as follows:

I. It sets forth a law for the expulsion of all free colored people who may have entered the state since the year 1807, and prohibits the entry of any person of this class into the state.

II. It establishes the penalty of public works for life for ail free colored persons who having returned to the state do not leave it.

III. It establishes that any white person who may be convicted of being the author, printer, or editor of any writing in the state, or even of using language, that has the purpose of disturbing the peace of the same with relation to the slaves or people of this state, or even to diminish the respect that the colored people should have for the whites, shall be fined the sum of $300 to $1,000 and condemned to prison for not less than six months and not more than three years. But if the persons who commit these offenses should be colored they shall suffer a fine of not more than $1,000 and be condemned to public works for from three to five years, and banishment forever after that time.

IV. It establishes that in these cases it shall be the obligation of the public prosecutor or the general attorney, and of the private attorneys of the districts, under the pain of loss of job, to prosecute the colored persons who may have violated this law, or *as often as they may be required to prosecute the said colored persons by any citizen of the state.*

These laws were signed by Mr. Roman, president of the House of Representatives, Mr. Smith, president of the Senate, and Mr. Dupré, governor of the state at that time. Today Mr. Roman is governor.

Sad indeed is the situation of a state where its legislators consider necessary such offensive measures of repression against the rights of man. Those who know the spirit of liberty that prevails in all the deliberations of those who guide the United States can only think, in view of these acts of notorious injustice towards a group of individuals of the human race, that very strong motives, that an inevitable necessity, *dura necessitas,* obliges these people to sanction such laws. There are those among these legislators who go from the halls of their sessions to pay homage and adoration to the beautiful quadroons, with whom they would bind themselves in the sacred bonds of matrimony if an invincible prejudice did not interpose itself to prevent such unions. I have known respectable persons who lived condemned to an involuntary celibacy because they could not unite with the women who because of their charms, beauty and affectionate solicitude had made captive their wills. There are several examples of these clandestine concessions in the state of Louisiana.

This type of exceptional laws has an extraordinary influence on the moral progress and the civilization of the states that permit slaves, such as Georgia, South Carolina and Louisiana. It is sufficient to cast a glance over the present state of publishing in those parts, compared to that of other states free of slaves, and one will notice immediately the advantages of the latter. Let us pick out three free states and three where slavery is permitted. In 1810 there were published in the state of New York sixty-six newspapers; in 1830 there were two hundred twelve. In 1810 there were published in Pennsylvania sixty-one; in 1830, eighty-five. In 1810 there were fourteen published in Ohio; in 1830, sixty-six. Let us see now the slave states. In 1810 in South Carolina ten newspapers—were published; in 1830, sixteen. In Georgia in 1810, thirteen; in 1830, an equal number. In Louisiana *ten* were published; today the number has gone down to *nine*. It is to be noted that while the population of this last state has increased from the 20,854 that it had at that time to the 115,262 that it had reached in 1830, the newspapers have decreased in number, following a course that is contrary to the progress of civilization and trade.

The sugar cane plantations, the lemon and orange and other aromatic trees of our hot lands that are to be found on the plantations reminded me of the beautiful holdings of Cuautla and Cuernavaca in the state of Mexico. But here agriculture is more advanced, and the ease of export and locomotion, with the advantage that the planters have in cultivating with slaves, makes it possible for them to sell their sugar at very low prices. The quality of the sugar is never as fine as that which we have in the states of Veracruz, Puebla and Mexico. There is always a greater amount of dirt in the sugars from Louisiana and Havana. The same thing happens with our sweets from Yucatan, which bring even less than those of Havana.

The heat was excessive at the time when I arrived in New Orleans; there were some days when the thermometer went up to 98° and even 100° Fahrenheit. All the well-to-do people traveled up the river in search of a better climate.

I was very glad to find in New Orleans some old friends with whom I had traveled in Europe previously, or whom I had met in this city. Among these were Mr. Charles Black, city treasurer, and Mr. Fleytas, a rich planter, the ex-count of Montezuma, the family of Mr. Duncan and other important people of the country. Mr. Curson, a man of much education who had traveled a great deal in America and Europe, favored me with his advice and reflections. He gave me letters of recommendation for several people, among them the English minister to Washington, Mr. Vaughn. In Mexico Mr. A. Butler, the business attaché of the United States, gave me letters that were very useful to me.

On June 15, General Mejía and I took passage on the steamer *Louisiana*. This is one of the better steamboats of the line that offers all the comforts compatible with a floating home. Most of these boats are of four to five hundred tons, and they are constructed with the triple purpose of carrying poor people and a cargo of sugar, coffee and rum when they go up; cotton, flour, meat, hides, etc., when they come down. On the upper deck they are like our bullrings, or like the baths that are found in Paris on the Seine. They have their balconies which serve for the travelers to amuse themselves, and their inside cabins where there are a bed, washstand and mirror for sleeping and dressing. There are staterooms for different classes. The passage from New Orleans to Louisville costs forty dollars. The distance is close to 1,200 miles.

The 16th we went aboard at 12:00 noon, and a little before the departure of the boat the sheriff presented himself asking for Mr. Zavala. The sheriff was accompanied by a man whom I did not know. The officer told me that that individual's name was Browerman and that he had presented himself at the city court asking that I pay ninety—four dollars that he said that I owed him for repairing a coach when I was governor of the State of Mexico. Note the evil workings of this man who waited until the moment of the departure of the steamer, which made it necessary for me either to be delayed, which would put me terribly behind schedule, or to pay him, although I was certain that I did not owe that amount, for I had paid him in Mexico when it was due. But I had not kept the receipt, and I cannot imagine how there can be any right for such a demand in a foreign country, far from the place where the debt is supposed to have been contracted. The only recourse that I had was to get Mr. Breadlove, Mexican vice-consul, who fortunately was on the boat, to stand good for me. Thus I got out of this small and unpleasant embarrassment.

After two years of travel in which this matter was forgotten I had to pay in Mexico on October 4, 1833, the sum of $105.50, which included court costs, with judgment without my consent, which receipt I still have, as well as those of all the artists, innkeepers, and others that I have paid, in order to avoid another similar happening. I have with me a trunk full of receipts.

CHAPTER III

The day was beautiful, the sun was shining with all its splendor, and its rays, reflected by the waters of the river, multiplied its effect and increased the fire that seemed to burn the earth. The wind blew hot, and the only comfort was found in the sight of the clumps of trees along the banks and the hope of a more temperate atmosphere at the end of the day. There were six ladies, and among them one from Guatemala, who was following her husband Don Mariano de Aycinena, exiled from his country for political matters, like so many others.

Also on board was a man from Yucatan, Don Joaquín Gutiérrez, a young man with refined manners, pleasant ways, and that easy and friendly lack of shyness that is found among educated people who have traveled and lived in good society. Count Cornaro, a person distinguished because of his birth and elegant manner, who was coining from Mexico, was also on the boat. There were a number of other people, all capable of making a truly interesting company.

In the navigation of the Mississippi there are not the risks of storms, hurricanes and coral reefs that cause so much and such terrible damage to the ships that sail the ocean. But the frequent encounters with the enormous tree trunks that come down the river are apt to cause trouble for the steamers. There is another greater risk, but it has lessened a great deal because of the precautions that have been taken. I speak of the explosions of the receptacles or boilers for the steam that is confined to move the machinery. When this happens, and frequent cases have been seen on the Mississippi steamboats, many people perish, either directly from the scalding water, or because with the shipwreck the passengers are exposed to the turbulent river, or finally, from the force with which the exploding machinery strikes people in its path. The boats also are apt to run aground on banks of sand or mud, but they are easily pulled free by other steamboats that pass frequently.

One hundred miles from New Orleans is a small place called Baton Rouge, where they manufacture sugar, syrups and rum. In this town there are a military garrison and a fortress. We passed by there on June 18. The climate is very little different from that of the capital. The 19th we passed by Natchez, famous for M. de Chateaubriand's interesting novel which bears that title.

Mrs. Trollope, who has written of her trip to the United States with the spirit of satire and sarcasm that often leads to excess, speaks of the steamboats on this run and of the associations to be found on them:

> I advise those who wish to get a favorable impression of the manners and customs of the Americans that they not begin a trip on the Mississippi because I declare in all sincerity that I would give my preference to a well cared for pigsty with a herd of pigs to the cabins on these boats. I know of scarcely anything so repugnant for an Englishman as the incessant spitting of the Americans.

Elsewhere, when she speaks of the passengers, of whom she says that most of them use the title of colonel, general or major:

> Their absolute lack of table manners, the voracious speed with which they grab their plates to devour their food, the strange and unusual expressions that they use, the frequent spitting, from which it was hard to keep our clothes free, the horrible habit of eating by putting their knives into their mouths up to the handle, and the most

horrible habit yet of picking their teeth with their penknives after eating, led us to believe immediately that we were not surrounded by generals, colonels and majors of the Old World, and that meal time was not a time for pleasure.

Those who have traveled on steamboats from the Thames to Calais, to Ostend, Boulogne, etc., after having done so in the United States, cannot help being surprised that Mrs. Trollope should use this language, when evidently those in the United States are much more comfortable, more respectable, cleaner, and in every respect better. What shall we say of those of the Seine, the Gironde and other rivers of France? It is impossible to conceive how these countries so civilized and advanced in every type of social comfort can maintain boats that are so filthy and disgusting.

As for the habit of the North Americans to spit frequently, we should not hide the fact that it is a disgusting fault in good society and is due to a habit that they have generally of chewing tobacco, as we Americans of the South have the habit of smoking it. What would Mrs. Trollope say if she were to see our charming Mexican women continually blowing smoke through their mouths and noses, staining their small and well-shaped hands with the oil from the cigarette paper, contaminating their clothing with tobacco smoke and giving their breath a disagreeable odor? On the boats smoking is not allowed except in a place designated for it, in order to avoid the discomfort that the ladies have from the smoke, as well as many delicate people who neither smoke nor chew tobacco.

Although for miles and miles the banks of the Mississippi offer only a constant and uniform view without the interruption of towns, or mountains or hills, there is always a surprising spectacle presented by the pleasant sight of the continual passing of palmettos, palm trees, the great oak trees, firs, sycamores and other gigantic productions of the vegetable kingdom all intertwined with the vines that serve as the nests and perches for a varied multitude of birds that raise their songs in those eternal and solitary rural settings.

How the spirit is transported as it contemplates the inner being of these infinite places of solitude where no human footstep has ever fallen. Those trees, like our great mountains, seem like contemporaries of creation itself! Looking at all this one is able to get an idea of how still life could be brought alive under the romantic brush of Chateaubriand and could lift up his ardent heart to the degree of enthusiasm that made it possible for him to bring his readers to have a part in his brilliant pages. The Mississippi, like the Nile, the Marathon and the Orinoco and other great rivers of America and Asia, cannot fail to produce strong impressions and ideas of the grandeur and majesty of the Creator as one contemplates them. Nature in her primitive state with all her rough spots, her air of abandon, to put it thusly her silence, her languor, but at the same time with all her fertility, her riches, her magnificence, her hopes, is always for the eyes of the sensitive man an object worthy of profound reflections.

The Mississippi is joined and augmented by the Red River, the White River, the Arkansas, Ohio, Missouri and many other rivers of lesser importance. The Mississippi varies in depth and width according to the places through which it passes, and naturally becomes smaller as one approaches its headwaters. In New Orleans it is about 120 feet deep; in Natchez, 80; this is 300 miles upstream. From the Balize to Pittsburgh, to which one travels by steamboat along the Ohio, there is a distance of 2,012 miles, which amounts to more than 700 leagues in Mexico. The impetus to growth in commerce and civilization as a result of the introduction of steamboats is tremendous.

Formerly it took three or four months to make this trip from New Orleans. Today one arrives in Louisville in ten days, 1,100 miles; another day to Cincinnati, 120 miles; in four to Wheeling, 380 miles, and in a day and a half to Pittsburgh, about 280 miles. It is not uncommon to see families go to visit one or another of these places, 100, 200, or 300 leagues, to return home in two or three days. It is as though one were going from Mexico City to Zacatecas or to Durango. The trip from New Orleans to Pittsburgh is a greater distance than from Veracruz to Sinaloa.

Every twenty-four hours our boat would stop to take on wood to keep the fire going that was necessary to run the machinery. The daily consumption of firewood according to my calculations amounted to twenty-eight or thirty dollars. On the swampy banks there are wretched settlements of small wooden houses, standing on stilts that sustain them and preserve them from the dampness and the lizards, and these miserable huts are the homes of the men who provide the wood for the three hundred boats that traverse the mighty river. The Americans call them *squatters,* no doubt because their houses are so small that they cannot stand up Mrs. Trollope paints a very melancholy picture of these people:

> From time to time [says this traveler], there come into view a few cabins of the woodcutters who provide the steamboats with the necessary fuel, and they live in this traffic at the risk, or rather I will say, with the certainty of a premature death in exchange for dollars and whiskey. These dismal houses are for the most part flooded during the winter, and the best of them are on stilts that keep the inhabitants from drowning when the waters of the river rise. These unfortunate beings are the victims of high fevers that they face

without fear, helped along by the stimulus of spirituous liquors of
which they make use. The sallow appearance of their wretched
children and women is a cause for horror, and although this sight
was repeated frequently, it never ceased to make the same impression upon me. Their color is a bluish pallor, and they all look drop-
sical. A cow with two or three pigs, with water almost up to their
knees, distinguish those that are better off among these hapless
people, and one thing I can tell you is that never did I see human
nature reduced to such a state of degradation as appears among
the woodcutters of the unhealthful banks of the Mississippi.

Indeed Mrs. Trollope's description is exact. But I have seen several of
these small settlements increase in size in places where the height of the
land along the banks permitted it and form villages in which they are beginning to build houses of some comfort. Our own Indians along Lake Chalco
and the swamps of the Valley of Toluca find themselves in the same situation as these squatters. But there is a difference in that our Indians can
improve the lands a great deal, build their houses on solid ground, raise animals and harvest crops; while these cannot leave the small circles in which
they have set up their courtyards of lumber and firewood because the flooding of the river will not permit it. In a small town three leagues from Toluca called San Pedro de los Petates the Indians live in the waters that come
down from the river at flood time. They die very young, and the last cholera
epidemic that caused so many deaths in the capital of the state almost put
an end to that small village.

In the navigation of this river one encounters a great number of rafts
that bring goods down to New Orleans—especially lumber for homes and
buildings. These rafts are often five or six hundred feet in length and twelve
to fifteen feet wide, made of wooden planks nailed and joined, upon which
they put others and then the animals, seeds and other goods. In the middle
there is a room where they sleep and prepare their meals. They come down
with the current, which runs at four or five miles an hour after the Missouri
and the Ohio have joined the river. In New Orleans they break these rafts
up and sell the lumber. A few years ago to make a round trip to Louisville
took eight months. Today they do it in two weeks. Could there be anything
more fitting than to erect in each town a bronze statue to the immortal Fulton who applied steam to navigation? Such is the greatness of a man of
genius who brings about a revolution beneficial to humankind! Gioya, John
Guttemberg, Columbus and Fulton will live eternally.

One of the great rivers that flows into the Mississippi is the Arkansas;
its course is known for more than nineteen hundred miles, and it is navigable for more than six hundred. The banks of this river have so much lime-

stone that some people say that the stock die when they eat the soil. In the rainy season small steamboats can even get close to the mountains. On this side is the White River, which is navigable for more than four hundred miles in the Arkansas Territory which borders the lands of New Mexico and California. The inhabitants of this part of the United States are generally not very civilized, and there are many who are much like our Indians, although they are always more proud. They always carry knives shaped like a cutlass, which they use against wolves, bears and other wild beasts.

In our most remote small towns, one can feel the effects of the slavery under which we lived under the old regime. Civilization is nothing more than the effects of terror impressed upon the minds of the inhabitants, which causes them not to show themselves hostile to travelers, nor to live together in a state of open war with continual reprisals.

In the places of which I am speaking where there is neither civilization, nor fear, nor religion, men only respect each other for their individual strength and power. It would not be out of line to relate in this work a few anecdotes that often give a better idea of the character of a people than do exact descriptions. "April 10, 1830," says Mr. Stuart in his trip to the United States,

> in one of the places where the boat stopped to take on wood, the captain urged me to get off in order to hear from the mouth of the mayor himself an event that he did not think that I would believe if he told me himself. The justice of the peace was a respectable American of good manners; he lived in a house that was neat and comfortable, and he invited me to enjoy a rye whiskey, which in his opinion was the best of that kind in the United States. He told me that some small boats which were coming down the river loaded with different goods of the country had stopped nearby during the night, and that on one of these boats a murder had been committed, and that the murderer had been surprised in the act. This caused great excitement among the passengers, among whom were friends of the murdered man. Since the punishment would be delayed for many days if the guilty man were sent to Arkansas to be judged by the court, and there would be no witnesses to the deed there, they decided to hold the trial right on the boat. Having tried him, they sentenced him to be hanged, which was done a few hours after the crime was committed. The mayor could not have prevented it even if he had tried.

There is another curious affair which gives an idea also of the civil situation of those remote lands, and which I wish to relate because I think it would not be strange to find it repeated in some parts of Mexico such as Texas, California, and New Mexico.

A little above the town of Memphis there is a place that is called Little Prairie in the state of Missouri. At that point we found a cultivated field cleared by a colonist named Brown. This fellow had bought those lands from the government, paying $2.50 or $3.00 an acre for them. He had not yet received the title when a certain man named Eastwood had taken possession of some adjacent lands that also belonged to Brown. Eastwood was busy plowing them when Brown, accompanied by two daughters that he had, decided to oust that intruder. He sent his older daughter to bring a rifle or American musket. He was held back, however, from carrying out such a desperate decision by the fear that his daughter would be held equally guilty as an accomplice if he fired on Eastwood. The action of this man was not, however, as absurd as might be imagined by a reader from a civilized place. It is very common in the western states and territories of the United States, and in Texas, California and New Mexico of our republic, that those who get there first take possession of lands without any title, cultivate them and live on them until a legal owner may come to occupy them. In such a case the one who cultivated the land is reimbursed for his work according to some agreement. There is no law for such a claim, but it has become the custom in many places.

A few miles beyond the confluence of the Ohio and the Mississippi there are a considerable number of islands that are being settled and must be wonderfully fertile. Among them is one called Wolf Island, about one mile square, that belongs to Mr. James Hunter. In a book which contains directions for travelers on the Mississippi, printed in Pittsburg, is the following curious statement: "Mr. James Hunter, the only man that I have known that has the pleasure of being called a professional gambler, is the only one who lives on Wolf Island." He carries on a lucrative trade in hogs, cows, chickens, milk, etc., which he sells to the boats that ply the river.

The small town of Memphis, in the state of Tennessee, is on the left bank of the river on one of the few hills along the swampy banks. There are not many places on the Mississippi so lovely and majestic. At that spot the river looks like a beautiful lake, and an island that divides its abundant waters gives a picturesque aspect because of the trees which cover it. The town is on an elevated point about three hundred feet above the Wolf, which is one of the innumerable tributaries of the Mississippi. Memphis is a modern town that is growing rapidly and carries on trade in lumber, dried beef, cheeses, and other foodstuffs with the boats; as well as with the nearby state of Louisiana.

The constitution of Tennessee was written in Knoxville in 1796. The legislative power resides in a general assembly composed of a senate and a house of representatives. The members of these bodies are elected biennially the first Thursday and Friday of the month of August.

The number of representatives is sixty, which are apportioned according to the number of taxpayers of each county. The number of senators cannot be more than half nor less than a third of the number of representatives.

The executive power is given to the governor, who is elected at the same time as the senators and representatives by the people; his term runs for two years, and he cannot be reelected more than three times.

The sessions are convened in Nashville the third Monday of the following September, each two years. But the assembly can be called into session by the governor on suitable occasions. The right of suffrage is given to all free men twenty-one years of age who have any property in the county in which they vote, or to anyone other than a slave who has lived in the county for six months prior to the election. The judicial power is the same as that in other states.

Before leaving the state of Tennessee, I must speak of a religious ceremony that is observed in all the states, but the broad lands of Tennessee offer a vaster field for carrying it out. I wish to speak of the Camp Meetings, which have been described differently by English travelers, among them the celebrated Mrs. Trollope, whose work has been so popular in England I shall relate what I have seen and what I have been told by impartial and educated people so that the reader may form a precise opinion. This is one of the most imposing religious practices that have a remarkable influence on the manners and customs of the country, as will be noted from the faithful account that I am going to give of it.

Unless one has seen it, he cannot have any idea of the excitement and enthusiasm in a district of more than fifty miles radius with the approach of these religious gatherings, and unless one has been a witness, he cannot imagine how thoroughly the preachers have understood the effects that they have, and how well they have been able to take advantage of it. Let us suppose the spot and setting where for the past two years these have been held most frequently, and that by its silence offers truly interesting scenes—one of the most beautiful and fertile valleys in the mountains of Tennessee. The news circulates two or three months in advance. On the day indicated coaches, carts, chairs, people on horseback, countless on foot, wagons with provisions of bedding, camp tents and utensils, necessary for a week's stay begin to arrive. Those who have seen our fairs of San Juan de los Lagos, Chalma and Guadalupe in our Mexican republic can have some sort of hazy idea of these numerous assemblies. In order to provide themselves with the necessary water, the people scatter out among the somber forests and dark woods of Tennessee, on the banks of one of those streams that wind among the trees.

"Attending this religious assembly are the rich, the ambitious," Mr. Flint goes on,

> because public opinion, all powerful in that country, dictates it. They also go there to extend their influence, or so that their failure to attend may not reduce it. Aspirants for public office attend also to gain followers and popularity. Many are there out of curiosity, and there are also those who go for the fun of it. Youth and beauty are also mysterious motives which it is wise not to examine too closely. Then there are children, whose curious eyes take in with remarkable speed everything that surrounds them, middle-aged men, fathers and mothers of families, whose way of life is already settled, waiting in holy expectation to hear the divine word, and finally the old people of both sexes with their white hair, with the thought of the eternity that they are approaching. These types of persons make up these congregations that count their numbers in the thousands.
>
> A swarm of preachers, who under diverse denominations explain the gospel, hasten to show off their eloquence, their learning and their piety to the congregation. Young preachers who in the vigor of their age, aided by sonorous and powerful voices, struggled to shine. Others who have proclaimed the gospel as pilgrims of the cross from the most remote areas of the north to the shores of the Gulf of Mexico, ready to offer words that express profound feelings, the fruits of their experience garnered in their long and painful journeys, exercising for fifty years their ministry, whose trembling accents and appearance produce a greater impression than their words, announce that for the last time they are directing their terrible exhortations to mortals. Such are the ministers who occupy the attention of the immense audience.
>
> A line of campaign tents is set up on the banks of the streams, and the religious city is raised in a few hours among the trees. A multitude of lamps and torches hung in the branches cause a magic effect amidst that somber rural setting. The state of the most brilliant theater of Europe is a feeble painting beside this wondrous spectacle. In this setting those attending, among the sweetest transports of social feeling, added to the general enthusiasm of the expectation, go from one tent to another to exchange greetings and embraces of apostolic congratulations and to speak of the solemn occasion that brings them together. They have tea and supper, and by this time the peaceful rays of the moon are beginning to cut through the branches of the trees.
>
> It should be noted that the time is always calculated for when there will be a moon to enhance the majesty of these solemn occasions. A clear sky permits one to see a few stars that shine feebly.

All this together produces a natural atmosphere that is worthy of the grandeur of the Creator.

A venerable old man, dressed with elegant simplicity, mounts to the pulpit, cleans his dust-covered spectacles, and in a voice that expresses the emotion of his soul intones the hymn so that the entire congregation can repeat it, and so that all voices are joined with his. We would consider sad indeed the heart that did not beat violently as it comes to this song similar to the "sound of many waters" whose echo is sent back by the nearby mountains and forests. Such are the scenes, the associations, and such the influence of things eternal upon a nature that is so impressionable and so constituted as is ours that a small effort is sufficient in a matter such as religion to fill the heart and the eyes.

The honored speaker talks of God, of Eternity, of the final judgment, and of everything that can cause a strong impression. He speaks of his experiences, his works, his travels, his persecutions and good receptions, and of all that he has seen in hope, in peace, in triumph, in the fruit of his predecessors. When he talks of the short space that is left to him of life, he says that he regrets it only "because he will not in the silence of death be able to proclaim the benefits and goodness of his crucified Redeemer."

One does not have to be an accomplished orator to produce in those surroundings profound religious feelings. Nor should it be a cause for wonder that when the preacher pauses a few times to dry his eyes his whole audience dissolves into tears and breaks into demonstrations of penitence. Nor should it cause surprise that many whose pride persuades them of their superiority to the common mass of society and of a noble lack of sensitivity to such objects, should be dragged in spite of themselves towards that general feeling, that they should become women and children in their turn, and that although they have come to be amused, they should acknowledge repentance.

In spite of all that has been said to expose to laughter and public ridicule these spectacles that are so common in our parts, it cannot be denied that when everything is considered their influence is salutary, and the general result of their practice upon social interests is good. It will be a long time, if the day ever comes, when the ministry will be supported by the community. Instead of this, nothing is more fitting to make up for the lack of influence that results from the constant duties of the established ministers than recourse to this sort of simultaneous explosion of religious feelings that shake the moral world and purify its atmosphere until the accumulated seeds of moral sickness demand a new purification.

Whatever may be the cause, it is evident that these religious spectacles have brought about a noticeable improvement in the customs, manners, ways and habits of the people in the states of Tennessee, Mississippi, Missouri, Kentucky, Ohio, Indiana, and Illinois. In many places taverns and gambling halls have decreased in number or disappeared, and those who formerly frequented these places go to religious assemblies. The Methodists have also brought great and incalculable benefits to the way of life.

The picture which I have just presented, taken from a work by Mr. Flint, one of the best educated of Americans and one worthy of esteem because of his brilliant qualities, gives an exact idea of what goes on in these gatherings. Those of the Methodists in the eastern states are almost the same, and perhaps I shall have occasion to speak of them.

Compare this religious festival with those that we have in the republic, which are more or less like those of Spain and all of Italy, an hour or two in the temple, where the people take very little part in the religious feelings that should occupy them in those circumstances. The pomp of our Catholic worship, so imposing and from which one could take so much good in the improvement of moral character, loses all its effect because of the absolute lack of communication between the priesthood and the people. The mass is said in Latin in a low voice, hurriedly and according to formula; the preaching generally speaking is a weaving of words without coherence, without conscience and without divine comfort. The rest of the day, after the ceremonies, the lower classes eat and drink; those of the upper class play and dance. Look at our religious festivals. And what shall we say of the Indians in Chalma, in Guadalupe and in other shrines. Ah! The pen falls from the hand in order not to expose to the civilized world a horde of idolaters who come to deliver into the hands of lazy friars the fruits of their year's work to enrich them, while they, their women and children have no clothing, not even a bed. And the Spaniards, our fathers, have dared call this religion!!!

On June 27 we arrived at Shippingport, a small town a mile from Louisville. At this point we took coaches which were ready, and they took us to Louisville. During the course of our sailing we had lived in an agreeable society. Some ladies played the harpsichord, others the guitar, and they sang very charmingly and without having to be begged.

There was tea or coffee early in the morning, a good breakfast nine o'clock, lunch at noon, dinner at four, and tea or supper in the evening. In this way there was a very short interval from one meal to the next, in addition to the serving of beer, champagne, cider, etc. On these trips, according to the observation of M. Fare one meets on the same boat gentlemen, merchants, workers, congressmen and legislators, captains, generals and judges, all seated around one table in a truly republican simplicity. One does not note uncouthness in the conduct of the most humble person of those at the table, and in truth the refinement of their manners is remarkable that is when compared with people of the same class in France or England.

What is true is that when a worker finds himself in this count with a certain importance in the social scale, he makes an effort show himself worthy of being in the same society and at the same table with rich people and those of first rank. It is true that the upper classes lose something of their refinement by their continued contact with less polished people, but the latter gain a great deal at the same time. All are well dressed, and in the United States there are no ragged people.

Louisville is located on the left bank of the Ohio, in the state of Kentucky. The opposite bank belongs to Indiana. The city has probably twelve thousand inhabitants and is growing considerably although not to the same extent as Cincinnati and New Orleans. Its principal north-south street must be about one mile long, and it has only four streets in this direction. It is the depot for many foreign goods that are imported to the interior through that city; it also serves as a port for exporting flour from wheat, barley and other grains as well as corn meal.

From Louisville I wrote to Mr. McClure asking him about a young Indian boy that I had entrusted to his care when he was Mexico and I was governor of the state in 1828. Mr. McClure was in charge of the educational establishment that Mr. Owen found in New Harmony, Indiana, about thirty leagues from Louisville. I shall speak of Mr. McClure and of the reason that I had for delivering to him the boy to whom I gave the name of Toribio Zavala.

Mr. Owen, so well known in literary circles for his vast knowledge, his eloquence and the singularity of his doctrines, formed the project of starting in the United States his system of instruction under Mr. McClure. It was a practical school of crafts, trades, reading and writing, the object of which was to be to occupy the boys in work that would give them enough to support themselves. Mr. Poinsett, United States minister to Mexico, introduced me to Mr. Owen and Mr. McClure when I was governor of the state of Mexico, and I confess that I was much taken by the project of those two philosophers. Later we shall see how their establishment was dissolved.

In the same year they presented to me an Indian boy from the town of Zempoala in Mexico about eight years old, more or less, who, as I was told by the schoolmaster who brought him to my house, was an orphan that he had taken in and whose prodigious memory he had developed. I examined him in the presence of a few people asking him several questions on geography, astronomy, spelling, versification and grammar, religion and morals, to all of which the boy answered with ease and without embarrassment. He had given him the name of Toribio Pauper because of his poverty, and I substituted my own family name. Thinking that the young fellow could have a better career in Mr. McClure's establishment, I turned the boy over to him, paying only for the expenses of the trip to New Harmony. I found out later that the establishment was dissolved and that my Zempoala lad had already found a way to make a living in the country.

In the state of Indiana the executive power resides in a governor who is elected by the people every three years and can be reelected one time. The lieutenant governor is elected at the same time; he presides over the senate, and exercises the duties of the governor in his absence.

There is a senate and a house of representatives. The members of the first are elected every three years; those of the second each year. The number of representatives cannot be less than thirty-six nor more than one hundred. This arrangement is based on the number of white males twenty-one years of age. The number of senators in the same proportion cannot be less than one third nor more than one half the number of representatives.

These and a third of the members of the senate are elected annually the first Monday in August. The governor and the lieutenant governor are elected every three years on the same day.

The legislature convenes in Indianapolis the first Monday in December.

The right of suffrage is granted to every citizen twenty-one years of age who has resided in the state for one year.

The judicial power is administered by a supreme court of justice and circuit courts. The supreme court consists of three judges, and the circuit courts of one presiding judge and two associates. All the judges serve for a term of seven years. The governor names those of the supreme court with the consent of the senate. The presiding judges of the circuit courts are named by the house of representatives and the associates by the people.

In Louisville there is a small theater where, it is curious to note, they have separate entrances and seats for the women who are not received into society. When I passed through this city, the famous actress Mrs. Drake was playing; she is one of the best comediennes in the United States and can hold her own in the theaters of Europe.

Besides Louisville, there are two other important cities in the state of Kentucky; they are Lexington and Frankfort. The second one is the capital of the state. Both are beautiful towns according to what I have been told by several persons.

The state of Kentucky was the favorite land of several tribes of Indians that had set it aside for hunting. It is said that in the remote forests where they are at the present time on the other side of the Missouri they sigh for their ancient lands and the graves of their forefathers and have songs about their migration. Indeed, few states offer the appearance of abundant fertility as does Kentucky. Its beautiful forests covered with sturdy trees, oaks, sugar maples, sycamores, firs, chestnuts, etc., delight the eye of the traveler. Its products are wheat, tobacco, corn, barley and other valuable crops. Its people are notable for their height and large build, as well as for the beauty and regularity of their proportions.

In 1790 Kentucky separated from the state of Virginia, of which it was a part, and the constitution that was adopted then lasted until 1799, when it was replaced by the one now in force. Its legislative power consists of two houses, that of the representatives and the senate. The representatives are elected annually, and every four years they adjust the number according to the number of electors in each county. The present number is one hundred, which is the maximum, and it cannot go below fifty-eight. Senators are elected every year, one quarter at a time. The present number is thirty-eight, the maximum, and twenty-four is the minimum.

The executive power is in the hands of a governor elected for four years, who cannot be reelected within a period of seven years. A lieutenant governor is elected at the same time, and his duties are to preside over the senate and act in the absence of the governor.

The representatives and a fourth of the senators are elected annually by the people the first Monday in August. The governor and lieutenant governor are elected likewise by the people on the same day every four years and take office on the fourth Tuesday of the same month. Voting is open for three days, and it is done by voice vote and not by written ballot. The sessions are convened annually in Frankfort on the first Monday in December.

The constitution grants the right of suffrage to all male citizens (with the exception of colored people) who have reached the age of twenty-one and have resided in the state for two years.

The judicial power is administered by a supreme court of justice called the appellate court, and other lesser tribunals or courts that the assembly establishes. The judges and justices of the peace serve as long as they are on good behavior.

To the southwest are the states of Indiana and Illinois and the territory of Missouri.* The Mississippi River which runs along these states has on its banks cities that carry on trade with our territory of New Mexico, and from St. Louis numerous caravans leave for as far away as Santa Fe and California. Before many years those vast lands will be populated by strangers in search of a better climate and vacant lands to set up new establishments, and then one will see descending the Rio Grande travelers who will have come by the St. Lawrence, through New York or along the Mississippi and have made across the country a journey of six thousand or eight thousand miles. While the states to the south in the Mexican republic are occupied with civil wars and domestic quarrels, those of the north, dedicated to trade, agriculture and navigation, will give examples of morality and useful work to their quarrelsome brothers who will be fighting for power and supremacy.

On June 27 we continued our journey to Cincinnati on a smaller steamboat the *B. Franklin* that was very comfortable. We paid five dollars per person and sailed for thirty hours. We arrived in Cincinnati as the people were celebrating the arrival of General Jackson, president of the United States. It is easy to imagine that there were no battalions in line, nor artillery, nor armed people, nor priests, bishops or canons who were coming ceremonially to receive the chief of the government of the Union. There was none of that. But what one did see was a numerous crowd of people running along the banks of the river to receive and to see their first citizen, the honorable old man who had liberated New Orleans and given Florida to the United States and who today was guiding the destinies of the country with prudence, care and purity of intentions. There was music with banners, flags, shouts and cries of joy. Everything was natural and spontaneous. It was more like the fiestas in our towns when people are celebrating some saint than those ceremonies set up on days of homage in which one does not see in people's faces any vestige of true interest or a feeling of sympathy. Jackson was received with enthusiasm, especially by the workers, laborers and craftsmen.

The next day General Mejía and I went to visit the patriarch president. I had for him a letter of recommendation from Mr. Butler, chargé of business affairs from the United States to our government, and Señor Mejía had known him since the time that he was in Washington as secretary to the Mexican legation. The honorable elderly man was staying in a modestly furnished house and was seated in an armchair and surrounded by twenty-five or thirty persons who by their dress seemed to be workmen and craftsmen, thus making for him the simplest court in the world. He appeared to be one of those ancient heroes of Homer, who after having performed great deeds in war had retired to live among their fellow citizens whom they governed as children. The general received us cordially and asked us about his friend General Guerrero. He regretted his fate and had no doubt that the people's cause which he was defending would have a complete triumph.

Cincinnati is a city of twenty-five thousand inhabitants situated on the banks of the Ohio River in the state of the same name. It is not threatened by the waters of the river like New Orleans; its elevated position protects it even from those periodic overflows that cause so much disaster in towns that are not so elevated. Before the introduction of the steamboat twenty years ago Cincinnati had at the most six thousand inhabitants, and ten years before that ten or twelve houses. Its rapid growth has been due to the ease of communication, the fertility of the soil and the numbers of immigrants that come from Europe and even from the eastern states. Many colonists who came and established themselves in Massachusetts, Vermont, Maine and New England, generally, after having cleared and cultivated the land, built new homes and set up valuable establishments, put their real and personal property up for sale, weary, as they say, of hearing for so many years the barking of the neighbor's dog and the village bell. With their families and no belongings they came to establish new homes in the western states. Some come to Arkansas, others to Missouri, Ohio, Indiana, Illinois, and finally today many are going to Texas, New Mexico, and even Chihuahua. The places that they are leaving are filled by new immigrants from Europe. In this manner North America and following that the Mexican republic are enriched by the crafts, industry and elements of European civilization, while that part of the Old World is relieved of a part of its population that cannot maintain its land because the aristocracy needs gardens, woods, meadows and huge terrain from which to reap large rentals. In other places such as Switzerland and Wurtemberg it is because there is not sufficient land for the population.

Cincinnati is surrounded by beautiful hills covered with trees that in the summer offer the most picturesque scenes. The view of the city from the river, and that of the river and nearby banks from the elevated hill where the city is, are likewise pleasing and varied. There are eighteen churches, of which two are Episcopal, one a Roman Catholic cathedral, one a synagogue, another Unitarian, another Universalist, another Lutheran, Reformed Quaker, and the others are Presbyterian, Methodist, and Anabaptist. Many houses are beautiful with the first story of granite and white marble and the rest of brick. Generally they are small compared to our houses in Mexico, but they have all possible conveniences. The streets are not as clean as should be expected in a city founded on the slope of a hill on the banks of a great river. The lack of underground pipes and sewers causes the accumulation of filthy materials and the formation of mudholes, which are made even worse by the hogs. Food is very cheap as can be seen from the list made up by Mr. Bullock whom we knew in Mexico. Forty-five cents for a turkey, fifty cents for a roast pig, ten cents a pound for beef and three cents for a pound of pork. Other articles cost proportionately.

In Cincinnati there are cotton and woolen factories, as there are installations for the manufacture of articles of lead which is brought in in great quantities from the state of Illinois. But the prime elements of its amazing social progress and growth in population are to be found in the fertility, the ease of communication with the other states, and the form of government which makes it easy for a man to develop all his intellectual and material faculties. What would Cincinnati be without the constitutional provision which permits the free exercise of all forms of worship?

Mrs. Trollope, when she speaks of this prodigious multiplication and increase of inhabitants, wealth and prosperity of Cincinnati, says that it cannot be otherwise in a country where idleness is not welcome, and where one who does not work does not eat. "During my stay in this city," says this lady,

> or in its environs, which was close to two years, I never saw a beggar, nor even a man who although he had considerable wealth did not work actively to increase it. Like bees they are ever eagerly in search of that Hybla honey called money. Neither fine arts, nor the sciences, nor the attractions of pleasures can separate them from their labors. This singleness of purpose, favored by the spirit of enterprise, together with sharpness and lack of ethics when it is a matter of self-interest, can obtain the object under consideration with advantage.
>
> I have read much [she continues] about *the few and simple necessities of man,* and until now I had given a certain indulgent acquiescence to those who feel that each new necessity is a new enemy. Those who give themselves over to reasoning of this nature in their comfortable boudoirs of London or Paris know little about the subject. If it were food that nourishes a man, all that he would need, the faculties of a pig would be sufficient for him. But if we analyze the hour of pleasure, we will find that it is produced by pleasant sensations, occasioned by a thousand delicate impressions on as many nerves. When these nerves are inactive because they have never been touched, exterior objects are less important because they are perceived less. But when the whole machine of the human body is fully active, when each sense gives to the brain testimony of its impressions of pleasure or of pain, then each object that is presented to our senses comes to be a cause of wretchedness or of happiness. Let people who are made like that carefully avoid traveling in the United States; or if they do, let them not remain longer than is necessary to deposit in the memory those images that by force of contrast can appear pleasant to them in the future.
>
> Look and pass by and then we shall reason concerning them.

The traveler continues, as she gives a very unflattering description of the manners and civility of the people of the western states, with such acrimony that she seems to have set out to hold up to ridicule the industrious colonists and their beautiful daughters, and to paint a melancholy picture of the whole country, with the purpose of discouraging her fellow countrymen and other Europeans from emigrating to those parts. But, is it fair to compare London with Cincinnati, Liverpool with New Orleans, Birmingham with Pittsburgh, in brief England with the United States? The strangest thing is that in order to measure the civilization of Cincinnati one should speak of the society of London and Paris. It is not surprising thus to find the Catholic cathedral small and insignificant when compared with Notre Dame of Paris, and the same with the Protestant church when compared with St. Paul's of London.

There is no doubt that generally speaking the people of the United States are self-centered, uncommunicative and distrustful. In addition they have a certain harshness in their dealings that makes their society unpleasant when one has not established relations in the country. It has often happened with me that I have traveled in the same coach, on the same boat with Americans without speaking a single word during the trip. Business people who have dedicated their whole lives to improving their lot with work, accustomed to seeing in all dealings of human life nothing more than the exchange of one product for another or for money, may be said not to make a single move or to come to any decision that does not have as its object pecuniary advancement. They make no move to get into conversation with a man whom they do not know, and they even avoid it unless their penetrating eye perceives that they can gain some advantage from knowing him, or at least that it will not be to their disadvantage.

On the other hand, one may be sure that there are no more moral people than those of the United States of the North. Constant application to work makes men virtuous or independent, but at the same time proud and distrustful. A shoemaker, a tailor, a blacksmith who sets himself up in one of those new towns with a capital of twenty-five dollars, rents a wooden room and buys the raw materials of his trade at the end of ten years of work and rigorous economy has a house, a garden, and his well-equipped workshop. Such a man (and there are tens of thousands of these in the United States) fears that a loafer will come along and swindle him out of the fruits of his labor, or that a man without a conscience will seduce his daughter or his wife, and as a consequence he holds back from close communication with any person that is not very well known to him.

One can imagine that this excessive precaution leads naturally to extreme incivility, and indeed, the traveler who arrives in that country without connections lives in isolation in the midst of human kind. What a difference between these people and those of Mexico! We are essentially outgoing; it seems that we are impelled to become involved with all those about us, of whatever class and condition they may be. Our forefathers the Spaniards did not hand down to us that harsh and haughty character that they made us feel so strongly under their domination. I do not know whether or not in our extreme amiability there is a touch of servility or of the habit of passive obedience. I am inclined to suspect there is because we are not always sincere in our flattery or in our compliments, and we have a saying that "one kisses hands that he would like to see burned."

"I visited one house," says Mrs. Trollope,

that attracted my attention because of its solitary and rustic location, and interested me because of the dependence of the family upon their own resources. It was a cultivated spot in the midst of the forest. The house was built upon an elevated hill so steep that they needed a long set of steps to get to the frontier style front door, while the back opened out upon a large patio on the same level.

At the foot of this steep rise was a waterfall of clear water that ran into a pond formed in front of the dwelling. At one side there was a plot planted in corn, and on the other a corral for hogs, chickens, cows, etc. There was also near the house a small garden planted with potatoes, a few apple and peach trees. The house was made of logs and consisted of two rooms besides a small kitchen. The two rooms were well furnished with good beds, chairs, wardrobes, etc. The farmer's wife and a young girl who seemed to be her sister were spinning, and three boys were playing about outside. The woman told me that they spun and wove all that they needed in the home made of cotton and wool, and they knit their stockings. The husband, although he was not a shoemaker by profession, made the shoes. In the home they made soap, candles, and even sugar, taken from a sugar tree that they called the maple tree, which is found in those forests. "The only thing that we need money for," she said, "*is for tea, coffee and whiskey, and we provide that easily by sending each week to the market a bar of butter and some chickens.*" They did not use wheat, and from the corn which they harvested from their planting they made their bread and several kinds of pastries; they used it also for the animals in the winter. The women did not seem healthy, and they said that they had had intermittent fevers, but that they were better. The mother seemed satisfied and proud of her independent state, although she said in a somber tone: "It is very rare that we see people, and my greatest pleasure is the hope of seeing the sun rise and set a hundred times without seeing any other human being besides those of the family."

I believe that this minute description deserves the attention of the readers because there are a great many like this family in the woods and forests of Indiana, Tennessee, Ohio, Illinois, Missouri, and other states. They are to be found also in our Mexican republic, although they are generally poor Indians who have no other dwelling than a straw hut, for a bed the ground and a petate or straw mat, a tortilla, salt and chili for food, and for clothing a piece of old rag around the body. What a difference!

I am of the same opinion as Mrs. Trollope that this manner of living is a little savage and not natural. That solitude—that isolation from the rest of mankind, that eternal silence of the forests in which they live—does not seem to befit the noble attributes of man. They never hear the sound of a bell that unites mortals in places set aside for prayer, where men find the goodwill of their brothers; there is no consecrated cemetery to receive their remains when they die; no canticles of religion come to breathe their sweet breath in a last farewell over their tomb; the husband, the father or the son opens with his hands the grave that will cover them forever beside a tree near the house; they themselves bury the body, and the sound of the wind as it moves in the branches of the trees is their only requiem.

Upon our arrival in Cincinnati there was much talk in the public papers and in society of the famous philosopher Miss Wright, whose vehement eloquence and seductive doctrines in a person of her seat, set forth in assemblies where were gathered all who could get into the halls and theaters in which she gave her lectures, attracted the attention of the Americans. This lady received an outstanding education in England and let her talents shine in many notable gatherings.

She had the farfetched idea of becoming the head of a sect; since there was no revelation in her system, she did not follow the direction of Saints Teresa and Agreda, but she did plunge into the philosophical doctrines of Rousseau and of Owen. She preached the absolute equality of classes and conditions, religious scepticism, voluntary divorce and other similar things. If there were anyone who doubted our spirit of tolerance in the United States of the North, Mr. Owen's establishments and Miss Wright's lectures would be enough to convince the least disposed to believe it. This apostle of philosophism was listened to by all classes of society in all the cities in which she saw fit to present herself to the public. She left the United States in 1829 without having made any converts.

Among the notable things in the domestic society of the United States, especially in the interior, should be listed the false modesty that degenerates into hypocrisy in conversation. A person who at the table might ask for *a chicken leg* would offend the *chaste and virtuous* ears of the ladies, and anyone who was so imprudent as to put forth the profane words of lady's chemise, shift, underskirt, petticoat, or corset would be held in very low esteem in society. These scruples remind me of those of our nuns who find themselves embarrassed to pronounce certain words. It is impossible, for example, to persuade an American woman to go out on the street when she is pregnant, unless it be at night.

The reader will not be averse to hearing the story of the memorable literary-philosophical-religious challenge given by Mr. Owen in Cincinnati the year before my arrival in that city. The object was to provoke a debate with all who might wish, setting forth as a conclusion that *there was no true religion,* and that all of them were based on imposture and deceit. Mr. Owen had circulated his challenge everywhere for more than a year. The preacher Alexander Campbell, a Presbyterian, had publicly accepted it with the same solemnity. The appointed day was the second Monday of May in 1829, and indeed a Methodist church was readied for the noisy discussion. The building was filled with people of both sexes, seated on opposite sides.

Both debaters spoke with eloquence, decorum and mutual and fitting respect. After the discussion, Mr. Campbell asked the audience to be seated. Then he addressed them and said: "Those who profess the Christian religion, of whatever denomination they may be, stand up."

Nine out of ten stood up, and with that he declared the triumph of his cause. Mr. Owen protested saying that many people did not make known their opinion because they feared that credulous people would not buy their goods and would cut off trade with them. Thus ended the famous debate, which is another proof of the philosophical tolerance of the United States in one of the least civilized places of that republic.

This is the same Mr. Owen who founded the school of *mental independence* of New Harmony. He bought the establishment and lands from some fellow members who under the supervision of Mr. Rapp had constructed buildings and cultivated more than ten thousand acres of land on the banks of the Wabash River, one of the tributaries of the Ohio. Mr. Robert Owen put more than two hundred thousand dollars into this enterprise.

At the beginning of his establishment in 1824 he aroused great interest in the United States. Many distinguished people of all classes of society wrote to him asking for information concerning the rules, method, principles and objectives of the founder, indicating a desire to join his society. A year later Mr. Owen left for Europe, leaving his two sons and Mr. McClure in charge of the college.

In 1826 the society had about a thousand members who lived under a regimen of perfect equality and had to eat at one table. A respectable traveler says that Mr. Owen showed him the complete establishment and relates things worthy of knowing. At night a concert was given in a large hall in which all the members of the establishment were gathered. The music was perfectly executed. In the intermissions some piece of William Shakespeare or some other poet was recited, and then there were dances. In the daytime some exercised themselvese at fencing, others were engaged in making shoes and chairs, others in blacksmithing, tailoring and other mechanical trades. Most off the young women were busy making straw hats.

On Sunday morning all the members met together, and Mr. Owen, pastor of this philosophical church, delivered a discourse on the advantages of the society. In the visits that he had with the ladies he found one that was playing the piano with great perfection. After a little while a man came in and told her that it was her turn to milk the cows for the community.

The doctrines of the society were: that it is absurd to promise conjugal love for a lifetime; that children should not be an impediment to separation, and that they should belong to the community after the age of two years; that the society endorsed no religion, leaving each member to maintain his own belief; that all were equal, etc. Mr. Owen was so infatuated with his system that he seriously thought that he could establish it throughout the world. I remember having read the proposal that he made to Mr. Poinsett, calling him to be the reviver of the New World on those principles, while he (Mr. Owen) returned to Europe to busy himself in converting the Old World, in order to cut off *at the root all crime, abolish all punishment, equalize needs and desires, and avoid all dissension.* He was so thoroughly convinced concerning his system that it never occurred to him that anyone could doubt it.

Already by 1827 discontent had appeared in the community. Many people, especially the women, did not adjust to absolute equality and avoided contact with the tatterdemalions or ragged ones. The major charge brought against Mr. Owen was that he had from the beginning taken into the society without any distinction people of all classes, without examining their character, their mode of life, their previous education, qualities, etc., consequently producing a mixture *so heterogenous that assimilation was impossible.* I am going to extract a few paragraphs from the famous declaration of political independence, or as he called it *mental independence,* proclaimed by Mr. Owen on June 4, 1826.

> My friends, we have before us a noble objective that should be won by one party or another in this or in some other country. It is a matter of nothing less than the destruction of the triple cause which deprives man of his mental liberty, compels him to commit crime and to suffer all the woes that that crime brings with it. Permit me now to ask you whether you are inclined to imitate the example of your forefathers and wish to run the risks to which they were exposed. Are you disposed to carry out a mental revolution as superior in its benefits and results to the first revolution in this country as the mental powers of man exceed his physical powers?
>
> If you are so disposed, with the greatest satisfaction I will join you in this arduous undertaking, the latest and boldest which mortals in the irrational state in which they found themselves have dared to carry out.
>
> But, my friends, knowing as I do the immeasurable magnitude of the benefits that this mental revolution must bring and secure per-

manently for the human race of future ages, I judge the continued stay here for a little longer of a few individuals as a thing worthy of little consideration in comparison with the goal that we propose. Therefore, since I cannot know the present disposition of your souls, and since on the other hand the prolongation of my life at the age which I now have is very uncertain, I have calmly and deliberately determined on this portentous and happy occasion to break completely what remains of the mental chain which for so many years has unfortunately afflicted our nature, and for this time human understanding shall stand in complete liberty.

As the fruits of forty years of experience, due to a very peculiar set of widely varying, extensive and unusual circumstances that are perhaps not to be found in any other man, during which period my understanding has been continually occupied with investigating the cause of every human suffering, whose knowledge has come to me from its true origin; I declare to you and to the whole world that man has until this moment been in all parts of the globe a slave to the most monstrous trinity that has ever been put together to cause ill to the physical and mental faculties of the human race.

I denounce to you as such: 1. Individual or private property. 2. The absurd and irrational religious systems. 3. Marriage as an individual property combined with one of these irrational systems of religion.

It is very difficult to say which of these great sources of all crime should be placed first or last because they are so intimately connected and consecrated together by time that they cannot be separated without being destroyed. Each one of them supports the other two.

This formidable trinity composed of ignorance, superstition and hypocrisy is the only demon or devil that has ever existed and is the eternal torment of the human race. It is calculated in all its consequences to produce the most frightful wretchedness to which nature is susceptible in the soul and in the body. The division of property among individuals has prepared the seeds, cultivated the increase and led to the maturity of all the evils of poverty and wealth that exist in a people at one and the same time. The industrious fellow undergoes privation, and the idler finds himself loaded with wealth that he does not deserve.

Religion or superstition, which is the same thing, for all religions are superstitious, have as their objective the destruction of reason and the rationalization of all the mental faculties of man and to make him the most abject slave by means of imaginary entities created solely by disordered imaginations. Superstition obliges him to believe and to say that he believes that there exists a Supreme Being who possesses all power, infinite goodness and infinite wisdom; that he has been able to make and has made all things; that evil and sufferings abound everywhere; that this Being who makes and produces all things is not the direct or indirect author of evil and suffering. Such is the foundation upon which all the mysteries of superstition are erected in the whole world. Its inconsistency and inconceivable madness have been such that they have occasioned continual wars and massacres throughout the world, have caused private divisions and have led to all imaginable evils. It is possible that superstitions have caused more than a third of the crimes and misfortunes of the human race.

The forms and rituals of matrimony, in the manner that up until now they have been celebrated and later maintained, point out that they were invented and introduced among people during the same period that property was divided among a few chiefs with superstition coming to their support, since this was the only device that they could put forth in order to authorize retaining their division of the public spoils and creating among themselves an aristocracy of wealth, power and doctrine.

As the fruit of the experience of a lifetime consecrated to the investigation of these important objectives, I declare to you without any fear because of a conviction as deep and as intimate as can exist in the human mind that this composite of ignorance and fraud is the only and the real cause of crime and of all the miseries that emanate from it and that are spread about in human society.

For forty years I have dedicated my heart and my soul, day after day without ceasing, to preparing the means and combining the circumstances that have enabled me to give the kiss of death to tyranny and despotism that for years without number have held human understanding bound with chains and fetters of mysterious forms from which no mortal has dared to undertake to liberate the unfortunate prisoners. The time had not yet come for the fulfillment of this great event until this very hour. Such has been the extraordinary course of events that the declaration of political independence in 1776 has produced this result, to wit: the declaration of mental independence of 1826, half a century after the first one. Rejoice with me, my friends because your mental independence is now as well assured as your political independence.

With the circumstances in which this mental revolution has been realized no human power can destroy or bring to naught what has already been done. This truth has passed from me beyond the possibility of any revocation, and has been received in your hearts; within a short time it will be heard throughout America, and from there it will pass to the north and to the south, to the east and to the west as far as the word of man is heard. And with the same swiftness with which it circulates human nature will give it acceptance and universal approval. Rejoice then once more with me, my friends, because this light is now placed upon the mountain; from there it will become ever greater day by day until it is seen, felt and understood throughout all the nations of the earth.

For the fulfillment of this great objective we are preparing the means by educating our children in useful and industrious habits, with natural and consequently rational ideas and points of view, with sincerity in all that they do, and lastly inspiring in them tender and affectionate feelings one for another—charity in all the meaning of this word for all their fellow beings.

By these means, uniting your separate interests, abandoning the use of money in your business transactions, adopting the exchange of the articles of your industry on the basis of work for equal work, providing that the surplus of your wealth be distributed among those who do not have the wherewithal to put them in a position to improve their lot and to acquire the same advantages, and finally by the abstention from spirituous liquors you will promote in a special manner the objective of all wise governments and of all men who are truly enlightened.

This prayer and its publication in some newspapers were sufficient to complete the dissolution of the society. The same thing happened in France with the St. Simonians who preached the same doctrines, although accompanied by more religious apparatus.

CHAPTER IV

Appearance of the people.—Constitution of Ohio.—Celebration of July 4.—Arrival in Wheeling.—Allegheny Mountains.—Pittsburg.—Journey to Lake Erie.—Buffalo. —Niagara Falls.—Chateaubriand.—Battlefield.—Departure from Niagara.—Queenston.—Fort Niagara.

For a Mexican who has never left his country, or who has not done so in a long time, the first impression as he arrives at any point in the United States or England is that of seeing all classes of people dressed. They say that when the Emperor Alexander visited London in 1814, he said to those about him that he found no common people in that capital. What a pleasant spectacle to the eye of the beholder is that of a society that announces by its appearance of decorum and decency the industry, the comforts and even the morality of a people! On the contrary, how unpleasant is the aspect of nudity and lack of cleanliness and what a sad idea a nation gives of the state of its civilization and of its morality when it is inhabited by such people! In a work on Spain that he published in Paris a certain M. Faurefour years ago put on the title page of the book an engraving of a student wearing a torn cloak and other rags, with a staff in his hand, begging alms for the love of God. This alone gave an idea of the object which most attracted the attention of the French traveler in the Pyrenean Peninsula.

If I were trying to produce a work that was a luxury item with engravings, I would have prepared immediately beautiful plates on which would be pictured steamboats, workmen leveling the land and laying planks of wood and iron to form roads, meadows bathed by streams, cities divided by navigable rivers, cities being born of the earth and dedicating themselves to improving it immediately, rooms filled with children of both sexes learning to read and to write, workers and craftsmen with plow or instrument in one hand and the newspaper in the other, six thousand temples of diverse cults in which man raises his vows to the Creator in accordance with the dictates of his heart, in short tranquility and abundance bringing happiness to fifteen million people. Such is the idea that 'I have of the United States of the

North and the impressions that I received from New Orleans to Cincinnati.

The constitution of the state of Ohio was drawn up in the town of Chillicothe in 1802. There are two chambers as in the others. The representatives are elected annually the second Tuesday in October, and the number is proportional to the white population of males above the age of twenty-one years, but should never exceed seventy-two members, nor fall below thirty-two. The senators are elected every two years in the same manner, with the number proportioned to half that of the other chamber.

There is a governor who exercises the executive power, elected by the people every two years, the second Tuesday in October. He begins his term the first Monday of the following December.

The capital is Columbus, where the general assembly of the state convenes the first Monday of December.

The right of suffrage is universal within the white class.

The judicial power rests in the supreme court of justice, in the Courts of Common Pleas of each county, and others that the legislative power may establish from time to time for the expediting of justice. The judges are elected by secret vote every seven years in a joint session of both houses. There are juries as in the other states.

On June 29, I embarked upon the steamer Magnolia that was leaving for Wheeling. On board the boat, the day of July 3 was designated for celebrating the anniversary of the independence of the United States because the fourth, which is the legal day, fell on Sunday, and it could not be celebrated then since that day was consecrated by religion for worshiping the creator, each man according to his sect. There were fifteen or twenty persons on board, certainly not a sufficient number to give an idea of what a great nation, infused on that solemn day with the noble feeling of its liberty, does in such august circumstances. I shall not speak then on this occasion of what happens on this day of general enthusiasm in the United States; I have only recalled this circumstance in order to indicate that even in the most isolated and remote places, the North Americans celebrate with religious and patriotic rejoicing the anniversary of the declaration of their independence, and I shall mention the toast that I gave on that day, which was as follows:

> Mexican citizens express their good wishes for liberty wherever they may be. On this solemn day dedicated to celebrating that of the United States of North America, I dare to join my own to those of free men who are celebrating the anniversary of their independence. Hear then my wishes: That providence maintain this people in its present institutions for many centuries, and that Mexico may imitate it successfully.

Señor Mejía spoke in the same vein, and the Americans joined their good wishes to ours.

On the afternoon of that day we arrived in Wheeling, a manufacturing city where they make fine and everyday crystal, in the state of Virginia, where passengers disembark to go to the states of Virginia, Pennsylvania, Maryland, New York, etc. Here I separated from Señor Mejía, who was to continue his journey to Washington across the Alleghenies. These mountains, which play a great role in the climatology of the United States, deserve special mention in this work.

From Wheeling there is a road that leads to the states of the East and the North, as I have said, passing through Little Washington, Laurel Hill, Brownsville, Hagerstown and Baltimore. From this latter city they had begun to build a railroad, which in 1830 was only thirteen miles long, and today in 1834 is about one hundred miles in length.

The Allegheny Mountains, which in some parts they call the Appalachians, are entirely separated from the general system of the Andes. At no point do they rise to more than 6,112 feet above sea level. Their principal ranges extend from the northeast to the southwest, from the St. Lawrence to the Alabama, and the Yarou Rivers. The eastern chain is known as the Blue Ridge Mountains. These extend from the state of Georgia to the northeast as far as the state of New York. A little farther north, to the west of the Hudson River, there is a small group of mountains known as the Catskills, which the North Americans point out to the travelers from Albany from the steamboats as a marvel for altitude. Farther on are the Green Mountains. The western chain is the Alleghenies, and they are known in the vicinity of Wheeling by the name of the Cumberland Mountains; they cross Tennessee, Virginia and a part of Pennsylvania. Beyond the Susquehanna River this range of mountains takes a more easterly direction and joins the chain of those in the state of Vermont.

There are several small rivers on the way to Wheeling, and a rather deep creek on the first day crosses the road thirty times, making necessary as many bridges among which there are some of great taste and elegance. The views of the mountains are enchanting for the variety of the trees, the fragrance of the flowers and aromatic herbs, broken rocks, valleys, landscapes, cultivated areas, country homes, cattle, plains, etc.

While Señor Mejía was taking this road, I continued my journey to Pittsburg, the manufacturing city of the states of the west. Pittsburg is located at the confluence of the Monongahela and Allegheny Rivers that form the Ohio. The coal smoke that covers the city night and day makes it a little sad. The great number of factories of porcelain and glass of all kinds, as well as every sort of instrument of iron, steel, lead and other metals in common use, place this city among the most progressive in the United States. Its location at the head of the Ohio River and at a point that puts it in a position to be in touch by water with any place in the world after a two-thousand-mile trip down the river offers a unique advantage of this sort. In Pittsburg ocean-going vessels are built and it seems as something out of a fairy tale to see such things being done at such a distance. Perhaps the day will come when our own Rio Grande of the North will see steamships coming down to carry the products of Chihuahua to London or Bordeaux.

When I passed through Pittsburg workmen were digging a canal to connect the Ohio River with Lake Erie, thus making it possible to go to New York by water, and to leave by the same means for the Mississippi, traveling along the Hudson, the Clinton Canal, Lake Erie, the Ohio Canal and the rivers as far as the Balize. This work was finished in 1833.

Another undertaking of greater importance, and one which General Bernardo figured would be worth twenty-five million dollars, was a proposed canal that would cross from the Chesapeake Bay at the lighthouse of Baltimore, following the Potomac that flows by Washington, and Pittsburg, crossing the Allegheny Mountains to the Ohio River. This canal would be 341 miles long, 60 feet wide and 6 feet deep. The general preference for the railroad has caused this great enterprise to be suspended for the present.

The city of Pittsburg is in the state of Pennsylvania; it has about thirty to thirty-five thousand inhabitants. There are Germans, English, French, Irish, Scots, in short all that wish to live by the fruits of their industry. If in these states they were to adopt a law like the one lately proposed by Señor Tornel in Mexico to prohibit foreigners from engaging in retail trade, never would one see such progress, such prosperity. What did Señor Tornel learn on his trip and his long stay in Baltimore and Philadelphia?

I left Pittsburg by stagecoach taking the Erie Road through the towns of Butler, Mercer, Meadville, all new, but all of them witnessing the spirit of life that animates their inhabitants. Always to be found are schools, newspapers, and three or four churches or chapels where they gather on Sunday to pay tribute to the Supreme Being with their worship. In Meadville there is also a college where they teach moral philosophy, physics, Greek and Latin grammar and the elements of mathematics. I arrived in Erie on July 8, and in that port we embarked on a steamer on the beautiful lake of the same name that receives its waters from several rivers and from Lakes Superior, Huron and Michigan.

The next day I arrived in Buffalo which is situated on the right bank of the famous Niagara River as it leaves Lake Erie to flow into Lake Ontario. I stopped at an inn called The Eagle, one of the most cheerful buildings that I have ever seen in my life, all of wood and capable of lodging two hundred persons with comfort. Buffalo is one of the prodigies of the United States, one of those cities that were born in this century and are already competing with the older ones because of their beauty and their trade. In 1814 it was completely reduced to ashes by the English, and today it has ten thousand inhabitants, five churches and more than two thousand houses, although almost all of them are of wood. According to general information that I have received and continue to receive 120,000 persons pass through Buffalo annually, and there is not a day on which there are not at least 1,000 travelers in the city. It is one of the principal trade centers of this small Mediterranean Sea called Erie, surrounded by new towns, arid the vehicle of communication between Canada, the states of the east, Europe, and the states and territories of the west which are called to play a great role within the next century.

I will copy what I wrote in my travel diary on Saturday, July 10, 1830:

> We left Buffalo at nine thirty in the morning, and we arrived, after an hour's travel at Black Rock, which is a town located on the right bank of the Niagara River. This river flows from Lake Erie to empty into Lake Ontario after having run thirty-five miles and having formed the most amazing falls that bears its name. Black Rock is opposite Waterloo, the English town that is on the other bank of the river. One leaves the coach in Black Rock and crosses the river on what they call a horse ferry because one or two horses move the oars by means of a machine. In Black Rock begins the famous canal of the state of New York which connects with the river of the north or the Hudson at the city of Albany.
>
> We continued our trip in stagecoaches which were waiting for us, traveling along the banks of the river through the beautiful plains of English Canada, Near Chippewa, which is a town two miles from Niagara Falls, is the field where the Americans and the English did battle in 1814. I went over these places with the book which gives a description of all these beautiful spots in my hand, and I felt an indescribable respect at the sight of the monuments erected to the memory of those who died in battle. The same thing happened to me in Mexico when I passed by the crosses and the Calderon bridge. In this small village near the Falls, a woman who had a shop in her tavern took out to show us two skulls of persons who had died in action there and which she kept very carefully.
>
> We arrived at the great cataract of Niagara at noon. One cannot conceive the surprise that this spectacle causes, a mighty river that dashes down from a height of 170 feet into an unknown depth. The force of the waters causes clouds to be formed from the vapor into which these waters are converted. A thick column rises up over the cataract; the noise is deafening; the gaze remains fixed involuntar-

ily for some time upon this phenomenon, this marvel of nature. The precipices which surround it; the movement of the waters that give vista and perspective and warn of the danger; the broken sides of the neighboring hills; the variety of trees such as chestnuts, cherries, acacias, firs, poplars, and the evergreen pines; in short the swift currents that before plunging into that abyss seem to stop on the rocks that they encounter, all produce sensations of wonder, pleasure, horror and melancholy. It seems that the soul feels itself oppressed by feelings that it cannot resist. The waters of the torrent smother all ideas in the imagination; it is a giant of a hundred arms that presses the mortal against its body with irresistible force. Such was the effect that the presence of Niagara had on me.

On the English side there is a good inn from which can be seen what is called Horseshoe Falls, and on the other side that they call the American side, is another inn; the falls are not as magnificent, nor is there as great a mass of water as on the English side. At this point the river is divided by an island called Goat Island, located right on the edge of the abyss of the cataract. Between this and the American side they have built a wooden bridge that trembles all over when walked upon. From this point the spectator sees the torrent that runs beneath his feet and plunges with indescribable swiftness into the unknown depths to continue its course then peacefully into Lake Ontario, which receives this mighty river, and afterwards it continues further down under the name of the St. Lawrence.

Many unfortunate things have happened at this cataract. Some persons have sought and found in its abyss a quick death; others have escaped. Well known is what happened to the famous Chateaubriand who was miraculously rescued when his horse, frightened by a snake, plunged toward the main cataract. Well known also is the beautiful description of Niagara at the end of his *Atala*.

All the banks of the Niagara River as far as Lake Ontario have been the theater of a deadly war in the years 1812, 1813, and 1814, between the Americans and the English. On the left bank of the river ten miles below the falls there is a column of granite one hundred feet high, erected on a hill in memory of the English General Brock, who died in an action against the American militia in October of 1812.

It is worthy of note that the English troops were all regulars commanded by war generals educated on the battlefields of Europe such were General Freeddale who was mortally wounded in the battle of Chippewa, General Drummond wounded likewise in another action that took place two weeks later in Bridgewater, and General Riall who was taken prisoner. The American generals Brown, Scott and Ripley showed themselves to be worthy of such enemies although they had never been in any war action. General Scott, who gave brilliant proofs of bravery and intelligence in action at Chippewa and at Bridgewater, was not long before the campaign a famous lawyer in the state of Virginia. The first action in which he took part was at Queenston, where General Brock of whom I have spoken died.

✦   The Niagara River and the lakes form a very weak barrier to prevent Canada from one day being a part of the United States of the North. Although that English colony has no reason to complain of its mother country in the matter of its political constitution, there are, nevertheless, some trade restrictions that are always an obstacle to progress. The capital of Upper Canada is York.

From Niagara I went to Queenston, an English town on the left bank of the river and on the shores of Lake Ontario. Opposite it is Lewiston on the American side, where there is an inn that is large and comfortable. I went up again to visit the falls on the side of Manchester. Although I may seem to repeat myself, I am going to copy what I wrote about the same places on Monday, July 12, 1830:

> There is a very beautiful inn, and the view of the falls from this side reveals it in all its perfection. The Americans have built a bridge over to Goat Island, an island that became theirs after the last war. It is wonderful to see how they have been able to tame the terrible current that plunges down from the rocks. Genius and desire for gain have united to perform miracles of the art. On the island there is an inn where they have set up a sort of museum, and various curious objects can be seen, such as fossils, minerals, animals, etc. Among those there is a dead swan perfectly preserved that was caught in the cataract in 1828. Everything is surprising and magnificent; to walk over the suspension bridge high above the falls gives one a feeling of horror.

All these places were uninhabited when M. de Chateaubriand made his journey among the savages in 1792.

> The sky is pure above my head, the waves are clear beneath my canoe which glides before a light breeze. To my left I see hills cut off sharply and flanked with rocks from which hang vines with blue and white flowers, festoons of wild roses, grasses of all kinds; to the right vast meadows. As the canoe advances, more and more new perspectives open up. Some times there are smiling and solitary valleys, at others hills bare and without vegetation. Here there is a forest of cypress trees that form shady porticos, farther on a grove of sugar maples where the sun penetrates as through a blond lace. Yes, primitive liberty, at last I have found you!

I travel like that bird that flies before me, that takes its course by chance and that is only worried about the selection of the tree in which it will build its dwelling. Here I am such as the Almighty has created me, sovereign over nature, carried in triumph upon the waters, while the inhabitants of the rivers accompany my course, the denizens of the air sing me their hymns, the beasts of the earth greet me, and the trees bow their heads as I pass by. Is it upon the forehead of the man of society or upon mine that is engraved the seal of our noble origin? Run, shut yourselves up in your cities; go subject yourselves to your strict laws; earn your bread by the sweat of your brow or devour the food of the poor. Kill because of an argument, to have one chief instead of another; doubt the existence of God or worship him under superstitious forms; for my part, I shall wander at will through these solitary places, in which my heart will beat freely, and my thoughts will run unshackled and unchained. I shall be as free as nature; I shall recognize no other sovereign than the one who gave light and existence to so many suns and who with one impulse of his arm caused so many worlds to rotate.

With an ineffable pleasure I read these pages when I was traveling through those same places then covered with towns, where civilization and the hand of man have not breathed the deadly breath of slavery or of superstition. I was leaving the anarchy of Mexico where I had seen myself so often exposed to being the victim of parties, and now wandered freely along the delightful banks of the Niagara, among the eternal forests of Canada, getting away as much as I could into those solitary places where as a man unknown in countries so remote, I gave myself over entirely to my meditations. Oh Niagara! With my eyes fixed upon your swift currents, they seemed to indicate that I was completely engrossed in the grandiose spectacle, I was seeing in you the most melancholy representation of our disastrous revolutions. I was reading in the succession of your waves the generations that hasten on to eternity, and in the cataracts that proceed to your abyss the strength of some men that impels others to succeed them in their places.

In Fort Niagara there is a detachment of American troops, and in Fort George English troops. Borders and fortresses are the only places where regular troops are seen in the United States. It goes without saying that they are well dressed and well fed. There are few desertions, while they are rather frequent among Canadian troops, or so I am told.

CHAPTER V

In Queenston I took passage on a steamboat called the *Alciope,* which although comfortable was not comparable to those of the Ohio and the Mississippi. The passage cost me ten dollars to Montreal, one of the largest arid richest cities of Canada. We traveled the day and the night of the thirteenth across Lake Ontario, and after having covered 150 miles we stopped in Kingston to take on firewood. From this town which is situated on the east bank of the lake they have begun the construction of a canal which they call the Rideau Canal, and which is to terminate in Montreal. The object is to facilitate the navigation of the St. Lawrence River below, which cannot be passed, at least not without considerable danger, because of the small cataracts that are encountered between this point and Montreal. The cost of this canal is reckoned at £500,000 ($2,500,000).

There is also another canal already begun in Upper Canada between Lakes Erie and Ontario to overcome the roughness of the Niagara River and to make possible communication by water between the two sides. This is the Welland Canal where there is a cut that approximates our outlet at Huehuetoca, although it is not so immense nor so deep. The cut is twenty-seven feet across. This canal must be about forty-five miles long. Our canal at Huehuetoca is probably ten miles long at the most; but the cut of Nochistongo is considerably longer. Here is the real beginning of the St. Lawrence River, which is famous for its width and its thousand islands.

Montreal, a city of 25,000 to 30,000 inhabitants, is located on the left bank of the St. Lawrence River, on a high bluff and surrounded by fertile hills that are well cultivated and that give a pretty view. There is a considerable going and coming of Indians, most of whom are savages that come to trade their beaver, nutria, buffalo, deer, panther and other skins and hides for foreign merchandise such as glass, crystal, clothing, brandy, powder, lead, etc. Most of the houses are built of brick and stones with square cut masonry and also granite. There are some monuments worthy of attention such as that erected to the memory of Admiral Nelson on which in bas relief the Nile is represented by a crocodile and the sea by well-designed boats.

Most of the people are Catholic, and there is a rather large cathedral in very bad taste, Gothic style, of limestone. The houses have their roofs covered with tin, which causes them to present a beautiful view from the hills when the sun or the moon shines upon them. The people are strangely dressed; they speak a mixed French which scarcely resembles the speech of Paris. Most of the merchants and large landowners are English. The inn in which I stayed, that was called Good Enough, has very good service, although more expensive than the inns of the United States.

There are several convents in Montreal, founded during the time when it belonged to the French. There has been no change in their establishments since the Government considers them only as companies or associations. The nuns go out on the street when they wish, but they generally keep their vows and serve the sick.

As travelers who have written on the United States have never failed to draw a parallel between the St. Lawrence and the Mississippi Rivers because of the visible and remarkable contrasts that are to be found between them, I think that I should follow the same example so that the reader may get some idea of the diverse manifestations of nature. The St. Lawrence is quite varied in its banks and presents diverse scenes. The Mississippi is uniform, the same and monotonous; the former has a swift and tumultuous stream; the latter runs majestically and does not appear to be carrying the immense volume of water that it discharges into the ocean; the former has pure crystalline ripples; the latter is turbulent and muddy; the former has its source in Lake Ontario, so great and majestic as it empties into the gulf of the same name; the latter is fed by mighty rivers that increase its volume; the former runs for three thousand miles; the latter does not exceed five hundred;* the St. Lawrence is neither increased nor decreased in volume; the Mississippi floods, rises and threatens with its overflow the towns, villages, and cities that are nourished by its waters. The St. Lawrence passes through many lakes; the Mississippi runs through the midst of forests; the first is great and beautiful; the second is somber and sublime; in short the St. Lawrence brings pleasant impressions to the imagination; the Mississippi oppresses it with its immensity.

In twenty-four hours of sailing on the St. Lawrence River in a steamboat we went from Montreal to Quebec, the capital of Lower Canada. We arrived at the hour when they were sounding retreat at the fort, and the military music produced a very pleasant feeling.

Quebec consists of the upper city and the lower city because it is erected on the hills that rise gradually in some places and suddenly in others, forming a wall on the river. The lower part is unhealthful, dirty, inhabited by poor people with wretched houses; the upper part does not have so many or such beautiful buildings as does Montreal, but it is not lacking in beauty and in houses that are comfortable and of good appearance. The cathedral is a formless mass, without architectural taste or form. The fortress, which is now being finished on Cape Diamond, is without doubt one of the most grandiose works of military art, both for its location and for its architecture. It must have cost the English government more than two million dollars. The Fields of Abraham is a plain that dominates the city, and it has been the theater of glorious actions, both in the war with France and in the war of independence. At different times the English General Wolfe and the American Colonel Montgomery died there, and their ashes were later transported to St. Paul's Church in New York. This whole plain is filled with the vestiges of war, and there are some monuments erected to the memory of the English leaders.

On my trip to Quebec I talked with Mr. Coveocy, a respectable elderly man of that city who was born in Boston. Few, very few, Americans hold Mr. Coveocy's opinions with regards to the future destiny of Canada. He thinks that within a period of time a part of the state of Vermont and even of Maine will unite with Canada in order, as he says, to complete their territory. I on the contrary indicated to him that I believed that all the English part of that area would be independent, or would form states in the American confederation in the course of time.

He spoke to me very enthusiastically of a M. Bailli, a reformer of the Catholic Church in Lower Canada in the years from 90 to 94 of the past century, who reduced the number of holidays by cutting them to six per year, not counting Sundays, which he accomplished with a great deal of difficulty and amid clamors of fanaticism. He brought to my attention that only the coasts were populated, as happens with new countries, where the colonists naturally seek the river banks and the shores of the sea.

As far as the addition of Upper Canada to the United States, I am going to transcribe here the reflections of an English traveler, who under the title of *Men and Manners in America,* has given a not very impartial description of the United States, although the force of truth often causes him to confess to its rapid progress and local advantages. "The legislative chambers were not meeting when I passed through Canada," says the traveler, and consequently I know little of the questions under consideration. However, I have some information from a M. Papineau, who represents with much decorum the role of the O'Connell of the colonies. The field is not vast, but he does what he can, and he enjoys the dignity of being the perpetual thorn stuck in the side of the governors. M. Papineau and his party show themeslves always unhappy with English domination. But, what more do they want? They pay no taxes. John Bull (the English people) spends his money with great liberality among the Canadians, as they themselves can see in the magnificent fortifications of Cape Diamond and the Rideau Canal: This latter should bring immense benefits to both provinces—benefits that the Canadians would never have had if left to their own devices.

What would they have then? At least Lower Canada would not join the United States, and it is very poor and destitute of means to be able to subsist by itself. Take away English capital from this colony, and there would remain only poverty and solitude.

With respect to Upper Canada, we see rapidly approaching the time of its union with the United States. All things tend to the consummation of this matter. The canals that put that long pipeline of lakes in communication with the Ohio and Hudson Rivers will accelerate the accomplishment of this. The workers of Upper Canada have easier trade with the markets of New York and New Orleans than with that of Quebec. The masses of the people are republican in their political ideas and anarchist in their morals. Let's admit it then—the loss for England does not count for that much. The eagle's wing is not diminished because one of its feathers falls out.

When I was in Quebec (July of 1830), the heat was much greater than I had experienced in Yucatan or Veracruz. The thermometer stood at 102° F., and never in my life have I felt more miserable. The heat lasts two months, and already in September one begins to feel the cold which increases considerably until the end of January when the country is all covered with snow and ice. The summer passes so quickly that it does not permit corn to mature, and consequently this precious grain is not planted in Canada. They have wheat, barley, rye, buckwheat from which they make delicious pancakes, and oats. The fruits are not good, although they do have cherries, mulberries of various types, apples and peaches.

There are two noteworthy falls near Quebec. One of them is Montmorency Falls, which although it is higher than that of Niagara did not give me the pleasant impression that the other one did, even though its appearance is more rustic. The quantity of water that falls from 148 feet is not a sixth of the other, but it makes more noise, no doubt because the vast receptacle does not have sufficient water to diminish the force of the falling mass. The other cascade is the *Chaudiére* or Cauldron, which has a hundred-foot perpendicular fall and produces the effect of causing the water to boil furiously and plunge into the St. Lawrence River.

The village of Loreto which is nearby offers, as in many of our very old towns, the melancholy sight of ruins. The last remains of a powerful tribe of Huron Indians live there. Brandy and gunpowder have done their work, and only two hundred persons are left of this people, noble and warlike in another day. They have adopted the religion and the language of their conquerors. There is a church in this town, and a priest who lives among his parishioners who love him. Christianity is the only benefit that the Indians have received from the whites. The latter have cheated, robbed, corrupted and ruined them in this world, and then they do them the favor of providing them with salvation in the next. The benefit is in truth sublime, but the poor Indians must mistrust a gift that comes from such people.

In the two provinces of Canada there are legislative chambers, and the laws receive their sanction from the governor who is named by the king of England. There are also certain laws of property and of special importance that require the approval of the government of His Britannic Majesty. Otherwise, there is freedom of the press, trial by jury, and the other same great social guarantees as in England. The French language is that of the public registers in Lower Canada, and the discussions are in this language.

I left Quebec and returned to Montreal, passing through the town of Sorel on the Richelieu River which has its source in Lake Champlain and empties into the St. Lawrence. This would be an excellent means of communication with the state of New York through Lake Champlain and Lake George, of which I shall speak later. I returned to Montreal and was there for only an hour.

In Montreal I crossed the river and set foot on land in a very beautiful place called La Prairie, where there is a convent of the Sisters of Charity, and I continued by stagecoach as far as St. Jean, a place located on the east bank of Lake Champlain. There I boarded the steamer *B. Franklin,* on which I again found the cleanliness and comforts of American vessels of this type. Since leaving Niagara I had been associated in making the trip to Canada with Mr. M. Evans, a merchant of New Orleans, and Laville de Beau, a landowner of Louisiana. In Fort Niagara we joined a friendly family from Pittsburg called Simpson and Dahra, and in this company we continued the pleasant crossing of Lake Champlain. After traveling thirty-four miles one comes to Black Island, beautiful, fertile and unhealthful, and three miles farther up again enters the territory of the United States, where a guard asks very courteously if one has any contraband material, and without further formality allows the travelers to proceed.

We passed through Plattsburgh, a town of considerable size in the state of New York which gave its name to a naval battle between the American and English fleets in 1814 when the Americans overcame the British, and ten thousand Englishmen had to retreat under the orders of General Provost, whose plan was nothing less than cutting the communications between New England and the rest of the United States.

After 142 miles of traveling on Lake Champlain, we landed in White-hall, which is on the western side of the lake, from where Lake George is scarcely more than the distance of one mile. On this isthmus are the remains of the old fortress called Ticonderoga, the theater of bloody war-fare, both when the French held Canada and later in the two wars between the English and the Americans. I visited these ruins where there is now nothing more than piles of stones and sand with some old walls.

Lake Champlain is in no place more than five miles wide. On the west side it has to the south the mountains of Vermont that are called the Green Mountains, among the highest of this cordillera. Between the two lakes there is a small town called Alexandria with a cascade that tumbles gradu-ally, something like fifty feet to form a brilliant spectacle. We ate there and took the steamer on Lake George, which is even more narrow than the other lake, deep, with clear transparent waters, and closed in on both sides by high rocks so that it appears to be a channel. All these mountains and forests are sparsely populated; from time to time one sees a few houses high up that inspire the desire to occupy them in men weary of the world and of busi-ness, who seek in vain the illusions of the country and of solitude after hav-ing uselessly pursued a happiness that ever escapes from their hands.

Few places indeed have inspired in me so burning a desire to retire to the country life as those delightful and romantic shores of the Niagara River and Lake George. What solitude so well accompanied by the beauties of nature! Cliffs, streams, crystalline and navigable waters, exquisite fish, magnificent vistas, even the ruins of Crown Point and Ticonderoga, every-thing inspires sublime, simple and natural ideas.

The lake ends at Caldwell. One cannot pass these places without remembering two terribly tragic events that took place in the vicinity of these lakes. In the war between the French and the English in 1759, at the capture of Quebec for the second time, Mr. Schoonhoven and seven Amer-icans were taken prisoners by a band of savages near Sandy Hill. Taken to a meadow they were made to sit down in a row upon a tree trunk, and then an Indian armed with an axe killed them one by one by breaking their heads. When they came to Mr. Schoonhoven, the chief ordered the bloody scene to stop, and addressing him he said:

> Do you remember one day when you were at a dance and several of us Indians presented ourselves at the affair, and when your companions were opposed to letting us in, you commanded that we be permitted to take part in the festivities? I believe I find in your face the same traces of affinity with the Indians; now you will see that we know how to appreciate these acts.

He then ordered that they free Mr. Schoonhoven and one of his companions who was still alive. *Sunt bic etiam praemia laudis* ("Such indeed are the rewards of a praiseworthy action").

During the War for Independence, in 1777, a young American named Jones, captain of the English troops, was engaged to a young lady named Miss McCrea. Her house was between the contending armies. Captain Jones, in order to get married, dispatched a party of Indians who were in the service of the English to escort his bride to the fort, which was the general headquarters. Not content with the first escort, he sent another also of Indians, offering a barrel of brandy as a reward to those who went. Both parties joined ranks and argued as to which ones would conduct the lady. The sad result was that the young lady was killed and fell victim to a fight begun to honor her.

In Caldwell we took the stagecoach to go to Saratoga. After a few miles we came upon Glens Falls, famous for its high cliffs, rock formations and great numbers of fossils. This cataract is on the famous Hudson River, which pours its great waters into New York Bay. We went on to Saratoga, which at that time was filled with travelers who come from all over the United States to take the celebrated mineral waters in the springs there, to dance, and to make acquaintances that may later decide the fate of the persons involved.

Saratoga is a town of the state of New York which has four excellent inns, each of which may lodge two hundred persons at least, not to mention a large number of smaller houses that they call boardinghouses. The principal inns are the Congress Hotel and the United States Hotel. More than one thousand persons go and come daily in this delightful place during the months of June, July, and August. As a center for mineral waters, the people there have tried to beautify it with groves, walks, gardens and everything that they can to make it pleasant for those who for pure pleasure or for their health go to drink the waters at the Congress.

There are fourteen springs of different combinations of salts, gases and minerals. Most of them contain sodium chloride, sodium carbonate, calcium carbonate, magnesium carbonate and iron carbonate in varying proportions. In the one which they call "Congress Water" there is a large quantity of carbonation, and the travelers drink two or three glasses every morning before breakfast to cleanse their stomachs gently. It is not distasteful like the water of the springs in our village of Guadalupe or the city of Hidalgo, which contain sulphur, petroleum, and much carbonation. When I passed through Saratoga, I was presented to the Count of Survilliers, José Bonaparte, ex-king of Spain, of whom I shall speak on another occasion.

In the vicinity there are still to be seen relics of campaigns of the War for Independence. The English General Burgoyne, after having taken Fort Ticonderoga, made his way with ten thousand regular soldiers and many thousands of savage Indians whom he had as auxiliaries towards Saratoga and Albany, in the center of the state of New York. In a proclamation which he published in June of 1777, he said that what he would be doing was more of a military passage than a campaign. Such was the pride that the easy taking of Fort Ticonderoga had inspired in him. He had conceived the idea of taking Albany, which seemed easy enough to him because of the terror that had been created by his sudden appearance on the left bank of the Hudson, the object of his desires as a barrier between the states of the west and New England. But the victory at Bennington, accomplished by the American Colonel Stark against the British troops commanded by Colonel Baun who was killed in battle, opened the eyes of the English general to the fact that he had to fight with a formidable enemy.

Worthy of attention is the discourse of Colonel Stark to his troops before the battle: "Today we must rout the enemy," he said to them, "otherwise, Mary Stark (his wife) will be a widow before the sun goes down."

After this action General Burgoyne fought two very bloody battles and was forced to surrender October 17 of the same year, leaving the field to the Americans. This campaign was directed by General Gates, who was born in England but was a faithful and noble defender of the American cause.

Subsequent to the expedition of the English General Burgoyne many incidents took place that are worthy of relating because of their unusual nature. This leader had received no communications from General Henry Clinton, who was to come to his aid by coming up the Hudson River. The courier named Taylor, who was carrying information on this important news to General Burgoyne, was taken prisoner by the advanced forces of the American General George Clinton. Poor Taylor swallowed something that he took from the bag, but he was observed. They gave him a strong dose of tartar emetic, whereupon he threw up a small hollow silver ball, and in it was found the letter from Clinton to Burgoyne. Taylor was tried and executed.

In the first attack of September 27 it was noted that a greater number of officers died than was in proportion to the number of troops. The American sharpshooters had stationed themselves in the branches of the trees, from where they aimed at the officers by choice. In the action of October 7 the principal leaders of the English army died. General Fraser, Colonel

Breytman and Mr. Clarke, aid to General Burgoyne, fell victims to the American riflemen.

General Fraser was an active officer, a man of bravery and ability. General Morgan was the one charged to make first contact with a body of American *chasseurs*. In the fiercest part of the action the American general chose six of his best riflemen and said to them: "You see that man? I admire him for his valor and his energy, but he must die, do what you must and carry out your duty."

This was the sentence of death for the brave English general; within a quarter of an hour he was dead. The account of this event and the tragic action is taken from the description written by a German lady who found herself on the same battlefield or in the vicinity where her husband Baron de Reidesdel served under the command of the British general:

> Harsh and severe tests awaited us the seventh day of October when our misfortunes began. I was having breakfast with my husband, and I realized that some serious business was at hand. I was expecting to dine with Generals Burgoyne, Tillips and Fraser. I saw much movement among the troops. My husband said that it was only a review, which told me nothing. I met many armed Indians, who to my questions only answered *guerre, guerre,* giving me to understand no doubt that they were going into battle. This made me hasten my retreat to the house where I had scarcely arrived when I began to hear cannon shots and gunfire that became louder and louder. At four o'clock in the afternoon, instead of the guests whom I was expecting to come to eat. I saw a litter enter bearing General Fraser mortally rounded. I had his bed placed in the same room that was to have been used far dining with him and the others. I sat down sadly in one corner waiting from one moment to the next for news of my husband.
>
> General Fraser said to the surgeon: "Tell me if my wound is mortal: I don't wish you to be easy with me," The surgeon told him that the bullet had pierced the stomach and had cut the principal tendons of that organ. The general was buried the next day in the midst of the bullets and the fire of the two opposing armies. Colonel Wilkinson whom we met in Mexico where he died, and with whom I had a special friendship, took part in this action. He says in his history that he was following a party of the enemy when he discovered near a fence a man stretched out who said to him: "Protect me my colonel from the bullets of this boy." He turned his head and saw a lad of fourteen or fifteen years pointing his rifle at the poor Major Ackland, who, gravely wounded, had been carried to that point by a corps officer who, was with him, and Colonel Wilkinson delivered both of them from the deadly shot of the small American.

Most interesting is the story that Baroness de Reidesdel tells of the efforts of the wife of Major Ackland, who accompanied her husband in all his perils and was with him in the enemy camp itself. We also have the same sort of examples of conjugal love and feminine heroism in our Mexican war.

CHAPTER VI

Departure from Saratoga.—Trip to New York.—Hudson River.—Arrival in New York.—Description of the bay and the city.—Its population.—Trade.—City Hall.—Theaters.—Reflections.—Inns.—Newspapers.—Religious sects.—Bishop Hobart.—Catholics.—Popular assemblies.—Banks.—Packages.—Class of population.—Manners and customs.

On July 24 I left Saratoga for Ballston which is on the way to Albany. This is also a town of mineral waters of about two thousand inhabitants and with good inns. I did not stop there except for the time that it took to visit its springs, and journeyed on to the capital of the state of New York, the city of Albany on the right bank of the Hudson River. Six miles before you get to Albany is Troy, a pleasant village pleasantly located on the opposite bank of the river which has about tour hundred inhabitants. On another occasion I shall turn my attention to Albany when I speak of my travels to New England in this same work.

July 25, 1830, I boarded the steamer United States, on which were traveling at least three hundred passengers, both men and women, all well dressed, especially the women, whose neatness and elegance were a real pleasure. In spite of the large number of people, all of them were very much at ease; some wished to stroll upon the deck, some to go below to the salons. For everyone there was a place at the tables set up for eating and dining. At dinner the food was plentiful, well seasoned, with good service, in short, with all the enticing comforts. We went down the picturesque Hudson River at a rapid pace and at West Point we had the pleasure of meeting Señor Mejia, and his family who were on their way down to New York, from where they had come to see the fatuous military establishment of this place. We arrived in New York at seven o'clock in the evening, having sailed 148 miles from Albany in twelve hours.

I stayed at Mrs. Street's Boarding House, No. 36, Broadway. This is one of the numerous stopping places that are neither public nor private, and in which a certain number of persons lodge under stipulated conditions. Those established on the street called Broadway in New York are the best, and one lives there in great comfort, in a select social group, and without the noise and confusion and going and coming of the large places.

Three times I have gone into New York by the bay, four by the Raritan, once from the east coming from Boston, and three or four by the Hudson River from the north. As I shall speak of the latter ones on another occasion, I shall begin now with the entrance of the magnificent bay of this great trade center.

As one approaches the coasts of New York there come into sight the heights of the state of New Jersey on the left side, and those of Long Island to the right. On Sandy Hook, which is a small sand hill on the southwest coast, there is a magnificent lighthouse, besides others that may be seen along the coast. The entrance becomes more narrow in about fifteen miles at Staten Island, which extends from the Raritan River as far as the straits which are called the Narrows, at the end of which a fortress has been built and is under the command of General Bernard.

The view is at once picturesque, magnificent and imposing; beautiful country homes on both sides surrounded by trees planted symmetrically on land that rises gradually and displays a prodigious fertility; the sight of the two rivers that descend leaving the city in the middle; a multitude of ships of all types and sizes that come and go taking different directions with full sail; steamships that cross each other's paths, and like great whales make their way lifting with their prows mountains of foaming water and leaving behind thick black smoke from their stacks; five hundred boats anchored on both sides of the angle formed by the rivers between which is located the city. This apex is covered with groves of trees, and the whole makes a pleasant ensemble that inspires the imagination and lifts up the spirit. New York is no doubt one of the most beautiful and most convenient ports in the world, and is also after London and Liverpool the city with the greatest maritime trade.

The city is located on the island of Manhattan formed by the North River, the Passaic and the East River, which is rather an arm of the sea. Long Island is a tongue of land separated on the south and is an island one hundred miles long and five or six miles wide. On this portion of land there are some rather large towns, among them Brooklyn, which is opposite the city, Jamaica, Flushing and other small towns and villages that are increasing in population and wealth in an extraordinary manner that is noted throughout the United States.

The state of New York has a population of two million inhabitants. In the city there are more than one hundred churches or chapels of different denominations; among these are eighteen Episcopal churches, twenty-five Presbyterian, twenty Methodist, nineteen Anabaptist, five Catholic, and the rest are Quakers, Unitarians and other sects. New York has approximately 220,000 inhabitants.

The city is irregular in form, and the streets are generally crooked. There are some, however, that can compare with the best of London or Paris. Such are Broadway, which divides the city and runs from the northwest to the southeast for about four miles, more than eighty feet wide, with stone sidewalks about six feet wide, made beautiful by quite handsome buildings, stores, shops, and all the brilliant things that there are in New York; Chatham, likewise made up of many very good buildings; Canal, Bowery, Blekery, Bonn, Greenwich, and others. Broadway is the place where all the best—dressed people promenade—ladies, young sports, strangers; it is at one and the same time a park, a street, and a promenade. More crowded than Regent Street in London, cleaner and more beautiful than the Boulevards of Paris, straighter and longer than Alcalá Street in Madrid. In New York there are no public promenades, with the exception of the small park at the Battery. There are no public fountains, and the drinking water is rather bad.

The advantageous location of New York, and more than anything else the system of liberty without petty passport restrictions, under the protection of just and wise laws, with absolute freedom of worship, have led this city to such a degree of prosperity and greatness in forty years that it is today the metropolis of the New World. In 1778 New York had only 22,000 inhabitants; in 1795 it had grown to 33,000; in 1800 it had 60,000; in 1820 it had increased to 123,000; in 1825 it had 166,000; and today, as I have said, it has 220,000. What city in the world has had such rapid growth?

The value of the merchandise that is imported and exported through this city is calculated to amount to $100,000,000; the income from the mails gives the treasury annually $120,000. What movement is necessary to produce such vast and extensive exchange!

There are more than seventy steamboats that leave the wharves to cross the bay. Some serve for crossing the Hudson and East Rivers to carry people that are going and coming from Brooklyn, Hoboken, Staten Island, and they are running all day long until twelve o'clock at night. Others leave for Flushing, New Haven, Hartford, Albany, Raritan, etc. During the summer up into the fall that bay appears to be one perpetual fair.

One of the most beautiful buildings of New York is the one called the City Hall, which is where the courts are held also. This is located in the midst of a tree—covered plaza called the Park, in the center of the city. It is 216 feet long and 105 feet wide. The facade is of beautiful white marble, and this building would be very elegant if it were better proportioned. But it is lower than it should be for its size. There are two other famous plazas in this city—one, Hudson Square, where there is a park surrounded by a high iron fencing with lots of scrolls; the other, Washington Square, which is outside the city, and which within a few years will be surrounded by buildings, shops, stores and houses.

In New York there are three theaters, and these are the Park, the Bowery and the Opera. Generally speaking North Americans are not very fond of this sort of entertainment which presupposes a degree of urbanity that cannot be said to be most noticeable among those people. Where taste for society and amusements has increased in the cities, such as Boston, Philadelphia, New York and a few others, one notices always that the people are not very enthusiastic about attending these functions. What a difference from the eagerness with which people rush to the doors of the theaters, balls and concerts in the cities of Europe, especially in France! The fifteen theaters of the city of Paris are filled nightly, and the managers make a living with good profits. In New York one theater of Italian opera cannot support itself at the same time as the other two in which they present separate bits of song and drama. I have noted a much greater inclination to the theater in the people of the Mexican republic than in the states of the North. The reason for this difference must be sought in the diverse circumstances under which these two peoples have developed. The North Americans are made up for the most part of agricultural immigrants who, because they were obliged in the beginning to work in the fields, have not had the time or the stimulation to dedicate their hours of rest to any exciting pastime. On the other hand, the spirit of sectarianism, which at first tended to a rigorous asceticism among the Presbyterians who migrated to those parts, left in its wake an insurmountable aversion to such presentations since they were prohibited by religion.

In the Spanish colonies there was an absolute separation between the conquerors and the conquered. The former had the wealth, privileges and the pleasures that provide both the inclination and the tastes that they engender. The descendants of the conquerors inherited from their parents the Spaniards the taste for music and entertainment, which were in accord with the Catholic religion, whose head in Rome gave encouragement to all sorts of spectacles. Instead of dedicating themselves to working the land or to other arduous occupations, they gave themselves over to noisy festivals to which on the other hand their warm or temperate climates invited them. Furthermore, there was not the dire necessity of accumulating for the winter provisions, firewood and clothing. The prime mover for work is necessity, then come pleasures. Thus then one sees a Mexican spend a peso which he had obtained without much difficulty in the theater, on the bullfight, or at a dance; while a North American would be afraid to take one dollar out of a hundred for such an investment.

In New York there are more than five hundred coaches for hire, not as comfortable as those of Mexico and Paris, but fast and elegant. There is scarcely room for four persons in a coach, and it costs one dollar per hour. A host of foreigners from every country keep these carriages continually occupied.

The principal hotels or public inns in this city are the City Hotel, Congress Hall, the National Hotel, the American Hotel, the Washington Hotel, the Franklin Hotel, all on Broadway. The rate is twelve dollars per week for room and meals, which consist of breakfast, dinner, tea and supper. The Washington Hotel is in a building that is quite large with a beautiful facade. Nearby are the Arcade Baths which are the best in the city, established by a Spaniard named Quesada. There are also many others that are second-rate, in addition to the boardinghouses of which I have spoken, which number more than eight hundred.

In no country in the world is there as great a number of newspapers in proportion to the population as in the United States of the North. In New York in 1831 there were twenty—eight newspapers, most of them rather large. In every town that has as many as two thousand inhabitants, the first thing that the people do is to build a small church, construct one or two buildings for schools and set up a print shop. When I read some days past of a project presented to the senate of Mexico by Señor Pacheco Leal on March 21 of this year, according to which there was to be set up a credit of $100,000 for the publication of a newspaper, I remembered the distance that exists between liberty that strives for thought and the publication of opinions and ideas in the country that we have taken as a model and our poor republic in which those who try to direct public affairs, far from moving openly towards the emancipation of our past servitude, try to maintain a monopoly on thought and put obstacles in the way of the intellectual progress of their fellow citizens. I cannot understand how men who profess popular republican principles can, even for a moment, adopt such projects that are in direct conflict with popular sovereignty.

I have said that in New York there were one hundred churches, but I have not spoken of the manner in which the clergy is supported, and this deserves a special explanation.

The American people are most religious, even to the extent of being fanatic in some places and congregations; but worship is entirely in the hands of the people. Neither the general government nor that of the states intervenes in any manner in religious matters. The need for having a church or chapel to meet in on the Sabbath, as they say, according to the precepts of Genesis, brings together these assemblies of the same denomination, who are in agreement as to how their worship is to be carried out. They name their ministers, support them, and exercise over them the authority that a company would have that pays its workers. To facilitate the exercise of their liturgical and economic government they elect a certain number of persons who have the powers of administration delegated by the congregation. Among the Protestants, Lutherans, Presbyterians, Episcopalians, etc., the people elect their ministers, and they dismiss them for bad conduct. Among Catholics the same thing occurs, but they go through the form of asking the bishop, and he never refuses them. Catholic bishops are appointed by the Pope, and the people receive these or not as they please. The Episcopalians, when they have a vacancy, meet to name their prelates. All of this is in accordance with the first centuries of Christianity, and compatible with the system of popular equality. *Any other method in which the government has a part in the affairs of worship is destructive to liberty.*

I cannot resist the desire to insert here a document that gives a clear and perceptive idea of the whole political system of the United States of the North as it concerns religious matters. The one who is speaking is an Episcopal bishop, Mr. Hobart, who died in a town in New York while carrying out his holy ministry during the time that I was in that state. Upon the death of Governor DeWitt Clinton, one of the most beneficent and honored men of the United States, the mayor of the city of New York sent a note to Bishop Hobart asking him to please make known in a solemn manner in the churches of his denomination the regrettable death of the governor of the state. Here is what the bishop replied on February 16, 1828:

> Sir, I have received today from the secretary of the city corporation a copy of the resolution of the city council, in which the request is made of the reverend clergy of the city that they publish tomorrow in corresponding and solemn form in their churches the very regrettable misfortune suffered by our common fatherland in the death of our first magistrate and fellow citizen De Witt Clinton.
>
> Since I find it necessary to refuse to comply with this demand in Trinity Church and in St. John's and St. Paul's chapels, I hope that you permit me to set forth the reasons that I have for this in order to avoid a bad interpretation in this particular.
>
> The prostitution of religion to secular political use has worked great harm, and I conceive that the careful separation of the Church from the intervention of the State, which characterizes our republican constitution, has been for the purpose of preventing and avoiding that religion and its ministers should become instruments that some might use for political gain. All right, if the municipal authority wishes the clergy to communicate "in a solemn and proper manner" the death of the first magistrate of the state, this same petition can be extended successively to all distinguished citizens in public office, and in this manner the intervention of the clergy can be made to increase the influence of political men and of their political measures. The regrettable results of this danger have been seen in the

ancient world, and against it we should strive to free ourselves in our fortunate country.

Whatever may be the character of the individual, he can never be worthy of this sacred religious distinction. In the circumstances of great political excitement an individual can be hated by some and the idol of others, and in this case the clergy, whose province is to administer to all in its spiritual functions, would be obliged to take sides between the parties and to experience dire conflicts. In almost all cases the ministers of religion, in their capacity as eulogists, find themselves embarrassed among the diverse opinions of their listeners, among which there are persons who wish for extraordinary eulogies, while there are others to whom moderate praise will seem excessive. Therefore, there is no point of view, as I see it, from which serious objections will not be met with in fulfilling the demands of the municipality.

As far as my own feelings are concerned, it would afford me great satisfaction to give public testimonial to the eminent talents, civic 'services and private virtues of the first magistrate whom we mourn. Very worthy of consideration also are the petitions of the municipal dignitaries of the city in which I carry out my ministry. But superior considerations of duty prevent me from complying with a demand which in the principle involved and the precedents that it establishes, seem to me a dangerous tendency with respect to the spirit of our free constitution, to the spirit of religion and to the character and influence of its ministers. I have the honor, etc.

J. J. HOBART

Among ministers respectable for their learning and their virtues that I have known in the United States special mention is due Father José Maria Varela, a native of the island of Cuba, who emigrated from his country because of his liberal principles during the period of the persecutions of Ferdinand VII. Another is Doctor Power; both of there are Catholics, both well educated and examples of Christian virtues. The Catholic religion is making considerable progress in the United States, especially in the states of Maryland, Louisiana, and Mississippi. The most extensive are the Presbyterians, Methodists, Episcopalians and Anabaptists. The people on the whole are religious and moral.

In New York, as in the other cities of the United States, the people come together when they think it necessary to discuss political questions of general interest. There are not only assemblies to inform public opinion concerning elections; we have seen them also deliberate concerning difficult banking theories, tariffs and duties, and other issues that have been debated recently in the United States.

In New York they meet regularly in Tammany Hall, the Masonic Hall, the City Hall and in the Stock Exchange, which are the largest and most convenient buildings for the purpose. It is surprising to see the order with which they convene and dismiss these assemblies, which always begin by naming a president, two vice-presidents and secretaries to direct the discussions. Very seldom does one see excesses or hear boisterous voices and much less disorders of any other sort. When the discussion begins the president proposes the questions that are to be dealt with and grants the floor to whoever asks to be recognized. Usually they have already written the resolutions that the individuals that are directing them consider to be the consensus of those present. As each party has its determined location, it is already known more or less what the resolutions will be. Thus we have seen that the backers of General Jackson always meet in Tammany Hall, just as those on the other side meet in the Masonic Hall. Consequently, the resolutions of the first group have always been against the Bank of the United States, against the election of Mr. Clay, etc.

On the following day they publish the resolutions in the newspapers and on posters that are put up in public spaces. Thus they are made known throughout the other states, in which assemblies are formed in the same manner, and at the end of a couple of months it can be stated mathematically how many citizens think one way, and how many the other. When the majority has spoken, the question is considered settled, and no one thinks of appealing the decision by force of arms to undo what has been done. In some complicated questions as that of the Bank, in which great interests are opposed, what usually happens is to delay the resolution because the people cannot understand it in the first discussions, and the complication makes it difficult to know what is best.

In one of these meetings held in the month of January of this year on the question of the Bank of the United States, the following resolutions were passed:

1) The opinion of this assembly is that the prejudices suffered by all classes are due to the unconstitutional intervention of the president of the United States to arrange for the circulation of securities.

2) The manner in which the executive power has taken upon itself the disposition of the government's funds indicates a tendency to arbitrary action and proves that it intends to govern without any consideration for the constitution or the laws off this country.

3) Thirty persons shall he mined to form a commission of public

welfare whose duty shall be to come to an agreement with the commision of the Union; engage in correspondence with the other commissions organized to apply opportune remedies to the ills that affect the country, and finally to take suitable measures to the end that the public administration shall operate ire conformity with the constitution.

4) The unworthy and brutal manner in which General Jackson has conducted himself with the commission of workers and craftsmen of this city debases the high rank that he occupies in his capacity as the president of the United States, and offends the entire body of the signatories, of whom the commissioners were the representatives. Concerning Martin Van Buren, the highly imrpoper reception that he gave the commissioners themselves is an indication off the low esteem in which he holds the working and industrious class of this city.

This fiery accord, the product of the assembly held in the Stock Exchange, was contradicted three days later by another of a more numerous gathering held in Tammany Hall, in which they approved the resolutions of the president. Thus the most troublesome questions were aired, but they never arrived at a plan of action.

The state of New York has eighty banks whose total capital amounts to $27,800,000. There are $43,712,958 in circulation in discounts issued by these banks, for the most; part in paper, and this produces an unbelievable activity in all branches of industry. Among these banks there exist some small ones whose funds are in the range of $104,000 and they circulate $200,000 or $300,000; as soon as a city of any size is organized, people begin to think about starting a bank. In the state legislature there were petitions for granting a charter to fifty new banks, or to renew those of existing ones . These banks have a solid basis for existence in that the lenders take the funds to invest in productive uses such as raising crops, purchasing cattle, building houses, boats, and other always useful enterprises that produce profits greater than the interest paid. This is the reason why one has seen these speculations prosper when they create imaginary values and put into circulation capital that does not exist.

From New York packet boats depart regularly three or four times per month for Liverpool, London, Le Havre, New Orleans, Charleston; and others not so regularly and frequently for Veracruz, Jamaica, Havana and the Spanish Main. Among the first there are boats that are outstanding for the comfort, cleanliness and even elegance of their cabins. The service is generally good, the food plentiful and the wines according to one's own choice. Always in greater numbers are the passengers on the return trip from

Europe, especially of poor people who are emigrating. There is no packet boat that does not carry forty or fifty emigrants bound for America to seek lands, work, and liberty.

The greater part of the inhabitants of New York City and the state are descendants of the Dutch. They preserve their ways, customs, and in many places their language. To this is due the fact that most of the houses are painted in bright colors, which gives to the city and smaller towns an air of happiness that is pleasing to the traveler.

CHAPTER VII

Colonization of Texas.—Formation of the company.—Type of inhabitants in that area.—Its future destiny.—Meeting my son in New York.—Persons that I dealt with. —The fair sex.—Museums.—Public education.—Participation of the people in public affairs.—Courts.

One of the first things that I did when I arrived in New York was to bring about the formation of a company to carry out the conditions of an agreement entered into by me with the government of the State of Coahuila and Texas relative to colonizing lands that lie between the Sabine River, Galveston Bay, the town of Nacogdoches and the sea. I could not carry out such an undertaking alone because it required considerable funds, and as a consequence I solicited persons that might wish to have a part in the enterprise. Don José Vilhein, from Mexico, who has a grant adjoining mine, gave me complete authority to establish a colony for both of us, and Mr. David Barnet, who has another grant in the interior where ours end, also joined with us, with the result that the three colonies provide a great extension of land that can be colonized where we should in a given time establish close to two thousand families.

This undertaking was carried out among more than fifty persons from various states, and we had named as trustees of this vast enterprise Messrs. Dey, Curtis, and Summer, who were in charge of the funds and all that was necessary to fulfill the colonization laws of the State of Coahuila and Texas concerning the grants made by the government of the State to the citizens Lorenzo de Zavala. José Vilhein and David G. Barnet.

My enemies in Mexico had many disagreeable remarks to make concerning this action, not only innocent but beneficial to the country; they said that I had sold a part of Texas to the United States, and that I had made myself rich by that sale. Time and my own poverty have caused all this slander to disappear. The government of the State has made a fair disposition of my patriotic efforts and has granted me an extension of time in consideration of the obstacles that the administration of General Bustamante placed in the way of the enterprise, and the persecution that General Teran directed against my young colony by not permitting the colonists sent by the company to disembark, or by taking them to other points. All of this is public knowledge in those parts, and the supreme government of the State itself lodged a complaint against Teran.

In my *Historical Essay* on the revolutions of Mexico I have set forth my opinions concerning that beautiful and rich portion of land known formerly as the province of Texas and today as an integral part of the State of Coahuila and Texas. Once the way was opened to colonization, as it should have been, under a system of free government, it was necessary that a new generation should appear within a few years and populate a part of the Mexican republic, and consequently that this new population should be entirely heterogenous with respect to the other provinces or states of the country. Fifteen or twenty thousand foreigners distributed over the vast areas of Mexico, Oaxaca, Veracruz, etc., scattered among the former inhabitants cannot cause any sudden change in their ways, manners and customs. Rather they adopt the tendencies, manners, language, religion, politics and even the vices of the multitude that surrounds them. An Englishman will be a Mexican in Mexico City, and a Mexican an Englishman in London.

The same thing will not happen with colonies. Completely empty woods and lands, uninhabited a dozen years ago, converted into villages and tows suddenly by Germans, Irish, and North Americans, must of necessity form an entirely different nation, and it would be absurd to try to get them to renounce their religion, their customs and their deepest convictions. What will be the result?

I have stated it many times. They will not be able to subject themselves to a military regime and an ecclesiastical government such as unfortunately have continued in Mexican territory in spite of the republican-democratic constitutions. They will point out the institutions that should govern the country, and they will want it not to be a deceit, an illusion, but a reality. When a military leader tries to intervene in civil transactions, they will resist, and they will triumph. They will organize popular assemblies to deal with political matters as is done in the United States and in England. They will build chapels for different faiths to worship the Creator according to their beliefs. Religious practices are a social necessity, one of the great consolations for the ills of humanity. Will the government of Mexico send a legion of soldiers to Texas to enforce Article 3 of the Mexican constitution which prohibits the exercise of any other faith than the Catholic? Within a few years this fortunate conquest of civilization will continue its course through other states towards the south, and those of Tamaulipas, Nuevo Leon, San Luis, Chihuahua, Durango, Jalisco and Zacatecas will be the freest ones in the Mexican confederation. Meanwhile, those of Mexico, Pueblo, Veracruz, Oaxaca, Michoacan and Chiapas will have to experience for some time the military and ecclesiastical influence.

When I arrived in New York I had the pleasure of embracing my son Lorenzo at the literary establishment of Mr. and Mrs. Peugne, where I had sent him five years before. Nothing can compare to the pleasant and gentle impression that one gets when after a long absence he meets the object of his affection and love. But these feelings become even more pleasing when a man sees in them the heir of his name, his name image and his representatives, to put it thusly, in posterity. The seeds of virtue and instruction that the worthy directors of that school planted in the soul of my son had taken hold and sent out deep roots. All this was sufficient reward for my past sufferings. A little while later I sent him to another school in Round Hill in the state of Massachusetts, under the direction of Mr. Cogswell, a man who was very respected for his learning and excellent character.

In New York I came to know the famous Albert Gallatin, one of the best educated and most respectable men in the United States, although born in Switzerland. He has been secretary of the treasury, and one of the companions of the first founders of the constitution and of the institutions. I also became friends with Don Tomás Gener, a Spanish immigrant, who had been a member of the Chamber of Deputies in 1823, and was held in high esteem in New York for his learning, his honesty and respectable manners. There was General Laight, with whose friendly family my son found the comfort and favors of a generous hospitality; Mr. James Prentiss; Mr. Webb, editor of the morning *Courier and Enquirer;* Mr. Fisher, editor of the *Advertiser and Advocate;* Mr. Dwight, editor of the *Daily Advertiser.*

Later on I shall mention other persons that I had the satisfaction of coming in contact with and that are important in that country. In the same boardinghouse or pension where I stayed there was a Dane named Sigmund Leidesdorf, who had lived for many years in Santa Fé de Bogotá as an agent of one of the loan companies of London. This individual with whom I have since been a close friend is a person who knows of many things, has a very pleasant disposition, correct manners and is well informed in the matter of credits, banks and even of finance. General Bolívar had ordered him to leave the country because of his friendly relations with General Santander, with our chargé d'affaires Don Anastasio Torrens, and the British consul Mr. Henderson, all of whom Bolívar ordered to be relieved of their passports. Mr. Leidesdorf's opinion concerning the Liberator of Colombia was not very favorable. .

Among the causes for surprise to a Mexican who travels for the first time in the United States, one is the beauty of the women. All travelers speak of this great advantage of those parts, and a Mexican has much more reason to do so. Indeed, among us the fair sex possesses charm, regular proportions, is endowed generally with much spirit and an irrepressible friendliness. But there is not that multitude of beauties that one encounters at every step in the states of the North. Even in the Mexican republic it is noted that the women of the north are more beautiful than those of the south; those of Sonora and New Mexico are famous for their beauty throughout the country. North American women have very good color, large bright eyes, well-shaped hands and feet; but they are very far from the elegance and voluptuous manner of walking of our Mexican women, of whom it may be said *incessu patent deae* (by their walk they reveal themselves to be goddesses).

In New York there are two museums that, as others in the United States and England, are privately owned. The one belonging to Mr, Peels is the oldest, although there are in the other one a larger number of very well-preserved animals. Mr. Peels' museum has rather the usual pictures, portraits of the principal persons of North America and a self-portrait of the founder of the museum. There is also a lyceum to which foreigners are admitted when presented by one of its members, and here they can read newspapers from this and foreign countries. The lyceum which they call American Lyceum, and of which I am a member, is for the purpose of promoting primary education.

This field is one of those receiving the most attention in that city. New York has more than three hundred schools, most of them free, in which are enrolled more than forty thousand children of both sexes. I have never seen a man who does not know how to read, and there are very few who do not know how to write among those in the cities of the United States. This accounts for the fact that they read newspapers, take part in the discussions of great interest and make up a mass of powerful public opinion. There is not nor has there been any country where the citizens have or have had so decisive and direct an influence on the decisions of its government. In Athens and in Rome a public directed by ambitious or salaried orators apparently made their decisions after the examination of matters that were subjected to their deliberation. Everything was the work of party enthusiasm or spirit, from which resulted those acts of injustice which posterity has condemned, and which led those republics to their ruin. Pericles in Athens and Cicero in Rome were not the only ones who dominated and directed the multitude by their eloquence. Aristophanes began the misfortune of Socrates, and Anytus aroused the feelings of the people against that wisest of men. Claudius began the troubles of the great Roman orator Cicero, and Anthony bore him to his death.

In the United States of the North although the people govern, and the chambers are their faithful interpreters, the decisions come from long and deep discussions. The meetings or popular assemblies in which political questions are debated do not settle anything definitely. They only set forth the opinion of a small fraction of the country, which finds or does not find sympathy and cooperation from other gatherings in the Union. Meanwhile the same questions are discussed in the newspapers, and the North American under a tree if he be a farmer or a shepherd, or in his office if a lawyer, or behind his counter if a merchant, or in his shop if a craftsman, reads and clarifies his ideas calmly and maturely. Such a government is the Utopia sought by political writers.

The administration of justice in the United States, is not entirely free of judicial chicanery. Nevertheless, everywhere one observes the admirable simplicity of their government. "It is difficult to conceive," says an English traveler,

> less ceremony in the administration of justice than in the United States. Judges and lawyers without wigs or robes, dressed as they wish or as they go out on the street. There are no maces nor any, symbol of authority, with the exception of various staffs which I observed that some constables or bailiffs of the court had in their hands. The witnesses gave their declarations with the appearance of the greatest ease or indifference as they do in England. No one seemed to think that he was in the presence of the court or should therefore maintain a certain decorum.
>
> The judges were probably about fifty years of age and went through no special ritual in the performance of their duties. The lawyers, although younger insofar as I could tell, did their part with zeal and ability in defense of their clients. The only disagreeable thing; about the whole procedure—in which I was happy to see justice done with purity and good faith—was the continual spitting on the part of everyone present.
>
> When I had satisfied my curiosity in this court, [the traveler continues] I went to another which I found to be the supreme court of the state. At the moment it was occupied with a case concerning bank bills. The dryness of the subject matter caused me to leave, but before I did I noticed the jurors were called in to give their verdict. I must admit that I was surprised to see three fourths of them busy eating bread and cheese, and that their foreman announced the sentence with his mouth full, getting the syllables out in between his chewing. To tell the truth, an American seems to see a judge just as any other craftsman, such as a carpenter, a tailor or a shoemaker, and it does not occur to him that one who administers justice is worthy of any more respect than one who manufactures hair dressing or candles. The judge and the candlemaker are both paid for their work, and *Jonathan* firmly believes that as long as he has money in his pocket there is no reason to fear that he won't have laws or skillets.

I cannot, however, persuade myself concerning this matter that legislation is founded upon solid and brilliant principles. A very learned lawyer asked me the other night if the visits that I had made to the courts had not cured me of my fondness for the formulas of John Bull (the English) and the togas, wigs, maces and other inconsequential apparatus and ridiculous insignia that they use there and that could only be imposed upon weak minds. I answered no, and that on the contrary, since my arrival in New York I had been even more convinced of the propriety of that apparatus. There followed a long discussion on the subject during which each one maintained his own opinion, and it must be said with due regard to fairness that my opponent used arguments based upon liberty that were expressed with force and energy. I refrain from giving this discussion in detail because a protocol signed by one of the parties is evidently only a partial document, and when a casuist enjoys the privilege of bringing forth the arguments of both parties, he must be endowed with a superhuman detachment in order not to present those against him as weak, putting himself on the side of the gods while he leaves his adversary that of Cato.

It is usual in these countries to ask, and generally with a certain air of triumph, if it is believed in England that wisdom consists of a wig, and if a few ounces of horsehair placed upon the heads of judges plastered with pomades and starch can be imagined to increase the knowledge of the individuals done up in so bothersome a manner. The answer is no—no Englishman believes that the head in its natural state or decorated with these things can be more or less disposed to judgment and legal criteria, and still I do not hesitate to admit that in some parts a judge in shirt sleeves seated upon a simple wooden bench can be as effective and useful an administrator of right as one who is bewigged and covered with a toga of ermine and scarlet.

But this does not necessarily indicate that Americans do not consider these apparatuses useful. If a man were a being of pure reason, forms would not be necessary; but whoever passes laws under such a concept would prove that he does not know human nature. Man is a being of feelings and imagination, and even in religious matters the constant experience of the world has shown the necessity of certain external rites and solemn observances in order to stimulate devotion and to accustom one to finding his faculties for worship of a mysterious and incomprehensible being "whose kingdom is where there is no time or space." It is difficult to conceive upon what principle those who approve of the stole on the priest and the chevrons on the general can condemn as irrational the insignia of judges. Let the Americans be consistent by adorning their judges with titles of honor; they should protect them from the rusticity and common familiarity of their people.

Thus this traveler explains himself, and he does not seem to be very logical since he wishes to make a precedent out of the fact that judges should be dressed in court with trappings that were used four hundred years ago, upon the principle, with which I agree, that certain symbols of dignity are necessary to impose respect. Indeed, these symbolic vestments used by the judges in England and by the presiding officers of their chambers can contribute nothing to the majesty of the laws or to the inviolability of the oracles of justice. The English parliament is respected and obeyed intrinsically because of the justice of its agreements and the wisdom of its deliberations, and considered extrinsically for the profound policy of its decisions. Thus, like magistrates of that same nation, it is worthy of the praises given it by all the writers that speak of it because of the integrity, learning, and purity of its members. If the judges of England were to present themselves in their courts with the ordinary dress of society, they would not be therefore less respected. It is done that way in most of the courts of France and in those of the United States where the judges justly enjoy the most distinguished consideration.

If I could but transport my fellow citizens to these free lands to witness the simple and natural manner by which they reach their judgments, I should certainly succeed in seeing established in my country trial by juries, without which there can be no true liberty nor judicial independence. In some states of the Mexican republic some attempts were made, and their legislators stopped short at the beginning of their philosophical considerations because they found no oracles of Areopagus in the first deliberations of inexperienced men little accustomed to this type of judgments. In all countries the same thing happened at the beginning, and only the constancy and the conviction that this system was the only method of judging according to the principles of liberty caused the legislators to maintain this holy institution of trial by jury,

"The penalties against robbery were severe," says Mr. Hallan in his *Constitutional History* of *England,* "but they were nevertheless effective in deterring these acts of violence that arise naturally out of the gross and licentious customs of that period and from the imperfect dispositions that had been taken to insure the public peace. These acts were committed or advised often by persons whose fortune and power placed them beyond the laws."

Here then is the situation in which we find ourselves at the present time in Mexico, and the time most apropos for establishing the jury. I shall never tire of saying it. Under whatever form of government the Mexican republic may be, in the end, it will be a grave charge against its directors not to establish trial by jury.

CHAPTER VIII

Washington Irving.—His writings.—New York's hospitality.—Anniversary of Mexico's independence.—Object of conversations with the Americans.—Inclination to the English.—Mr. Adams' account of recognition by Great Britain.—His speech to the king.—The reply of George III.—Celebrations in New York on the occasion of the revolution in France.—Master Burke.—Colored population.—England's conduct with reference to the slaves.—Reflections.—Anecdote.—Fires.—Aristocracy in the United States.—Mr. Livingston.

While I was in New York, Washington Irving arrived in the city on his way back from Europe. He was received by his fellow citizens with the enthusiasm inspired naturally by the presence of a compatriot whose works have merited approval in literary circles and deserved to be placed beside the classical authors. Washington Irving has written a considerable number of novels and other works that have elevated him to the rank of Goldsmith, Addison, and Robertson. It has been said of him that his *Braceridge Hall* was comparable to the *Vicar of Wakefield* by Goldsmith, his *Sketch Book* to the *Spectator* by Addison, and his history of Columbus to the histories of Robertson. His style is that of the Burkes and the Gibbons. He is, moreover, a true painter of customs such as Walter Scott. Cooper, another American writer, should not be passed over in silence. His novels are written with elegance, naturalness, and verisimilitude. The interest that they inspire is a real one that is not dissipated and does not disappear when the book leaves the hand, as happens generally. It leaves great and deep reflections.

In New York I received the most cordial hospitality from all the people to whom I was introduced. Many did me the honor of inviting me to their dinners and their tea parties. In the United States, as in England, the ladies retire after the dessert, and the men remain at the table for some time longer.

The tea parties are in fact social gatherings where generally there is singing and sometimes dancing. They serve fruits, tea, wines, sweets, cookies, pastries, or other similar things. Businessmen are not overlooked on these occasions. In September of 1830 we celebrated in New York at a banquet the anniversary of the independence of Mexico. Those present included Generals Negrete, Echavarry y Mejía, Count Cornaro, Don José Armaro Ruiz, the consul of Colombia Medina, several well-known North Americans and myself.

In no country in the world do they deal more constantly with mercantile business and how to make money. Very few people speak of abstract questions or matters without including some material interest. An American will ask a Mexican whether there are steamboats, whether there are factories, whether there are mines, whether money is to be found easily in such and such a state. A Mexican will ask what kind of government, what religion, what customs and what theaters, if any, he can expect to find in this or the other place. The North Americans are essentially grasping and hardworking. In England during the meal people talk about the quality of the wines, how the food is seasoned, the elegance of the table and other things having to do with what they are engaged in. In the United States the conversation will likely be about the price of cotton, of lumber, etc.

Although it is generally thought that the North Americans have, with respect to the English, the same averse feelings that have developed in the former Spanish colonies against the Spanish, this is not entirely true. The North Americans do detest royal authority, and everything that has any connection with monarchial institutions, and they do perhaps carry to the extreme their aversion to certain formulas and items of etiquette of the British; but as far as people are concerned, I am certain that the English find among North Americans the best of good feelings in treatment and hospitality, as well as in language and popular customs.

The pride of primogeniture and the advantages that the English have because of their antiquity sometimes brings about disagreeable differences between those on one side and the other; differences where the Americans always make a great show, with much justice, of their admirable progress and of their unquestionable liberty. But it must be agreed that the open and philosophical policy of the British government with respect to its former colonies has played a large part in keeping down these national hatreds, to which purpose the admonitions and good offices of Washington and his successors contributed constantly.

Although after the peace between Great Britain and the United States in 1783 the government of the former sent no minister nor agent to the new republic, the respectful and attentive manner with which George III received the minister John Adams, first American envoy to His Britannic Majesty, gave occasion to continue in the most perfect harmony in those thorny beginnings. Mr. Adams, who had been in Europe on other occasions with missions of an important nature, received in 1785 the delicate and prickly one of being representative at the Court of St. James in London as the first minister from the liberated colonies. I shall copy the account that this distinguished American dispatched to the secretary of state of his government because I think the reading of it will be interesting in the circumstances in which the Mexican republic finds itself at the moment of establishing the same sort of relations with its former mother country. "During my interview with the Marquis of Carmarthen," says Mr, Adams,

he informed me that it was the custom for all the ministers on their first presentation to His Majesty to pay him a courtesy in keeping with his credentials, and when Sir Clement Dormer, master of ceremonies came to inform me that the secretary of state of the court would accompany me, he added that new Ministers should also pay their respects to the queen. On Tuesday night Baron de Lynden, ambassador from Holland, came to see me and told me that he had come from the home of the ambassador from Sweden, Baron de Nolkin, and that they had spoken of the singular situation in which I found myself, and they both agreed on the need for my pronouncing a complimentary discourse to the king. All of this agreed with what Count de Vergennes had recently said to Mr. Jefferson. Since that was the way things were, and since I saw that it was the established custom in these two great courts, and that the Court of St. James and the ministers of the other nations were of the same opinion, I thought that I could not get out of it, although my first intention had been to deliver my credentials without saying anything and then withdraw at once.

Finally on Wednesday, June 1, the master of ceremonies came to my house for me, and we went together to the ministry of foreign affairs, where the Marquis de Carmarthen received me and introduced me to Mr. Frazier, the subsecretary. After a short conversation concerning the fact that they would take my luggage from France and Holland without duty, Lord Carmarthen invited me to get into his coach to go to the court. When we arrived at the antechamber, the master of ceremonies came out to receive me and stayed with me while the secretary of state went in to receive his orders from the king. While I was in this room, where all the ministers wait on such occasions, and which was full this time, you may imagine that I was the center of attention, and that all looks were turned in my direction.

Fortunately the ministers of Sweden and Holland lessened the embarrassment in which I found myself as they stayed close to me and kept up a pleasant conversation. Other gentlemen whom I had met previously likewise favored me with their conversation until the return of the minister, who advised me that His Majesty awaited us. I went with his lordship into the king's chamber. The door was closed, and I was left alone with His Majesty and the secretary of state. I made three bows, one at the door, another half way there, and another before His Majesty, according to the protocol of the courts of Northern Europe, and then as I addressed the king, I said to him:

"Sir, the United States has named me as its minister plenipotentiary to Your Majesty, and I have the honor of delivering the credentials that declare this. In obedience to its express commands, I have the satisfaction of assuring Your Majesty of the unanimous disposition on the part of the citizens of those States to cultivate the most friendly and open relations with Your Majesty, and of their most sincere wishes for the health of Your Majesty and of his royal family.

"The naming of a minister from the United States to the court of Your Majesty will mark an epoch in the history of England and America. I consider myself the most fortunate of my fellow citizens for having had first the distinguished honor of presenting myself to Your Majesty in a diplomatic role, and I shall hold myself to be the happiest of men if I can be a useful instrument for recommending repeatedly to my country the royal benevolence of Your Majesty, and continuing to restore complete confidence, esteem, and affection, or in other words, the former good feelings, and the former good humor between peoples who, although separated by an ocean and with different governments, have the same language, the same religion, and blood ties. I beg Your Majesty to permit me to add that although I have received the confidence of my country on numerous occasions, at no time has it been so pleasing and flattering as now."

The king listened to my whole discourse with dignity, but with a certain emotion. I do not know whether that was the effect of the nature of such an interview or perhaps of the visible agitation with which I delivered my discourse; what is certain is that he was very much moved and answered me with greater spirit than I had used as he said to me:

"Sir, the circumstances of this audience are very unusual, the language that you have used is so adequate, and the feelings that you have expressed are so opportune on this occasion that I must say that not only do I receive with pleasure the assurances of the friendly disposition of the people of the United States, but also it is a great satisfaction to me that the mission to represent them has fallen to you. I desire, sir, that you be persuaded and that the American people understand that anything that I have done in the recent conflict has been done only as my conscience has persuaded me was for the good of my people. I must speak to you frankly; I have been the last to come to terms with the separation, but now that it has been accomplished I have always said, and I repeat now that I will be the first to seek the friendship of the United States as an independent power. The moment that I see that the feelings that you have expressed are those of that people, in that moment I shall be able to say that the great sympathies that are born of one same religion, one same tongue, and one same blood will have their full effect."

It must not be forgotten that the declaration of independence was made in July of 1776, and that in 1783 the United States was recognized as a sovereign nation by the mother country. Our republics of America, formerly Spanish, declared their independence more than twenty years ago, and for more than twelve years have been completely independent, without any obstacle or opposition on the part of Spain, nor even the capacity on her part to do anything. They are recognized as independent nations with duly constituted governments by the civilized nations, and the Spanish cabinet and its new Cortes are still considering whether they will do *us the favor of recognizing us.* Such a policy is mean and little in accord with the liberal principles that they have claimed to profess.

I was in New York when the news came about the famous revolution and the three days in July in Paris and its happy results. It is hard to believe the enthusiasm displayed by the people of the United States for an event that it would seem should not affect a commercial and agricultural nation dedicated to its profits and material improvement. But the feeling for liberty is deeply rooted in those independent souls who can never forsake their sympathies for the progress that other countries make to come closer to their social position. Mr. Monroe, who had been president of the United States, was the one who presided over the assembly or meeting of the workers, craftsmen, businessmen, and other classes gathered in Tammany Hall to take the necessary steps to put on a function worthy of the thing that was being celebrated. The procession was one of the most brilliant gatherings that I have ever seen. To understand the number of those who took part in it, suffice it to say that although they proceeded at a normal pace, the spectator could be in one place for three hours watching them go by.

It started off with a squadron of cavalry, then came the general in chief, Mr. Swartswout, with his aides-de-camp and a detachment of French residents of New York, with uniforms of the national guard of France. There followed an open coach in which rode ex-President Monroe, Mr. Gallatin and the speaker. After that came the commissions of the different trades and occupations with their corresponding emblems, banners, instruments, and then the musicians, singers, comedians.

There were printers carrying the type from their printshops, tailors, shoemakers, silversmiths, ironworkers, blacksmiths, businessmen, sailors, lawyers, doctors, students, every class beneath its own banner. Finally came the legislators, mayors, consuls, all of the most brilliant and respectable people. The procession began at Canal Street at nine o'clock in the morning and ended at Washington Square at six o'clock in the evening. There were more than one hundred thousand persons in the procession. The order, good behavior, decorum and general good manners that were evident from the beginning to the end corresponded to the wealth of the people, to the great occasion which they were celebrating, and to the majesty of the American nation.

During those days performing at the Park Theater was the prodigious Master Burke, an Irish lad of eleven years who played, sang, gave readings and did pantomime with the grace, finesse, strength and naturalness of the leading masters of the art. I was spellbound, as were the others in the audience, as I watched a boy three feet tall, with his feminine voice and delicate features, present himself upon the stage and show forth his prodigious abilities.

In the city of New York there are a considerable number of blacks and colored people, although as in the other states to the north of Maryland slavery is not permitted. But in spite of this emancipation of the African class and its descendants, it is excluded from all political rights, and even from the common trade with the others, living to a certain degree as though excommunicated. This situation is not very natural in a country where they profess the principles of the widest liberty. Nothing, however, can overcome the concern that exists with respect to this particular subject.

The colored people have their separate homes, hotels, and churches; they are the Jews of North America. This rejection by society degrades them and takes from them the incentive to work; they resign themselves to idleness and do not try to improve a hopeless situation, circumscribed within limits so narrow that there is scarcely room to calculate self-interest. Hence the vices and laziness which with very few exceptions holds this whole class down to the lowest ranks of society. This is the great argument against the emancipation of the slaves, an argument that discourages its most ardent supporters and that would make their efforts useless if the abolition of slavery were not demanded by a necessity that within a short time will admit no further delay.

England, in the midst of economic difficulties, contrary to its mercantile way of doing things, has just paid, with the high price of $100,000,000, a debt to humanity and national honor that for forty years, has been maintained by the futile efforts of a powerless philanthropy. While isolated acts of violence—although one of these irrational happenings has no consequence—raises protests in an American city in favor of slavery, an assembly in London composed of all parties, where O'Connell sat on the side of the minister of colonies, where proud aristocracy fraternized with colored men, celebrated the anniversary of freeing of the slaves. Lord Murgrave, recently arrived from Jamaica where he presided over the first sessions of the emancipation, has declared that two more years of slavery would have caused the same disasters as in Santo Domingo. The whole noble example that was carried out peacefully with the best of order in the islands of British America cannot fail to have a good effect on the United States of the North.

All men who are aware of the fact that worry about the future must take into account the questions of the present are easily persuaded that society must give consideration to slavery before slavery produces its bloody eruptions in society. Abolition already has many supporters in the state legislatures. But how does one remedy that embarrassing situation of free colored people in the center of American society? Will the day come when they will be incorporated into the state and form an integral part of the community? We must hope so. The New York legislature took the first step when in 1829 it extended the right of suffrage to colored people who owned real property valued at $250, free of all debt.

I shall end this discussion with a story told by a traveler. The son of a general of Haiti, a very good friend of President Boyer, decided to make a trip to New York for the purpose of having a good time while he was learning something. This young man, although a mulatto, had very good manners and a neat and pleasant appearance and had a better education than is generally found in his country. Accustomed in his homeland to receiving the respect due his station, he expected to find in New York the consideration that money and fortune give, together with the pleasures that a rich and civilized city provides.

When he got off the ship, he ordered that his luggage be taken to the best hotel. But he found that they would not admit him because of his color. He went to another and another; but everywhere he met with the same result, until he found it necessary to take a room in the home of a black woman. The pride of the young Haitian was humiliated, all the more since he was dressed with elegance and adorned with gold chains, rings and diamond buttons, etc. Unfortunately he continued to experience the same insults everywhere he went; in the theater he was not admitted to the seats of the white people, nor in the churches, nor in any society. At the first opportunity he went back to his country vowing never to visit the United States again. If this young man had gone to Europe, he would certainly have found all the comforts and entertainment that he would have desired and that he could buy, sitting in the theater, in the hotel and in church next to the whitest and blondest English, French, or German lady.

"One cannot be in New York for twenty-four hours without hearing alarming shouts of fire," says one traveler.

Indeed, a fire in that city is so common an occurrence that it never causes that anxiety and upset that it does in other parts less accustomed to this calamity. The *firemen* of New York are famous for their quick action and forcefulness, and since it is interesting to witness the exercise of these qualities, I decided to go to all the fires that might occur while I was in the city. The first four were of little consequence since three of them were already extinguished when I got there, and I only got to see the smoke of the fourth one. On the fifth I had better luck. Since I had gotten into the scene of the action farther than was proper, thinking that it was the same as the others, I finally had the satisfaction of witnessing the appearance of a respectable volume of flames coming out of the windows, chimneys and doors of the four stories of the house, accompanied by smoke, alarms, noise and confusion captable of fulfilling my reasonable desires.

Then a fire truck arrived, and the shouts and the grinding of the wheels of the machines announced the approach of help. Some time was spent in getting water, on which matter it is to be desired that the city improve the situation. Nevertheless, in a few minutes it was coming out in torrents, and the two elements began their battle. Those who perform this service are young citizens who because they dedicate themselves to this, and it is very severe, are exempt from serving in the militia. Their activity and daring are truly surprising. At once ladders were put in place, they climbed up to the chimneys, began to take out furniture which they threw into the street without much consideration for those who were there, at the risk of breaking their heads.

The traveler continues giving an animated description of the progress of the fire, the brilliant spectacle that it presented at night, of the confusion and alarm in neighboring houses, and he makes the observation that in these cases they should do as in London, where in order to avoid the crowds of idle people that hinder the operations and increase the difficulties, they are supposed to close the entrances and have them guarded by the police.

"When I suggested this idea for improvement to an American friend," he continues,

he replied that it would be desirable, but that such means were not calculated for the American scene where exclusion of any sort is always contrary to popular sentiment. In this matter I cannot persuade myself that the exclusion of a group of idlers from the scene of a fire because they increase the difficulty of saving the property and the lives of some, can be considered as an attack upon liberty.

I have heard many people say that in the United States there is a true *aristocracy,* and others say that it is the country of liberty and of absolute equality. No law, no custom, no historical record exists in that country whose tendency would be to form an aristocratic class. Civil law calls all citizens before the same courts; political law clothes them with the same rights. But there is a law superior to human institutions, a law of inequality that nature has established, and that no legislator can do away with: a law that has more sway in free peoples than with despotic governments, but that always exercises a powerful influence. This law is that of mental capacity, the superiority of talent. What disposition, what rule can indeed cause a man of talent, of instruction and capacity to remain at the same social level, at the same degree of consideration and of influence as another man who is not endowed with the same qualities? Consequently, the second one cannot choose the same employment nor be received in society with the same esteem, nor attract the same respect and attention as the first one. This is already an inequality, and this exists in the United States as it does everywhere. Webster, Clay, Calhoun, Van Buren, Jackson, Forsythe, Poinsett and others are personages who are very superior to the rest of their fellow citizens.

There is another superiority which, although it is not natural, is a necessary consequence of the state in which society finds itself constituted in general, and that various Utopian philosophers have tried to modify without success. It is that of wealth. A rich man must have more concessions, must offer more hopes, must spend more than another one who is poor. He has more means of influence and a greater capacity for doing good and evil than another in whom wealth and talent are not found together. Such a man considers himself lifted up above the rest, and to a certain degree it is true because many depend upon him, because he does not need to work to live, because he can satisfy his necessities and his pleasures.

Here are two classes of people that in the United States of the North maintain a kind of habitual hierarchy whose natural privileges depend in no way whatsoever upon legislation. I remember that as I was going from Europe to the United States in 1831 on the beautiful packetboat *Francis I* there was at the same time on the boat a family of Mr. Francois Depau, a millionaire merchant of New York and one of the partners of the packetboat company. There were many distinguished passengers, among them General Santander, Señor Acosta, at the present time chargé d'affaires from Nueva Granada to the United States, a noble Italian named Suzarelli, in short all of them people of education and high principles. Notwithstanding this, Mr. Depau and his family ate by themselves in the ladies' section, thus perhaps having to associate less with us. I confess that that conduct was offensive to me in such circumstances. But whom did it offend, or what right could there be to say anything against their ridiculous isolation? I looked at him with scorn, the same as my companions. Many from the United States of the North do this also.

Compare this with the Mexican aristocracy, and you will note the difference. Arnong us the laws and the former concerns maintain a true *aristocracy,* an *aristocracy* of privilege, in short an *aristocracy* of *exceptional* laws and therefore a dying one in a popular republican society. How can people who recognize entire classes as superior to others because of legal privileges convince one of their sincere and true love of liberty? In the United States the statesmen can pass on their venerable names to their children and grandchildren if these maintain with their own intelligence, patriotism, and honor the luster of their forebears. But it is seen that this is not a prerogative of the law; it is that of personal merit.

In this city I had the satisfaction of being presented to Mr. Edward Livingston, an illustrious legal authority in the United States, the author of the codes of Louisiana and senator at that time, then secretary of state and today minister plenipotentiary to the king of the French. Mr. Livingston himself has told me that after twelve years of continuous work in getting the codes completed to his satisfaction he retired at twelve o'clock at night and said to his wife: "Now I am going to sleep with the satisfaction of having concluded my work at the end of twelve years."

At two o'clock he heard a noise and then warning cries of the servants who were shouting fire. The room in which Mr. Livingston had the papers and books was the scene of a roaring fire. The fire consumed everything, and Mr. Livingston began his task anew the following day with the same constancy, until once more he finished his work worthy of a profound jurisconsult.

Mr. Livingston has likewise played a very distinguished part in the development of the office of the secretary of state which he held during the delicate questions of the *nullificantionists* of Carolina. The skill with which he was able to manage the negotiations led things to a happy ending. The proclamation of President Jackson in the month of December in 1832, the work of Mr. Livingston, is a document of major importance in the annals of republican governments. In this paper are developed the principles of the form of government of those states with an insight and mastery worthy of the majesty of a great people.

CHAPTER IX

Trip to Philadelphia.—Iron road.—New Jersey.—Its constitution.—Bordentown.
—Joseph Bonaparte.—Delaware River.—William Penn.—Philadelphia.—Water
reservoir.—Theaters.—Miss Wright.—Pennsylvania navy.—Sea trade.—Independence Hall.—Washington Square.—Quakers.—Sundays.—Banks.—Their history.
—Penitentiary.—Public education.—Respectable subjects.—Mr. Girard.

In August I left for Philadelphia and took passage for four dollars on the steamboat *Swan,* which is one of those of the line. The trip is made by going to the southwest through Raritan Bay, then into the Raritan River and landing at a small town called Washington, in the state of New Jersey. This is crossed by coach, and again one boards a steamer at Bordentown or Trenton. Today the course has been changed since the railroad was laid from Amboy to Camden. The journey lasts three hours through Raritan Bay, three hours by land, and three on the Delaware River to Philadelphia. The distance is about thirty-five leagues.

The state of New Jersey, which one crosses, lies between the ocean, the river on the north called the Hudson, the Delaware, and the states of New York and Pennsylvania. The principal cities are Burlington, New Brunswick and Trenton. The latter is the capital of the state. The constitution of New Jersey was written in 1776 and has not been revised since that time, with the exception of a few changes made by the legislature. The executive power, as in the other states, is exercised by the governor. There is a legislative council and a general assembly. The members of each are selected annually the second Tuesday in October. These two bodies make up the *legislature.*

The number of members in the council is fourteen, with one selected from each county. The general assembly is composed of forty-three individuals. But a law passed in 1828 added seven more members, and today the council is composed of fifty members taken from the counties in the following order: three from Bergen, five from Essex, four from Morris, three from Sussex, three from Sommersett, four from Monmouth, five from Burlington, four from Gloucester, three from Salem, three from Cumberland, one from Cape May. The legislature meets annually in Trenton the fourth Tuesday in October. The governor is named annually by the vote of the council and of the assembly. The governor is president of the council, which in its first session names a vice-president from its own body, who exercises the functions of the governor in his absence.

The governor and the council make up the court of appeals in all cases of law in the final instance and have the power of pardon.

The constitution gives the right of suffrage to all persons who have property in the value of two hundred dollars and have resided for one year in the place of the county where they vote. The legislature declared in 1829 that every citizen twenty-one years of age with a capital of two hundred dollars could vote provided he were of the white race. By another decree blacks and women are deprived of the right to vote. In Canada the latter do have that right. The judges are named by the legislature—those of the supreme court for seven years, those of the lower courts for five years.

In Bordentown, a small town on the Delaware, is the beautiful country home of Joseph Bonaparte, ex-king of Naples and of Spain, today the Count de Survilliers. This famous personage, whom Spanish papers painted in such ugly colors, is very well educated, has a very pleasant personality and elegant and natural manners, and is endowed with social qualities that have brought him respect in the United States of the North, where he retired after the catastrophe of the Emperor Napoleon his brother. A respectable amount of money, which he was able to salvage from the political shipwreck, has put him in a brilliant situation in that country of trade and business. His magnificent house, gardens and parks on the banks of the delightful Delaware would be enough to make him happy if other pursuits did not take him away from the modest and peaceful sphere to which he has been reduced by the misfortunes of the great personage who elevated his whole family to the rank of kings.

The Delaware is a broad and beautiful river, navigable for steamboats as far as Trenton. The views on both sides, especially in the vicinity of Philadelphia, are magnificent and picturesque: country homes with presumptions of Greek architcture of very good style and placed in the midst of groves artistically planted and watered by many streams; new villages made up of buildings of beautiful appearance, stores and factories. The vegetation is earlier than in New York. On the left side of the river the railroad runs now; in March of 1834 it reached Camden, and will probably extend as far as across from the city of Philadelphia within two more years.

This great city founded by William Penn, inhabited in the beginning by a few Quaker families, today presents the appearance of one of the illustrious cities of Europe, with greater beauty and much greater hopes of prosperity. From four leagues away on the river are discovered its towers, its tall buildings, its observatories, and the smoke that rises in a colossal column toward the sky.

I stayed in the Mansion House, one of the better hotels in the United States. There I found Mr. Poinsett, my old friend, who was busy writing an article about English politics for the *Quarterly Review.*

The city of Philadelphia is cut perfectly in parallel lines that form streets in the figures of parallelograms. There are numbers 1 to 11 from East to West; and from North to South the streets have the names of plants or fruits—such as Mulberry, Chestnut, etc. But in addition to the street No. 11, the city has already been extended five or six streets more that are not yet numbered. The sidewalks are of brick and are two yards wide. The streets are from fifteen to twenty yards wide, most of them with a border of acacia, chestnut, or walnut trees, which give a beautiful view and a pleasant shade in the summer.

There are magnificent buildings in the city. The stock exchange is being completed and is much better than the one in New York. The Bank of the United States is of beautiful white marble, an imitation, although imperfect, of the Parthenon in Athens. The facade is beautiful, but it lacks the lateral columns. Another bank opposite the one of Mr. Girard (Bank of Pennsylvania) has six beautiful columns of Ionic order, likewise of marble.

The reservoir and machinery for the provision of waters for the city on the banks of the delightful Schuylkill River are works of considerable size. They are built on one side of the river where the scene is truly interesting, and the works, whose utility has corresponded to the enterprise, are solid and beautiful at the same time. No stranger should fail to visit them. The river is at that point about nine hundred feet wide and twenty-five feet deep. A dam has been placed across it, a dike that leads a great part of the waters into the reservoir, and more to the mills that move the wheels destined to raise the water by means of pumps to an open tank in a rock elevated 270 feet above the level of the city, at a distance of one league. Eleven million gallons of water are raised daily to the receptacle. Not only is the water taken to the public fountains, and utilized for irrigating and other common use, but few houses in Philadelphia do not have the advantage of running water on the upper floor. The undertaking cost $1,600,000, and the company today receives an interest of at least twelve percent per year.

In Philadelphia there are two theaters, one on Walnut Street, and another on Chestnut Street. Both are small, but of regular dimensions, each capable of seating six hundred people. Next to the second one is the museum, surely the richest and most abundant in all types of curious objects of any to be found in America. Exhibited there is ancient clothing of the Indians of the country, very similar to that of the Egyptians, and also the complete skeleton of the biggest mammoth that I have seen up to this time. Each one of the tusks is eight feet in length. In the museum are the portraits of the principal American personages, of many ladies, and of some wise European generals.

In one of these theaters Miss Wright gave her lessons in philosophy a short time before my arrival. The theater was filled with persons of both sexes, and they were listening to the philosopher preaching with an attention uninterrupted by signs of approval or disapproval. The main purpose of her preachings was to persuade her hearers that instead of employing the first day of the week in religious exercises and spending twenty million dollars a year supporting preachers, in building churches, and in enriching idle people, they should use their time and employ their money in discovering the hidden secrets of nature.

"Take as masters," she said emphatically, "experimental philosophers; convert your temples into halls of science, and dedicate your feast days to the study of your own bodies and to the examination of the beautiful material world."

The doctrines of Miss Wright, as I have said another time, are founded in philosophical deism, and they cannot suit a society. But in a free people, truly free, and not free by *proclamations and theoretical constitutions,* all thinking beings have the right to express their opinions, their systems, and their ideas, without the authorities or the mob's opposing this exercise of mental faculties.

One of the things that attracts the attention in Philadelphia is the amazing ship *Pennsylvania,* which without a doubt is the largest boat built up to the present time. It has, or is supposed to have, 150 cannons and 1,400 men. Its main anchor weighs 10,171 pounds. The length of the ship is 220 feet, and it is 58 feet wide. It has thirty-four beams on each deck; the main beam is two feet in diameter. It has five bridges. This boat as well as others and the war frigates that are built in the United States are covered with superstructures of wood that are taken down when they are launched.

The United States Navy has given unequivocal proofs during the last war with England of its capability, bravery, and discipline. What nation has been able to compete with the proud Albion, exclusive mistress of the ocean, except her emancipated daughter, that enterprising nation which lifts itself up each year to a greater height, that some day shall surpass the other powerful nations? The North Americans count with pride among their naval men the names of Stephen Decatur, the American Nelson, Patterson, Bainbridge, and Porter.

In this city was written the famous Declaration of Independence on July 4, 1776, and the hall still stands where the illustrious Americans signed it. In this hall is the statue of General Washington with this inscription at its base:

FIRST IN WAR
FIRST IN PEACE
FIRST IN THE HEARTS OF
HIS COUNTRYMEN

At the back of this building is a small plaza, one corner of which adjoins the beautiful Washington Square, one of the best places to walk in Philadelphia, marked off by iron railings very well made.

As we speak of a city founded by Quakers, and in which the major part of the people are of that faith, we should not pass in silence over the manner in which they observe their worship.

This famous sect, founded by George Fox in the seventeenth century in England, had as its object to follow strictly the doctrines of the gospel. Thus it is that the counsel to present the other cheek when one is struck, that of St. James to say *yea, yea, nay, nay* and never go beyond that, that of humility, and others similar formed the body of their doctrine, so that they did not admit war, nor oaths, nor any manner of luxury, etc.

Such people who on the other hand reproved other religious sects as profanations suffered cruel persecution from the beginnings of their church. Their opposition to taking oaths before courts, to taking up arms in defense of their country, and their hatred for the dominant sects were plausible pretexts for presenting them as enemies of religion and the community. The fantastic differences in their dress, in their language, and in their manners seemed to be the symbol of their sharp and perpetual separation from human society. Proscribed by law and by prejudice, they gladly accepted the mercy of King Charles II of England. They were the most consistent adherents of passive obedience which the gospel prescribes, because they resisted no affront, nor disarmed their enemies otherwise than by kindness and by their submission to the injustice of tyrants.

William Penn, one of the illustrious converts of this religious doctrine, after having employed all his talents without results for systematizing religious liberty under Charles II, saw himself obliged to come to America to seek asylum for his persecuted brothers, and he founded the city of Philadelphia and other towns of the state of Pennsylvania, a name derived from that of its founder. The admirable Locke, his friend, gave him the first laws for his colony. Charles II granted him all those lands for the debts of the crown to the admiral his father, and then he entered into treaties with the other provinces. Treaties made without oaths, says Voltaire, are the only ones that have not been broken. William Penn died in London in 1718 while negotiating for certain privileges for the trade of his colony.

The worship of the Quakers, like their dress, is extremely simple.

There are no sacraments, there are no prayers, there are no saints. All of them keep their hats on, the women separated from the men. Any one who feels inspired goes up to the pulpit, or from his bench preaches, or counsels, or says some sentences. When a person begins to speak, he takes off his big hat, if a man, if a woman, she speaks with her hat on. It is a singular manner of worshiping God; but perhaps they say the same thing about our mass and our ceremonies. The important thing is that in general they are charitable, hardworking, and honorable. The women are modest and simple.

In Philadelphia Sunday is even sadder than in New York. All the women go to the churches of their respective sects, and they are there two hours in the morning and two more in the afternoon at least. Many men go also, but not all of them. On these days there is no music, nor games, nor any other type of entertainment. The streets where there are churches are closed with chains to prevent the passage of carriages whose noise would interrupt the worship service.

Philadelphia is the city of capital as New York is of commerce. In the former is the main branch of the Bank of the United States. This bank was created in 1816, with a charter for twenty years. It began its operation January 1 of that year with a nominal capital of thirty-five million dollars. The general government is a shareholder in this bank to the sum of seven million dollars, but in reality it has not delivered to the bank more than the two million dollars that it had deposited formerly, with the result that the shares that it has are the capital from a debt that has been opened for it on the books of the bank.

The other $28,000,000 in capital, divided into 280,000 shares at $100 each, were subscribed by individuals and were to be settled in three payments, to wit: $5 in money and $25 in specie or public paper at will at the time of the subscription, and the other $70 in two equal payments of $35 each, of which $10 would be paid in cash and $25 in public paper or in coin. The $5 per share of the first payment is the only payment that the bank has received in coin of gold and silver. The directors thought that it was not necessary to demand more.

"It is clear," one of them said, "that when the bank had begun its operations and put its paper into circulation, it could not oblige its shareholders to buy gold or silver coin to make the payment of $10 that was supposed to be made in cash when the second and third payments became due."

As a result a memorial was presented to Congress in 1819 that the bank had not really received more than $324,000 in cash, instead of the $2,800,000 that the shareholders were to have put in on the second payment, and that the third brought in an even smaller amount. The shareholders paid with paper and in part with bills of the bank itself that they had received, taking the legal discount and received guaranteed titles to the shares. Thus, instead of the bank's capital being, as required by the charter granted, $7,000,000 in cash and $28,000,000 in public funds, after making the three payments it was only $2,000,000 in silver or gold and $21,000,000 in public funds; the balance of $12,000,000 was satisfied with titles of shares of the first shareholders.

In a work that has as its principal purpose presenting to Mexicans the customs, manners, institutions, and establishments of the United States as a nominal model, to put it thus, for Mexican legislators, it should not appear as beyond its scope to give an extensive idea of the system of banks established in that country, which moreover can be rather useful for their financial system. Therefore, I am going to continue to indicate what has happened and what is happening among our neighbors to the north in this interesting area.

I have pointed out the manner in which the Bank of the United States was set up, and the reader will be surprised at the manner in which a State Bank called the Sulton Bank was founded in Boston in 1828. It can be affirmed that most of the banks of that country have been created on more or less the same basis. By a decree of the legislature of the State of Massachusetts, in March of 1828, the directors of the new Sulton Bank were authorized to establish it under the obligation that the capital would be $100,000 in gold or silver, divided into 1,000 shares at $100 each; that half of this sum would be paid before October 1 of that year, and the other half during the following six months; that the bank would not begin its discounts, loans or issuing of bills until there capital of $50,000.

To assure the execution of these clauses, it was added that the bank could not begin its operations until a commission of six members named by the governor of the State had verified the existence in the coffers of the bank of the sum expressed of $50,000 in hard money. The directors should declare under oath that that capital was the product of the payments made by the shareholders for the funds of the bank, and that it would remain as half of the total.

On September 26, 1828, the governor named the commission at the request of the directors. On the day that the visit was to be made the directors of the new bank asked the loan of the sum of $50,000 on bills from another bank called the City Bank, for just one day. This sum was counted and its existence verified by the commissioners as though coming from payments made by the shareholders, on the sworn statement of the directors, all according to the law that granted the charter.

When the formality was concluded, the money was returned to the lenders, and the bank had left only the small sum coming from the shareholders. This was the matter of an hour's time. The truth of this affair is set forth in a memorial directed to the senate of Massachusetts in January of 1830. In it is stated furthermore that the second payment was no more precisely made than the first; and in this manner the Sulton Bank, instead of a capital of $100,000, could scarcely count on a fourth of that amount.

Among the present stockholders of the State banks there are many who have paid in whole the total amount for the shares that they possess, especially those that have bought the original titles, with the result therefore that the first founders have made a great profit.

It is evident that the real capital of American banks differs greatly from the nominal capital, and since far from directing their operations regularly on this basis, they do not hesitate to issue bills of circulation or credit for sums that double or even triple the figures, the result is that the total of the obligations contracted by the banks with the public is always greater than the real assets that they have for fulfilling them. In ordinary times, as long as there is no sudden event, an unforeseen circumstance that produces in people's minds an uneasiness sufficiently great to cause the multitude to decide to go to the banks to demand payment in cash of the great mass of circulating bills in their hands, the directors of these establishments are always in a position to satisfy the ordinary demands. Having a knowledge of the daily flow of deposits and other payments, by very approximate calculations they are careful to keep in the cash reserves a sum in gold or silver equivalent to the amount of the bills that may be presented for cash.

But the moment that a grave circumstance such as a war or a commercial crisis is felt to be approaching, the confidence is weakened to the degree that it impels the holders to rush to the banks for money, and the latter find themselves with a sum three or four times greater than their cash reserves. With the impossibility of satisfying such demands the banks suspend payment and often take bankruptcy.

These crises, from which European banks established upon more solid bases and much more rational principles are not entirely exempt, are repeated frequently in the United States, and since 1828 have been the cause of 144 of the 544 banks in the country being declared in complete bankruptcy. Fifty suspended their payments and ceased their operations entirely. Even the Bank of the United States several times found itself embarrassed and compromised. The years 1814, 1819, 1825 and 1828 are the periods when these institutions found themselves in the hardest straits. The crisis of 1814, occasioned by a war that the Americans were then carrying on with the British, obliged all the banks of the Union, including the former Bank of the United States, whose time had not yet run out, to suspend redemption of their respective bills.

In 1816 and 1817 when the issuance of bills was considerable, there was so great an export of coin that the banks were not able to procure what was necessary to redeem their notes. The new Bank of the United States found itself obliged (as this year) to cause money to be brought from Europe to the United States, and in spite of all its efforts, at that time it could not get together in cash reserves more than three million dollars, a sum completely insufficient to maintain its operations and those of its eighteen branches in the states. It had to take recourse then in a partial suspension of payments in cash, fortunately coming out of this crisis in a short time. This did not happen with several private banks that closed their doors and dragged to ruin a considerable number of families.

Likewise the issuance of a large amount of notes was what brought about the difficulties in 1828. In this last period the directors of the Bank of the United States, in an effort to rid themselves of the competition of other banks, made every effort to extend the operations of their former branches in order to establish new offices. They issued a larger number of bills and authorized their different dependant banks, whose number had now reached twenty-four, to discount private bills. They had calculated that their bills and those of their branches would enjoy more consideration than those of the local banks, and it would be easy for them to substitute in circulation their own notes for those of the others by taking them. Then they could present all at once the notes for payment, or retain them on deposit, thus lessening their operations and drafts. They succeeded indeed in diminishing the operations of some banks, but they could not prevent others from increasing their discounts, which led to a new exportation of money from the country, and to its consequent scarcity, so that the banks could not find sufficient funds to meet their daily needs.

At the beginning of 1830 the total amount of gold and silver in circulation was valued at \$10,000,000, \$55,000,000 in bank notes, and in bank credits an equal amount. The existing sum in cash for assuring the payment of notes and bank credits, that is to say \$110,000,000, consisted of only \$22,000,000 in hard money.

The banking system, with the extension that it has been given in the United States, had in its beginning an extremely beneficial effect on the progress of industry in that country. However, as a consequence of the excessive issuance of bills, metal coinage has been exported, thus leaving in circulation the representative symbols in too large a proportion to maintain credit for very long. Indeed, the bills that the banks issued appeared to have the advantage of increasing the wealth of the country by raising the nominal value of all goods and property. But since the result of an abundant circulation is to raise the prices of merchandise in the country, it is clear that the time will come when they will not be able to export goods in exchange for foreign products because with the expense of transportation, duties and other things, they will not be able to meet the competition of foreign merchants. Then it will be necessary to resort to the export of hard cash to secure consumer goods in a nation where there are no mines, or where the products of the mines do not furnish a quarter of the cash necessities; it will bring about the scarcity that has caused the bankruptcies of which I have spoken.

These ideas on the banking system in the United States that I have taken from a book entitled *History of Paper Money and Banks in the United States* can give the readers an understanding of the great question that is being argued between the government of President Jackson and the supporters of the Bank of the United States. The president has believed that a renewal of the charter of the bank referred to would be a great disservice to the country, as much because it creates a sort of monetary aristocracy as because the system of banks is harmful to the nation.

There is an establishment in Philadelphia that it would be well to adopt in Mexico, if not on as extensive a scale, at least to a lesser degree. A league from the city is the penitentiary, which is a building with thick walls of gray granite thirty feet high. It incloses a space a mile in circumference, and in the center of it the prison is located. This consists of a rotunda from which there project seven radials that form as many corridors, each about eleven feet wide. Between one radial and another are distributed the small rooms where the prisoners are. Each one has a small courtyard where he goes out to get some fresh air three hours each day. Beneath the rooms runs a sewer with water for sanitary purposes. From the corridor which controls all the cells, through a small hole, can be seen what the prisoner is doing, and from the rotunda the only watchman they have, seated in the center, can look along all the corridors that converge upon the center. There are no guards or watchmen; there are only four helpers to take the meals to the prisoners, the number of which was 350 when I was there. Their food is plentiful and healthful, but if they resist working, the amount is cut down. There are connecting pipes that heat their rooms in the winter.

The sentenced prisoner is brought into the prison blindfolded. Then he is taken to a small room where they cut his hair, he goes into another to bathe, and here he gets his prison garb which consists of a jacket, a cap, a shirt and a pair of trousers. The old clothes are put away until he leaves. The director of the establishment who is an honored and respected Englishman, Scotch I *think,* told me that the work done produces all that is necessary to support the institution. Smoking is not permitted, nor can they drink anything besides water. They can only have the Bible or some book of devotion according to the sect of the prisoner. Many men who have been in this prison have gone out afterwards rehabilitated to continue a normal life.

Men that have been imprisoned three, four, or six years without communication with anyone, when they come out into the world, arrive with new clothes, with the reflective character that should be contracted in society, and without inclinations to vices, or at least with them very much lessened. The same thing does not happen with persons who have been in a prison with others, where unfortunately they do not acquire virtuous habits.

In the state of Pennsylvania there is a university where moral philosophy, history, Latin, Greek, Hebrew, metaphysics, ideology and mathematics are taught. The course is four years, a very short time to come out thoroughly educated in any branch. But generally speaking, in that republic they have preferred to promote primary education rather than to build establishments such as Oxford or Cambridge that contain the elements of advanced science, of those sciences that absorb the whole life in profound and elevated meditations. The prime necessity is to read and write. This the North Americans try to satisfy by giving to primary education all the general character that is compatible with the other social necessities. The basis of education in that country is to "extend the sphere of thought and to elevate the conscience by means of useful knowledge that makes man apt for dealing ably with the affairs of life and not to make himself ridiculous or the object of scorn because of a noticeable ignorance."

This does not mean that in the United States there are not men of great knowledge and scientific ability. Evidently there are, but not in the number corresponding to the population, as occurs in England, France and the other civilized nations of northern Europe. The translation that has just been published in Boston of the works of M. LaPlace is an unmistakable proof of the great advances of that city.

In Philadelphia I met Mr. Sergeant, a distinguished lawyer of the United States who was in Mexico as minister to the Congress of Tacubaya, where the ministers of the republics of America were supposed to be gathered, according to the agreement of the Congress of Panama in 1826. It is well known that this project was never carried out. Mr. Sergeant is an American very learned in his profession, and has a rather wide reputation, to the extent that it took him to the candidacy for the vice-presidency against Mr. Van Buren. I also spoke with Mr. Walsh, editor of the *National Gazette* and of the *Quarterly Review,* periodicals respected in both hemispheres for the ability with which they are written and the material that they contain, especially the second, with M. DuPonceau, a Frenchman of literature and patriarch of the literary societies of Philadelphia because of his age and vast education.

Mr. Girard, the richest banker that has lived since M. Rothschild, died this year (December of 1831); he was French, born in Bordeaux. Since in

1811 the former Bank of the United States ceased operations, Mr. Girard took advantage of the building and the credits with the lack of discounts that were no longer made, and extended his drafts and business. He left about eight million dollars, and the greater part of his fortune he distributed in the United States, especially in Pennsylvania and New York. In his will he placed an express clause that in none of the colleges that were to be established with his funds should any ecclesiastic of any religion be admitted. He detested any exclusive doctrine.

CHAPTER X

In 1830 I visited the widow of Señor Don Agustín de Iturbide in Georgetown near Washington, where she was living and looking after the education of her children. In 1834 I had the pleasure of seeing this respectable Mexican family for a second time in Philadelphia, after the president of the Mexican republic, General Santa Anna, had lifted the banishment which condemned her to live outside her own country, although with a good pension. Señora Iturbide had achieved in good part the fruits of her endeavors; her older daughters, receiving an education according to the culture of the country, have followed the wishes of their teachers and have augmented the charms of their sex with the advantages of the mind and with the physical perfection of a material education.

The market of Philadelphia is one of the best that I have seen. It is on a street at least one hundred feet wide and one mile long, in the midst of which they have built a wooden shed open on both sides and covered with a roof overhead. A large crowd of people comes there in the mornings to buy necessary provisions from an abundant market, to which come contributions from the sea, the rivers, the land and the air. Indeed, one finds there fresh and salt water fish, wild animals, birds, vegetables, flowers, fruits, seeds, meats prepared with care and everything that the gourmet could wish to provide for his kitchen and to set a good table.

Four miles from Philadelphia is a small town called Frankfort, the home of Colonel Burnt, an old friend of Mr. Poinsett. The latter invited me to pay a visit to his friend, and I had the pleasure of a day in the home of Mr. Burnt. He commanded a body of calvary in the last war with England, and he had retired to live peacefully in a country home that he has in the town; it is very well cared for, well laid out, although small, but with all the comforts for a man alone. He had his principal holdings in Scotland, where after his death Mr. Poinsett, his executor, went to get them together. Mr. Burnt was a man of pleasant disposition, had a good education and was extremely modest. Some travelers in America have spoken of him in the same vein.

In Philadelphia I embarked on the steamboat *William Penn,* in company with Señor Mejía, who as I have said was secretary to the Mexican legation in the United States. After traveling down the river for three hours we disembarked upon an isthmus that is formed between the Delaware River, Chesapeake Bay and a canal that leads to the latter in the state of Delaware. This is one of the states that formed the first confederation which numbered thirteen. Its population will scarcely reach two hundred thousand inhabitants, but it prospers like the others because of the wisdom of its government, the industry of its inhabitants, its liberal institutions, economics and other circumstances that distinguish the fortunate states. The schools are established in Delaware upon the same basis as those of Boston, of which I shall speak later.

The constitution of this small state was written in 1792 and revised in 1831. The legislature is called the General Assembly, and is composed of a senate and house of representatives. It has nine senators, with three named from each of its counties, a third of them elected every four years.* There are twenty-one representatives, seven from each county, and all are elected every two years. The General Assembly meets in Dover, capital of the state, biennially, the first Tuesday in the month of January, unless the governor calls it into session before that time. The general election is held the second Tuesday in November of the preceding year.

The executive power is held by the governor elected by the people every four years, and he cannot be reelected for an immediately succeeding term. The judicial power resides in a Court of Errors and Appeals, a Supreme Court, another of Chancellery, another of orphans, another of hearing of last resort, another of general sessions of peace, liberty, prisoners, and one of registry, etc.

The right of suffrage is held by all male citizens who are white and twenty-one years of age, provided they have resided for one year in the state prior to the elections, and for one month in the county in which they are held, and in which they have paid taxes.

On the canal that leads from the Delaware River to Chesapeake Bay one travels fourteen miles and then walks twenty or thirty yards to take the steamer on the second. I boarded the *Charles Carroll,* of four hundred tons, with room for three hundred passengers and baggage. I arrived in Baltimore at five o'clock in the afternoon of the same day.

Baltimore, a city of one hundred thousand inhabitants, is located between the Patapsa, Potomac, and Susquehannah Rivers and almost in the life stream of the United States. It is the largest city in the state of Maryland, whose capital is Annapolis. Lord Baltimore, an English gentleman and a Catholic, was the founder of this colony, and the principles of tolerance and philosophy of that venerable colonizer were in contrast to the persecutions of the Puritans of New England.

I stayed at the City Hotel, which they call by another name, Barnum, because he is the owner of the hostel. It is the largest one in Baltimore, and its central location on the corner of the square where is located the monument to the memory of the victims of the war of 1814, together with the good service that is to be found there, make it one of the more popular ones. The service is usually by blacks and colored people and some Irish.

The monument of which I just spoke, called the Battle Monument, a sort of trophy erected in memory of the resistance to the attack which under the orders of General Ross the English made against the city, contains the names of the most notable persons who died in the action. The column rises to about fifty feet, represents the Roman fasces, the symbol of union, and at each corner there is a spigot. On top is located the statue of Victory. Nobler and simpler is the monument erected to the memory of the immortal Washington on a hill that overlooks the city. It consists of a white marble column 150 feet high, upon which is placed the statue of the hero.

The Catholic cathedral is considered as one of the best churches in the United States. It is a very small one compared with our cathedrals of Mexico City, Puebla, Merida and Jalisco and much more so when compared to those of the great and ancient cities of Europe. However, the interior aspect of this church is very pleasant for its cleanliness and for some of its images and pictures. It is in the form of a Greek cross with its cupola in the center. The type of architecture is irregular with leanings towards the Gothic. Another Catholic building attracts the attention of the traveler in Baltimore, and it is the chapel of St. Mary's College. Although located in the heart of the city, this building is as solitary and silent as though it were in the desert. It is surrounded by a small garden where there is a Mount of Calvary with a very tall cross. A narrow lane among the shrubs and cedars leads to a small chapel, comparable in its smallness and beauty to that of Santa Teresa in Mexico. A lamp, whose dim light filters through the glass that covers it, sheds upon the darkness a melancholy clarity, fitting for a soul that comes to lift its entreaties and prayers in a self-communion that should not be interrupted by any strong emotion. The light of day comes in through the windows that are covered with glass of crimson color which gives an aspect of sublimity and grandeur to that sacred place.

There is another well-known building in Baltimore, and it is the church of the Unitarians. This sect, more philosophical than religious, is making extraordinary progress in all parts of the United States, especially in New England. The Unitarians are as opposed to the trinity of the persons in the divinity, as the reformers to the mass. It is a modification of the doctrines of the Socinians, enlightened by the progress that philosophy has made in the nineteenth century.

The *infant school* of Mr. Ibberson is one of the most useful establishments, not only in Baltimore, but even in the United States. Children from the age of two years begin to receive by means of agreeable sensations and material lessons instruction which serves later as a basis for a more thorough knowledge of geography, natural history, botany and arithmetic. Instead of entertaining the children with dolls, tops, whistles and other childish toys, they are made familiar with the different kinds of animals painted in natural colors—birds, fishes, quadrupeds. A large map is placed on the wall with the rivers, seas, isthmuses, islands, continents; they make pictures which contain the letters of the alphabet. In short, they prepare the first elements of instruction in different pleasant ways, and when they get through, the children already know the letters and their combinations. They know the names of the animals, plants, flowers; they can pick out the continents, rivers, etc. Mr. Ibberson has about one hundred children of both sexes who will later spread the teaching abroad in their country.

The constitution of the state of Maryland was written in 1776. Since then it has been amended many times. The legislative power is exercised by the senate, which contains fifteen members, and by the House of Delegates composed of eighty members. Both together form the body called the General Assembly of Maryland. The members of the House of Delegates, four from each county, two from Baltimore and two from Annapolis, are elected annually by the people the first Monday in October. Those of the senate are elected every five years the third Monday in September, in the capital Annapolis by electors chosen by the people the first Monday of the same month of September. These electors, voting by written ballot, elect nine senators from the west shore and six from the east shore, and these serve for five years.

The executive power is in the hands of the governor, who is named by the two houses by a majority vote each year on the first Monday in January; he cannot be reelected more than twice so that one person cannot direct the destinies for more than three years; he is eligible to be elected for the same job after having been out of office for four years. The governor has a council of five delegates named by both houses.

The General Assembly meets in regular session the last Monday in

ember. The governor appoints the employees, and the council confirms
1. According to the constitution the right of suffrage is held by all white
twenty-one years of age who have lived one year in the state and six
iths in the county, or in the cities of Annapolis or Baltimore. The chan-
or and the judges are named by the governor with the approval of the
incil.

From Baltimore to Washington it is forty miles, which is covered by
land. I took a private coach to make this journey more slowly and with
greater comfort. I was accompanied by Don Anastasio Zercero, who met
me in Baltimore, and who was at that time exiled by the Mexican republic
for political matters.

Washington is a city erected upon the ashes to which it was reduced by
the British troops and British navy in 1814 under General Ross and Admiral Cockburn. For many years Congress met in a provisional building until
the Capitol was constructed, a magnificent work, which does no discredit
to this venerable word. Built upon the highest point in the city, it dominates
the whole place as does the Potomac River, which at that point is half a mile
wide. It seems that from its superb cupola freedom and liberation of
thought and ideas are announced to humanity, while in that original Capitol in Rome subjection, slavery and blind obedience were preached.

Who does not feel inspired with these noble feelings as he mounts the
steps that lead to those chambers where discussions have as their purpose
the true interests of the masses? There one finds no hereditary privileges,
no lifetime incomes, no sacred persons. That assembly is judged also by the
people who have the faculty of subjecting to examination in the press, in the
clubs, in assemblies, the opinions and decisions of those mandated. I had
come from Mexico when I visited the Capitol in Washington. What should
I think of all that I saw, that I heard, that I felt, in the capital city of the
AngloSaxon Union, in the very building where the legislators of the human
race gather?

In this magnificent building the two chambers of the general congress
meet, have their offices, and here are located the supreme court and the
offices attached to it. The home of the president is on the opposite side of
the city, a mile from the Capitol. It is a beautiful building 175 feet long and
85 feet wide. It has only two stories, and although there are included in it
all the comforts for a family, it is not a palace. On the same terrain, at some
distance, there are four buildings that correspond to the four corners of the
president's house, which are the offices of the state department.

Mr. Van Buren, who was secretary of state when I went to Washington
the first time, did me the honor of inviting me to dinner. At the dinner were
the foreign ministers and many of the more distinguished representatives

and senators. Señor Tornel, the minister from Mexico to the United States at that time, had his residence in Baltimore.

Mr. Van Buren is a man about fifty years of age, small in stature, blond, with a very spiritual face and well educated. He is from the state of New York where he was governor when called to be secretary of state. After my departure from Washington he was sent to London as minister plenipotentiary while the chambers were in recess. The Senate did not approve his nomination, and the Democratic party, of which he was the head, to avenge him for this insult, named him vice-president in 1832.

Since I was near Mount Vernon, the residence of General Washington, I decided to cross the Potomac and make this little journey of fifteen miles in order to have the pleasure of walking in the same places where the venerable patriarch of liberty had lived and to meet his nephew, the heir to his home and virtues. I took a coach for hire, went over the very long bridge across the Potomac and arrived after five hours at Mount Vernon, a very pleasant place associated with such interesting memories. There I met Mr. Washington, one of the individuals of the Supreme Court of the United States, who with the greatest politeness showed me all of his uncle's rooms, which they have tried to keep just as he left them, out of a religious respect for his memory.* In the vestibule one can see hanging the keys to the Bastille which General Lafayette sent to his venerable friend.

General Washington was the oldest son of the second marriage of Augustine Washington of Virginia, grandson of John Washington, a gentleman of a respected family in the north of England, from where he migrated. Lawrence Washington, the oldest son of the father of George Washington by the first marriage, left the lands of Mount Vernon to George, who was born February 22, 1732, and after a glorious life died December 11, 1800.

The state of Virginia, founded as an English colony under the direction of Mr. Smith, has become the second state after having been the first one of the Federation. The extraordinary character and amazing adventures of Smith will make an interesting episode on this journey.

Captain John Smith was born in 1579 in Willoughby, in the County of Lincoln. From a very tender age he astonished his companions and even his school master by the boldness of his pranks. He was thirteen years old when he got the desire to see the ocean. With this in mind he sold his books and toys, which brought him a small sum. He was getting ready to leave when his father died, and he fell under the tutelage of positive men to whom the romantic bent of the youth seemed a bitter madness, and although he was the object of a kindly watchfulness on their part, nevertheless, it was so narrow that it became unbearable to his independent spirit. As soon as he was fifteen years old, so that he might occupy his intellectual faculties he was placed in the store of a merchant who was not economical either in the lessons that he gave nor in the work that he had for him.

The merchant with whom Smith was learning was one of the principal ones of Lynn. He had much maritime business, and the young Smith hoped that his master would let him travel, and travel on the sea. However, since he heard nothing concerning his shipping out, and weary of that monotony, without taking leave he left the merchant and his business, and departed with only two or three dollars. His lucky star caused him to fall in with a young lord who was going with his numerous company on a trip to Europe. Smith settled down to his service, but this was not for long.

After some months he became displeased with his new master and went to enlist in the army in Holland. He spent three or four years there, and inspired by a Scottish gentleman who offered him excellent recommendations to the court of King James, he crossed the sea again and went to Scotland. When his hopes were dashed, he left the court and took the road again to his native country. There in horror at the fanatical patriotism of his fellow countrymen he went to live alone in the midst of the forest with some books on tactics and military history, a horse and a lance. Thus he divided his time between the study of war and the exercise of arms without seeing another person besides an Italian servant from the house of the Count of Lincoln.

While engaged in these pastimes he came into possession of a part of his father's fortune. With the means to travel, he again had the desire to see the world. So here is Smith once more launched upon the ocean. He arrived in Flanders, and there he was robbed by four French swindlers; he followed them, found one of them, fought him, wounded him, made him confess his crime, and set out on the road again with some money that an old friend of the family had given him. He followed the coastline of France from Dunkirk to Marseilles, visiting the arsenals and fortifications. Then he set sail for Italy.

An Englishman and a heretic, he found himself to his misfortune in the midst of a crowd of pilgrims who were going to fulfill their promises to our Lady of Loreto and to Rome. The boat was overtaken by a storm; the pilgrims overpowered the heretic, and the new *Jonah* Smith was thrown into the sea. He had the good fortune to be able to swim to St. Mary's Island near Nice. He stopped there just long enough to take another boat that was leaving for Alexandria.

This ship, after completing its voyage, got into a dispute with another boat from Venice with a rich cargo, attacked it, captured it and stripped it. He had them let him off in Antibes with his part of the booty, went to Italy, crossed the Gulf of Venice, arrived in Styria and wound up by volunteering in the service of the emperor, who was at that time at war with the Turks.

Smith was not only brave and enterprising; he was also a resourceful man. He found the means to force the Turks to lift the siege of Olympach and thus earn the rank of captain in the regiment of the Count of Meldritch, a distinguished man from Transylvania. After many deeds, Smith found himself at the siege of Regal in Transylvania; the siege was long, and one day a herald presented himself in the Christian camp and announced that the lord *Turbashaw*, a famous Turk, challenged the bravest among them to singlehanded combat, for the purpose, he said, of amusing the ladies and passing the time. By lot it was decided that from the Christian warriors Smith should be the one who must answer the Turk's challenge. The combat was solemnly held; the Turkish ladies adorned the parapets of Regal; the besiegers were stationed along their lines; the music sounded. Smith killed the Ottoman; another Turk undertook to avenge *Turbashaw;* Smith killed him also. A third one presented himself, the terrible Bonny-Mulgro of gigantic stature. At the first charge Smith was almost dismounted by a blow from the axe. The Turks burst into shouts of joy, and the Turkish women clapped; they even shouted and applauded when Bonny-Mulgro, run through by a sword thrust, lay stretched out on the ground and Smith cut off his head. A short time later the city was taken.

But the fortunes of war are changeable. Some time later the Christians were beaten; Smith was left for dead on the field of battle; the richness of his armor caused the Turks to take him for a distinguished personage; he was treated as a man worth a considerable ransom; cured quickly he was taken to the slave market of Axiopolis; there he was bought by a pasha, who sent him to the lady of his thoughts in Constantinople, saying (despicable show-off) that he was a Bohemian gentleman that he had taken in battle. This pretense turned out badly for the pasha; Charatza Tragabigzanda (this was the lady's name) knew Italian, and Smith spoke it also; he told her his adventures, his glory and his misfortunes; Tragabigzanda began to get angry at the boasting of the pasha; she was moved by Smith's misfortunes, and later she was inflamed by his noble actions and his perils like Desdemona, says one of the captain's biographers. Smith hoped for a little rest and happiness when the lady, either to circumvent the suspicions of her mother or to make Smith learn Turkish, sent him to her brother Timur-Pasha, whose residence was on the shores of the Sea of Azov.

The instructions from Tragabigzanda were very insistent; to her brother she confessed her feelings for the captive; but the pasha of the Sea of Azov was angry that a *Christian dog* should have engaged his sister's heart. Smith, who expected a cordial reception, had not been an hour in Timur's house when he had been beaten, stripped and shaved. They put an iron collar on him, covered him with a heavy horsehair cloak and sent him to work the land with the other Christian slaves of the pasha. Every day this barbarian master inspected the prisoner's work and flayed him with insults and blows.

Once when Smith was alone with him, and the pasha was berating him for the way he was threshing the grain, Smith killed him with a blow from the harrow, hid the body under the straw, and mounting the Ottoman's Arabic horse, fled at top speed. When he reached deserted country, he got his directions as best he could and after traveling for six days he arrived at Hexapolis on the Don River; there he met a Russian vanguard. The Russians received him generously; a charitable or merciful lady, the Princess or Baroness of Palamata, showered Smith with evidence of interest. After resting he set out for Transylvania where his friends wept for joy when they saw him, giving him generous help. From there he returned to England, passing through Germany, France, Spain, and the kingdom of Morocco.

He got to England just at the moment when an expedition was leaving for America to found a colony. Invited to participate, he accepted. Smith was then twenty-eight years old. The expedition left the Thames December 19, 1606, and entered Chesapeake Bay April 26, 1607. On May 13 he disembarked on a peninsula where the colony of Jamestown was founded. The traveler who goes up the James River today in a steamer will see on this peninsula a tower in ruins and the remains of a corner of a cemetery. That is all that is left of this first establishment.

As companions, Smith had mediocre men that could not forgive him his superiority; scarcely had they left the Thames when he was accused of plotting to have himself crowned in the colony. Under this absurd pretext he was put in prison during the crossing. After they disembarked, when they read the instructions given to the expedition, it was found that the government of the colony was entrusted to a council of seven persons, among whom was Smith. His companions excluded him under the pretext of his pretended aims. Smith asked for a trial, but he could not get one.

He armed himself with patience and went out to explore the areas around Jamestown, going up the rivers, getting acquainted with the Indian tribes, and paying visits to Powhatan, the most powerful of the Indian princes. During this time the colony was badly governed; nothing was planned in advance; no houses were built for winter which was approaching; there were little or no provisions, no military precautions against the savages, who because of some hostility had made known their dissatisfaction. One day the colony was suddenly attacked by Powhatan's warriors, a man was killed and seventeen wounded, there was discontent against the council and principally against President Wingfield. Smith took advantage of the occasion to insist upon his petition concerning the trial; he obtained it, was absolved of all charges, and Wingfield was condemned to pay him £200 sterling in damages, which Smith generously turned over for the benefit of the colony. At once there was a sort of reconciliation. All the colonists took communion the same day as a sign of forgetting what had happened, and Captain Newport, who had brought them from England, returned with his fleet, leaving the colony composed of 105 persons.

But then came scarcity and with it illnesses, and afterwards what is worse than the plague, discord. Fifty colonists perished miserably. In the midst of the general despair President Wingfield, in agreement with some of his companions, decided to take over secretly the only boat that the colony possessed and flee to England. The plot was discovered; Wingfield was deposed, and another president elected in his place. He had the good sense to be guided by Smith whose moment had come. Smith laid out a work plan and gave each one his task; he was obeyed. Houses were built, the colony was fortified and covered. He himself gave the example to the workers by working harder than they did.

It was not enough to have houses for the winter; it was necessary to have provisions also. Smith set about looking for these, and especially corn which the Indians cultivated. On one of these excursions he encountered a large tribe, took their idol, demanded as ransom for their god several bushels of corn as well as venison and hastened back to Jamestown with this food. He arrived just in time because Wingfield had again planned his flight, and this time it was necessary to fight to bring the conspirators to order. From that time on the authority remained firmly in Smith's hands.

Scarcely had he straightened things out in the colony when, allowing himself to be carried away by his enterprising imagination—perhaps more than was proper for a man upon whose shoulders the health of the colony depended—he set out to explore the Chickahominy River. He went up as far as he could in his boat, and leaving it with the greater part of the crew, hidden in a cove protected against all danger, he went even farther upstream in a canoe, taking with him two white men and two Indians. Unfortunately those that he had left behind forgot their orders as soon as he was out of sight. Against his command they disembarked and were attacked by a group of Indians under Opechancanough, brother of Powhatan, who was spying on Smith. One of them was taken prisoner and forced to tell where the captain had gone; the others were able to get back to the boat and save themselves.

During this time Smith had arrived at the swamps that were the source of the river. Opechancanough surprised him in the night and killed the two Englishmen. Smith was surrounded by two hundred barbarians; an arrow wounded him in the thigh, and he defended himself with the *wisdom of a serpent* and the *strength of a leopard.* He killed three of his enemies and tying one of his two Indians to his arm with thongs, he used him as a shield. His enemies were frightened and separated; he had gained ground and was going back to his boat, but as he crossed he fell into the midst of a swamp that he could not get through and sank with his Indian up to his waist. Such was the fear that he instilled in the savages that even under these circumstances none of them dared to approach him until he threw them his arms. He was half dead with cold. The Indians pulled him out of the swamp, put him by the fire and rubbed him down until he recovered the use of his limbs.

Smith considered himself lost. The bodies of his companions were lying to one side quartered. It occurred to him to take from his bag a compass and show it to Opechancanough. The savage could not get over his amazement caused by this needle that moved all the time. As he had no notion of transparency, he was even more surprised that it was impossible for him to take hold of the needle with his fingers although he could see it perfectly (it was covered with glass). Smith, in an effort to excite even more the wonder of the barbarian chief and his warriors, began to talk to them about the movement of the heavenly bodies, about the sun and the moon, all that he knew about astronomy. His listeners heard him in amazement. Savage instinct took over again. After Smith had finished his speech, they tied him to a tree. The savages made a circle around him and aimed their arrows at him. Smith was going to die.

When the time came to give the signal to let fly the arrows at his chest, Opechancanough ordered that he be pardoned. He wanted to show off his prize at the court of the neighboring princes, and especially at that of Powhatan, the lord and master of all, because all the chieftains had formed a confederation of the James River, as the German princes formed the Rhine Confederation some twenty years ago, and Powhatan was the protecting Napoleon.

Smith's bravery, his physical strength and active mind caused the savages to consider him as an extraordinary man, superhuman. His imprisonment was celebrated with endless ceremonies in which the savages heaped all manner of attentions upon him that they could imagine. So careful were they to furnish him with fresh food that Smith thought immediately that they were trying to get him fat in order to eat him later. Charlatans came to cast a spell upon him, the great spirit was consulted to know the depths of the captain's intentions. Powhatan brought out all his forest luxury to receive him. When Smith appeared before the first chief, a queen it was who washed his hands, and another presented him with a feather material as a sort of napkin. Smith was handed from tribe to tribe, and they wound up by proposing to him that he become a savage and direct the government of Jamestown. With this condition they offered him all the women and lands that he might want. At his negative reply there was a council of chieftains and kings in which it was decided that Smith should die, and that they should proceed immediately to the execution of the sentence.

This time everything was done. Two stones were brought to the feet of the great king, and the victim laid there. The chiefs took their places around him. The people were behind them in complete silence. Powhatan himself had wished to be the high priest. He approached with his mace and raised it to give the fatal blow. There was no hope!

Suddenly a woman—everywhere women were Smith's guardian angels—a woman had pushed through the crowd. She put her head between Smith's head and Powhatan's mace; she was the first-born daughter of the king, his most beloved daughter, the beautiful Pocahontas. Stretching out her arms to her father she begged him to pardon the captive. The king was angry at first, but he loved Pocahontas too much not to be moved by her tears. He looked around at his warriors, seeking in their eyes the resolve that he lacked; he saw that they were moved with compassion.

"Let him live," he said. The next day Smith was on his way to Jamestown with two guides. He was to send Powhatan as a peace testimonial two rifles and a grindstone.

Now that Smith was safe, he busied himself with the business of the colony, and when he had everything in order, he resumed his excursions. He ascended the Potomac and discovered in his course a thousand dangers—the small creeks, most of them backed up by the Chesapeake Bay. His presence of mind, the religious terror that he inspired in the savages, and especially the noble assistance of Pocahontas always saved him and the colony as if by a miracle.

Pocohontas, to be as famous as Atala, only needed to find a Chateaubriand. As young and as beautiful as the Muskogean daughter, she was more heroic, and it was not just one man that she saved. Weak as she was (she was fourteen or fifteen years old at the time), it happened many times that during the night she made long journeys through forests and across swamps, in the midst of hurricanes that are terrible in Virginia, to warn Smith and his colonists of the plottings of the savages. Other times when they were short of food, Pocohontas appeared as a kindly benefactor with a group loaded with provisions, and disappeared immediately after having supplied them.

Until that time no colony had been successfully founded on the American continent north of the Gulf of Mexico. Providence made use of the hands of that mysterious virgin to plant one at last. Greece would have erected altars to her or would have made her a goddess halfway between

Diana, goddess of the forests, and Minerva, the wise and farseeing one. The colonists managed things differently. When Smith separated from them, they took control of Pocohontas, intending to hold her as a hostage against her father Powhatan. After holding her for some time and treating her with the greatest of care, they agreed to marry her with her consent and that of her father to one of them, to Mr. Rolfe, who took her to England.

Pocohontas—the beautiful, the modest, the heroic Pocohontas—thus became Madame Rolfe, a resident of London and Brentford. At the age of twenty-two she died of consumption in Gravesand, just when she was going to take a ship for America. It may be that had her end been more tragic, she would have become the heroine of twenty epic poems.

The great deeds of Captain John Smith are as numerous and as amazing as those of Hercules. According to what he relates simply (like Caesar he wrote his memoirs) about a festival that the women of the court of Powhatan gave for him, it would not be going too far to believe that not a one of the adventures of Jupiter's son were missing, even those that belong to the domain of the secret chronicle. Once he surpassed Antheus' destruction by garroting single—handed a chief of gigantic proportions, the king of the Pashipsays, who had laid an ambush for him; he carried the chief into Jamestown on his shoulders. Again Opechancanough had besieged him with seven hundred men, and Smith took the chief by the hair, dragged him trembling and humiliated into the midst of the Indians frozen with stupor and made them give up their arms.

The difficulties that he had to overcome were endless. Against him he had hunger and pestilence, the cleverness and the arrows of the savages, violence on the part of the colonists, and the complaints and feelings of the others who sighed afterwards for the *fleshpots of Egypt,* the laziness and ignorance of the adventurers who poured in on the colony in search of gold there, the treachery of some, Germans and Swiss, who had gone over to Powhatan's kingdom because there was better food there—everything was against him, even rebellion and assassination by sword and poison.

There was no extremity to which he had not been reduced, and one day when his companions saw him in agony, they had already dug his grave. His perserverance and bravery triumphed over all else. Thanks to his tireless efforts the colony was established definitely; many towns were founded; and after remaining two years in Virginia, gravely wounded by the explosion of a barrel of powder, he left Jamestown never to return. After his departure, the colony still had much to suffer, but it had already put down its roots.

Such were the origins of Virginia. It was the most powerful state when the war for independence broke out. It would still be in the forefront without the institution of slavery, which holds it back like a great weight upon its feet. It is the one that gave the revolution Washington, Jefferson, Madison, Monroe and many less illustrious statesmen. It is evident that there are in the character of those men of Virginia generous and gentlemanly traits that like the example and lessons of Smith left a lasting mark upon the hearts of their companions.

If I recount thus in detail the life of John Smith, it is not because of the interest that is aroused by an extraordinary man, but it is indeed because of the analogy that our epoch presents with his.

It was a time of political and religious crisis, of civil war and revolution. It was the time of the reconstruction of Europe by the Treaty of Westphalia. It was then that Charles I lost his head; then another dynasty was on the eve of occupying the throne of England. It was the time when the Protestant party was trying to set up a republic in France. Imaginations were excited and unloosed; brains were working. Wise men believed then that the world was coming to an end. It was not, however, a world that was ending, but the new one that was being born, and the pains that the old one felt were the pangs of birth.

Let us suppose that men of the temperament of Smith had been obliged to remain in England. With that active imagination, that fiery energy, that determined will, inevitably they would have been launched into politics, at that time seething with interests and movements. And how many men of that temperament at the head of the parties would have been needed to turn the country upside down?

Let us say rather: England was indeed rocked upon her foundations then, and it may be said that it would not have been if two men, endowed as Smith was with a burning imagination and an iron will, had not been detained. Those two were John Hampden and Oliver Cromwell. They wanted to come to America; the king refused to let them. A few years later one of them struck down the royal power, at least as the Stuarts understood it; the other one killed the king.

CHAPTER XI

In Washington in 1830 a question was being aired, the discussion of which and the decision of the commission of the House of Representatives, as well as the final resolution of Congress, are a new proof of the generous, liberal and independent policy of the United States of the North. A large number of groups, especially Presbyterians, sent general representations to Congress asking that on Sunday, a day set aside for rest and prayer, the post offices not be opened and that the post routes not be run. The commission's decision is worthy of being included in this work, the main purpose of which is that the Mexicans and all the republics of that part of America formerly Spanish may take examples and lessons from that practical school of free and independent politics, which is today the model of all civilized peoples.

Later on I shall also include another no less interesting document that is the representation of several citizens of Virginia, made by Mr. Madison in 1784 on a similar subject, and in which the same principles are developed. For these documents and many items that I have made use of in this book I am indebted to the most valuable work of Mr. James Stuart entitled *Three Years in North America.*

The Committee on Post-offices and Post-roads, to whom the memorials were referred, for prohibiting the transportation of mails, and the opening of Post-offices on Sunday, report:—

That the memorialists regard the first day of the week as a day set apart by the Creator for religious exercises, and consider the transportation of the mail, and the opening of the post-offices on that day, the violation of a religious duty, and call for a suppression of the practice. Others, by counter memorials, are known to entertain a different sentiment, believing that no one day of the week is holier than another. Others, holding the universality and immutability of the Jew-

121

ish decalogue, believe in the sanctity of the seventh day of the week as a day of religious devotion; and by their memorial now before the committee, they also request that it may be set apart for religious purposes. Each has hitherto been left to the exercise of his own opinion; and it has been regarded as the proper business of government to protect all, and determine for none. But the attempt is now made to bring about a greater uniformity, at least in practice; and as argument has failed, the government has been called upon to interpose its authority to settle the controversy.

Congress acts under a constitution of delegated and limited powers. The Committee look in vain to that instrument for a delegation of power, authorizing this body to inquire and determine what part of time, or whether any, has been set apart by the Almighty for religious exercises. On the contrary, among the few prohibitions which it contains, is one that prohibits a religious test; and another, declares that Congress shall pass no law respecting an establishment of religion, or prohibiting the free exercise thereof. The Committee might here rest the argument, upon the ground that the question referred to them does not come within the cognizance of Congress; but the perserverance and zeal with which the memoralists pursue their object seems to require further elucidation of the subject. And, as the opposers of Sunday mails disclaim all intention to unite church and state, the committee do not feel disposed to impugn their motives; and whatever may be advanced in opposition to the measure, will arise from the fears entertained of its fatal tendency to the peace and happiness of the nation. The catastrophe of other nations furnished the framers of the constitution a beacon of awful warning, and they have evinced the greatest possible care in guarding against the same evil.

The law, as it now exists, makes no distinction as to the days of the week, but is imperative, that the post-masters shall attend at all reasonable hours in every day to perform the duties of their offices; and the post-master-general has given his instructions to all post-masters, that, at post-offices where the mail arrives on Sunday, the office is to be kept open one hour or more after the arrival and sorting of the mail; but in case that would interfere with the hours of public worship, the office is to be kept open for one hour after the usual time of dissolving the meeting. This liberal construction of the law does not satisfy the memoralists. But the Committee believe that there is not just ground for complaint, unless it be conceded that they have a controlling power over the consciences of others. If Congress shall, by the authority of the law, sanction the measure recommended, it would constitute a legislative decision of a religious controversy, in which even Christians themselves are at issue. However suited such a decision may be to an ecclesiastical council, it is incompatible with a republican legislature, which is purely for political, and not religious purposes.

In our individual character we all entertain opinions, and pursue a corresponding practice, upon the subject of religion. However diversified these may be, we all harmonize as citizens, while each is willing that the other shall enjoy the same liberty which he claims for himself. But in our representative character our individual character is lost. The individual acts for himself,—the representative acts for his constituents. He is chosen to represent their religious views,—to guard the rights of man,—not to restrict the rights of conscience. Despots may regard their subjects as their property, and usurp the Divine prerogative of prescribing their religious faith; but the history of the world furnishes the melancholy demonstration, that the disposition of one man to coerce the religious homage of another, springs from an unchastened ambition rather than a sincere devotion to any religion. The principles of our government do not recognise in the majority any authority over the minority, except in matters which regard the conduct of man to his fellow-man. A Jewish monarch, by grasping the holy censer, lost both his sceptre and his freedom. A destiny as little to be envied may be the lot of the American people who hold the sovereignty of power, if they, in the person of their representatives shall attempt to unite, in the remotest degree, church and state.

From the earliest period of time, religious teachers have attained great ascendancy over the minds of the people; and in every nation, ancient or modern, whether Pagan, Mahomedan, or Christian, have succeeded in the incorporation of the religious tenets with the political institutions of their country. The Persian idols, the Grecian oracles, the Roman auguries, and the modern priesthood of Europe, have all in their turn been the subject of popular adulation, and the agents of political deception. If the measure recommended should be adopted, it would be difficult for human sagacity to foresee how rapid would be the succession, or how numerous the train of measures which might follow, involving the dearest rights of all,—the rights of conscience. It is perhaps fortunate for our country that the proposition should have been made at this early period, while the spirit of the revolution yet exists in full vigour. Religious zeal enlists the strongest prejudices of the human mind, and when misdirected, excites the worst passions of our nature under the delusive pretext of doing God service. Nothing so infuriates the heart to deeds of rapine and blood. Nothing is so incessant in its toils, so perservering in its determinations, so appalling in its course, or so dangerous in its consequences. The equality of rights secured by the constitution may bid defiance to mere political tyrants, but the robe of sanctity too often glitters to deceive. The constitution regards the conscience of the Jew as sacred as that of the Christian, and gives no more authority to adopt a measure affecting the conscience of a solitary individual, than that of a whole community. That representative who would violate this principle would lose his delegated character, and forfeit the confidence of his constituents. If Congress shall declare the first day of the week holy, it will not convince the Jew nor the Sabbatarian. It will dissatisfy both, and consequently, convert neither. Human power may extort vain sacrifices, but Deity alone can command the affections of the heart. It must be recollected, that, in the earliest settlement of this country, the spirit of persecution, which drove the pilgrims from their native homes, was brought with them to their new habitations; and that some Christians were scourged, and others put to death, for no other crime than dissenting from the dogmas of their rulers.

With these facts before us, it must be a subject of deep regret, that a question should be brought before Congress which involves the dearest privileges of the constitution, and even by those who enjoy its choicest blessings. We should all recollect that Cataline, a professed patriot, was a traitor to Rome; Arnold, a professed Whig, was a traitor to America; and Judas, a professed disciple, was a traitor to his Divine Master.

With the exception of the United States, the whole human race, consisting, it is supposed of 800,000,000 rational human beings, is in religious bondage; and in reviewing the scenes of persecution which history everywhere presented, unless the Committee could believe that the cries of the burning victim, and the flames by which he is consumed, bear to Heaven a grateful incense, the conclusion is inevitable, that the line cannot be too strongly drawn between church and state. If a solemn act of legislation shall in one point define the law of God, or point out to the citizen one religious duty, it may with equal propriety define every part of divine revelation and enforce every religious obligation, even to the forms of ceremonies of worship, the endowment of the church, and the support of the clergy.

It was with a kiss that Judas betrayed his Divine Master, and we should all be admonished, no matter what our faith may be, that the rights of conscience cannot be so successfully assailed as under the pretext of holiness. The Christian religion made its way into the world in opposition to all human governments. Banishment, tortures, and death, were inflicted in vain to stop its progress. But many of its professors, as soon as clothed with political power, lost the meek spirit which their creed inculcated and began to inflict on other religions, and on dissenting sects of their own religion, persecutions more aggravated than those which their own apostles had endured. The ten persecutions of Pagan emperors were exceeded in atrocity by the massacres and murders perpetrated by Christian hands; and in vain shall we examine the records of imperial tyranny for an engine of cruelty equal to the holy inquisition. Every religious sect, however meek in its origin, commenced the work of persecution as soon as it acquired political power. The framers of the constitution recognised the eternal principle, that man's relation with God is above human legislation, and his rights of conscience inalienable. Reasoning was not necessary to establish this truth: we are conscious of it in our own bosoms. It is this consciousness which, in defiance of human laws, has sustained so many martyrs in tortures and in flames. They felt that their duty to God was superior to human enactments, and that man could exercise no authority over their consciences; it is an inborn principle which nothing can eradicate.

The bigot, in the pride of his authority, may lose sight of it; but strip him of his power; prescribe a faith to him which his conscience rejects; threaten him in turn with the dungeon and the fagot; the spirit which God has implanted in him rises up in rebellion and defies you. Did the primitive Christians ask that government should recognise and observe their religious institutions? All they asked was toleration; all they complained of was persecution. What did Protestants in Germany, and the Huguenots of France, ask of their Catholic superiors? Toleration. What do the persecuted Catholics of Ireland ask of their oppressors? Toleration.

Do not all men in this country enjoy every religious right which martyrs and saints ever asked? Whence, then, the voice of complaint? Who is it that, in the full enjoyment of every principle which human laws can secure, wishes to wrest a portion of these principles from his neighbor? Do the petitioners allege that they cannot conscientiously participate in the profits of the mail contracts and post-offices, because the mail is carried on Sunday? If this be their motive, then it is worldly gain which stimulates to action, and not virtue and religion. Do they complain that men, less conscientious in relation to the Sabbath obtain advantages over them, by receiving their letters and attending to their contents? Still their motive is worldly and selfish. But if their motive be, to make Congress to sanction by law their religious opinions and observances, then their efforts are to be resisted, as in their tendency fatal both to religious and political freedom. Why have the petitioners confined their prayer to the mails? Why have they not requested that the government be required to suspend all its executive functions on that day? Why do they not require us to exact that our ships shall not sail,—that our armies shall not march,—that officers of justice shall not seize the suspected, or guard the convicted? They seem to forget that government is as necessary on Sunday as on any other day of the week.

It is the government, ever active in its functions, which enables us all, even the petitioners, to worship in our churches in peace. Our government furnishes very few blessings like our mails. They bear, from the centre of our republic to its distant extremes, the acts of our legislative bodies, the decisions of the justiciary, and the orders of the executive. Their speed is often essential to the defence of the country, the suppression of crime, and the dearest interests of the people. Were they suppressed for one day of the week, their absence must often be supplied by public expresses, and, besides, while the mail-bags might rest, the mail-coaches would pursue their journey with the passengers. The mail bears, from one extreme of the union to the other, letters of relatives and friends, preserving a communion of heart between those far separated, and increasing the most pure and refined pleasures of our existence; also the letters of commercial men convey the state of markets, prevent ruinous speculations, and promote general as well as individual interest; they bear innumerable religious letters, newspapers, magazines, and tracts, which reach almost every house throughout this wide republic. Is the conveyance of these a violation of the Sabbath? The advance of the human race in intelligence, in virtue and religion itself, depends, in part, upon the speed with which knowledge of the past is disseminated. Without interchange between one country and another, and between different sections of the same country, every improvement in moral or political science, and the arts of life, would be confined to the neighborhood where it originated. The more rapid and the more frequent this interchange, the more rapid will be the march of the intellect, and the progress of improvement. The mail is the chief means by which intellectual light irradiates to the extremes of the republic. Stop it one day in seven, and you retard one-seventh the improvement of our country. So far from stopping the mail on Sunday, the Committee would recommend the use of all reasonable means to give it a greater expedition and a greater extension. What would be the elevation of our country, if every new conception could be made to strike every mind in the union at the same time! It is not the distance of a province or state from the seat of government which endangers its separation, but it is the difficulty and unfrequency of intercourse between them. Our mails reach Missouri and Arkansas in less time than they reached Kentucky and Ohio in the infancy of their settlements; and now, when there are 3,000,000 people, extending 1,000 miles west of the Alleghany, we hear less of discontent than when there were a few thousands scattered along their western base.

To stop the mails one day in seven would be to thrust the whole western country, and other distant parts of this republic one day's journey from the seat of government. But were it expedient to put an end to the transmission of letters and newspapers on Sunday, because it violates the law of God, have not the petitioners begun wrong in their efforts? If the arm of government be necessary to compel man to respect and obey the laws of God, do not the state governments possess infinitely more power in this respect? Let the petitioners turn to them, and see if they can induce the passage of laws to respect the observance of the Sabbath; for if it be sinful for the mail to carry letters on Sunday, it must be equally sinful for individuals to write, carry, receive, or read them. It would seem to require that these acts should be made penal to complete the system. Traveling on business or recreation, except to and from church; all printing, carrying, receiving, and reading of newspapers; all conversations and social intercourse, except upon religious subjects, must necessarily be punished, to suppress the evil. Would it not also follow, as an inevitable consequence, that every man, woman, and child should be compelled to attend meeting; and, as only one sect, in the opinion of some, can be deemed orthodox, must the law not determine which that is, and compel all to hear these teachers, and contribute to their support? If minor punishments would not restrain the Jew, or the Sabbatarian, or the infidel, who believes Saturday to be the Sabbath, or disbelieves the whole, would not the system require that we should resort to imprisonment, banishment, the rack, and the fagot, to force men to violate their own consciences, or compel them to listen to doctrines which they abhor? When the state governments shall have yielded to these measures, it will be time enough for Congress to declare that the rattling of the mail-coaches shall no longer break the silence of this despotism. It is the duty of this government to affirm to all,—to Jew or gentile,—Pagan or Christian,—the protection and the advantages of our benignant institutions on Sunday as well as every day of the week. Although this government will not convert itself into an ecclesiastical tribunal, it will practice upon the maxim laid down by the founder of Christianity, that it is lawful to do good on the Sabbath Day.

This opinion filled with such brilliant principles, written with an irresistible logic and upon the basis of one of the freest and most philosophical of constitutions that is known, concludes by declaring the petition unconstitutional and was approved unanimously. Will not this be a useful lesson to the supporters of intolerance in Mexico, and other governments that make the pretense of being free? What was the Mexican congress thinking when it passed a law obliging ecclesiastical governments to provide parishes with property after having passed philosophical laws on monastic tithes and vows in which they limited themselves to withdrawing coercion? These are the great inconsistencies of our legislators. But even worse is what followed.

The second document that I am going to include is an exposition by several citizens of the state of Virginia made to the legislature of the state asking that it should suspend the project of establishing teachers of Christian religion as they considered doing in 1784. The author of this memorial [James Madison] was later president from 1808 to 1816.

To the Honorable General Assembly of the Commonwealth of Virginia

We the subscribers, citizens of the said commonwealth, having taken into serious consideration a bill printed by the last session of the General Assembly, entitled "A bill establishing a provision for teachers of the Christian religion,"—and conceiving that the same, if finally armed with the sanction of a law, will be a dangerous abuse of power, are bound, as faithful members of a free state, to remonstrate against it, and to declare the reasons by which we are determined. We remonstrate against the said bill,—

1st. Because, We hold it for a fundamental and undeniable truth, "that religion, or the duty which we owe to our Creator, and the manner of discharging it, can be directed only by reason and conviction, not by force or violence." The religion, then, of every man must be left to the conviction and conscience of every man; and it is the right of every man to exercise it, as these may dictate. This right is in its nature an unalienable right. It is unalienable, because the opinion of men, depending only on the evidence contemplated in their own minds, cannot follow the dictates of other men. It is unalienable also, because what is here a right towards men is duty towards the Creator. It is the duty of every man to render to the Creator such homage, and such only, as he believes to be acceptable to Him. This duty is precedent, both in order of time and in degree of obligation, to the claims of civil society. Before any man can be considered a member of society, he must be considered as a subject of the Governor of the Universe: And if a member of civil society, who enters into any subordinate association, must always do it with a reservation of his duty to the general authority, much more must any man who becomes a member of any particular civil society do it, with a saving of his allegiance to the Universal Sovereign. We maintain, therefore, that in matters of religion, no man's right is abridged by the institution of civil society, and that religion is wholly exempt from its cognizance. True it is, that no other rule exists by which any question which may divide a society can be ultimately determined but by the will of a majority; but it is also true that the majority may trespass on the rights of the minority.

2nd. Because, If religion be exempt from the authority of the society at large, still less can it be subject to that of the legislative body. The latter are but the creatures and viceregents of the former. Their jurisdiction is both derivative and limited. It is limited with regard to the co-ordinate departments; more necessarily is it limited with regard to the constituents. The preservation of a free government requires not merely that the metes and bounds which separate each department of power be invariably maintained, but more especially that neither of them be suffered to overleap the great barrier which defends the rights of the people. The rulers who are guilty of such an encroachment exceed the commission from which they derive their authority, and are tyrants. The people who submit to it are governed by laws made neither by themselves nor by any authority derived from them, and are slaves.

3rd. Because, It is proper to take alarm at the first experiment of our liberties. We hold this prudent jealousy to be the first duty of citizens, and one of the noblest characteristics of the late revolution. The free of America did not wait till usurped power had strengthened itself by exercise, and entangled the question in precedents. They saw all the consequences in the principle, and they avoided the consequences by denying the principle. We revere this lesson too much soon to forget it. Who does not see the same authority which can establish Christianity, in exclusion of all other religions, may establish with the same case any particular sect of Christians in exclusion of all other sects? That the same authority which can force a citizen to contribute threepence only of his property for the support of any one establishment, may force him to conform to any other establishment, in all cases whatsoever.

4th. Because, The bill violates the equality which ought to be the basis of every law, and which is more indispensable in proportion as the validity or expediency of any law is more liable to be impeached. If "all men are by nature equally free and independent," all men are to be considered as entering into society on equal conditions,—as relinquishing no more, and therefore retaining no less than another of their rights. Above all are they to be considered as retaining an "equal title to the free exercise of religion, according to the dictates of conscience." While we assert for ourselves a freedom to embrace, to profess, and to observe the religion which we believe to be of Divine origin, we cannot deny an equal freedom to those whose minds have not yet yielded to the evidence which has convinced us. If this freedom be abused, it is an offence against God, not against man: To God, therefore, not to man, must an account be rendered. As the bill violates equality, by subjecting some to peculiar burdens, so it violates the same principle by granting to others peculiar exemptions. Are the Quakers and Menonists the only sects who think a compulsive support of their religion unnecessary and unwarrantable? Can their piety alone be entrusted with the care of public worship? Ought their religions to be endowed, above all others, with extraordinary privileges, by which proselytes may be enticed from all others? We think too favourably of the justice and good sense of these denominations to believe that they either covet pre-eminence over their fellow-citizens, or that they will be seduced by them from the common opposition to the measure.

5th. Because, The bill implies either that the civil magistrate is a competent judge of religious truth, or that he may employ religion as an engine of civil policy. The first is an arrogant apprehension, falsified by the contradictory opinions of rulers in all ages, and throughout the world; the second an unhallowed perversion of the means of salvation.

6th. Because, The establishment proposed by the bill is not requisite for the support of the Christian religion. To say that it is, is a contradiction to the Christian religion itself; for every page of it disavows a dependence on the powers of this world. It is a contradiction to fact; for it is known that this religion both existed and flourished, not only without the support of human laws, but in spite of every opposition from them and not only during the period of miraculous aid, but long after it had been left to its own evidence, and the ordinary care of Providence. Nay, it is a contradiction in terms; for a religion not invented by human policy must have pre-existed and been supported before it was established by human policy. It is, moreover, to weaken in those who profess this religion pious confidence in its innate excellence, and the patronage of its author; and to foster in those who still reject it a suspicion, that its friends are too conscious of its fallacies to trust to its own merits.

7th. Because, Experience witnesseth that ecclesiastical establishments, instead of maintaining the purity and efficacy of religion, have had contrary operation. During almost fifteen centuries has the legal establishment of Christianity been on trial. What have been its fruits? More or less, in all places, pride and indolence in the clergy; ignorance and servility in the laity; in both, superstition, bigotry, and persecution. Inquire of the teachers of Christianity for the ages in which it appeared in its greatest lustre, those of every sect point to the ages prior to its incorporation with civil policy. Propose a restoration of this primitive state, in which the teachers depended on the voluntary rewards of their flocks, many of them predict its downfall. On which side ought their testimony to have greatest weight, when for, or when against their interest?

8th. Because, The establishment in question is not necessary for the support of civil government. If it be urged as necessary for the support of civil government only, it is as a means of supporting religion; and if it be not necessary for the latter purpose, it cannot be necessary for the former. If religion be not within the cognizance of civil government, how can its legal establishment be said to be necessary to civil government? What influence, in fact, have ecclesiastical establishments had on civil society? In some instances, they have been seen to exert a spiritual tyranny on the ruins of the civil authority; in many instances, they have been seen upholding the thrones of political tyranny; in no instance have they been seen guarding the liberties of the people. Rulers, who wished to subvert the public liberty, may have found an established clergy convenient auxiliaries. A just government, instituted to secure and perpetuate it, needs them not. Such a government will be best supported by protecting every citizen in the enjoyment of his religion, with the same equal hand which protects his person and his property; by neither invading the equal rights of any sect, nor suffering any sect to invade those of another.

9th. Because, The proposed establishment is a departure from that generous policy which, offering an asylum to the persecuted and oppressed of every nation and religion, promised a lustre to our country, and an accession to the number of its citizens. What a melancholy mark is the bill, of sudden degeneracy! Instead of holding forth an asylum to the persecuted, it is itself a signal of persecution. It degrades from the equal rank of citizen, all those whose opinions in religion do not bend to those of the legislative authority. Distant as it may be in the present form from the inquisition, it differs from it only in degree. The one is the first step, the other the last, in the career of intolerance. The magnanimous sufferer under this cruel scourge in foreign regions must view this bill as a beacon on our coast, warning him to seek some other haven, where liberty and philanthropy, in their due extent, may offer a more certain repose from his troubles.

10th. Because, It will have a like tendency to banish our citizens. The allurements presented by other situations are every day thinning their number. To superadd a fresh motive to emigration, by revoking the liberty which they now enjoy, would be the same species of folly which has dishonoured and depopulated flourishing kingdoms.

11th. Because, It will destroy that moderation and harmony which the forbearance of our laws to intermeddle with our religion has produced amongst its several sects. Torrents of blood have been spilt in the Old World, by vain attempts of the secular arm to extinguish religious discord, by proscribing all difference in religious opinions. Time has at length revealed the true remedy. Every relaxation of narrow and rigorous policy, wherever it has been tried, has been found to assuage the disease. The American system has exhibited proofs, that equal and complete liberty, if it does not wholly eradicate it, sufficiently destroys its malignant influence on the health and prosperity of the state. If, with the salutary effects of this system under our eyes, we begin to contract the bonds of religious freedom, we know no name that will too severely reproach our folly. At least, let warning he taken at the first fruits of the threatened innovation. The very apperance of the bill has transformed "that Christian forbearance, love, and charity," which of late mutually prevailed, into animosities and jealousies, which may not soon be appeased. What mischiefs may not be dreaded, should this enemy to the public quiet be armed with the force of a law?

12th. Because, The policy of the bill is adverse to the diffusion of the light of Christianity. The first wish of those who enjoy this precious gift ought to be, that it may be imparted to the whole race of mankind. Compare the number of those who have as yet received it, with the number still remaining under the dominion of false religions, and how small is the former. Does the policy of the bill tend to lessen the disproportion? No: it at once discourages those who are strangers to the light of Revelation from coming into the region of it; and countenances, by example, the nations who continue in darkness, in shutting out those who might convey it to them. Instead of levelling, as far as possible, every obstacle to the victorious progress of truth, the bill, with an ignoble and unchristian timidity, would circumscribe it with a wall of defence against the encroachments of error.

13th. Because, Attempts to enforce by legal sanctions, acts obnoxious to so great a portion of citizens, tend to enervate the laws in general, and to slacken the bonds of society. If it be difficult to execute any law which is not generally deemed necessary or salutary, what must be the case where it is deemed invalid and dangerous? And what may be the effect of so striking an example of impotency in the government, on its general authority?

14th. Because, A measure of such singular magnitude and delicacy ought not to be imposed without the clearest evidence that it is called for by a majority of citizens. And no satisfactory method is yet proposed by which the voice of the majority in this case may be determined, or its influence secured. "The people of the respective counties are indeed requested to signify their opinion respecting the adoption of the bill to the next session of the Assembly." But the representation must be made equal, before the voice either of the representatives, or of the counties, will be that of the people. Our hope is, that neither of the former will, after due consideration, espouse the dangerous principle of the bill. Should the event disappoint us, it will still leave us in full confidence that a fair appeal to the latter will reverse the sentence against our liberties.

15th. Because, finally, "The equal right of every citizen to the free exercise of his religion, according to the dictates of conscience," is held by the same tenure with all our other rights. If we refer to its origin, it is equally the gift of nature;—if we weigh its importance, it cannot be less dear to us;—if we consult the "declaration of those rights which pertain to the good people of Virginia as the basis and foundation of government," it is enumerated with equal solemnity, or rather studied emphasis. Either, then, we must say, that the will of the legislature is the only measure of their authority, and that, in the plenitude of this authority, they may sweep away all our fundamental rights; or that they are bound to leave this particular right untouched and sacred. Either we must say, that they may control the freedom of the press,—may abolish the trial by jury,—may swallow up the executive and judiciary powers of the state,—nay, that they may despoil us of our very right of suffrage, and erect themselves into an independent and hereditary assembly; or we must say, that they have no authority to enact into law the bill under consideration. We, the subscribers, say, that the general assembly of this commonwealth has no such authority. And, that no effort may be omitted on our part against so dangerous an usurpation, we oppose to it this remonstrance, earnestly praying, as we are in duty bound, that the Supreme Lawgiver of the Universe, by illuminating those to whom it is addressed, may, on the one hand, turn their counsels from every act which would affront his holy prerogative, or violate the trust which may be worthy of his blessing, may redound to their own praise, and may establish more firmly the liberties, the prosperity, and the happiness of the commonwealth.

Mr. Van Buren was kind enough to accompany me on my visit to President Jackson, whom I saw for a second time since I had seen him before in Cincinnati as I have said. The famous chief invited me to dinner, and I had the satisfaction of sitting beside one of the great historical personages of the Anglo-American republic, and hearing from his mouth the account of some important events. Our conversation turned particularly to events in Mexico, and the honorable old man expressed himself with a tact and discernment that gave me a good idea of his mental ability and of his correct judgments.

"You have to pass through many tests," he said to me, "before ridding yourselves of the vices and prejudices of your earlier education and form of government. For a long time after a political change nations follow the impulses and direction of their former habits, and to change them training and popular education are needed more than laws."

When I was there, they were celebrating in Washington the triumphs of the liberals in the three days of July in Paris. After a long and gala procession in which artisans and other classes of society were divided with their respective banners, the crowd made its way to the home of the president of the United States; he came out and accompanied them to the Capitol (more than a mile) where he made a speech. That night there was a ball which was very well attended and very popular.

The question of the Tariff of 1828 began to heat up from 1830 on, and ended happily in 1833 after heated discussions between the supporters of South Carolina and the states of the North. The former claimed that it was not fair that import taxes on goods manufactured in Europe should be placed at high levels only to increase their prices for the purpose of protecting the processors and manufacturers of the states of New England while a portion of luxury items were subject to extremely low rates. The result of this was, said the *nullificationists* (a name adopted by those of South Carolina), that in attempting to protect the manufacturing companies of the states of the North, our working classes who raise sugar and cotton have to pay higher prices for goods to clothe their families. This tariff had been put into effect under the administration of Mr. Adams while Mr. Clay was secretary of state.

The defenders of the tariff said that the Northern states consumed the cotton, sugar, and other products of the states of the South and the West, and that these should contribute to promoting their manufacturing, which within a few years would have no need of this extra tax upon foreign goods. The question became very heated as always happens in matters of large interests, to the point that a dreadful collision was feared in that happy republic.

In November of 1832 the convention of South Carolina published a decree nullifying the tariffs of the general congress, a curious document that should not be omitted from this book. It reads as follows:

Whereas the Congress of the United States, by various acts, purporting to be acts laying duties and imposts on foreign imports, but in reality intended for the protection of domestic manufactures, and the giving of bounties to classes and individuals engaged in particular employments, at the expense and to the injury and oppression of other classes and individuals, and by wholly exempting from taxation certain foreign commodities, such as are not produced or manufactured in the United States, to afford a pretext for imposing higher and excessive duties on articles similar to those intended to be protected, hath exceeded its just powers under the Constitution, which confers on it no authority to afford such protection, and has violated the true meaning and intent of the Constitution, which provides for equality in imposing the burthens of taxation upon the several States and portions of the Confederacy: And whereas the said Congress, exceeding its just power to impose taxes and collect revenue for the purpose of effecting and accomplishing the specific objects and purposes which the Constitution of the United States authorizes it to effect and accomplish, hath raised and collected unnecessary revenue for objects unauthorized by the Constitution:—

We, therefore, the people of the State of South Carolina in Convention assembled, do declare and ordain, . . . that the several acts and parts of acts of the Congress of the United States, purporting to be laws for the imposing of duties and imposts on the importation of foreign commodities, . . . and, more especially . . . the tariff acts of 1828 and 1832 . . . , are unauthorized by the Constitution of the United States, and violate the true meaning and intent thereof, and are null, void, and no law nor binding upon this State, its officers or citizens; and all promises, contracts, and obligations, made or entered into, or to be made or entered into, with purpose to secure the duties imposed by the said acts, and all judicial proceedings which shall be hereafter had in affirmance thereof, are and shall be utterly null and void.

And it is further Ordained, That it shall not be lawful for any of the constituted authorities, whether of this State or of the United States, to enforce the payment of duties imposed by the said acts within the limits of this State; but it shall be the duty of the Legislature to adopt such measures and pass such acts as may be necessary to give full effect to this Ordinance, and to prevent the enforcement and arrest the operation of the said acts and parts of acts of the Congress of the United States within the limits of this State, from and after the 1st day of February next. . . .

And it is further Ordained, That in no case of law or equity, decided in the courts of this State, wherein shall be drawn in question the authority of this ordinance, or the validity of such act or acts of the Legislature as may be passed for the purpose of giving effect thereto, or the validity of the aforesaid acts of Congress, imposing duties, shall any appeal be taken or allowed to the Supreme Court of the United States, nor shall any copy of the record be printed or allowed for that purpose; and if any such appeal shall be attempted to be taken, the courts of this State shall proceed to execute and enforce their judgments, according to the laws and usages of the State, without reference to such attempted appeal, and the person or persons attempting to take such an appeal may be dealt with as for a contempt of the court.

And it is further Ordained, That all persons now holding any office of honor, profit, or trust, civil or military, under this state, members of the Legislature excepted, shall, within such time, and in such manner as the Legislature shall prescribe, take an oath well and truly to obey, execute, and enforce this Ordinance, and such act or acts of the Legislature as may be passed in pursuance thereof, according to the true intent and meaning of the same; and on the neglect or omission of any such person or persons so to do, his or their office or offices shall be forthwith vacated . . . and no person hereafter elected to any office of honor, profit, or trust, civil or military, (members of the Legislature excepted), shall, until the Legislature shall otherwise provide and direct enter on the execution of his office, . . . until he shall, in like manner, have taken a similar oath; and no juror shall be empanelled in any of the courts of this State, in any cause in which shall be in question this Ordinance, or any act of the Legislature passed in pursuance thereof, unless he shall first, in addition to the usual oath, have taken an oath that he will well and truly obey, execute, and enforce this Ordinance, and such act or acts of the Legislature as may be passed to carry the same into operation and effect, according to the true intent and meaning thereof.

And we, the People of South Carolina, to the end that it may be fully understood by the Government of the United States, and the people of the co-States, that we are determined to maintain this, our Ordinance and Declaration, at every hazard, Do further Declare that we will not submit to the application on the part of the Federal Government, to reduce this State to obedience; but that we will consider the passage, by the Congress, or any act . . . to coerce the State, shut up her ports, destroy or harass her commerce, or to enforce the acts hereby declared to be null and void, otherwise than through the civil tribunals of the country, as inconsistent with the longer continuance of South Carolina in the Union; and that the people of this State will thenceforth hold themselves absolved from all further obligation to maintain or preserve their political connexion with the people of the other States, and will forthwith proceed to organize a separate Government, and do all other acts and things which sovereign and independent States may of right to do.

Here we have a *pronunciamiento,* or uprising, which resembles those that take place on a monthly basis in the Mexican republic. Fortunately this act found no echo in any one of the other states as they did not consider the claims as having foundation and much less the manner of making them. There is, however, more openness and frankness than in those absurd plans of the revolutionaries of Mexico, who always begin by pleading and end up killing or banishing.

November 14 of the same year 180 citizens met in the capital of the same state (Columbia), and signed a declaration in contradiction to the previous resolution, and it was stated in these terms:

The supporters of the Union and of the rights of the State of South Carolina set forth and protest solemnly against the resolution passed by the convention of the same State on November 24, last.

1st. Because the people of South Carolina elected their delegates to said convention with the solemn assurances that these delegates would not propose other than peaceful and constitutional remedies and measures in order to avoid the evils of the tariffs without compromising the union of these States. Instead of acting in this manner, the convention has published an *ordinance that directly violates all these principles*.

2nd. Because the above mentioned *ordinance* has attacked one of the inalienable rights of man by attempting to shackle all freedom of conscience by the tyrannical intervention of the power of the *oath*.

3rd. Because the resolution that those who do not wish to swear such an oath *shall be deprived of their civil and military* posts has *attacked and proscribed* about half the free men of South Carolina only because they hold an honest and legal opinion that is different.

4th. Because it has trampled upon the *great principles of liberty guaranteed to the citizens* by the constitution of this State, *depriving free men of this country of the right of impartial trial by jury*, thus violating the clause of the constitution which is to be *perpetual* that declares that *trial by jury as has been done in this State, as well as freedom of the press, shall be forever preserved inviolate*.

5th. Because it has violated the independence of the *judicial* power by ordaining that all judges shall swear the absurd oath, or that they shall be *removed arbitrarily from their positions,* thus depriving them of the privilege of trial by proper accusation, which by the constitution of the State is the safeguard for the security of these positions.

6th. Because by prohibiting the payment of imposts within the boundaries of the State the ordinance *has directly violated the constitution of the United States* which authorizes the Congress to impose taxes.

7th. Because it *has violated the constitution of the United States* itself in the article which ordains that it shall not give preference to one port over another, when the ordinance declares that goods that are brought into the ports of South Carolina shall pay no duty whatsoever.

8th. Because it *violates the constitution itself* and attacks the rights of the citizen by denying him the right of appeal in cases of *law and equity* that are granted by *the constitution and laws of the Union.*

9th. Because *it has virtually destroyed the Union* by opposing the decisions of the general government being put into effect by placing obstacles in the way of the execution of the laws by means of the courts of the States and proclaiming that if the government uses means of repression then it will separate therefrom.

10th. Because *tyranny and oppression,* effects of the ordinance, are of a character so repulsive and ruinous that they have already weakened the *trade and credit* of the State, which will lead these areas to their destruction since industrious and peaceful citizens will find themselves obliged to seek peace and tranquility in other states.

The Union supporters of South Carolina meeting in convention protest solemnly, furthermore, against the plan for a *permanent army* proposed by the party in power as dangerous to the *liberties of the people.* They respectfully ask their fellow citizens whether, if such an army is not capable by their confession of protecting the *nullification party* against the people of the United States, they will resolve to restrain it. What other purpose if it cannot hold back that force but to serve as an instrument of tyranny against its fellow citizens?

This *convention protests* also against all efforts made to put into effect a system of *conscription* which will oblige citizens to abandon their homes and occupations to take up *arms* under penalty of *treason,* in order to uphold doctrines that the people were sure did not need the aid of force and whose triumph could and should be obtained by constitutional means.

Solemnly declaring, as at the present it does declare, against the aforesaid resolutions the *Union Party* can do no less than to set forth its firm determination to support the same principles of conduct which have directed it thus far, and while on the one hand they will continue in forceful opposition to the vicious tariff act, on the other they will never separate themselves from the joys of those inalienable rights which by inheritance belong to every *American citizen.* Disavowing consequently all intention of revolutionary and extra-legal violence, *they proclaim* here and now their resolution to protect their rights by all constitutional means, and in so doing they wish to continue to maintain the character of peaceful citizens unless they be compelled to rise up against an intolerable oppression.

Thomas Taylor, president.—Henry Middleton.—David Johnson.—Richard I. Manning.—Starling Tuckec.—Vice-presidents (180 signatures follow). Given in Columbia Friday December 14, 1832, in the year fifty-five of the independence of the United States of America.—Authorized.—Franklin J. Moses.—James Edward Henry.—

Secretaries of the Convention.

This dispute which brought fear of ill-fated results for the cause of liberty and the republic was brought to an end by the prudent and moderate conduct of President Jackson and the enlightened and patriotic agents whom he chose for so delicate an undertaking. He pointed out to the general congress the propriety and even the necessity that existed to moderate the tariffs, which was carried out upon the bases proposed by the excellent Mr. MacLane and with the cooperation of Mr. Livingston, secretary of state, and Mr. Poinsett, member of the legislature of South Carolina.

Those who know the distance that exists between the manner of handling matters in the United States of North America and in the United Mexican States will look in vain for the causes of the different organization of powers. In their ways, in the enormous distance that exists between material and mental capacities of the two countries, in their customs, in their interests, in their very beliefs, is where the legislator-philosopher must find the origins and the divergent directions that negotiations take with respect to the descendants of the English and the descendants of the Spanish.

CHAPTER XII

Washington is a new city in the District of Columbia ceded to the general government by the State of Maryland. Its area is two square leagues as is that of Mexico City. The city has a sad appearance although it has some very pleasant views. But the streets are too wide, and there is a great distance between the houses. A town has grown into isolated groups of buildings so that it does not yet present that combination of houses and people that gives one at once the aspect of a city. There is a small theater in Washington and several hotels. The Gadsby, which is the one where I stayed and surely considered the best, is rather expensive and does not offer the comforts of those of Baltimore, Philadelphia, and Boston.

The principal street which is called Pennsylvania Avenue extends through the center of the city from the president's home to the Capitol. It is more than a mile and a half long. The president, as I have said, has no guards, nor halbardiers nor other trappings. He goes to the Presbyterian Church on Sunday as any other citizen and takes his seat among the others without any distinction. When in the first months of the year 1833 we in Mexico saw Señor Pedraza and later Señor Farias in their roles as presidents present themselves with the same simplicity in public places and live their private lives in the same manner, we thought that there was being introduced the informality of our neighbors in their first magistrates, and that never again would we see the pompous ways of the vice-royalty. Sweet but vain illusion!!

A mile from Washington is a place called Georgetown, where there is a convent named the Sisters of the Visitation. There are probably sixty nuns whose principal occupations are to give free education to the young girls intrusted to their care. The free school is under the instruction of the

140

youngest nuns who have more than four hundred little girls in attendance. The most important establishment consists of a pension or boarding place which is in a rather flourishing condition. These convents are not like those of Spain where the victims of an ill-considered and premature vow are shut up for their whole life. When their inclinations have changed, or their interests require it, the law does not force them to remain cloistered, living in perpetual torment which the Divinity cannot accept. They leave to better their conditions and to live in society as mothers or in some other respectable manner. Two daughters of General Iturbide were in this convent when I visited his widow.

Each year there is held in Washington a convention of the famous society founded about thirty years ago with the philosophical object of redeeming slaves and sending them to Liberia, the name given to a colony established on the coast of Africa to receive these unfortunate beings. In the memorial presented by Mr. Clay in December of 1829 one reads that one of the first acts of the society was to dispatch an agent to explore the coast of Africa and find a place that was suitable for the colony. The selection fell upon a person capable of carrying out so weighty a commission. The purchase of good fertile land was made in 1822, and more was added later.

The land bought from the authorities extends as far as two hundred miles inland from the coast, in some places advantageous for trade, and the climate is analogous to the complexion of the blacks. The society founded this colony under the name of Liberia; it established towns, farmed lands, and built fortresses in order to defend them from the natives. Each year, or more often if the financial circumstances of the society permitted, ships were sent from the United States loaded with emigrant slaves with the tools of agriculture or of some trades for their work, as well as things necessary for their establishment. There has never been any difficulty in transporting colonists when the funds of the society have permitted it. Rather there have not been sufficient funds to take care of all who sought aid so eagerly. The travel expenses were greater in the first years; today the cost is only twenty dollars per person, and it is likely that it will be even less.

During the first period of their existence the colonists had to struggle with the native tribes even to open warfare. It all had a happy ending as soon as the natives were convinced of the greater ability, bravery, and discipline of the colonists.

The colonists have a government adequate to protect their rights, their persons and property, as well as for maintaining good order. The society's agent is governor, commanding general and supreme judicial chief. The colonists participate in the government through the election of various officials and minor employees. Annually they select commissions for public works, agriculture, health and sanitation, which are charged with overseeing these important areas.

The colony has established schools for the instruction of the youth and built churches for public worship which is held with great regularity. Finally they have a public library with more than twelve thousand volumes and their printshop where they publish the regular newspaper. The colonists work in trade, agriculture or mechanical trades according to their knowledge and inclination. The lands produce rice, corn, yucca, coffee, potatoes and all kinds of vegetables. In a short while they will have sugar, indigo, and other tropical products. Trading is carried on effectively by exchanging their goods with the natives of the country who have ivory, gums, ink plants, medicinal drugs and other articles which account for the sum of seventy thousand dollars; this amount is increasing year by year.

This society has branches in many of the states of the American union where there is a truly philosophical enthusiasm for the gradual abolition of slavery and the formation of a nation of civilized blacks on the coast of Africa.

"It is impossible longer to maintain the abuse of slavery in some of our states," said Mr. North, president of Union College of New York.

It will not take a domestic revolution nor foreign intervention to bring down an institution that is so repulsive to our sentiments and so contrary to our institutions. Public opinion has already declared itself on this issue, and the moral energy of the nation will sooner or later carry out its abolition. But the question that arises then is what will be the situation of this class restored to liberty? In other nations the races have blended with each other forming a general mass. Here we do not have the same situation. Our freed slaves in the third, fourth, and ever so many generations would still be what they are today—that is a distinct, degraded and unfortunate class.

Consequently when their chains have been broken, and this will happen evidently, either all at once or by degrees, it is clear that this country will find itself covered with a population as useless as it is miserable, a population which with its increase will lessen our strength, and its numbers will only bring crime and poverty. Slave or free it will always be for us a calamity. Why then must we hesitate one moment in promoting their departure from the country? It is prudent and praise worthy to restore to Africa as citizens the children of that region, who as slaves and bound in chains we have brought here with grave affront to their humanity.

 Such is the general feeling of the people of the United States concerning this class as different in color as they are in moral qualities from the others. It is not certain that once the castes were mixed the natural stigma would never disappear. The quadroons in Louisiana and Carolina give the lie to the assertion. But how many centuries would be needed for this to take place? And in the meantime the difficulties of the permanent residence of the black people in the United States are a matter of too much concern for a farsighted people that look well to their interests to fail to make provisions to free themselves from the ills or at least to lessen them. Recent events in New York and Philadelphia between whites and blacks are forerunners of what that nation may fear in the future.

I returned to New York by the same road that I had taken to Washington. Before my arrival in the United States a group known as the Temperance Society had begun to spread. Every establishment that has for its purpose the promoting of a principle, some particular virtue, or of some doctrine, always winds up by going to the extremes and often to the extravagant and the ridiculous. Seldom does it fail to gain the enthusiasm of its members and followers, and the consequences are sometimes harmful.

What is apparently more reasonable and useful than the establishment of societies whose purpose will be to preach and set examples of sobriety and temperance? However, the first ones professed to renounce all spirituous liquors; the second ones then added wine, beer, cider and other fermented liquors; the third group proscribed the use of coffee, tea, chocolate and all types of stimulants. Heaven knows where we will be led by this new sect that happily until now is not associated with any mysteries of religious dogma. In one of the sermons that Dr. Beecher of Boston has published on this new doctrine we read the following remarkable advice:

> I know that many defend the moderate use of spirituous liquors, but this is the same thing as speaking of the prudent use that may be made of the plague. Others have recommended beer as a cordial that can be a substitute for those in the habit of drinking spirituous liquors, but although beer may not nurture habits of intemperance so quickly, it does not have the power to dislodge them. In the end it produces the same effects with the sole difference that it does not weaken the vital organs with the same harshness and swiftness as does whiskey and only leads its victims to the grave more slowly, gradually making them stupid idiots, without the frenzied fury of the former. Some have proposed wine as an innocent thing for distracting the habits of intemperance and to maintain the health, but habits cannot be gotten rid of, just as a voracious appetite is not satisfied with a sober and temperate table. Useless precautions that are successful one time in a thousand! They are the efforts of a child against a giant—the efforts of a lap dog against a lion.

Evidently habits of intemperancce have visibly decreased. But there have been many harmful results from that absolute abandonment of spirituous and fermented liquors. There have been very frequent sudden deaths of people who in the heat of summer, after some exercise, drink pure cold water straight from the pump, and all the doctors are agreed that if this were mixed with a little brandy, it would not cause such dire effects. What would those of the societies say if they were to see our pulque shops on fiesta days, and even more the Indians of Yucatan fallen here and there along the public roads, in the streets and in the plazas? Such scenes are never found in the United States, nor in the civilized cities of Europe.

Often in the course of my travels I come upon travelers' descriptions concerning the same places and persons that I have visited. Such is the one that I am going to deal with at this time, and it is the visit that I made to Hyde Park, which belonged to Dr. Hosack on the Hudson River. This is a country home built on the high hills on the left bank of the beautiful river, and from where one can look out upon picturesque views. Dr. Hosack is a learned American educated in Scotland and married to a very rich landowner of the state of New York. He has beautified that spot with man-made groves, gardens and plantings of trees and Scottish fruit trees. I must make mention of the friendliness, of the pleasant treatment at the hands of the entire family of Dr. Hosack. There I met the daughter of the famous Fulton, a young girl of eighteen at the time, full of charm, and one of the beauties of the state of New York.

A short time later I left with Mr. Poinsett for New England, going by way of the Hudson River. I shall speak later of various points along this river that deserve special mention when I relate my trip to West Point with Señor Salgado.

Albany on the right bank of the river is 148 miles from New York, and the trip takes ten hours by steamboat. The cost is two dollars, although this varies up to four dollars. We stopped at the Citendew Hotel, one of the most popular in the city, frequented by both working people and great merchants. It is located on one of the highest hills in the city and dominates a greater part of it. Mr. Poinsett introduced me to Mr. Cambreleng, a member of Congress, one of the most learned and eloquent of men. At that time he was busy laying out the project of the decree concerning tariffs—the project that was later adopted in the noisy question of the nullificationists.

The Statehouse, where the two bodies meet, is a newly constructed building and has two chambers for the two assemblies of senators and representatives with their corresponding offices, all very well laid out and arranged. The view from the cupola of this building is picturesque. The river dominates the whole city, and in the distance can be seen the high

Catskill Mountains; of which I shall speak later.

The constitution of the state of New York was written in 1821. The executive power rests with the governor, who is elected by the people every two years, at the same time as the lieutenant governor who presides over the senate and performs the duties of the governor in case of death, or separation for any reason. The legislative power is exercised by the two chambers—the senate which is made up of thirty-two members elected every four years; and the assembly of twenty-eight representatives, and they steer annually. The members of this body are elected by divisions called counties, in numbers proportionate to the population. For the election of senators the state is divided into eight districts, each one of which elects four senators, of whom one is chosen each year.

The election of the governor; lieutenant governor, senators, and members of the assembly is held the first Monday of the month of November, and continues for three days The legislature can vary these days by legal arrangements. The political year begins with the New Year, and the legislature meets annually the first Tuesday in January. The constitution gives the right of suffrage for political offices to all white male citizens above the age of twenty-one that have lived one year prior in the state and six months in the county where the election is held. Citizens of African descent must have real property in the value of at least $250 free of lien in order to have the right to vote. The governor names the chancellor and judges with the approval of the senate. The judges and the chancellor remain in office during good behavior, but only to the age of sixty years. The other county judges hold office for five years.

I have already spoken elsewhere about the famous canal that starts from this city and for a distance of more than 120 leagues runs to Lake Erie; it gets its water from there and from several streams that it crosses. It is worth noting that in this part of the state of New York one finds the names of ancient Greek or Roman cities, such as Rome, which is a small town on the canal, Troy, a town near Albany, Utica. There are a number of waterfalls on this road. The one at Genesee is about 160 feet high, the one at Trenton, the one at Mohawk, or Little Falls, and others. At the first one a maniac named Sam Patch died; he amused himself jumping from waterfalls. On another occasion he jumped from the one at Leucade easily; on the second occasion he fell and was never heard from again. I remember hearing of a certain Rodriguez, also crazy, from Merida, Yucatan, who was continually climbing on church steeples and the highest buildings, jumping with great agility, and he died in one of his undertakings.

For the most part the people of Albany are of Dutch descent. One of the most outstanding persons of this city is General Van Rensselaer, known as the "Patroon" of Albany. I made the acquaintance of him and his family through Mr. Poinsett. His daughter, seventeen years of age (1830), spoke Spanish, French, Italian and her own language perfectly. General Rensselaer is extremely wealthy, and his fortune consists principally of real estate inherited from his grandfather, to whom the legislature of the state had given full possession of the lands which the king of England had granted him for colonization. He has done many good things for the state, and there is a town that bears the name of the family. My wife's birthplace is in the vicinity of this town.

We left Albany in a stagecoach which in order to cross the river went aboard a vessel called a *ferry boat,* a general name given to those boats designed to go from one side of a river to the other in the United States, sometimes propelled by steam and sometimes by horses. We were going towards Lebanon, a town of the same state about twenty-five miles from Albany where there are mineral waters and baths; consequently it is quite crowded in the summer, as are the baths of Ems, Wiesbaden, and others in Europe. On the way there is nothing of note other than some lands called Greenbush, where the general congress has decreed the cultivation of mulberry trees for silkworm culture, which has gotten under way with success.

We arrived at Lebanon on the same day, and we lodged in one of the large hotels of that small town. Lebanon is located in a gorge surrounded by hills and woods that give it a somber aspect, in addition to the fact that the poor and meager population have done nothing to beautify it. The hotels are all of wood and very large. The thermal waters are not good to drink, and their temperature is constantly 75°F. The town overlooks a small valley, which gives it a pleasant view in that direction. One league from Lebanon there is a community of the Shakers, an unusual sect which I shall describe briefly.

This new religion had its beginnings in Manchester, England, in 1747. A woman by the name of Anna Lee came to be received as the mother of the Society in Christ as its prophetess, teacher and director. Consequently she received revelations from the spirit of Christ, of whom she was a second representation, and she conversed with them frequently, as did many others, with which our legends are filled. Because of persecutions by the authorities and other sects Anna Lee emigrated to the United States with her disciples in 1774 sixty years ago, and there she was joined by others from New York and New England. They bought lands in order to live as a community, and there they founded their first establishment. Anna Lee died ten years later, giving with her last breath testimony of the firmness of her faith and the sanctity of her doctrine.

The group is called the Millennial Society; its first religious principle is the Unity of God. Jesus Christ, according to them was not the son of God, nor coeternal with the Divinity, but an outflowing of that Divinity in time through the operation of divine power. They say that religion consists rather of the practice of virtue than of faith or of speculative doctrines; that man was created innocent, although free to choose between good and evil; but that having lost his original uprightness, no one can be saved until the coming of Christ; that Christ took upon himself the burden of lifting fallen human nature and overruling the power of death—which indeed he did; but that the Church departed from the true spirit of Christ, involving itself in worldly interests, and then the Anti-Christ placed himself at the head of it; that the manifestations of the second coming of Christ began again in the person of Anna Lee, and that through her the same divine spirit that had dwelled in Christ announced itself. The confession of sins is one of the principle articles of faith, following the gospel text, "He who hides his sins shall not prosper, but he who confesses and abandons them shall have mercy."

Its principal commandments are:

1. Duties to God. "Thou shalt love the Lord with all thy heart and all thy faculties."

2. Duties to man. "Thou shalt love thy neighbor as thyself." In this rule are included all the obligations of man to his fellow beings.

3. Separation from the world. "My kingdom is not of this world." Hence the obligation to abstain from all participation in politics and the renunciation of any worldly honor or pomp.

4. Peace. Christ is the prince of peace; therefore, his disciples must maintain this spirit. "If my kingdom were of this world, then my followers should fight."

5. Simplicity of speech. "Guard your tongue from evil and your lips from deceit." All kinds of profane language, idle and false conversation, are to be avoided. "Flee from all titles of honor or distinction. Do not call yourself Doctor (learned)."

6. The legitimate use of property. Christ asked that his disciples be one with him. This unity should be understood with regards to temporal and spiritual things. The primitive church was established upon these principles—the apostles lived in common.

7. A virgin life. They invoke the example of our Saviour. "Married persons take care for the things of the world and the manner of pleasing their husbands and wives, but the unmarried person takes care for the things of the Lord and the way in which he can be holy in body and in soul.—The children of this world marry and are given in marriage, but those who are

counted as worthy of the other world and the resurrection from the dead neither marry nor are given in marriage." The Shakers consider marriage as a purely civil institution with which true Christians have nothing to do.

They believe that freedom of conscience is the most sacred right that God has given to man. They recommend that everyone should live according to the dictates of his conscience as the only means of making himself acceptable in the eyes of God. Their worship is quite different and must seem very unusual to those who judge only by what they have seen in their own country. One Sunday on August 15, 1830, I attended their church, which is a square building without any sort of decoration, altar, or pulpit, and only in the form of a large room with a number of benches for strangers or spectators. Their worship began with a brief talk made by one of their ministers to the spectators, which was simply to ask them to maintain the composure and decorum due the assembly of a religious people who were worshiping the Supreme Being in the way that they thought would be most pleasing to him.

"Reason and the sacred scriptures support our manner of praising God," said the Millennial pastor.

> The Israelites danced after crossing the Red Sea; David danced, and likewise the people of Israel, before the holy ark; and Jeremiah says let the virgins rejoice in the dance, and that the young and the old shall dance together. Jesus Christ in the parable of the prodigal son says that on his return home there was music and dance. Therefore, we have the scriptures on our side. Reason dictates likewise that both the body and the soul exercise themselves in acts of devotion before the Creator; and that since God has created all the active powers of man for his honor and glory, let not the tongue alone pay him homage. The hands and the feet which are useful to man in their proper utilization and service should also offer their worship to the Divinity. In other rites people sing; others have made use of the dance; we use the one and the other.

After this discourse the service began. The men and women, separated on two different sides and in line, began a dance reduced to a few simple and easy movements, at the same time singing in unison to not unpleasant music. All the while they moved their hands as in a gesture of beckoning to some one, and thus they were dancing and singing for the space of an hour and a half. The sermon came next and was simply an attempt to prove the truth and the divinity of the sect and of their dogma.

As for the dress of the Shakers, the women wear a tunic of fine wool held in at the waist with a leather belt, wool or cotton stockings, a cape, or else a cap, all very well fitted and very neat. I saw these people eating together—the farmers under the trees, the craftsmen in their workshops, and the women in charge of the storerooms in their large refectories or dining halls. They have about five hundred acres of land which they cultivate and harvest the seed, which they sell throughout the United States. I bought some and sent them to Veracruz to Don Alejandro Troncoso of that city, to send to President Santa Anna in 1830. They also sell brushes, baskets, feather fans, brooms, handbags and a number of domestic utensils. The funds that they have left over they deposit in the banks of the United States and now have more than half a million. The men and women live separately and maintain the strictest chastity—evidently stricter than that of our friars. Generally they are pale and do not appear to be in very robust health. It seems that they must thus be going contrary to the strongest inclination of human nature.

The authorities do not bother about their affairs, nor do they avail themselves of their political rights to vote or to be elected. They live under their own rules without any other policing or authority. Later we shall see a manufacturing town, which without following a religious sect and only under the control of the manufacturing companies, lives in almost the same manner—although more naturally. Agriculture and horticulture are the principal occupations of the members of this sect. The visible head of their church is a ministry composed of four pastors, two men and two women, selected from among them.

CHAPTER XIII

From New Lebanon, Mr. Poinsett and I continued along a road that was mountainous but rather good. After twelve hours we arrived at Northampton at eight o'clock at night. This is a town in the state of Massachusetts in New England on the Connecticut River, where there are some cotton factories, and where they raise excellent crops of wheat, barley, potatoes, green beans and other vegetables and grains. About a mile away, on a hill called Round Hill, is the literary establishment of Mr. Codswell, where I had placed my son, and at the same time another Yucatecan named Don Juan Cano had sent his son. This boy's talent, application and conduct will within a few years make him one of the leading men of Mexico. The Connecticut River is navigable from this point for steamboats, and they go as far as Hartford, a port and the capital of the state of the same name.

During the morning we visited Mt. Holyoke which is on the other side about a thousand feet above the level of the river. The views from here extend to the boundaries of the states of Connecticut, New Hampshire and New York. Beautiful valleys, rivers and springs, meadows, and towns recently started among the forests—all present a surprising spectacle.

From the moment that one enters New England one notes an improvement in the roads, inns, agriculture, beauty of houses and gardens, in short in everything that surrounds the traveler and that can be perfected with the aid of hard work. All these small towns—Northampton, Worcester, Belcherton, and others up to the outskirts of Boston—appear to be country homes built expressly for recreation and pleasure. Such is the cleanliness, the beauty, and such the charm of these small towns. The roads for the most part are macadamized.

Boston, today the capital of the state of Massachusetts, was before

150

independence the capital of New England, which was composed of the states of New Hampshire, Vermont, Maine, Rhode Island, Connecticut and Massachusetts. The diversity of sects in England and the intolerance of the predominant ones obliged a portion of the English in 1620 to come to colonize this part of North America in search of liberty. This purpose and not the spirit of commerce nor of material advantages prompted the first settlers to abandon their native land and to seek refuge in the inhospitable forests of the new continent. Their great sufferings, the endless tasks that they underwent in a harsh climate, in a country without resources, beset by hostile savage Indians, and obliged to live at first in their boats while they constructed their first houses—all this caused them to be called Pilgrims. A few years later the famous Cromwell tried to come to this colony with all of his followers the Puritans, but Charles I opposed that emigration because of the large numbers, holding back in this manner, without dreaming of it, the very man who some years later would cause him to lose his throne and to be led to the scaffold.

The city of Boston is located on a peninsula in the great Massachusetts Bay. It has two suburbs which are Charleston and South Boston. In Charleston, which is reached by a wooden bridge about half a mile long, there is a great glass factory which competes with the best of England, although the product is more expensive and can only meet the competition from Europe because of the import duties. In Charleston also is the penitentiary, where when I was there they had three hundred prisoners and only fourteen jailers, without there having been any case of an escape or an attempt, although as is to be presumed the greater part of them are daring people with very intemperate habits. But the rigorous discipline and the constant watchfulness of the guards is sufficient to keep them quiet and docile while hoping for an end to their confinement. During the clay they are busy at their trades, lining up at mealtime to go to the kitchen to get their plates which they take to their rooms where they eat. Twice a day they pray or listen to a religious and moral exhortation, and at night they are locked up in their small cells. A melancholy example for humanity is the following anecdote taken from the work of Mr. Hamilton to whom it was told by the prison warden.

Many years ago before the establishment of the present state prison or penitentiary, a man with honorable connections but of rough character and unbridled habits was convicted of the crime of robbery at night and sentenced to life imprisonment in the Charleston jail in the state of Massachusetts. His pride was not taken down with the disgrace and the punishment— his conduct was arrogant and insubordinate with his jailers, so that it was necessary to separate him from the other prisoners and subject him to harsh discipline. The first year he remained silent and scowling; the clergyman who visited him found him unteachable and unbelieving. But during the following months he changed gradually in manners and ideas. His disposition was more friendly; he was seen reading the scriptures regularly; and the chaplain and the jailer congratulated themselves on such a healthy change in the prisoner. He would talk of his past life and of the terrible offenses that he had committed against God and men, full of grief and repentance; and he gave thanks to the Creator for having preserved his life so that he might have time to ask for his mercy. Now the prisoner's conduct was edifying, and his conversation evangelical; all who saw him became interested in the fate of so good a Christian, so that a number of wellknown people interceded with the governor of the state to pardon him. This magistrate was inclined to do so, when one day with the greatest trust the jailer and other persons were talking with the prisoner, and he threw himself upon the jailer, wounded him several times, and tried to flee, although without success.

He was taken to a solitary cell with bars where he remained for some years without the slightest hope of getting out. Finally a brother-in-law of his, a person of influence and wealth in South Carolina, went to Boston and accepted responsibility for the prisoner if he were pardoned. They granted his request, and to remove from him all temptation to commit the same crimes they provided him with everything necessary in the city of Charleston, South Carolina.

The prisoner got out after twenty years, during which time he had not breathed the pure free air of the heavens nor seen the splendor of the sun. During this time Boston, which was a small town when he was locked up, had changed into a rich and beautiful city. At every step he took he had to marvel at some new thing that he saw. The physical and moral appearance, the customs, clothing, thoughts, worries and opinions of the generation that he saw were very different from those of the generation that he had known. The wooden houses that he had seen standing alone and unadorned had been replaced by magnificent buildings of marble, granite or brick; he saw plazas and promenades in places that had been wooded and sylvan when he left them. In short he felt like the inhabitant of another planet that had come to an unknown world. At the sight of such new things, of a spectacle so alive and interesting, surrounded by so many strange and unknown objects, this man dissolved into tears thinking that he had been transported to an unknown land.

He arrived in Charleston, South Carolina, where his brother-in-law found him good lodgings and the comforts of life. The first year his conduct was above reproach, but the evil hour induced him to visit New York.

There he ran into people of evil ways, associated with them, again robbed by night and was condemned to life imprisonment in Sing Sing, the penitentiary of the state of New York, from where he will go forth as a corpse. Can human nature be so incorrigible as is shown by this sad example? Are there in the physical makeup of man irresistible tendencies? These are questions that concern phrenologists and their adversaries. There is no doubt that our material composition has much to do with our moral character.

Commodore Morris, an old friend of Mr. Poinsett, was good enough to go with us to the arsenal where they are building a granite dry dock for constructing and repairing war ships. It is three hundred feet long, twenty-five feet deep, and fifty feet wide. It is elliptical in form, and the water comes and goes at discretion as it is needed. The cost is figured to be five hundred thousand dollars.

The next day we went to visit Mr. Adams at his home in Quincy. This illustrious American is the son of the president who followed Washington, and he himself was president for the four-year term of 1824 to 1828. He had been secretary of state in Mr. Monroe's administration, and minister to the English government. I never saw a man so cold and circumspect of character. During the visit which lasted more than half an hour we scarcely said more than what would in other circumstances take five minutes. "What do you hear from Mexico?" he asked me. After some silence I related to him briefly the series of revolutions that had occurred.

"You won't be at peace," he said to me, "for any period of time until you adopt institutions fitting to the circumstances. These circumstances must be created also."

We said goodbye and left this strange man in his lonely house seven miles distant from Boston. We went to see Mr. Perkins, one of the richest persons in New England, the owner of rich granite quarries which furnish this valuable stone for buildings, docks, stone pavements, columns, etc., of the nearby towns. We had tea in his famous country home which is enhanced by a great number of exotic plants and fruit trees, flowers and vegetables. Mr. Perkins has the particular pleasure of eating pineapples from his garden, pears and peaches in the winter time, by means of conservatories kept at various temperatures.

As one of the richest manufacturing impresarios of Lowell, Mr. Perkins invited us to go with him to see that remarkable town which had sprung up among the trees in the short space of seven years. Nowhere does the power of hard work and liberty make one feel so forcefully its beneficial effects as in the United States of America. I shall give a description of this amazing progress with the aid of the able pen of a young man named M. Chevalier, who when he visited this place felt himself inspired at the sight of the order, prosperity and good customs of the workers of Lowell.

It is not war, that last rationale of kings, that can lift a people or a nation up to prosperity. A battlefield will excite horror, or feverish enthusiasm, or piety and fear. The strength of man applied to production is more majestic than human strength applied to killing. The pyramids and the temples of colossal dimensions of Thebes, the Coliseum, or St. Peter's Church in Rome, disclose more grandeur than a battlefield covered with dead men and ashes, even when there were three hundred thousand corpses lying about as in those battles in which Napoleon carried fear to the world and covered France with glory. The power of man is thus like that of God, visible in small things as in large ones. There is nothing in the material order of which our species has more right to boast than the mechanical inventions by means of which man curbs the unordered vigor of nature or develops its hidden energy. By means of mechanics man, weak and wretched in appearance, by extending his hand over the immensity of the world, takes possession of its floods, of its unleashed winds, of the ebb and flow of the sea, of metals and combustibles scattered about over the surface of the earth, or hidden in its depths, of the liquids that are converted into steam to be the most powerful agent in the hands of man.

Is there indeed anything that gives a more exalted idea of the power of man than the steam machinery in the forms that have been given to him for application to transport, either in ships upon the sea and the rivers, or in trains across the surface of the earth. It is a living being rather than a machine. It goes by itself, runs like a horse; more than that, it breathes. In fact the steam that comes out of the stacks regularly and that condenses into white smoke truly looks like breath, the violent respiration of a horse running a race.

Anyone in the midst of these forests a short time ago when they were inhabited by a few wandering tribes, and today dotted here and there by a few recently built houses—anyone who with no knowledge of these prodigious machines—that happened one night to see a body moving along showering millions of sparks, breathing loudly and frequently running with an unknown speed without a horse or other animal to move it, would no doubt think that he was seeing one of those dragons or fabulous monsters that spew flames out of their mouths and threaten to devour the unfortunate mortal that happens to get in their way. A few years ago when the Brahmans saw a steamboat struggling and conquering the currents of the sacred Ganges, in good faith those fathers of ancient knowlede believed that it was an unknown animal recently discovered by the English in a distant land.

In modern societies mechanical progress has produced factories that promise to be for the human race an inexhaustible source of prosperity and well-being. English factories produce today about eight hundred million yards of cotton textiles that are equivalent to one yard for every individual upon the earth. If all the men living were to set to work on these products with only the help of their fingers it is probable that in a year they would produce only a part of what Great Britain does. Thus the labors of the human race would be engaged in a work which, thanks to mechanization and factories employs at the most a million and a half in that nation.

We must infer from this that when manufacturing is developed and well planned, the moderate work of a portion of the human race will be sufficient to provide for all the comforts of material life. There seems to be no doubt that that day will come, but up until this time it has not been possible to set up this wonderful order of things, and a long time will pass before it is accomplished. The system of manufacturing is a new discovery; it is developing more every day, and as it develops it will improve. Here is an example. The cotton imported into England for manufacturing in 1785 weighed 11 million English pounds. In 1816 it amounted to 9 million and in 1831 to 245 million. These three numbers are in this ratio: 1:9.5:22.25. However, this progress is slow, and in those countries where these skills are just beginning it must be much slower still.

In this North America the development of manufacturing is, however, surprising. Who is not amazed at the sight of the town of Lowell, a forest village ten years ago, and today a town of seven thousand people with factories that are competing with those of Europe.

"I had scarcely recovered from the sight of this improvised city," says M. Chevalier,

scarcely had I seen and touched it to assure myself that it was not a cardboard city like those that Potemkin had had built on Catherine's dressing table, in order to find out to what extent the factories in this place had stirred up, with respect to the wellbeing and morality of the working class with relation to the security of the rich and that of public order, the dangers that had been experienced in Europe. Thanks to the supervising agents of the two principal companies (Merrimack Corporation and Lawrence Corporation) I have been able to satisfy my curiosity.

The cotton factories alone employ six thousand persons in Lowell. Of this number about five thousand are young single women from seventeen to twenty-four years of age, daughters of tenant farmers from the different states of New England, particularly Massachusetts, New Hampshire and Vermont. There they are far from their families and on their own. As I saw them in the morning or in the afternoon in the streets dressed neatly and cleanly, leaving the shops and taking from the hangers covered with flowers their hats, caps, shawls and kerchiefs, I said to myself, "This is not like Manchester." Here are the average general salaries such as were paid during the recent month of May per week—that is, for six days of work:

	$3.00
Preparatory operations (ginning and cleaning)	3.12
	2.50
Spinning	3.25
Weaving of various types	3.25
Dyeing and sizing	3.75
	4.00
Measuring and packing	3.25

The salaries of skilled workers are notably higher and are as much as $6.00 per week.

Let us now compare the situation of these workers with those of Europe, and an enormous difference will be noted in favor of those of the United States of the North. There are few women in Europe of that class who earn more than eighteen or nineteen cents per day, or $1.08 to $1.14 per week. Bear in mind also that articles of prime necessity such as bread, meat, sugar, coffee, rice, etc, are much cheaper in the United States. Thus, a large number of the women workers of Lowell can save up to $1.50 per week. At the end of four years they will have $300, and that is the dowry with which they go out to establish themselves by marrying a young man who has an equal amount, and they apply themselves to the exercise of a profession.

In France, and much less in Mexico, one cannot even imagine the position of pretty young girls, most of them twenty to thirty leagues from their parents' homes, with only their virtue. In spite of this one does not notice deplorable effects in Lowell, with the exception of a very limited number of cases which do not break down the general rule. The English race has customs very different from the Spanish and the French. Other habits, other ideas. Protestant education draws around each individual a circle much more difficult to penetrate than that drawn by Catholic education. For one thing there is, indeed, more coldness, less communication in social relations, more or less an absolute absence of free expression and confidence. But on the other hand, one finds more respect, more consideration for the personality of others. What among us would be considered as a bit of mischief, an insignificant adventure, would be reproached severely in England or in the United States of the North. Let no one be surprised then in this country to see the daughters of farmers and landowners leave their parents to go to a city where they know no one and remain there in their work for three or four years until they have made a small fortune. They are under the safeguard of public faith.

This presupposes in customs an extreme reserve, and in public opinion a watchful and unrelenting sternness and this reserve give society a certain coloring of sadness and tedious monotony which wearies those who are not used to it, but when one reflects upon the perils to which the opposite system exposes unwitting young girls who rush into pleasure, when one counts the victims that have resulted from that ease of communication and that abandon in other countries, it is difficult not to agree that the coldness and the Anglo-American incommunicative manner are a great deal better than the friendly and easygoing sociability of the French and the Mexicans.

The manufacturing companies watch over the habits of these young working women. Each company has constructed a building that has a number of rooms sufficient to house the women in what they call boardinghouses. There they are under the protection and sponsorship of the landladies who run the places, for which the women pay each week only one dollar for their board and room. The landladies keep the company informed of the conduct of the young women in their care, and they live by rules that are laid down for them. Here is an excerpt from these rules:

1st. All persons employed by the company must be busy at their tasks during the hours of work. They must also be capable of doing the job to which they are assigned or to make efforts to be so. On all occasions and under all circumstances either in speech or by conduct they are to demonstrate a love of temperance and all the virtues, and to be motivated by a feeling for their moral and social obligations. The company's agent will strive to set for all a good example. Any person who is notoriously lazy, dissolute or intemperate, or who is in the habit of missing divine worship, who violates Sunday rest, or who is given over to gambling, will be dismissed from the company.

2nd. No spirituous liquor is allowed on the premises of the company unless it be by a doctor's orders. Nor is any game of chance or of cards allowed. Article 13 requires that all workers must live in the boardinghouses.

Since Lowell is a workers' town where everybody is subject to company rules, it is evident that it is like a vast monastery where civil authority is little concerned. They are like large families or school groups under special constitutions, whose object is to stimulate work and maintain good habits as the basis of every social establishment. Just as at the end of ten or twelve years young people come out of literary institutes with a wealth of knowledge and learning, so the working men and women leave these shops after some years with the monetary capital which is the fruit of their savings, and furthermore with the habits of love of work, respect for virtue, and horror towards vice. Sunday, which among us is a day of pleasure and fiesta, in these places is dedicated to prayer, meditation and rest. This is one of the many aspects in which the Anglo-American and the Mexican peoples are different. In the moral and religious aspect among South Americans there is a relaxation and contempt that is in direct contradiction with our religious profession and the hypocritical zeal which we manifest in support of our exclusive worship. This reflection leads to very sad consequences for the new republics, but it is no less the truth. These consequences are that since the source of political authority among us could not be found, as it should have been in a republic, in that severe restraint of North American customs, in the inflexibility of life habits, and in the religious sternness of the people, alongside a multiplicity of sects, we have found ourselves obliged to find such source in material force, in terror on the same basis as before independence, in open conflict with the institutions and openly incompatible with republican principles.

So certain is it that the need for order and for liberty is essential to human nature, and that it is impossible to found a society with only one of these elements. If you give one portion of social institutions over to liberty, be assured that the principle of order will play a part no less exclusive on another point. Unfortunately among us the laws of equilibrium between order and liberty have not yet been established.

The company rules are religiously observed in Lowell. In the factories which are buildings of great extent there are bells to call the people to work so that they resemble the convents of one of our cities. But in Lowell there are no supplicants with saints, there are no beggars, there are no ragged and poverty stricken people. These nineteenth-century nuns, instead of keeping busy making relicaries, scapularies and shrouds, are employed in spinning cotton and weaving textiles of all qualities. In Lowell there are no pastimes nor entertainment, but a peaceful town inhabited by people dressed with charm, neatness and decency.

CHAPTER XIV

Battle of Lexington.—Monument.—Tremont House.—Constitution of the State.—The education of its people.—Review.—Observations on this periodical.—Schools. —State of instruction in New England.—Comparison with the states of Mexico. —Advantages of popular education.—Cambridge College.—Boston society.—Nahant Island.—Rhode Island.—New Providence.—Its constitution.—Character of the Yankees.—Equal distribution of wealth.—State of Connecticut and its government.—New Haven.—Hartford Convention.

On the way from Boston to Lowell we went by Lexington, the town where the first action between Americans and English occurred in the War of Independence. General Cage had sent eight hundred soldiers to occupy the warehouses of war materials that the Massachusetts assembly had ordered to be set up, and as the British troops passsed through Lexington they were attacked by civilian troops there, and eight men were killed. They continued their march, but on their return they encountered a large number of militiamen, and there was a hard fought action in which 273 Englishmen and 88 North Americans died. The first blood was shed between the two nations. In the public square of that small town there is a monument erected in 1799 in granite with the following inscription:

Sacred to the liberty and rights of mankind; the freedom and independence of America, sealed and defended by the blood of her sons.

This monument is erected by the inhabitants of Lexington, under the patronage and at the expense of the commonwealth of Massachusetts, to the memory of their fellow citizens, Ensign Robert Munroe, Messrs. Jonas Parker, Samuel Hadley, Jonathan Harrington, junior, Isaac Muzzey, Caleb Harrington, and John Brown of Lexington, and Asahel Porter of Woburn, who fell on this field, the first victims to the sword of British tyranny and oppression, on the morning of the ever-memorable 19th of April, 1775.

The die was cast. The blood of these martyrs, in the cause of God and their country, was the cement of these states, their colonies, and

gave the spring to the spirit, firmness and resolution of their fellow citizens. They rose, as one man, to revenge their brethren's blood, and
at the point of the sword to assert and defend their native rights. They
nobly dared to be free. The contest was long, bloody, and affecting.
Righteous Heaven approved the solemn appeal. Victory crowned
their arms, and the peace, liberty, and the independence of the United States of America were their glorious reward.

After the Battle of Lexington the English general fortified Boston, and
both parties prepared for war. The Americans immediately occupied the
heights around the city where they set up fortifications. The English dis-
lodged them after a fierce battle in which they lost a third of their troops. The
theater of this action was Bunker's Hill, famous in these parts since that day.
On this hill there is a monument 220 feet high which was erected in 1825.

The inn where I stayed in Boston is the best there is in the United
States. It is called Tremont House, in front of the theater. The building is of
that beautiful micah-granite which is so plentiful in the northern states,
especially in New England. There is room for four hundred persons to stay
in this hotel, and there were at least three hundred of both sexes when I was
there. Everyone eats at a common table, or else privately if one wishes to
pay a little more. The service is prompt; the food is very well seasoned; the
beds comfortable and clean; that large house is lighted with gas, and in all
the hallways there is sufficient light to get around. The charge is thirteen
dollars per week with wine extra.

Boston streets are mostly crooked, and most of them rather narrow;
some are stone paved, others are beautiful and comfortable with
Macadam's method. There are very notable buildings of white marble and
granite. The State House built on a small hill rises up to a height so that one
looks out from the cupola over all parts of the city and the bay. The two
chambers that make up the legislative body meet there.

The constitution of this state was written in 1780 and revised in 1821.
The legislative power rests in the senate and house of representatives, and
both are called the General Court of Massachusetts. The members of the
house of representatives are elected each year the second Monday in
November. Each town that has 150 voters listed names a representative,
above that, another one for each 225 increase. The senate has forty members elected by the districts annually the second Monday in November. The
governor is also elected annually by the people the second Monday in
November, and likewise the lieutenant governor. There is a governor's
council composed of nine members taken from among the senators and
selected by both houses. The legislative body meets in Boston the first
Wednesday in January each year.

All citizens twenty-one years of age or older can vote, provided they have lived for one year in the state and six months preceding the time of the election, and that they have paid taxes to the state for two years, unless the law makes an exception.

The judicial power rests in judges named by the governor in agreement with the council. Their term of office is *ad vitam aut culpam* ("for life during good behavior").

Boston is one of the best-educated cities in the United States, and the State of Massachusetts is one that has produced a large number of learned men, eloquent orators, well-educated lawyers and famous statesmen. The Adams, Franklins, Hancocks, Ticknors, Quincys, Everetts and other similar names occupy a distinguished place in the literary and political annals of that area. The last of these is the principal editor of a tri-monthly review known as the *North American Review,* comparable to the most classical reviews of Europe. When I arrived in the United States in 1830, I found discussed in that review events of Mexico of December 1828, in which unfortunately I had a part under the colors that Mr. Ward had pictured them in his writings in a supplement on his trip to Mexico. The same subject, although from a very different point of view, had been treated by the skillful hand of Mr. Walsh in his *Quarterly Review.*

The editors of these periodicals imitate the English reviews, and they prefer more extensive articles and analytical discussions to a greater number of superficial items or simple accounts. In one of the numbers of this review, when analyzing the work of Father Guasi on the United States, there are, he says, a Jesuit college in Georgetown near Washington, and a literary institution of the same order in New York, a college for priests of St. Sulpice in Baltimore, and a school in Emmetsburg. In Kentucky the English Dominicans have a school and a church under the tutelage of Santa Rosa of Lima. In the western states there are missionaries of St. Francis of Paula and a convent of Carmelite nuns of Santa Teresa. In Georgetown another one of the Visitant Sisters.

The abbott Dubois founded another convent in Emmetsburg for the education of young women, and himself started another in Philadelphia, in which he had the double purpose of education and caring for the sick. This establishment is supported not only by the charity of the Catholics but of the Protestants as well. The abbott Nerina has founded in Kentucky a convent for nuns who go under the name of Sisters of Mary at the Foot of the Cross, and finally a Protestant minister converted to the Catholic faith has brought to Boston, his birthplace, the Ursulines and has left them sufficient funds for their establishment.

Although this progress of Catholicism caused some alarm to the friends of religious independence, the editor of the *Review* sets forth his own alarm with the expression of a sincere tolerance as religious as it is philosophical. In a country where the force of law does not come to the support of an exclusive religion there is nothing to fear.

In Boston there are sixty-eight free schools besides twenty-three Sunday schools. It is true that in this state and in Connecticut education is most advanced. According to figures compiled by official reports coming to the capital in 1830, among 60,000 persons there were only 400 who did not know how to read or write, and of 131 towns that sent in reports on education there were 12,393 children of both sexes learning to read and write, do arithmetic and algebra, the principles of geography, history, drawing, and religion, and there were only fifty-eight who did not know how to read and write among all the children between fourteen and twenty years of age. The annual sum of public funds dedicated to this sacred object in the city of Boston is from $50,000 to $70,000.

The method of arranging these establishments in the United States deserves the attention of Mexicans. Each year the representatives of the respective wards meet and name ten or twelve commissioners that are called Trustees, who are charged with the collection of funds, their distribution, the examination of the state of the schools, the conduct of the teachers, the number of children, instruments, books, etc. They collect the income from legacies, donations, legislative grants and others set aside for education. When the year has ended, they make a report in which they give an accounting to the public of all that they have observed, the improvement that they think should be made, the expenses, number of children, etc. As I write this I have before me the twenty-fourth annual report of the Trustees of the public society of New York, *Twenty-fourth Annual Report of the Public School Society of New York.*

It can be stated on very approximate calculations that a third of the inhabitants of the states of Massachusetts and Connecticut attend schools, and that with the exception of two thousand persons in a population of two million of these states, all know how to read and write at least. Compare this moral situation of the people of the United States with one or two of our states, and it will be clear as to the true reason why it is impossible at the present time to bring our institutions up to the level of those of our neighbors, *particularly in some states.* Of those of the state of Mexico, for example, and of Yucatan, which I know best, it may be said that among 1,200,000 inhabitants in the first and 700,000 in the second, there will probably be at the most one in twenty [who can read]. And something more—among the five in a thousand that know how to read and write two fifths do not know arithmetic, and three fifths do not even know the meaning of the words geography, history, astronomy, etc. Four fifths do not know what the Bible is, and the names of Genesis, Paralipomenon, Gospel, Apocalipsis are entirely unknown. Add to this that in Yucatan there are at least a third of the people who do not speak Spanish, and in the state of Mexico one fifth. Those who consider the degree of civilization of the masses as no reason to give institutions to the people are either dismally ignorant or they are extremely perverse.

This state of public education in the United States can well justify the call made to all classes of citizens to take part in the elections and other governmental functions. I remember having read that one of the big arguments that were made for extending the electoral census in France and England was the ignorance of a large part of the people in some provinces. In the county of Wales, for example, one in twenty knows how to read and write; in Scotland one in ten. In the southern departments of France there are some where one out of twenty-five knows how to read and write. But in these places there are many persons who compensate in some degree for the roughness or ignorance of the masses by their learning, experience and general knowledge.

Mr. Otis was the mayor when I was in Boston. I had the honor of being invited to his table where there were several people well known for their knowledge and long services. Mr. Otis has made sacrifices for the cause of liberty, although he did not belong to the democratic party. His connections with Adams, Webster, Everett and other men of the former Federalist group cause him to be placed in their lineage.

Cambridge College is one of the most famous in the United States. On the visit which I made to this establishment under the guidance of Mr. Quincy I had reason to be satisfied with the intelligence of the rector, the beauty of the place, the elegance of the building, the literary wealth of its library and museum of antiquities. At Cambridge College they teach the humanities, physical sciences, mathematics, history, the Greek, Latin, French, Spanish and German languages, ideology and political economy.

In the same town I visited Mr. Gros, a man who has made a great fortune in the tannery trade. He uses a considerable part of it to acquire beautiful pictures and original paintings or good copies of the best artists. The Atheneum in Boston is an establishment that attracts the attention of the educated traveler because of the great number of well-chosen books and curious monuments. Mr. Everett, junior, did me the honor of introducing me to this society.

In Boston there is a beautiful marble statue of General Washington made by Mr. Chantry, and in a cemetery near the public park is the tomb of Franklin and his family. The park is a beautiful grove on a level spot in front of the State House, and the only adornment, if such it can be called, is a pool 120 feet long and half as wide. No statues, no fountains, no pavilions, etc. In the United States they look for the necessary and the useful. There are not even any establishments of pleasure and luxury.

Boston society is generally educated and one might say has good taste. In the winter there are dances and tea parties where the people of different classes of society get together according to their different tastes, inclinations, and professions.

Eight miles from Boston there is an island in the very mouth of the bay known as Nahant, very popular in the summer for sea bathing. The views are magnificent over the sea, the coasts, small towns and towers of Boston. On the island, which is about a mile long, there are two or three good hotels, baths and places of entertainment.

From Boston I went to the state of Rhode Island, taking a seat on a stagecoach. As in the state of Massachusetts, this is one of those with the least navigation because of the lack of rivers. It is also the one where there are more carriages proportionally, and in which the roads are kept up better and railroad lines are undertaken with the most enthusiasm. The roads generally are much better than in the other states of the Union. From Boston to Providence is about forty-five miles; we had dinner in Dedham and got to Providence, the capital of the state of Rhode Island on the Providence River. This is a manufacturing city as are all those of New England. It has fifteen to sixteen thousand people, and a college where they teach physics, geometry, history, Greek and Latin, ideology and penmanship.

The government of the state is based on the charter granted by Charles II at the time of the establishment of the colony in 1683, and this is the only state in the Union which does not have a written constitution. The legislative power is exercised by the General Assembly which consists of a senate and a house of representatives. The latter is composed of seventy-two members taken six from New Port, four from each of the cities of Providence, Portsmouth, and Warewich, and two from each of the towns of the state. They are elected every six months in April and August. The senate is composed of ten members elected annually in April.

There is a governor, popularly elected each year in April, and a lieutenant governor elected at the same time who stands in for the governor when necessary. The assembly meets four times a year—in New Port the first Wednesday in May, which is the beginning of the civil year, and is the first session, until the first Wednesday in June; the first Wednesday in October in Providence, until the first Wednesday in November; those of January and March in the towns of South Kingston, East Greenwich, and Binsol.

From New Providence to New York the distance is 180 miles by the maritime canal the Sound. The first colonization of Providence recalls one of those sad effects of the intolerance of religious sects that wish the exclusive dominion of their beliefs. The Puritans, pursued in England under the government of Charles I, leaving their native land under the name of the Pilgrim Fathers, came to the New World in search of the liberty that they did not find in the Old World. But scarcely were these victims of persecution settled in New England than, contradicting not only their former principles, but even those of universal morality, and especially that of the gospels which is the most tolerant, they in turn became persecutors. The Socinians, the Quakers, in a word all those who did not hold to their religious opinions and beliefs were run out of the colony violently with offense against their property. Among these was Roger Williams, a Puritan clergyman, who was bold enough to expose what he considered evidence of apostasy in the churches of Massachusetts.

At first the clergy proposed to fight him with theological arguments and demonstrations. Since they were not able to make him or the others disappear, they had recourse to civil authority so that by force they might throw out of the midst of the true believers so able and learned an enemy. Roger Williams was banished, and accompanied by his followers he wandered through the wilderness until he came to a place called Moohausic by the Indians, and here he placed his settlement and named it Providence.

When nature made the people of New England, according to Mr. Hamilton, it seemed to be her wish to give them *twice the amount of brains* and *half a heart*. Indeed, they are perhaps the most intelligent and astute people known. When one says *Yankee*, which is what they are commonly called, it is understood that one means a man who knows his business; that the odds of his being cheated or cheating are nineteen to one in favor of the latter. The character of these people, says the same writer, is not friendly, does not inspire confidence; but it is also far from being scornful. They have a degree of energy, strength and independence that does not allow one to look down upon them.

Wealth is better distributed in New England than in any other part of the globe. Although there are great capitalists, there are no huge fortunes. There are no poor, and it is very rare to find families in poverty. Regularly beside great palaces there is the unfortunate fellow who is begging for bread for his children. Although there are some beggars, they are always foreigners, especially Irishmen who have recently arrived and are looking for a way to get along.

The state of Connecticut has three hundred thousand inhabitants and lies between the maritime canal called the Sound, the states of Rhode Island, Massachusetts, and New York. The capital is Hartford, a city of about nine thousand inhabitants on the Connecticut River, and it has a very busy port. The constitution of Connecticut was granted by Charles II in

1662 and revised in 1818 by the General Assembly. There are a senate and a house of representatives. The latter is composed of 208 members who receive no pay. There are thirty-four senators, and both groups are elected for one year. The governor is elected by the people annually. He receives three hundred dollars per year. The assembly meets one year in Hartford and the other in New Haven. There is universal suffrage for whites among those citizens aged twenty-one years or over.

New Haven is one of the beautiful cities of the United States, because of its location and the elegance of its buildings. The population is nine thousand, it is built on an extensive bank, and extends about two miles from north to south and three from west to east. The children's academy run by Mr. Dwight is notable for its size and would surprise anyone who did not know that in that small state the whole attention of the people is directed to the education of the young. Yale College is another educational institution that competes with the University of Cambridge in the state of Massachusetts. The number of students is about five hundred. The cemetery of this city is the best in the United States because of its size, symmetry, beauty of monuments, trees and location.

Before leaving the state of Connecticut I shall include an interesting document which is the manifesto of the famous Hartford Convention held in 1814, when Mr. Madison was president of the United States and during the critical moments of the second war with England, when the states suffered great bankruptcies because of the interruption of trade, and the general congress passed some laws that did not meet with the approval of many. The delegates to the convention were from the legislatures of Massachusetts, Connecticut and Rhode Island, from the counties of Grafton and Cheshire in the state of New Hampshire, from Winthrop County in the state of Vermont. The total number was twenty-five. Here is the manifesto:

> The convention is deeply impressed with a sense of the arduous nature of the commission which they were appointed to execute, of devising the means of defence against dangers, and of relief from oppressions proceeding from the acts of their own government, without violating constitutional principles, or disappointing the hopes of a suffering and injured people. To prescribe patience and firmness to those who are already exhausted by distress, is sometimes to drive them to despair, and the progress towards reform by the regular road, is irksome to those whose imaginations discern, and whose feelings prompt, to a shorter course. But when abuses, reduced to a system, and accumulated through a course of years, have pervaded every department of government, and spread corruption through every region of the state; when these are clothed

with the forms of law, and enforced by an executive whose will is their source, no summary means of relief can be applied without recourse to direct and open resistance. This experiment, even when justifiable, (p. 311) cannot fail to be painful to the good citizen; and the success of the effort will be no security against the danger of the example. Precedents of resistance to the worst administration, are eagerly seized by those who are naturally hostile to the best. Necessity alone can sanction a resort to this measure; and it should never be extended in duration or degree beyond the exigency, until the people, not merely in the fervour of sudden excitement, but after full deliberation, are determined to change the constitution.

It is a truth, not to be concealed, that a sentiment prevails to no inconsiderable extent, that administration have given such constructions to that instrument, and practised so many abuses under colour of its authority, that the time for a change is at hand. Those who so believe, regard the evils which surround them as intrinsic and incurable defects in the constitution. They yield to a persuasion, that no change, at any time, or on any occasion, can aggravate the misery of their country. This opinion may ultimately prove to be correct. But as the evidence on which it rests is not yet conclusive, and as measures adopted upon the assumption of its certainty might be irrevocable, some general considerations are submitted, in the hope of reconciling all to a course of moderation and firmness, which may save them from the regret incident to sudden decisions, probably avert the evil, (p. 312) or at least insure consolation and success in the last resort.

The constitution of the United States, under the auspices of a wise and virtuous administration, proved itself competent to all the objects of national prosperity comprehended in the views of its framers. No parallel can be found in history, of a transition so rapid as that of the United States from the lowest depression to the highest felicity—from the condition of weak and disjointed republics, to that of a great, united, and prosperous nation.

Although this high state of public happiness has undergone a miserable and afflicting reverse, through the prevalence of a weak and profligate policy, yet the evils and afflictions which have thus been induced upon the country, are not peculiar to any form of government. The lust and caprice of power, the corruption of patronage, the oppression of the weaker interests of the community by the stronger, heavy taxes, wasteful expenditures, and unjust and ruinous wars, are the natural offspring of bad administrations, in all ages and countries. It was indeed to be hoped, that the rulers of these states would not make such disastrous haste to involve their infancy in the embarrassments of old and rotten institutions. Yet all this have they done; and their conduct calls loudly (p. 313) for their dismission and disgrace. But to attempt upon every abuse of power to change the constitution, would be to perpetuate the evils of revolution.

Again, the experiment of the powers of the constitution to regain its vigour, and of the people to recover from their delusions, has been hitherto made under the greatest possible disadvantages arising from the state of the world. The fierce passions which have convulsed the nations of Europe, have passed the ocean, and find their way to the bosoms of our citizens, have afforded to administration the means of perverting public opinion, in respect to our foreign relations, so as to acquire its aid in the indulgence of their animosities, and the increase of their adherents. Further, a reformation of public opinion, resulting from dear—bought experience, in the southern Atlantic states, at least, is not to be despaired of. They will have felt, that the eastern states cannot be made exclusively the victims of a capricious and impassioned policy. They will have seen that the great and essential interests of the people are common to the south and to the east. They will realize the fatal errors of a system which seeks revenge for commercial injuries in the sacrifice of commerce, and aggravates by needless wars, to an immeasurable extent, the injuries it professes to redress. They may discard the influence of visionary theorists, and recognize the benefits of a practical policy. (p. 314) Indications of this desirable revolution of opinion, among our brethren in those states, are already manifested. While a hope remains of its ultimate completion, its progress should not be retarded or stopped, by exciting fears which must check these favourable tendencies, and frustrate the efforts of the wisest and best men in those states, to accelerate this propitious change.

Finally, if the Union be destined to dissolution, by reason of the multiplied abuses of bad administrations, it should if possible, be the work of peaceable times, and deliberate consent. Some new form of confederacy should be substituted among those states which shall intend to maintain a federal relation to each other. Events may prove that the causes of our calamities are deep and permanent. They may be found to proceed, not merely from the blindness of prejudice, pride of opinion, violence of party spirit, or the confusion of the times; but they may be traced to implacable combinations of individuals, or of states, to monopolize power and office, and to trample without remorse upon the rights and interests of commercial sections of the Union. Whenever it shall appear that these causes are radical and permanent, a separation, by equitable arrangement, will be preferable to an alliance by constraint, among nominal friends, (p. 315) but real enemies, inflamed by mutual hatred and jealousy, and inviting, by intestine divisions, contempt and aggression from abroad. But a severance of the Union by one or more states, against the will of the rest, and especially in a time of war, can be justified only by absolute necessity. These are among the principal objections against precipitate measures tending to disunite the states, and when examined in connection with the farewell address of the Father of his country, they must, it is believed, be deemed conclusive.

Under these impressions, the convention have proceeded to confer and deliberate upon the alarming state of public affairs, especially as affecting the interests of the people who have appointed them for this purpose, and they are naturally led to a consideration, in the first place, of the dangers and grievances which menace an immediate or speedy pressure, with a view of suggesting means of present relief; in the next place, of such as are of a more remote and general description, in the hope of attaining future security.

Among the subjects of complaint and apprehension, which might be comprised under the former of these propositions, the attention of the convention has been occupied with the claims and pretensions advanced, and the authority exercised over the militia, by the executive and legislative departments of the national government. Also, upon the destitution of the means of defence in which the eastern states are left; (p. 316) while at the same time they are doomed to heavy requisitions of men and money for national objects.

The authority of the national government over the militia is derived from those clauses in the constitution which give power to Congress "to provide for calling forth the militia to execute the laws of the Union, suppress insurrections and repel invasions;"—Also "to provide for organizing, arming, and disciplining the militia, and for governing such parts of them as may be employed in the service of the United States, reserving to the states respectively the appointment of the officers, and the authority of training the militia according to the discipline prescribed by Congress." Again, "the President shall be commander in chief of the army and navy of the United States, and of the militia of the several states, *when called into the actual service of the United States.*" In these specified cases only, has the national government any power over the militia; and it follows conclusively, that for all general and ordinary purposes, this power belongs to the states respectively, and to them alone. It is not only with regret, but with astonishment, the convention perceive that under colour of an authority conferred with such plain and precise limitations, a power is arrogated by the executive government, and in some instances sanctioned by the two houses of congress, of control over the militia, which if conceded will render nugatory the rightful authority of the individual states over that class of men, and by placing at the disposal (p. 317) of the national government the lives and services of the great body of the people, enable it at pleasure to destroy their liberties, and erect a military despotism on the ruins.

An elaborate examination of the principles assumed for the basis of these extravagant pretensions, of the consequences to which they lead, and of the insurmountable objections to their admission, would transcend the limits of this report. A few general observations, with an exhibition of the character of these pretensions, and a recommendation of a strenuous opposition to them, must not, however, be omitted.

It will not be contended that by the terms used in the constitutional compact, the power of the national government to call out the militia is other than a power expressly limited to three cases. One of these must exist, as a condition precedent to the exercise of that power—Unless the laws shall be opposed, or an insurrection shall exist, or an invasion shall be made, congress, and of consequence the President as their organ, has no more power over the militia than over the armies of a foreign nation.

But if the declaration of the President should be admitted to be an unerring test of the existence of these cases, this important power would depend, not upon the truth of the fact, but upon executive infallibility. And the limitation of the power would consequently be nothing more than merely nominal, as it might always be eluded. [p. 318] It follows therefore that the decision of the President in this particular cannot be conclusive. It is as much the duty of the state authorities to watch over the rights *reserved,* as of the United States to exercise the powers which are *delegated.*

The arrangement of the United States into military districts, with a small portion of the regular force, under an officer of high rank of the standing army, with power to call for the militia, as circumstances in his judgment may require; and to assume the command of them, is not warranted by the constitution or any law of the United States. It is not denied that Congress may delegate to the President of the United States the power to call forth the militia in the cases which are within their jurisdiction—But he has no authority to substitute military prefects throughout the Union, to use their own discretion in such instances. To station an officer of the army in a military district without troops corresponding to his rank, for the purpose of taking command of. the militia that may be called into service, is a manifest evasion of that provision of the constitution which expressly reserves to the states the appointment of the officers of the militia; and the object of detaching such officer cannot be well concluded to be any other than that of superseding the governor or other officers of the militia in their right to command. (p. 319)

The power of dividing the militia of the states into classes, and obliging such classes to furnish by contract or draft, able-bodied men, to serve for one or more years for the defence of the frontier, is not delegated to Congress. If a claim to draft the militia for one year for such general object be admissible, no limitation can be assigned to it, but the discretion of those who make the law. Thus, with a power in Congress to authorize such a draft or conscription, arid in the Executive to decide conclusively upon the existence and continuance of the emergency, the whole militia may be converted into a standing army disposable at the will of the President of the United States.

The power of compelling the militia, and other citizens of the United States, by a forcible draft or conscription, to serve in the regular armies as proposed in a late official letter of the Secretary of War, is not delegated to Congress by the constitution, and the exercise of it would be not less dangerous to their liberties, than hostile to the sovereignty of the states. The effort to deduce this power from the right of raising armies, is a flagrant attempt to pervert the sense of the clause in the constitution which confers that right, and is incompatible with other provisions in that instrument. [p. 320] The armies of the United States have always been raised by contract, never by conscription, and nothing more can be wanting to a government possessing the power thus claimed to enable it to usurp the entire control of the militia, in derogation of the authority of the state, and to convert it by impressment into a standing army.

It may be here remarked, as a circumstance illustrative of the determination of the Executive to establish an absolute control over all descriptions of citizens, that the right of impressing seamen into the naval service is expressly asserted by the Secretary of the Navy in a late report. Thus a practice, which in a foreign government has been regarded with great abhorrence by the people, finds advocates among those who have been the loudest to condemn it.

The law authorising the enlistment of minors and apprentices into the armies of the United States, without the consent of parents and guardians, is also repugnant to the spirit of the constitution. By a construction of the power to raise armies, as applied by our present rulers, not only persons capable of contracting are liable to be impressed into the army, but those who are under legal disabilities to make contracts, are to be invested with the capacity, in order to enable them to annul at pleasure contracts made in their behalf by legal guardians. Such an interference with the municipal laws and rights of the several states, (p. 321) could never have been contemplated by the framers of the constitution. It impairs the salutary control and influence of the parent over his child—the master over his servant—the guardian over his ward—and thus destroys the most important relations in society, so that by the conscription of the father, and the seduction of the son, the power of the Executive over all the effective male population of the United States is made complete.

Such are some of the odious features of the novel system proposed by the rulers of a free country, under the limited powers derived from the constitution. What portion of them will be embraced in acts finally to be passed, it is yet impossible to determine. It is, however, sufficiently alarming to perceive, that these projects emanate from the highest authority, nor should it be forgotten, that by the plan of the Secretary of War, the classification of the militia embraced the principle of direct taxation upon the white population only; and that, in the house of representatives, a motion to apportion the militia among the white population exclusively, which would have been in its operation a direct tax, was strenuously urged and supported.

In this whole series of devices and measures for raising men, this convention discern a total disregard for the constitution, and a disposition to violate its provisions, demanding from the individual states a firm and decided opposition. An iron despotism can impose no harder servitude upon the citizen, than to force him from his home and his occupation, (p. 322) to wage offensive wars, undertaken to gratify the pride or passions of his master. The example of France has recently shown that a cabal of individuals assuming to act in the name of the people, may transform the great body of citizens into soldiers, and deliver them over into the hands of a single tyrant. No war, not held in just abhorrence by the people, can require the aid of such stratagems to recruit an army. Had the troops already raised, and in great numbers sacrificed upon the frontier of Canada, been employed for the defence of the country, and had the millions which have been squandered with shameless profusion, been appropriated to their payment, to the protection of the coast, and to the naval service, there would have been no occasion for unconstitutional expedients. Even at this late hour, let government leave to New England the remnant of her resources, and she is ready and able to defend her territory, and to resign the glories and advantages of the border war to those who are determined to persist in its prosecution.

That acts of Congress in violation of the constitution are absolutely void, is an undeniable position. It does not, however, consist with the respect and forbearance due from a confederate state towards the general government, to fly to open resistance upon every infraction of the constitution. The mode and the energy of the opposition, should always conform to the nature of the violation, the intention of its authors, the extent of the injury inflicted, (p. 323) the determination manifested to persist in it, and the danger of delay. But in cases of deliberate, dangerous, and palpable infractions of the constitution, affecting the sovereignty of a state, and liberties of the people; it,is not only the right but the duty of such a state to interpose its authority for their protection, in the manner best calculated to secure that end. When emergencies occur which are either beyond the reach of the judicial tribunals, or too pressing to admit of the delay incident to their forms, states which have no common umpire, must be their own judges, and execute their own decisions. It will thus be proper for the several states to await the ultimate disposal of the obnoxious measures recommended by the Secretary of War, or pending before Congress, and so to use their power according to the character these measures shall finally assume, as effectually to protect their own sovereignty, and the rights and liberties of their citizens.

The next subject which has occupied the attention of the convention, is the means of defence against the common enemy. This naturally leads to the inquiries, whether any expectation can be reasonably entertained, that adequate provision for the defence of the eastern states will be made by the national government? Whether the several states can, from their own resources, provide for self-defence and fulfil the requisitions which are to be expected for the national treasury? and, generally, what course of conduct ought to be adopted by those states, in relation to the great object of defence. (p. 324)

Without pausing at present to comment upon the causes of the war, it may be assumed as a truth, officially announced,that to achieve the conquest of Canadian territory, and to hold it as a pledge for peace, is the deliberate purpose of administration. This enterprize, commenced at a period when government possessed the advantage of selecting the time and occasion for making a sudden descent upon an unprepared enemy, now languishes in the third year of the war. It has been prosecuted with various fortune, and occasional brilliancy of exploit, but without any solid acquisition. The British armies have been recruited by veteran regiments. Their navy commands Ontario. The American ranks are thinned by the casualties of war. Recruits are discouraged by the unpopular character of the contest, and by the uncertainty of receiving their pay.

In the prosecution of this favourite warfare, administration have left the exposed and vulnerable parts of the country destitute of all the efficient means of defence. The main body of the regular army has been marched to the frontier. The navy has been stripped of a great part of its sailors for the service of the lakes. Meanwhile the enemy scours the, sea-coast, blockades our ports, ascends our bays and rivers, makes actual descents in various and distant places, holds some by force, and threatens all that are assailable with fire and sword. (p. 325) The sea-board of four of the New England states, following its curvatures, presents an extent of more than seven hundred miles, generally occupied by a compact population, and accessible by a naval force, exposing a mass of people and property to the devastation of the enemy, which bears a great proportion to the residue of the maritime frontier of the United States. This extensive shore has been exposed to frequent attacks, repeated contributions, and constant alarms. The regular forces detached by the national government for its defence are mere pretexts for placing officers of high rank in command. They are besides confined to a few places, and are too insignificant in number to be included in any computation.

These states have thus been left to adopt measures for their own defence. The militia have been constantly kept on the alert, and harassed by garrison duties, and other hardships, while the expenses, of which the national government decline the reimbursement, threaten to absorb all the resources of the states. The President of the United States has refused to consider the expense of the militia detached by state authority, for the indispensable defence of the state, as chargeable to the Union, on the ground of a refusal by the Executive of the state to place them under the command of officers of the regular army. Detachments of militia placed at the disposal of the general government, have been dismissed either without pay, or with depreciated paper. The prospect of the ensuing (p. 326) campaign is not enlivened by the promise of any alleviation of these grievances. From authentic documents, extorted by necessity from those whose inclination might lead them to conceal the embarrassments of the government, it is apparent that the treasury is bankrupt, and its credit prostrate. So deplorable is the state of the finances, that those who feel for the honour and safety of the country, would be willing to conceal the melancholy spectacle, if those whose infatuation has produced this state of fiscal concerns had not found themselves compelled to unveil it to public view.

If the war be continued, there appears no room for reliance upon the national government for the supply of those means of defence which must become indispensable to secure these states from desolation and ruin. Nor is it possible that the states can discharge this sacred duty from their own resources, and continue to sustain the burden of the national taxes. The administration, after a long perseverance in plans to baffle every effort of commercial enterprize, had fatally succeeded in their attempts at the epoch of the war. Commerce, the vital spring of New England's prosperity, was annihilated. Embargoes, restrictions, and the rapacity of revenue officers, had completed its destruction. The various objects for the employment of productive labour, in the branches of business dependent on commerce, have disappeared. The fisheries have shared its fate. Manufactures, which government has professed an intention to favour and to cherish, (p. 327) as an indemnity for the failure of these branches of business, are doomed to struggle in their infancy with taxes and obstructions, which cannot fail most seriously to affect their growth. The specie is withdrawn from circulation. The landed interest, the last to feel these burdens, must prepare to become their principal support, as all other sources of revenue must be exhausted. Under these circumstances, taxes, of a description and amount unprecedented in this country, are in a train of imposition, the burden of which must fall with the heaviest pressure upon the states east of the Potomac. *The amount of these taxes for the ensuing year cannot be estimated at less than five millions of dollars upon the New England states, and the expenses of the last year for defence, in Massachusetts alone, approaches to one million of dollars.*

From these facts, it is almost superfluous to state the irresistible inference that these states have no capacity of defraying the expense requisite for their own protection, and, at the same time, of discharging the demands of the national treasury.

The last inquiry, what course of conduct ought to be adopted by the aggrieved states, is in a high degree momentous. When a great and brave people shall feel themselves deserted by their government, and reduced to the necessity either of submission to a foreign enemy, or of appropriating to their own use those means of defence which are indispensable to self-preservation, they cannot consent to wait passive spectators of approaching ruin, which it is in their power to avert, and to resign the last remnant of their industrious earnings to be dissipated in support of measures destructive of the best interests of the nation. (p. 328)

This convention will not trust themselves to express their conviction of the catastrophe to which such a state of things inevitably tends. Conscious of their high responsibility to God and their country, solicitous for the continuance of the Union, as well as the sovereignty of the states, unwilling to furnish obstacles to peace-resolute never to submit to a foreign enemy, and confiding in the Divine care and protection, they will, until the last hope shall be extinguished, endeavor to avert such consequences.

With this view they suggest an arrangement, which may at once be consistent with the honour and interest of the national government, and the security of these states. This it will not be difficult to conclude, if that government should be so disposed. By the terms of it these states might be allowed to assume their own defence, by the militia or other troops. A reasonable portion, also, of the taxes raised in each state might be paid into its treasury, and credited to the United States, but to be appropriated to the defence of such state, to be accounted for with the United States. No doubt is entertained that by such an arrangement, this portion of the country could be defended with greater effect, and in a mode more consistent with economy, and the public convenience, than any which has been practised. (p. 329)

Should an application for these purposes, made to Congress by the state legislatures, be attended with success, and should peace upon just terms appear to be unattainable, the people would stand together for the common defence, until a change of administration, or of disposition in the enemy, should facilitate the occurrence of that auspicious event. It would be inexpedient for this Convention to diminish the hope of a successful issue to such an application, by recommending, upon supposition of a contrary event, ulterior proceedings. Nor is it indeed within their province. In a state of things so solemn and trying as may then arise, the legislatures of the states, or conventions of the whole people, or delegates appointed by them for the express purpose in another Convention, must act as such urgent circumstances may then require.

But the duty incumbent on this Convention will not have been performed, without exhibiting some general view of such measures as they deem essential to secure the nation against a relapse into difficulties and dangers, should they, by the blessing of Providence, escape from their present condition, without absolute ruin. To this end a concise retrospect of the state of this nation under the advantages of a wise administration, contrasted with the miserable abyss into which it is plunged by the profligacy and folly of political theorists, will lead to some practical conclusions. On this subject, it will be recollected, (p. 330) that the immediate influence of the Federal Constitution upon its first adoption, and for twelve succeeding years, upon the prosperity and happiness of the nation, seemed to countenance a belief in the transcendency of its perfection over all other human institutions. In the catalogue of blessings which have fallen to the 1t of the most favoured nations, none could be enumerated from which our country was excluded—a free Constitution, administered by great and incorruptible statesmen, realized the fondest hopes of liberty and independence—The progress of agriculture was stimulated by the certainty of value in the harvest—and commerce, after traversing every sea, returned with the riches of every clime. A revenue, secured by a sense of honour, collected without oppression, and paid without murmurs, melted away the national debt; and the chief concern of the public creditor arose from its too rapid diminution. The wars and commotions of the European nations, and their interruptions of the commercial intercourse afforded to those who had not promoted, but who would have rejoiced to alleviate their calamities, a fair and golden opportunity, by combining themselves to lay a broad foundation for national wealth. Although occasional vexations to commerce arose from the furious collisions of the powers at war, (p. 331) yet the great and good men of that time conformed to the force of circumstances which they could not control, and preserved their country in security from the tempests which overwhelmed the old world, and threw the wreck of their fortunes on these shores. Respect abroad, prosperity at home, wise laws made by honoured legislators, and prompt obedience yielded by a contented people, had silenced the enemies of republican institutions. The arts flourished—the sciences were cultivated—the comforts and conveniences of life were universally diffused—and nothing remained for succeeding administrations but to reap the advantages and cherish the resources flowing from the policy of their predecessors.

But no sooner was a new administration established in the hands of the party opposed to the Washington policy, than a fixed determination was perceived and avowed of changing a system which had already produced these substantial fruits. The consequences of this change, for a few years after its commencement, were not sufficient to counteract the prodigious impulse towards prosperity, which had been given to the nation. But a steady perseverance in the new plans of administration, at length developed their weakness and deformity, but not until a majority of the people had been deceived by flattery, and inflamed by passion, into blindness to their defects. Under the withering influence of this new system, the declension of the, nation has been uniform and rapid. (p. 332) The richest advantages for securing the great objects of the constitution have been wantonly rejected. While Europe reposes from the convulsions that had shaken down her ancient institutions, she beholds with amazement this remote country, once so happy and so envied, involved in a ruinous war, and excluded from intercourse with the rest of the world . . . .

The convention ended its long declaration with propositions that subsequent events and the rising prosperity of that fortunate nation have shown not to have been in conformity with the spirit of its wise institutions, and this noisy happening had no further consequences, with the brilliant victory in Louisiana one month later. This changed the political and mercantile aspect of the United States of the North and brought an advantageous peace with Great Britain.

CHAPTER XV

Return to New York.—Colonel Burr.—General Santander.—Elections.—Popular meetings.—Reflections.—Trip to West Point.—Idea of the military college.—Reflections.—Shelters for juvenile delinquents, deaf and dumb and the insane in New York.—Prisons.

Since my return to New York after my trip to New England was followed by the one that I made to Europe, in the account I shall continue of the United States I shall not follow the order of dates, but will talk about New York, which I also visited in 1832 on my return from Europe. During this time I met the famous Colonel Burr, a lawyer of great knowledge in his profession, an enterprising and remarkable man in the United States in the first years following independence.

Colonel Burr was introduced to me by Dr. Johns who had been for some time in the state of Tabasco. One day I saw this doctor come into my living room with a small man about seventy years old, with a very spiritual countenance, and in whom, in spite of the fact that he was half-paralyzed, there could be seen mental strength and vigorous character. Colonel Burr speaks French after a fashion and likes to use this language in conversation. He was vice-president of the United States during the administration of the elder Mr. Adams,* and at the time of the election of Mr. Jefferson as president he was tied twenty-three times in the voting by the chamber. Aaron Burr lost the esteem of his fellow citizens because of a noisy duel with the virtuous General Hamilton which resulted in the death of the latter. After that Mr. Burr went to Europe to give his fellow citizens time to forget the bloody catastrophe.

The British government did not allow him to remain in England long, because he became greatly involved with the radicals and maintained close communication with the French revolutionaries. Later he tried to gain possession of the province of Texas; some say that he had the idea of proclaiming himself emperor. What is certain is that there was a scandalous trial, and although he was absolved by successive juries, public opinion did not consider that he was proven not guilty. Today he makes his living as a lawyer, and his forensic ability would give him sufficient to live on even if he had not acquired a fortune to which he has recently added by his marriage to a rich lady of New York.

In New York at this time was Don Francisco de Paula Santander, the present president of New Granada. He had been banished from Colombia under the dictatorship of Bolivar, who had had him sentenced to death for a conspiracy against the life of the dictator, in which he was supposed to have taken part. Bolivar, out of mercy, commuted the death sentence to banishment for six years. From the trial, of which General Santander gave me a copy, it was brought out only that some one had revealed to him confidentially the secret of the conspiracy against the usurper. On such a charge Santander was condemned to death because he had not denounced the plot. This general was feted by the leading people of New York, and I recall that they gave him a public dinner at which there were at least one hundred fifty present.

I had occasion to be with him considerably in France, during the voyage and in the United States. At his hotel in Philadelphia I met General Don Manuel G. Pedraza, who had not been allowed to land on the coast of Mexico for reasons of state. General Santander is an honorable man who loves liberty and is able to discern the true road to happiness for his fellow citizens. Perhaps he is a little more fond of his own judgment than is good. But his moderation and tact in business correct this fault.

During this time the election of the president of the United States was going on. General Jackson had been elected in 1828 against Mr. Adams, in whose reelection the old Federalist Party was quite active in opposition to the Democratic Party. Quite worthy of note are two public documents of that time among a thousand others because they give an idea of the character of the parties in the United States. The first is the one that supported the election of General Jackson, and the second that of Mr. Adams. It should be kept in mind, as I have said before in this work, that anyone can announce through the newspapers that there is going to be a Convention or a meeting on this subject or that when public opinion is divided.

REPUBLICAN CONVENTION IN EDINBURG
(State of New York)

In a well-attended and respectable convention of Republicans of the town of Edinburg, held in the restaurant of Mayor Weeks Copeland in said town, September 13, 1828, to name the delegates that would go to the county convention for the purpose of dealing with the nomination of a president for the following year. John

Rhodes was named to preside over the meeting, and Martin Butler was named secretary. The committee appointed for the purpose reported the followed resolutions, which were indeed approved unanimously.

We Resolve: That it is not only the right but the duty of Republicans to investigate the conduct of those who are placed at the head of the government, to discover and put an end to their arbitrary acts, and to repress examples of corruption and disorder. The convention is of the opinion that in the present crisis it is urgently called to make this investigation.

We Resolve: That we cannot support the conduct of the present administration with our future votes because of their disorderly handling of affairs, their lack of respect for many of our more distinguished citizens, the profusion of rewards showered upon their favorites, the abandonment of their obligations because of involvement in the elections, the very unbecoming means that they have employed to maintain themselves in power and assure their reelection.

We Resolve: That we are persuaded that General Andrew Jackson is the man that has covered his country with glory, and that his services to the nation cause him to be due the highest recompense, that because of his solid principles, his ardent love for his country manifested in the days of greatest danger, his devotion to democracy, his simple life free of all pomp, his incomparable services to the nation, he is a citizen fitted to check the progress of prodigality, halt the march of corruption, and reinstate the government in the purity of its former principles.

We Resolve: That for these and other considerations we approve the nomination of Andrew Jackson for the presidency, and that we shall employ our efforts to secure his election.

We Resolve: That this confidence is increased because we believe that he wishes to rise to this elevated post by the voice of the people, without the aid of public funds, the influence of the cabinet, or by intrigue, begging, or threats.

We Resolve: That we approve the nomination of John C. Calhoun for the office of vice-president, persuaded that during the course of his public life he has conducted himself in a manner that makes him worthy of our votes.

We Resolve: That we should not thank any of our representatives or senators for having abused in a bastardly manner their franking privilege to send throughout all the states innumerable printed pamphlets and papers that contain absurd declarations to support an election that is disapproved by civilized men and even more so by knowledgeable Republicans.

We Resolve: That we are not in agreement with the opinion set forth in Utica which supports the party of the present administration and proposes for governor and lieutenant governor persons of that party.

We Resolve: That these resolutions shall be signed by the president and the secretary and be published in the newspaper in Saratoga.

John Rhodes, president.
M. H. Butler, secretary.

THE AMERICAN SYSTEM
Convention of the Republican Administration

In this convention of delegates supporting the administration of the present national government, gathered from all the towns of the County of Saratoga, held in the Town Hall of the town of Ballston Spa, on Wednesday, October 22, 1828, General John Prior was called to the chair, and John House and James McCrea were named secretaries.

It Was Resolved that the outstanding and patriotic present administration of our national government is worthy of our most ardent votes and that we shall use all honorable means in order to procure the reelection of John Quincy Adams to the presidency, and the election of Richard Bush for the office of vice-president.

It Was Resolved that we cordially approve the nomination of Smith Thompson for the position of governor of the state, and of Francis Granger for lieutenant governor, and we are ready to support their nominations by our votes.

It Was Resolved that we have complete confidence in the talents and integrity of John McLean, junior, of Washington, and heartily united with the Republican convention of this district we recommend him for senator.

It Was Resolved that the delegates from each town shall name one from among their group to compose a committee chosen with instructions to inform the convention about the persons that should be the candidates for the county offices.

The said committee having withdrawn and then returned to the convention hall, they reported that they had unanimously agreed to recommend the following candidates: for elector John Child, for deputy John Taylor, for sheriff John Dunning, for county clerk Thomas Palmer, for members of the legislature Gilbert Waring, Joshua Mandeville and Calvin Wheeler, for coroner Herman Rockwell, Dirck L. Palmer, Hugh Alexander and Nathan D. Sherwood.

After which, having read and approved each recommendation individually and unanimously, it was resolved that Salmon Child, Samuel Treeman, Edward Watrous, James McCrea, Amon Brown, Increase W. Child and Moses Williams shall be the ones to compose the central committee for the coming year, and that the delegates elected by the people to this convention shall be the ones who compose a watch committee in their respective places to carry out the elections referred to above; finally it was resolved that these minutes be signed by the president and the secretaries.

The proclamation is as follows:

Citizens: in a government such as ours in which each of the citizens has in his hands a portion of the sovereign power, it is all important that he make use of the authority with which he is vested with clear judgment. The coming presidential election is of the most vital importance for the happiness and the progress of the United States, and consequently it will determine whether a virtuous and illustrious administration shall remain or be overthrown, and whether measures that profoundly affect the interests of this vast majority of our fellow citizens are to be promoted or abandoned.

The present administration of the general government is at the head of a great political system that promises to put into effect undertakings that will extend the resources, increase the wealth, and promote all those principles that will assure the independence of the country. For many years now Great Britain has refused to receive into her ports goods produced in the states of the North and the South while this country receives annually from that nation the value of many millions of dollars of her manufactured goods; from this has come the result that all our gold and silver have taken that road to pay for her merchandise. From this has resulted the fact that our workers have not found a market for their surplus products, and all classes of society have found themselves in dire straits because of this slowing down of circulation. Our government has provided for a remedy for these ills—while American industry continues in the competition which it offers to foreigners—by means of a law of the country concerning the maxim of buying from them only the equivalent of what they buy from us, putting into effect Jefferson's doctrine of setting the manufacturer and the worker opposite each other, and thus creating a domestic market for the surplus at our ports. The adoption of this economic system, so fitting for our situation, so inseparable from our prosperity, and so honorable for our character, is the reason that the present administration has been attacked. Our fellow citizens of the South have abandoned themselves to factious and illegal threats to dissolve the Union in the event that Mr. Adams should be reelected. We trust that our fellow citizens are not ready to abandon their interests by abandoning the present government in order to please an ill—starred faction. If you are all prepared to assert your own rights against the violent Southern faction, unite your votes in the upcoming elections and support the cause of the principles of your country. The candidates that we have presented to be elected have been well known to you. They are staunch friends of the administration, and no one doubts their qualities and capacity for carrying out the duties of the respective offices for which we have chosen them.

John Prior, president
John House, James McCrea, secretaries.

The latter part of this proclamation makes reference to the noisy question of tariffs, concerning which I have had enough to say to my readers by including the documents in their proper places. This is the way they treat elections in the United States, but the saving principle of the country is that when the election has been carried by the majority, then all are silent before the law. Much of this is due to the fact that the election of the president comes directly from the people, and consequently is not subject to the intrigues and maneuvering which take place where the election is carried out by the legislatures in a country in which the elections are indirect. When done in this manner, the president is far from his legitimate origins, which should be the will of the majority of the citizens.

In New York at this same time was Don José Salgado, banished from Mexico for political reasons. With him I made a trip to West Point, one of the most picturesque spots in the world.

West Point is the place where the military school is located, on a vast plateau that is a part of the Allegheny chain, and at its foot runs the majestic Hudson River. The level area is more than three hundred feet above the river, and consequently the air is fresh, and the students enjoy good health. The very isolated location of this institute gives them protection against the corruption of the city, and at the same time obliges them to give themselves over to their studies without distractions. Teaching and habits both gain by this. There are 220 students, and they attend without charge since the secretary of war of the United States transmits the order of the president. The qualifications that the young men must have are that they be from fifteen to eighteen years of age, have a good education and a perfect knowledge of the English language and possess the first principles of arithmetic. The course of study is four years, in which period they learn mathematics, astronomy, experimental physics, military science, natural history, geography, French, history, drawing, moral philosophy and the laws of the Union.

At the same time they are taught the handling of arms, field exercise, and the practice of military art in general. With this in mind they devote two months out of the year to making excursions into the surrounding areas, where the students make surveys, take positions and become accustomed to the fatigues of the campaign.

The mathematical sciences are the ones that they are most actively involved with. The students are expected to show a very broad knowledge much superior to what is required in Europe to make a good infantry or cavalry officer. Great importance is given to mathematics in the United States certainly because there is still and will be for a long time to come a great amount of territory to explore and develop, for which purpose knowledge of mathematics is very useful.

The staff of the school consists of a commander in chief of the institution, which must have an officer of artillery or engineering, a professor of natural history and physics with an assistant, a professor of mathematics with a second, a professor of engineering with a second, an ecclesiastical professor of eloquence and literature, a teacher of drawing, a professor of French, a fencing master and a physician.

The library is well chosen. It is composed of works on statistics, natural history, civil and military history. Among the latter are all the letters from the French campaigns, enhanced by very rich engravings. Also included are the campaigns of Frederick the Great and the plans of the fortifications of Vauban. The collection of maps, which is very valuable, contains among others the Baltic and North Sea ports by Beautemps and Beaupré.

West Point was during the revolution an important point which the English tried to get control of several times. Still to be seen are the ruins of some of the fortifications of that period. There travelers see the place where the tents of Washington were pitched, Kosciuzko's gardens cultivated by his own hands, and the cenotaph of this famous Pole. It would be difficult to select a place richer in memories, more appropriate for bringing out in the hearts of the young the love of patriotic virtues and a noble desire for studies that contribute to maintaining national glory and independence. The views across the Hudson River are romantic, filled with natural beauties and capable of firing the imagination.

Throughout the whole institution things are orderly and clean, and the instruction is rather advanced. A few years ago a young Indian from the Creek tribe named Moniac held a distinguished place among the students. I have heard praises of his mathematical knowledge from persons that saw him solve varied questions of geometry and analysis with great ease. This example and many that I could cite of Mexican Indians who do honor to their country give the lie to the statement by Buffon and Reynal that the natives of the Americas cannot attain the degree of intelligence of the inhabitants of the Old World.

The students in this institute are divided into companies, and they perform military service under the orders and direction of an army officer who gives them lessons in tactics. Each one receives a degree according to the merits and progress of his studies in accordance with the special rules of each class. The cadets are in camp during two months each year, during which time they are only concerned with military exercises. Then they receive rations twice a day and sixteen dollars per month, which amounts to about twenty-eight dollars. When he leaves school each student receives a commission or place in one of the military branches according to his ability and merit. Some come out to continue their studies and receive broader instruction in the great colleges of Europe, with their same salary.

A great part of the prime policy of governments is to favor a literary, scientific, and industrial direction suitable to impress the natural movement of the human mind. The activity, the very ferment of the minds of our new republics, favor the progress of civilization, and that abundance of life that produces long and violent political and military shakeups which have stirred up the social structure in the new states, have had, from some points of view, salutary effects like the flooding of the Nile that spreads fertility over the lands that its waters have covered. This activity, which cannot appear dangerous, except to those who have plans of tyranny and oppression, who wish to do away with superior men of sound character and capable of thoughts and plans of general interest, will become useful and advantageous when it receives proper direction. Its effects will be beneficial to public morality, the free development of intellectual faculties, the stability of philanthropic institutions, bringing glory to the directors.

In New York there is a house of refuge for delinquent youths of both sexes where they are taught trades suitable to their dispositions, and they are not exposed to being corrupted by the bad examples of the criminals in the other jails. There is also a school for the deaf and dumb and an asylum for the insane. In these establishments there is the best order, and nothing is lacking for the unfortunate ones whom fate has condemned to suffer. The interest which those in charge take in watching over the direction of these institutions and the perfect cooperation that they meet with in all their agents are truly laudable and worthy of being proposed as models. Those who may compare this establishment with our San Hipólito in Mexico will note in the Mexican hospice the magnificence of the buildings, great staffs of employees and administrators, a spacious temple, many rules and ample incomes, by the side of the lack of cleanliness and little attention for the troubled ones. In the North American institution the building is proportionate to the need, there is a chapel, the care and attention for the insane are admirable, and the neatness and cleanliness of beds and clothing leaves nothing to be desired, and the salaries are very moderate.

In the state of New York there are two large prisons more or less on the model of those of the states of Massachusetts and Pennsylvania of which I have already spoken. These are Sing Sing on the Hudson River and Auburn on the Oswego. The latter has 550 cells with a prisoner in each one. Their imprisonment is not such as to keep them solitary for the whole time of confinement as is true at the penitentiary at Philadelphia.

Since the state legislature has felt that physical exercise is necessary to maintain health, they are put to work during the day under the strictest of rules. As soon as the convict comes in he is given prison clothing, they read him the rules and instruct him as to his duties. These consist solely of obeying orders and working diligently and silently, speaking respectfully to the prison guards, not speaking except when necessary even to the guards, not dancing or singing or making any sort of noise whatsoever, not going away from the area where they are assigned without permission, not becoming distracted from their work nor resting for a moment. Nor are they permitted to receive letters, nor have any sort of communication with the outside. Anything of this nature must be through their custodians. Each prisoner has a Bible furnished by the state.

Any infractions against the rules or verbal admonitions are immediately punished by the penalty of lashing with a leather whip. Punishment is so swift and immediate for breaking the rules that there are very few cases of this. Early in the morning a bell rings, and the jailers open the cells of the prisoners. These come out into a common courtyard in the summertime or into a great hail in the winter; they wash their hands and faces in basins provided, and then continue in line like soldiers to their respective jobs. The new prisoners, if they have a trade, work at it; if not, they are taught one that they choose. They regularly work twelve hours. They eat in a refectory and always with their backs to each other in the greatest silence. When they need something, they raise their hands and are served what they want. The time allotted for each meal is regularly half an hour. When they retire for the night they wash their hands and faces again. Their clothes are always kept clean.

On Sunday, after washing, instead of working they go to the chapel where the chaplain has the divine service. Those who know how to read and write, who are very few, go to Sunday School where they receive suitable instruction.

The daily rations for each prisoner are ten ounces of pork or sixteen of beef, ten ounces of wheat flour, twelve of cooked cornmeal hot potatoes and half a quart of barley made in the form of coffee and sweeted with molasses. At noon they are served soup made with beef broth thickened with cornmeal bread, potatoes and cold water. For supper there is a sort of cornmeal porridge that they call mush, and cold water. This amount of food has been considered as sufficient for keeping the prisoners in perfect health.

The daily earnings of each prisoner are calculated at twenty-five to thirty-five cents. From this fund come the expenses of the prison, which is so neat and clean that one could not ask more. Before the prisoners leave, they are obliged to relate their lives, and tell what trade they have followed and intend to follow. This will make an interesting collection of case histories from which may be drawn useful observations concerning the national character, and even about human nature. Of 170 who have gone forth, 112 have straightened up completely, and 26 have continued in their evil ways; the others were indifferent. The prisoners say that the greatest penalty is not to be able to talk or to have news of what is going on outside. One must confess that these precautions are necessary and weep over the fate of the man condemned to suffer such great privations. Here one cannot say with Dante: *Qui vive la pieta quand' e ben morta.* ("Here mercy dwells when it is quite dead").

CONCLUSION

"The United States," Mr. Hamilton says very well, "is perhaps the people least exposed to revolutions today. But its stability," he adds, "consists of the unique circumstances that the great majority of the inhabitants are property owners."

There is no doubt that it is one, but not the only cause for the unchanging tranquility of that fortunate people. In social systems a question cannot be resolved by the explanation of a single circumstance. Spain, for example, remained peaceful until the year 1808 under the tyrannical yoke of monarchy, inquisition and military government. And this peace of the tomb could not be explained solely by one single cause, to wit, the *terror inspired* by the established forms. There were in addition ignorance, superstition, the tremendous influence of friars and clergy, support of the grandees, in short an order of things established and coordinated in such a manner that they upheld each other. Set up in that same Spain or in Mexico *the agrarian law,* distribute properties equally, and the result will be to throw all classes into confusion, debase values, nourish and foster laziness and multiply disorders.

It is true that one of the principal causes of the stability of the institutions of the United States of North America is the fortunate situation of the great majority of the people. But side by side with those material enjoyments the people place the sacred right of taking part in all transactions that have as their purpose the organizing of public powers, individual guarantees that assure them their laws, freedom to write and publish their opinions, freedom that they have to worship God according to their own consciences, and the deep and indestructible conviction of all the citizens that the law is equal for all, and that there are no institutions set up to favor one class, nor a hierarchy of privilege.

As he casts a rapid glance over this gigantic nation which was born yesterday and today extends its arms from the Atlantic to the Pacific and the China Sea, the observer stands in deep thought and naturally asks himself

188

the question, "What will be the final outcome of its greatness and prosperity?" It is not the power of conquests nor the force of arms; nor is it the illusions of a cult that unites the rules of morality with the mysteries of dogma; it is a new social order, brilliant, positive; a political system that has excluded all privilege, all distinctions consecrated by previous centuries, that has produced this prodigious creation. Standing before this political phenomenon statesmen of all countries, philosophers, economists have stopped to contemplate the rapid march of this amazing people, and agreeing with one accord on the never before seen prosperity of its inhabitants side by side with sobriety, love of work, unlimited liberty, domestic virtues, a creative activity, and an almost fanatical religious feeling, they have made an effort to explain the causes of these great results.

What have the ancient republics, the anarchies of the Middle Ages, or the European confederations been in comparison with this extraordinary nation? Athens was a turbulent democracy, four leagues in extent, dominated by skillful orators who knew how to exploit it to their own advantage. Sparta, a vast community subject to rules rather than laws, a family rather than a society, without individual independence, without stimulation for the arts, the sciences, or virtues, a religious order similar to the Templars, that cannot serve as a model to any modern people.

Rome! In what period did that proud republic ever do anything for the well-being of the masses? The Roman people were oppressors of others and oppressed themselves by their patricians, even in their days of greatest liberty. Turbulent tribunals, often victims of their demagogic furies and of the hatreds of the patricians, they kept in ferment the common people who were content with a lessening of their debts, with occasional distributions of wheat, or with an apologue told with wisdom. Miserable attempts, although useful lessons, in order one day to arrive at the establishment of the American system!

Indeed, the political school of the United States is a complete system, a classic work, unique, a discovery such as that of printing, the compass, steam power, but a discovery that applies moral force to individual intelligences to move the great social machine, which until our day has been dragged rather than directed, driven by factious springs composed of heterogenous combinations, a monstrous mosaic of gathered bits of feudalism, superstition, caste privilege, legitimacies, sanctities, and other elements against nature, and ruins of that flood of shadows that inundated the world for twelve centuries.

Political experts of Europe may well turn to interpretations, prophecies, conjectures, and doleful commentaries upon the constitutions, future, stability, and laws of the United States. What they cannot deny is that there is not nor ever has been a people where the rights of the citizens were more respected, where individuals had more participation in government, where the masses were more perfectly equal in all social pleasures. What sort of argument against its institutions is it to announce to a nation an unhappy future, melancholy catastrophes, when the present is filled with life, happiness, and good fortune?

Those who cannot resist the conviction of obvious facts of daily experience resort to doleful prophecies and predict now the dissolution of the great republic. We shall answer them that the present good is better than hopes unrealized; that there is probably no man or people who would prefer living under oppression or in poverty to the happy and independent existence of that republic; only because some dyspeptic politicians tell them that that prosperous situation will not last two hundred years. No, never will the strength of that living and perservering example of social Utopia be weakened by such arguments. Be welcome to spy out their small and fleeting mob scenes; exaggerate the heat of their public debates, the turmoil of their elections, their most curious aberrations of Presbyterian fanaticism, their aversion to the black caste, their difficulties because of their system of slavery, their questions of tariffs, momentary difficulties with their banks, make the most unfavorable comments concerning these political and economic crises; a positive solution, a happy and quick insight comes forward to answer all your arguments. That nation, full of life and movement continues its course towards a goal, and from the frontiers of Nova Scotia to New Mexico the North American labors only upon these principles: *work and the rights of the citizen.* His code is concise, but clear, pure and easily perceived. Complicated questions, which they cannot decide since they are beyond the grasp of the less-educated classes, they refer entirely to that part of the people that has seemed to them to have best deserved their confidence because of a series of upright actions and decisions with beneficial results.

All those who are trying to make social improvements in the peoples that are marching towards progress look to Great Britain or the United States of the North, true and original types of social organizations that are solid and progressive. But the first one, a great nation, mistress of the seas, the depository of great wealth, with an abundance of outstanding and profound men, still has many steps to take in the direction of an order that is more liberal, more economical, in short more independent of the ancient feudal shackles; and her *Whigs* and *radicals,* after their triumphs of the Catholic emancipation, their bill of parliamentary reform, of ministerial organization, demand new improvements to put themselves in some degree at the same level as the latter. Still pending are questions of high political interest that were resolved in the United States since its birth. The tithes, the privileges of the nobles, the absolute separation of worship and administrative functions, primogeniture and others less essential, consequences of the former, are points that have been tossed about for a long time in the newspapers, in the tribunals, in the clubs and in the cabinet. What sort of shake-up will the colossal Albion have to undergo before seeing a definite end to these matters! Her great political experts, her ministers, have said so recently. "Much has been done," one of them was saying not long ago to his fellow citizens who were flattering him, "but we still have much left to do." Words filled with good sense and great hopes.

After the struggle that took place in the United States of the North a few years after independence between aristocratic and democratic parties, the latter came out victorious, to the point that the former disappeared completely, which is another phenomenon in the history of peoples; since then all the questions that have been aired on the rostrum, in the newspapers, and popular meetings have been purely economic. The Hartford Convention, which in 1814 attempted to revive the old Federalist principles, found no support anywhere, and since then there has been no single statesman who has dared to come forth to defend the system of Hamilton and Adams. Popular power in all its fullness, governing a nation powerful and of vast extent, taking its course with wisdom, moderation, and care, seeing the elements of a great territorial, industrial, and commercial prosperity develop under its administration, is perhaps the most powerful argument that can be put up against the eternal declamations of the absolutists and aristocrats.

In such a state of affairs two hundred thousand Europeans come to the United States every year seeking refuge in their wretchedness, and recompense for their work and weariness, free from the deductions to which the taxes of the Old World subject them, and from the shackles placed upon them by their systems more or less arbitrarily; with active and robust arms they find work immediately, and within, a few months, owners of land made fertile by their sweat, they found towns in spots a short time before inhabited only by wolves, bears and other wild animals.

Populous cities spring up overnight, steamboats ply rivers and lakes thousands of leagues from the sea in lands just discovered and unknown to the civilized world, manufactured goods are transported by skillful craftsmen from Europe, flying printing presses that multiply thoughts and ideas spreading education, missionaries of sects that from Italy, Germany, France, England, and other places come to preach their gospel beliefs, each one as he understands and professes it, and that agree completely in moral principles. The love of God and a fellow man is the basis of all religions. Immigrants from Ireland, France, Mexico, Colombia, Spain, Italy, from both hemispheres, who in the political upheavals in their own countries, obliged to leave their fatherland, come to find out what the enviable tranquility of that people consists of. Here you have the spectacle that the United States of the North presents. Add its maritime cities; that of New York, third port in the world, receiving in its bay three thousand boats each year that come loaded with products from the four corners of the world; that of New Orleans, the depot for a hundred cities that send to it their fruits by the boundless Mississippi, and by means of which a thousand communities are provided with foreign articles. Philadelphia, the city of peace, brotherhood and monotony, surrounded by country houses as beautiful as its daughters, founded upon the pleasant Delaware and the delightful Schuylkill, occupies a distinguished place on the commercial ladder. Baltimore, Charleston, Boston, remarkable cities because of the education of their inhabitants, their trade activity, the advantageous situation of their ports, the hospitality of their people, in short that openness, that assuredness, that liberty that all men enjoy, without the hindrances of passports, without the apparatus of soldiers, without the troublesome police, are circumstances that cannot fail to lead to prosperity and progress in all areas.

Those who accuse the North American people of being rude and unsociable fail to think about the elements that have gone into the makeup of that unusual nation. Persecuted families who came to seek liberty and a living in the frozen and uncivilized forests of northern America were forced to devote themselves to harsh and difficult tasks, to suffer painful privations, and to accustom themselves to a monotony of foods, words and communication, to which the needs of their continual work condemned them. So here you have the forefathers of the North Americans. To these have been added the farmers and artists that have come later from Holland, Germany, and Ireland, people who are generally hard working, economical, taciturn, dedicated exclusively to their undertakings; and think then how there have come the Washingtons, the Jeffersons, the Franklins, the Adams, the Clintons, the Madisons, the Clays, the Websters, the Livingstons, the Hamiltons, the Monroes, the Jacksons, the Van Burens, the Dwights, and many other statesmen, famous writers, profound sages, distinguished literary men, economists, and illustrious generals who have lifted the country to its high degree of prosperity and glory.

The people of the United States are wise, economical and fond of accumulating capital for the future. That is the way it should be naturally. Because, in addition to their origins from which they inherit these qualities, in a climate like that, where man is obliged to work half the year for a severe season that confines him to his hearth and home, he cannot abandon himself to chance, confident in the fertility of the land and the cooperation of the seasons. The peoples of the south of Europe and of Asia were always the least industrious, and in Spain one notes that the Galicians, the Catalans, and the Basques are better farmers than the peoples of Andalucia and Castilla; besides, they have a more serious and less communicative and less flexible character. The progress of primary education, to which Americans give a great deal of interest, and the ease of their communications will with time make the manners of that people better and more sociable.

Before bringing this book to a close, I must not overlook the political relations that should progressively increase between the United States of the North and the United Mexican States, and the influences that the first undoubtedly exercises over the second. There is not a more seductive example for a nation that does not enjoy complete liberty than that of a neighbor where are found in all public acts, in all writings, lessons and practices of an unlimited liberty, and in which instead of the disastrous cataclysms that have overwhelmed some peoples in their anarchial revolutions, or in their bloody despotic systems, one sees the spectacle of the peaceful joys of a numerous segment of the human race, lifted up by the simultaneous energy of its popular intelligence to an eminently free and happy social rank. Could the legislators of the Mexican nation resist so strong an influence when they had in their hands the arranging of the destinies of their constituents? The model was sublime, but not to be imitated. Those who set themselves to copy a painting of Raphael or of Michael Angelo at times succeed in imitating some of the shadows, some of the characteristics that bring them somewhere within range of the original. However, they never manage to equal those sublime concepts. Original artists do not copy or imitate others; they invent, they create upon the models of nature, and they study her secrets and divine mysteries.

One of the political plagues that have brought many ills to some peoples has been the false persuasion of their legislators that such an organization or such laws would have their effect, and would be put into practice only because the majority of their representatives favored them. A similar error was fought against by the doctrines of all the great writers and by the experience of the centuries. But the example of thirteen republics born at the end of the last century in the New Continent, that have not only maintained themselves but by growing progressively have become twenty— four, thus forming a great confederation, produced so great and universal a sensation in minds that forthwith ancient doctrines were considered to have been destroyed by such an event. The reasoning appeared to be conclusive. English colonies with which at that time the political and commercial world little concerned itself, which with just the name of colonies were supposed to be degraded, ignorant and enslaved, suddenly elevated to the rank of free nations, in consequence of a well—written declaration of the rights of man and of peoples. "Why should we not do the same thing," said many writers, politicians and philosophers of the Old World, "we the depositories of the sciences, masters of the human race, proprietors of the commerce of nations, heirs to the glory of the Greeks and the Romans, fathers of those emancipated peoples?" Great events that have come to pass subsequently in both hemispheres have provided sufficient proof of the irresistible impulse given to the social movement by the appearance of that bright star in the firmament of nations.

What should be then the consequences of the constant example near at hand presented by the United States of the North 'to the Mexican nation, young and inexperienced, full of life and desirous of shaking off the remains of its ancient chains? In the narrow circle of continental Europe public right is that of the conservation of certain monarchial principles, the basis of all European political activity. Upon this code, sketched out for the first time in Pilnitz forty years ago, modified several times according to the diverse interests of the high contracting parties, European governments model themselves and change in different ways. In America things are different. Although the monarchial principle is not proscribed, it is evident that the opinion as it can be applied to the emerging republics is almost exclusively democratic. There one finds no interventions nor alliances, no diplomatic maneuvering, no money bags, not a single element with sufficient influence to determine the monarchial form. The only one that exists to some degree is ecclesiastical power, whose weakness is demonstrated by the experience of its fruitless endeavors up to now.

Consequently the influence of the United States upon Mexico will with time be a power of opinion, of teaching by guidance, all the stronger because it is purely moral, founded upon its doctrines and lessons. But there is more. Ten thousand citizens of the United States settle each year in the territory of the Mexican republic, especially in the states of Chihuahua, Coahuila and Texas, Tamaulipas, Nuevo Leon, San Luis Potosi, Durango, Zacatecas, Sonora, Sinaloa, and the Territories of New Mexico and the Californias.

These colonists and businessmen along with their hard work carry with them habits of freedom, economy, industry, their austere and religious ways, their individual independence and their republicanism. What change must these enterprising guests not make in the moral and material existence of the former inhabitants? Carthage was a Carthaginian people, Cadiz a Phonician people, Marseilles a Greek people for many centuries, because their colonists were from those nations. The Mexican republic then within a few years will come to be molded to a combined regimen of the American system and Spanish customs and traditions.

But it is necessary to distinguish in the Mexican nation that part populated, disciplined, founded, to put it thusly, in the mold of its former mother country, from that part bare of inhabitants, and consequently susceptible to a new population, completely different from the other one. In the first there will exist for many years yet the struggle of opposing principles that have been planted in their institutions, and civil war will be inevitable, while in the second the American, German, Irish, and English colonies are establishing completely free settlements that will prosper peacefully under the influence of their democratic institutions, and even more of their work habits, their ideas and convictions concerning the dignity of man and the respect that is due the law. Thus, while the states of Puehia, Chiapas, Oaxaca, Mexico, Queretaro, Michoacan, and Guanajuato continue in the grip of the military and ecclesiastical arm as a penalty for their prejudices, their ignorance, and their superstition; while in the bosom of these states a few generous and enlightened patriots will make efforts to lift their fellow citizens up to the level of the adopted institutions and will seek to give them lessons in liberty and tolerance; while these opposing elements light the fires of combat among an ardent youth that loves progress and civilization and an ignorant clergy strongly attached to their privileges and income, supported by a few generals and officers of the former Spanish army, without faith, without honor, without patriotism, possessed of a sordid greed and given over to degrading vices; while this is happening in these states, the others will be populated, will become rich, striving to avoid being contaminated by the disastrous things happening to their brothers in the south.

The net result, however, will be the triumph of liberty in these states, and upon the Gothic ashes and the remains of untenable privileges there will be raised up a glorious and enlightened generation that will put into motion all the sources of wealth that abound and will bring into association with the civilized family that indigenous group, until today debased and vilified, and will teach them to think and to hold in esteem their dignity by lifting their thoughts to a higher level.

What barrier can oppose this torrent that was born twenty-four years ago in a small town in the Bagio, obscure in its origins, without direction or channel, destroying everything in its path, today a majestic river that receives pure crystalline waters from other countries that will make fertile the entire Mexican territory? Unsuccessful efforts will oppose a debased generation, heir to Castilian traditions and beliefs and defender without great results of their antisocial doctrines. The American system will obtain a complete though bloody victory.

Viaje ᵃ ˡᵒˢ Estados Unidos del Norte de América

VIAGE

A LOS

ESTADOS-UNIDOS

DEL NORTE DE AMERICA,

Por D. Lorenzo de Zavala.

PARIS,

IMPRENTA DE DECOURCHANT,

CALLE D'ERFURTH, Nº 1, JUNTO A LA ABADIA.

—

1834

VIAGE

A LOS

ESTADOS-UNIDOS.

DEL NORTE DE AMERICA.

—

Despues de la caida del general Guerrero, en
diciembre de 1829, arrojado de la silla presidencial
por el general D. Anastasio Bustamante, yo habia
permanecido en Méjico espuesto á todos los furores
del partido dominante. Esta posicion era tanto mas
peligrosa para mí, cuanto que uno de los pretestos

1

CONCLUSION.

Los Estados-Unidos, dice muy bien M. Hamilton, son el pueblo quizá menos espuesto á revoluciones en el dia. Pero su estabilidad consiste, añade, en la única circunstancia de que la *gran mayoría de los habitantes son propietarios*. No hay duda en que esta es una, pero no la única causa de la tranquilidad inalterable de aquel dichoso pueblo. En los sistemas sociales no puede resolverse una cuestion por la esplicacion de una sola circunstancia. La España, por ejemplo, se mantuvo tranquila hasta el año de 1808, bajo el yugo tiránico de la monarquía, inquisicion y gobierno militar; y esta paz sepulcral no podia esplicarse solamente por una sola causa, á saber, el *terror que inspiraba* la forma establecida. Habia ademas la ignorancia, la supersticion, el inmenso influjo de los frailes y clérigos, apoyo de los grandes, en suma, un órden de cosas establecido, y coordinado de modo que unas sostenian á las otras. Estableced en esa misma España ó en Méjico la *ley*

23

PRÓLOGO

Dos causas me han estimulado a escribir este viaje. La primera porque he creído que nada puede dar lecciones más útiles de política a mis conciudadanos, que el conocimiento de las costumbres, usos, hábitos y gobierno de los Estados Unidos, cuyas instituciones han copiado servilmente. Segundo, porque habiendo ofrecido, en mi Ensayo histórico, *publicar mis Memorias, es ya tiempo de que comience, aunque sea por partes incoherentes según lo permitan las circunstancias.*

No he podido, porque no he debido ni continuar la Historia de México, posterior al año de 1830, ni publicar la parte de mis Memorias anterior a esta época, porque en mi calidad de ministro del gobierno mexicano en Francia, no sería conforme a las conveniencias públicas un libro escrito por mi en que calificase la conducta de los gobernantes de la República, con más o menos severidad, según mi conciencia. Por otra parte yo no había de publicar una obra de partido, ni mucho menos una colección de panegíricos. La verdad histórica deberá salir de los documentos oficiales, de los impresos de la era y de las publicaciones concienzudas de los pocos hombres que se desnudan de las afecciones de las personas y de los partidos, para trasmitir a la posteridad las cosas conforme se las presenta un examen crítico de los sucesos a su entendimiento. Ya que hemos cometido tantos errores que han sido tan fatales a nuestros conciudadanos, hagamos siquiera el servicio de confesarlos, y de presentarnos como hemos sido. Las generaciones venideras se aprovecharán de estas terribles lecciones.

Este libro no tiene ningún mérito en cuanto a originalidad. Puedo decir que no me ha costado mucho trabajo mental; porque la mayor parte de las descripciones, de los documentos y aun muchas reflexiones, o las he sacado de otros, o de mis apuntes hechos sobre los lugares. He añadido al tiempo de coordinarlo algunas consideraciones que nacían de las circunstancias o hechos que yo refería. Sin embargo debe ser de mucha utilidad para los mexicanos, que son a los que le dedico. En él encontrarán una descripción verdadera del pueblo que sus legisladores han querido imitar. Un pueblo laborioso, activo, reflexivo, circunspecto, religioso en medio de la multiplicidad de sectas, tolerante, avaro, libre, orgulloso y perseverante. El mexicano es ligero, perezoso, intolerante, generoso y casi pródigo, vano, guerrero, supersticioso, ignorante y enemigo de todo yugo. El norteamericano trabaja, el mexicano se divierte; el primero gasta lo menos que puede, el segundo hasta lo que no tiene: aquél lleva a efecto las empresas más arduas hasta su conclusión, éste las abandona a los primeros pasos: el uno vive en su casa, la adorna, la amuebla, la preserva de las inclemencias; el otro para su tiempo en la calle, huye la habitación, y en un suelo en donde no hay estaciones poco cuida del lugar, de su descanso. En los Estados del Norte todos son propietarios y tienden a aumentar su fortuna; en México los pocos que hay la descuidan y algunos la dilapidan.

Al hablar así debe entenderse que hay honorables excepciones, y que especialmente entre la gente de educación se encuentran virtudes sociales y domésticas muy recomendables. También hay en los Estados Unidos personas pródigas, perezosas y despreciables. Pero no es ésta la regla general.

Parece que oigo a algunos de mis paisanos gritar: ¡Qué horror! ved cómo nos desacredita este indigno mexicano, y nos presenta a la vista de los pueblos civilizados. Tranquilizaos, señores, que ya otros han dicho; eso y mucho más de nosotros y de nuestros padres los españoles. ¿Queréis que no se diga? Enmendaos. Quitad esos ochenta y siete días de fiesta del año que dedicais al juego, a la embriaguez y a los placeres. Acumulad capitales para vuestra decente manutención y la de vuestras familias, para dar garantías de vuestro interés en la conservación del orden social: tolerad las opiniones de los demás: sed indulgentes con los que no creen lo que vosotros creéis: dejad a los huéspedes de vuestro país ejercer libremente su industria, cualquiera que sea, y adorar al supremo autor del Universo, conforme a su conciencia. Dedicaos al trabajo útil: componed vuestros caminos, levantad casas para vivir como racionales, vestid a vuestros hijos y a vuestras esposas con decencia, no excitéis tumultos para apoderaros de lo ajeno, por último, vivid del fruto de vuestro trabajo, y entonces seréis dignos de la libertad y de los elogios de los hombres sensatos e imparciales.

El pueblo mexicano es mi Mecenas; pero no sigo el camino de los otros, que llenan una página con los elogios de las personas cuyo patrocinio solicitan. Esta es la ventaja de los que escriben sin esperar recompensa. Dicen lo que sienten, y son más creídos y respetados. En mis escritos no he buscado nunca más que la verdad; cualquiera que los haya leído, a no ser que esté mal prevenido, encontrará naturalidad, franqueza, buena fe, un deseo inextinguible del bien público y un amor insaciable de libertad. Si la pasión o la afección se han mezclado alguna vez, seguramente ha sido sin advertirlo ni sospecharlo.

Tú, amigo lector, procura leer este libro con atención, y espero que cuando lo hayas concluido habrás cambiado muchas de tus ideas; no en perjuicio de la razón, ni mucho menos de la moral, ni de tu religión, cualquiera que sea, sino en favor de ellas.

CAPÍTULO I

Salida del autor de la capital de México y los motivos.—Llegada a Puebla, e indicaciones sobre el estado de los caminos.—Golpe de vista rápido acerca de las diferentes temperaturas.—Llegada a Veracruz.—Salida precipitada de este puerto y los motivos.—Breves reflexiones acerca de los sucesos de México.—Llegada a la baliza.—Descripción de ésta.—Continuación en buque de vapor hasta Nueva Orleans.—Periódico realista que publicaban unos españoles.—Su objeto.—Clases de población de Nueva Orleans y descripción rápida de la ciudad.—Su comercio. —Su rápido incremento.—Pintura hecha por M. Flint de esta ciudad.—Los lagos. —Mercado.

Después de la caída del general Guerrero, en diciembre de 1829, arrojado de la silla presidencial por el general don Anastasio Bustamante, yo había permanecido en México expuesto a todos los furores del partido dominante. Esta posición era tanto más peligrosa para mí, cuanto que uno de los pretextos que habían alegado contra la administración de Guerrero, era el ser yo uno de los secretarios, y que mis abusos y dilapidaciones llevaban la nación al precipicio. No podían tampoco olvidar que yo había tenido una grande parte en la revolución popular de la Acordada; revolución cubierta de ignominia por el saqueo que la acompañó y por la ilegalidad de su principio, pues tenía por objeto sustituir al presidente legítimamente electo don Manuel G. Pedraza, por otro individuo que tenía menor número de votos; aunque evidentemente era más popular, y que si se hubiera hecho la elección por sufragios individuales, habría reunido una mayoría inmensa en su favor. Este es uno de los grandes defectos de la actual Constitución de los Estados Unidos Mexicanos.

Yo era pues el objeto del odio del partido victorioso, y don Lucas Alamán me lo repetía diariamente en las visitas que me hacía para observarme. No había diario del Gobierno o del partido que no contuviese una diatriba, una calumnia, una excitación contra mí; y yo, encerrado en mi casa, entregado enteramente a la lectura y al trabajo privado, veía amenazada mi existencia, después de varios asesinatos cometidos y la persecución desecha contra los partidarios de la precedente administración. Por último, el ministro Alamán me manifestó que yo debería salir del país y que éste sería el único medio de asegurarme.

El día 25 de mayo de 1830, cuatro años de la fecha en que hoy comienzo a escribir este libro, salí de la ciudad de México, en compañía del general don José Antonio Mejía, entonces coronel y secretario de la legación mexicana cerca del gabinete de Washington. No tomamos escolta, porque varios amigos me habían afirmado que yo no estaría muy seguro en manos de gentes que podían librarse de mí a poca costa, y quisimos más bien exponernos a ser asaltados por bandoleros, que al fin se contentarían con quitarnos lo que teníamos, y cuando mucho darnos algunos golpes.

Llegamos a Puebla de los Angeles y paramos en casa de don Domingo Couto, vecino rico de la ciudad, cuya familia, llena de urbanidad, nos consoló en parte de los pasados sufrimientos. Aún no se había establecido la carrera de diligencias que hoy existe entre México, Puebla, Jalapa y Veracruz, y se hacía entonces el camino en diez o doce días con las mayores incomodidades; pues no había ninguna posada en que pudiese descansar el pasajero, no digo con decencia, pero ni aun con las comodidades más comunes, como cama, sillas, mesas, vasos, platos, etc. Mucho han variado las cosas de entonces acá, y es de esperar que mejorarán cada día más. En Jalapa ya había una posada francesa bien servida, y ciertamente es un consuelo, después de un viaje penoso, encontrar un alojamiento aseado, y en el que el hombre reconoce las ventajas de la civilización.

Al bajar a las playas de Veracruz se comienza a sentir el aire abrasador de las tierras bajas entre los trópicos. Las inmensas llanuras de la meseta no presentan, es verdad, esa vegetación vigorosa, ese aire embalsamado, esa variedad de flores, frutas, aves y aguas que causan emociones vivas al viajero en la tierra caliente. Pero una atmósfera ardiente, nubes de mosquitos y otros insectos volátiles, reptiles venenosos y la mortal fiebre amarilla que amenaza a los nacidos en climas fríos o templados, son plagas terribles que deben causar mayor impresión desfavorable que las dulces emociones de sus ventajas. Mas los que han disfrutado de la admirable igualdad del delicioso clima del valle de Puebla, de la salubridad constante y uniforme frescura del de Toluca, suave y casi divino de Querétaro, ¿qué impresiones tan fuertes no deben experimentar al entrar en esa tierra caliente, que San Agustín creyó era inhabitable, sin duda porque sentía venir los vientos sures de los arenales del Africa, en donde estaba su obispado? Yo, como nacido en Yucatán, no tenía que temer la fiebre amarilla. Llegamos a Veracruz el 30 de mayo.

Comiendo en casa de M. Stone, vicecónsul americano entonces, al día siguiente de mi llegada recibí cartas y papeles públicos de México por los que se anunciaba la noticia de que debería ser pasado por las armas, en aquella ciudad, el capitán don Mariano Zerecero, por habérsele acusado, pocos días antes, de hallarse implicado en una conspiración. Tal fue el terror que nos inspiró esta noticia que resolvimos el señor Mejía y yo dar al capitán de la goleta *United States*, quinientos pesos, con tal que saliese con nosotros al día siguiente para Nueva Orleans, a donde habíamos determinado dirigirnos para viajar por el Misisipí.

Por haber habido norte se detuvo la salida de la goleta hasta el día 2 de junio en que nos hicimos a la vela, en un buque que no ofrecía ningún género de comodidades; pero que me sacaba de un país en el que entonces no había garantías, y mucho menos para mí que había corrido tantos riesgos y azares en los días aciagos en que el poder militar gobernaba aquella desventurada nación. La vista del océano, cuya majestad imponente causa siempre una profunda sensación a los que no le han visto, o han dejado de verle por algún tiempo, o le contemplan con ojos filosóficos; este espectáculo grandioso me condujo a profundas meditaciones sobre los sucesos de que había sido testigo, y en muchos parte, desde mi entrada en México, en abril de 1822, cuando vine por la primera vez a desempeñar el encargo de diputado por el Estado de Yucatán, mi patria nativa, después de haber cumplido igual misión en España el año anterior. Ocho años habían transcurrido y había visto representar los más importantes dramas históricos; levantarse una grande nación desde su nulidad colonial; formarse un imperio; congregarse una asamblea nacional; coronarse un general mexicano, descender del trono y disolverse el imperio; elevarse de los escombros de la monarquía una república federativa; darse este pueblo una constitución, y organizarse sus Estados, soberanos e independientes; establecer relaciones diplomáticas con las primeras potencias, y figurar entre las naciones del globo. Pero ¡ah! ¡qué gérmenes de disenciones civiles!!!

A los seis días de navegación (7 de junio) el capitán nos anunció que nos acercábamos a la Baliza de Nueva Orleans. La primera impresión que se recibe es la variación notable del color de las aguas del Golfo de México, algunas leguas antes de entrar en las bocas del caudaloso Misisipí. Este inmenso río lucha con las aguas del océano y las hace retrogradar de manera que más de seis leguas el gusto de ellas no es el de las aguas del mar. Las playas son tan bajas que no se perciben, aun entrando por la Baliza, más que unos montones de tierra al nivel de las aguas, sobre los que hay unas miserables chozas en donde apenas puede concebirse cómo habitan seres racionales. Se ven desembocar grandes trozos de madera, árboles enteros que la fuerza de los huracanes arranca a dos o tres mil millas y que vienen arrastrados por las corrientes impetuosas de los ríos tributarios del Misisipí. El aspecto de esta entrada y aun el curso del río hasta el fuerte Placamino es desagradable, pues sólo se ven juncos y arbustos miserables, cuya vista aparece tanto más fastidiosa cuanto que sólo presenta montones de lodo y una innumerable cantidad de lagartos que semejan trozos de madera seca.

Tuvimos necesidad de anclar a doce millas de la Baliza dentro del río, esperando un viento favorable o la subida de algún buque de vapor de los que se emplean en remolcar las embarcaciones que llegan al puerto y quieren pagar a razón de dos reales por tonelada. Por la noche la luna se levantó clara y hermosa, y su luz, lánguidamente reflectada por las aguas turbias del río, hacía agradable aquella noche, cuyo silencio interrumpía el zumbido de infinidad de mosquitos que nos chupaban la sangre. Al día siguiente, 9 de junio, continuamos hasta el fuerte Placamino, en donde nos trasbordamos al vapor que subía a Nueva Orleans remolcando dos bergantines y una goleta. Llegué a Nueva Orleans a las siete de la tarde, jueves 10 de junio.

Publicaban en esta ciudad algunos españoles un periódico titulado *El Español,* pagado por el gobierno de Fernando VII, y que fue establecido con el objeto de servir de vanguardia a la expedición de Barradas, cuyo éxito fue, como se sabe, correspondiente a la extravagancia del proyecto. Mi llegada a Nueva Orleans la anunciaron con insultos groseros, mientras que la *Abeja* y el *Louisiana Advertiser* hablaron de mí con elogio y respeto debido siempre al infortunio. Me alojé en la posada francesa de madame Herries, una de las mejores de la ciudad, en donde se encontraba todo género de comodidades; buenos cuartos, camas decentes, comida abundante y bien sazonada, aunque algo cara la paga, pues no baja de tres pesos diarios por persona.

Nueva Orleans es una ciudad habitada por pequeños restos de antiguas familias españolas, una parte considerable de familias francesas, una mitad de la población de negros y cuarterones y el resto de americanos del Norte, que, como se sabe, son un compuesto de hijos y descendientes de ingleses, alemanes, irlandeses y otros pueblos de Europa. Se habla en la ciudad muy poco el español, mucho más el francés y generalmente el inglés, en cuyo idioma se escriben los registros públicos de las autoridades. El aspecto de la ciudad no ofrece nada que pueda agradar la vista del viajero, no hay cúpulas, ni torres, ni columnas, ni edificios de bella apariencia y arquitectura exquisita. Su situación, más baja que la superficie del río y rodeada de lagunas y pantanos, la hace sombría y en extremo malsana; el carácter del pueblo es enteramente desemejante al de las otras poblaciones de los Estados Unidos del Norte. El río tiene en aquella parte cerca de una milla de ancho, y una muralla de arena forma un dique poderoso que se extiende por muchas leguas, y tiene el nombre de *Levée,* que impide que las aguas del gigantesco río inunden la ciudad y los lugares comarcanos. En Nueva Orleans apenas se percibe la marea.

La situación de Nueva Orleans es admirable para una ciudad comerciante. Un bosque de mástiles se descubre al acercarse a la Levée, y como es profundo el río en aquella parte, permite a las embarcaciones fácil acceso a la orilla, pudiéndose descargar fácilmente por medio de planchas de madera aplicadas a los buques. No hay en el globo ciudad que tenga la ventaja de una navegación interior tan extensa; pues pasa de veinte mil millas el espacio navegable no solamente por el Misisipí, Misuri, Ohio y otros grandes ríos tributarios de aquél, sino por lagos y bahías que la hacen comunicable con las Floridas y otros puntos.

A mi llegada había más de mil buques entre grandes y pequeños, y a lo menos cinco mil marineros. Cuando estuve en aquella ciudad, en diciembre de 1821, había a lo más cuarenta mil habitantes, y en el día se calcula por lo menos a setenta mil. El comercio ha crecido considerablemente y los derechos de aduana ascienden hoy a cerca de dos millones de pesos. Los principales artículos de exportación son algodón y azúcar, y se asegura que su valor anual asciende a veinticinco millones de pesos. Si las calenturas amarillas, las intermitentes, los mosquitos y un calor insoportable en el estío no ofreciesen tan graves inconvenientes al aumento de la población, ciertamente que Nueva Orleans vendría a ser, bajo el gobierno libre y popular que hoy tiene, una de las más ricas y distinguidas ciudades del globo. A pesar de las plagas referidas, adelanta rápidamente y llegará a ser una de las primeras ciudades del Nuevo Mundo.

No será desagradable al lector ver la descripción que hace M. Flint de esta ciudad. "A cien millas de distancia de las bocas del Misisipí y a más de un mil de las del Ohio, en un ángulo agudo sobre los bancos orientales del río, está situada Nueva Orleans, la gran capital comercial del valle del Misisipí. Su posición como ciudad comercial no tiene igual en el mundo, según creo. A corta distancia del Golfo de México, sobre las márgenes de un río que puede decirse riega el Universo, a seis millas del lago Ponchartrain y en comunicación con él por un canal navegable; el inmenso aluvión de aguas que descienden a todas direcciones y forman estanques que facilitan la comunicación por canales naturales; centenares de buques de vapor que frecuentan el puerto de cincuenta puntos diferentes; producciones de agricultura de su mismo Estado y de los otros que pueden competir con las más ricas de cualquiera otro país del globo. Su posición es muy superior a la de Nueva York. Tiene sin embargo un reverso espantoso: la insalubridad de su situación. Si pudiesen desecarse los inmensos pantanos que hay entre la ciudad y los eternos bosques, y completarse las mejoras que se han emprendido en la ciudad; en suma si pudiese conseguirse que el aire atmosférico no fuese tan húmedo, Nueva Orleans vendría a ser indudablemente la primera ciudad de la Unión.

"Muchos esfuerzos se están haciendo para conseguir estos grandes resultados. Desgraciadamente cuando la constelación del Can está sobre el zénit la fiebre amarilla comienza a aparecer sobre el oriente. Mas a pesar de que anual o al menos bienalmente esta plaga pestilencial visita el país; a pesar de que su fatal guadaña destruye una multitud de infelices no aclimatados y obliga a los ricos a buscar un suelo más sano a distancias considerables, y por último a pesar del terror que en todas partes acompaña la aparición de estas plagas y que en cierta manera está asociado al nombre de la ciudad, su población se aumenta considerablemente. Por donde quiera se ven nuevos edificios que se levantan con rapidez, y el aspecto de la ciudad mejora mensualmente. Los americanos vienen aquí de todos los Estados, su objeto es acumular riquezas y pasar a disfrutarlas a otros puntos; pero la muerte que no están dispuestos a cargar en sus cuentas, les obliga a abandonar el sitio antes de llenar sus deseos".

Nueva Orleans está en una isla formada por un lado por el Misisipí, y por los otros por los lagos Borgue, Ponchartrain y Maurepas, y el pequeño río Iberville, que se separa del Misisipí ciento veinte millas arriba de la ciudad, y fluye en el lago Maurepas.

La plaza del mercado es abundante y barata. En el mes que estuve escaseaban las verduras, que abundan en los de marzo, abril y mayo. El mercado es la Torre de Babel, porque allí se oyen negros, mulatos, franceses, españoles, alemanes y americanos pregonando sus mercancías en idiomas diferentes. Las *cuarteronas* se visten con mucha gracia y aseo, y como generalmente son bien formadas y hermosas, presentan un contraste muy singular con los negros de que descienden, y el filósofo no puede dejar de fijar su atención sobre esta variedad de castas que forma matices sorprendentes.

Hay dos ciudades distintas divididas no por algún río, ni barrio, ni otro objeto semejante, sino por el género de edificios, costumbres, idioma y clase de sociedad. Se sabe que ésta fue una colonia francesa, en su origen, que pasó por algún tiempo a manos de los españoles, y que en tiempo de Carlos IV, el gobierno español la cedió a la Francia por un convenio sobre amortización de ciertas deudas y ocupación de todas las Floridas. Napoleón la vendió a los Estados Unidos del Norte por diez millones de pesos, y desde esa época, data la progresión rápida de la Luisiana. De aquí nace esa diversidad de costumbres y de modo de vida que en aquella ciudad es uno de los caracteres peculiares de su población.

CAPÍTULO II

Excursión de los franceses y fundación de la colonia.—Ocupación del Canadá por los ingleses.—Pasa a mano de los españoles.—Vuelve a las de los franceses en tiempo de la república.—Marina de los americanos del norte.—Negociaciones entabladas con este objecto.—Mm. Livingston y Monroe ministros por parte de aquella república.—M. Barbe.—Marbois por la de la francesa.—Conclusiones del tratado.—Progresos rápidos de la Luisiana después de este convenio.—Tierras cultivables en poder del gobierno de los Estados Unidos.—Dificultades de la demarcación de límites en aquéllos inmensos territorios.—Reflexiones de M. Barbe.—Marbois.—Producciones y comercio de la Luisiana.—Su gobierno.—Teatro.—Bello sexo.—Días festivos.—Católicos y protestantes.—P. Cedella.—Cementerio.— Campo de batalla en 1815.—Disposiciones del general Jackson.—Ataque del general inglés Pakenam.—Pérdida de los ingleses.—Triunfo glorioso de los americanos.—Confianza y medidas del general americano.—Tropa de línea de este país.—Opinión sobre ella de los príncipes de Sajonia.—Weimar y Wurtemberg.— Método de reemplazos.—Breves reflexiones sobre la esclavitud—Decreto del general Guerrero que la abolió en México.—Duro tratamiento que experimentan los esclavos en la Luisiana.—Leyes antifilosóficas en el mismo estado sobre esta clase infeliz.—Reflexiones.—Influencia de la esclavitud sobre el progreso de la civilización.—Breve recuerdo de las haciendas de tierra caliente de la República Mexicana.—Suceso desagradable antes de mi partida de Nueva Orleans.

En 1672, los franceses que poseían el Canadá, hicieron una excursión por el Misisipí y le bajaron hasta el río Arkansas, cerca del grado 33 latitud N. En 1682, el gobernador de Canadá descendió hasta el Golfo de México, y dio el nombre de Luisiana a los países que corrió en honor de Luis XIV. Los franceses tomaron posesión de aquellas comarcas desde la desembocadura del río Mobila hasta la bahía de San Bernardo, que dista cerca de ciento veinte leguas más allá de las bocas del Misisipí. Luis XIV concedió a Crozat, rico financiero, el comercio exclusivo de estas colonias por doce años. Estos cesaron en 1719, y transferida la colonia a la compañía de las Indias Occidentales, ésta envió un número considerable de colonos.

El padre Charlevoix, jesuita instruido que viajó por la Luisiana en 1722, ridiculizaba a los escritores que habían ponderado mucho las riquezas metálicas de esta provincia, y al mismo tiempo vaticinaba su futura prosperidad, por la fertilidad de su terreno y abundancia de aguas y de ríos. La colonia estaba mal gobernada: la compañía hacía guerra a los indios, y en 1731, el comercio fue declarado libre. Poco tiempo después de este período fue cuando el gobierno francés quiso realizar el proyecto de unir el Canadá con la Luisiana, con el objeto de cerrar toda comunicación a los colonos ingleses, con las partes occidentales del continente. En aquella época, los ingleses aun no habían penetrado al oeste de los montes Aleghanys. Muchos franceses habían trasladado sus familias y fortunas a los Ilineses, país de infinita fertilidad, regado por varios ríos navegables, y dotado de uno de los climas más dulces del mundo. Los colonos, en lugar de elegir los puntos que debían ocupar como propiedad, cercarlos y cortarlos, para asegurarla como debe ser, se colocaron indistintamente sin ninguna designación o límite.

En la guerra entre Francia e Inglaterra, en 1754, la segunda conquistó el Canadá, y la primera convino en ceder todo el territorio existente en toda la orilla oriental del Misisipí, a excepción únicamente de la Luisiana. Una línea tirada en medio del Misisipí, separaba las posesiones inglesas de las francesas. En 1764, la Luisiana pasó a manos del gobierno español por un tratado secreto; pero la administración permaneció en manos de los franceses hasta 1768. Ocurrieron posteriormente las dos grandes revoluciones de América y Francia, y Napoleón, elevado al poder con miras extensas sobre todos los puntos del globo, formó el proyecto de ocupar la Luisiana, para de esta manera tener un influjo poderoso en las grandes transacciones de América, que ya comenzaba a llamar la atención de la Europa. Acertó a conseguir que Carlos IV, por un tratado secreto en 1800, restituyese la Luisiana a la república francesa; no transpirándose este convenio hasta que se firmaron los preliminares de paz entre la Gran Bretaña y la Francia, y fue completamente conocido cuando la paz de Amiens, en 29 de marzo de 1802. Pero en el momento que se divulgó en Inglaterra, por todas partes se levantaron reclamos enérgicos contra la cesión de la Luisiana a Francia. El lord Haw-Kesburry decía en la Cámara de los Comunes "que la Francia había poseído bastante tiempo la Luisiana, sin haber sacado de esta colonia ninguna ventaja". En esta ocasión profirió aquella frase atrevida e imprudente: "nosotros sólo queremos hacer una paz experimental".

El general Bernardote, hoy rey de Suecia, fue nombrado primer gobernador de la colonia; pero rehusó el mando, y nombrado en su lugar el general Víctor, estaba al punto de partir cuando comenzaron de nuevo las hostilidades entre la Inglaterra y la Francia.

En este intervalo, informado el Congreso de los Estados Unidos de la cesión de la Luisiana hecha a la Francia, y que ésta se preparaba a tomar posesión, no creyó deber mantenerse indiferente al ver establecerse en sus límites y en puntos tan importantes una nación guerrera que no había de mantenerse en la inacción de los españoles, y que pronto principiaría a establecer cuestiones acerca de la navegación del Misisipí. El alarma fue tan grande en la parte occidental de los Estados Unidos, que el Presidente M. Jefferson tuvo muchas dificultades para pacificar a sus habitantes que se disponían a ocurrir a vías de hecho; lo que hubiera ofrecido obstáculos a la negociación que el gobierno americano intentaba entablar con la Francia, primero para mantener libre la navegación del Misisipí; lo segundo para que continuase Nueva Orleans como puerto de depósito para los productos de los Estados interiores; y último para conducir las cosas al punto en que pararon que fue la traslación del dominio.

En este período M. Livingston, hermano del actual ministro de los Estados Unidos en Francia, y muy conocido como cooperador de *Fulton* en el establecimiento de los buques de vapor, ejercía el mismo encargo que hoy desempeña el honorable Edward Livingston. Había hecho representaciones al Presidente Jefferson acerca de la crisis que amenazaba a los Estados Unidos si la república francesa ocupaba la Luisiana, y Jefferson no podía desconocer las consecuencias de semejante ocupación. Entonces encargó la misión de enviado extraordinario, para tratar con Napoleón, a M. Monroe, dándole instrucciones para que en el caso de no obtener un convenio satisfactorio y conforme a los intereses de los Estados Unidos, entrase en comunicaciones con los gabinetes de San James y de Madrid. M. Monroe, que fue después presidente en los Estados Unidos, había sido enviado en tiempo del directorio, y su conducta dejó establecida en Francia una reputación apreciable.

La misión cometida a los señores Monroe y Livingston era la de obtener del gobierno francés, mediante la indemnización correspondiente en numerario, la cesión de Nueva Orleans y todo el territorio perteneciente a la Francia en la banda oriental del Misisipí, en medio del cual se consideraba la línea divisoria entre los territorios americano y francés. Tenían instrucciones de que en el evento de no poder conseguir esto, o en último caso la libre navegación del Misisipí, y la circunstancia de quedar Nueva Orleans como puerto de común depósito, negociasen con la Inglaterra con el fin de hacer con ella causa común contra la Francia. En la carta escrita a M. Livingston por el Presidente Jefferson se encuentran estas notables palabras: "El día en que la Francia tome posesión de Nueva Orleans pronuncia la sentencia de su baja para siempre con respecto de los Estados Unidos, y sella la alianza de dos naciones que unidas, pueden mantener la posesión exclusiva del Océano. Desde aquel momento nos enlazaremos íntimamente con la nación inglesa, su marina, etc". M. Monroe salió de Nueva York, en 8 de marzo de 1803, día mismo en que se remitió al Parlamento británico el mensaje de la Corona que anunciaba la proximidad de una ruptura con

Francia; de manera que a su llegada encontró M. Monte al gobierno francés en buena disposición para tratar con los Estados Unidos. Napoleón conoció que estando en guerra con la Inglaterra debía cambiar sus miras y su política con respecto a la posesión de la Luisiana. No podía ocultársele que siendo 'Os ingleses tan poderosos en el Océano, cortarían todas sus relaciones comerciales con la colonia, y que la ocuparían en la primera oportunidad para venderla a los americanos del Norte. Por uno de aquellos golpes maestros que eran en él una cosa casi natural, determinó vender la colonia a los Estados Unidos. De esta manera no solamente prevenía la conquista que podían hacer los ingleses de aquella comarca, recibía además una cantidad cuantiosa de dinero por el pago de ella, cuya suma sería de mucha utilidad a la Francia en las circunstancias en que se encontraba exhausta de recursos y en vísperas de una guerra continental.

Hubo dos opiniones en el gabinete del primer cónsul. M. Marbois opinaba en favor de la medida por las razones expuestas, y M. Talleyrand era de sentir que la posesión de la Luisiana debía con el tiempo indemnizar a la Francia de sus grandes pérdidas por la riqueza y fertilidad de su suelo, por su posición dominante del Misisipí y por su comercio, y en el caso de que los ingleses la ocupasen, la Francia podría hacer otro tanto con el Hanover que sería una prenda de restitución. El primer cónsul no mudó de dictamen y al día siguiente llamó a M. Barbé Marbois y le dijo: "Señor ministro, yo renuncio a la Luisiana, no solamente quiero que la Francia se desprenda de Nueva Orleans, sino también de toda la colonia sin ninguna reserva. Os comisiono para tratar este delicado asunto con los agentes de los Estados Unidos. Yo necesito mucho dinero para esta guerra y no quiero dar principio a ella por nuevas contribuciones. Si hubiese de arreglar los términos de la indemnización en vista de las ventajas que resultarán de esta cesión a los Estados Unidos, ciertamente no habría suma equivalente para el pago. Yo seré moderado por la necesidad en que estoy de hacer la venta: quiero cincuenta millones de francos (poco más de nueve millones de pesos), en inteligencia de que por menos no entraré en ningún tratado. M. Monroe está al llegar, comenzad por hacerle la propuesta sin preliminar alguno: me daréis cuenta día por día, hora por hora del progreso de la negociación. El gabinete de Londres sabe las resoluciones del de Washington, pero ignora las mías: guardad el mayor secreto y exigidle de los ministros americanos".

Las conferencias comenzaron al siguiente día, y los ministros de ambos países, que tenían un mismo interés en la pronta conclusión, condujeron la negociación hasta el punto en que podían, conforme a las instrucciones y poderes de los americanos. Pero como he dicho, sólo los tenían para tratar acerca del lado izquierdo del río inclusive Nueva Orleans, y no sobre la otra banda del Oeste.

Les era imposible ocurrir a su gobierno sobre una distancia tan larga, un asunto tan delicado y cuando ya habían comenzado o debían comenzar luego las hostilidades entre la Inglaterra y la Francia, de consiguiente los ministros americanos no vacilaron en tomar sobre sí la responsabilidad de tratar sobre esa vasta porción de la América del Norte perteneciente a la Francia, que se extiende sobre las márgenes de los más caudalosos ríos del Universo. Sobre estas bases se firmó el tratado. En una carta escrita por M. Jefferson a M. Monroe le decía: "Nuestro proyecto de adquirir por compra Nueva Orleans y las Floridas está sujeto a tantas combinaciones y trabajos diversos, que no podemos dar instrucciones determinadas: era necesario enviar un ministro extraordinario, para que en unión del ordinario obrasen con poderes discrecionarios". Esta cláusula indica que los enviados americanos tenían confianza en que su conducta sería aprobada, como en efecto lo fue. La negociación se concluyó sobre ochenta millones de francos, quedando veinte millones en depósito para satisfacer los reclamos de los Estados Unidos contra la Francia. El tratado fue ratificado en Washington, y la Luisiana vino a ser una provincia de los Estados Unidos.

De entonces acá se han formado dos Estados de aquel territorio. El de *Luisiana* que comprende Nueva Orleans y contiene cuarenta y ocho mil millas cuadradas, y *Misuri,* parte del extensísimo territorio de Misuri, en la parte occidental del Misisipí, cuya extensión es de sesenta y tres mil millas cuadradas. Aun no se ha formado estado del gran territorio de Arkansas, parte también de la que era antes provincia francesa. Tiene como quinientas cincuenta millas de largo y doscientas veinte de ancho. La parte N. O. del Missouri, hasta las márgenes del Pacífico es de inmensa extensión. El río corre por más de dos mil millas.

Al contemplar la prodigiosa extensión de estas partes y las demás posesiones de los Estados Unidos del Norte en la parte del N. O., así como los territorios de Floridas y Michigan aun poco poblados, no es muy aventurado el cálculo de M. de Chateaubriand de que la población de los Estados Unidos *aún ocupa una decimoctava parte de su territorio.* M. de Marbois, empleado largo tiempo en los Estados Unidos, escribía: "Que en estas ilimitadas regiones, la raza humana puede multiplicarse con toda libertad. Allí por *muchas centurias* no se opondrán obstáculos a los matrimonios, y los padres no temerán que falte a sus descendientes tierra para alimentar los frutos de la dulce y honesta unión conyugal". Este cálculo y estas reflexiones son igualmente aplicables a nuestros Estados Unidos Mexicanos, en donde incuestionablemente la Naturaleza ha sido más próvida en cuanto a la fertilidad del terreno y facilidad de subsistir.

En los Estados Unidos del Norte hay en efecto trecientos millones de acres de tierras cultivables, sin contar las inmensas regiones del Oeste y Noroeste. Una gran porción de estas tierras permanecen en manos del Gobierno de la Unión, y en el curso de algunos años, producirán a su territorio muchos millones de pesos. No hay cálculo que pueda alcanzar su valor.

Todos los terrenos que no estaban ocupados vinieron a ser, en consecuencia de los tratados hechos con la Francia o con la España, una propiedad de los Estados Unidos. Mucha dificultad tuvo el gobierno de Washington para demarcar los países que se iban a ocupar conforme al tratado hecho con la Francia; pues aun no están clasificados en la geografía sino bajo la denominación de países desconocidos. El comisionado fue M. Jacob Astor de Nueva York, quien fundó una población en las márgenes del río Colombo, llamada, de su nombre, *Astoria*.

"Los conquistadores, dice M. Marbois, extienden sus estados por la fuerza de las armas; se hacen notables por la sangre que derraman y la desolación que reparten en los países que ocupan. La República de los Estados Unidos se ha extendido enviando geómetras y hombres sabios a distancias de mil quinientas leguas. Establecen sin fuerza los límites de sus pacíficas conquistas, y aseguran por buenas leyes la prosperidad duradera de las comunidades para las que se formaron".

Al hablar de la ciudad de Nueva Orleans parece llenarse de entusiasmo por sus rápidos progresos, cuya población era en 1803 sólo de ocho mil personas. "Nueva Orleans, fundada en 1707, y que ha permanecido en estado estacionario durante una centuria, ha venido a ser en el corto espacio de veinticinco años, una de las más florecientes ciudades, tan luego como entró en la gran comunidad de los Estados Unidos del Norte. Pocos años de un gobierno bueno han producido lo que muchas generaciones no pudieron efectuar bajo el imperio de *leyes prohibitivas y restricciones mezquinas*. La población, que en tiempo de aquellas leyes estaba sin movimiento, se ha quintuplicado: sus tierras producen desde lo más necesario hasta los más delicados artículos de lujo y comodidad".

En los Estados de Luisiana y Misisipí se fabrica azúcar suficiente para proveer una mitad del consumo de los Estados Unidos. Las otras producciones de aquellos terrenos aumentan proporcionalmente. Se ven almacenes de pieles de castor, hermina, martas, lobos marinos y de otros animales. Las tierras vendidas en tiempo de los gobiernos francés y español subieron a un precio extraordinario. Yo conocí a un antiguo colono español, llamado don José Vidal, que había hecho una fortuna considerable con tierras que tenía en Natches adquiridas en tiempo que era colonia española.

En el Estado de Luisiana hay dos cámaras legislativas. Es el único en donde he visto que las discusiones se hagan en dos idiomas; de manera que muchas veces el representante criollo que habla en francés, no es entendido por el representante americano que habla en inglés. Sin embargo, al fin se imprimen las discusiones en los dos idiomas. Muchos periódicos publican mitad en francés y la otra en inglés. Hay también un intérprete que reproduce los discursos en el idioma respectivo para ser entendido, por todos, y aunque esto tiene el inconveniente de que nunca puede ser trasladado como se pronuncia, y se pierde mucho tiempo, es ventajoso bajo el aspecto de que cuando hay alguna personalidad en la discusión, es modificada por el intérprete.

En Nueva Orleans hay teatro francés y teatro inglés. El primero es bastante bueno y he visto en él algunos *vaudevilles* bien cantados y representados. Del teatro inglés hablan muy mal los viajeros ingleses. Yo creo que en efecto no debe ser muy exquisito, porque generalmente hablando los norteamericanos no son amantes de esta clase de diversiones, y como dice Mrs. Trollope, piensan mucho antes de sacar los shillings de la bolsa para pagar la entrada.

Las criollas son generalmente bonitas y graciosas. Aunque no son tan blancas como las americanas del Norte, tienen mejores cuerpos, y visten con más gracia, andan mejor, y su trato es más franco y agradable.

Como en todos los países católicos, el domingo es el día de las diversiones en Nueva Orleans. Las tiendas de los católicos están abiertas; hay bailes, músicas y fiestas. Por la mañana corren a la catedral a oír misa en donde se reúnen gentes de todos colores. La catedral es un pequeño templo que no tiene un orden regular de arquitectura y que en nada se parece a nuestras iglesias de México. Los altares son como los de nuestros pueblos, a excepción de las imágenes que son mucho mejores.

Aunque los católicos y los protestantes convienen en que todos los hombres son hijos de Dios, hermanos entre sí y herederos de la gloria con iguales títulos, sólo los primeros dan ejemplos prácticos de esta profesión de fe. En un templo católico, el negro y el blanco, el esclavo y su señor, el noble y el plebeyo se arrodillan delante de un mismo altar, y allí hay un olvido temporal de todas las distinciones humanas: todos vienen con el carácter de pecadores y no hay otro rango que el de la jerarquía eclesiástica. En este sagrado recinto no recibe inciensos el rico, no se lisonjea el orgullo de nadie ni el pobre se siente abatido; desaparece el sello de la degradación de la frente del esclavo al verse admitido con los libres y ricos en común para elevar sus cánticos y ruegos al autor de la Naturaleza. En los templos protestantes no es así. Todas las gentes de color son excluidas, o separadas en un rincón por enrejados o barandales; de manera que aun en aquel momento tienen que sentir su condición degradada.

El más miserable esclavo recibe de manos del sacerdote católico todos los consuelos de la religión. Es visitado en su enfermedad, consolado en sus aflicciones; sus labios moribundos reciben la hostia consagrada, y en el último momento de su agonía, la voz postrera que escucha es el sublime apóstrofe que dirige el católico al moribundo: *Proficiscere, anima christiana*. Parte en paz, alma cristiana. ¿Cómo no han de ser así católicos todos los esclavos y negros de la Luisiana? La congregación de la iglesia protestante consiste en algunas damas bien vestidas, en sus bancos adornados, mientras que todo el pavimento de la catedral está lleno de gentes de todos colores. Tengo presente que el padre Fray Antonio de Cedella, religioso capuchino, con quien tuve amistad en 1822, muerto ya, era el oráculo de las gentes de color, y respetado por todas las clases de la población. Este eclesiástico español se había hecho estimar por su amabilidad, por su tolerancia y otras virtudes.

En Nueva Orleans, como en México, no se pueden ahondar sus sepulturas sin encontrar agua. El cementerio, en una porción de terreno no distante media milla de la ciudad, rodeado de pantanos, aunque de grande extensión, apenas es suficiente para las necesidades de la población.

No puede un viajero curioso e interesado en las glorias de la América visitar Nueva Orleans, sin pasar a ver el campo de la célebre acción dada por el general Andres Jackson a las tropas inglesas, bajo el mando del general Eduardo Pakenham, en enero de 1816. El llano en que se dio la acción dista cuatro millas de la ciudad: tiene cerca de una milla de extensión, y cuando el desembarco de los ingleses estaba cubierto de callas de azúcar. En el día está destinado a la pastura. Por la parte del Oeste le corta el Misisipí; por el Este un bosque espeso de cipreses y pinos. Aun permanecen los vestigios del foso mandado hacer por el general americano entre el río y el pantano. La excavación no podía ser profunda, porque a poco que se excave se llena de agua. Las trincheras que se formaron fueron de sacos de algodón, que eran ciertamente muy a propósito al objeto, por la blandura del algodón que amortiguaba el efecto de las balas. Detrás de estas trincheras el general Jackson colocó los tiradores de rifles, poniendo a las espaldas de cada uno otro que cargase en el momento, para no perder tiempo.

Una o dos semanas se pasaron en escaramuzas hasta el 8 de enero en que sir Edward Pakenham comenzó el ataque de la línea. El campo intermedio hasta el punto de defensa estaba completamente descubierto, y así el general inglés exponía su tropa a recibir todo el fuego del enemigo sin ninguna defensa. Expuestos a las terribles descargas de la artillería hasta medio tiro de cañón, y luego al certero fuego de los rifles, no pudieron conservar el orden de ataque los invasores y rompieron sus columnas. Los defensores en algunos puntos tenían seis de centro y hacían estragos horrosos. El osado Pakenham se dirigió en persona a conducir las tropas al ataque, esforzándose a restablecer el orden; pero fue herido por la metralla de la artillería que le llevó las dos piernas, y luego muerto por las balas de los rifles. Los generales Gibbs y Kean que le sucedieron con el mismo ardor, corrieron igual suerte; y el general Lambert, que últimamente conoció la imposibilidad de sacar ventaja alguna, ordenó la retirada y el reembarque de las tropas.

El número de los invasores era de cerca de diez mil hombres y el de los americanos de tres a cuatro mil. El general Jackson dando parte de su triunfo decía a su Gobierno: "No hay ejemplo en la historia de una victoria más completa, y que haya costado menos sangre a los vencedores. Nuestra pérdida ha sido de *seis muertos y nueve heridos;* la del enemigo pasa de tres mil muertos y otros tantos heridos". Esta defensa la hizo el bravo general americano con *voluntarios de Tennessee y milicia nacional de Kentucky con algunos otros de Nueva Orleans,* y muy poca tropa de línea.

El gran mérito del general Jackson en esta crítica circunstancia, además del de su valor que nadie le disputa, estuvo en haber podido inspirar confianza a los habitantes de Nueva Orleans por la energía de su carácter. La legislatura de la Luisiana había estado vacilante, y los vecinos de la ciudad llegaron a manifestar síntomas de querer entrar en tratados con los ingleses. Al momento que llegó a la ciudad puso fin a todas las incertidumbres. En un mensaje dirigido al gobernador decía: "El que no es con nosotros es contra nosotros. Los que han salido en suerte deben ser obligados con penas a ir a la línea. Más debemos temer a los enemigos ocultos que a los descubiertos. La patria debe ser defendida, y lo será". En estas penosas circunstancias el general no tenía tropas; y es fácil imaginarse las dificultades en que se encontraría con el terror que inspiraba un ejército numeroso y disciplinado a las puertas de la ciudad, a las madres, esposas e hijas de los que eran llamados a un combate al parecer tan desigual. Cuando salió de la ciudad para el campo de batalla con unos pocos centenares de hombres, escribía al señor Eduardo Livingston, auntor de los códigos de la Luisiana, hoy ministro plenipotenciario en Francia, diciéndole: "Asegurad a esos habitantes que el enemigo no penetrará a la ciudad, y procurad tranquilizarlos". Pero en la difícil situación en que se encontraba se revistió de las facultades de Dictador, publicó la ley marcial; castigó con pena capital varios desertores; internó a ciento veinte millas al interior muchos franceses que se negaron a tomar las armas; arrestó al cónsul francés que quiso resistir la ejecución de la ley marcial; desterró un juez que proveyó un acto del *habeas corpus* para poner en libertad al cónsul francés, en suma obró como lo exigía la emergencia de las grandes circunstancias de un hombre capaz de tal empresa, y el pueblo de Nueva Orleans, convencido de que la energía de su carácter y la oportunidad de sus providencias habían salvado la ciudad, le recibió, después de la victoria, en triunfo, y como el libertador de todo el país.

No debo terminar este capítulo sin hacer mención de la tropa de línea de los Estados Unidos, citando el testimonio de viajeros respetables en aquella dichosa comarca. El ejército de la Unión americana se compone únicamente de seis mil hombres; pero el orden, la disciplina, el aseo, las buenas costumbres, son como naturales en aquellos soldados. No hay un oficial que no sepa sus deberes como militar y como ciudadano. Su educación es digna de respeto, y sobre este particular quiero citar el testimonio respetable del duque de Sajonia Weimar que escribe acerca de algunos oficiales que encontró en Washington, en estos términos: "La mayor parte de los hombres que aquí he tratado son oficiales del ejército. Con dificultad se encontrará un ejército en Europa que tenga un cuerpo de oficiales mejor compuesto que el de este pequeño ejército americano. Ninguno puede ser oficial si no ha recibido una educación distinguida. Casi todos son tomados de la Academia Militar de West Point: no hay esas promociones rápidas en Europa. Cuando se ve un oficial americano se puede asegurar que tiene todas las prendas capaces de hacerle estimar en la sociedad más selecta". El príncipe que esto escribe es hermano político del rey de Inglaterra actual.

El príncipe de 'Wurtemberg, que viajó en los Estados Unidos el año de 1828, escribía acerca de la misma materia: "No hay país en el mundo, decía, en donde los soldados sean empleados con mayor utilidad. En Europa el soldado consume el día en ejercicios, en paradas, en limpiar sus vestidos y armas, o en la ociosidad. El soldado americano está constantemente ocupado en la labranza. La rigurosa disciplina a que está sujeto le mantiene al nivel de las disposiciones en que a fuerza de trabajos se conserva a las tropas en otros países. *Ningún soldado en el mundo está mejor alimentado, más bien vestido y pagado que los de los Estados Unidos*. El Gobierno de este país ha injertado sus instituciones militares, en la administración civil, y el resultado ha sido no sólo la mejora del ejército, sino una obra maestra de sistema militar".

La manera de hacer los enganches de los reclutas se conoce por la siguiente advertencia que se ve en los papeles públicos: "Se necesitan para servicio de tierra de los Estados Unidos tantos cientos de hombres de edad de entre diez y ocho a treinta y cinco años, sanos y que tengan cinco pies, seis pulgadas de alto. Se dan de gratificación cinco pesos, abundante socorro de comida y vestido, con cinco pesos de sueldo al mes. Los que quieran pueden ocurrir a tal parte".

El sistema de sorteos, que hasta mi salida de México estaba adoptado en nuestra república, es sumamente odioso, y cuando yo era gobernador del Estado de México, confieso que muchas veces disimulé el que no se practicase, en vista de las reiteradas y dolorosas representaciones de los labradores y artesanos. Sólo en las circunstancias angustiadas, como en las que se encontró el general Jackson, como hemos visto, todo el mundo está obligado a hacer el servicio de las armas. El método de conscripciones en Francia enajenó mucho los espíritus de la causa de Napoleón. Al pasar de la República Mexicana a los Estados que permiten la esclavitud en nuestra hermana y vecina, no puede dejar el filósofo de sentir el contraste que se advierte entre ambos países, ni dejar de experimentar una agradable memoria por los que han abolido este degradante tráfico y hecho desaparecer entre nosotros los vestigios de tan humillante condición de una especie humana. El general Guerrero dio un decreto en 16 de septiembre de 1829, en virtud de facultades extraordinarias, por las generosas inspiraciones de don José María Tornel. A mi pasada por Nueva Orleans había en venta más de un mil esclavos. Esta pobre gente es tratada con mucha severidad en la Luisiana. Ellos hacen el servicio de las casas y posadas, y generalmente duermen en el suelo. Cuando un amo quiere castigar a su esclavo o esclava, los manda a la cárcel con un billete que contiene la orden del número de azotes que debe darles el carcelero. El pobre hombre o mujer vuelve a su casa con la nota que participa habérsele aplicado el castigo prevenido. Cuando el amo lo estima conveniente ordena que se aten las manos del esclavo por otras, se le eche a tierra boca abajo, y se le azote de esta manera. Muchas veces se oyen los gritos y lamentos de estos infelices, al pasar por las cárceles por la mañana.

Voy a trasladar un hecho que refiere el duque de Weimar, de quien he hablado ya, y que posó en la misma casa en que yo estuve en Nueva Orleans, con la diferencia de que él viajó en 1826. "No puedo pasar en silencio, dice este príncipe, una escena que presencié en 22 de marzo, y que excitó mi más profunda indignación. Había en la posada una joven esclava de Virginia empleada como recamarera, y cuya limpieza y exactitud en el servicio la hacían querer de todos. Un francés que estaba alojado en la posada pidió agua en la mañana temprano. La muchacha no pudo servir con la presteza que aquel hombre quería, por estar ocupada en otras atenciones; bajó las escaleras y encontrándola en el patio en otras diligencias, la golpeó ferozmente hasta hacerle salir sangre por la boca y nariz. La pobre criatura, queriendo defenderse, echó mano al cuello del agresor, quien comenzó a dar fuertes gritos. Escapado de las garras de la muchacha, pasó a su cuarto, recogió su ropa y baúles, y se determinaba a partir, cuando la dueña de la posada, madame Herries, queriendo satisfacer al cruel huésped, mandó que se aplicasen a la esclava veinticinco azotes con un látigo de cuero, y para hacer doble el tormento de la víctima este castigo fue infligido por su mismo amante, que era un esclavo de la misma casa. No satisfecho el francés con esta pena, ocurrió a la policía, en donde, conducida la infeliz esclava por dos ministriles, fue azotada de nuevo por ellos en presencia del demandante.

Siento mucho, añade el ilustre viajero, no haber tomado el nombre de este mal cristiano para publicarle y denunciarle a la exsecración pública".

Pocos meses antes de mi llegada, en 7 de marzo de 1830, la legislatura de la Luisiana había pasado dos leyes que contienen principios sumamente antiliberales; y son los siguientes. 1° Cualquiera que escriba, publique o distribuya un escrito que *tenga una tendencia* a crear el descontento entre la población de color libre en este Estado, o a introducir la insubordinación entre los esclavos, sufrirá, según la gravedad del hecho a juicio del tribunal de justicia, la pena capital, prisión perpetua, o trabajos públicos a vida. 2° Cualquiera que en los discursos públicos, en el foro, en los parages concurridos, en el púlpito o en cualquiera otra parte, o sea en conversaciones privadas o por signos o acciones, haga o diga alguna cosa que *tenga tendencia a producir el descontento* entre las gentes de color libre de la población de este Estado, o a excitar la insubordinación entre sus esclavos, o cualquiera que a sabiendas haya traído a él papeles, folletos o libros que tengan la misma tendencia, sufrirá, a juicio del tribunal, la pena de trabajos públicos, no menos de tres años, ni más de veinte, o la muerte. 3° Toda persona que enseñare, o fuese causa de que se enseñe a un esclavo a leer o escribir, sufrirá la pena desde uno a doce meses de prisión.

La otra ley es como sigue: 1° Da una ley de expulsión a todas las gentes de color libres que hubieren entrado al Estado desde el año de 1807, y prohíbe la entrada de cualquiera persona de esta clase al Estado. 2° Establece la pena de trabajos públicos perpetuos a todas las personas de color que habiendo regresado al Estado no salgan de él. 3° Establece que toda persona blanca que fuese convencida de ser autor, impresor o editor de cualquiera escrito en el Estado, o bien de usar un lenguaje que tenga por objeto perturbar la paz o seguridad del mismo, en relación a los esclavos o pueblo de este Estado, o *bien a disminuir el respeto que el pueblo de color debe tener por los blancos,* será multada con una suma de trecientos hasta mil pesos, y condenada a prisión que no baje de seis meses, ni exceda de tres años. Pero si las personas que cometieren estas faltas fuesen de *color* sufrirán una multa que no pase de mil pesos, y condenadas a trabajos públicos de tres a cinco años, y exportación, después de cumplido el término, para siempre. 4° Establece que en estos casos será obligación del fiscal o procurador general, y de los procuradores particulares de los distritos, bajo la pena de perdida de empleo, el perseguir a las personas de color que hubieren violado esta ley o *cuantas veces fuesen requeridos a perseguir las expresadas personas libres de color por cualquiera ciudadano del Estado.* Estas leyes fueron firmadas por M. Roman, presidente de la Cámara de Diputados; Smith, presidente del Senado, y M. Dupré, gobernador del Estado entonces. Hoy lo es M. Roman.

Es lamentable a la verdad la situación de un Estado en donde sus legisladores juzgan necesarias medidas de represión tan ofensivas a los derechos del hombre. Los que conocen el espíritu de libertad que preside en todas as deliberaciones de los directores de los Estados Unidos, no pueden menos que pensar, a vista de estos actos de injusticia notoria hacia una porción de individuos de la clase humana, que motivos muy fuertes, que una necesidad inevitable, *dura necessitas,* obliga a éstos a sancionar tales leyes. No faltan entre estos legisladores quienes del salón de sus sesiones vayan a tributar homenajes de adoración a las bellas cuarteronas, con las que se enlazarían por los vínculos sagrados del himeneo, si una preocupación invencible no se interpusiese en medio de estos enlaces. Yo he conocido personas respetables que vivían condenadas a un celibatismo involuntario, porque no podían enlazarse con las mujeres que por sus gracias, belleza y afectuosa solicitud, habían cautivado su voluntad. Hay varios ejemplos de estas concesiones clandestinas en el Estado de la Luisiana.

Esta clase de leyes de excepción tiene una influencia extraordinaria sobre el progreso moral y la civilización de los Estados que permiten esclavos; tales como Georgia, Carolina del Sur y Luisiana. Basta echar una ojeada sobre el estado actual de la imprenta en estos países, comparativamente al que tiene en otros Estados libres de esclavos, y se advertirá desde luego las ventajas de los últimos. Escojamos tres Estados libres y los tres donde se permite la esclavitud. En 1810 se publicaban en el Estado de Nueva York sesenta y seis periódicos; en 1830 se publicaban doscientos doce. En 1810 se publicaban en el de Pensilvania sesenta y uno; en 1830 se publicaban ciento ochenta y cinco. En 1810 se publicaban en el de Ohio catorce; en 1830 sesenta y seis. Veamos ahora los estados de esclavos. En 1810 se publicaban en Carolina del Sur diez periódicos; en 1830 dieciséis. En Georgia en 1810 trece; en 1830 igual número. En la Luisiana se publicaban *diez;* en el día han bajado a *nueve.* Es de notar que mientras que la población de este último estado se ha aumentado desde veinte mil ochocientos cincuenta y cuatro que tenía entonces, hasta doscientos quince mil doscientos setenta y dos a que había ascendido en 1830, los periódicos hayan disminuido siguiendo un curso contrario al progreso de la civilización y comercio.

Las plantaciones de cañas de azúcar, los limoneros, los naranjos y otros árboles aromáticos de nuestras tierras calientes que hay en las haciendas de la Luisiana, me hicieron recordar las bellas posesiones de Cuautla y Cuernavaca, en el Estado de México. Pero aquí la agricultura está más adelantada, y la facilidad de la exportación y locomoción con la ventaja que da a los propietarios el hacer el cultivo con esclavos, hace que puedan dar las azúcares a precios muy bajos. La calidad de la azúcar nunca es tan exquisita como la que tenemos en los Estados de Veracruz, Puebla y México. Siempre hay mayor cantidad de parte térrea en las azúcares de la Luisiana y de La Habana. Lo mismo sucede con nuestros dulces de Yucatán, que son aun menos valiosos que los de La Habana.

El calor era excesivo en la estación en que llegué a Nueva Orleans; pues había día en que el termómetro de Farenheit ascendía noventa y ocho, hasta cien grados. Todos los individuos acomodados viajaban para buscar mejor clima subiendo el río.

Tuve mucho placer en encontrar en Nueva Orleans antiguos amigos con quienes había viajado en Europa anteriormente, o tenido relaciones en esta ciudad. Tales fueron los señores Charles Blacke, tesorero de la municipalidad, Fleytas, propietario rico, el ex-conde de Montezuma, la familia de M. Duncan y otras personas respetables del país. M. Curson, sujeto de vasta instrucción y que había viajado mucho en América y Europa, me favoreció con sus consejos y reflexiones. Me dio cartas de recomendación para algunas personas, entre ellas el ministro inglés en Washington M. Vauwhon. En México me había favorecido igualmente con cartas que me fueron muy útiles, el encargado de negocios de los Estados Unidos M. A. Butler.

El día 15 de junio tomamos pasaje en el buque de vapor Luisiana, el general Mejía y yo. Este es uno de los mejores *steamboats* de la línea que ofrece todas las comodidades compatibles en una casa flotante. La mayor parte de estos barcos son de cuatrocientas a quinientas toneladas, y están construidos con el triple objeto de llevar pasajeros pobres y cargamento de azúcar, café y aguardiente cuando suben; algodones, harinas, carnes, pieles, etcétera, cuando bajan. En la parte superior son como nuestras plazas de toros, o como los baños que hay en París sobre el Sena. Tienen sus balcones que sirven para que se diviertan los viajeros, y sus gabinetes interiores en donde hay cama, aguamanil y espejo, para dormir y vestirse. Hay cuartos de diferentes órdenes. El pasaje de Nueva Orleans a *Louis Ville* cuesta cuarenta pesos. La distancia es de cerca de mil doscientas millas.

El día 16 nos embarcamos a las doce del día, y poco antes de la partida del buque se presentó un sherif preguntando por M. Zavala. El *sherif* venía acompañado de un hombre que yo no conocía. El ministril me dijo que aquel individuo se llamaba Browerman y que se había presentado al *city court*, o tribunal de la ciudad, pidiendo que yo le pagase noventa y cuatro pesos que decía deberle yo por la composición de un coche cuando yo era gobernador del Estado de México. Adviértase la malicia de este hombre que esperó el momento de la salida del buque de vapor, lo que me ponía en la necesidad o de detenerme, lo que me causaba un atraso terrible, o de pagarle, aunque estaba cierto de que no debía aquella cantidad; pues la había pagado en México a su tiempo; pero yo no había conservado el recibo, y no puedo concebir cómo haya derecho para semejante demanda en un país extranjero, lejos del lugar en que se supone contraída la deuda. El único recurso que tuve fue dejar de fiador a M. Breadlove, vicecónsul mexicano, que se hallaba felizmente en el buque. Así salí de este pequeño y desagradable embarazo. Después de dos años de peregrinación en que este asunto fue olvidado tuve que pagar en México, en 4 de octubre de 1833, la suma de ciento cinco pesos, cuatro reales a que ascendió la cantidad en los gastos del proceso, juzgado sin mi consentimiento, cuyo recibo conservo, así como los de todos los artistas, posaderos y demás que yo haya pagado para evitar otro lance igual. Tengo conmigo un baúl lleno de recibos.

CAPÍTULO III

El día era hermoso, el sol brillaba con todo su esplendor, y sus rayos, reflejados por las aguas del río le hacían multiplicarse y aumentar el incendio en que parecía abrasarse la Tierra. El viento soplaba caliente y sólo se encontraba consuelo en la vista de las arboledas de las orillas, y en la esperanza de una atmósfera más templada a la caída del día. Había seis damas y entre ellas una de Guatemala que seguía a su esposo don Mariano de Aycinena, desterrado de su país por materias políticas, como otros muchos. Iba también a bordo un yucateco, llamado don Joaquín Gutiérrez, joven apreciable por sus maneras delicadas, su trato, y aquel fácil y amable desembarazo que se encuentra entre las gentes de educación que han viajado y vivido en buena sociedad. El conde Cornaro que venía de México, sujeto distinguido por su nacimiento y elegante trato, se hallaba igualmente en el buque. Había otra porción de gentes, todas capaces de formar una compañía verdaderamente interesante.

En la navegación del Misisipí no hay los riesgos de las tempestades, huracanes y arrecifes que causan tantos y tan espantosos estragos en los buques que surcan el Océano. Pero los frecuentes encuentros con los enormes troncos que descienden el río, suelen causar desgracias en los buques de vapor. Hay otro riesgo mayor, pero que ha disminuido mucho su repetición por las precauciones que se han tomado. Hablo de las explosiones que hacen las pailas o recipientes del vapor encerrado para dar movimiento a la máquina. Cuando esto acontece, de lo que se han visto frecuentes ejemplos en los steamboats del Misisipí, perecen muchas gentes, ya por los estragos que directamente hacen con el agua caliente, ya por el naufragio a que están expuestos los pasajeros en el caudaloso río, ya por último por la fuerza con que rompiéndose las máquinas ofenden a las personas que encuentran. Suelen también bararse los buques sobre bancos de arena o limo; pero los remolcan con facilidad otros stemboats que pasan con frecuencia.

A cien millas de Nueva Orleans está un pequeño lugar llamado *Bâton rouge* en el que elaboran azúcares, mieles y aguardiente. Hay en este pueblo una guarnición militar y una fortaleza. Pasamos por él el día 18 de junio. El clima es con poca diferencia como el de la capital. El 19 pasamos por Natches, célebre por la interesante novela de M. de Chateaubriand que lleva ese título.

Mrs. Trollope que ha escrito su viaje a los Estados Unidos con el espíritu de sátira y sarcasmo que muchas veces lleva al exceso, hablando de los buques de vapor de esta carrera y del trato que se da en ellos, dice: "Aconsejo a los que desean recibir agradables impresiones de los usos y trato de los americanos que no comiencen un viaje por el Misisipí; porque declaro con toda sinceridad que daría preferencia a un chiquero bien cuidado en que estuviese una piara de cerdos, que los gabinetes de estos buques. Apenas conozco una cosa tan repugnante para un inglés, como el incesante escupir de los americanos". En otra parte hablando de los pasajeros, de los cuales dice que la mayor parte se denominaban coroneles, generales y mayores: "Su absoluta falta de modales en la mesa, la voraz rapidez con que se apoderaban de los platos para devorarlos, las extrañas y desusadas frases de que se servían, la frecuente expectoración, de que con dificultad podíamos libertar nuestros vestidos, la horrible manera de comer metiéndose el cuchillo hasta el puño en la boca, y la más horrible todavía de excavarse los dientes después de comer con sus cortaplumas, nos obligaron desde luego a creer que no estábamos rodeados de generales, coroneles y mayores del antiguo mundo, y que la hora de la comida no era un rato de placer".

Los que han viajado en los buques de vapor del Támesis a Calais, a Ostende, Boulogne, etc., después de haberlo hecho en los de los Estados Unidos, no pueden menos de admirarse de que Mrs. Trollope use de este lenguaje, cuando evidentemente los segundos son mucho más cómodos, más decentes, más aseados y bajo todos aspectos mejores. ¿Qué diremos de los del Sena, del Gironda y otros ríos de Francia? Es imposible concebir cómo en estos países tan civilizados y adelantados en todo género de comodidades sociales, se puedan mantener buques tan asquerosos y repugnantes.

En cuanto a la costumbre de los norteamericanos de escupir con frecuencia, no debemos disimular que es defecto repugnante en la buena sociedad, debido a la costumbre que tienen generalmente de mascar tabaco, así como lo tenemos los americanos del Sur de fumar. ¿Qué diría Mrs. Trollope si viese a nuestras graciosas mexicanas arrojar continuamente humo por la boca y narices, manchar sus pequeñas y bien formadas manos con el aceite que despide el papel del cigarro, contaminar sus vestidos con el humo del tabaco y dar a su aliento un olor desagradable? En los buques de vapor no se permite fumar, sino en un lugar destinado al efecto, para evitar la mortificación que las señoras tendrían con el humo, y muchas gentes delicadas que ni fuman ni mastican tabaco.

Aunque por muchas millas las orillas del Misisipí sólo ofrecen una vista constante y uniforme sin interrupción de poblaciones, ni montañas, ni colinas, es siempre un espectáculo sorprendente y una perspectiva agradable el cuadro continuado de lataneros, palmas, de grandes árboles de encinos, abetos, sicómoros y otras gigantescas producciones del reino vegetal, entrelazadas por las enredaderas que sirven de lechos y asientos a una multitud variada de aves, que hacen resonar sus cantos en aquellos bosques solitarios y florestas eternas. ¡Cómo se enajena el espíritu al contemplar el interior de esas inconmensurables soledades en donde jamás pasó la huella humana! ¡Aquellos árboles, como nuestras grandes montañas, parecen contemporáneos a la creación! A su aspecto se acierta a concebir cómo se pudo animar la Naturaleza muerta bajo el pincel romántico de Chateaubriand y elevar su alma ardiente al grado de entusiasmo de que hace participar a sus lectores en sus brillantes páginas. El Misisipí, como el Nilo, el Marañón y el Orinoco y otros grandes ríos de América y Asia no pueden dejar de producir impresiones fuertes e ideas de la grandeza y majestad del Creador al contemplarlos. La Naturaleza en su estado primitivo con toda su aspereza, su abandono por decirlo así, su silencio, su languidez; pero con toda su fecundidad, sus riquezas, su magnificencia, sus esperanzas, es siempre a la vista del hombre sensible un objeto digno de profundas reflexiones.

El río Misisipí recibe en su seno, o se forma de los ríos Rojo, Red River, Blanco, White River, Arkansas, Ohio, Misuri, y otros muchos de menor importancia. El Misisipí varía de profundidad y de anchura según los parajes por donde pasa, y disminuye naturalmente conforme se aproxima a su origen. En Nueva Orleans tiene cerca de ciento veinte pies de profundidad, en Natches tiene ochenta: esto es a trecientas millas de distancia. Desde la Baliza hasta Pitsburgo, en que se navega por buques de vapor por el Ohio hay la distancia de dos mil doscientas doce millas, que son más de setecientas leguas de México. Es prodigioso el impulso que ha recibido el comercio y la civilización con la introducción de los buques de vapor. Anteriormente se necesitaban tres y cuatro meses para hacer este viaje desde Nueva Orleans. En el día se llega en diez días a *Louis Ville,* mil cien millas; en un día a Cincinati, ciento veinte millas; en cuatro a Wheeling, trecientas ochenta millas; y en uno y medio a Pitsburgo, cerca de doscientas ochenta millas. Nada es más frecuente que ver a las familias pasar a visitarse de uno a otro de estos puntos, ciento, doscientas o trecientas leguas, para regresar a su casa a los dos o tres días. Es como si se fuese de México a Zacatecas o Durango. El viaje de Nueva Orleans a Pitsburgo es de más distancia que de Veracruz a Sinaloa.

Cada veinticuatro horas se detenía nuestro buque a cargar leña para mantener el fuego necesario a la máquina. El consumo diario de leña según mi cálculo ascendía de veintiocho a treinta pesos. En los bancos menos cenagosos de las orillas hay *rancherías* o pequeñas casas de madera, montadas sobre estacas que las sostienen y preservan de la humedad y de los lagartos, y en estas miserables chozas habitan los proveedores de leña para los trecientos barcos que viajan en aquel caudaloso río. Los americanos los llaman *squatters,* que creo quiere decir *agachados:* será sin duda porque no pueden estar en pie en sus habitaciones por ser muy pequeñas. Mrs. Trollope hace una pintura muy melancólica de estas pobres gentes. "De tiempo en tiempo, dice esta viajera, aparecen unas cabañas de cortadores de leña, que proveen a los buques de vapor de la necesaria, y que viven en este tráfico a riesgo, o mejor diré, con la certidumbre de una muerte prematura, a cambio de pesos y de whiskey (aguardiente de maíz). Estas tristes habitaciones están en la mayor parte inundadas durante el invierno, y las mejores están sobre estacas que preservan a los habitantes de ahogarse cuando suben las aguas del río. Estos desgraciados seres son víctimas de calenturas agudas, que ellos desafían sin miedo alentados por el estímulo de licores espirituosos de que hacen uso. El aspecto maciliento de sus miserables hijos y mujeres causa horror, y aunque se repetía este espectáculo con frecuencia jamás dejó de causarme la misma impresión. Su color es pálido azulado y todos parecen hidrópicos. Una vaca y dos o tres puercos, con el agua hasta las rodillas, distinguen a los más acomodados entre estos desventurados, y lo que puedo asegurar es que nunca vi la naturaleza humana reducida a tanta degradación como aparece en los leñeros de los malsanos bancos de Misisipí".

En efecto es exacta la descripción de Mrs. Trollope. Pero yo he visto varias de estas pequeñas rancherías aumentarse en los lugares en donde lo permitía la altura de las tierras litorales, y formar ya aldeas en que se comienzan a establecer casas de alguna comodidad. Nuestros indios de la laguna de Chalco y de los pantanos del Valle de Toluca se hallan en la misma situación de estos *squatters*. Pero hay esta diferencia, que nuestros indios pueden mejorar mucho las tierras, establecer sus casas sobre un suelo sólido, criar animales y coger cosechas; mientras que éstos no pueden salir del pequeño círculo en que han establecido sus cortes de madera y leña, porque los aluviones del río no se lo permiten. En un pueblo a tres leguas de Toluca, llamado *San Pedro de los Petates*, los indios viven dentro de las aguas que se derraman del río de Lerma en tiempo de lluvias. Mueren muy jóvenes, y la última peste del cólera, que hizo tan pocos estragos en la capital del Estado, acabó casi con aquella pequeña población.

En la navegación de este río se encuentra una gran cantidad de balsas que bajan efectos a Nueva Orleans, especialmente maderas de construcción y para casas. Estas balsas son muchas veces de doscientas varas de largo sobre doce a quince de ancho, formadas de planchas de maderas clavadas y juntas, sobre las que ponen otras, y luego los animales, semillas y demás efectos. En el medio hay una habitación en que duermen y hacen su comida. Bajan con la corriente que es de cuatro a cinco millas por hora, cuando se han reunido los ríos Misuri y Ohio. En Nueva Orleans deshacen estas balsas y venden la madera. Hace pocos años que para hacer un viaje redondo hasta *Louis Ville* se necesitaban ocho meses. En el día se hace en quince días. ¿Habría cosa más justa que erigir en cada población de aquellas una estatua de bronce al inmortal Fulton que aplicó el vapor a la navegación? ¡Tanta es la grandeza de un hombre de genio, que hace una revolución benéfica al género humano! Gioya, Juan de Guttemberg, Colón y Fulton vivirán eternamente.

Uno de los ríos caudalosos que alimentan el Misisipí es el de Arkansas. Aún no se ha descubierto su origen, y se conoce su curso por más de mil novecientas millas, siendo navegable hasta más allá de seiscientas. Los bancos de este río tienen en algunas partes tanta cantidad de cal, que aseguran algunos que los ganados mueren comiendo la tierra. En tiempo de lluvias los buques de vapor pequeños pueden acercarse a las montañas. Por este lado corre el *White River* o río blanco, que es navegable más de cuatrocientas millas en el territorio de Arkansas, que es limítrofe con las tierras de Nuevo México y California. Los habitantes de esta parte de los Estados Unidos son generalmente poco civilizados, y hay muchos que se aproximan a nuestros indios, aunque siempre son más orgullosos. Llevan siempre unos cuchillos en forma de alfanges de que usan contra los lobos, osos y otras bestias feroces. En nuestros pueblos los más recónditos, se palpan los efectos de la esclavitud en que hemos vivido bajo la antigua dominación. No es la civilización sino los efectos del terror impreso en los ánimos de los habitantes el que hace que no se manifiesten hostiles a los viajeros, ni vivan entre sí en una guerra abierta de continuas represalias. En los lugares de que voy hablando en donde no hay ni civilización, ni temor, ni religión, los hombres sólo se respetan por su fuerza y poder individual. No será fuera del caso de esta obra referir algunas anécdotas que muchas veces dan mejor a conocer el carácter de un pueblo que las exactas descripciones.

"El 10 de abril de 1830, dice M. Stuard en su viaje a los Estados Unidos, en una de las paradas del buque para proveerse de leña, el capitán me instó a bajar a tierra para oír de boca del mismo alcalde un suceso a que él juzgaba no daría yo crédito refiriéndomelo él mismo. El juez de paz era un americano respetable y de buenos modales; habitaba una casa aseada y cómoda, y me convidó a gustar su whiskey de centeno, que en su opinión era lo mejor en los Estados Unidos de aquel género. Me contó que hace pocos días que pasando algunos botes pequeños, que venían del río arriba cargados con efectos del país, se habían detenido durante la noche en las cercanías; que en uno de estos botes se había cometido un asesinato, y que el asesino había sido sorprendido *in fraganti*. Esto causó una excitación grande en los viajeros, entre los cuales tenía muchos amigos el difunto. Considerando que el castigo sería dilatado por muchos días, si se remitía al culpable a Arkansas para ser juzgado por el tribunal, y que no habría allí testigos del hecho, resolvieron formar el proceso en los mismos botes, y habiéndole juzgado le sentenciaron a ser ahorcado, lo que se ejecutó a las pocas horas de cometido el delito. El alcalde no hubiera podido evitarlo aun cuando lo hubiese intentado".

Hay otro hecho curioso que da idea asimismo de la situación civil de aquellos remotos países y que quiero referir, porque creo que no será extraño se repita en algunos puntos de México, tales como Tejas, California y Nuevo México.

Poco más arriba del pueblo Memphis hay un lugar que se llama la *Pequeña Pradería, Little Praire,* en el Estado de Misuri. En aquel punto encontramos un campo cultivado y cortado por un colono llamado *Brown.* Este había comprado aquellas tierras al gobierno, pagando el acre por diez o doce reales. Aun no había adquirido los títulos, cuando un tal, llamado *East-*

wood, había tomado posesión de unas tierras adyacentes que también pertenecían a Brown. Se ocupaba en ararlas Eastwood cuando Brown, a quien acompañaban dos hijas que tenía, resolvió deshacerse de aquel invasor, a cuyo efecto mandó a su hija mayor a traer un rifle o escopeta americana. Le contuvo sin embargo para llevar a efecto aquella desesperada resolución, el temor de que su hija sería igualmente procesada como cómplice si tiraba sobre Eastwood. La acción de éste no era sin embargo tan absurda como puede figurarse el lector de un pueblo civilizado. Es muy común en los estados y territorios occidentales de los Estados Unidos, y en Texas, California y Nuevo México de nuestra República, el que los primeros venidos tomen posesión de un terreno sin ningún título, le cultiven y vivan en él hasta que un propietario legal venga a ocuparle, y en este caso se indemniza al cultivador por su trabajo mediante un convenio. No hay un derecho para semejante reclamo; pero se ha hecho costumbre en muchos puntos.

Pocas millas después de la confluencia del Ohio y del Misisipí, hay una porción considerable de islas que comienzan a ser habitadas y deben ser de una admirable fertilidad. Entre ellas está una llamada *Wolf Island* (Isla del Lobo), de cerca de una milla cuadrada, que pertenece a M. James Hunter. En un libro que contiene la dirección de los viajeros del Misisipí impreso en Pitsburgo, se ve la siguiente curiosa nota: "M. James Hunter, el sólo hombre que yo haya conocido que tenga placer en ser llamado jugador de profesión, es el único que ocupa la Isla del Lobo". Hace un comercio muy lucrativo con los puercos, vacas, gallinas, leche, etc., que vende a los buques que trafican en el río.

La pequeña Villa de Memphis en el Estado de Tennessee, está al lado izquierdo del río sobre una de las pocas colinas de sus pantanosas márgenes. Pocos puntos de vista hay en el Misisipí tan bellos y majestuosos. En aquel sitio parece el río un lago hermoso, y una isla que divide sus caudalosas aguas, da un aspecto pintoresco por los árboles que la cubren. La villa es un punto elevado como trecientos pies sobre el nivel del Wolf, que es uno de los innumerables tributarios del Misisipí. Memphis es una población moderna que aumenta rápidamente y hace comercio de maderas, cecinas, quesos y otros comestibles con los buques y la Luisiana.

La Constitución de Tennessee fue hecha en Knox Ville en 1796. El poder legislativo reside en una asamblea general compuesta de senado y cámara de representantes. Los miembros de estos colegios son elegidos bienalmente los primeros jueves y viernes del mes de agosto.

El número de diputados es de sesenta, que es proporcionado al número de contribuyentes de cada condado. El de senadores no puede ser más que una mitad, ni menos que un tercio del de diputados.

El poder ejecutivo lo tiene el gobernador que es nombrado al mismo tiempo que los senadores y diputados, por el pueblo, cuyas funciones duran dos años sin poder ser reelectos más que tres veces.

Las sesiones se abren en Nashville el tercer lunes de septiembre siguiente, cada dos años. Pero puede ser convocada la asamblea por el gobernador en los casos convenientes. El derecho de sufragio es concedido a todos los hombres libres de veintiún años de edad que tengan una propiedad cualquiera en el condado en que votan; o a cualquiera que no siendo esclavo, haya residido seis meses antes de las elecciones en el condado. El poder judicial es lo mismo que en los otros Estados.

Antes de salir del Estado de Tennessee, o Tenesi, según nuestra pronunciación, debo hablar de una ceremonia religiosa que se practica en todos los Estados; pero que las llanuras del Tennessee ofrecen un campo más vasto para su ejecución. Quiero hablar de los *Campos Meetings* de que han dado tan diferentes descripciones los viajeros ingleses, entre ellos la célebre Mrs. Trollope, cuya obra ha tenido tanto consumo en Inglaterra. Yo me referiré a lo que he visto, y a la relación de personas imparciales e instruidas para que el lector pueda formar un juicio exacto. Esta es una de las prácticas religiosas más imponentes y que tienen una influencia notable sobre las costumbres y usos del país, como se advertirá por la noticia fiel que paso a dar de ella.

Ninguno que no haya visto puede formarse una idea de la excitación y entusiasmo en un distrito de más de cincuenta millas de extensión, a la aproximación de estas reuniones religiosas, y ninguno que no haya sido testigo puede imaginarse cuán profundamente han comprendido los predicadores los efectos que producen y que bien saben sacar fruto de esto. Supóngase el lugar de la escena en donde de dos años a esta parte se han celebrado con más frecuencia, y que por su silencio ofrece cuadros verdaderamente interesantes; uno de los bellísimos y fértiles valles, entre las montañas de Tennessee. La noticia circula con dos o tres meses de anticipación. En el día señalado comienzan a llegar coches, carros, sillas, gentes de a caballo, innumerables a pie, carretas con provisiones, con colchones, tiendas de campaña y utensilios necesarios para una semana de residencia. Los que han visto nuestras ferias de San Juan de los Lagos, Chaima y Guadalupe en nuestra República Mexicana, podrán formarse una idea imperfecta de estas numerosas asambleas; se reparten entre los sombríos bosques y oscuras florestas del Tennessee, a las márgenes de uno de los arroyos que serpentean entre los árboles, para proveerse del agua necesaria.

"Concurren a esta asamblea religiosa el rico y el ambicioso, continúa M. Flint, porque la opinión, todopoderosa en aquel país, los obliga a ello; también van allá para extender su influencia, o para que la nota de su falta no la disminuya; asimismo concurren los aspirantes a las plazas públicas, para hacerse prosélitos y ganar popularidad. Muchos asisten por curiosidad y no faltan quienes vayan por divertirse. Allí están la juventud y la belleza por motivos misteriosos, que es prudente no examinar con severidad. Se ven allí niños cuyos ojos volubles recorren con admirable rapidez todos los objetos que les rodean, hombres de media edad, padres y madres de familia, cuyo método de vida está ya arreglado, esperando con santo recogimiento oír la palabra divina: por último ancianos de ambos sexos con sus cabellos enblanquecidos con el pensamiento en la eternidad a que se aproximan. De estas clases de personas son estas congregaciones que cuentan muchos millares de almas.

Una turba de predicadores que bajo diversas denominaciones explican el evangelio corren a ostentar su elocuencia, su saber y su piedad a aquella congregación. Sacerdotes jóvenes que en el vigor de la edad, ayudados de una voz sonora y poderosa, se esfuerzan a brillar: otros que han proclamado el evangelio como peregrinos de la cruz desde las más remotas comarcas del norte hasta las playas del Golfo de México, dispuestos a proferir palabras que expresan sentimientos profundos, frutos de su experiencia, atesorados en sus largos y penosos viajes, ejerciendo su ministerio por cincuenta años, y cuyos débiles acentos y aspecto tembloroso, producen más impresión que sus palabras, anuncian que por última vez dirigen a los mortales sus terribles apóstrofes. Tales son los ministros que ocupan la atención de este inmenso auditorio.

Una línea de tiendas de campaña se forma sobre las orillas de los arroyos, y la religiosa ciudad se levanta en pocas horas entre los árboles. Multitud de lámparas y faroles colgados en las ramas causan un efecto mágico entre aquellas florestas sombrías. La escena del más brillante teatro de Europa, es una débil pintura respecto de este admirable espectáculo. En este intermedio los concurrentes, entre los más dulces transportes de sentimiento social, añadido al entusiasmo general de la expectación, pasan de unas tiendas a otras a darse mutuos abrazos de congratulación apostólica, y a hablar sobre la solemnidad que los reúne. Toman el té y cena, y en este tiempo los apacibles rayos de la luna comienzan a penetrar entre las ramas de los árboles. Debe advertirse que siempre se calcula el tiempo en que la luna venga a aumentar la majestad de estas solemnidades. Un cielo claro deja percibir algunas estrellas que centellean débilmente. Este conjunto hace un tiempo digno de la grandeza del Creador. Un anciano venerable, vestido con elegante simplicidad, sube a un púlpito, limpia sus anteojos cubiertos de polvo, y en una voz que expresa las emociones de su alma, entona el *himno* de manera que toda la asamblea pueda repetirle, y que todas las voces se junten a la suya. Muy triste idea tendríamos del corazón que no palpitase violentamente al llegar a este cántico semejante al "sonido de muchas aguas" cuyo eco reproduce por las montañas y bosques contiguos. Tales son las escenas, las asociaciones y tal la influencia de las cosas eternas sobre una naturaleza tan excitable y portentosamente constituida, como la nuestra, en que un pequeño esfuerzo es suficiente en una materia tal como la religión, para llenar el corazón y los ojos. El respetable orador habla de Dios, de la eternidad, del Juicio Final y de cuanto puede causar fuertes impresiones. Habla de sus experiencias, de sus trabajos, de sus viajes, de sus persecuciones y buenos recibimientos, y de cuanto ha visto en esperanzas, en paz, en triunfos, fruto de la predicación de sus predecesores: y cuando habla del corto espacio que le queda de vida, sólo dice sentirlo, "porque no podrá en el silencio de la muerte, proclamar los beneficios y bondades de su redentor crucificado".

No se necesita ser un consumado orador para producir en aquel teatro los profundos sentimientos religiosos. Ni debe maravillar que, mientras el predicador hace algunos pausas para enjugar algunas lágrimas, todo su auditorio se deshaga en llanto, y aun en demostraciones de penitencia. Tampoco debe causar sorpresa el que muchos a quienes su amor propio les persuade de su superioridad sobre la masa común de la sociedad, y de una noble insensibilidad sobre objetos semejantes, sean arrastrados, a pesar suyo, hacia este sentimiento general, y se hagan niños y mujeres a su vez, y aunque hayan venido con el fin de divertirse, se hagan penitentes.

A pesar de cuanto se ha dicho para exponer a la burla y risa pública estos espectáculos, tan comunes en nuestras comarcas, no puede negarse que su influencia, considerado el todo, es saludable, y el resultado general de su práctica sobre los grandes intereses sociales, bueno. Mucho tiempo ha de ser necesario, si llegase el día alguna vez, para que el ministerio sacerdotal sea mantenido por la comunidad. En lugar de esto nada es más conveniente, para suplir la falta de la influencia que resulta de los constantes deberes de ministros establecidos, como el recurso a este género de explosión simultánea de sentimientos religiosos, que sacuden el mundo moral y purifican su atmósfera, hasta que las semillas acumuladas de las enfermedades morales exijan otra vez una nueva lustración.

Cualquiera que pueda ser la causa, es evidente que estos espectáculos religiosos han producido una palpable mejora en los hábitos, maneras, usos y costumbres del pueblo en los Estados de Tennessee, Misisipí, Misouri, Kentucky, Ohio, Indiana y los ilineses. Se han disminuido y desaparecido en muchos puntos, las tabernas y casas de juego, y los que anteriormente concurrían a estas casas van a las asambleas religiosas. Los metodistas también han hecho grandes e incalculables beneficios a las costumbres".

El cuadro que acabo de presentar, traducido de una obra de M. Flint, uno de los americanos más instruidos y dignos de aprecio por sus brillantes cualidades, da una idea exacta de lo que pasa en estas reuniones. Las de los metodistas en los Estados del Este son casi semejantes, y quizá tendré ocasión de hablar de ellas.

Comparárese esta fiesta religiosa con las que tenemos en la República, que son, poco más o menos, como las de España y toda la Italia, una o dos horas de concurrencia en el templo, en donde el pueblo participa muy poco de los sentimientos religiosos que deben ocuparle en aquellas circunstancias. La pompa de nuestro culto católico, tan imponente y de que se podía sacar mucho provecho en beneficio de la moral, pierde todo su efecto por la absoluta incomunicación entre el ministerio sacerdotal y el pueblo. La misa dicha en latín en voz baja, aprisa y como por fórmula; la predicación, generalmente hablando, es un tejido de palabras sin coherencia, sin conciencia y sin unción. El resto del día, después de estas ceremonias, el pueblo bajo bebe y come; la gente de categoría juega y baila. Ved aquí nuestras fiestas religiosas. ¿Y qué diremos de las de los indios en Chalma, en Guadalupe y en los otros santuarios? ¡Ah! la pluma se cae de la mano para no exponer a la vista del mundo civilizado, una turba de idólatras que vienen a entregar en manos de frailes holgazanes, el fruto de sus trabajos anuales para enriquecerlos, mientras ellos, sus hijos y sus mujeres no tienen un vestido, ni una cama. ¡Y a esto han osado llamar religión los españoles nuestros padres!!!

En 27 de junio llegamos Shippingport, pueblo pequeño distante una milla de Louis Ville. En este punto tomamos coches que estaban prontos, y nos condujeron a Louis Ville. Durante el curso de nuestra navegación hemos vivido en una sociedad agradable. Algunas señoras tocaban el clave, otras la guitarra, y cantaban con mucha gracia y sin hacerse de rogar. Había te o café por la mañana, almuerzo a las nueve, *lonch* a las once, al mediodía, comida a las cuatro, y té o cena por la noche. De esta manera había muy corto intervalo de una comida a otra, además de otros intermedios de cerveza, champaña, sidra, etc., etc. En estos viajes se encuentran en un mismo buque, según la observación de M. Farel, caballeros, tratantes, labradores, diputados, capitanes, generales y jueces todos sentados alrededor de una misma mesa, en una simplicidad verdaderamente republicana. No se advierten groserías en el manejo de la más humilde persona de las que están en la mesa; y en realidad es notable la urbanidad de su trato, esto es, comparado con las personas de la misma clase en Francia o Inglaterra. Lo cierto es que un menestral encontrándose asimismo en este país con cierta importancia en la escala social, hace esfuerzos para manifestarse digno de estar en la misma sociedad y mesa con personas ricas, y de los primeros rangos. Es cierto que las clases altas pierden alguna parte de su finura por su contacto continuo con este pueblo menos civilizado, pero éste gana notablemente al mismo tiempo. Todos están bien vestidos y no hay en los Estados Unidos gente andrajosa.

Louis Ville está situado sobre la orilla izquierda del Ohio, en el Estado de Kentucky. El lado opuesto pertenece al de Indiana. Tendrá la ciudad cerca de doce mil habitantes, y aumenta considerablemente, aunque no en la progresión que Cincinati y Nueva Orleans. Su calle principal de N. a S. tendrá cerca de una milla, y sólo tiene cuatro calles en esta dirección. Es el depósito de muchos efectos extranjeros que se importan en el interior por aquella ciudad; también sirve de conducto para exportar harinas de trigo y maíz, cebada y otros granos.

Desde Louis Ville escribí a Mr. M. Clure, pidiéndole razón de un joven indígena que confié a su cuidado cuando estuvo en México, y yo era gobernador del Estado en 1828. Mr. M. Clure era el encargado de este establecimiento de educación que fundó M. Owen en New Harmon, Estado de Indiana, a cosa de treinta leguas de Louis Vile. Hablaré del establecimiento de Mr. M. Clure, y del motivo que tuve para entregarle el muchacho a quien di el nombre de Toribio Zavala.

M. Owen, tan conocido en el orbe literario por su vasta instrucción, su elocuencia y la singularidad de sus doctrinas, formó el proyecto de plantar en los Estados Unidos su sistema de enseñanza bajo la dirección de Mr. M. Clure. Era una escuela práctica de artes, oficios y primeras letras, cuyo objeto debía ser ocupar a los muchachos en trabajos que les diese lo suficiente para mantenerse. M. Poinsett, ministro de los Estados Unidos en México, me hizo conocer a los señores Owen y M. Clure, cuando yo era gobernador del Estado de México y confieso que me aficioné al proyecto de aquellos dos filósofos. Después veremos cómo se disolvió su establecimiento.

En el mismo año me presentaron un niño indígena del pueblo de Zempoala de México, de edad poco más o menos de ocho años, quien, según me dijo el maestro de escuela que le condujo a mi casa, era un huérfano que había recogido y cultivado su prodigiosa memoria. Le examinó a presencia de algunas personas haciendo varias cuestiones de geografía, de astronomía, de ortología, prosodia y gramática, de religión y moral, a todas las que el muchacho contestaba con desembarazo y facilidad. Le había dado el nombre de Toribio *Pauper* por su pobreza y yo le sustituí el de mi casa. Considerando que este joven podría hacer mejor carrera en el establecimiento de Mr. M. Clure, se lo entregué pagándole únicamente gastos del viaje hasta New Harmony. Supe posteriormente que el establecimiento se disolvió y que mi zempoalteca había buscado ya un modo de vivir en el país.

El Poder Ejecutivo reside en el Estado de Indiana en un gobernador nombrado por el pueblo cada tres años y que puede ser reelecto una vez. El vicegobernador es electo al mismo tiempo; preside el Senado y ejerce las funciones de gobernador en su falta.

Hay un Senado y una Cámara de representantes. Los miembros del primero son nombrados cada tres años; los de la segunda cada año. El número de diputados no puede ser menor que treinta y seis ni mayor que de ciento. Este arreglo se hace sobre una base del número de varones de vintiún años entre los blancos. El de senadores en la misma proporción no puede bajar de un tercio ni subir de una mitad sobre el número de los representantes.

Estos y una tercera parte de los miembros del Senado son nombrados anualmente el primer lunes del mes de agosto. El gobernador y el vicegobernador son elegidos cada tres años en el mismo día.

El Congreso se reúne en *Indianápolis* el primer lunes de diciembre.

El derecho de sufragios es concedido a todo ciudadano de veintiún años de edad para arriba que haya residido un año en el Estado.

El Poder Judicial lo administra una Suprema Corte de Justicia y Cortes de Circuito. La Corte Suprema consiste en tres jueces, y las de Circuito en un juez presidente y dos asociados. Todos los jueces son por el término de siete años. El gobernador nombra los de la Suprema Corte con el consentimiento del Senado. Los presidentes de las Cortes de Circuito son nombrados por la Cámara de Diputados y los asociados por el pueblo.

En Louis Ville hay un pequeño teatro en el que se encuentra la particularidad de tener una entrada y lugares separados para las mujeres que no son recibidas en la sociedad. Cuando pasé por esta ciudad, representaba la célebre actriz Mrs. Drake, una de las mejores cómicas de los Estados Unidos y que puede hacer papel en los teatros de Europa.

Además de Louis Vile hay dos ciudades importantes en el Estado de Kentucky, y son Lexiton y Frankfort. Esta segunda es la capital del Estado. Ambas son muy hermosas poblaciones, según me han asegurado algunas personas.

El Estado de Kentucky era el terreno predilecto de varias tribus de indios que le habían destinado para la caza. Se dice que en los remotos bosques en que actualmente se hallan más allá del Misuri, suspiran por sus antiguas tierras y los sepulcros de sus padres, y tienen cánticos análogos a su emigración. En efecto, pocos Estados ofrecen el aspecto de abundancia y fertilidad que el de Kentucky. Sus hermosos bosques, cubiertos de árboles robustos, encinos, azucareros, sicomoros, cedros, abetos, castaños, etc., etc., deleitan la vista del viajero. Sus producciones, trigo, tabaco, maíz, cebada y otras semillas apreciables. Sus habitantes son notables por la altura y corpulencia, al mismo tiempo que la hermosura y regularidad de sus proporciones.

Kentucky se separó del Estado de Virginia, de que era parte, en 1790, y la constitución que entonces formó, duró hasta 1799, reemplazándola por la que ahora está en vigor. Su poder legislativo existe en dos Cámaras de representantes y del Senado. Los diputados a la primera son nombrados anualmente, y en cada cuatro años se arregla en los diversos condados al número de electores que le corresponden. Su número actual es el de ciento, del cual no puede pasar como ni bajar de cincuenta y ocho. Los senadores son elegidos cada año, renovándose por cuartas partes. Su número actual es de treinta y ocho, el *maximum,* y de veinticuatro, el *minimum.*

El Poder Ejecutivo está en manos de un gobernador elegido por cuatro años, quien no puede ser reelecto sino pasados siete años. Un vicegobernador es elegido al mismo tiempo, y sus funciones son presidir el Senado y suplir las faltas del gobernador.

Los diputados y una cuarta parte de los senadores son nombrados anualmente por el pueblo, el primer lunes de agosto. El gobernador y vicegobernador son nombrados igualmente por el pueblo el mismo día cada cuatro años, comenzando a ejercer sus oficios el cuarto martes del mismo mes. La votación está abierta por tres días y los votos son dados *viva voce,* y no por cédulas. Las sesiones se abren en Frankfort anualmente el primer lunes de diciembre.

La Constitución concede el derecho de sufragio a todos los ciudadanos varones (a excepción de la gente de color) que han cumplido veintiún años y han residido en el Estado dos años.

El Poder Judicial es administrado por una Suprema Corte de Justicia, llamada Corte de Apelaciones, y en otros tribunales o juzgados inferiores que la asamblea legislativa establece. Los jueces y justicias de paz duran el tiempo que se porten bien.

Por el lado del sudoeste se hallan los Estados de Indiana, Tilines y territorio de Misuri. El río Misisipí, que corre hacia aquellos Estados, tiene en sus márgenes ciudades que hacen comercio con nuestro territorio de Nuevo México, y desde San Luis salen caravanas numerosas que van hasta Santa Fé y las Californias. Antes de muchos años aquellas vastas comarcas serán pobladas por extranjeros que buscan mejores climas y tierras baldías para formar sus establecimientos, y entonces se verá descender por el Río Bravo del Norte, viajeros que habrán entrado por el de San Lorenzo, por Nueva York o el Misisipí haciendo por el interior del país un curso de seis a ocho mil millas. Mientras los Estados del Sur de la República Mexicana se ocupen de guerras civiles y querellas domésticas, los del Norte, dedicados al comercio, a la agricultura y a la navegación, darán ejemplos de moralidad y de trabajos útiles a sus hermanos desidentes, que pelearán por la dominación y la supremacía.

El día 27 de junio continuamos nuestro viaje embarcándonos para Cincinati en un buque de vapor *B. Franklin* más pequeño; pero muy cómodo.

Pagamos cinco pesos por persona y navegamos treinta horas. Llegamos a Cincinati cuando se celebraba la venida del general Jackson, Presidente de los Estados Unidos. Es fácil imaginarse que no había batallones en línea, ni artillería ni gente armada, ni tampoco curas, obispos o canónigos que venían en ceremonia a recibir al jefe del Gobierno de la Unión. Nada de esto había. Pero sí se veía un concurso numeroso de todo el pueblo que corría a las márgenes del río a recibir y ver a su primer conciudadano; al respetable anciano que había libertado a la Luisiana, y dado las Floridas a los Estados Unidos, y que hoy regía los destinos del país con prudencia, tino y pureza de intenciones. Había músicas, banderas, cortinas, vítores y gritos de alegría. Todo era natural, todo espontáneo: más bien parecía a las fiestas de nuestros pueblos y ciudades cuando celebran algún santo, que a esas ceremonias formuladas en los días de besamanos en que no se advierte en los semblantes ningún vestigio de verdadero interés, de un sentimiento de simpatía. Jackson fue recibido con entusiasmo, especialmente por los obreros, los labradores y artesanos.

Al día siguiente pasamos el general Mejía y yo a visitar al patriarca Presidente. Yo tenía para él una carta de recomendación de M. Butler, encargado de negocios de los Estados Unidos cerca de nuestro gobierno, y el señor Mejía le conocía desde que fue empleado cerca del gabinete de Washington como secretario de la legación mexicana. El respetable anciano estaba alojado en una casa medianamente amueblada, sentado en un sillón y rodeado de veinticinco a treinta personas que por su traje parecían labradores y artesanos, haciéndole la más sencilla corte del mundo. Parecía uno de aquellos antiguos héroes de Homero que después de haber hecho grandes acciones en la guerra, se retiraban a vivir entre sus conciudadanos, a quienes gobernaban como hijos. El general nos recibió cordialmente: nos preguntó por su amigo el general *Guerrero;* lamentó su suerte, y no dudaba que la causa del pueblo que defendía tendría un triunfo completo.

Cincinati es una población de veinticinco mil habitantes, situada sobre las márgenes del Río Ohio, en el Estado del mismo nombre. No está como Nueva Orleans amenazada por las aguas del río; su posición elevada la garantiza aun de esos aluviones periódicos que causan tantos desastres en las poblaciones menos altas. Cincinati tenía antes de la introducción de buques de vapor sobre el Misisipí, hace veinte años, cuando mucho seis mil habitantes y diez años antes diez o doce casas; su aumento rápido es debido a la facilidad de sus comunicaciones, a la feracidad de su suelo y al número de emigración que viene de Europa, y aun de los Estados del Este. Muchos emigrados colonos que se establecían en Masachussets, Vermont, Maine y generalmente en la Nueva Inglaterra, después de haber desmontado, cultivado y fabricado habitaciones y formado establecimientos valiosos, ponían en venta sus bienes muebles e inmuebles, cansados, como ellos dicen, de oír después de muchos años el ladrido del perro del vecino y la campaña del lugar; y metiéndose en un cerro con toda su familia venían y vienen a levantar nuevos establecimientos en los Estados del Oeste. Unos van a Arkansas, otros a Misuri, Ohio, Indiana, Tilines, en fin muchos en el día a Texas, Nuevo México y hasta Chihuahua. En los lugares que dejan son reemplazados por nuevos emigrados de Europa. De esta manera la América del Norte y sucesivamente la República Mexicana se enriquecen con las artes, industria y elementos de civilización europea, mientras esta parte del antiguo mundo se descarga de una parte de su población que no puede mantener su terreno, porque la aristocracia necesita jardines, bosques, praderías y un terreno grande para sacar rentas cuantiosas. En otros puntos, como en Suiza y Wurtemberg, porque no hay tierra bastante para la población.

Cincinati está rodeada de hermosas colinas pobladas de árboles que en el estío ofrecen las vistas más pintorescas. El aspecto de la ciudad desde el río, y el del río y riberas fronterizas desde la elevada colina en que está la ciudad, son igualmente agradables y variados. Hay dieciocho templos, de los cuales dos son episcopales, una catedral católica romana, una sinagoga, una de unitarios, otra de universalistas, otra de luteranos, de cuaqueros reformados, y las otras son de presbiterianos, metodistas y anabaptistas. Muchas casas son bellas, siendo el primer piso de granito y de mármol blanco y el resto de ladrillo. Generalmente, son pequeñas, comparadas con nuestras casas de México, pero tienen todas las comodidades posibles. Las calles no son tan aseadas como debía esperarse en una ciudad fundada sobre la pendiente de una colina a la orilla de un río caudaloso. La falta de cañerías subterráneas y de cloacas, hace que se acumulen materias inmundas y se formen lodazales que los puercos aumentan; pues andan sueltos muchos en las calles. Los víveres son sumamente baratos, como puede verse por la lista que formó M. Bullock, a quien hemos conocido en México. Tres reales y medio un pavo, cuatro reales un puerco asado, tres cuartillas la libra de carne, y una cuartilla la de cerdo. En esta proporción están los demás artículos.

En Cincinati hay manufacturas de algodón y de lana; las hay también de plomo que traen en abundancia del Estado Tilines. Pero los principios de su admirable progreso social y de población son su fecundidad, la facilidad de sus comunicaciones con los otros Estados, y la forma de gobierno que facilita al hombre desenvolver todas sus facultades intelectuales y materiales. ¿Qué sería Cincinati sin el artículo que permite el libre ejercicio de todos los cultos?

Mrs. Trollope, hablando de esta prodigiosa multiplicación y aumento de habitantes, de riqueza y prosperidad de Cincinati, dice que no puede menos de ser así en un país en donde la ociosidad no tiene acogida, y en donde el que no trabaja no come. "Durante mi mansión en esta ciudad, dice esta señora, o en sus cercanías, que fue cerca de dos años, jamás vi un limosnero, ni tampoco un hombre, que aun cuando tuviese bastante fortuna, dejara de trabajar activamente para aumentarla. Semejantes a las abejas se afanan sin cesar en busca de esa miel de *hybla*, que se llama moneda. Ni las bellas artes, ni las ciencias, ni los atractivos de los placeres pueden separarlos de sus trabajos. Esta uniformidad de propósito, favorecido con el espíritu de empresa, junto a la agudeza y *falta de probidad* cuando media el interés, puede conseguir el objeto meditado con ventajas.

"Yo he leído mucho, continúa, acerca *de las pocas y sencillas necesidades del hombre,* y hasta ahora había yo dado cierta indulgente aquiescencia a los que sientan que cada nueva necesidad es un enemigo nuevo. Los que se entregan a raciocinios de esta naturaleza en sus cómodas alcobas de Londres o París, conocen poco de la materia. Si fueran los alimentos que nutren al hombre, todo lo que pudiera necesitar, le bastarían las facultades de un cerdo. Pero si analizamos una hora de placer, encontraremos que es producido por sensaciones agradables, ocasionadas por mil impresiones delicadas en otros tantos nervios. Cuando estos nervios están en inacción por no haber sido jamás tocados, los objetos exteriores son menos importantes, porque se les percibe menos. Pero cuando toda la máquina del cuerpo humano está en plena actividad, cuando cada sentido viene a dar al cerebro el testimonio de sus impresiones de placer o dolor, entonces cada objeto que se presenta a nuestros sentidos viene a ser una causa de miseria o de felicidad. Que las personas así organizadas, se guarden bien de viajar por los Estados Unidos; o en el caso de hacerlo, que no permanezcan más tiempo que el necesario para depositar en la memoria las imágenes que por la fuerza de los contrastes, puedan hacérselos agradables en lo venidero".

"Guarda e passa (e poi) ragioniam di bor".

Continúa la viajera haciendo una descripción poco ventajosa de las maneras y urbanidad de los habitantes de los Estados del Oeste, con tanta acrimonia que parece haberse propuesto poner en ridículo los industriosos colonos y sus hermosas hijas, y hacer una pintura melancólica de todo el país, con el objeto de desalentar a sus paisanos y demás europeos a emigrar a aquellas comarcas. Pero ¿habrá justicia en comparar Londres con Cincinati, Liverpool con Nueva Orleans, Birmingham con Pitsburgo, en suma la Inglaterra con los Estados Unidos? Lo más raro es que para medir la civilización de Cincinati, hable de las sociedades de Londres y París, y no es extraño que así encuentre mezquina la catedral católica, comparada con *Notre Dame* de

París: y la iglesia protestante, comparada con San Pablo de Londres.

No hay duda en que, generalmente hablando, la población de los Estados Unidos es egoísta, incomunicativa y desconfiada. Tiene, además, cierta aspereza en su trato, que hace desagradable su sociedad cuando no se han hecho relaciones en el país. Muchas veces me ha sucedido caminar en un mismo coche, en un mismo buque con americanos, sin hablar una sola palabra durante el viaje. Personas de negocios, que han dedicado toda su vida a mejorar su suerte con el trabajo, acostumbradas a no ver en todas las transacciones de la vida humana, más que cambios de productos por productos, o por dinero, se puede decir que no dan ningún paso ni se proponen otro objeto que los adelantos pecuniarios. Un hombre a quien no conocen se abstienen de buscar su comunicación, y aun la evitan, a no ser que con ojo penetrante no perciban que pueden sacar de su trato alguna ventaja, o que a lo menos no les sea de carga en algún evento. En cambio de esto se puede asegurar que no hay pueblo más moral que el de los Estados Unidos del Norte. La aplicación constante al trabajo hace a los hombres virtuosos o independientes; pero al mismo tiempo orgullosos y desconfiados. Un zapatero, un sastre, un herrero que se establece en una de esas poblaciones nuevas, y con un capital de veinticinco pesos, alquila un cuarto de madera, y compra los primeros materiales de su obrador, al cabo de diez años de trabajo y economía rigurosa, ya tiene una casa, un jardín, y su taller bien montado. Semejante hombre (y de éstos hay millares en los Estados Unidos), teme que un holgazán venga a estafarle los productos de su industria, o que un hombre desmoralizado venga a seducirle su hija o su mujer, y de consiguiente se abstiene de entrar en comunicación íntima con ninguna persona que no le sea perfectamente conocida.

Ya se podrá conjeturar que esta precaución excesiva conduce naturalmente al extremo de la incivilización, y en efecto, el viajero que llega a aquel país sin conexiones, vive aislado en medio del género humano. ¡Qué diferencia entre esta y la población mexicana! Nosotros somos comunicativos por esencia; parece que somos impelidos a entrar en relaciones con todos los que se nos acercan, de cualquiera clase y condición que sean. Nuestros padres los españoles no nos transmitieron ese carácter duro y altanero que nos hicieron sentir tan fuertemente en su dominación. Yo no sé si en nuestra amabilidad extremada hay un poco de servilismo, o de hábito de obediencia pasiva. Me lo hace sospechar el que no siempre son sinceros nuestros obsequios ni nuestros cumplimientos, y solemos decir que *manos besa uno que quisiera verlas quemadas*.

"Yo visité una casa, dice Mrs. Trollope, que me llamó la atención por su situación solitaria y agreste, y me interesó por la dependencia de la familia sobre sus mismos recursos. Era un punto cultivado entre el bosque.

La casa estaba construida sobre una colina elevada y tan pendiente que se necesitaba de una escalera alta para subir a la puerta fronteriza, mientras que la posterior daba a un patio grande a su nivel. Al pie de esta repentina eminencia cae un caño de agua hermosa que recibe un estanque formado al frente de la habitación. A un lado había un terreno cubierto de maíz y al otro un corral para cerdos, gallinas, vacas, etc. Había también cerca de la casa un pequeño huerto sembrado de papas, algunos manzanos y árboles de duraznos. La casa era de troncos de árboles, y consistía en dos piezas además de la cocinita. Las dos piezas estaban bien amuebladas, con buenas camas, sillas, roperos, etc. La mujer del paisano y una joven que parecía su hermana, estaban hilando, y tres muchachos traveseando fuera. La mujer me dijo que ellas hilaban y telaban todo lo que se necesitaba de algodón y lana en la casa, y tejían las medias; el marido, aunque no era zapatero de profesión, hacía los zapatos. En su casa se elaboraba el jabón, las velas y aun el azúcar que sacan del árbol de azúcar llamado *mapple tree,* que hay en aquellos bosques. Para lo único que necesitamos dinero, decía, *es para el té, café y aguardiente, y nos proveemos con facilidad mandando cada semana una barrica de manteca de leche y unas gallinas al mercado.* No usaban trigo, y del maíz que recogían de su siembra hacían su pan y varios géneros de pasteles, sirviéndole también para sus animales durante el invierno. Las mujeres no parecían sanas, y decían que habían tenido calenturas intermitentes; pero que estaban mejor. La madre parecía satisfecha y orgullosa de su estado independiente; aunque decía en un acento sombrío: 'Es muy extraño para nosotros ver gentes, y mi mayor placer es la esperanza de ver salir y ponerse el sol cien veces, sin ver otro ser humano que los de la familia'".

Creo que merece la atención de los lectores esta minuciosa descripción, porque, como esta familia, hay muchísimas en los bosques y florestas de Indiana, Tennessee, Ohio, Tilines, Misuri y otros Estados. No faltan tampoco en nuestra República Mexicana, aunque generalmente son indios pobres que no tienen más habitación que una choza de paja, por cama el suelo y un *petate* o estera, por alimento tortilla, sal y chile, y por vestido un pedazo de trapo viejo alrededor del cuerpo. ¡Qué diferencia!

Yo opino con Mrs. Trollope que esta manera de existir es un poco salvaje y fuera de lo natural. Esa soledad, ese aislamiento del resto de los hombres, ese eterno silencio de los bosques en que viven, no parecen convenir a los nobles atributos del hombre. No oyen nunca el sonido de la campana que reúne a los mortales en los lugares destinados a la oración, en donde los hombres encuentran las congratulaciones de sus hermanos: no hay un cementerio consagrado que reciba sus restos cuando mueran: no vienen los cánticos de la religión a respirar su dulce aliento en su último adiós, sobre su sepultura; el marido, el padre o el hijo abren con sus manos la hoya que debe cubrirlos para siempre junto a un árbol, cercano a la habitación: ellos mismos entierran el cadáver, y el ruido que hace el viento moviendo las ramas de los árboles, es su único *requiem.*

A nuestra llegada a Cincinati se hablaba mucho en los papeles públicos y en las sociedades de la célebre filósofa Miss Wright, cuya vehemente elocuencia y cuyas doctrinas seductoras en una persona de su sexo, enseñadas en asambleas a donde concurrían todos cuantos podían caber en los salones y teatros en que hacía sus lecturas, llamó la atención de los americanos. Esta señorita había recibido en Inglaterra una educación distinguida y hecho brillar su talento en muchas concurrencias notables. Le ocurrió la extravagante idea de hacerse cabeza de sexta, y como no encontraba en su sistema ninguna revelación, no siguió el rumbo de las Santas Teresa y Agreda, sí se lanzó en las doctrinas filosóficas de Rousseau y de Owen. Predicaba la absoluta igualdad de clases y condiciones, el escepticismo religioso, el divorcio voluntario y otras cosas semejantes. Si hubiese quien dudare del espíritu de nuestra tolerancia en los Estados Unidos del Norte, los establecimientos de M. Owen y las lecturas de Mrs. Wright bastarían para convencer al menos dispuesto a creerlo. Esta apóstol del filosofismo era escuchada por todas las clases de la sociedad en todas las ciudades en que tuvo por conveniente presentarse al público. Salió de los Estados Unidos para Inglaterra en 1829, sin haber hecho prosílitos.

Entre las cosas notables de la sociedad doméstica en los Estados Unidos, especialmente en los internos, debe enumerarse la falsa delicadeza que degenera en hipocresía en la conversación. Una persona que en la mesa pidiere una *pierna de pollo* ofendería los *castos y virtuosos* oídos de las señoras, y el que cometiese la imprudencia de proferir las palabras profanas de camisa de mujer, *shift,* guardapiés, *petticoat,* corsé, *corset,* sería muy mal considerado en la sociedad. Estos escrúpulos me hacían recordar los de nuestras monjas que se ven embarazadas al pronunciar ciertas palabras. Es imposible, por ejemplo, persuadir a una americana que salga a la calle cuando está embarazada, a menos que sea de noche.

No será desagradable al lector la historia del memorable desafío literario-filosófico-religioso, hecho por M. Owen en Cincinati, el año anterior a mi llegada a esta ciudad, cuyo objeto era provocar a combate en discusión a todos los que quisiesen, asentando como conclusión, *que no había ninguna religión verdadera,* y que todas estaban formadas sobre la impostura y el engaño. Hacía más de un año que M. Owen había circulado su desafío por todas partes. Le había aceptado públicamente y con la misma solemnidad el padre Alejandro Cambpell, presbiteriano. El día señalado era el segundo lunes de mayo de 1829, y al efecto se preparó una iglesia de metodistas para la ruidosa discusión. El edificio estaba lleno de gentes de uno y otro sexo separados en los dos lados. Ambos contendientes hablaron con elocuencia, con decoro, con respeto recíproco y conveniente. Después de la discusión, el padre Cambpell suplicó al auditorio que se sentase. Luego le dirigió la palabra y dijo: "Los que profesan la religión cristiana de cualquiera secta que sean, pónganse en pie". Se levantaron las nueve décimas partes; y con esto declaró el triunfo por su causa. M. Owen protestó diciendo que muchas personas no manifestaban su opinión porque temían que las gentes crédulas no les comprarían después sus efectos, y les cerrasen su comercio. Así terminó esta célebre discusión, que es otra prueba de la tolerancia filosófica de los Estados Unidos en uno de los lugares menos cilivilizados de aquella república.

Este es el mismo M. Owen, fundador de la escuela de *independencia mental* de New Harmony. Compró el establecimiento y las tierras de unos cófrades que, bajo la dirección de M. Rapp, habían levantado edificios y cultivado más de diez mil acres de tierras a las orillas del río Wabash, uno de los tributarios del Ohio. M. Robert Owen empleó más de doscientos mil pesos en esta empresa.

Al principio de su establecimiento en 1824 excitó un grande interés en los Estados Unidos. Muchas personas distinguidas en todas las clases de la sociedad escribieron a la dirección pidiendo informes acerca de las reglas, método, principios y objetos del fundador, manifestando deseo de incorporarse a su sociedad. Un año después partió para Europa M. Owen, dejando encargado el colegio a sus dos hijos y a Mr. M. Clure.

En 1826 tenía la sociedad cerca de mil miembros que vivían bajo un pie de perfecta igualdad y debían comer en una misma mesa. Un viajero respetable dice, que M. Owen le manifestó todo el establecimiento y refiere cosas dignas de conocerse. Por la noche se daba concierto en un gran salón en que se hallaban todos los miembros del establecimiento. La música era perfectamente bien ejecutada. En los intermedios se declamaba alguna pieza de William Shakespeare, u otro poeta, luego había bailes. En el día se ejercitaban unos en la esgrima, otros en hacer zapatos, sillas; otros en herrería, sastrería y demás oficios mecánicos. La mayor parte de las jóvenes se ejercitaban en hacer sombreros de paja.

En la mañana del domingo todos los miembros se reunieron y M. Owen, sacerdote de esta iglesia filosófica, pronunció un discurso acerca de las ventajas de la sociedad. En las visitas que hizo a las señoras encontró una que estaba tocando el piano con mucha perfección. A poco rato entró uno y le dijo que a ella tocaba ordeñar las vacas para la comunidad.

Las doctrinas peculiares de la sociedad eran: que es un absurdo prometer amor conyugal durante la vida; que los hijos no deben ser impedimento para la separación, y que debían pertenecer a la comunidad desde que tuvieron dos años: que la sociedad no profesaba ninguna religión, pudiendo cada miembro conservar su creencia; que todos eran iguales, etc. M. Owen estaba tan infatuado en su sistema que pensaba seriamente poderle establecer en todo el globo. Me acuerdo haber leído la propuesta que hizo a M. Poinsett, llamándole a ser regenerador del Nuevo Mundo sobre aquellos principios, mientras él (M. Owen) volvía a Europa a ocuparse de convertir el Antiguo, para cortar de *raíz todo crimen, abolir todos los castigos, uniformar las necesidades y los deseos, y evitar así toda disensión*. Estaba tan profundamente convencido de su sistema que jamás le ocurría que pudiese uno dudarlo.

Ya en 1827 se había introducido el descontento en la comunidad. Muchas personas, especialmente mujeres, no se avenían con la absoluta igualdad y evitaban juntarse con los *tatterdemalions* o andrajosos. El mayor cargo que hacían a M. Owen era el de haber recibido sin distinción en aquella sociedad, desde el principio, gentes de todas clases, sin examinar su carácter, su género de vida, educación anterior, calidades, etc., resultando por consiguiente una mezcla tan *heterogénea que no era posible amalgamar*. Voy a extractar algunos párrafos de la célebre declaración de independencia política, o como él llamaba *independencia mental*, hecha por M. Owen en 4 de junio de 1826.

"Mis amigos, tenemos a nuestra presencia un objeto noble que debe ser conquistado por uno u otro partido en éste o en otro país. Trátase nada menos que de la destrucción de la triple causa que priva al hombre de su libertad mental, le compele a cometer el crimen y a sufrir todas las miserias que el mismo crimen trae consigo. Permitidme ahora que os pregunte ¿si os halláis dispuestos a imitar el ejemplo de vuestros antepasados y queréis correr los riesgos a que ellos se expusieron? ¿Estáis dispuestos a completar una revolución mental tan superior en sus beneficios y resultados a la primera revolución de este país, cuando los poderes mentales del hombre ceden a sus poderes físicos?

"Si os halláis dispuestos, yo con la mayor satisfacción me juntaré a vosotros en esta ardua empresa; la última y la más atrevida que hayan osado consumar los mortales en su estado irracional en que se encontraban.

"Pero, amigos míos, conociendo como conozco la inconmensurable magnitud de beneficios que esta revolución mental debe traer y asegurar permanentemente para la humana naturaleza por las futuras edades, yo juzgo la continuación de la permanencia por un poco más de tiempo aquí de algunos individuos, como cosa de poca consideración en comparación con el objeto que nos proponemos; y por esto como no puedo conocer la presente disposición de vuestras almas y como por otra parte la prolongación de mi vida en la edad en que me hallo es muy incierta, he determinado, con calma y deliberación sobre esta portentosa y feliz ocasión romper completamente los restos de la cadena mental, que por tantos años ha desgraciadamente afligido nuestra naturaleza, y que por esta vez va a quedar en plena libertad el entendimiento humano.

"Como fruto de una experiencia de cuarenta años, debida a una muy peculiar combinación de circunstancias todas variadas, extendidas y singulares, que quizá no se han reunido en ningún otro hombre, durante el cual período mi entendimiento se ha ocupado continuamente en investigar la causa de cada miseria humana, cuyo conocimiento me ha venido de su verdadero origen, yo os declaro y al mundo entero que el hombre hasta este momento ha sido en todas las partes del globo un esclavo de una trinidad la más monstruosa que haya podido combinarse para causar males a las facultades físicas y mentales de la raza humana.

"Os denuncio como tal: 1° La propiedad individual o privada. 2° Los absurdos e irracionales sistemas de religión. 3° El matrimonio fundado corno una propiedad individual combinado con uno de estos irracionales sistemas de religión.

"Es muy difícil decir cuál de estas grandes fuentes de todo crimen debe ser colocada en primero o último lugar, porque están tan íntimamente conexionadas y consagradas juntas por el tiempo que no se pueden separar sin ser destruidas. Cada una de ellas sostiene a las otras dos. Esta formidable trinidad compuesta de ignorancia, superstición e hipocresía es el solo demonio o diablo que haya existido jamás y el tormento eterno de la raza humana. Ella está calculada en todas sus consecuencias para producir la más espantosa miseria de que sea la naturaleza susceptible en el alma y en el cuerpo. La división de propiedad entre los individuos ha preparado las semillas, cultivado el aumento y llevado hasta la madurez todos los males de la pobreza y de la riqueza que existen en un pueblo al mismo tiempo: el industrioso experimenta privaciones y el ocioso se ve cargado con riquezas que no merece.

"La religión o superstición, que es lo mismo, pues todas las religiones son supersticiosas, teniendo por objeto destruir el juicio y racionalizar todas facultades mentales del hombre y hacerle el más abyecto esclavo por medio de entidades imaginarias creadas solamente por imaginaciones desordenadas. La superstición le obliga a creer o decir que cree que existe un Ser supremo que posee todo poder, infinita bondad e infinita sabiduría: que ha podido hacer y que ha hecho todas las cosas; que los males y las miserias abundan por todas partes; y que este Ser que hace y produce todas las cosas no es el autor directo ni indirecto del mal y de la miseria. Tal es el fundamento en que todos los misterios de la superstición están levantados en todo el mundo. Su inconsistencia e inconcebible locura ha sido tal que ha ocasionado continuas guerras y matanzas en todo el mundo, formado divisiones privadas y conducido a todos los males imaginables; siendo probable que las supersticiones han causado más de un tercio de los crímenes y desgracias de la raza humana.

"Las formas y ceremonias del matrimonio, en la manera con que hasta hoy se han celebrado y después mantenido, demuestran que fueron inventadas e introducidas entre el pueblo en el mismo periodo que la propiedad fue dividida entre unos pocos jefes viniendo la superstición en su apoyo, siendo ésta la única divisa que pudieron introducir para autorizarse a retener su división de los despojos públicos y crear entre si mismos una aristocracia de riqueza, de poder y de doctrina.

"Como fruto de la experiencia de una vida consagrada a la investigación de estos importantes objetos, os declaro sin ningún temor por una convicción tan profunda y tan íntima como puede existir en el entendimiento humano, que esté compuesto de ignorancia y fraude es la única y verdadera causa de todo crimen y de todas las miserias que emanan del crimen y que están repartidas en la sociedad humana.

"Por cuarenta años he dedicado mi corazón y mi alma, día por día sin intermisión, en preparar los medios y combinar las circunstancias que me hicieran capaz de dar un soplo de muerte a la tiranía y al despotismo que por innumerables años han tenido al entendimiento humano ligado con cadenas y grillos de misteriosas formas, que ningún mortal se ha atrevido a emprender libertar a los desgraciados prisioneros. Aún no se había llenado el tiempo para el cumplimiento de este gran suceso hasta esta misma hora; y tal ha sido el extraordinario curso de los acontecimientos que la declaración de independencia política en 1776 ha producido este resultado, a saber: la declaración de la independencia mental en 1826, medio siglo después de la primera. Regocijaos conmigo, amigos míos, porque vuestra independencia mental está ahora tan asegurada como vuestra independencia política.

"En las circunstancias en que se ha realizado esta revolución mental, ningún poder humano puede destruir ni hacer nugatorio lo que ahora ha sido hecho. Esta verdad ha pasado de mí más allá de la posibilidad de una revocación, y ha sido ya recibida en vuestras almas: dentro de poco será escuchada en toda la América, y de ésta pasará al Norte y al Sur, al Este y al Occidente tan lejos como la palabra del hombre sea escuchada; y con la misma rapidez con que circula, la naturaleza humana le dará el acogimiento y la aprobación universal. Regocijaos, pues, otra vez conmigo, amigos, porque esta luz está ahora colocada encima de la montaña; desde aquí ella se aumentará diariamente más y más hasta que sea vista, sentida y entendida por todas las naciones de la Tierra.

"Para el cumplimiento de este grande objeto estamos preparando los medios, educando a vuestros hijos con industriosos y útiles hábitos; con naturales y de consiguiente racionales ideas y miras; con sinceridad en todos SUS procedimientos; y por último inspirándoles tiernos y afectuosos sentimientos recíprocos, la caridad, en toda la extensión de esta palabra, por todos sus semejantes.

"Por estos medios, uniendo vuestros intereses separados, abandonando el uso de la moneda en vuestras transacciones mercantiles, adoptando los cambios de los artículos de vuestra industria sobre la base de un trabajo por trabajo igual, proveyendo el que el sobrante de vuestras riquezas se distribuya entre los que no tienen para ponerlos en la posición de poder mejorar su suerte y adquirir las mismas ventajas, y por último absteniéndonos del uso de los licores espirituosos, promoveréis de una manera particular el objeto de todos los gobiernos sabios y de todos los hombres verdaderamente ilustrados".

Esta oración y su publicación en algunos periódicos fueron suficientes para acabar de disolver la sociedad. Lo mismo sucedió en Francia con los sansimonianos que predicaban las mismas doctrinas, aunque acompañadas de más aparato religioso.

CAPÍTULO IV

La primera impresión que recibe un mexicano que no ha salido de su país, o que ha estado mucho tiempo sin haberlo hecho, al llegar a cualquiera punto de los Estados Unidos, o de Inglaterra, es el ver a todas las clases del pueblo vestidas. Dicen que cuando el emperador Alejandro visitó Londres, en 1814, decía a los que le rodeaban, que no encontraba plebe en aquella capital. ¡Qué espectáculo tan agradable a la vista de un observador es el de una sociedad que anuncia por sus apariencias de decoro y decencia, la industria, las comodidades y aun la moralidad de un pueblo! Por el contrario, ¡cuán desagradable es el aspecto de la desnudez y falta de limpieza, y qué melancólica idea da una nación del estado de su civilización y de su moralidad cuando está habitada de un pueblo semejante! En una obra sobre España que publicó en París, un tal M. Faure, hace cuatro años, puso a la portada del libro la estampa de un estudiante, vestido de un manteo roto y otros andrajos, con un bordón en la mano, *pidiendo una limosna por el amor de Dios*. Esto sólo daba idea del objeto que más llamó la atención del viajero francés en la península pirenaica.

Si yo tratase de hacer una obra de lujo y con estampasa, desde luego, haría grabar hermosas láminas en que se representasen buques de vapor; obreros nivelando el terreno y colocando planchas de madera y hierro para formar caminos; praderas bañadas de arroyos; ciudades divididas por ríos navegables; poblaciones naciendo de la tierra y dedicándose a mejorarla luego; salones cubiertos de niños de ambos sexos aprendiendo a leer y escribir; labradores y artesanos con el arado o el instrumento en la mano y el periódico en la otra; seis mil templos de diversos cultos en que el hombre eleva al Creador sus votos, conforme se lo dicta el corazón; en suma la tranquilidad y la abundancia haciendo felices a quince millones de habitantes. Tal es la idea que tengo de los Estados Unidos del Norte y las impresiones que recibí desde Nueva Orleans a Cincinati.

La Constitución del Estado de Ohio fue formada en el pueblo de Chilicote en 1802. Hay dos cámaras, como en los otros. Los representantes son nombrados anualmente el segundo martes de octubre, y el número es correspondiente a la población blanca de varones desde la edad de veintiún años; pero nunca debe exceder de setenta y dos diputados, ni bajar de treinta y seis. Los senadores son elegidos cada dos años, en la misma forma, y en número proporcionado a una mitad de la otra Cámara.

Hay un gobernador que ejerce el Poder Ejecutivo, electo por el pueblo, cada dos años, el martes segundo de octubre. Comienza a desempeñar el primer lunes de diciembre siguiente.

La capital es Columbus, en donde se reúne la asamblea general del Estado el primer lunes de diciembre.

El derecho de sufragio es universal entre la clase blanca.

El Poder Judicial reside en la Suprema Corte de Justicia, en las Cortes de *Common pleas* de cada condado, y otras que el Poder Legislativo puede establecer, de cuando en cuando, para la expedición de la justicia. Los jueces son nombrados por votos secretos, cada siete años, en asamblea de ambas Cámaras. Hay jurados como en todos los otros Estados.

El día 20 de junio me embarqué en el steamboat o vapor *Magnolia* que salía para Wheeling. El día 3 de julio fue señalado para celebrar a bordo del buque el aniversario de la independencia de los Estados Unidos, porque cayendo en domingo el 4, que es el legítimo día, no podía celebrarse siendo éste consagrado por la religión para adorar al Creador, cada hombre según su culto. Quince o veinte personas que éramos en el buque no son ciertamente un número suficiente para dar una idea de lo que una gran nación, penetrada en aquel día solemne del noble sentimiento de su libertad, hace en tan augustas circunstancias. No hablaré pues en esta ocasión de lo que pasa en este día de general entusiasmo, en los Estados Unidos; y sólo he hecho recuerdo de esta circunstancia, así para manifestar que, aun en los más aislados y remotos lugares, los americanos del Norte celebran con religioso y patriótico regocijo el aniversario de la declaración de su independencia, como para hacer mérito del brindis que dije en aquel día, y fue el siguiente: "Los ciudadanos mexicanos hacen votos por la libertad en cualquiera parte en que se hallan. En este día solemne, consagrado a celebrar la de los Estados Unidos de Norteamérica, me atrevo a unir mis votos a los de hombres libres que hoy celebran el aniversario de su independencia; oíd mis deseos: 'que la providencia mantenga este pueblo en sus actuales instituciones por muchos siglos, y que México lo imite con suceso'. El señor Mejía habló en el mismo sentido, y los americanos unieron sus votos a los nuestros".

En la tarde de este día llegamos a Wheeling, pueblo fabricante de cristalería fina y ordinaria en el Estado de Virginia, en donde regularmente desembarcan los viajeros para internarse a los Estados de Virginia, Pensilvania, Maryland, Nueva York, etc. Aquí me separé del señor Mejía, que debía continuar para su destino en Washington, atravesando los aleghanys. Estas montañas, que hacen un gran papel en la climatología de los Estados Unidos, merecen mención particular en esta obra.

Desde Wheeling hay un camino que conduce a los Estados del Este y Norte, como he dicho, pasando por *Little Washington, Laurel Hill, Brownsville, Haggerstown y Baltimore.* Desde esta última ciudad había comenzado a hacerse un camino de hierro, que en 1830 tenía sólo trece millas, y ahora, 1834, ya llega a cerca de ciento.

Las montañas Aleghanys, que en algunas partes llaman Apalaches, están enteramente separadas del sistema general de los Andes. En ninguna parte se elevan más de seis mil ciento doce pies sobre el nivel del mar. Sus brazos principales se extienden del N. E. al S. O. desde el San Lorenzo hasta el Alabama y el Yarou. Su cadena oriental es conocida bajo el nombre de Montaña Azul, *Blue Ridge.* Estas montañas se extienden desde el Estado de Georgía, en dirección Nordeste, hasta el Estado de Nueva York. Poco más al Norte, a la derecha del río Hudson, hay un pequeño grupo de montañas que pertenecen a esta categoría, y llaman *Catts Hills;* que muestran los norteamericanos a los viajeros desde Albany, y en los steamboats como un prodigio de elevación. Más allá están las Montañas Verdes, *Green Mountains.* La cadena occidental son propiamente los aleghanys, y son conocidas en las cercanías de Wheeling con el nombre de *Cumberland Mountains;* atraviesan el Tennessee, la Virginia y una parte de Pensilvania. Más allá del río Susquehannah toma este brazo de la montaña una dirección más oriental, y se une a la cadena de las del Estado de Vermont.

Hay varios ríos pequeños en el camino de Wheeling, y un arroyo bastante profundo en la primera jornada, atraviesa treinta veces el camino, y necesita de otros tantos puentes entre los cuales hay algunos de mucho gusto y elegancia. Las vistas de las montañas son encantadoras por la variedad de árboles, fragancia de flores y yerbas aromáticas; quebradas, rocas, valles, paisajes, tierras cultivadas, casas de campo, ganados, vegas, etc.

Mientras el señor Mejía tomaba este camino yo continué mi viaje a Pitsburgo, la ciudad manufacturera de los Estados del Oeste. Pitsburgo está situada en la confluencia de los ríos Monongahela y Aleghany que forman el Ohio. El humo de carbón de piedra que cubre la ciudad noche y día la hace un poco triste. La gran cantidad de fábricas de porcelana y vidrios de todas clases, así como de toda especie de instrumentos de hierro, acero, plomo y otros metales de uso común, colocan a esta ciudad entre las más progresivas de los Estados Unidos. Su situación en el principio del Ohio y en un punto capaz de entrar en comunicación por agua con cualquiera puerto del mundo, después de una navegación río abajo de más de dos mil millas, ofrece la única ventaja de este género. En Pitsburgo se construyen buques para el Océano, y parece cosa de encanto el ver que a tanta distancia se hagan estas obras. Quizá llegará un día en que nuestro Río Grande del Norte vea bajar embarcaciones para conducir los productos de Chihuahua a Londres o Burdeos.

Cuando pasé por Pitsburgo se trabajaba un canal que comunicaba el Ohio con el lago Erié; pudiéndose de esta manera entrar por agua a Nueva York, y salir del mismo modo por el Misisipí, navegando el Hudson, el Canal de Clinton, el Lago Erié, el Canal del Ohio y los ríos hasta la Baliza. Esta obra ya estaba terminada en 1833. Otra más importante y que el general Bernardo calculó valdría veintidós millones de pesos, era otro canal que debería atravesar desde el Chesapeake, en donde está la Baliza de Baltimore, el Potomac, Río de Washington, y Pitsburgo atravesando los montes Aleghanys hasta el Río Ohio. Este canal debe tener trecientas cuarenta y una millas de largo, sesenta pies de ancho y seis de profundidad. La generalidad con que se han preferido los caminos de hierro ha hecho suspender por ahora esta grande empresa.

La ciudad de Pitsburgo está en el Estado de Pensilvania; tendrá de treinta a treinta y cinco mil habitantes. Hay alemanes, ingleses, franceses, irlandeses, escoceses, en suma de cuantos quieren trabajar y vivir del fruto de su industria. Si en estos Estados se adoptase una ley como la que últimamente ha propuesto el señor Tornel en México, prohibiendo el comercio de menudeo a los extranjeros, no se vería nunca tanto progreso, tanta prosperidad. ¿Qué aprendió el señor Tornel en su viaje y larga mansión en Baltimore y Filadelfia?

Salí de Pitsburgo en diligencia tomando el camino de Erié por las poblaciones Buttler, Mercer, Mead Ville, todas nuevas; pero todas anunciando el espíritu de vida que anima a sus habitantes. Nunca faltan escuelas, imprenta y tres o cuatro templos o capillas, en donde se reúnen los domingos a tributar al Ser supremo sus adoraciones. En Mead Ville hay además un colegio en donde se enseña filosofía moral, física, gramática griega y latina, y elementos de matemáticas. Llegué a Erié en 8 de julio, y en este puerto tomamos el buque de vapor embarcándonos en el hermoso lago de este nombre, que recibe sus aguas de varios ríos y de los lagos Superior, Huron y Míchigan. Al día siguiente llegué a Búfalo, situado a la orilla derecha del famoso Río Niágara, al salir del Lago Erié, con dirección al Ontario. Paré en la posada llamada el Águila, uno de los más alegres edificios que yo haya visto en mi vida, todo de madera y capaz de alojar doscientas personas con comodidad. Búfalo es uno de los prodigios de los Estados Unidos, de esas ciudades que nacieron en este siglo y ya compiten con las más antiguas por su belleza y su comercio. En 1814 fue enteramente reducida a cenizas por los ingleses, y en el día tiene diez mil habitantes, cinco templos y más de dos mil casas, aunque casi todas de madera. Según las relaciones uniformes que recibí y he continuado teniendo, pasan por Búfalo anualmente ciento veinte mil personas, y nunca hay día en que a lo menos no haya en la ciudad mil pasajeros. Es uno de los principales puntos de comercio de ese pequeño mar mediterráneo llamado Erié, rodeado de nuevas poblaciones, y vehículo de comunicación entre el Canadá, los Estados del Este, y la Europa, con los Estados y territorios del Oeste, que están llamados a hacer un gran papel en el mundo dentro de una centuria.

Copiaré aquí lo que escribí en mi Diario de viaje, el sábado 10 de julio de 1830. "Salimos de Búfalo a las nueve y media de la mañana y llegamos, después de una hora de camino, a Black Rock, que es una villa situada a la orilla derecha del Río Niágara. Este río sale del Lago Erié para echarse en el Ontario, después de haber corrido treinta y cinco millas, y formado la admirable catarata que lleva este nombre. Black Rock está enfrente de Waterloo, pueblo inglés situado al lado opuesto del río. Se dejan después los coches en Black Rock y se atraviesa el río en lo que llaman *horse boat*, o bote de caballo; porque uno o dos caballos mueven por medio de una máquina los remos. En Black Rock comienza el famoso canal del Estado de Nueva York que comunica con el río del Norte o Hudson en la ciudad de Albany.

"Continuamos nuestro viaje en coches que nos esperaban, caminando sobre las márgenes del río en las hermosas llanuras del Canadá inglés. Cerca de Chippewa, que es un pueblo distante dos millas de la catarata de Niágara, está el campo en que los americanos y los ingleses se batieron en 1814. Yo recorrí estos lugares con el libro en que se hace la descripción de todas estas bellas comarcas, en la mano, y sentía no se qué respeto a la vista de los monumentos levantados a la memoria de los muertos en la campaña. Lo mismo me había sucedido en México cuando pasaba por las cruces y el puente de Calderón. En esta pequeña aldea cerca de las Caídas, una mujer que vendía en su taberna, sacó para manifestárnoslas dos calaveras de personas muertas en la acción y que guardaba con cuidado.

"Llegamos a la gran catarata de Niágara a las doce del día. No puede concebirse la sorpresa que causa este espectáculo. Un río caudaloso que se precipita desde la altura de ciento setenta pies en una profundidad desconocida. El choque de las aguas hace formarse nubes del vapor en que se convierten estas aguas: una columna espesa se eleva sobre la catarata; el ruido es sordo, la vista queda fija involuntariamente por algún tiempo sobre este fenómeno, esta maravilla de la naturaleza. Los precipicios que le rodean, el movimiento de las aguas que dan cierta vista a la perspectiva y avisan del peligro; las quebradas laderas de las colinas vecinas; la variedad de árboles tales como castaños, cerezos, acacias, abetos, álamos, y el *pinus semper virens;* en fin las corrientes rápidas que antes de precipitarse en aquel abismo parece que se detienen en las rocas que encuentran, todo produce sensaciones de admiración, placer, horror y melancolía. Parece que el alma se siente oprimida por sentimientos que no puede resistir: las aguas del torrente ahogan en la imaginación todas las ideas: es un gigante de cien brazos que estrecha al mortal entre su cuerpo con una fuerza irresistible. Tal efecto produjo en mí la presencia del Niágara".

En el lado inglés hay una buena posada desde donde se ve la caída que llaman la herradura, *Horse Shoe,* y al otro lado, que llaman americano, hay otra posada, y la caída no es tan magnífica, ni tiene la gran masa de agua que la inglesa. En este punto el río está dividido por una isla que llaman *Goat Island,* Isla de Cabra, situada precisamente en la misma orilla del abismo de la catarata. Entre esta isla y el lado americano han construido un puente de madera que tiembla todo cuando se pasa sobre él. Desde este punto ve el espectador el torrente que corre bajo sus pies y va a precipitarse con una rapidez inexplicable en la profundidad desconocida, para continuar luego pacíficamente su curso al Lago Ontario, que recibe este caudaloso río, y después continúa más abajo con el nombre de San Lorenzo.

Muchas desgracias han ocurrido en esta catarata. Algunas personas han buscado y encontrado en sus abismos una muerte pronta; otras han escapado. Bien conocidos son los sucesos del célebre Chateubriand libertado maravillosamente cuando su caballo, espantado por una culebra de cascabel que salía del bosque, se desbocó hacia la caída principal. También es conocida su bella descripción del Niágara al fin de su Atala.

Todas esas márgenes del Niágara hasta el Lago Ontario han sido el teatro de una guerra mortal en los años de 1812, 1813 y 1814, entre los americanos y los ingleses. En el lado izquierdo del río, diez millas de la catarata abajo, hay una columna de granito de más de cien pies, elevada sobre una colina en memoria del general inglés Brock, muerto en una acción contra las milicias americanas, en octubre de 1812. Es de notar que las tropas inglesas eran todas de línea, mandadas por generales aguerridos educados en las campañas de Europa, tales eran los generales Freeddale, herido mortalmente en la batalla de Chippewa; Drummond, herido igualmente en otra acción habida quince días después, en *Bridgewater,* y Riall hecho prisionero. Los generales americanos Brown, Scott y Ripley se manifestaron dignos de tales enemigos, aunque nunca habían estado en acción alguna de guerra. El general Scott, que dio brillantes pruebas de valor e inteligencia en las acciones de Chippewa y Bridgewater, era poco antes de la campaña un abogado de fama en el Estado de Virginia. La primera acción en que se vio fue en la de Queenston, en que murió el general Brock de que he hablado.

Muy débil barrera es el Niágara y los lagos para evitar que el Canadá sea un día parte de los Estados Unidos del Norte. Aunque esta colonia inglesa no tiene por qué quejarse de su metrópoli en cuanto a su constitución política, hay, sin embargo, algunas restricciones comerciales que siempre son un obstáculo a su progreso. La capital del Alto Canadá es York.

Desde Niágara pasé a Queenston, población inglesa a la orilla izquierda del río y en las márgenes del Lago Ontario. Frente a ella está Lewiston en la parte americana, en donde hay una posada grande y cómoda. Subí de nuevo a visitar la catarata por el lado de Manchester. Aunque parezca repetirme, voy a copiar lo que escribí sobre los mismos lugares el lunes 12 de julio de 1830. "Hay una posada hermosísima, y vista la cascada por este lado se descubre en toda su perfección. Los americanos han fabricado un puente hasta *Goat Island,* isla que les quedó después de la última guerra. Admira cómo han podido dominar la terrible corriente que se precipita desde las rocas. El genio y la codicia se han unido para hacer milagros del arte. En la isla hay una fonda en que han hecho una especie de museo, y se ven varios objetos curiosos, tales como fósiles, minerales, animales, etc. Entre éstos hay un hermoso cisne muerto y perfectamente conservado, cogido en la catarata en 1828. Todo es sorprendente y magnífico; causa horror caminar sobre el puente pendiente elevado en la cascada".

Todos estos lugares estaban inhabitados cuando M. de Chateaubriand hizo su viaje entre los salvajes en 1792. "El cielo es puro sobre mi cabeza, las ondas son limpias bajo mi canoa que huye delante de una brisa ligera. A mi izquierda, veo colinas cortadas a pico y flanqueadas de rocas desde donde penden enredaderas de flores blancas y azules, festones de rosas silvestres, gramas y plantas saxsátiles de todas especies: a la derecha descubro vastas praderas. A medida que la canoa avanza se abren nuevas y nuevas perspectivas. Unas veces son valles risueños y solitarios, otras colinas desnudas y sin vegetación. Aquí hay un bosque de cipreses que forman pórticos sombríos, más allá es una floresta de azucareros en donde el sol penetra como por entre una blonda. ¡Sí, libertad primitiva, al fin te encuentro! Yo viajo y ando a la manera de esa ave que vuela delante de mi, que se dirige a la casualidad y que sólo se embaraza en la elección del árbol en que hará su mansión. Véme aquí tal como el Todopoderoso me ha creado, soberano de la Naturaleza, llevado en triunfo sobre las aguas, mientras que los habitantes de los ríos acompañan mi curso, que los pueblos del aire me canten sus himnos, que las bestias de la Tierra me saluden, que las florestas inclinan sus cabezas a mi pasaje. ¿Es sobre la frente del hombre de la sociedad o sobre la mía en donde está grabado el sello de nuestro noble origen? Corred a encerraros a vuestras ciudades; id a someteros a vuestras estrechas leyes; ganad el pan con el sudor de vuestra frente o devorad el alimento del pobre. Mataos por una disputa, por tener un jefe en lugar de otro: dudad de la existencia de Dios, o adoradle bajo formas supersticiosas; yo por mi parte vagaré errante por estas soledades, en donde mi corazón palpitará libremente, y mis pensamientos correrán sueltamente sin ser encadenados. Yo seré libre como la Naturaleza; no reconocerá otro soberano que el que dio luz y existencia a tantos soles y que con un solo impulso de su brazo hizo girar tantos mundos".

Con un placer inefable leía estas páginas cuando yo viajaba por esos mismos lugares ya cubiertos de poblaciones, en donde la civilización y la mano del hombre no han dado el soplo mortal de la esclavitud, ni la superstición. Salía de la anarquía de México en donde me vi tantas veces expuesto a ser víctima del furor de los partidos, y ahora vagaba libremente en las deliciosas márgenes del Niágara, entre las eternas florestas del Canadá, alejándome cuanto podía hacia esos lugares solitarios en donde el hombre, desconocido como yo era en países tan remotos, me entregaba enteramente a mis meditaciones. ¡Oh Niágara! mientras mis ojos fijos en tus rápidas ondas parecían dar indicio de que me ocupaba enteramente el grandioso espectáculo, yo veía en ti la representación más melancólica de nuestras desastrosas revoluciones. Yo leía en la sucesión de tus olas, las generaciones que corren a la eternidad; y en las cataratas que preceden a tu abismo, los esfuerzos de unos hombres que impelen a los otros para sucederlos en sus lugares.

En *Fort Niagara* hay guarnición de tropas americanas, y en *Fort George* inglesas. Las fronteras y fortalezas son los únicos lugares en que se ven tropas de línea en los Estados Unidos. Es excusado decir que están muy bien vestidas y alimentadas. Hay pocas deserciones, en ocasión que son muy frecuentes en las del Canadá, según me informaron.

CAPÍTULO V

En Queenston tomé pasaje a bordo de un buque de vapor llamado *Alciope,* que aunque cómodo, no es comparable a los del Ohio y Misisipí. El pasaje me costó diez pesos hasta Montreal, una de las mayores y más ricas ciudades del Canadá. Navegamos el día y noche del 13 por el Lago Ontario, y después de haber hecho ciento cincuenta millas, nos detuvimos en Kingston para proveer de leña el buque. Desde este pueblo que está situado a la orilla oriental del lago, se ha emprendido la construcción de un canal, que llaman *Rideau Canal,* que debe terminar en Montreal. El objeto es facilitar la navegación del Río San Lorenzo abajo, el cual no puede pasarse, al menos con mucho riesgo, en las pequeñas cascadas que se encuentran entre este punto y Montreal. Los gastos de este canal se supone montarán a quinientas mil libras (dos y medio millones de pesos).

También hay otro canal ya principiado en el Alto Canadá, entre el Lago Erié y el Ontario, para corregir las desigualdades del Niágara y hacer comunicables por agua ambos lagos. Este es el *Welland Canal,* en donde hay una cortadura que se aproxima a nuestro desagüe de Huehuetoca, aunque no es tan grandioso ni profundo. Tiene veintisiete pies de cortadura. Este canal deberá tener cuarenta y cinco millas. Nuestro Canal de Huehuetoca tendrá a lo más diez millas; pero la obra de la cortadura de Nochistongo es mucho más considerable. Aquí comienza propiamente el Río San Lorenzo, notable por su anchura y sus mil islas.

Montreal es una ciudad de veinticinco a treinta mil habitantes, situada a la izquierda del Lorenzo, sobre un banco elevado y rodeado de colinas fértiles, bien cultivadas y vistosas. Hay una concurrencia numerosa de indios, la mayor parte salvajes, que vienen a cambiar sus pelleterías de castor, nutrias, cíbolos, ciervos, panteras, etc., con las mercancías extranjeras, cristales, ropas, aguardientes, pólvora, plomo, etc. La mayor parte de las casas son de ladrillo y piedra de sillería y granito. Hay, algunos monumentos dignos de atención, tal es un trofeo levantado a la memoria del almirante Nelson, en donde se representa, en bajo relieve, el Nilo por un cocodrilo, y el mar por buques bien dibujados.

La mayor parte de los habitantes son católicos y hay una catedral bastante grande de muy mal gusto, género gótico, de piedra calcárea. Las casas están en su parte superior cubiertas de hoja de lata, lo que hace que desde las colinas vecinas o las alturas, den un golpe de vista hermoso con el sol o la luna. El pueblo está extrañamente vestido; habla un francés mixto que apenas se parece a la lengua de París. La mayor parte de los comerciantes y grandes propietarios son ingleses. La posada en que paré, que se llama *Good Enough,* es muy bien asistida, aunque más cara que las de los Estados Unidos.

Hay varios conventos de monjas en Montreal, fundados desde que pertenecía el país a los franceses. No ha habido ninguna alteración en sus establecimientos, porque el Gobierno no los considera sino como compañías o asociaciones. Las religiosas salen a la calle cuando quieren; pero generalmente guardan sus votos y sirven a los enfermos.

Como los viajeros que han escrito sobre los Estados Unidos nunca han dejado de hacer un paralelo entre los ríos San Lorenzo y Misisipí, por los visibles y notables contrastes que se encuentran entre ellos, creo que debo seguir el mismo ejemplo para que el lector forme idea de las diversas fisonomías de la Naturaleza. El Río San Lorenzo es muy variado en sus márgenes y presenta escenas diversas. El Misisipí es uniforme, igual y monótono: el primero lleva un curso rápido y bullicioso; el segundo corre majestuosamente y no parece llevar la inmensa mole de agua que descarga en el Océano; aquél tiene las ondas puras y cristalinas; éste turbias y lodosas; aquél nace en el Ontario, tan grande y majestuoso como desemboca en el Golfo del mismo nombre; éste se aumenta con ríos caudalosos que lo enriquecen; aquél corre por tres mil millas; éste no excede de quinientas; el San Lorenzo no aumenta ni disminuye su volumen; el Misisipí se infla, se eleva y amenaza con sus inundaciones los pueblos, villas y ciudades que se alimentan de sus aguas. El San Lorenzo atraviesa muchos lagos; el Misisipí corre en medio de florestas: el primero es grande y hermoso; el segundo sombrío y sublime; en fin el San Lorenzo causa impresiones agradables en la imaginación; el Misisipí la oprime con su inmensidad.

En veinticuatro horas de navegación sobre el Río San Lorenzo, en buque vapor, nos pusimos de Montreal a Quebec, capital del Bajo Canadá. Llegamos a la hora que se tocaba la retreta en el fuerte, y la música militar causaba una agradable sensación. Quebec se compone de ciudad alta y ciudad baja, porque está levantada sobre las colinas que se elevan gradualmente en algunas partes y repentinamente en otras, formando un muro sobre el río. La parte baja es insana, sucia, habitada por gente pobre, casas miserables; la alta no tiene tantos y tan hermosos edificios como Montreal, pero no carece de belleza y de casas cómodas y de buena apariencia. La catedral es una masa informe, sin gusto ni orden de arquitectura. La fortaleza, que se estaba ya concluyendo en la punta Diamante, es sin duda una de las más grandiosas obras del arte militar, por su posición y arquitectura. Habrá costado al gobierno inglés más de dos millones de pesos.

El campo de Abrahan es una llanura que domina la ciudad, y ha sido el teatro de acciones gloriosas, tanto en la guerra con la Francia, como en la de la independencia. Allí murieron en diversas épocas el general inglés, Wolfe, y el coronel americano, Montgomery, cuyas cenizas fueron después trasladadas a la iglesia de San Pablo, en Nueva York. Todo este llano está aun lleno de los vestigios de la guerra y hay algunos monumentos erigidos a la memoria de los jefes ingleses.

En mi viaje a Quebec tuve relación con M. Coveocy, anciano respetable, vecino de aquella ciudad y nacido en Boston. Pocos, muy pocos americanos tienen las opiniones de M. Coveocy en orden a los futuros destinos del Canadá. El cree que dentro de algún tiempo, una parte del Estado de Vermont y aun de Maine se agregará al Canadá, para completar, dice, su territorio. Yo le manifesté que por el contrario creía que toda la parte inglesa de aquel continente sería independiente, o compondría Estados de la Confederación Americana con el tiempo. Me habló con mucho entusiasmo de un M. Bailhi, reformador de la iglesia católica, en el Bajo Canadá, en los años de 90 a 94 del siglo pasado, que disminuyó los días festivos reduciéndolos a seis al año, fuera de los domingos, lo que consiguió con mucha dificultad y en medio de los clamores del fanatismo. Me hizo observar que las costas eran las únicamente pobladas, como sucede en las nuevas poblaciones, en donde los colonos buscan naturalmente las márgenes de los ríos o las playas del mar.

En cuanto a la agregación del Alto Canadá a los Estados Unidos, voy a transcribir aquí las reflexiones de un viajero inglés, que, bajo el título de *Men and manners in America,* ha hecho una descripción no muy imparcial de los Estados Unidos; aunque la fuerza de la verdad le obliga muchas veces a confesar sus rápidos progresos y ventajas locales.

"Las Cámaras Legislativas no estaban reunidas cuando pasé por el Canadá, dice el viajero, y de consiguiente conozco poco de las cuestiones pendientes. Sin embargo, tengo conocimiento de un M. Papineau, que representa con mucha propiedad el papel del O'Connell de las colonias. El campo no es vasto, pero hace cuanto puede, y goza de la dignidad de ser la espina perpetua clavada en el costado de los gobernadores. M. Papineau y su partido se manifiestan siempre descontentos de la dominación inglesa. Pero ¿qué desean tener de más? Ellos no pagan contribuciones. *John Bull* (el pueblo inglés) gasta su dinero con mucha liberalidad entre los canadienses, como lo pueden ver ellos mismos en la magnífica fortificación del Cabo Diamante y el Canal Rideau. Este último debe traer inmensos beneficios a ambas provincias: beneficios que jamás hubieran tenido los canadienses, abandonados a sus solos recursos. ¿Qué tendrían entonces? A lo menos el Bajo Canadá no se agregará a los Estados Unidos; y es sumamente pobre y destituido de medios para poder subsistir por sí solo. Quitad los capitales ingleses de esta colonia y sólo quedará miseria y soledad.

"Con respecto al Alto Canadá vemos venir con rapidez el período de su agregación a los Estados Unidos. Todas las cosas tienden a la consumación de esta obra. Los canales que ponen en comunicación esa larga cañada de lagos con el Ohio y el Hudson acelerarán este acontecimiento. Los labradores del Alto Canadá tienen más fácil comercio en los mercados de Nueva York y Nueva Orleans, que en el de Quebec. La masa del pueblo es republicana en sus ideas políticas y anarquista en su moral. Váyanse pues: la pérdida de la Inglaterra es de poca monta. El águila no disminuye sus alas porque se le caiga una pluma".

Cuando estaba en Quebec (julio de 1830), había un calor mucho más fuerte que los que haya yo experimentado en Yucatán o Veracruz. El termómetro de Farenheit estaba a ciento dos grados, y jamás en mi vida me sentí más atormentado. El calor dura dos meses y ya en septiembre comienza a sentirse frío, que aumenta considerablemente hasta fines de enero, y el país todo está cubierto de nieves y hielos. La rapidez con que pasa el estío no permite que se madure el maíz y de consiguiente no se siembra esta preciosa semilla en el Canadá. Se da trigo, cebada, centeno, trigo sarraceno, con el que hacen unas tortillas muy gustosas, y avena. Las frutas no son buenas; aunque no faltan cerezas, moras de diversas calidades, manzanas y duraznos.

Hay dos cascadas notables en las cercanías de Quebec. La una es la de Montmorency, que si bien es más alta que la de Niágara no me causó la impresión agradable que aquélla, aunque sí su aspecto es más selvático. La cantidad de agua que cae de ciento cuarenta y ocho pies no es la sexta parte de la otra; pero hace más ruido sin duda porque el vasto recipiente no tiene agua suficiente para disminuir el choque de la masa. La otra cascada es la de *Chaudiere* o Caldera, que tiene cien pies de caída perpendicular y produce el efecto de hacer hervir el agua que corre con rapidez a arrojarse en el San Lorenzo.

La aldea de Loreto, que está cerca, ofrece, como en muchas de nuestras antiguas poblaciones, el aspecto melancólico de ruinas. Allí habitan los últimos restos de una poderosa tribu de indios hurones. El aguardiente y la pólvora han concluido su obra, y solamente quedan doscientas personas de este pueblo noble y belicoso en otro tiempo. Han adoptado la religión y hablan el idioma de sus conquistadores. Hay una iglesia en este pueblo y un cura que vive entre sus feligreses que le aman. El cristianismo es el solo beneficio que los indios han recibido de los blancos. Estos los engañan, los roban, los corrompen y los arruinan en este mundo, y después hacen un mérito de procurarles la salvación en el otro. El beneficio es sublime a la verdad; pero los pobres indios deben desconfiar de un don de que viene de tales gentes.

En las dos provincias del Canadá hay Cámaras Legislativas y las leyes reciben su sanción del gobernador que nombra el rey de Inglaterra. Hay también ciertas leyes de hacienda y de trascendencia que necesitan la aprobación del gobierno de S. M. Británica. Por lo demás hay libertad de imprenta, juicio por jurados, y las demás garantías sociales que en Inglaterra. El idioma francés es el de los registros públicos en el Bajo Canadá, y las discusiones son en este idioma.

Salí de Quebec y regresé a Montreal, pasando de paso por el pueblo de Sorel, sobre el Río Richelieu, que nace en el Lago Champlain y desagua en el San Lorenzo. Este sería conducto utilísimo de comunicación con el Estado de Nueva York por los lagos Champlain y George, de que hablaré luego. Regresé a Montreal en donde sólo estuve una hora.

En Montreal atravesé el río, salté a tierra en un pueblo bellísimo llamado la *Prairie,* en donde hay un convento de religiosas de la Caridad, y continué en diligencia hasta San John, lugar situado en la banda oriental del Lago Champlain. Allí me embarqué en el buque de vapor B. Franklin, en el que volví a encontrar la limpieza y comodidades de los transportes americanos en este género. Desde Niágara me había asociado para hacer el viaje del Canadá con Mr. M. Evans, comerciante de Nueva Orleans, y Laville de Bean, propietario de la Luisiana. En Fort Niagara nos juntamos con una amable familia de Pitsburgo llamada Simpson y Dahra, y en esta compañía continuamos la agradable travesía del Lago Champlain. A las treinta y cuatro millas de navegación se encuentra la Isla Negra, hermosa, fértil y malsana, y a tres millas más arriba se entra de nuevo en el territorio de los Estados Unidos, en donde un guarda pregunta con mucha cortesía si tiene uno algunos efectos de contrabando, y sin más formalidad deja pasar a los viajeros. Pasamos enfrente de Platsburgo, villa considerable del Estado de Nueva York, y que dio nombre a la batalla naval que entre las flotillas americanas e inglesas se dio en 1814, habiendo quedado la última en poder de los americanos. Diez mil ingleses tuvieron que retirarse bajo las órdenes del general Prevost, cuyo proyecto era nada menos que cortar las comunicaciones entre la Nueva Inglaterra y el resto de los Estados Unidos. Después de ciento cuarenta millas de navegación en el Lago Champlain, tomamos tierra en *White Hall,* que está a la parte occidental del lago, desde donde al Lago George habrá apenas la distancia de una milla. En este istmo están los vestigios de la antigua fortaleza llamada Ticonderoga, teatro de guerras sangrientas, tanto en tiempo en que los franceses tuvieron el Canadá como posteriormente en las dos guerras habidas entre los ingleses y los americanos. Yo visité estas ruinas, en donde no quedan más que montones de piedras y de arena con algunos viejos paredones.

El Lago Champlain nunca excede de cinco millas de anchura. En su parte occidental tiene al sur las montañas de Vermont que se llaman Green Hills, de las más elevadas de esta cordillera. Entre ambos lagos hay un pequeño pueblo llamado Alejandría, en donde existe una cascada que se precipita gradualmente, como de cincuenta pies de altura, y forma un espectáculo brillante. Comimos allí y tomamos el buque de vapor sobre el Lago George, aún más angosto que el anterior, profundo, de aguas transparentes y claras, y costeado por rocas elevadas en ambos lados, de manera que parece un caño. Todas estas montañas y bosques están muy escasamente poblados; de cuando en cuando se ven algunas casas sobre las alturas, que inspiran el deseo de ocuparlas a los hombres cansados del mundo y de los negocios, que buscan en vano las ilusiones del campo y de la soledad, después de haber andado inútilmente tras de una felicidad que siempre se escapa de las manos. Pocos lugares, en efecto, me han inspirado un deseo más vehemente del retiro a la vida campestre, que esas deliciosas y románticas márgenes del Niágara y del Lago George. ¡Qué soledad tan acompañada de las bellezas de la Naturaleza! Peñascos, arroyos, aguas navegables y cristalinas, peces exquisitos, vistas magníficas; hasta las ruinas de Crown Point y Ticonderoga, todo inspira ideas sublimes, sencillas y naturales.

El lago termina en Caldwell. No se puede pasar por estos lugares sin recordar dos sucesos extremadamente trágicos, acaecidos en las cercanías de estos lagos. En la guerra entre los franceses y los ingleses, en 1759, cuando la toma de Quebec por los segundos, M. Schoonhoven y siete americanos fueron hechos prisioneros por una partida de salvajes en las cercanías de Sandy Hill. Conducidos a un prado se les hizo sentar en hilera sobre un tronco de árbol, y a continuación un indio, armado de una hacha, iba sucesivamente matándolos rompiéndoles el cerebro. Al llegar a M. Schoonhoven el jefe mandó suspender la sangrienta escena, y dirigiéndose a éste le dice: "¿Te acuerdas de un día en que estando en un baile nos presentamos a la función varios indios, y cuando tus compañeros se oponían a recibirnos, tú mandaste que se nos permitiese tomar parte en la fiesta? Yo creo descubrir en tu fisonomía los mismos rasgos de afinidad con los indios; ahora verás cómo sabemos apreciar estos actos". Mandó luego dejar ir libre a M. Schoonhoven y a uno de sus compañeros que aun había sobrevivido. *Sunt hic etiam proemia laudis.*

En la guerra de la independencia, en 1777, un joven americano, llamado Jones, capitán en las tropas inglesas, había contraído esponsales con una señorita llamada Miss. M. Crea. Su casa estaba en el centro de los ejércitos contendientes. El capitán Jones, para poder verificar su matrimonio, despachó una partida de indios de los que estaban al servicio inglés, para escoltar a su novia al fuerte, que era el cuartel general. No satisfecho con la primera escolta, manda otra igualmente de indios, ofreciendo un barril de aguardiente de recompensa a los conductores. Ambas partidas se reunieron y se disputaron cuál de ellas conduciría a la dama. El triste resultado fue que la señorita fue asesinada, y cayó víctima de una contienda comenzada en su obsequio.

En Caldwell tomamos la diligencia para dirigirnos a Saratoga. A pocas millas encontramos la Cascada de Glens, notable por sus inmensos peñascos, petrificaciones y cantidad de fósiles. Esta catarata es del famoso Río Hudson, que desemboca tan caudaloso en la bahía de Nueva York. Continuamos a Saratoga, que entonces estaba llena de los viajeros que de todos los Estados Unidos vienen a tomar las celebradas aguas minerales en sus mismas fuentes, a bailar y a contraer conexiones que después suelen fijar la suerte de las personas.

Saratoga es una villa del Estado de Nueva York que tiene cuatro posadas magníficas, en cada una de las que pueden alojarse doscientas personas a lo menos, fuera de un grande número de casas más pequeñas que llaman *boarding house*. Las principales posadas son *Congress Hotel, United States Hotel*. Más de mil personas entran y salen diariamente de esta deliciosa mansión, durante los meses de junio, julio y agosto. Como plaza de aguas minerales, los habitantes han procurado embellecerla con arboledas, paseos, jardines, bosques y cuanto pueda hacerla agradable a los que por puro placer o por su salud van a beber las aguas del *Congreso*. Hay catorce fuentes de diferentes combinaciones de sales, gases y minerales. Las más contienen muriate de sosa, carbonate de sosa, carbonate de cal, carbonate de magnesia y carbonate de hierro en diversas proporciones. En la que llaman Congress Water hay mucha cantidad de aire fijo, y los viajeros van todas las mañanas en ayunas a tomar dos o tres grandes vasos para purgar ligeramente el estómago. No es desagradable como la del manantial de nuestra Villa de Guadalupe o Ciudad de Hidalgo, que contiene azufre, petróleo y mucho aire fijo. A mi pasada a Saratoga fui presentado al conde de Survilliers, José Bonaparte, ex rey de España, de quien hablaré en otra ocasión.

En estas cercanías se ven todavía vestigios de las campañas de la guerra de la independencia. El general inglés Burgoyne, después de haber tomado el fuerte de Ticonderoga, se dirigió con diez mil hombres de tropa de línea y muchos miles de indios salvajes que tenía de auxiliares, hacia Saratoga y Albany, centro del Estado de Nueva York. En una proclama que publicó en junio de 1777, decía que era más bien un paseo militar que una campaña, la que tendría que hacer. Tal era el orgullo que le había inspirado la fácil toma del fuerte de Ticonderoga. Había concebido el proyecto de apoderarse de Albany, lo que le parecía fácil por el terror que había inspirado su repentina aparición sobre la orilla izquierda del Hudson, objeto de sus deseos, como una barrera entre los Estados del Oeste y la Nueva Inglaterra. Pero la victoria de Bennintong, conseguida por el coronel americano Stark, sobre las tropas británicas mandadas por el coronel Baun, muerto en la acción, hicieron ver al general inglés que tenía que luchar con un enemigo temible. Es muy digna de atención la alocución del coronel Stark a sus tropas antes del combate. "Hoy debemos derrotar al enemigo, les dijo, de lo contrario, María Stark (su mujer) será viuda antes de ponerse el sol".

Después de esta acción el general Burgoyne sostuvo dos combates muy sangrientos, y tuvo necesidad de capitular en 17 de octubre del mismo año, dejando a los americanos el campo. Esta campaña fue dirigida por el general Gates, inglés de nacimiento; pero fiel y noble defensor de la causa americana.

Muchos incidentes ocurrieron después de la expedición del general inglés Burgoyne, que merecen referirse por su singularidad. Este jefe había estado sin recibir ninguna comunicación del general Henrique Clinton, que debía venir a su socorro subiendo el Río Hudson. El correo llamado Taylor, que conducía los avisos de esta importante noticia al general Burgoyne, fue hecho prisionero por las avanzadas del general americano George Clinton. El pobre Taylor tragó una cosa que sacó de la bolsa, pero fue observado. Se le dio una fuerte dosis de tártaro emético, con la que arrojó una pequeña bola de plata, que estando hueca, se halló en ella la carta de Clinton a Burgoyne. Taylor fue juzgado y ejecutado.

En el primer ataque de 27 de septiembre, se advirtió que murió un número mucho mayor de oficiales que el que debía en proporción a la tropa. Los tiradores americanos se habían puesto en las ramas de los árboles, desde donde apuntaban a los oficiales de preferencia. En la acción de 7 de octubre murieron los principales jefes del ejército inglés. El general Fraser, el coronel Breytman y M. Clarlle, ayudante del general Burgoyne, cayeron víctimas de los tiradores americanos.

El general Fraser era un oficial activo, de valor y de capacidad. El general Morgan era el encargado de hacer frente al primero con un cuerpo de cazadores americanos. En lo más fuerte de la acción, el general americano escogió seis de sus mejores tiradores de rifle y les dijo: "Ved a ese hombre, yo le admiro por su valor y energía; pero es necesario que muera; tomad vuestras medidas y cumplid vuestro deber". Esta fue la sentencia de muerte del bravo general inglés: al cuarto de hora ya había caído muerto. La relación de este suceso y de la trágica acción es sacada de la que hizo una señora alemana que se halló en el mismo campo de batalla o sus cercanías, en donde su esposo, el barón de Reidesdel, servía bajo las órdenes del general británico: "Severas y duras pruebas nos esperaban el día 7 de octubre en que comenzaron nuestros infortunios. Yo estaba almorzando con mi marido, y percibí que había entre manos algún negocio serio. Esperaba a comer a los generales Burgoyne, Tillips y Fraser. Vi un gran movimiento entre las tropas. Mi esposo me dijo que sólo era una revista, no dándome conocimiento de nada. Encontré muchos indios armados que a mis preguntas sólo contestaron *guerre, guerre,* dando a entender sin duda que iban a batirse. Esto me hizo apresurar mi retirada a casa, en donde apenas había llegado que comencé a oír tiros de cañón y de fusilería que aumentaban más y más. A las cuatro de la tarde, en lugar de los huéspedes que esperaba a comer, veo entrar una litera que traía herido mortalmente al general Fraser. Hice colocar su cama en la misma pieza destinada a comer con él y los otros. Yo me senté tristemente en un rincón, esperando de un momento a otro noticias de mi marido.

El general Fraser dijo al cirujano: "Dígame usted si mi herida es mortal; no quiero ser lisonjeado". El cirujano declaró que la bala le había atravesado el estómago y cortado los principales tendones de esta entraña. El general fue enterrado al día siguiente en medio de las balas y fuego de los dos ejércitos beligerantes. El coronel Wilkinson, que conocimos en México en donde murió, y con quien tuve una particular amistad, se halló en esta acción. Dice en su historia que perseguía una partida de enemigos, cuando descubrió junto a una cerca un hombre tendido que le decía: "Protéjame usted, señor coronel, de los tiros de este muchacho". Volvió la vista y descubrió un joven de catorce a quince años, que apuntaba con su rifle al pobre mayor Ackland que, gravemente herido, había sido llevado a aquel punto por un oficial de su cuerpo que estaba con él, y el coronel Wilkinson libertó a ambos de los tiros mortales del pequeño americano. Es muy interesante la relación que la baronesa de Reidesdel hace de los trabajos de la esposa del mayor Ackland, que acompañó a su esposo en todos los riesgos, y le asistió en el mismo campo enemigo. También tenemos iguales ejemplos de amor conyugal y heroísmo femenil en nuestra guerra mexicana.

CAPÍTULO VI

El 24 de julio salí de Saratoga para Baliston, que está en el camino hacia Albany. Este es un pueblo también de aguas minerales, de cerca de dos mil habitantes y con buenas posadas. No me detuve en él más que el tiempo suficiente para visitar sus fuentes y continué a la capital del Estado de Nueva York, la ciudad de Albany o Albania a la orilla derecha del Río Hudson. A seis millas antes está Troya, villa agradablemente situada al lado opuesto del río, que tendrá cuatro mil habitantes. En otra ocasión me ocuparé de Albany cuando hable de mis viajes a la Nueva Inglaterra en esta misma obra.

El día 25 de julio de 1830 me embarqué en el buque de vapor *Estados Unidos,* en el que iban a lo menos trecientos pasajeros entre hombres y mujeres, todos decentemente vestidos; especialmente las damas cuyo aseo y elegancia causaban un verdadero placer. A pesar de este crecido número de gentes, todos están desahogados, ya quieran pasearse sobre cubierta, ya bajarse a los salones. Para todos había campo en las mesas dispuestas para almorzar y comer. La comida era abundante, bien sazonada, buen servicio, en suma, con todas las comodidades apetecibles. Bajamos rápidamente el pintoresco Río Hudson, y en West Point tuve el placer de encontrar al señor Mejía y su familia que bajaban a Nueva York, de donde habían venido a ver el famoso establecimiento militar de este lugar. Llegamos a Nueva York a las siete de la tarde, habiendo navegado en doce horas ciento cuarenta y ocho millas desde Albany.

Me alojé en el *boarding house* de *Mrs. Street,* número 36, en Broadway. Esta es una de esas innumerables posadas que ni son públicas ni privadas, y en que se aloja cierto número de personas bajo condiciones estipuladas. Las establecidas en la calle llamada *Broadway,* en Nueva York, son las mejores, y se vive en ellas con mucha comodidad, en medio de una sociedad escogida, y sin el concurso y bullicio de las posadas grandes. Tres veces he entrado a Nueva York por la bahía, cuatro por el Raritan, una por el este, viniendo de Boston, y tres o cuatro por el Río del Norte o Hudson. Como en otra ocasión tendré que hablar de los últimos, comenzaré ahora por la entrada de la magnífica bahía de este emporio comercial.

Al aproximarse a las costas de Nueva York se descubren las tierras elevadas del Estado de Nueva Jersey a la izquierda, y las de la Isla Larga o *Long Island* a la derecha. En *Sandy Hook,* que es un montecillo de arena en la costa al sudoeste, hay un faro magnífico, fuera de otros que se descubren por las costas. La entrada se hace más estrecha a quince millas con la isla del Estado, o *Staten Island,* que se extiende desde el Río Raritan hasta los estrechos que llaman *Nar Rows,* en cuyo punto hay una fortaleza elevada bajo la dirección del general Bernard.

La vista entonces es al mismo tiempo pintoresca, magnífica e imponente, hermosas casas de campo por ambos lados, rodeadas de árboles plantados con simetría, en terrenos que se elevan sucesivamente y ostentan una fecundidad prodigiosa; la vista de dos ríos que a derecha e izquierda bajan dejando la ciudad en el medio: multitud de embarcaciones de todas clases y tamaños que salen y entran tomando diversas direcciones a velas desplegadas: buques de vapor que se cruzan, y semejantes a las grandes ballenas, van levantando por su proa montones de agua espumosa, y despidiendo un humo espeso y negro por sus vértices: quinientos buques anclados en los lados del ángulo que forman los ríos entre los que está colocada la ciudad, cuyo vértice está cubierto de arboledas, forma todo un conjunto admirable que arrebata la imaginación y enajena el espíritu. Nueva York es sin duda uno de los más bellos y más cómodos puertos del Universo, y es también después de Londres y Liverpool, la ciudad de mayor comercio marítimo.

La ciudad está situada en la Isla de Manhatan formada por los ríos del Norte, el Pasaie y el Río del Este que es más bien un brazo de mar. Long Island es una lengua de tierra separada por el sud y forma una isla de cerca de cien millas de longitud con cinco o seis de latitud. En esta porción de terreno hay poblaciones bastante grandes, entre ellas Brooklyn, que está enfrente de la ciudad, Jamaica, Flushing y otras aldeas y villas que aumentan en población y riqueza con una rapidez extraordinaria que se advierte en toda la extensión de los Estados Unidos.

El Estado de Nueva York tiene una población de dos millones de habitantes. En la ciudad hay más de cien templos o capillas de diferentes cultos; entre éstas se encuentran dieciocho episcopales, veinticinco presbiterianas, veinte metodistas, diecinueve de anabaptistas, cinco católicas, y el resto de cuaqueros, unitarios y demás sectas. Nueva York tiene al pie de doscientos veinte mil habitantes.

La ciudad tiene una forma irregular, y las calles son generalmente torcidas. Hay sin embargo algunas que pueden competir con las mejores de Londres y París. Tales son Broadway, que divide la ciudad y corre de noroeste a sudoeste por cerca de cuatro millas; de más de ochenta pies de ancho, con embanquetado de piedra labrada a lo menos de seis pies; hermoseada por edificios bellísimos; tiendas, almacenes, y cuanto hay de más brillante en Nueva York. Chatham, igualmente formada por muy buenos edificios: Canal, Bowery, Blekery, Bonn, Greenwhich y otras. Broadway es el lugar en que se pasean todas las gentes mejor vestidas, las damas, los petimetres, los extranjeros, es al mismo tiempo alameda, calle y paseo. Más concurrida que *Regen's Street* de Londres; más aseada y bella que los *boulevards* de París; más regular y larga que la calle de Alcalá de Madrid. En Nueva York no hay paseos públicos, a excepción de la pequeña arboleda de la Batería. No hay fuentes públicas, y el agua que se bebe es bastante mala.

La ventajosa situación de Nueva York y más que todo el sistema de libertad sin restricciones mezquinas de pasaportes, bajo la protección de leyes justas y sabias, con absoluta libertad de cultos, ha conducido a esta ciudad a un grado de prosperidad y grandeza en cuarenta años, que es hoy la metrópoli del Nuevo Mundo. En 1778 Nueva York tenía sólo veintidós mil habitantes; en 1795 ascendió a treinta y tres mil; en 1800 tenía sesenta mil; en 1820 aumentó hasta ciento veintitrés mil; en 1825 subió a ciento sesenta y seis mil; y hoy tiene, como he dicho, doscientos veinte mil. ¿Qué ciudad en el mundo ha tenido un incremento tan rápido?

El valor de las mercancías que se importan y exportan en esta ciudad se calcula ascender a cien millones de pesos fuertes, la renta de correos da anualmente ciento veinte mil pesos a la tesorería. ¡ Qué movimiento no es necesario para un giro tan vasto y extenso!

Hay más de setenta buques de vapor que salen de los muelles para cruzar la bahía. Los unos sirven de puentes en los ríos Hudson y del Este, para llevar y traer las gentes que van y vienen de Brooklyn, Hobboken, Staten Island, y éstos están cruzando todo el día hasta las doce de la noche. Los otros salen para Flushing, New Haven, Hardfort, Albany, Raritan, etc. En el verano hasta el otoño parece aquella bahía un lugar de perpetua feria.

Uno de los más bellos edificios de Nueva York es la casa del ayuntamiento, que llaman *City Hall,* que es donde se reúnen también los tribunales. Está colocado en medio de una plaza cubierta de árboles, que llaman del Parque, en el centro de la ciudad. Tiene doscientos dieciséis pies de longitud y cientocinco de latitud. La fachada es de hermoso mármol blanco, y este edificio sería muy elegante si tuviese mejores proporciones. Pero es más bajo que lo que permite su magnitud. Hay otras dos plazas notables en esta ciudad: la una, *Hudson Square,* en donde se ve una arboleda rodeada de un enrejado de fierro elevado y bien trabajada; y la otra, *Washington Square,* que se halla estramuros, y que dentro de pocos años estará rodeada de edificios, almacenes y casas.

En Nueva York hay tres teatros, que son el Park, el de Browery y el de la Opera. Generalmente hablando los americanos del Norte son poco afectos a esa clase de diversiones que suponen un grado de civilización urbana que no se puede decir es la parte más prominente entre aquellos habitantes. En las ciudades en que el gusto por la sociedad y las diversiones ha tomado incremento, tales como Boston, Filadelfia, Nueva York y otras pocas, se advierte siempre que el pueblo no toma mucho empeño en la asistencia a ellas. ¡Qué diferencia de la ansiedad con que corren a las puertas de los teatros, a los bailes, a los conciertos en las ciudades de Europa, especialmente en Francia! Quince teatros que hay en toda la ciudad de París se llenan todas las noches, y se sostienen los empresarios haciendo buenas ganancias. En Nueva York no puede mantenerse un teatro de ópera italiana, en concurrencia de los otros dos en que se representan piezas sueltas de canto o dramáticas. Yo he advertido mucha mayor inclinación al teatro en el pueblo de la República Mexicana, que en el de los Estados del Norte. La razón de esta diferencia debe buscarse en las diversas circunstancias en que se han formado ambos pueblos. El de los norteamericanos se compone en su mayoría de emigrados agricultores que, obligados en su principio a trabajar en el campo, no tenían ni el tiempo ni los estímulos para dedicar las horas del descanso a ningún pasatiempo bullicioso. Por otra parte el espíritu de secta, que tendía en su origen a un ascetismo riguroso entre los presbiterianos emigrados a aquellas comarcas, dejó tras sí una aversión insuperable a los espectáculos, como prohibidos por la religión.

En las colonias españolas se hizo una separación absoluta de conquistadores y conquistados. Los primeros tenían las riquezas, los privilegios y los goces que ambos procuran, así como las inclinaciones y gustos que engendran. Los descendientes de los conquistadores heredaban de sus padres los españoles el gusto por la música y las diversiones, que se conciliaban con el culto católico, cuya cabeza en Roma daba el impulso a todo género de espectáculos. En vez pues de dedicarse al trabajo de la tierra o a otras ocupaciones penosas, se entregaban a las bulliciosas fiestas a que por otra parte convidan sus climas cálidos, o templados. No había además esa imperiosa necesidad de acumular para el invierno provisiones, leña y ropa. El primer móvil para el trabajo es la necesidad, luego entran los placeres. Así pues, se ve un mexicano hacer el gasto de un peso que ha adquirido sin mucha dificultad, en el teatro, en los toros, o en el baile; mientras que un norteamericano temería sacar uno entre cien pesos, para una inversión semejante.

En Nueva York hay sobre quinientos coches de alquiler, no tan cómodos como los de México y París, pero más ligeros y elegantes. Apenas caben cuatro personas en un coche, y se paga a peso la hora. Una multitud de extranjeros de todos los países mantienen en continua ocupación estos carruajes.

Los principales *hoteles* o posadas públicas en esta ciudad son *City Hotel, Congress Hall, National Hotel, American Hotel, Washington Hotel, Franklin Hotel,* todos en la calle Ancha o Broadway. Se pagan regularmente doce pesos cada semana por cuarto y comida, que consiste en almuerzo, comida, té y cena. El edificio de Washington Hotel es amplio y de hermosa fachada. En sus cercanías están los baños de la Arcada que son los mejores de la ciudad, establecidos por un español llamado Quesada. Hay además otros muchos de segundo orden fuera de los *boarding houses* de que he hablado, cuyo número es de más de ochocientos.

En ningún pueblo del globo hay tan grande cantidad de periódicos proporcionalmente a la población, que en los Estadas Unidos del Norte. En Nueva York había en 1831, veintiocho periódicos, la mayor parte de una grande dimensión. En todas las poblaciones que llegan a dos mil habitantes, lo primero que hacen los vecinos es levantar un pequeño templo; hacer uno o dos edificios para escuelas, y poner una imprenta. Cuando leí días pasados un proyecto presentado en el Senado de México por el señor Pacheco Leal, en 21 de marzo de este año, por el que se debía dar una fianza de cien mil pesos para poder publicar un periódico, recordé la distancia que había entre la libertad que se procura al pensamiento y a la publicación de las opiniones y de las ideas, en el país que nos hemos propuesto por modelo, y nuestra pobre república, en donde los que pretenden dirigir los negocios públicos, lejos de caminar francamente a la emancipación de nuestra pasada servidumbre, procuran mantener el monopolio del pensamiento, y oponen obstáculos al progreso intelectual de sus conciudadanos. Yo no entiendo como hombres que profesan principios republicanos y populares puedan, ni aun momentáneamente, adoptar semejantes proyectos que pugnan diametralmente con la soberanía popular.

He dicho que en Nueva York había cien templos; pero no he hablado de la manera en que el clero es mantenido, y esto merece una particular explicación.

El pueblo americano es sumamente religioso, hasta el grado de fanático en algunos pueblos y congregaciones; pero el culto está enteramente en manos del pueblo. Ni el gobierno general, ni el de los Estados tienen género alguno de intervención en las materias religiosas. La necesidad de tener un, templo o capilla para juntarse los *sábados,* como ellos dicen, conforme al precepto del Génesis, forma esas asambleas de gentes de un mismo culto, quienes convienen en los términos en que se ha de arreglar el culto: nombran sus ministros, los mantienen, y ejercen sobre ellos la jurisdicción que debe tener una compañía que paga sus dependientes. Para facilitar el ejercicio de su gobierno litúrgico y económico, se eligen cierto número de personas que tienen las facultades de administración delegadas por la Congregación. Entre los protestantes, luteranos, presbiterianos, episcopales, etc., el pueblo elige sus ministros, y los despide cuando tienen mala conducta. Entre los católicos sucede lo mismo; pero usan la forma de pedirlo al obispo, que jamás se lo niega. Los obispos católicos son enviados por el Papa; y ellos los reciben o no según les parece conveniente. Los episcopales, cuando tienen vacante, se reúnen a nombrar sus prelados. Todo esto es conforme a la disciplina de los primeros siglos del cristianismo, y *compatible con el sistema de igualdad popular. Otro cualquier método, en que el gobierno tenga parte en los negocios del culto, es destructivo de la libertad.*

No puedo resistir al deseo de insertar aquí un documento, que da una idea clara y perceptible de todo el sistema político de los Estados Unidos del Norte, en lo concerniente a materias religiosas. El que habla es un obispo de la Congregación Episcopal, Mr. Hobart que murió en un pueblo del Estado de Nueva York, ejerciendo su santo ministerio, cuando yo me hallaba en aquel Estado.

A la muerte del gobernador De Witt Clinton, uno de los hombres más benéficos y honrados de los Estados Unidos, el corregidor de la ciudad de Nueva York pasó una nota al obispo Hobart suplicándole hiciese publicar de una manera solemne en los templos de su culto, la lamentable muerte del gobernador del Estado. Ved aquí lo que contestó el obispo en 16 de febrero de 1828.

"Señor, he recibido hoy del secretario de la corporación de la ciudad una copia de la resolución del consejo común (ayuntamiento), por la que se suplica a los reverendos eclesiásticos de la ciudad respetuosamente publiquen mañana, en forma correspondiente y solemne, en sus iglesias, la muy lamentable desgracia sufrida por nuestra patria común con la muerte de nuestro primer magistrado y conciudadano De Witt Clinton.

"Como yo me veo en la necesidad de negarme a cumplir con esta demanda en la Iglesia de la Trinidad y capillas de San Juan y San Pablo de que estoy encargado como párroco, espero me permitirá exponer las razones en que me fundo, para evitar mala inteligencia en el particular.

"La prostitución de la religión en usos de la política secular ha producido muchos perjuicios; y ya concibo que la estudiada separación de la Iglesia de la intervención del Estado, que caracteriza nuestra constitución republicana, ha tenido por objeto prevenir y evitar el que la religión y sus ministros puedan venir a ser instrumentos de que usen algunos en sus miras políticas. Ahora bien, si la autoridad municipal desea que el clero comunique 'de una manera solemne y propia' la muerte del primer magistrado del Estado, esta misma petición puede extenderse sucesivamente a todos los ciudadanos distinguidos en empleos públicos, y de esta manera la intervención del clero puede hacer aumentar la influencia de hombres políticos y de sus medidas políticas. Peligro del cual se han visto los más lamentables resultados en el antiguo mundo, y contra el cual debemos de todos modos procurar libertarnos en nuestra feliz patria.

"Cualquiera que sea el carácter del individuo, no puede nunca ser digno de esta sagrada distinción religiosa. En circunstancias de grandes excitaciones políticas, un individuo puede ser aborrecido por unos y el ídolo de otros, y en este caso el clero, cuyo instituto es administrar a todos en sus funciones espirituales, sería obligado a tomar un rango entre los partidos, y experimentar rudos conflictos. En casi todos los casos, los ministros de la religión, en su capacidad de eulogistas, se encuentran embarazados entre las diversas opiniones de su auditorio, entre el que hay personas que quieren elogios extraordinarios, y hay otros a quienes parecerá excesivo un panegírico moderado. De manera que no hay aspecto, en mi modo de ver, por donde no se encuentren serias objeciones al cumplimiento de la demanda de la corporación.

"Por lo que mira a mis sentimientos privados, sería de mucha satisfacción para mí dar un testimonio público de los eminentes talentos, servicios civiles y virtudes privadas del primer magistrado que lloramos. Son, además, muy dignas de consideración las peticiones de los funcionarios municipales de la ciudad en que ejerzo mi ministerio. Pero consideraciones superiores de deber me prohiben cumplir con una demanda que en el principio que envuelve y en los precedentes que establece, me parece de una peligrosa tendencia, con respecto al espíritu de nuestra libre constitución, al espíritu de la religión y al carácter e influencia de sus ministros. Tengo el honor, etc.

"J. H. HOBART"

Entre los ministros respetables por su saber y sus virtudes, que he conocido en los Estados Unidos, merece particular mención el padre don José María Varela, hijo de la isla de Cuba, emigrado de su país por sus principios liberales en la época de las persecuciones de Fernando VII. Otro es el doctor Power, irlandés, ambos católicos, ambos instruidos y ejemplo de virtudes cristianas. El culto católico hace, bastantes progresos en los Estados Unidos, especialmente en los estados de Maryland, Luisiana y Misisipí. Los más extendidos son los presbiterianos, metodistas, episcopales y anabaptistas. El pueblo es por lo general religioso y moral.

En Nueva York, como en las demás ciudades de los Estados Unidos, el pueblo se reúne cuando lo estima conveniente para discutir sobre las cuestiones políticas de interés general. No solamente hay asambleas para uniformar la opinión en las elecciones, las hemos visto también formarse para deliberar sobre las difíciles teorías de los bancos; de las tarifas o aranceles; y otras que se han agitado últimamente en los Estados Unidos. En Nueva York se reúnen por lo regular en *Tamany Hall, Masonic Hall, City Hall*, en la *Bolsa*, que son los edificios más amplios y acomodados al efecto. Admira ver el orden con que se reúnen y disuelven estas asambleas, que siempre dan principio nombrando un presidente, dos vicepresidentes y secretarios para dirigir las discusiones. Muy raras veces se ven en ellas excesos, ni se oyen voces tumultuosas, ni mucho menos desórdenes de otro género. Cuando se abre la discusión el presidente propone las cuestiones que se van a tratar, y se concede la palabra al que la pide. Regularmente ya llevan escritas las resoluciones que los individuos que las dirigen consideran ser la opinión de los concurrentes. Como cada partido tiene sus localidades determinadas, ya se sabe poco más o menos cuáles serán las resoluciones. Así hemos visto que en *Tamany Hall* se reunieron constantemente los partidarios del general Jackson, así como en *Masonic Hall* los contrarios. Por consiguiente las resoluciones de la primera han sido siempre contra el banco de los Estados Unidos, contra la elección de M. Glay, etc. Al día siguiente se publican las resoluciones en los periódicos y en carteles que fijan en los parajes públicos. Así se difunden por todos los demás Estados, en los que se forman asambleas de la misma manera, y al cabo de dos meses ya se puede decir aritméticamente cuántos ciudadanos opinan por un lado, y cuántos por el otro. Cuando ha hablado la mayoría, la cuestión se considera resuelta, y ninguno piensa apelar de su decisión, a mano armada, para deshacer lo hecho. En algunas cuestiones complicadas, como la del *Banco*, en que se cruzan grandes intereses, lo más que sucede es dilatarse la resolución; porque el pueblo no puede entenderla en las primeras discusiones, y la complicación dificulta mucho el conocimiento de lo mejor.

En una de esas asambleas, tenida en el mes de enero de este año sobre la cuestión del Banco de los Estados Unidos, se tomaron las resoluciones siguientes: "1° La opinión de esta asamblea es que los perjuicios que sufren todas las clases, son debidos a la intervención anticonstitucional del Presidente de los Estados Unidos para arreglar la circulación de valores. 2° La manera con que el Poder Ejecutivo se ha arrogado la disposición de los fondos del Gobierno, indica una tendencia al arbitrario, y prueba que tiene la intención de administrar sin ningún miramiento a la constitución ni a las leyes del país. 3° Se nombrarán treinta personas que formarán una comisión de salud pública, cuyo encargo será el de entenderse con la comisión de la Unión; ponerse en correspondencia con las demás comisiones organizadas para aplicar remedios oportunos a los males que affligen el país, y en fin tomar las medidas convenientes para que la administración pública obre conforme a la Constitución. 4° La manera indigna y brutal con que el general Jackson se ha conducido con la comisión de obreros y artesanos de esta ciudad, envilece el rango elevado que ocupa en calidad de Presidente de los Estados Unidos, y ofende el cuerpo entero de los signatarios, de quienes los comisionados eran los representantes. En cuanto a Martín Van Buren, la recepción poco conveniente que hizo a las mismos comisionados, manifiesta el poco aprecio que hace de la clase obrera e industriosa de esta ciudad".

Este acuerdo acalorado, fruto de la asamblea tenida en la Bolsa, fue contrariado a los tres días por otro de una junta más numerosa tenida en *Tamany Hall,* en el que aprobaban las resoluciones del Presidente. Así se ventilaban las cuestiones más arduas; pero jamás se llega a vías de hecho.

El Estado de Nueva York tiene ochenta Bancos, cuyos capitales ascienden a veintisiete millones ochocientos mil pesos. Hay en circulación cuarenta y tres millones setecientos doce mil novecientas cincuenta y ocho pesos, de descuentos que facilitan estos bancos, la mayor parte en papel, y esto da una actividad increíble a todos los ramos de industria. Entre estos bancos existen algunos pequeños cuyos fondos son de cien mil pesos, y circulan dos o trecientos mil, y apenas se forma una ciudad de alguna consideración, empiezan a pensar en levantar un banco. En la legislatura del Estado había peticiones para conceder carta a cincuenta bancos nuevos, o renovar las de los antiguos. Estos bancos tienen la base sólida de su existencia en que los prestamistas toman los fondos para invertirlos en usos productivos, como son laboríos de tierras, compras de ganados, construcción de casas, de buques, y otras empresas siempre útiles y que dan ganancias superiores a los intereses. Esta es la razón por qué se ha visto prosperar estas especulaciones que crean valores imaginarios y ponen en circulación capitales no existentes.

De Nueva York salen paquetes regulares tres o cuatro veces al mes, para Liverpool, Londres, Havre, Nueva Orleans, Charleston; y otros, no tan regulares y frecuentes, para Veracruz, Jamaica, La Habana y Costa Firme. Entre los primeros hay buques notables por la comodidad, aseo y aun elegancia de sus cámaras. El trato es generalmente bueno, la comida abundante y los vinos a discreción. Siempre es mucho mayor el número de pasajeros al regreso de Europa, especialmente de las gentes pobres que emigran. No hay paquete que deje de llevar de cuarenta a cincuenta emigrados, que van a buscar a las Américas tierras, trabajo y libertad.

La mayor parte de los habitantes de Nueva York y del Estado son descendientes de holandeses. Conservan sus usos, costumbres, y en muchas partes el idioma. De aquí proviene que la mayor parte de las casas estén pintadas de colores vivos, lo que da a la ciudad y poblaciones más pequeñas un aire de alegría que agrada al viajero.

CAPÍTULO VII

Colonización de Texas.—Formación de la compañía.—Clase de habitantes de aquella comarca.—Su futuro destino.—Encuentro de mi hijo en Nueva York.—Personajes con quienes traté.—Bello sexo.—Museos.—Instrucción pública.—Intervención del pueblo en los negocios públicos.—Tribunales.

Una de las primeras cosas que hice luego que llegué a Nueva York fue llevar a efecto la formación de una compañía para cumplir con las condiciones del convenio celebrado por mí con el gobierno del Estado de Coahuila y Texas, relativo a colonizar las tierras que existen entre el Sabina, la bahía de Galveston, el pueblo de Nacodoches y el mar. Semejante empresa no podía yo llevarla a efecto solo, porque requería fondos de consideración, y en consecuencia solicité personas que quisiesen entrar en la empresa. Don José Vilhein, vecino de México, que tiene una concesión limítrofe a la mía, me confirió su poder amplio para establecer una colonia de ambas, y M. David Burnet, que tiene otra concesión en la parte interior en donde terminan las nuestras, se asoció igualmente con nosotros; resultando de las tres colonias una grande extensión de terreno colonizable, en cuyas tierras debíamos, en un espacio dado, establecer cerca de dos mil familias.

Esta empresa se realizó entre más de cincuenta personas de varios estados, habiendo nombrado nosotros *fideicomisarios o trustees,* de esta vasta empresa, a los señores Dey, Curtís y Summer encargados de los fondos y de cuanto fuese conveniente para dar cumplimiento a las leyes de colonización del Estado de Coahuila y Texas, en lo concerniente a las concesiones hechas por el gobierno del Estado a los ciudadanos Lorenzo de Zavala, José Vilheín y David G. Burnet. Mis enemigos de México comentaron este paso, no solamente inocente sino benéfico al país, de una manera odiosa, diciendo que yo había vendido la parte de Texas a los Estados Unidos, y que me había enriquecido con aquella venta. El tiempo y mis pobrezas han hecho desaparecer todas estas calumnias. El gobierno del Estado ha hecho justicia a mis esfuerzos patrióticos, y me ha concedido prórroga de tiempo, en consideración a los obstáculos que opuso la admi-

275

nistración del general Bustamante a la empresa, y la persecución que declaró el general Terán a mi colonia naciente, no permitiendo desembarcar a los colonos enviados por la compañía, a tomándolos para otros puntos. Todo esto es público en aquellos lugares, y el mismo gobierno supremo del Estado elevó quejas contra Terán.

En mi *Ensayo histórico* de las revoluciones de México he manifestado mis opiniones acerca de esa bella y rica porción de terreno, conocido antes por provincia de Texas, y hoy como una parte integrante del Estado de Coahuila y Texas. Abierta la puerta a la colonización, como debía ser, bajo un sistema de gobierno libre, era necesario que una generación nueva apareciese dentro de pocos años poblando parte de la República Mexicana, y de consiguiente que esta nueva población fuese enteramente heterogénea, respecto de las otras provincias o Estados del país. Quince o veinte mil extranjeros distribuidos en las vastas comarcas de México, Oaxaca, Veracruz, etc., diseminados entre los antiguos habitantes, no pueden causar ningún cambio súbito en sus usos, costumbres y hábitos. Más bien ellos adoptan las inclinaciones, maneras, idioma, religión, política y aun los vicios de la multitud que les rodea. Un inglés será mexicano en México, y un mexicano inglés en Londres. No sucederá lo mismo con las colonias. Lugares enteramente desiertos, bosques y florestas, inhabitadas hace doce años, convertidos en villas y pueblos repentinamente por alemanes, irlandeses y norteamericanos, deben por necesidad formar una nación enteramente diversa, y sería absurdo pretender que renunciasen a su religión, a sus costumbres y a sus más profundas convicciones. ¿Cuáles serán los resultados?

Ya lo he anunciado muchas veces. Ellos no podrán sujetarse al régimen militar y gobierno eclesiástico, que por desgracia ha continuado en el territorio mexicano, a pesar de las constituciones republicodemocráticas. Alegarán las instituciones que deben gobernar el país, y querrán que no sea un engaño, una ilusión, sino una realidad. Cuando un jefe militar intente intervenir en sus transacciones civiles, resistirán y triunfarán. Formarán asambleas populares para tratar los asuntos públicos, como se practica en los Estados Unidos y en Inglaterra. Levantarán capillas de diferentes cultos para adorar al Creador conforme a sus creencias. Las prácticas religiosas son una necesidad social, uno de los grandes consuelos a los males de la humanidad. ¿El gobierno de México enviará a Texas una legión de soldados para hacer cumplir el artículo 3° de la Constitución mexicana, que prohibe el ejercicio de otro culto que el católico? Dentro de pocos años esta feliz conquista de civilización continuará su curso por los otros Estados hacia el sudoeste, y los de Tamaulipas; Nuevo León, San Luis, Chihuahua, Durango, Jalisco y Zacatecas serán los más libres en la confederación mexicana; mientras que los de México, Puebla, Veracruz, Oaxaca, Michoacán y Chiapas tendrán que experimentar, durante algún tiempo, la influencia militar y eclesiástica.

A mi llegada a Nueva York tuve el placer de poder estrechar en mi seno a mi hijo Lorenzo, en el establecimiento literario de los señores Peugne, a donde le había enviado hacía cinco años. Nada puede igualarse a la agradable y dulce impresión que se recibe cuando después de una larga ausencia encuentra el hombre los objetos de su cariño y de su amor. Pero estas sensaciones vienen a ser más gratas cuando ve en ellos los herederos de su nombre, su misma imagen y sus representantes, por decirlo así, en la posteridad. Las semillas de virtud y de instrucción que los dinos directores de aquel colegio sembraron en el alma de mi hijo, habían prendido y echado raíces profundas. Todo esto me indemnizaba de mis pasados sufrimientos. Poco después le pasé a otro colegio, en Round Hill, en el Estado de Massachusets, bajo la dirección de M. Cogswell, sujeto respetable por sus luces y excelente carácter.

En Nueva York tuve relaciones con el célebre Alberto Gallatin, uno de los hombres más instruidos y respetables de los Estados Unidos, aunque nacido en Suiza. Ha sido Ministro de Hacienda, y uno de los compañeros de los primeros fundadores de la Constitución y de las instituciones. Tuve igualmente relaciones de amistad con el señor don Tomás Gener, español emigrado, diputado en las Cortes de 1823, muy apreciado en Nueva York por su ilustración, su honradez y relaciones respetables; con el general Laihtg; en cuya amable familia encontró mi hijo los consuelos y favores de una generosa hospitalidad; M. James Prentis, M. Web, editor del *Morning Courier and Enquirer;* M. Fisher, editor del *Advertiser and Advocate;* M. Dwithg, editor del *Daily Advertiser.* Después haré mención de otras personas que tuve la satisfacción de tratar, y figuran en aquel país. En el mismo *boarding house* o pensión en que me alojé, estaba un dinamarqués llamado Segismundo Leidesdorf, que había residido muchos años en Santa Fé de Bogotá, como agente de una de las casas prestamistas de Londres. Este individuo, con quien posteriormente he tenido amistad, es un sujeto de muchos conocimientos, de un trato agradable, de maneras decentes y bastante instruido en materia de créditos, bancos y aun de finanzas. El general Bolívar le había mandado salir del país por sus relaciones de amistad con el general Santander, con nuestro encargado de negocios don Anastasio Torrens, y el cónsul británico M. Handerson, a todos los que mandó Bolívar librar pasaporte. La opinión de M. Leidesdorf sobre el Libertador de Colombia no le era muy favorable.

Entre los objetos que sorprenden a un mexicano que viaje por la primera vez en los Estados Unidos, uno de ellos es la belleza de las mujeres: Todos los viajeros hablan de esta gran ventaja de aquellos países, y con mucha más razón debe hacerlo un mexicana. En efecto, entre nosotros el bello sexo tiene gracia, proporciones regulares, está dotada generalmente de mucho espíritu y de una amabilidad inestinguible. Pero no hay esa multitud de bellezas que a cada paso se encuentran en los Estados del Norte. Aun en la misma República Mexicana se advierte que las mujeres del Norte son más bellas que las del Sur; así que las de Sonora y Nuevo México tienen fama de hermosas en el país. Las norteamericanas tienen colores muy buenos, ojos vivaces y grandes, manos y pies bien formados; pero están muy distantes de la elegancia y voluptuoso modo de andar de nuestras mexicanas, de las que puede decirse *incessu patent deoe*.

En Nueva York hay dos museos que, como en los Estados Unidos y en Inglaterra, son de compañías particulares. El de M. Peels es el más antiguo, aunque en el otro hay más abundancia de animales muy bien conservados. El de Peels tiene cuadros bastante regulares, los retratos de los principales personajes de la América del Norte y el del fundador del museo, hecho por él mismo. También hay un liceo en el que son admitidos los extranjeros presentados por alguno de sus miembros, en donde se leen los papeles públicos del país y extranjeros. El liceo, que llaman *American Lyceum,* y del que soy miembro, tiene por objeto promover la enseñanza primaria.

Este ramo es uno de los más atendidos en aquella ciudad. Nueva York tiene más de trecientas escuelas, la mayor parte gratuitas, en que aprenden cerca de cuarenta mil niños de ambos sexos. No he visto ningún hombre que no sepa leer, y muy pocos son los que no sepan escribir entre los que habitan las ciudades de los Estados Unidos. De aquí proviene el que lean los papeles públicos, tomen parte en las cuestiones de grande interés, y formen una masa de opinión irresistible. Ningún pueblo hay ni ha habido en donde los ciudadanos tengan o hayan tenido una influencia tan decisiva y directa en las resoluciones de su gobierno. En Atenas y en Roma un pueblo dirigido por oradores ambiciosos o asalariados, tomaba al parecer sus resoluciones después del examen de las materias que se sujetaban a su deliberación. Toda era obra del entusiasmo o del espíritu de partido, de donde resultaban esos actos de injusticia, que la posteridad ha condenado, y que condujeron aquellas repúblicas a su ruina. Pericles en Atenas, y Cicerón en Roma, no fueron los únicos que dominaron y dirigieron la multitud por su elocuencia. Aristófanes comenzó la desgracia de Sócrates, y Anito sublevó los sentimientos del pueblo contra el más sabio de los hombres. Clodio dio principio a la desgracia del grande orador romano, y Antonio le llevó al suplicio. En los Estados Unidos del Norte aunque el pueblo gobierne, y las Cámaras sean su fiel intérprete, las resoluciones vienen de largas y profundas discusiones. Los *Meetings* o asambleas populares en que se debaten las cuestiones políticas, no resuelven nada definitivamente. Manifiestan únicamente la opinión de una fracción pequeña del país, que encuentra o no encuentra simpatías o cooperación en las otras asambleas de la Unión. Entretanto se discuten las mismas cuestiones en los periódicos, y el norteamericano al pie de un árbol si es labrador o pastor, o en su bufete si es abogado, o en su mostrador si negociante, o en su taller si artesano, lee y fija sus ideas con calma y madurez. Un gobierno semejante es la utopía buscada por los escritores políticos.

La administración de justicia en los Estadas Unidos no está enteramente libre de las chicanas judiciales. Sin embargo, en todo se observa la admirable simplicidad de su gobierno. "Es difícil concebir, dice un viajero inglés, menos fórmulas en la administración de justicia, que la de los Estados Unidos. Jueces y abogados sin pelucas ni togas, vestidos como quieren o pueden salir a la calle. Allí no hay mazas ni símbolo alguno de autoridad, a excepción de unas varillas que observé tenían en las manos algunos alguaciles, o porteros del Tribunal. Los testigos daban sus declaraciones con apariencia de la mayor flema o indiferencia que la que se acostumbra en Inglaterra. Ninguno parecía pensar que se hallaba delante del Tribunal, y que debía por consecuencia mantener cierto decoro. Los jueces serían de cincuenta años de edad, y no tenían nada de afectación en el modo de desempeñar sus funciones. Los abogados, aunque más jóvenes, según puedo alcanzar, cumplían con su deber, con celo y capacidad en la defensa de sus clientes. La sola cosa desagradable de aquel espectáculo, en el que me complacía de ver administrarse la justicia con pureza y buena fe, era el continuo salivar de toda la concurrencia".

"Habiendo satisfecho mi curiosidad en este Tribunal, pasé a otro, continúa el viajero, el que me informé ser el Supremo Tribunal del Estado. En este momento estaba ocupado de un proceso sobre billetes de banco. La aridez de la materia me hizo salir; pero antes de retirarme advertí que se llamó a los jurados para pronunciar. Debo confesar que me causó admiración el ver las tres cuartas partes de los jurados ocupados en comer pan y queso, y que el presidente de éstos anunciase la sentencia con la boca llena emitiendo las sílabas cortadas en los intervalos que se lo permitía la masticación. A la verdad que un americano parece ver en un juez un artesano cualquiera, como ve un carpintero, un sastre o un zapatero, y no le ocurre que un administrador de justicia es digno de más respeto que un fabricante de pomadas o de velas. El juez y el velero son igualmente pagados por su trabajo, y Jonatan firmemente cree que mientras tenga dinero en la bolsa, no hay miedo de que le falten ni leyes, ni sartenes".

"No puedo sin embargo persuadirme que, con respecto a esta materia, la legislación esté fundada en este país sobre sólidos y luminosos principios. Un abogado muy instruido me preguntó la otra noche si las visitas que yo había hecho a los Tribunales, no me habían curado de mi adhesión a las fórmulas de *John Bull* (inglesas), y a las togas, pelucas, mazas y demás aparatos insustanciales y ridículas insignias que allí se usaban, y sólo podían imponer a almas débiles. Yo le contesté que no: y que por el contrario, después de mi llegada a Nueva York, me había yo confirmado más en la conveniencia de aquel aparato. Siguió una larga discusión sobre la materia, en la que cada uno sostenía su propia opinión, debiendo decir en obsequio de la justicia, que mi contendiente usaba de argumentos apoyados sobre la libertad, y expresados con fuerza y energía. Me abstengo de dar el detalle de esta discusión, porque un *protocolo* firmado por una de las partes es evidentemente un documento parcial, y cuando un casuista goza del privilegio de aducir los argumentos de ambas partes es necesario que esté dotado de un desprendimiento de sí mismo sobrehumano, para no presentar los de su contrario débiles, colocándose él mismo al lado de los dioses, mientras que deja al opositor el de Caton".

"Es uso en estos países el preguntar, y generalmente con cierto aire de triunfo, si en Inglaterra se cree que la sabiduría consiste en una peluca, y si unas cuantas onzas de crines puestas en la cabeza de los jueces, apelmasadas con pomada y polvos de almidón, pueden imaginarse que aumenten los conocimientos de las personas cuyos cráneos están tan molestamente envueltos. La respuesta es que no: ningún inglés cree que la cabeza al natural, o bien guarnecida con estas cosas, pueda ser más o menos dispuesta para sus juicios y criterio legal, y aún no tengo inconveniente en admitir que en algunas regiones un *juez en cuerpo,* y sentado en un banco simple y llano de madera, puede ser tan eficaz y útil administrador del derecho, como uno empelucado y cubierto de una toca de armiño y escarlata. Pero esto no da la consecuencia que quieren inferir los americanos de la inutilidad de estos aparatos. Si el hombre fuese un ser de pura razón, las formas serían innecesarias; mas quien legislase bajo tal concepto, probaría que no conoce la humana naturaleza. El hombre es un ser de sentidos y de imaginación, y aun en las materias religiosas la constante experiencia del mundo ha manifestado la necesidad de ciertos ritos exteriores y de observancias solemnes, para estimular su devoción y habituarle a encontrar sus facultades para el culto de un ser misterioso e incomprensible, 'cuyo reino está en donde no hay tiempo ni espacio'. Es difícil concebir sobre qué principio aquellos que aprueban la estola en el sacerdote, y los galones en el general, podrán condenar como irracional las insignias de los jueces. Sean consecuentes los americanos, revistiendo a sus jueces con títulos de honor, deben protegerlos de la rusticidad y vulgar familiaridad de su pueblo".

Así se explica este viajero, quien no parece ser buen lógico, queriendo sacar la consecuencia de que los jueces deben estar vestidos en el Tribunal con ropajes que se usaban hace cuatrocientos años, sobre el principio en que convengo, de que es necesario cierto aparato de dignidad para imponer respeto. En efecto, nada pueden contribuir a la majestad de las leyes, ni a la inviolabilidad de los oráculos de la justicia, esas vestimentas mímicas que usan los jueces en Inglaterra, y los presidentes de sus Cámaras. El Parlamento inglés es respetado y obedecido en el interior, por la justicia de sus acuerdos, y sabiduría de sus deliberaciones, y considerado en el exterior por la política profunda de sus resoluciones; así como la magistratura de la misma nación, es digna de los elogios que le tributan todos los escritores que hablan de ella, por la integridad, instrucción y pureza de sus miembros. Si los jueces de Inglaterra se presentasen en su tribunal con los vestidos comunes de la sociedad, no serían por eso menos respetados. Así se hace en los más de los Tribunales de Francia y en los de los Estados Unidos, en donde la magistratura goza justamente de la más distinguida consideración.

Si yo pudiese transportar a mis conciudadanos a estos pueblos libres para presenciar la manera simple y natural con que hacen sus juicios, lograría ciertamente ver establecido en mi patria el juicio por *jurados,* sin el cual no puede haber verdadera libertad ni independencia judicial. En algunos Estados de la República Mexicana se hicieron algunos ensayos, y sus legisladores se pararon en el principio de su carrera filosófica, porque no encontraron los oráculos del Aréopago en las primeras deliberaciones de hombres inexpertos y poco acostumbrados a este género de juicios. En todas partes aconteció lo mismo en su principio, y la constancia y la convicción de ser éste el único método de enjuiciar conforme a los principios de la libertad, hizo a los legisladores mantener tan santa institución. "Las penas contra el robo eran severas, dice M. Hallan en su *Historia constitucional de Inglaterra;* pero eran sin embargo ineficaces para reprimir esos actos de violencia que nacen naturalmente del seno de las costumbres groseras y licenciosas de aquella época y de las disposiciones imperfectas que se habían tomado para asegurar la tranquilidad pública. Estos actos eran cometidos o aconsejados muchas veces por personas cuya fortuna y poder los ponía fuera del alcance de las leyes". Ved aquí el caso en que nos hallamos actualmente en México, y el tiempo más a propósito para establecer el jurado. Jamás me cansaré de decirlo. Bajo cualquiera forma de gobierno que haya de quedar definitivamente la República Mexicana, será un grave cargo a sus directores, no establecer el juicio por jurados.

CAPÍTULO VIII

Washington Irving.—Sus escritos.—Hospitalidad de Nueva York.—Aniversario de la independencia de México.—Objeto de las conversaciones de los americanos.—Inclinación a los ingleses.—Relación de M. Adams sobre el reconocimiento de la Gran Bretaña.—Su discurso al rey.—Contestación de Jorge III.—Fiestas en Nueva York por la Revolución Francesa.—Masthen Burke.—Población de color.—Conducta de Inglaterra sobre los escalvos.—Reflexiones.—Anécdotas.—Incendios.—Aristocracia en los Estados Unidos.—M. Liwingston.

Estando en Nueva York llegó a aquella ciudad el ilustre escritor americano, Washington Irving, de regreso de Europa. Fue recibido por sus conciudadanos con el entusiasmo que inspira naturalmente la presencia de un compatriota, cuyas obras han merecido la aprobación del orbe literario, y ser colocado al lado de los autores clásicos. Washington Irving ha escrito un crecido número de novelas y otras obras que le han elevado al rango de Goldsmith, Addison y Robertson. Se ha dicho de él que su *Bracebridge Hall* era comparable al *Vicario de Wakefield* de Goldsmith: su *Sketch Book* al *Spectator* de Addison y su historia de Cristóbal Colón a las historias de Robertson. Su estilo es estilo de los Burkes, de los Gibbons. Es además un verdadero pintor de las costumbres como Walter Scott. Cooper, otro escritor americano, no debe ser pasado en silencio. Sus novelas están escritas con elegancia, naturalidad y verosimilitud. El interés que inspiran, es un interés real que no se disipa ni desvanece cuando se ha dejado el libro de la mano, como acontece generalmente. Deja grandes y profundas reflexiones.

En Nueva York recibí la más cordial hospitalidad de todas las personas a quienes fui presentado. Muchas me hicieron el honor de convidarme a sus comidas y partidas de té. En los Estados Unidos, como en Inglaterra, las señoras se retiran después de los postres, y los hombres permanecen a la mesa por algún tiempo más. Las partidas de té se reducen a tertulias en que por lo regular hay canto y algunas veces baile. Se sirven frutas, té, virgos, dulces, bizcochos, pasteles u otras cosas semejantes. Los hombres de negocios, no los olvidan en estas ocasiones. En septiembre de 1830 celebramos en Nueva York, en un banquete, el aniversario de la independencia de México. Los concurrentes fuimos los generales Negrete, Echavarry y Mejía, el conde Cornaro, don José Armaro Ruiz, el cónsul de Colombia Medina, varios norteamericanos respetables y yo.

En ningún país del mundo se trata más constantemente de negocios mercantiles y modo de hacer dinero. Entre muy pocas gentes se habla de cuestiones abstractas, o de materias en que no se verse algún interés material. Un americano preguntará a un mexicano, si hay buques de vapor, si hay manufacturas, si hay minas, si busca el dinero con facilidad en tal o tal Estado. Un mexicano preguntará qué clase de gobierno, qué religión, cuáles son las costumbres y si hay teatros en éste o en el otro lugar. Los norteamericanos son esencialmente codiciosos y trabajadores. En Inglaterra en el tiempo de la comida se habla de la calidad de los vinos, de la sazón de las viandas, de la elegancia de la mesa, y de otras cosas análogas a lo que se hace. En los Estados Unidos casi siempre quizá la conversación acerca del precio del algodón, de la madera, etc.

Aunque generalmente se cree que los americanos del Norte tienen, respecto de los ingleses, la misma aversión que se ha desenvuelto en las antiguas colonias españolas contra los españoles no es enteramente exacto. Es verdad que los norteamericanos detestan la autoridad real, y todo lo que tiene conexión con las instituciones monárquicas, y que llevan quizá hasta el exceso su aversión a ciertas fórmulas y etiquetas británicas; pero en cuanto a las personas, estoy cierto de que los ingleses encuentran entre los norteamericanos las simpatías más dulces y agradables en el trato y hospitalidad, así como en el idioma y costumbres populares. El orgullo de primogenitura, y de ventajas que da a los ingleses su antigüedad hace nacer algunas veces cuestiones desagradables entre unos y otros; cuestiones en las que los americanos hacen siempre ostentación, con mucha justicia, de sus admirables progresos, y de su incuestionable libertad. Mas debe convenirse en que la política franca y filosófica del gobierno inglés, respecto de sus antiguas colonias, ha sido mucha parte para disminuir estos odios nacionales, a cuyo objeto contribuyeron constantemente las providencias y exhortaciones de Washington y sus sucesores.

Aunque después de la paz entre la Gran Bretaña y los Estados Unidos, en 1783, el gobierno de la primera no envió ningún ministro ni agente a la nueva república, la manera urbana y atenta con que Jorge III recibió al ministro John Adams, primer enviado americano cerca de S. M. B., dio ocasión para continuar en la más perfecta armonía, en aquellos principios espinosos. M. Adams, que había estado en Europa otras ocasiones con encargos de naturaleza importante, recibió en 1785 el delicado y espinoso de representante en la Corte de Londres, como primer ministro de las colonias emancipadas. Copiaré la relación que este distinguido americano remitió al Secretario de

Estado de su Gobierno, porque me parece que será interesante su lectura, en circunstancias en que la República Mexicana se halla en los momentos de establecer iguales relaciones con su antigua metrópoli.

"Durante mi entrevista con el marqués de Carmarthen, dice M. Adams, me manifestó que era costumbre el que todos los ministros en su primera presentación al Rey hiciesen a S. M. un cumplido conforme al espíritu de sus credenciales, y cuando sir Clement Cottrel Dormer, maestro de ceremonias, vino a informarme que él me acompañaría con el Secretario de Estado a la Corte, me añadió que los nuevos ministros debían hacer también sus cumplimientos a la Reina. El martes por la noche el barón de Lynden, embajador de Holanda, vino a verme y me dijo que venía de la casa del embajador de Suecia, barón de Nolkin, y que habían hablado acerca de la singular situación en que yo me hallaba, y ambos convinieron en la necesidad de que yo hiciese un discurso de cumplimiento al Rey. Todo esto era conforme a lo que últimamente había manifestado el conde de Vergennes a M. Jefferson. Siendo esto así, y viendo que ésta era la costumbre establecida en estas dos grandes Cortes, y que ésta de St. James y los ministros de las otras naciones opinaban lo mismo, creí que no podía evitarlo, aunque mi primera intención había sido entregar mis credenciales sin decir nada y retirarme luego. Por fin el miércoles 1° de junio, el maestro de ceremonias pasó a mi casa por mí y fuimos juntos al ministerio de negocios extranjeros, en donde el marqués de Carmarthen me recibió y me introdujo a M. Frazier, subsecretario. Después de una conversación corta acerca de que se me condujesen mis efectos de Francia y Holanda libres de derechos, el lord Carmarthen me invitó a entrar en su coche para ir a la Corte. Cuando llegamos a la antesala, el maestro de ceremonias salió a recibirme y me entretuvo, mientras el Secretario de Estado iba a tomar las órdenes del Rey. Mientras estuve en esta sala, en donde todos los ministros esperan en tales ocasiones, y que se hallaba llena en esta vez, debe usted suponer que yo era el foco en que se reunían todas las miradas".

"Felizmente me disminuyeron el embarazo en que me hallaba los ministros de Suecia y Holanda que se acercaron a mí y me mantuvieron una conversación agradable. Otros caballeros a quienes había tratado antes me favorecieron igualmente con su conversación hasta la vuelta del ministro, quien me avisó que S. M. nos esperaba. Fui con su señoría hasta el gabinete del Rey. Se cerró la puerta y yo quedé solo con S. M. y el Secretario de Estado. Hice las tres reverencias, una en la puerta, otra en la mitad y otra cerca de S. M., conforme al ceremonial de las Cortes del Norte de Europa, y luego dirigiendo la palabra al Rey, le dije:

"Señor, los Estados Unidos me han nombrado su ministro plenipotenciario cerca de V. M, y tengo el honor de entregar la credencial que lo manifiesta. En obediencia a sus órdenes expresas, tenga la satisfacción de asegurar a V. M. de la unánime disposición de los ciudadanos de aquellos Estados de cultivar las más amistosas y liberales relaciones con V. M., y de sus más sinceros deseos por la salud de V. M. y de su real familia.

"El nombramiento de un ministro de los Estados Unidos cerca de la Corte de V. M. formará época en la historia de Inglaterra y América. Yo me tengo por el más afortunado de mis conciudadanos, por haber tenido el primero el honor distinguido de presentarme a V. M. con carácter diplomático, y me tendré por el más feliz entre los hombres si puedo ser un útil instrumento para recomendar más y más a mi país a la real benevolencia de V. M. y conseguir restaurar una entera confianza, estimación y afecto, o en otros términos, la antigua buena naturaleza, y el antiguo buen humor entre pueblos que, aunque separados por el Océano y por diferentes gobiernos, tienen el mismo idioma, la misma religión y la sangre de familia. Yo suplico a V. M. me permita añadir que aunque he recibido bastantes confianzas de mi país, ninguna ha sido tan agradable y lisonjera como la presente.

"El Rey oyó todo mi discurso con dignidad; pero con cierta emoción. Yo no sé si ella ha sido efecto de la naturaleza de una entrevista semejante, o quizá de la visible agitación con que pronuncié mi discurso; lo cierto es que estaba bastante afectado y me contestó con más vivacidad que la que yo empleé diciéndome:

"Señor, las circunstancias de esta audiencia son muy extraordinarias, el lenguaje que habéis usado es tan adecuado, y los sentimientos que habéis expresado tan oportunos en esta ocasión que debo decir, que no solamente recibo con agrado las seguridades de las amistosas disposiciones del pueblo de los Estados Unidos, sino también que me es muy satisfactorio el que haya recaído en vos el encargo de representarle. Yo deseo, Señor, que os persuadais y que el pueblo americano entienda, que nada he hecho en la última contienda que no haya sido por persuasión de conciencia que no estuviese obligado a hacer en bien de mi pueblo. Debo hablaros con franqueza; yo he sido el último en conformarme con la separación; pero ya verificada, he dicho siempre y ahora repito que yo seré el primero en buscar la amistad de los Estados Unidos como poder independiente. En el momento en que yo vea que los sentimientos que habéis expresado son los de aquel pueblo, en aquel momento podré decir que tendrán su efecto pleno, las grandes simpatías que nacen de una misma religión, un mismo idioma y una sangre misma".

No debe olvidarse que la declaración de independencia se hizo en julio de 1776 y que en 1783 se reconoció como nación soberana por la metrópoli. Nuestras Repúblicas de América, antes española, llevan más de veinte años de haber hecho sus declaraciones de independencia, y más de doce de estar enteramente independientes, sin ningún obstáculo, ni oposición, ni aun capacidad por parte de la España de hacerla; reconocidas como naciones independientes con gobiernos constituidos, por las naciones civilizadas, y el gabinete español y sus nuevas Cortes están todavía pensando si nos harán *la gracia de reconocernos*. Semejante política es mezquina y poco conforme con los principios liberales que han declarado profesar.

Me hallaba en Nueva York cuando llegó la noticia de la famosa revolución de los tres días de julio en París, y de sus felices resultado. Parece increíble el entusiasmo que manifestó el pueblo de los Estados Unidos por un suceso que parecía no deber afectar a una nación comerciante y agricultora dedicada a sus ganancias y mejoras materiales. Pero el sentimiento de libertad está profundamente arraigado en aquellas almas independientes, que jamás pueden renunciar a sus simpatías por el progreso que hacen los demás pueblos para acercarse a su posición social. M. Monroe, Presidente que fue de los Estados Unidos, fue el que presidió la asamblea o *meeting* de los obreros, artesanos, negociantes y demás clases reunidas en *Tamany Hall,* para tomar las disposiciones convenientes a hacer una función grande digna del objeto que se celebraba. La procesión fue una de las más brillantes concurrencias que he visto. Para poder comprender el número de los asistentes a ella basta decir que aunque llevaba un paso regular, el espectador podía estar tres horas en un lugar viéndola pasar. Daba principio con un escuadrón de caballería, seguía el general en jefe, M. Swartswout con sus cuatro edecanes y un destacamento de franceses, residentes en Nueva York, con el uniforme de guardias nacionales de Francia. Seguía un coche abierto en el que iba el ex Presidente Monroe, M. Gallatin y el orador. Después venían las comisiones de los diferentes oficios y ocupaciones con sus correspondientes emblemas, banderas, instrumentos, y luego los músicos, cantores, cómicos. Allí se veían impresores llevando los tipos de la imprenta; sastres, zapateros, plateros, fundidores, herreros, negociantes, marinos, abogados, médicos, estudiantes, cada clase bajo su bandera. Por último los diputados, corregidores, cónsules, todo lo más brillante y respetable. La procesión comenzó en Canal Street, a las nueve de la mañana, y concluyó en *Washington Square* a las seis de la tarde. Había más de cien mil personas en el cuerpo de la procesión. El orden, la decencia, el decoro, la circunspección que reinó desde el principio hasta el fin, fueron correspondientes a la riqueza de la población, al grande objeto que se celebraba, y a la majestad de la nación americana.

En aquellos días representaba en el teatro del Parque el prodigioso Master Burke, irlandés de once años, que tocaba, cantaba, declamaba y hacía la pantomima con la gracia, delicadeza, fuerza y naturalidad que los primeros maestros del arte. Yo he quedado absorto, así como los demás espectadores, al ver un niño de una vara de altura, su voz femenil, sus facciones delicadas, presentarse sobre las tablas y hacer ostentación de sus prodigiosas habilidades.

En la ciudad de Nueva York hay un considerable número de negros y gentes de color; aunque felizmente, así como en los otros Estados del Norte desde el Maryland, no es permitida la esclavitud. Pero a pesar de esta emancipación de la clase africana y su posteridad, existe una especie de proscripción social, que la excluye de todos los derechos políticos, y aun del comercio común con los demás, viviendo en cierta manera como excomulgados. Esta situación es poco natural en un país donde se profesan los principios de la más amplia libertad. Nada puede, sin embargo, vencer la preocupación que existe sobre este particular. Las gentes de color tienen sus habitaciones, sus posadas, sus templos separados: son los judíos de la América del Norte. Esta repulsión de la sociedad los envilece y les quita los estímulos al trabajo: se entregan a la ociosidad, y no procuran mejorar una situación sin esperanzas, encerrada en tan estrechos límites en que apenas pueden tener lugar los cálculos del interés. De aquí los vicios y la pereza, que con muy pocas excepciones retienen a casi toda esta clase en los últimos rangos de la sociedad. Este es el grande argumento contra la emancipación de los esclavos, argumento que desalienta a sus más ardientes partidarios, y que inutilizaría sus esfuerzos si la abolición de la esclavitud no fuese la exigencia de una necesidad que dentro de poco no admitirá más dilación.

La Inglaterra, en medio de las severidades de sus economías, en despecho de sus hábitos mercantiles, acaba de pagar, con el subido precio de cien millones de pesos, una deuda de humanidad y de honor nacional que hace cuarenta años se ha estado manteniendo en esfuerzos inútiles de una impotente filantropía. Mientras que violencias aisladas, y que uno de esos movimientos irreflexivos que no tienen consecuencia, elevan protestas en una ciudad de la América en favor de la esclavitud, una asamblea en Londres *compuesta de todos los partidos,* en donde O'Conell se sentaba al lado del ministro de las colonias, en donde la fiera aristocracia fraternizaba con los hombres de color, celebraba el aniversario de la emancipación de los negros. Lord Murgrave, recientemente llegado de Jamaica, en donde ha presidido las primeras sesiones de la emancipación, ha declarado que la esclavitud por dos años más, hubiera causado los mismos desastres que en Santo Domingo. Este noble ejemplo que se cumple pacíficamente y en el mayor orden en las islas de la América inglesa, no puede dejar de causar un buen efecto en los Estados Unidos del Norte. Todos los hombres que se penetran de que la preocupación del porvenir, debe entrar en las cuestiones de lo presente, se persuaden fácilmente de que la sociedad debe preceder a las declaraciones de la esclavitud, antes que la esclavitud haga sus sangrientas irrupciones en la sociedad. La abolición cuenta ya numerosos partidarios en los congresos de los Estados. Pero ¿cómo se remedia esa situación embarazosa de las gentes de color libres en el centro de la sociedad americana? ¿Llegará un día en que se incorporen al Estado y formen una parte integrante de la comunidad? Debemos esperarlo. La legislatura de Nueva York ya dio el primer paso en 1829 extendiendo el derecho de sufragio a las gentes de color que tuvieren bienes raíces por el valor de doscientos cincuenta pesos, libre de toda carga.

Terminaré esta materia con una anécdota referida por un viajero. El hijo de un general haitiano, muy amigo del Presidente Boyen se propuso hacer un viaje a Nueva York con el objeto de divertirse y de instruirse al mismo tiempo. Este joven, aunque mulato, era de buenas maneras, trato agradable y decente, y de una educación más cuidada que lo que se encuentra en su país. Acostumbrado en su patria a recibir los respetos debidos a su rango, esperaba que en Nueva York encontraría las consideraciones que dan el dinero y la fortuna, con los goces que proporciona una ciudad opulenta y civilizada.

Al desembarcar ordenó que se llevase su equipaje a la mejor posada. Pero encontró que no se le admitía a causa de su color. Pasó a otra y a otra; mas en todas partes encontró el mismo resultado, hasta que se vio obligado a tomar habitación en la casa de una negra. El orgullo del joven haitiano se vio humillado, tanto más cuanto que se presentó vestido con elegancia y adornado con cadenas de oro, anillos y botones de brillantes, etc. Desgraciadamente, continuó experimentando los mismos desaires en todos sus pasos; pues en el teatro no fue admitido en los palcos de los blancos, ni en los templos ni en ninguna sociedad. En la primera oportunidad regresó a su país jurando no visitar más los Estados Unidos. Si este joven hubiera ido a Europa ciertamente habría encontrado todas las comodidades y diversiones que hubiera deseado mediante su dinero, y sentándose en el teatro, en la posada y en el templo junto al más blanco y la más rubia inglesa, francesa o alemana.

"No puede uno estar veinticuatro horas en Nueva York, sin oír los gritos alarmantes de *fuego*, dice un viajero. En efecto, un incendio en aquella ciudad, es una ocurrencia tan común, que nunca causa aquella ansiedad y sobresalto que en otras partes menos acostumbradas a esta calamidad. Los *bombistas* de Nueva York son celebrados por su actividad y resolución; y como es agradable presenciar el ejercicio de estas cualidades, me propuse asistir a todos los incendios que ocurriesen mientras estuviese en la ciudad. Los cuatro primeros fueron de poca consideración, pues tres de ellos estaban ya extinguidos antes de mi llegada, y del cuarto sólo alcancé a ver el humo. En el quinto tuve mejor suerte. Habiendo entrado en el lugar de la escena más adentro de lo que convenía, creyendo que fuese lo mismo que anteriormente, tuve al fin la satisfacción de presenciar la aparición de un volumen respetable de llamas que asomaba de las ventanas, chimeneas y puertas de los cuarto pisos de la casa, acompañado de humo, clamores, ruido y confusión capaz de contentar mis razonables deseos. Luego llegó una bomba de agua, y los gritos y el rechinido de las ruedas de las máquinas anunciaron la aproximación del socorro. Algún tiempo se pasó en conseguir el agua, sobre lo cual es de desear que el ayuntamiento mejore sus disposiciones. Sin embargo, en pocos minutos ya venía a torrentes, y los dos elementos comenzaron su combate. Los que hacen este servicio son jóvenes ciudadanos que por dedicarse a él, y es sumamente severo, están exceptuados del de la milicia. A la verdad que es sorprendente su actividad y osadía. En el momento se pusieron escalas, montaron a las chimeneas, comenzaron a sacar los muebles que arrojaban a la calle sin mucha consideración por los que allí había, a riesgo de romperles los cascos". El viajero continúa haciendo una descripción animada de los progresos del incendio, del brillante espectáculo que presentó por la noche, de la confusión y alarma en las casas vecinas, y hace la observación de que en estos casos debería hacerse lo que en Londres, que para evitar el concurso de gente ociosa que embaraza las operaciones y aumentan las dificultades, deberían cerrarse las entradas y cuidarse por la policía. "Sugiriendo esta idea de mejora a un amigo americano, continúa, me contestó que sería de desear; pero que no estaban calculadas para el meridiano americano estas medidas, en donde la exclusión de cualquiera género es siempre opuesta a los sentimientos populares. En esta materia no puedo persuadirme que la exclusión de un grupo ocioso del teatro del incendio, por aumentar la dificultad de salvar la propiedad y la vida de algunos, pueda considerarse como un ataque a la libertad".

Yo he oído decir a muchas gentes que en los Estados Unidos había una verdadera aristocracia, y a otras que es el país de la libertad y de la *igualdad* absoluta. Unos y otros tienen razón, según el sentido que se dé a la voz *aristocracia*. Ninguna ley, ni costumbre, ni recuerdo histórico existe en aquel país cuya tendencia sea a formar una clase aristocrática. La ley civil llama a todos los ciudadanos delante de los mismos tribunales, la ley política los reviste de las mismos derechos. Pero hay una ley superior a las instituciones humanas, una ley de desigualdad que la Naturaleza ha establecido, y que ningún legislador puede abolir; ley que tiene más imperio en los pueblos libres que en los gobiernos despóticos, pero que siempre ejerce una influencia poderosa: esta ley es la de la capacidad mental, la superioridad del talento. ¿Qué disposición, qué reglamento podrá en efecto hacer que un hombre de talento, de instrucción y de capacidad permanezca al mismo nivel social, en el grado mismo de consideración y de influencia, que otro hombre que no esté dotado de las mismas cualidades? De consiguiente no puede el segundo optar a los mismos empleos, ni ser recibido en sociedad con la misma estimación, ni atraer el respeto y atenciones que el primero. Esta es ya una desigualdad, y esta existe en los Estados Unidos como en todas partes. Webster, Clay, Calhoum, Van Buren, Jackson, Forshyth, Poinsett y otros son personajes muy superiores al resto de sus conciudadanos.

Hay otra superioridad que, aunque no es de la naturaleza, es una consecuencia necesaria del estado en que se halla constituida la sociedad en general, y que han querido infructuosamente modificar varios filósofos utopianistas: esta es la de la riqueza. Un hombre rico debe tener más conexiones, debe ofrecer más esperanzas, debe hacer más gastos que otro pobre. Tiene más medios de influir, y más capacidad de hacer bien y mal, que otro en quien no concurren las circunstancias de riqueza o de talento. Semejante hombre se considera elevado sobre los demás, y en cierta manera lo está, porque de él dependen muchos, porque no necesita trabajar para subsistir, porque puede satisfacer sus necesidades y sus placeres.

Ved aquí las dos clases de gentes que en los Estados Unidos del Norte mantienen una especie de jerarquía habitual, cuyos privilegios naturales no dependen de manera alguna de la legislación. Yo me acuerdo que yendo de Europa a los Estados Unidos, en 1831, en el hermoso paquete Francisco I°, iba al mismo tiempo en el buque la familia de M. François Depau, comerciante millonario de Nueva York, y uno de los socios de la compañía de esos paquetes. Había muchos pasajeros de distinción, entre ellos el general Santander, el señor Acosta, actualmente encargado de negocios de la Nueva Granada, cerca de los Estados Unidos, un noble italiano llamado Suzarelli, en suma toda gente de educación y principios. Sin embargo de esto, M. Depau y su familia comían por separado en la cámara de las señoras, teniendo quizá a menos asociarse con nosotros. Confieso que me ofendía esa conducta, en tales circunstancias. Pero ¿a quién ofendía, o qué derecho podía haber para reclamar contra su ridículo aislamiento? Yo le miraba con menosprecio, lo mismo que mis compañeros. Esto hacen también muchos de los Estados Unidos del Norte.

Compárese ésta con la aristocracia mexicana y se notará la diferencia. Entre nosotros las leyes y las antiguas preocupaciones mantienen una *aristocracia* verdadera, una *aristocracia* de privilegio, en suma una *aristocracia* de leyes *excepcionales* y de consiguiente mortífera en una sociedad republicana popular. ¿Cómo podrán persuadir de su sincero y verdadero afecto a la libertad quienes reconocen clases enteras superiores a las otras por privilegios legales? Esto es lo que no he podido nunca entender, y esto explica también el origen de nuestras últimas revoluciones. En los Estados Unidos podrán transmitirse los venerables nombres de sus hombres de estado, a sus hijos y nietos, si éstos mantienen con sus luces, patriotismo y honor el lustre de sus ascendientes. Pero ya se ve que esta no es una prerrogativa de las leyes; es del mérito personal.

En esta ciudad tuve la satisfacción de ser presentada a M. Eduardo Livingston, ilustre jurisperito de los Estados Unidos, autor de los códigos de la Luisiana y senador entonces, luego Secretario de Estado y hoy ministro plenipotenciario cerca del rey de los franceses. M. Livingston me ha referido él mismo, que después de doce años de un trabajo continuado en la formación de los códigos terminados a su satisfacción, se retiró a las doce de la noche a su alcoba y dijo a su mujer: "Ahora voy a dormir con la satisfacción de haber concluido mi obra al cabo de doce años". A las dos horas sintió ruido y luego clamores de los criados que gritaban *fuego*. El cuarto en que M. Livingston tenía los papeles y libros era el teatro de un incendio voraz. Todo lo consumió el fuego, y M. Livingston dio principio a su tarea al día siguiente con la misma constancia, hasta que de nuevo concluyó su obra digna de un profundo jurisconsulta.

M. Livingston ha hecho un papel muy distinguido igualmente en el desempeño de la Secretaría de Estado que estuvo a su cargo, pendientes las delicadas cuestiones de los *nulificadores* de la Carolina. El tino con que supo manejar los negocios, condujeron las cosas a un feliz desenlace. El manifiesto del Presidente Jackson del mes de diciembre de 1832, obra de M. Livingston, es un documento de la mayor importancia en los anales de los gobiernos republicanos. En este papel se desenvuelven los principios de la forma de gobierno de aquellos Estados con una perspicuidad y maestría dignas de la majestad de un gran pueblo.

CAPÍTULO IX

En agosto salí para Filadelfia tomando pasaje por cuatro pesos en el buque de vapor *Swan*, o Cisne, que es uno de los de la carrera. El viaje se hace tomando al sudoeste por la bahía de Raritan, se entra luego a este río, y se toma tierra en un pequeño pueblo llamado Washington, Estado de Nueva Jersey, que se atraviesa en coches, y se toma otra vez el vapor en Bordentown o en Trenton. En el día se ha variado este curso, después de haberse conducido el camino de fierro, de Amboy a Camden. El viaje dura tres horas por la bahía de Raritan, tres horas por tierra, y tres en el Delaware hasta Filadelfia. La distancia es de cerca de treinta y cinco leguas.

El Estado de Nueva Jersey, que se atraviesa, está situado entre el Océano, el río del Norte, llamado Hudson, el Delaware, y los Estados de Nueva York y Pensilvania. Las principales ciudades son Burlington, N. Brunswick y Trenton. Esta es la capital del Estado. La Constitución de Nueva Jersey fue hecha en 1776 y no se ha revisado desde entonces, a excepción de algunas aplicaciones que ha dado la legislatura. El Poder Ejecutivo como en los demás Estados, lo ejerce el gobernador. Hay un consejo legislativo y una asamblea general. Los miembros de uno y otro son elegidos anualmente el segundo martes de octubre. Estos dos cuerpos forman la legislatura.

El número de miembros del consejo es de catorce, siendo elegido uno por cada condado. La asamblea general se componía de cuarenta y tres individuos. Pero por una ley dada en 1829 se añadieron siete diputados más, y en el día se compone de cincuenta miembros sacados de los condados en el orden siguiente: tres del de Bergen; cinco del de Essex; cuatro del de Morris; tres del de Sussex; tres del de Sommersett; cuatro del de Monmouth; cinco del de Burlington; cuatro de Gloucester; tres de Salem; tres de Cumberland; de uno Cap. May. La legislatura se reúne anualmente en Trenton, el cuarto martes de octubre. El gobernador es nombrado anualmente por el voto del consejo reunido y de la asamblea. El gobernador es presidente del consejo, el cual en su primera sesión, nombra un vicepresidente de su mismo seno, que ejerce las funciones de gobernador en su ausencia.

El gobernador y el Consejo forman tribunal de apelación en todos los casos de ley en última instancia, y tienen la facultad de indultar.

La Constitución concede el derecho de sufragio a todas las personas que tengan una propiedad de valor libre de doscientos pesos, y hayan residido un año en el lugar del condado en que votasen. La legislatura ha declarado en 1829 que todo ciudadano que tuviese veintiún años y un capital de doscientos pesos, pudiese votar siempre que fuese de raza blanca. Por otro decreto los negros y las mujeres son privados del derecho de sufragio. En el Canadá las segundas lo tienen. Los jueces son nombrados por la legislatura. Los de la Suprema Corte por siete de los tribunales inferiores por cinco años.

En Bordentown, pueblo pequeño sobre el Delaware, está la hermosa casa de campo de José Bonaparte, ex Rey de Nápoles y de España, hoy conde de Survilliers. Este célebre personaje, a quien los papeles españoles nos pintaban con tan feos coloridos, tiene mucha instrucción, es de un personal bastante agradable, de maneras elegantes y naturales, y está dotado de cualidades sociales que le han hecho respetable en los Estados Unidos del Norte, a donde se retiró después de la catástrofe del emperador Napoleón, su hermano. Un capital respetable que pudo salvar de su naufragio político, le ha colocado en una situación brillante en aquel país de comercio y de negocios. Su magnífica casa, jardines y parques a las márgenes del delicioso Delaware, bastarían para hacerle feliz, si otras *pretensiones* no le sacasen de la esfera modesta y pacífica, a que le habían reducido las desgracias del grande personaje que elevó toda su familia al rango de reyes.

El Delaware es un río ancho y hermoso, navegable en buques de vapor hasta Trenton. Sus vistas por ambos lados, especialmente en las cercanías de Filadelfia, son magníficas y pintorescas. Casas de campo con pretensiones de arquitectura griega muy limpias, y colocadas en medio de arboledas plantadas con arte, y fecundadas por las aguas de muchos arroyos; aldeas nuevas formadas de edificios de bella apariencia, almacenes y manufacturas. La vegetación es más temprana que en Nueva York. Al lado izquierdo del río se extiende ya el camino de fierro que en el mes de marzo de 1834 llegaba hasta Camden, y probablemente se extenderá hasta el frente de la ciudad de Filadelfia con dos años más.

Esta gran ciudad fundada por Guillermo Penn, habitada al principio por unas cuantas familias cuáqueras, hoy presenta el aspecto de una de las ilustres metrópolis de Europa, con mejor belleza y mucho mayores esperanzas de prosperidad. Desde cuatro leguas se descubren en el río sus torres, sus altos edificios, sus observatorios, y el humo que se eleva en una columna colosal hacia el cielo.

Me alojé en *Mansion House* una de las mejores posadas de los Estados Unidos. Allí encontré a M. Poinsett, mi antiguo amigo, que se ocupaba en escribir para el *Quarterly Review* un artículo acerca de la política inglesa.

La ciudad de Filadelfia está perfectamente cortada en líneas paralelas que forman calles en figuras paralelógramas. Hay desde el número 1 hasta el 11 de Este a Oeste; y de Norte a Sur las calles tienen nombres de plantas o frutas: como *Mulberry,* mora; *Chestnut,* castaño, etc. Pero además de la calle número 11 ya la ciudad se ha extendido cinco o seis calles más, que aún no están numeradas. Las banquetas son de ladrillo y de dos varas de ancho. Las calles son de quince a veinte varas de ancho, la mayor parte de ellas con una línea de árboles de acacia, castaños o nogales, lo que da una hemosa vista y agradable sombra en el estío.

Hay magníficos edificios en la ciudad. La bolsa que se está concluyendo, es mucho mejor que la de Nueva York. El banco de los Estados Unidos es de bello mármol blanco, imitación aunque imperfecto del Parthenon de Athenas; la fachada es bella; pero carece de las columnas laterales. Otro banco frente al de M. Girard *(Bank of Pensylvannia)* tiene seis hermosas columnas de orden jónico, igualmente de mármol.

El estanque y máquina para la provisión de aguas de la ciudad, en las márgenes del delicioso Río Schuytkill, son obras de mucha consideración. Están fabricadas en un lado del río en donde la escena es verdaderamente interesante, y la obra, cuya utilidad ha correspondido a la empresa, es sólida y bella al mismo tiempo. Ningún extranjero debe dejar de hacer su visita a aquella obra. El río tiene en aquella parte cerca de novecientos pies de anchura, con veinticinco de profundidad. Se ha formado una presa que lo atraviesa, un dique que conduce gran parte de las aguas al reservatorio, y otra a los molinos que hacen mover las ruedas destinadas a hacer subir el agua, por medio de bombas, a un estanque abierto en una roca elevada sobre el nivel de la ciudad doscientos setenta pies, a distancia de una legua. Once millones de gallones de agua se elevan diariamente al receptáculo, de donde no solamente se conduce el agua a las fuentes públicas, y sirve para regar y otros usos comunes, sino que pocas casas en Filadelfia no tienen la ventaja de naves de agua en el piso superior. Esta obra tuvo de costo un millón seiscientos mil pesos, y la compañía percibe hoy un interés a lo menos de doce por ciento al año.

En Filadelfia hay dos teatros, uno en *Warnut Street,* y otro en *Chestnut Street:* ambos son pequeños, pero de dimensiones regulares, capaces de con-tener seiscientas personas. Junto al segundo está el Museo, seguramente el más rico y abundante en todo género de objetos curiosos, que ninguno de América. Allí se ven antiguas vestiduras de indios del país, muy semejantes a las de los egipcios, y también se ve el esqueleto completo del *Mammout* más grande que yo haya visto hasta ahora. Los colmillos tienen ocho pies de longitud cada uno de ellos. Allí están los retratos de los principales personajes americanos, de muchas damas y de algunos sabios generales europeos.

En uno de esos teatros dio Miss Wright sus lecciones filosóficas, poco tiempo antes de mi llegada. El teatro estaba lleno de personas de ambos sexos, y oían a la filósofa predicante con una atención jamás interrumpida por signos de aprobación ni reprobación. El objeto principal de sus predicaciones, era persuadir a sus oyentes que en vez de emplear el primer día de la semana en ejercicios de religión, y de gastar veinte millones de pesos al año en mantener predicadores, en construir iglesias y enriquecer gente ociosa, deberían ocupar su tiempo y emplear su dinero en descubrir los arcanos de la Naturaleza. "Tomad por maestros, decía enfáticamente, filósofos experimentales; convertid vuestros templos en salones de ciencia, y dedicad vuestros días festivos al estudio de vuestros mismos cuerpos y al examen del bello mundo material". Las doctrinas de Miss. Wright, como he dicho otra vez, están fundadas en el deismo filosófico, y no pueden convenir a una sociedad. Pero en un pueblo libre, verdaderamente libre, y no libre por *proclamas y constituciones teóricas,* todos los seres pensadores tienen libertad para enunciar sus opiniones, sus sistemas y sus ideas, sin que la autoridad ni la canalla se opongan a éste ejercicio de las facultades mentales.

Una de las cosas que llaman la atención en Filadelfia, es el portentoso navío Pensilvania, que sin duda es el mayor buque construido hasta hoy. Tiene o debe tener ciento cincuenta cañones, y mil cuatrocientos hombres. Su ancla mayor pesa diez mil ciento setenta y una libras. El largo del navío es de doscientos veinte pies y cincuenta y ocho de ancho. Tiene treinta y cuatro baos en cada cubierta: la bao principal es de dos pies de diámetro. Tiene cinco puentes. Así éste como los otros navíos y fragatas de guerra que se construyen en los Estados Unidos, están cubiertos con edificios de madera, que se deshacen cuando se les arroja al agua.

La marina de los Estados Unidos ha dado pruebas inequívocas en la última guerra con la Inglaterra, de su capacidad, valor y disciplina. ¿Qué nación ha sido capaz de hacer frente a la orgullosa Albión, dueña exclusiva del Océano, sino su hija emancipada, esa nación emprendedora que se eleva anualmente a una altura, que algún día sobrepasará a las más poderosas naciones? Los norteamericanos cuentan con orgullo entre sus marinos los nombres de Stephen Decatur, el Nelson americano, Paterson, Bainbribge y Pórter.

En esta ciudad se hizo la famosa declaración de independencia en 4 de julio de 1776, y existe la sala en donde concurrieron los ilustres americanos que la firmaron. En este salón está la estatua del general Washington con esta inscripción al pie:

> Primero en la paz
> Primero en la guerra
> Primero en el corazón de
> Sus conciudadanos.

A la espalda de este edificio está una pequeña plaza, y uno de los ángulos de ella colinda con la bella plaza de Washington, *Washington Square,* uno de los mejores paseos de Filadelfia, acotado con verjas de fierro muy bien manufacturadas.

Al hablar de una ciudad fundada por *cuáqueros,* y en que la mayor parte de los habitantes lo son, no debe pasarse en silencio el modo como hacen su culto.

Esta célebre secta, fundada por Jorge Fox, en el siglo diez y siete en Inglaterra, tuvo por objeto seguir estrictamente y al pie de la letra, las doctrinas del evangelio. Así es que el consejo de presentar la otra mejilla, cuando se de un golpe en la una; el de Santiago, de decir, sí, sí; no, no; y nunca pasar de esto; los de humildad, y otros semejantes formaron el cuerpo de su doctrina, de manera que no admitían la guerra, ni el juramento, ni ningún género de lujo, etc. Semejantes gentes que por otra parte reprobaban las otras sectas religiosas como profanaciones, sufrieron desde el nacimiento de su iglesia crueles persecuciones. Su oposición a prestar juramento ante los Tribunales, a tomar las armas en defensa de su país, y su odio a las sectas dominantes, fueron plausibles pretextos para presentarlos como enemigos de la religión y de la comunidad. Las fantásticas singularidades de sus vestidos, de su lenguaje y de sus maneras, parecían ser la divisa de su acerba y perpetua separación de la sociedad humana. Proscritos por la ley y las preocupaciones, recibieron alegres la merced del Rey de Inglaterra Carlos II. Ellos eran verdaderamente los más consecuentes profesores de la obediencia pasiva, que prescribe el evangelio; porque no resistían a ningún agravio, ni desarmaban a sus enemigos de otra manera que por la benevolencia, y por su sumisión a la injusticia de los tiranos.

Guillermo Penn, uno de los ilustres prosélitos de esta doctrina religiosa, después de haber empleado inútilmente todos sus talentos para sistemar la libertad religiosa, bajo Carlos II, se vio obligado a pasar a la América a buscar un asilo para sus hermanos perseguidos, en donde fundó la ciudad de Filadelfia y otros pueblos en el Estado de Pensilvania, nombre derivado del de su fundador. El admirable Locke, su, amigo, le dio las primeras leyes para su colonia. Carlos II le concedió todas aquellas tierras por las deudas de la Corona al almirante su padre, y luego entró en tratados con las demás provincias. Tratados hechos sin juramento, dice Voltaire, y los únicos que no se han quebrantado. Guillermo Penn murió en Londres, en 1718, agenciando ciertos privilegios para el comercio de su colonia. El culto de los cuáqueros es, como su traje, sumamente sencillo. No hay sacramentos, no hay rezos, no hay santos. Todos están con sus sombreros, las mujeres separadas de los hombres. El que se siente inspirado sube al púlpito, o desde su banca predica, o aconseja, o dice algunas sentencias. Cuando toman la palabra se quitan su grande sombrero, el predicante, si es mujer, habla con el suyo puesto. Es un singular modo de adorar a Dios; pero quizá dirán lo mismo de nuestra misa y de nuestras ceremonias. Lo principal es que, en lo general, son caritativos, laboriosos y honrados. Las mujeres modestas y sencillas.

En Filadelfia el domingo es aún más triste que en Nueva York. Todas las mujeres van a los templos de su culto respectivo, y están dos horas por la mañana y otras dos por la tarde, a lo menos. También concurren muchos hombres, pero no todos. En estos días no hay música, ni juego, ni otra clase de diversión. Las calles en que hay iglesias están cruzadas por cadenas para impedir el paso de carruajes, cuyo ruido interrumpiría el culto.

Filadelfia es la ciudad de los capitales, así como Nueva York es la del comercio. En la primera está la caja matriz del banco de los Estados Unidos. Este banco fue creado en 1816, con carta de veinte años. Comenzó sus operaciones en 19 de enero de aquel año, con un capital nominal de treinta y cinco millones de pesos. El Gobierno general es accionista en este banco por la suma de siete millones de pesos: pero en realidad no ha pasado a este banco más de los dos millones que había depositado en el antigua, resultando que las acciones que tiene son del capital de una deuda que se le ha abierto en los libros del banco. Los otros veintiocho millones de capital, divididos en doscientas ochenta mil acciones de a cien pesos cada una, han sido suscritas por particulares y debieron ser satisfechas en tres pagos, a saber: cinco pesos en dinero, y veinticinco pesos en especies o efectos públicos, a voluntad, en el momento de hacerse la suscripción, y los otros setenta pesos en dos pagos iguales de treinta y cinco pesos cada uno, de los cuales diez pesos deberían pagarse en numerario, y veinticinco en efectos públicos o en metálica. Los cinco pesos por acción del primer pago son los únicos que el banco ha recibido en especies de oro y plata. Los directores creyeron que no era necesario exigir más. "Es claro, decía uno de ellos, que habiendo comenzado el banco sus operaciones, y puesto en circulación su papel, no podía obligarse a sus accionistas a comprar monedas de oro o plata para efectuar el pago de los diez pesos que debería hacerse en especies cuando llegase el plazo del segundo, así como del tercero". Resulta en efecto de una memoria presentada al Congreso, en 1819, que el banco no había verdaderamente recibido más de trecientos veinticuatro mil pesos en numerario, en lugar de dos millones ochocientos mil pesos que debieron haber ingresado de los accionistas en el segundo plazo, y que en el tercero aun entró menor cantidad. Los accionistas pagaron con efectos, y en parte con billetes del mismo banco que les había dado, haciéndoles el descuento legal, y recibiendo por garantía los títulos de sus acciones. Así es que en lugar de haber sido el capital del banco, como lo requería la carta de concesión, de siete millones de pesos en numerario, y veintiocho millones en fondos públicos, no fue realmente después de hechos los tres pagos, que de dos millones en plata u oro, y veintiún millones en fondos públicos; el resto de doce millones ha sido satisfecho con títulos de acciones de los primeros accionistas.

No debe parecer fuera de propósito en una obra que tiene por objeto principal presentar a los mexicanos las costumbres, los usos, instituciones y establecimientos de los Estados Unidos, modelo nominal, por decirlo así, de los legisladores mexicanos, el dar una idea extensa del sistema de bancos establecido en aquel país, lo que además podrá ser de bastante utilidad para su sistema financiero. Voy pues a continuar manifestando lo que ha pasado y pasa entre nuestros vecinos del Norte sobre esta interesante materia.

Ya he manifestado la manera con que se formó el banco de los Estados Unidos, y el lector se admirará del modo con que se fundó en Boston, en 1828, un banco del Estado, llamado *Banco de Sulton;* pudiendo asegurarse que la mayor parte de los bancos de aquel país han sido creados, poco más o menos, sobre las mismas bases. Por un decreto de la legislatura del Estado de Masachusets se autorizó, en marzo de 1828, a los directores del nuevo Banco de Sulton a establecerle bajo la obligación de que el fondo sería de cien mil pesos en oro o plata, divididos en mil acciones de a cien pesos cada una; que la mitad de esta suma sería pagada antes del 1° de octubre de aquel año, y la otra mitad en los seis meses siguientes: que el banco no comenzaría sus descuentos, préstamos, y emisiones de billetes, hasta que no hubiese en sus cajas el capital de cincuenta mil pesos. Para asegurar la ejecución de estas cláusulas, se añadió que el banco no podría dar principio a sus operaciones sin que una comisión de seis miembros nombrados por el gobernador del Estado, no hubiese verificado la existencia en los cofres del banco, de la suma expresada de cincuenta mil pesos en dinero efectivo, debiendo los directores declarar, bajo juramento, que aquel capital era el producto de los pagos hechos por los accionistas para fondos del banco, y que permanecería como una mitad del total. El 26 de septiembre de 1828, el gobernador nombró la comisión, a pedido de los directores. El día en que debió verificarse la visita, los directores del nuevo banco pidieron prestada la suma de cincuenta mil pesos sobre billetes de otro banco llamado *City Bank*, sólo para un día. Esta suma fue contada y testificada su existencia por los comisionados, como provenida de los pagos hechos por los accionistas, bajo la atestación jurada de los directores, todo conforme a la ley de concesión.

Concluida la formalidad, el dinero fue devuelto a los prestamistas, y el banco sólo quedó con una suma pequeña proveniente de los accionistas. Este fue asunto de una hora. La verdad de este suceso se halla consignada en una memoria: dirigida al Senado de Masachusets, en enero de 1830. En ella consta, además, que el segundo pago no fue más exactamente hecho que el primero, y que de esta manera el Banco de Sulton en vez de un capital de cien mil pesos en numerario apenas contaría con la cuarta parte.

Entre los actuales accionistas de los bancos de los Estados hay muchos que han pagado íntegramente la totalidad de las acciones que poseen, especialmente aquéllos que han comprado los títulos originales, resultando de aquí que los primeros fundadores han ganado mucho.

Es evidente que el capital real de los bancos americanos difiere mucho de su capital nominal; y como lejos de dirigir sus operaciones con arreglo a esta base, no temen emitir billetes de circulación o de crédito por sumas que duplican y aun triplican las cifras, resulta que el total de los empeños contraídos por los bancos para con el público, es siempre superior a los medios reales que tienen para llenarlos. En los tiempos ordinarios, mientras que un acontecimiento súbito, una circunstancia imprevista no viene a promover en los espíritus una inquietud bastante grande para decidir a la multitud a ocurrir a los bancos para exigir el pago en numerario de la gran masa de billetes circulante en sus manos, los directores de estos establecimientos están siempre en actitud de satisfacer las demandas ordinarias; porque teniendo conocimiento de los ingresos diarios por pagos, utilidades y otros ingresos por cálculos muy aproximados, tienen cuidado de mantener en caja una suma en oro o plata equivalente al monto de los billetes que se podrán presentar por numerario. Pero en el momento en que una circunstancia grave, tal como la guerra, o una crisis comercial, se anuncia con síntomas próximos, se debilita la confianza hasta el grado de impulsar a los tenedores a ocurrir a los bancos por dinero, éstos se encuentran con una suma triple o cuádruple superior de sus fondos en numerario. En la imposibilidad de satisfacer tales exigencias, suspenden sus pagos y aun muchas veces hacen bancarrota. Estas crisis, de que los bancos europeos establecidos sobre bases más sólidas y principios mucho más racionales, no están enteramente exentos, se repiten con frecuencia en los Estados Unidos, y fueron causa de que desde 1828 sobre quinientos cuarenta y cuatro bancos que había en el país, ciento cuarenta y cuatro hayan sido declarados en quiebra completa, y cincuenta hubiesen suspendido sus pagos y cesado enteramente sus operaciones. El banco mismo de los Estados Unidos se ha encontrado varias veces comprometido y embarazado. Los años de 1814, 1819, 1825 y 1828 son las épocas en que estos establecimientos se han encontrado más embarazados. La crisis de 1814, ocasionada por la guerra que entonces sostenían los americanos con los ingleses, obligó a todos los bancos de la Unión, inclusive el antiguo Banco de los Estados Unidos, cuyo plazo aún no había expirado, a suspender los reembolsos por sus respectivos billetes.

En 1816 y 1817 en que las emisiones de billetes fueron muy considerables, hubo una exportación de numerario tan grande, que los bancos no tuvieron capacidad de procurarse el necesario para el reembolso de sus vales. El nuevo Banco de los Estados Unidos se vio en la obligación (como en este año) de hacer pasar dinero de Europa a los Estados Unidos; y a pesar de todos sus esfuerzos, entonces no pudo reunir en sus cajas más que tres millones de pesos, suma enteramente insuficiente para sostener sus operaciones y las de sus dieciocho ramas en los Estados. Tuvo que ocurrir después a una suspensión parcial de pagos en numerario, saliendo felizmente al poco tiempo de esta crisis; no sucediendo lo mismo a varios bancos particulares que cerraron sus escritorios, y arrastraron en su ruina un número considerable de familias. Fue, asimismo, una emisión gruesa de vales la que ocasionó los embarazos de 1828. En esta última época los directores del Banco de los Estados Unidos, con el fin de desembarazarse de la concurrencia de los otros bancos, hicieron todos sus esfuerzos para extender las operaciones de sus antiguas ramas y para establecer nuevas oficinas. Emitieron mayor número de billetes y autorizaron a sus diversas dependencias, cuyo número ya había subido a veinticuatro, a descontar por billetes particulares. Habían calculado que sus billetes y los de sus anexos gozarían de más consideración que los de los bancos locales, y les sería fácil sustituir en la circulación sus propios vales a los de otros, apoderándose de ellos. Entonces podían o presentar de un golpe a la amortización los vales, o tenerlos estancados, disminuyendo así sus operaciones y giros. Consiguieron en efecto disminuir las operaciones de algunos bancos; pero no pudieron impedir que otros aumentasen sus descuentos, lo que condujo a una nueva exportación de numerario del país, y a su consiguiente escasez, de manera que los bancos no podían encontrar para ocurrir a sus necesidades diarias.

Se valuaba al principio de 1830, el monto total de especies de oro y plata circulante a diez millones de pesos; en billetes de banco a cincuenta y cinco millones; y en créditos de banco a igual cantidad. La suma existente en numerario para asegurar el pago de los vales y créditos de los bancos, es decir, ciento diez millones de pesos, consistía únicamente en veintidós millones de pesos fuertes.

El sistema de los bancos, en la extensión que se le ha dado en los Estados Unidos, ha tenido en su principio un efecto sumamente benéfico a los progresos de la industria de aquel país; pero la excesiva emisión de billetes ha tenido la consecuencia de que se exportara el numerario, quedando en circulación los signos representativos en una proporción incapaz de sostener su crédito por mucho tiempo. En efecto los billetes que emitían los bancos tenían en apariencia la ventaja de aumentar la riqueza del país, elevando el valor nominal de todos los efectos y bienes. Pero como el resultado de una abundante circulación es elevar los precios de las mercancías en el país, claro es que se llegará a un caso de no poder exportar los efectos para otros, porque con los gastos de transportes, aduanas y otros, no sufrirán la concurrencia en los mercados extranjeros. Entonces será necesario ocurrir a la exportación de numerario para procurarse las mercancías de consumo en una nación en que no hay minas, o en donde sus productos de minas no suministran una cuarta parte de las necesidades numerarias, vendrá a pararse en la escasez que ha producido las bancarrotas de que he hablado.

Estas ideas sobre el sistema de bancos en los Estados Unidos, que he sacado de un cuaderno titulado: *History of paper money and bank in the United States,* pueden poner a los lectores en estado de entender la gran cuestión que se agita entre el gobierno del Presidente Jackson y los partidarios del *Banco de los Estados Unidos.* El Presidente ha creído que la renovación de la carta al banco referido, sería un gran mal para el país, así porque crea una especie de aristocracia monetaria, como porque el sistema de bancos es perjudicial a la nación.

Un establecimiento hay en Filadelfia que sería de desear se adoptase en México, si no con la grandeza y extensión que en la primera, a lo menos en pequeño. A una legua de la ciudad está la Penitenciaría, que es un edificio murado con una pared gruesa de granito pardo, de treinta pies de elevación. Abraza un espacio de una milla de circunferencia, y en el centro de él está colocada la prisión. Esta se reduce a una rotunda de donde salen siete radios, formando otros tantos corredores de cuatro varas de ancho. Entre radio y radio están distribuidos los cuartos pequeños en que están los prisioneros. Cada uno tiene un patio pequeño en donde salen a tomar el aire tres horas al día. Por debajo de los cuartos pasa un caño de agua corriente en donde hacen sus necesidades. Desde el corredor que domina todas las prisiones se ve por un hoyo pequeño lo que hace el penitenciado, y desde la rotunda el único celador que hay, sentado en el centro, extiende la vista a todos los corredores que van a parar en líneas convergentes al centro. No hay guardias ni vigilantes, hay sólo tres o cuatro asistentes para llevar la comida a los presos, cuyo número ascendía a trecientos cincuenta cuando yo estuve. Su alimento es abundante y sano; pero cuando se resisten a trabajar se les acorta. Hay tubos comunicantes que en invierno calientan sus cuartos. La entrada de un sentenciado a la prisión se verifica vendándole los ojos antes de entrar. Luego es conducido a un pequeño cuarto en donde se le corta el pelo, pasa a otro a bañarse, y en éste toma sus vestiduras de penitencia, que son un jubón, una gorra, una camisa y un pantalón. Las antiguas quedan depositadas hasta su salida. El director del establecimiento, que es un honrado y respetable inglés, creo escocés, me dijo que el producto del trabajo daba lo suficiente para mantener el establecimiento. No se permite fumar, ni beber más que agua. Sólo pueden tener la *Biblia* o algún libro de devoción según el culto del preso. Muchos hombres que han estado en esta prisión han salido después corregidos, continuando una vida regular. Hombres que han estado encerrados tres, cuatro o seis años sin comunicar con nadie, cuando salen al mundo vienen con nuevos hábitos, con el carácter reflexivo que debe contraerse en la soledad, y sin inclinaciones viciosas, o a lo menos muy disminuidas. No sucede lo mismo con las personas que han estado en una prisión juntos con otros, en donde por desgracia no se contraen costumbres virtuosas.

En el Estado de Pensilvania hay universidad, en donde se enseña filosofía moral, historia; idiomas latino, griego y hebreo; metafísica, ideología y matemáticas. El curso es de cuatro años, tiempo muy corto para salir instruido profundamente en ningún ramo. Pero, generalmente hablando, en aquella república se ha preferido extender la enseñanza primaria, a levantar establecimientos que, como los de Oxford o Cambridge, contengan los elementos de la alta ciencia, de esas ciencias que absorben la vida entera en profundas y elevadas meditaciones. La primera necesidad es la de leer y escribir; a ésta procuran satisfacer los norteamericanos dando a la primera enseñanza toda la generalidad que es compatible con las otras necesidades sociales. La base de la educación en aquel país, es "extender la esfera del pensamiento, y elevar la conciencia por medio de útiles conocimientos que hagan al hombre apto para tratar con tino los asuntos de la vida, y no hacerse ridículo ni despreciable por una ignorancia notable".

Esto no quiere decir que en los Estados Unidos no haya hombres de grandes conocimientos y científicos. Los hay evidentemente, pero no en el número correspondiente a su población, como sucede en Inglaterra, Francia y demás naciones civilizadas del norte de Europa. La traducción que acaba de publicarse en Boston, de las obras de M. Laplace, es una prueba inequívoca de los grandes adelantos de aquella ciudad.

En Filadelfia encontré a M. Sergeant, abogado distinguido de los Estados Unidos, que estuvo en México como ministro al Congreso de Tacubaya, en que debieron reunirse los ministros de las repúblicas de América, según el acuerdo del Congreso de Panamá, en 1826. Se sabe que este proyecto nunca tuvo efecto. M. Sergeant es un americano muy instruido en su profesión, y tiene una reputación bastante extendida, hasta haberle llevado a la candidatura de la Vicepresidencia en concurso con M. Van Buren. Tuve igualmente relaciones con M. Walsh, editor del *Nacional Gazette* y del *Quarterly Review,* periódicos apreciados en ambos hemisferios por la capacidad con que están escritos y la materia que contienen, especialmente el segundo, con M. Du Ponceu, literato francés, y patriarca de las sociedades literarias de Filadelfia por su edad y vasta instrucción.

En este año (diciembre de 1831), murió M. Gerard, el banquero más rico que ha existido después de M. Rotschild; M. Gerard era francés, nacido en Bordeaux. Como en 1811 cesó el antiguo Banco de los Estados Unidos, se aprovechó del edificio y crédito con la falta de descuentos que dejaban de hacerse, y extendió sus giros y negocios. Dejó cerca de ocho millones de pesos, y la mayor parte de sus bienes la distribuyó entre los Estados Unidos, especialmente Pensilvania y Nueva York. En su testamento puso cláusula expresa para que en ninguno de los colegios que debían establecerse de sus fondos, se admitiese ningún eclesiástico de ningún culto. M. Gerard detestaba toda doctrina exclusiva.

CAPÍTULO X

Familia del general Iturbide.—Mercado de Filadelfia.—Coronel Burnt.—Salida de Filadelfia.—Estado de Delaware.—Su constitución—Llegada a Baltimore.—City Hotel.—Monumentos.—Catedral.—Unitarios.—Escuela de niños.—Constitución del estado de Maryland.—Salida para Washington.—Capitolio.—Casa del presidente.—M. Van Buren.—Viaje a Mont Vernon.—General Washington.—Estado de Virginia.—Aventuras de M. Smith.

En 1830 visité a la viuda del señor don Agustín de Iturbide, en George Town, cerca de Washington, en donde estaba viviendo al cuidado de la educación de sus hijos. En 1834 tuve el placer de ver por segunda vez esta respetable familia mexicana en Filadelfia, después de haberle el Presidente de la República Mexicana, general Santa Ana, suspendido el anatema que la condenaba a vivir fuera de su patria, aunque con una pensión decente. La señora Iturbide había conseguido en mucha parte el fruto de sus afanes; sus hijas mayores, recibiendo una educación conforme a la civilización del país, han correspondido a los deseos de sus maestros, y han aumentado las gracias de su sexo con las ventajas de la cultura del espíritu y con las perfecciones físicas de la educación material.

El mercado de Filadelfia es uno de los mejores que haya visto. Está en una calle de cien pies, por lo menos, de ancho, y una milla de largo, en medio de la cual se ha construido un tinglado de madera, abierta por ambos lados y cubierto con teja arriba. Allí se ve una concurrencia numerosa por las mañanas que se dirige a comprar las provisiones necesarias de un mercado abundante, al que contribuyen con sus producciones el mar, los ríos, la tierra y el aire. En efecto allí se encuentran peces de agua dulce y salada, animales de caza, aves, verduras, flores, frutas, semillas, carnes preparadas con aseo y todo cuanto puede desear el gastrónomo para proveer su cocina, y hacer buena mesa.

A cuatro millas de distancia de Filadelfia está un pueblo pequeño llamado Frankfort, en donde residía el coronel Burnt, antiguo amigo de M. Poinsett. Invitado por éste a hacer una visita a su amigo, tuve un día de placer en casa de M. Burnt. Mandó un cuerpo de caballería en la última guerra con Inglaterra, y se había retirado a vivir tranquilamente en una casa de campo que tiene en el pueblo, muy aseada, bien distribuida, aunque pequeña, pero con todas las comodidades para un hombre solo. Tenía sus principales fondos en Escocia, a donde vino después de su muerte, M. Poinsett, su albacea, a recogerlos. M. Burnt era hombre de buen trato; bastante instrucción y extremadamente modesto. Algunos viajeros en América han hablado de él en el mismo sentido.

En Filadelfia me embarqué en el buque de vapor *William Penn,* en compañía del señor Mejía, que, como he dicho, era secretario de la legación mexicana cerca de los Estados Unidos. Después de tres horas de navegación río abajo, desembarcamos en un istmo que se forma entre el río Delaware, Chesapeake y un canal que conduce a este último, en el Estado de Delaware. Este último es uno de los Estados que formaron la primera confederación, cuyo número era el de trece. Su población llegará apenas a doscientos mil habitantes; pero próspera como los otros por la sabiduría de su Gobierno, laboriosidad de sus habitantes, instituciones liberales, económicas, y demás circunstancias que distinguen estos felices Estados. Las escuelas están establecidas en Delaware sobre el mismo pie que las de Boston, de que hablaré después.

La Constitución de este pequeño Estado fue hecha en 1792 y reformada en 1831. La legislatura es llamada *Asamblea general,* y se compone de Senado y Cámara de representantes. Tiene nueve senadores nombrados tres por cada uno de sus condados, renovándose por terceras partes cada cuatro años. Los representantes son veintiuno, siete de cada condado, y se renuevan en su totalidad a los dos años. La asamblea general se reúne en *Dover,* capital del Estado, *bienalmente,* el primer martes del mes de enero, a menos que antes la convoque el gobernador. La elección general se verifica el segundo martes de noviembre del año anterior.

El Poder Ejecutivo le ejerce el gobernador nombrado por el pueblo cada cuatro años, sin poder ser reelegido en el período inmediato. El Poder judicial reside en una Corte de *errores* y apelaciones; una Corte superior; otra de Cancillería; otra de huérfanos; otra de audiencia y última instancia; otra de sesiones generales de paz, de libertad, de presos; y una de registros, etc.

El derecho de sufragio le tienen todos los ciudadanos varones, de la clase blanca, de veintidós años arriba, con tal que hayan residido un año en el Estado anteriormente a las elecciones, y un mes en el condado en que se verifican, habiendo pagado las contribuciones del dicho condado.

En el canal que conduce del Delaware al Chesapeake se navegan catorce millas, y se caminan a pie veinte o treinta varas para tomar el buque de vapor en el segundo. Yo me embarqué en el *Charles Caroll,* del porte de cuatrocientas toneladas, bastante como para trecientos pasajeros y cómodo. Llegué a Baltimore a las cinco de la tarde del mismo día.

Baltimore, ciudad de cien mil habitantes, está situada entre los ríos Patapsa, Potomac y Susquebannah, y casi en el curso de los Estados Unidos. Es la mayor ciudad del Estado de Maryland, cuya capital es *Annapolis.* Lord Baltimore, caballero inglés católico, fue el fundador de esta colonia, y los principios de tolerancia y de filosofía de aquel venerable colonizador formaban contraste con las persecuciones de los puritanos en la Nueva Inglaterra.

Yo paré en *City Hotel,* que llaman por otro nombre *Barnum,* porque es el dueño de la posada. Es la mayor de Baltimore, y su situación central, formando esquina con la plaza en que está el monumento en memoria de las víctimas de la guerra de 1814, juntamente con la buena asistencia que se da en él, hace que sea uno de los más concurridos. El servicio le hacen generalmente negros y gentes de color, y algunos irlandeses.

El monumento de que acabo de hablar llamado *Battle Monument,* especie de trofeo eregido en conmemoración de la resistencia al ataque que, bajo las órdenes del general Ross, dieron los ingleses a aquella ciudad, contiene los nombres de las personas más notables que murieron en la acción. La columna se eleva cerca de cincuenta pies, representa las faces romanas, símbolo de la unión, y tiene en cada ángulo un grifo. En el vértice está colocada la estatua de la Victoria. Más noble y sencillo es el monumento levantado a la memoria del inmortal Washington, en una colina que domina la ciudad. Consiste en una columna de mármol blanco de ciento sesenta pies, sobre la que está colocada la estatua del héroe.

La catedral católica es considerada como uno de los mejores templos de los Estados Unidos. Muy pequeña cosa es comparada con nuestras catedrales de México, Puebla, Mérida y Jalisco, y mucho más con las de las grandes y antiguas ciudades de Europa. Sin embargo, el aspecto interior de esta iglesia es muy agradable por su limpieza y algunas de sus imágenes y cuadros. La forma es de cruz griega con su cúpula en el centro. El orden es irregular con pretensiones de gótico. Otro edificio católico llama la atención del viajero en Baltimore y es la capilla del colegio de Santa María. Aunque situado en el centro de la ciudad, este edificio es tan solitario y silencioso como si estuviese en el desierto. Está rodeado de un pequeño jardín en donde hay un monte calvario con una cruz muy alta. Un camino estrecho entre arbustos y cedros conduce a la pequeña capilla, comparable en su pequeñez y belleza a la de Santa Teresa de México. Una lámpara, cuya luz amortiguada por los vidrios que la cubren, reparte por la noche una claridad melancólica, conveniente a la situación de una alma que viene a elevar sus ruegos y oraciones en un recogimiento que no debe ser interrumpido por ninguna emoción fuerte. La luz del día, penetra por las ventanas cubiertas por vidrieras de color carmesí, lo que da un aspecto sublime y de grandeza a aquel lugar sagrado.

Hay otro edificio notable en Baltimore, y es el Templo de los Unitarios. Esta secta, más filosófica que religiosa, hace progresos extraordinarios en todos los Estados Unidos, especialmente en la Nueva Inglaterra. Los unitarios son tan opuestos a la trinidad de las personas en la divinidad, como los reformistas a la misa. Es una modificación de las doctrinas de los socinianos, ilustrada con los progresos que ha hecho la filosofía en el siglo decimoctavo.

La escuela de niños, *Infant School,* de M. Ibberson, es uno de los más útiles establecimientos, no sólo de Baltimore, sino aun de los Estados Unidos. Niños desde la edad de dos años comienzan a recibir, por sensaciones agradables y lecciones materiales, instrucciones que sirven después de base para los altos conocimientos de geografía, historia natural, botánica y aritmética. En vez de entretener a los niños con la muñeca, el trompo, el pito y demás juguetes de la infancia, se les familiariza con los géneros diferentes de animales pintados al natural, aves, peces, cuadrúpedos. Se coloca un cuadro grande en la pared en que están los ríos, los mares, los istmos, islas, continentes: se hacen cuadrados que contienen las letras del alfabeto, en fin se preparan de diferentes modos agradables los primeros elementos de instrucción, y al cabo los niños ya conocen las letras y sus combinaciones; saben la nomenclatura de los animales, de las plantas, flores; distinguen los continentes, los ríos, etc. M. Ibberson tiene como cien niños de ambos sexos, que esparcirán después la enseñanza en su país.

La Constitución del Estado de Maryland fue hecha en 1776. Desde entonces ha sufrido muchas modificaciones. El Poder Legislativo se ejerce por el Senado, que tiene quince miembros, y por la Cámara de delegados compuesta de ochenta. Ambas reunidas forman el cuerpo que se llama *Asamblea general de Maryland.* Los miembros de la Cámara de delegados, cuatro por cada condado, dos por Baltimore y dos por Annapolis, son nombrados anualmente por el pueblo, el primer lunes de octubre; y los del Senado son elegidos cada cinco años el tercer lunes de septiembre, en la capital Annapolis, por electores elegidos por el pueblo, el primer lunes del mismo mes de septiembre. Estos electores eligen, votando por cédulas, nueve senadores de la costa occidental y seis de la casta oriental, debiendo ejercer sus oficios los senadores por cinco años.

El Poder Ejecutivo reside en el gobernador, el cual es nombrado por las dos Cámaras, a mayoría de votos cada año el primer lunes de enero, no pudiendo ser reelecto más que dos veces, de manera que sólo puede ejercer por tres años el destino una misma persona, y siendo elegible para el mismo encargo después de pasados cuatro años de haber cesado. El gobernador tiene un consejo de cinco delegados, nombrados por ambas Cámaras. La asamblea general se reúne en sesiones, el lunes último de diciembre. El gobernador confiere los empleos y el consejo confirma. Por la constitución ejercen el derecho de sufragio todos los hombres blancos desde veintiún años de edad, habiendo residido un año en el Estado, y seis meses en el condado, o en las ciudades de Annapolis o Baltimore. El canciller y los jueces los nombra el gobernador con aprobación del Consejo.

De Baltimore a Washington hay cuarenta millas, que se hacen por tierra. Tomé un coche particular para hacer este viaje con más despacio y comodidad. Me acompañó a él don Anastasio Zerecero, que estaba desterrado entonces de la República Mexicana por asuntos políticos, y me encontró en Baltimore.

Washington es una ciudad levantada de las cenizas a que quedó reducida por las tropas inglesas y armada británica, en 1814, bajo el general Ross y el almirante Cockburn. Muchos años se reunió el Congreso en un edificio provisional hasta que se erigió el Capitolio, obra magnífica que no desdice a la pompa de este nombre venerable. Edificado sobre la parte más elevada de la ciudad, la domina toda así como al río Potomac, que en aquella parte tiene media milla de ancho. Desde su soberbia cúpula parece que se anuncia al género humano la libertad y la emancipación del pensamiento y de las ideas, mientras que en otro Capitolio se predica la sujeción, la esclavitud y la obediencia ciega. ¿Quién no se sentirá inspirado de estos nobles sentimientos al montar los escalones que conducen a esas Cámaras, en donde las discusiones tienen por objeto los verdaderos intereses de las masas? Allí no hay privilegios hereditarios, no hay rentas vitalicias, no hay personajes sagrados. Aquella asamblea es juzgada también por el pueblo que tiene la facultad de sujetar a su examen por la prensa, por los *clubes,* por asambleas, las opiniones y resoluciones de sus mandatarios. Yo venía de México cuando visité el Capitolio de Washington. ¿Cómo debía parecerme todo lo que veía, lo que oía, lo que palpaba, en la capital de la Unión Angloamericana, el edificio mismo en donde se juntan los legisladores del género humano?

En este magnífico edificio se reúnen las dos Cámaras del Congreso general, están sus oficinas, la Corte Suprema de justicia y sus dependencias. La casa del Presidente está al lado opuesto de la ciudad, distante una milla del Capitolio. Es un hermoso edificio de ciento setenta y cinco pies de longitud, y ochenta y cinco de latitud. Tiene sólo dos altos, y aunque se encuentran en él todas las comodidades para una familia, no es un palacio. En el mismo terreno, a alguna distancia, hay cuatro edificios que corresponden a los ángulos de la casa del Presidente, en los cuales están las Secretarías de Estado.

M. Martin Van Buren, que era Secretario de Relaciones Exteriores, cuando fui la primera vez a Washington, me hizo el honor de convidarme a comer. Se hallaban los ministros extranjeros en la comida, y muchos de los diputados y senadores más distinguidos. El señor Tornel, ministro de México en aquella época orca de los Estados Unidos, tenía su residencia en Baltimore. M. Van Buren será un hombre de cincuenta años, de pequeña estatura, rubio, de una fisonomía muy espiritual, y de bastante instrucción. Es del Estado de Nueva York que era gobernador, cuando fue llamado al ministerio. Después de mi salida de Washington fue enviado a Londres como ministro plenipotenciario, en receso de las Cámaras. El Senado no aprobó su nombramiento, y el partido democrático, a cuya cabeza ha estado, por vengarle de este desaire le nombró Vicepresidente en las elecciones de 1832.

Hallándome cerca de Mont Vernon, residencia del general Washington, me resolví a atravesar el Potomac, y hacer este pequeño viaje de quince millas de distancia para tener el placer de pisar los mismos lugares en que habitó el venerable patriarca de la libertad, y conocer a su sobrino, heredero de su casa y de sus virtudes. Tomé un coche de alquiler, y pasando sobre un puente muy largo del Potomac, llegué al cabo de cinco horas a Mont Vernon, lugar muy agradable asociado a tan interesantes memorias. Allí encontré a M. Washington, uno de los individuos de la Suprema Corte de los Estados Unidos, quien con la mayor urbanidad me manifestó todas las piezas de la habitación de su tío, que se han procurado conservar en el mismo estado en que las dejó, por un religioso respeto a su memoria. En la antesala se ven colgadas las llaves de la Bastilla que el general Lafayette envió a su venerable amigo.

El general Washington era el hijo mayor del segundo matrimonio de Agustín Washington de Virginia, nieto de John Washington, caballero de una familia respetable en el norte de Inglaterra, de donde emigró. Lorenzo Washington, hijo mayor del padre del general Washington, en el primer matrimonio, dejó las tierras de Mont Vernon a George, que nació en 22 de febrero de 1732, y después de una vida gloriosa, murió en 11 de diciembre de 1800.

El Estado de Virginia, fundado por una colonia inglesa, bajo la dirección de M. Smith, ha venido a ser el segundo, después de haber sido el primer Estado de la Federación. El carácter extraordinario y las aventuras portentosas que ocurrieron a este hombre, harán un episodio interesante en este viaje.

El capitán John Smith nació el año de 1579 en Willonghby, en el condado de Lincoln. Desde su más tierna infancia admiraba a sus compañeros y aun a su maestra de escuela, por el arrojo de sus travesuras. Trece años tenía, cuando le vino el deseo de ver el mar. Con este objeto vendió sus libros y juguetes, lo que le proporcionó una pequeña suma. Se disponía a marchar, cuando murió su padre y cayó bajo la tutela de hombres positivos, a quienes el genio romántico del joven pareció una amarga locura: y aunque fue por parte de ellos el objeto de una vigilancia benéfica, era sin embargo demasiado estrecha para que fuese soportable a su espíritu independiente. Luego que tuvo quince años, se le colocó a fin de que ocupase su razón en el almacén de un comerciante, quien no le economizaba las lecciones ni el trabajo.

El comerciante en donde Smith aprendía, era uno de los principales de Lynn. Hacía muchos negocios marítimos, y el joven Smith esperaba que su patrón le haría viajar, y viajar en el mar. Sin embargo, no oyendo hablar de su embarque, y cansado de aquella monotonía, dejó sin despedirse al negociante y los negocios, marchándose con solos veinte reales. Su buena estrella le hizo encontrar a un joven lord que iba con séquito numeroso a hacer también un viaje a Europa. Smith se acomodó en su servicio, pero esto no fue por mucho tiempo. Después de algunos meses se disgustó con su nuevo amo y fue a engancharse en el ejército de Holanda. Allí pasó tres o cuatro años; y estimulado por un caballero escocés que le ofreció excelentes recomendaciones para la Corte del Rey Jacobo, volvió a pasar el mar y fue a Escocia. Frustradas sus esperanzas, se alejó de la Corte y volvió a tomar el camino de su país natal. Allí tomando horror al patriotismo fanático de sus compatriotas, se fue a vivir solo en el centro de los bosques, con algunos libros de táctica y de historia militar, un caballo y una lanza. Así dividía su tiempo entre el estudio de la guerra y el ejercicio de las armas, sin ver a otra persona que a un sirviente italiano de la casa del conde de Lincoln.

En estos pasatiempos entra en posesión de una parte de la fortuna de su padre. Con los medios de viajar, le vuelve el deseo de correr el mundo. Ved pues a Smith lanzado de nuevo en el Océano. Llega a Flandes y allí fue robado por cuatro franceses estafadores; los persigue, encuentra a uno de ellos, se bate con él, le hiere, le hace confesar su crimen, y se vuelve a poner en camino con algún dinero que le había dado un antiguo amigo de su familia. Sigue el litoral de Francia de Dunquerque a Marsella, visitando los arsenales y las fortificaciones; y se embarca para Italia.

Inglés y hereje, se hallaba por su desgracia en medio de una multitud de peregrinos que iban a cumplir sus promesas a Nuestra Señora de Loreto y a Roma. El buque es acometido por una tempestad; los peregrinos se apoderan del hereje, y el nuevo Jonás Smith es arrojado al mar. Tiene la fortuna de llegar a nado a la isla de Santa María, cerca de Niza. Allí se detiene justamente el tiempo necesario para embarcarse en otro buque que partía para Alejandría. Este buque, después de haber terminado su viaje, traba una disputa con otro buque venicio ricamente cargado, le ataca, le toma y le despoja. El se hace dejar en Antibo con su parte del botín, pasa a Italia, atraviesa el Golfo de Venecia, llega a Styria y dio fin entrando como voluntario al servicio del emperador, entonces en guerra con los turcos.

Smith no sólo era valiente y emprendedor, era también hombre de recursos. Encuentra medio de forzar a los turcos a levantar el sitio de Olympach, y de este modo gana el grado de capitán, en el regimiento del conde de Meldritch, hombre distinguido de Transilvania. Después de muchas hazañas, Smith se halló en el sitio de Regal, en Transilvania; el sitio iba largo, y un día un heraldo se presentó en el campo de los cristianos, anunciando que el señor *Turbashaw*, turco famoso, desafiaba al más valiente de entre ellos en un combate singular, a fin, decía, de divertir las damas y pasar el tiempo. La suerte decidió que de entre todos los guerreros cristianos Smith fuese el que debía responder al desafío del turco. El combate se celebró solemnemente; las señoras turcas adornaban los parapetos de Regal; los sitiadores estaban colocados a lo largo de sus líneas; la música resonaba. Smith mató al Osmanli; otro turco emprende vengar a *Turbashaw;* Smith le mata también. Se presenta un tercero, éste era el terrible Bonny Mulgro, de estatura gigantesca. Al primer choque, Smith es casi desmontado de un golpe de hacha. Los turcos prorrumpen en gritos de alegría, las damas turcas palmotean; aún gritaban y aplaudían, cuando Bonny Mulgro, pasado de un tiro de espada, queda tendido por tierra y Smith le cortaba la cabeza. Poco después fue tomada la ciudad.

Pero los sucesos de la guerra son variables. Poco tiempo después los cristianos fueron derrotados: Smith fue dejado por muerto en el campo de batalla; la riqueza de su armadura hizo que los turcos le hubiesen tomado como un personaje distinguido: fue tratado como un hombre que vale un rescate considerable; curado bien pronto fue conducido al mercado de esclavos de Axiópolis; allí fue comprado por un Rajá, que le envió de regalo a la dama de sus pensamientos en Constantinopla, diciendo (fanfarrón despreciable) que era un señor bohemio que había tomado en la guerra. Esta impostura salió mal al bajá; Charatza Tragabigzanda (éste era el nombre de la dama) sabía el italiano, Smith también le hablaba; éste contó sus aventuras, su gloria y sus desgracias; Tragabigzanda comenzó a indignarse de la fanfarronada del bajá, después se enterneció de las desgracias de Smith, se inflamó por sus nobles acciones y sus peligros como Desdémona, dice uno de los biógrafos del capitán; Smith esperaba un poco de reposo y dicha, cuando la dama, sea por burlar las sospechas de su madre, sea por hacer aprender el turco a Smith, le envió a su hermano Timur bajá, cuya residencia estaba en las playas del mar de Azof.

Las recomendaciones de Tragabigzanda eran empeñosas; hacia a su hermano la confesión de sus sentimientos por el cautivo; pero el bajá del mar Azof se indignó de que un *perro cristiano* hubiese interesado el corazón de su hermana. Smith que se esperaba un recibimiento cordial, no había pasado una hora en casa de Timur, cuando ya había sido apaleado, despojado y rapado. Se le puso un collar de fierro, se le cubrió de un capotón de crín, y se le mandó a trabajar la tierra con los demás esclavos cristianos del bajá. Diariamente este amo bárbaro iba a inspeccionar el trabajo de su prisionero, y le acababa a injurias y golpes. Una vez que Smith se hallaba solo con él, y que el bajá le reconvenía acerca del modo con que aventaba el grano, Smith le mató de un trillazo, escondió el cadáver bajo la paja, y montando sobre un caballo árabe del Otomano, se fugó a carrera abierta. Cuando hubo ganado el desierto, se orientó como pudo, y después de dieciséis días de viaje, llegó a Hexápolis sobre el Don; allí encontró una avanzada rusa. Los rusos le acogieron generosamente: una señora caritativa o tierna, la princesa o baronesa de Palamata, colmó a Smith de testimonios de interés. Descansado Smith, se puso en marcha para Transilvania, donde sus amigos derramaron lágrimas de gozo, viéndole, auxiliándole generosamente. De allí volvió a Inglaterra, pasando por Alemania, Francia, España y el reino de Marruecos.

Llegó a Inglaterra precisamente en el momento en que iba a partir una expedición para fundar una colonia para América. Invitado a hacer parte de ella, aceptó. Smith tenía entonces veintiocho años. La expedición dejó el Tamesis el 19 de diciembre de 1606, y entró en la bahía de Chesapeake al 26 de abril de 1607. El 13 de mayo desembarcó en una península, donde fue fundada la colonia de *James Town*. El viajero que hoy sube el *James River* en buque de vapor ve en esta península una torre en ruinas y los restos de un recinto de cementerio. Es todo cuanto queda de este primer establecimiento.

Smith tenía por compañeros hombres mediocres, que no le podían perdonar su superioridad: apenas habían salido del Tamesis, fue acusado de complots con objeto de coronarse en la colonia. Bajo este absurdo pretexto fue puesto en prisión durante la travesía. Cuando después del desembarque, se abrieron las instrucciones dadas a la expedición, se vio que el gobierno de la colonia se confiaba a un consejo de siete personas, entre las cuales entraba Smith. Sus compañeros, sin embargo, le excluyeron bajo el pretexto de sus pretendidas miras. Smith pidió que se le juzgase, y no pudo conseguirlo. Se armó de paciencia, y salió a descubrir los alrededores de *James Town,* subiendo los ríos, haciendo conocimientos con las tribus de indios, y haciendo algunas visitas al Rey Powhaltan, el más poderoso de los príncipes salvajes. Durante este tiempo la colonia estaba mal gobernada: nada se preveía; no se edificaban casas para el invierno que se acercaba; pocas o ningunas provisiones; ningunas precauciones militares contra los salvajes, quienes por algunas hostilidades habían dado a conocer su descontento. Un día fue atacada la colonia repentinamente por los guerreros de Powhaltan: un hombre fue muerto y diecisiete heridos: se manifestó el descontento contra el Consejo, y principalmente contra el Presidente Wingfield: Smith aprovechó la ocasión para insistir en su petición sobre el juicio; le obtuvo, fue absuelto sobre todos los cargos, y Wingfield fue condenado a pagarle doscientas libras esterlinas de daños y perjuicios que cedió generosamente en beneficio de la colonia. En seguida hubo una especie de reconciliación. Todos los colonos comulgaron el mismo día como en señal de olvido de lo pasado, y el capitán Newport, que los había conducido de Inglaterra, volvió con su flotilla, dejando la colonia compuesta de ciento cinco personas.

Pero sobrevino la carestía, y con ella las enfermedades, después la que es peor que la peste, la discordia. Cincuenta colonos perecieron miserablemente. En medio de la desesperación general, el Presidente Wingfield, de acuerdo con algunos de sus compañeros, resolvió apoderarse secretamente del único buque que poseía la colonia, y fugarse para Inglaterra. La trama fue descubierta; Wingfield fue depuesto, y otro Presidente se eligió en su lugar. Este tuvo la política de dirigirse por Smith, cuyo momento había llegado. Smith hizo un plan de trabajos y dio a cada uno su tarea; fue obedecido. Se levantaron las casas, la colonia fue fortificada y cubierta. El mismo daba el ejemplo a los operarios trabajando más que ellos. No era bastante tener casas para el invierno, eran necesarias también provisiones: Smith se dedicó pues a buscar algunos víveres, y particularmente maíz que cultivaban los indios. En una de estas excursiones, encontró una tribu numerosa, la quitó su ídolo, exigió por el rescate de su dios algunas fanegas de maíz y carne de venado, y se apresuró a volver a *James Town* con estos víveres. Llegó a tiempo, porque Wingfield había proyectado nuevamente su fuga, y esta vez fue necesario batirse para hacer entrar al orden a los conspiradores. Desde entonces la autoridad quedó asegurada en manos de Smith.

Apenas había restablecido en orden en la colonia, cuándo dejándose llevar de las inspiraciones de su imaginación emprendedora, quizá más de lo que convenía a un hombre sobre cuya cabeza descansaba la salud de la colonia un día salió a explorar el Río Chickahomini; le sube hasta donde le permite su buque, y dejándole con el mayor número de tripulación, oculto en un ancón al abrigo de todo peligro, sube aún más arriba en un bote llevando consigo dos blancos y dos indios. Desgraciadamente los que había dejado tras de sí, olvidaron sus órdenes luego que le perdieron de vista:

desembarcaron contra sus órdenes, y fueron atacados por un grupo de indios, bajo las órdenes de Opechancanough, hermano de Powhaltan, que espiaba a Smith. Uno de ellos fue hecho prisionero y obligado a declarar dónde había ido el capitán; los otros pudieron ganar el buque y salvarse. ⁊

Durante este tiempo Smith había llegado a las ciénagas donde nace el río. Opechancanough le sorprende en la noche y mata los dos ingleses. Smith es rodeado por doscientos bárbaros; una flecha le hiere en el muslo, se defiende con la *sabiduría de una serpiente* y el *vigor de un leopardo;* mata tres de sus contrarios, y atándose del brazo con sus ligas uno de sus dos indios, se sirve de él como de escudo. Sus enemigos espantados, se separan; ya él ha ganado terreno y va a alcanzar su barca; pero en su travesía cae en medio de un pantano impracticable, y se hunde con su indio hasta la cintura. Era tal el temor que inspiraba a los salvajes, que aun en esta situación ninguno de ellos se atrevió a acercársele, hasta que arrojó sus armas. Estaba medio muerto de frío. Los indios le sacaron del pantano, le acercaron al fuego, y le dieron fricciones hasta que recobró el uso de sus miembros.

Smith se veía perdido. Los cadáveres de sus compañeros estaban a su lado descuartizados. Ocurrióle sacar de la bolsa una brújula y mostrarla a Opechancanough. El salvaje no volvía en sí de la admiración que le causaba esta aguja que se movía siempre. Como no tenía noción de la transparencia, estaba aun más sorprendido de que le fuese imposible tomar la aguja con los dedos aunque la viese perfectamente (estaba cubierta de un vidrio). Smith por excitar todavía más la admiración del jefe bárbaro y de sus guerreros, se puso a hablarles sobre el movimiento de los cuerpos celestes, sobre la dimensión y figura de la Tierra y de los mares, sobre el Sol y la Luna, todo lo que sabía de astronomía. Su auditorio le escuchaba aturdido. El instinto salvaje volvió a predominar. Smith después de haber hecho su discurso, fue atado a un árbol. Los salvajes estaban formados circularmente a su alrededor, y le apuntaban con sus flechas. Smith va a morir.

Al momento de dar la señal que hiciera volar todas las flechas a su pecho, Opechancanough ordena que se le perdone. Quería hacer ostentación de su presa en la Corte de los príncipes sus vecinos, y sobre todo en la de Powhaltan, su señor y amo de todos: porque todos los capitanes formaban una confederación del *James River;* como veinte años ha, los príncipes alemanes formaban la confederación del Rhin, y Powhaltan era el Napoleón protector.

El valor de Smith, su fuerza física y la fecundidad de su espíritu, le hacían considerar por los salvajes como un hombre extraordinario, como un ser sobrehumano. Su prisión fue celebrada con algunas ceremonias sin fin, en que los salvajes le prodigaron las atenciones que puedan imaginarse.

Tanto cuidado se puso en proporcionarle alimentos frescos, que Smith creyó desde luego que trataban de engordarle para comérsele en seguida. Los charlatanes vinieron a conjurarle, se consultó el grande espíritu para conocer el fondo de las intenciones del capitán. Powhaltan desplegó todo su lujo montaraz para recibirle. Cuando Smith compareció ante el primer jefe, una reina fue quien le lavó las manos, y otra le presentó una estofa de plumas a modo de servilleta. Smith fue paseado de tribu en tribu, y concluyeron por proponerle que se hiciera salvaje y dirigiese el gobierno de *James Town*. Con esta condición le ofrecían tantas mujeres y tierras como quisiese. A respuesta negativa hubo un consejo de capitanes y reyes, en el que se decidió que Smith muriese, y que se procediera inmediatamente a la ejecución de la sentencia.

Esta vez todo es hecho. Se traen dos piedras a los pies del gran rey, y se tiende allí al paciente. Los jefes se colocan a su alrededor. El pueblo en sus espaldas en un profundo silencio. Powhaltan ha querido ser él mismo el gran sacerdote. ¡Se acerca con su maza, y la levanta para descargar el golpe fatal! ¡No hay esperanza!

Repentinamente una mujer —por todas partes las mujeres eran para Smith ángeles tutelares—, una mujer ha atravesado la multitud. Pone su cabeza entre la de Smith y la maza de Powhaltan: es la hija primogénita del Rey, su hija más querida, la bella Poucahousta. Tendiendo los brazos a su padre, le suplica perdone al cautivo. El Rey en el momento se indigna; pero amaba mucho a Poucahoutas para que no fuera conmovido de sus lágrimas. Extiende la vista sobre sus guerreros buscando en sus ojos la resolución que le falta: los ve movidos de compasión. "Que viva, dijo". Al día siguiente Smith estaba con dos guías en camino para *James Town*. Debía enviar a Powhaltan como testimonio de paz, dos fusiles y una piedra de amolar.

Salvo Smith, se ocupó de los negocios de la colonia, y cuando todo estuvo ordenado, volvió a emprender sus excursiones. Remontó el Potomac, y descubrió en la travesía mil peligros: las riberas, la mayor parte avenidas del Chesapeake. Su presencia de ánimo, el religioso terror que inspiraba a los salvajes, y sobre todo la noble asistencia de Poucahoutas le salvaron siempre, y a la colonia como por milagro. No ha faltado a Poucahoutas para ser tan célebre como Atala, que encontrar un Chateaubriand. Tan joven y bella como la hija Muscogulgue, tuvo más heroísmo, y no fue un sólo hombre a quien salvó. Débil como era (catorce o quince años tenía entonces) le acontecía muchas veces hacer durante la noche largas caminatas atravesando bosques y pantanos, en medio de huracanes, que son terribles en Virginia, con el objeto de advertir a Smith y sus colonos de las tramas de los salvajes. Otras veces cuando estaban escasos de víveres, Poucahoutas parecía como un genio bienhechor con un séquito cargado de víveres, y desaparecía inmediatamente después de haberlos nutrido. Hasta entonces ninguna colonia se había podido fijar en el continente americano hacia al Norte del Golfo de México. La providencia se sirvió de las manos de esta virgen misteriosa para plantar al fin una. La Grecia le hubiera erigido altares, o hubiera hecho de ella una diosa intermedia entre Diana, diosa de los bosques, y Minerva, la sabia y previsora. Los colonos se manejaron de otro modo. Cuando Smith se separó de ellos, se apoderaron de Poucahoutas, con el fin de tener un rehén contra su padre Powhaltan. Después de haberla retenido algún tiempo, tratándola con los mayores cuidados, convinieron en casarla con su consentimiento y el de Powhaltan con uno de ellos, con M. Rolfe que la condujo a Inglaterra. Poucahoutas, la hermosa, la modesta, la heroína Poucahoutas, vino de este modo a ser madame Rolfe, vecina de Londres o de Brentford. A la edad de veintidós años murió de consunción en Gravesand, en los momentos en que se iba a embarcar para América. Puede ser que si su fin hubiera sido más trágico, hubiese llegado a ser la heroína de veinte poemas épicos.

Los grandes hechos del capitán John Smith, son tan numerosos y admirables como los de Hércules. Según lo que él refiere sencillamente (escribió como César sus memorias) acerca de una fiesta que le dieron las damas de la corte de Powhaltan, no sería temerario creer que ninguna de las aventuras del hijo de Júpiter le ha faltado, aun aquéllas pertenecen al dominio de la crónica secreta. Una vez sobrepasó la destrucción de Anteón garroteando sólo a un jefe de talla gigantesca, el rey de los pashipsays, que le había tendido algunas emboscadas, conduciéndole sobre sus espaldas a *James Town*. Otra vez, Opechancanough le había sitiado con 700 hombres, y Smith tomó al jefe de los cabellos, le arrastró, tembloroso y humillado en medio de los indios helados de estupor, haciéndoles rendir las armas. Las dificultades que tuvo que vencer fueron innumerables. Tenía en contra la hambre y la pese, las astucias y las flechas de los salvajes, la turbulencia de una parte de los colonos, y las quejas y sentimientos de los otros que suspiraban después por las *cebollas de Egipto,* la pereza y la ignorancia de los aventureros que llovían en la colonia para buscar allí el oro, la traición de algunos, alemanes y suizos, que habían pasado al reino de Powhaltan porque allí se hacía mejor comida, todo tuvo contra sí, hasta la rebelión y el asesinato por el fierro y el veneno. No hay extremidad a la que no hubiese estado reducido, y un día viéndole en agonía sus compañeros habían ya cavado su sepulcro. Su perseverencia y valor triunfaron de todo. Gracias a sus infatigables esfuerzos, la colonia fue establecida definitivamente; muchos pueblos fueron establecidos; y después de dos años de permanencia en Virginia, herido gravemente por la explosión de un barril de pólvora, dejó a *James Town* para no volver más. Después de su partida, la colonia tuvo aún mucho que sufrir, pero ya había echado raíces.

Tal ha sido el origen de la Virignia. Era el Estado más poderoso cuando estalló la guerra de independencia. Estuviera todavía en el primer rango sin la institución de la esclavitud, que la detiene como un peso grande los pies. Ella es la que ha dado en la revolución americana a Washington, Jefferson, Madison, Monroe, y muchos hombres de Estado los más ilustres. Se advierte que hay en el carácter de los de Virginia, rasgos generosos y caballerescos que prueban cómo el ejemplo y lecciones de Smith, dejaron en el corazón de sus compañeros una marca duradera.

Si yo cuento así por menor la vida de John Smith, no es a causa del interés que se une a un hombre extraordinario, es sí, a causa de la analogía que presenta nuestra época con la suya.

Era un tiempo de crisis política y religiosa, de guerra civil, de revolución. Era el tiempo de la reconstrucción de Europa por el Tratado de Wesfalia. Entonces caía la cabeza de Carlos I; entonces otra dinastía estaba en vísperas de ocupar el trono de Inglaterra. Era el tiempo en que el partido protestante trataba de hacer una república en Francia. Las imaginaciones estaban excitadas y desencadenadas; los cerebros en movimiento. Los hombres sabios de entonces creían que el mundo iba a acabar. No era pues un mundo que acababa, era el nuevo que nacía, y los dolores que sentía el antiguo eran dolores de parto.

Suponed que hombres del género de Smith hubiesen estado obligados a permanecer en Inglaterra. Con esta imaginación activa, esta energía fogosa, esta voluntad firme, inevitablemente se hubieran lanzado en la política, entonces palpitante de intereses y movimientos. ¿Y cuántos hombres de este temperamento a la cabeza de los partidos, hubieran sido necesarios para trastornar al país?

Digamos mejor: la Inglaterra fue conmovida en sus fundamentos en efecto entonces, y puede ser que no lo hubiera sido si dos hombres, dotados como Smith de una imaginación ardiente y una voluntad de fierro, no hubiesen sido detenidos. Estos dos eran John Hampdem y Olivier Cromwell. Querían pasar a América, el rey se los impidió. Pocos años después uno de ellos mató al poder real, tal por lo menos como lo entendían los Stuarts; el otro mató al Rey.

CAPÍTULO XI

Discusión sobre oficinas de correos los domingos.—Dictamen de la comisión.—Fundamentos en que se apoyan.—Petición de algunos ciudadanos de la Virginia, contra un proyecto de escuelas religiosas.—Visita al general Jackson.—Fiestas en Washington por los acontecimientos de julio.—Cuestión de aranceles.

Se ventilaba en 1830 en Washington, una cuestión cuya discusión y el dictamen de la comisión de la Cámara de representantes, así como la final resolución del Congreso, son una nueva prueba de la política generosa, libre e independiente de los Estados Unidos del Norte. Una multitud de asociaciones, especialmente de presbiterianos, dirigieron al Congreso general representaciones, pidiendo que los domingos, días destinados al descanso y a la oración, no se abriesen las oficinas de correos, ni que las postas corriesen aquel día. El dictamen de la comisión merece insertarse en esta obra, cuyo principal fin es el que los mexicanos y todas las repúblicas de la América antes española, tomen ejemplos y lecciones de esa escuela práctica de política liberal e independiente, que hoy es el modelo a todos los pueblos civilizados. A continuación pondré también otro documento no menos interesante, que es la representación de varios ciudadanos de la Virginia, hecha por M. Madison en 1784 sobre un objeto análogo, y en la que se desenvuelven los mismos principios. De estos documentos y de muchas noticias de que he hecho uso en este libro, soy deudor a la preciosa obra de M. *James Stuart* titulada *Three years in North America*.

Documento 1° "La comisión de correos y caminos de posta, a la que se han pasado los memoriales en que se solicita la prohibición de la conducción de las malas y abertura de las oficinas de correos los domingos, expone: que los exponentes pretenden que el primer día de la semana es designado por el Creador para ejercicios religiosos, y consideran el transporte de las malas y la apertura de las oficinas de correos en este día como una violación, de los deberes religiosos, pidiendo en consecuencia la supresión de estos trabajos. Otros han pedido que el Congreso declare que no hay lugar a esta solicitud, fundados en que un día de la semana no es más santo que otro. Algunos apoyándose en la inmutabilidad y universalidad del Decálogo de los Judíos, creen que el día santificado no es el primero sino el séptimo de la semana, y por su exposición que tiene a la vista la comisión, piden que cese todo trabajo este día, que debe destinarse a la oración. Hasta aquí cada uno ha sido dejado en el ejercicio libre y pacífico de su propia opinión; y considerándose como el único deber del gobierno protegerlos a todos y no hacer distinción con ninguno. Pero ahora se ha querido hacer un esfuerzo para uniformarse, al menos en la práctica, y como no han bastado los argumentos, se ha ocurrido a la intervención del Gobierno para que con su autoridad decida la controversia.

"El Congreso obra en una esfera delineada y marcada por la constitución, con poderes limitados por ella. La comisión se ha esforzado inútilmente en buscar en este instrumento una autorización para que el Congreso pueda inquirir y determinar que parte del tiempo, si alguna lo ha sido, fue destinada por el Todopoderoso a ejercicios de religión. Por el contrario, entre las pocas reflexiones que contiene, una de ellas es la prohibición de un texto cualquiera religioso; y otra que declara que el Congreso no dará ley ninguna relativa al establecimiento de religión o prohibición del libre ejercicio de ella. Aquí podría terminar la comisión sus reflexiones, si la cuestión sometida a su examen no tuviese que ser sujetada a la deliberación del Congreso. Pero la perseverancia y celo con que los memorialistas sostienen su objeto, exige mayor dilucidación en la materia. La comisión está enteramente de acuerdo con los exponentes en la doctrina que sienta como base, la absoluta independencia del Estado respecto de los asuntos de la iglesia. Pero es claro que cualquiera medida en oposición de la solicitud, sólo tiene su origen en los temores que nacen de su fatal tendencia a perturbar la paz y felicidad de la nación. Las catástrofes de las otras naciones suministraron a los autores de nuestra constitución pruebas de melancólicos consejos, y ellos aplicaron su mayor atención en evitar estos peligros".

"La ley existente, sin hacer ninguna distinción en los días de la semana, manda que los maestros de posta sirvan con exactitud todos los días en sus respectivas oficinas, y el director general de correos ha dado todas sus instrucciones a todos los dependientes para que los oficios se mantengan abiertos los domingos hasta despachar las cartas; y que en el caso de que concurriere la llegada de la correspondencia con las horas del culto religioso, las oficinas deberán mantenerse abiertas una hora después de concluidas las asambleas religiosas. Esta aplicación liberal de la ley, no ha satisfecho a los memorialistas. Pero la comisión cree que no hay justa razón de queja, a menos que no se quiera conceder que éstos tienen un poder regulador sobre las conciencias de los otros. Si el Congreso sancionase por la autoridad de la ley la medida que solicitan, daría una decisión legislativa sobre una controversia religiosa, en la que aun los cristianos mismos están discordes. Por más que semejante resolución pudiese convenir a los consejos eclesiásticos, sería evidentemente incompatible con las facultades de una legislatura republicana, cuyos objetos son puramente políticos y bajo ningún aspecto religiosos".

"En nuestro carácter privado e individual, todos tenemos opiniones y seguimos las prácticas análogas sobre materias religiosas. Sin embargo, de su diversidad, todos conservamos una armonía perfecta como ciudadanos, mientras que cada uno quiera que los otros gocen de la misma libertad que reclama para sí mismo. Pero nuestro carácter individual desaparece en nuestro carácter representativo. Los actos individuales son para uno y por uno mismo: los actos representativos pertenecen a nuestros constituyentes. El representante es elegido para representar sus miras religiosas, para conservar los derechos del hombre, no para restringir los derechos de la conciencia. Los déspotas pueden mirar a sus súbditos como su propiedad, y usurpar la divina prerrogativa de prescribirles su fe religiosa. Pero la historia del mundo nos suministra melancólicas demostraciones de que las disposiciones *humanas que tienden a imponer coacción a los homenajes religiosos de los otros, emanan más bien de una ambición desmesurada que de sinceros sentimientos religiosos*. Los principios de nuestro gobierno no reconocen en la mayoría autoridad alguna sobre la minoría más que en los asuntos concernientes a la conducta del hombre como ciudadano. Un rey de Israel por echar mano del incensario, perdió el cetro y la libertad. Sería un destino poco envidiable la suerte del pueblo americano que ejerce el poder soberano, si el cuerpo de sus representantes se propusiese unir de cualquier modo la Iglesia al Estado".

"Desde la más remota antigüedad, los maestros de la religión tuvieron una grande influencia sobre el espíritu del pueblo: y en todas las naciones, tanto antiguas como modernas, paganos, mahometanos o cristianos, han conseguido incorporar sus dogmas religiosos a las instituciones políticas de su país. Los ídolos de Persia, los oráculos griegos, los augurios de Roma y el sacerdocio de la Europa moderna, han sido en su turno objetos de la adoración popular y los agentes de una política pérfida. Si se adoptase la medida que se solicita, sería difícil a la sagacidad humana prever la rápida sucesión y la numerosa cohorte de medidas que se seguirían después, envolviendo el más precioso de todos los derechos, los derechos de la conciencia. Sin duda que es un suceso feliz para nuestro país el que se haya agitado esta cuestión en este período de su reciente existencia política, cuando el espíritu revolucionario existe todavía en todo su vigor. El celo religioso tiene en su apoyo las más fuertes preocupaciones del entendimiento humano, y cuando es mal dirigido excita las peores pasiones del hombre bajo el engañoso pretexto de servir a la Divinidad. Nada es capaz de hacer más feroces las acciones, y conducir a los fanáticos a la rapiña y a las matanzas: nada más obstinado en sus empresas, más perseverante en sus determinaciones, más espantoso en su marcha y más peligroso en sus consecuencias. La igualdad de derechos establecida por la constitución, puede desafiar la tiranía política; pero el ropaje de la santidad, cubre con sus brillos el engaño".

"La constitución mira la conciencia del judío como la del cristiano igualmente sagradas, y no concede al Congreso más facultad para adoptar las ideas religiosas de una secta que de otra; el representante que violase este principio, perdería su carácter de delegado, y abusaría de la confianza de sus comitentes. Si el Congreso declarase *santo* el primer día de la semana, no por eso convencería al judío ni a los que santifican el *sábado*. Ambos quedarían ofendidos y nunca convertidos. El poder humano podrá forzar a hacer vanos sacrificios; pero la Divinidad sólo acepta los homenajes del corazón. Ni debemos olvidar que en los primeros tiempos de la formación de estas colonias, el espíritu de persecución que arrojó a los peregrinos de su suelo natal, les acompañó en la nueva patria, y que algunos cristianos fueron perseguidos y otros asesinados por el solo crimen de no pensar como sus gobernantes".

"A presencia de tales hechos no puede menos que ser un motivo de grande pena el ver que se intenta traer al seno del Congreso una cuestión que envuelve los más caros privilegios de la constitución, por aquellos mismos que gozan de sus más distinguidas bendiciones. Nosotros no podemos menos que recordar que mientras que Catalina hacía profesión de patriotismo, era traidor a los intereses de su patria. Arnolt, demócrata de profesión (whig), fue traidor, y Judas, discípulo, fue traidor a su divino maestro".

"A excepción de los Estados Unidos, toda la raza humana, cuyo número se calcula ser de ochocientos millones de seres racionales, gime bajo el peso del yugo religioso; y repasando las escenas de persecución que la historia presenta a cada paso, la comisión juzga que nunca *será bastante fuerte la línea que separe el Estado de la Iglesia,* a no ser que se crea que los gritos de las víctimas quemadas y las llamas que las consumieron eran un incienso grato al Creador. Si en un acto solemne de legislación se definiese en un solo punto la ley de Dios, o los deberes religiosos del ciudadano, ya no habría inconveniente en definir y aclarar otros de la revelación, y emplear la coacción en los deberes religiosos, aun en las formas y ceremonias del culto, y en dotar las iglesias y dar leyes para mantener el clero".

"El beso con que Judas entregó a su divino maestro, debía enseñarnos a todos, cualquiera que sea nuestra creencia, que los derechos de la conciencia sólo pueden ser invadidos bajo el pretexto de santidad. El cristianismo se propagó contra todo el poder humano. Los destierros, los tormentos y la muerte se opusieron inútilmente a sus progresos. Pero al momento en que sus corifeos fueron revestidos de poderes políticos, perdieron el espíritu de dulzura que les inculcaba su creencia, y comenzaron a perseguir a los profesores de otras religiones y de las sectas disidentes de la suya, con más rigor que el que lo habían sido los primeros apóstoles de sus dogmas. Las diez persecuciones de los emperadores paganos fueron mucho menos atroces que las matanzas y asesinatos cometidos por manos de los mismos cristianos, y buscaríamos inútilmente en los archivos de la tiranía imperial un instrumento de persecución tan horrible como la Santa Inquisición. Toda secta religiosa, dulce en su origen, comienza a perseguir en el momento que adquiere un poder político. Los autores de la constitución estaban profundamente convencidos del eterno principio, de que las relaciones del hombre con Dios, son sobre todas las leyes humanas, y sus derechos de conciencia inalienables. No es necesario el razonamiento para establecer esta verdad: tenemos todos la conciencia de su evidencia: esa conciencia que, desafiando las leyes humanas, sostuvo tantos mártires en los tormentos y en medio de las llamas. Sentían profundamente que sus deberes para con Dios eran superiores a los mandamientos humanos, y que el hambre no podía ejercer autoridad alguna sobre las conciencias. Estos son principios innatos al hombre; principios que ningún poder puede destruir".

"El hipócrita en el orgullo de su autoridad, puede perder de vista estas verdades; pero le desnudan de su poder. Prescribid una fe que la conciencia rechaza: armad al que resiste con la cárcel o el azote; el espíritu que Dios le ha inspirado se levanta y os desafía. ¿Pidieron los primeros cristianos que el gobierno los reconociese y adoptase su dogma? Nada de eso. Lo que únicamente querían era que se les tolerase: sólo se quejaban de las persecuciones que sufrían. Preguntad a los católicos que gobernaban la Francia y la Alemania, qué pidieron los hugonotes y los protestantes? Tolerancia. ¿Qué pedían los católicos perseguidos en Irlanda? Tolerancia".

"En nuestro feliz país ¿no disfrutan todos los hombres de esos mismos derechos religiosos que pedían con tanta justicia los santos y los mártices? ¿De dónde puede venir entonces una voz de queja racional? ¿Quién es aquél que en el pleno goce de todos los principios que las leyes pueden asegurar, desea arrancar una parte de estos principios de sus conciudadanos? ¿Pueden alegar los peticionarios que no participen de los beneficios de la correspondencia el domingo, porque sus escrúpulos religiosos se lo prohiben? Si es esta la razón, entonces será una utilidad mundana el que los estimula y no el celo de la religión. ¿Se quejarán porque otros hombres, menos escrupulosos en guardar el *sábado,* obtienen siempre ventaja sobre ellos, recibiendo sus cartas y sacando utilidad para sus negocios? Tal fundamento es también mundano y además egoísta. Pero si sus motivos son hacer que el Congreso sancione por una ley sus opiniones religiosas y sus ceremonias y observancias, entonces sus esfuerzos deben ser resistidos como fatales a la libertad política y religiosa. ¿Por qué han limitado su solicitud a la correspondencia? ¿Por qué no han pedido igualmente que se requiera al Gobierno suspenda todos sus actos en aquel día? ¿Por qué no solicitan que se prohíba la salida de los buques de nuestros puertos; que no marchen nuestras tropas de un punto a otro; que los alguaciles y demás oficiales de justicia no pongan en prisión a los delincuentes, o guarden a los presos? Parece que olvidaron que el Gobierno es tan necesario el domingo como en cualquiera otro día de la semana. El Gobierno es el que con la autoridad de su ministerio nos da garantías de paz a todos, inclusive los peticionarios, para celebrar su culto. El servicio de las postas y correos es uno de los más útiles. Ellos conducen desde el centro de la república hasta las extremidades las actas y resoluciones de nuestros cuerpos legislativos, las decisiones judiciales, y los decretos del ejecutivo. Su rapidez es muchas veces necesaria para la defensa de la patria, la supresión de muchos crímenes y la promoción de los más caros intereses del pueblo. Las *malas* llevan de un extremo a otro de la Unión cartas de unos a otros amigos y parientes, manteniendo la comunidad de afectos y amor recíproco entre personas separadas por largas distancias, aumentando los más puros y refinados placeres de nuestra existencia social. Además, las cartas de los comerciantes conducen el estado de los precios, evitan especulaciones ruinosas, y promueven los generales e individuales intereses: conducen innumerables cartas religiosas, papeles públicos, libros, discursos, contratos, etc., que se dirigen a todos los ángulos de esta vasta república. ¿Y podrá llamarse un servicio tan importante violación del domingo? Los adelantos del género humano en inteligencia, en virtud, y aun en religión, dependen en gran parte de la facilidad de las comunicaciones y de la consiguiente diseminación de las ideas. Sin esos cambios entre uno y otros países, entre las diferentes secciones de unas mismas naciones, todas las mejoras en moral y política, así como en las artes, se limitarían al país en que nacieron. Mientras más rápido y frecuente sea este comercio de ideas, más rápido será también el progreso del entendimiento humano. Detener un día entre siete estas comunicaciones, es retardar una séptima las mejoras de nuestro país; y tan lejos está la comisión de opinar por la supresión de los correos el domingo, que por el contrario, juzga oportuno recomendar todos los medios racionales de dar mayor rapidez y extensión a este ramo. ¿Cuál sería la elevación de nuestra patria, si cada nueva invención o nuevo proyecto pudiese comunicarse al mismo tiempo a todos los entendimientos? No es la distancia de un Estado al centro de su Gobierno lo que perjudica a su *bienestar,* es únicamente la dificultad y poca frecuencia de sus comunicaciones. Nuestra correspondencia es hoy recibida en el Misuri y en Arkansas en menos tiempo que se recibía en Kentucky y Ohio hace treinta años; y ahora que tres millones de habitantes se extienden en poblaciones a unas mil millas de los Alleghanis, se oyen menos rumores de descontento que cuando pocos miles de colonos estaban esparcidos en la base occidental de aquellos establecimientos. El suspender un día de la semana la correspondencia, sería retirar del centro del Gobierno todos esos Estados del oeste y demás distancias de la capital".

"Pero suponiendo que fuese conveniente suspender la correspondencia de los domingos, por ser contra la ley de Dios, y que el brazo del Gobierno debe emplearse en compeler a los hombres a obedecer las leyes de Dios, ¿no es evidente que los gobiernos de los Estados poseen un poder infinitamente mayor en este respecto? Diríjanse pues los solicitantes a ellos y hagan sus esfuerzos para inducirlos a que den leyes para santificar el domingo. Porque si es pecado conducir las cartas de unos a otros puntos, lo será también el escribirlas, recibirlas y leerlas. Parece que deberían requerirse leyes penales por estos actos para completar el sistema. Deberían ser castigados los que viajan por negocios o diversión aquel día; los impresores, conductores, receptores y lectores de los papeles públicos, con excepción de los relativos a cosas sagradas. La consecuencia inevitable sería obligar a todos los hombres, mujeres y niños a concurrir a la iglesia; y como sólo *una secta es la verdadera y ortodoxa,* la ley debería determinar cuál era, y compeler a los demás a concurrir a oír a sus sacerdotes y maestros, y contribuir para su manutención. Mas para ser consecuentes y formar un sistema completo, sería necesario aplicar algunas penas al judío, o al que cree que *sábado* es *sábado,* al infiel que nada cree, y obligar por el tormento, destierros, prisiones y otros castigos, a éstos que no quieren violar sus conciencias alistándose en las doctrinas religiosas que detestan. Cuando los gobiernos de los Estados hayan adoptado estas medidas, entonces el Congreso general tendrá tiempo para declarar que el ruido de los coches de pasta no deberá interrumpir el silencio de este despotismo horrible".

"El deber de nuestros gobiernos, es declarar a todos, al judío, al gentil, al cristiano y al mahometano, que tienen igual derecho a la protección y ventajas de nuestras benignas instituciones los domingos, así como en cualquier día de la semana; y sin que este gobierno se convierta en tribunal eclesiástico, obrará siempre sobre la máxima sentada del fundador del cristianismo, a saber: 'que es lícito hacer bien el sábado'".

Este dictamen lleno de principios tan luminosos, escrito con una lógica irresistible y sobre las bases de una constitución la más libre y filosófica que se conoce, concluye declarando inconstitucional la solicitud y fue aprobado por unanimidad. ¿No será esta una lección útil a los partidarios de la intolerancia en México, y demás gobiernos que tienen pretensión de ser libres? ¿Qué pensaba el Congreso mexicano cuando dio una ley, obligando a los gobiernos eclesiásticos a proveer curatos en propiedad, después de haber dado las leyes filosóficas de diezmos y votos monásticos, en que se limitaba a retirar la coacción? Estos son los grandes inconvenientes de nuestros legisladores. Pero aún es peor lo que sucedió después.

El segundo documento que voy a insertar es una exposición de varios ciudadanos del Estado de Virginia hecha al Congreso del Estado, para que suspendiese el proyecto de establecer maestros de religión cristiana, como se pensó hacer en 1784. El autor de este memorial fue después presidente desde 1808 hasta 1816.

A la honorable asamblea general del estado de Virginia

"Los abajo suscritos, ciudadanos del mismo Estado, habiendo tomado en seria consideración el proyecto de ley, impreso por orden de la asamblea en la sesión última, que lleva por título: *Proyecto para establecer maestros de la religión cristiana,* y convencidos de que si tal proyecto llega a recibir sanción legal, será un abuso peligroso del poder, se ven obligados, como fieles miembros de un Estado libre, a representar contra el proyecto, y a declarar las razones por las cuales se determinan a ser los representantes contra él".

"1° Porque tenemos como una verdad fundamental e innegable, *que la religión o los deberes del hombre para con su Creador, así como la manera de llenarlos, solamente pueden ser dirigidos por el raciocinio y el convencimiento, y no por la violencia y la fuerza.* Por consiguiente, la religión de cada hombre debe ser dejada a la convicción y conciencia de cada hombre, y es el más sagrado deber de cada hombre ejercerla según se lo dicte su conciencia. Este derecho es de la naturaleza, y no puede perderse ni enajenarse, porque dependiendo las opiniones de los hombres solamente de la evidencia reflejada en sus propios entendimientos, no pueden seguir ciegamente los dictámenes de otros. Es inalienable también porque lo que aquí es un derecho hacia los hombres, es un deber para con el Creador. Pues el deber de todo hombre, es tributar al Creador sólo aquel homenaje que en su juicio pueda serle aceptable. Este deber es precedente, tanto en el orden de tiempo como en el grado de obligación, a los títulos de la sociedad civil. Antes que ningún mortal pueda ser considerado como miembro de la sociedad, debe ser considerado como subordinado al gobernador del Universo. Y así como un miembro de la sociedad civil que se incorpora en alguna asociación subalterna, lo hace siempre bajo la reserva de sus obligaciones al gobierno general, con mayor razón todo hombre al constituirse miembro de la sociedad civil, es precisamente conservando sus deberes de obediencia y homenajes al Soberano universal. De aquí inferimos que en materias de religión ningún hombre pierde sus derechos por las instituciones civiles, y que la religión está totalmente exenta de su conocimiento. Es verdad que no existe otra regla por la que una cuestión que divide la sociedad pueda ser resuelta que las decisiones de la mayoría; pero también es verdad que la mayoría puede ofender los derechos de la minoría".

"2° Porque estando excluida la religión de la autoridad de la sociedad en general, mucho menos puede estar sujeta a la del cuerpo legislativo. Este no es más que la criatura y vicegerente de aquélla. Sus facultades son derivadas y sujetas a límites. Los tiene, en cuanto a cierta extensión de territorio, del mismo modo que en la autoridad que ejerce en sus comitentes. Las condiciones esenciales de todo gobierno libre, requieren no solamente que los límites que separan cada departamento del poder, sean mantenidos invariables; sino que más especialmente ninguno de ellos permita que alguno de los otros intente traspasar la gran barrera que defiende los derechos del pueblo. Los legisladores o gobernantes culpables de tal agresión, excediendo los límites de sus poderes legales, se convertirían en tiranos. El pueblo que se somete a las leyes que no ha hecho, él mismo o sus legítimos representantes, es pueblo esclavo".

"3° Porque es natural alarmarse en los primeros experimentos sobre nuestras libertades. Estamos persuadidos de que este celo prudente es el primer deber de los ciudadanos, y uno de los más notables caracteres de la última revolución. Los libres americanos nunca esperaron que el poder usurpador crease fuerzas y enredase la cuestión con los antecedentes. Vieron todas las consecuencias en el principio, y las evitaron negando el principio. Nosotros reverenciamos mucho esta lección para poderla olvidar tan pronto. ¿Quién no ve que la misma autoridad que puede establecer el cristianismo con exclusión de otras religiones, puede establecer una de las sectas del cristianismo, por ejemplo el catolicismo, con exclusión de las otras? ¿Qué la misma autoridad que puede obligar a un ciudadano a contribuir con medio real solamente de su propiedad para mantener tal establecimiento, puede obligarle a lo mismo con respecto de cualquiera otros?"

"4° Porque el proyecto viola aquella igualdad que debe ser la base de toda ley, y que es más indispensable cuando la validez o utilidad de alguna ley está más expuesta a ser inoculada. Si todos los hombres son por la naturaleza iguales, libres e independientes, todos deben ser considerados, al entrar en la sociedad, con iguales derechos y bajo iguales condiciones; no reteniendo ni abandonando más ni menos de sus respectivos derechos. Sobre todo, deben ser considerados con iguales títulos al libre ejercicio de su religión, con arreglo al dictamen de su conciencia. Al asegurar para nosotros mismos una perfecta libertad para abrazar, profesar y ejercer la religión que creemos ser de origen divino, no podemos sin injusticia negar la misma libertad a aquellos hombres cuyos entendimientos no están de acuerdo, con la evidencia de nuestra razón. Los abusos de esta libertad no son ofensas contra el hombre; a Dios únicamente deben dar cuenta de su ejercicio, y él da las recompensas o los castigos. El proyecto viola al mismo tiempo el principio de igualdad, concediendo a unos excepciones particulares, y cargando a otros de contribuciones para el pago de maestros de una religión que no profesan. ¿Son acaso las cuáqueros y metodistas las únicas sectas que deben ser sostenidas? ¿Debe confiarse a sola su piedad el cuidado del culto público? ¿Han de ser dotadas solamente sus iglesias con perjuicio de las otras? Nosotros pensamos más favorablemente respecto de la justificación y buen sentido de estas creencias, para juzgar que sean capaces de envidiar una preeminencia sobre las de sus conciudadanos, y que no vean la oposición grande que encuentra esta medida".

"5° Porque el proyecto envuelve la doctrina de que la magistratura civil es un juez competente sobre las verdades religiosas, o que puede hacer uso de la religión como instrumento de la política. La primera es uno presunción arrogante falsificada por las opiniones contradictorias de los directores en todos los siglos y por todo el mundo. Lo segundo un pernicioso abuso de los medios de salvación".

"6° Porque el establecimiento propuesto por el proyecto no es necesario para el mantenimiento de la religión cristiana. Decir lo contrario es una contradicción a lo que la misma religión enseña: cada página del Evangelio enseña la absoluta independencia de las cosas temporales y poderes mundanos. Es además una contradicción a los hechos; porque es sabido que esta religión nació y floreció no solamente sin la ayuda de las leyes humanas, sino a pesar de su oposición; no sólo también durante el período de la ayuda de los milagros, sino aun mucho tiempo después cuando quedó abandonada a su misma evidencia, y a los cuidados ordinarios de la Divina Providencia. Mas, es una contradicción en los términos. Porque una religión no inventada por la política humana debe preexistir y ser mantenida anteriormente a la política humana. Es de consiguiente debilitar en los que la profesan, la piadosa confianza en su nativa excelencia y en el patrocinio de su autor, y alimentar en aquellos que no la creen, la sospecha de que sus defensores tienen conciencia de su falibilidad, para poder confiar de su propio mérito y virtud".

"7° Porque la experiencia testifica que los establecimientos eclesiásticos en lugar de mantener la pureza y eficacia de la religión, tienen contrarios efectos. Por el espacio poco más o menos de quince siglos ha estado el establecimiento del cristianismo en disputas perpetuas. ¿Cuáles han sido los frutos? En todas partes, más o menos, la indolencia y el orgullo del clero; la ignorancia y envilecimiento de los legos; en unos y otros la superstición, la hipocresía y las más crueles persecuciones. Preguntad a los maestros del cristianismo cuáles fueron los tiempos de su mayor lustre y esplendor, y los de todas las sectas convendrán en que su más brillante período fue el anterior a su incorporación en el gobierno civil. Proponedles la restauración a aquel estado primitivo en que sus apóstoles dependían de las ofrendas voluntarias de sus ovejas, y veréis a muchos de ellos pronosticar su caída. ¿Por qué lado debe inclinarse el juicio, por el de la decisión interesada, o la desinteresada?"

"8° Porque el establecimiento en cuestión no es necesario a la conservación del gobierno civil. Pues si se considera que debe ser sostenida para coadyuvar al gobierno civil, luego se confiesa que necesita ser sostenida, y en este caso no es la sostenedora. ¿Qué influencia en realidad han tenido los establecimientos eclesiásticos en la sociedad? En algunos casos se les ha visto ejercer una tiranía espiritual sobre las ruinas de la potestad civil; en muchos sosteniendo los tronos sobre una política tiránica: jamás defendiendo la causa de la libertad y del pueblo. *Los gobernantes que han intentado destruir la libertad pública, encontraron siempre en los establecimientos eclesiásticos sus más poderosos auxiliares.* Un gobierno justo que se propone asegurar los derechos del pueblo, no tiene necesidad de tales apoyos. Semejantes gobernantes son siempre mucho mejor sostenidos por la protección que dispensan a cada ciudadano en el libre ejercicio de su religión, con la misma igualdad con que protege su persona y su propiedad, no permitiendo que ninguna secta invada los derechos de las otras: no sufriendo que alguna de ellas sea invadida por las demás".

"9° Porque el proyecto es contrario a esa política generosa que, ofreciendo protección y asilo a los hombres perseguidos y oprimidos de todas las naciones y cultos, dio tanto lustre a nuestro país, y un acceso fácil a numerosas generaciones de sus ciudadanos. ¡Qué aspecto melancólico el de un proyecto que nos aparta de esta senda! En vez de ofrecer un asilo a los perseguidos, se convierte en un lugar de persecución. Degrada del rango igual de ciudadanos a aquéllos que no ligan sus conciencias a las opiniones religiosas de sus autoridades. Especie de inquisición sólo diferente de la otra, en algunos grados de persecución. La una es el primer paso, la otra el último en la carrera de la intolerancia. Las almas magnánimas que sufren por la libertad de sus opiniones en otros países esclavos, verán en este proyecto una bandera plantada sobre nuestras costas, que les advierte se dirijan a otro suelo, en donde la libertad y la filantropía ejercen su imperio, a buscar un descanso y asilo a sus infortunios".

"10° Porque tiende a despoblar nuestra patria y sacar nuestros conciudadanos del país. Los atractivos presentados por las otras ventajas son muy pequeños, comparados con los inconvenientes que resultarán de esta medida que revoca la libertad de que gozan las conciencias, especie de locura igual a la que ha deshonrado muchos reinos, antes florecientes, que lamentan su despoblación".

"11° Porque destruiría esta feliz armonía que la prudente previsión de nuestras leyes, prohibiendo intervenir en materias de religión, ha producido entre las diversas sectas. Torrentes de sangre se han derramado en el antiguo mundo por los vanos esfuerzos del brazo secular para extinguir las discordias religiosas, prohibiendo las diferentes religiones. El tiempo sólo ha revelado el único y verdadero remedio. En cuantas naciones se ha probado el medio de abandonar esa estrecha y mezquina política de restricciones, se han experimentado luego felices resultados. El sistema americano ha dado las más evidentes pruebas de que una completa e igual libertad en esta materia, si no arranca en su raíz todo el mal, destruye su influencia maligna a la salud y prosperidad del Estado. Si con la experiencia de los saludables efectos de este sistema, intentamos ligarnos con lazos religiosos, no sabemos qué nombre dar a este absurdo proyecto. Tomemos al menos consejo de los primeros frutos de la innovación que nos amenaza. La sola aparición del proyecto ha transformado 'esa dulzura, amor y caridad cristiana' que antes prevalecía, en celos y animosidades cuyo término no sabemos cuál será. ¿Qué desgracias no habrá que temer si los enemigos de la paz pública se viesen armados contra la ley?"

"12° Porque la política del proyecto es opuesto a la de la fusión de la luz del cristianismo. El primer deseo de los que gozan de este precioso don, debe ser el que se difunda en toda la raza humana. Comparad el número de aquéllos que le han recibido con el de los que permanecen en las creencias de falsas religiones. ¡Cuán pequeño es el número de los primeros! Los efectos del proyecto ¿tienen tendencia a disminuir la desproporción? Nada de eso. Desalienta a los extranjeros que no están iluminados con la luz de la revolución a venir en la región en que existe, imitando a las naciones que continúan en el caos de la oscuridad, cerrando sus puertas a los que pueden ilustrarlos. En vez de quitar todos los obstáculos, en cuanto sea posible, a los victoriosos progresos de la verdad, el proyecto, con timidez innoble y poco cristiana, circunscribiría el país con una muralla de defensa contra las agresiones de éstos".

"13° Porque los esfuerzos para autorizar la sanción de la ley, actos perjudiciales a un gran número de ciudadanos, tienden a enervar la fuerza de las leyes en general y debilitar los vínculos sociales. Si es dificultoso poner en ejecución una ley que no se tiene generalmente por necesaria y saludable, ¿qué sucederá con la que es tenida por peligrosa e inútil? ¿Y cuáles serían los efectos de la impotencia del gobierno en toda su autoridad?"

"14° Porque no debe tomarse una medida de tal magnitud y delicadeza sin la más clara evidencia de que es reclamada por una mayoría de los ciudadanos. Y hasta ahora no se ha propuesto un método satisfactorio por el que se pueda determinar que se ha expresado el voto de la mayoría y asegurado su influencia. Porque aunque se ha pedido la opinión del pueblo de los respectivos condados, sobre la adopción del proyecto que deberá discutirse en las próximas sesiones, debió haberse remitido igualmente la representación de los que se oponen para que pudiese el pueblo juzgar con imparcialidad. Tenemos la esperanza de que ningún condado adoptará este proyecto peligroso, y en todo evento siempre estamos confiados en la sabiduría de nuestros representantes que nos libran de esta ignominia".

"15° Últimamente, porque la igualdad de derechos en todos los ciudadanos para el libre ejercicio de su religión, con arreglo al dictamen de su conciencia, está en el mismo caso que todos los otros derechos. Si recurrimos a su origen es un don de la Naturaleza; si pensamos su importancia no debe sernos menos caro. Si consultamos la declaración de aquellos derechos que pertenecen al buen pueblo de Virginia, como base y fundamento de su gobierno está colocado entre los otros con igual solemnidad, y aun con cierto énfasis. Entonces podemos decir, o que la legislatura tiene una autoridad sin límites y que de consiguiente puede derogar todos nuestros derechos fundamentales, o que sus facultades están limitadas a no tocar estas bases sagradas e inviolables: que o tiene facultad para derogar la libertad de imprenta, abolir el juicio por jurados, arrogarse los Poderes Ejecutivo y judicial, en fin despojarnos del derecho de sufragio, y erigirse en una asamblea independiente y hereditaria; o que no la tiene para adoptar como ley el proyecto en cuestión. Los que suscribimos decimos, que la legislatura no tiene tal autoridad, y que no omitiremos esfuerzo de nuestra parte contra tan peligrosa usurpación, rogando entre tanto al legislador supremo del Universo tenga a bien iluminar a las autoridades, a quienes nos dirigimos, para que con una mano las separe del proyecto de atentar a sus santas prerrogativas y violar la confianza que se les ha cometido, y con la otra las guíe a tomar las medidas que sean dignas de sus bendiciones, redunden en su elogio y puedan consolidar más y más las libertades, la prosperidad y felicidad de nuestra república".

El señor Van-Buren tuvo la bondad de acompañarme a visitar al Presidente Jackson, a quien vi por segunda vez, habiéndolo hecho antes en Cincinati, como llevo dicho. El ilustre jefe me invitó a comer y tuve la satisfacción de sentarme al lado de uno de los grandes personajes históricos de la república angloamericana, y oír de su boca la relación de algunos sucesos importantes. Nuestra conversación giró principalmente acerca de los sucesos de México, y el respetable anciano se explicó con un tacto y discernimiento que me dio una idea ventajosa de su capacidad mental y de su juicio recto. "Ustedes", me dijo, "tienen que pasar por muchas pruebas antes de purgarse de los vicios y preocupaciones de su anterior educación y forma de gobierno. Los pueblos siguen por mucho tiempo, después de un cambio político, los impulsos y dirección de sus anteriores hábitos, y para variarlos se necesita más que leyes, la enseñanza y la educación popular".

Se celebraba en Washington, cuando estuve, los triunfos de los liberales en los tres días de julio en París. Después de una procesión larga y lucida en que los artesanos y demás clases de la sociedad iban divididos, con sus respectivas banderas, se dirigió el concurso a la casa del Presidente de los Estados Unidos, el que salió y la acompañó hasta el Capitolio (más de una milla), en donde se pronunció un discurso. Por la noche hubo un baile muy concurrido y popular.

La cuestión del arancel de 1828 comenzó a tomar calor desde 1830, y terminó felizmente en 1833, después de discusiones acaloradas entre los partidarios de la Carolina del Sur y los Estados del Norte. Los primeros pretendían que no era justo que en los aranceles de importación se impusiesen derechos subidos a los efectos manufacturados de Europa, sólo para aumentar sus precios, con el objeto de proteger a los fabricantes y manufactureros de los Estados de la Nueva Inglaterra, mientras que una porción de artículos de lujo estaban sujetos a contribuciones sumamente ligeras. De aquí resulta, decían los *nulificantes* (nombre que adoptaron los de la Carolina), que por proteger a las compañías de manufactureros de los Estados del Norte, tienen nuestras clases obreras que cultivan el azúcar y el algodón, que comprar más caros los efectos que sirven para vestir a sus familias. Este arancel se había hecho bajo la administración de M. Adams y siendo primer ministro M. Clay.

Los defensores del arancel decían que los Estados del Norte consumían los algodones, azúcares y demás producciones de los Estados del Sur y del Oeste, y que éstos debían contribuir a fomentar sus manufacturas, que dentro de pocos años no tendrían necesidad de este sobrecargo en los efectos extranjeros; porque ya podrían sostener la concurrencia. La cuestión se acaloró extraordinariamente, como sucede siempre en las transacciones sobre grandes intereses, hasta el punto de temerse una colisión funesta en aquella feliz república.

En noviembre de 1832 la convención de la Carolina del Sur publicó un decreto anulando la ley de aranceles del Congreso general, documento curioso que no debo omitir en este libro. Es como sigue:

"Por cuanto el Congreso de los Estados Unidos, bajo el pretexto de dar leyes de contribuciones sobre importación de efectos extranjeros, pero en realidad intentando dar protección a algunas manufacturas del país y dispensar favor a ciertas clases e individuos empeñados en empresas con perjuicio, gravamen y opresión de otras clases e individuos, libertando de todo derecho otros artículos de lujo, porque no se manufacturan en los Estados Unidos, para aumentar los de aquéllos que se importan y se fabrican en el país, ha excedido los límites del poder que le concede la Constitución, la que no le permite dispensar semejante protección, y ha olvidado la verdadera inteligencia de la Constitución en los artículos que prescriben la igualdad de contribuciones e impuestos entre los Estados y territorios de la confederación; y por cuanto el referido Congreso, excediendo sus poderes de imponer contribuciones y derechos para las necesidades públicas, ha impuesto rentas innecesarias para objetos no autorizados por la Constitución. Por tanto, nosotros el pueblo del Estado de la Carolina reunido en convención, declaramos y ordenamos, y es ordenado y declarado por ésta, que todos los actos y las partes de los actos del Congreso de los Estados Unidos que tienen por objeto dar leyes para imponer derechos o contribuciones a los efectos que se importan en los Estados Unidos; y más especialmente la ley titulada: 'Acta relativa a alterar las leyes de impuestos a los efectos importados', aprobada en 19 de mayo de 1828, así como la ley 'que altera y enmienda muchos de los actos que imponen derechos a las importaciones', aprobada en 14 de julio de 1832, no están autorizados por la Constitución de los Estados Unidos, y violan la verdadera inteligencia de ella, y de consiguiente son nulos y de ningún valor: no obligando a ningún empleado ni ciudadano del Estado a obedecerlas: y todas las promesas, contratos y obligaciones hechos o comenzados con el objeto de asegurar los derechos impuestos por estas leyes, así como los actos judiciales que emanasen de ellas en lo sucesivo, se tendrán por absolutamente nulos y de ningún valor ni efecto. Ordenan, además, que no se tendrá por legal ningún acto de las autoridades de este Estado o de los Estados Unidos, que tenga por objeto obligar al pago de los derechos impuestos por las leyes referidas, en los límites de este Estado, y será un deber de la legislatura adoptar todos aquellos actos que considere necesarios para hacer efectivo este decreto, y evitar que se lleven a efecto las resoluciones del Congreso de los Estados Unidos, entre los límites de este Estado, desde el primero de febrero próximo en adelante, siendo una obligación de todas las autoridades, así como de todas las personas que residen en el Estado, obedecer y contribuir a que esta ordenanza tenga todo su efecto del mismo modo que los actos de la legislatura que puedan expedirse para que esta ley tenga su efecto".

"Se ordena además que en ningún caso en que las decisiones de la Corte de este Estado que recaigan sobre esta ordenanza, y los actos de la legislatura que tiendan a llevarla a efecto, ó bien sobre la validez de los referidos actos del Congreso que imponen los derechos en que sean puestas en juicio de apelación ante la Suprema Corte de los Estados Unidos, se permitirá sacar copias ni testimonios de los protocolos públicos a este efecto, y en el evento de que se intente la tal apelación, la Corte del Estado procederá a ejecutar y llevar a efecto sus sentencias con arreglo a las leyes y usos del mismo, sin atender a la mencionada apelación, y las personas que osasen hacerla serán castigadas como delincuentes de menosprecio de la Corte".

"Se ordena además que todas las personas que en la actualidad ejercen empleos de honor, sueldo y confianza, ya sean civiles o militares bajo la autoridad de este Estado, prestarán en la manera y forma que lo prescriba la legislatura, juramento de obedecer y ejecutar esta ordenanza y todos los actos de la legislatura que tiendan a su cumplimiento, y en el caso de resistencia, se considerarán vacantes sus empleos, y se proveerán como si hubiesen muerto y renunciado, no eligiéndose de aquí en adelante para ningún empleo de honor, sueldo o confianza sea civil o militar, persona que no preste este mismo juramento; ni tampoco será inscrito en las listas de jurados, en las causas que tengan relación con esta ordenanza, los que no presten el mismo juramento".

"Y nosotros, el pueblo de la Carolina del Sur, con el fin de que llegue a conocimiento del gobierno de los Estados Unidos, y al del pueblo de los coestados que estamos determinados a mantener esta nuestra ordenanza y declaración en todo evento; declaramos igualmente que no nos someteremos a la fuerza que empleará el gobierno general para obligar este Estado a la obediencia, y que consideramos como incompatibles con la Constitución de la unión del Estado de la Carolina del Sur con los Estados Unidos cualquiera decreto del Congreso general que tienda a autorizar el empleo de la fuerza militar o naval contra este Estado, sus autoridades o ciudadanos, o cualquiera acto que tenga por objeto cerrar sus puertos, obstruir la libre entrada y salida de buques de cualquiera de ellos, paralizar su comercio o que destruya los derechos dados por esta ordenanza; y que en este caso el pueblo de este Estado se considera absuelto de toda obligación de mantener o conservar su lazo político con el pueblo de los otros Estados, y procederá en adelante a organizar un gobierno separado, y a hacer todos los actos y cosas que los Estados soberanos e independientes tienen derecho de hacer".

Ved aquí un *pronunciamiento* que se parece a los que se representan mensualmente en la República Mexicana. Por fortuna este acto no encontró eco en ninguno de los otros Estados que no consideraron fundadas las reclamaciones y mucho menos el modo de hacerlas. Hay, sin embargo, más franqueza y candor que en esos planes absurdos de los revolucionarios de México que siempre comienzan suplicando y concluyen matando o desterrando.

El 14 de diciembre del mismo año, ciento ochenta ciudadanos se reunieron en la capital del mismo Estado (Columbia), y firmaron una acta en contradicción de la resolución anterior concebida en estos términos:

"Los partidarios de la unión y de los derechos del Estado de la Carolina del Sur *representan y protestan solemnemente* contra la resolución tomada por la convención del mismo Estado en 24 de noviembre último".

"1° Porque el pueblo de la Carolina del Sur eligió sus diputados a dicha Convención bajo la seguridad solemne de que estos delegados no propondrían más que remedios y medidas pacíficas y constitucionales para evitar los males de los aranceles sin comprometer la unión de estos Estados. En vez de hacerlo así, la Convención ha publicado una *ordenanza que viola directamente todos estos principios*".

"2° Porque la referida *ordenanza* ha atacado uno de los derechos inalienables del hombre, intentando encadenar toda libertad de conciencia por la tiránica mediación del poder del *juramento*".

"3° Porque el resolver que aquéllos que no quieran prestar juramento *sean privados de sus destinos civiles y militares,* ha *atacado y proscrito* cerca de una mitad de los hombres libres de la Carolina del Sur, sólo porque tienen una honesta y legal opinión diferente".

"4° Porque ha hollado los *grandes principios de libertad asegurados al ciudadano* por la Constitución de este Estado, *privando a los hombres libres de este país del derecho del juicio imparcial del jurado,* violando en consecuencia la cláusula de la Constitución que debe ser *perpetua* que declara que el *juicio por jurado como se ha usado en el Estado, así como la libertad de la imprenta, serán por siempre inviolablemente conservados*".

"5° Porque ha violado la independencia del *Poder judicial* ordenando que todos los jueces presten el absurdo juramento, o que sean *removidos arbitrariamente de sus destinos,* privándolos así del privilegio del juicio por acusación intentada, la que por la Constitución del Estado es la salvaguardia para asegurar estos destinos".

"6° Porque al prohibir el pago de las rentas en los límites del Estado la ordenanza *ha violado directamente la Constitución de los Estados Unidos* que autoriza el Congreso a imponer contribuciones".

"7° Porque ha *violado la misma Constitución de los Estados Unidos* en el artículo que ordena que no se de preferencia a un puerto sobre otro; al resolver la ordenanza que los efectos que se introduzcan en los puertos de la Carolina del Sur no paguen derecho alguno".

"8° Porque *viola la misma Constitución y ataca* los derechos del ciudadano negándole el recurso de apelación en los casos de *ley y equidad* nacido de la *Constitución y leyes de la Unión*".

"9° Porque ha *destruido virtualmente la Unión* oponiéndose a que las disposiciones del gobierno general tengan efecto, poniendo trabas a la ejecución de las leyes por medio de los Tribunales del Estado, y proclamando que si el gobierno de la Unión usa de los medios de represión entonces se separará de él".

"10. Porque la *tiranía y opresión,* efectos de la odenanza, son de un carácter tan repugnante y ruinoso que ya se resienten en el *comercio y crédito* del Estado; lo que conducirá estos ramos a su *aniquilamiento,* pues los industriosos y pacíficos ciudadanos se ven obligados a buscar la paz y la tranquilidad en otros Estados".

"*Los partidarios de la unión de la Carolina del Sur reunidos en Convención* protestan además solemnemente contra el proyecto de un *ejército permanente* propuesto por el partido que tiene el poder, como peligroso a las *libertades del pueblo.* Preguntan respetuosamente a sus conciudadanos que si tal ejército no es capaz por confesión de ellos de proteger el *partido de los nulificantes* contra todo el pueblo de los *Estados Unidos,* se resolverán a contenerle. Qué otro objeto si no puede tener aquella fuerza sino servir de instrumento a la tiranía contra sus conciudadanos?"

"Esta *convención protesta* también contra todos los esfuerzos hechos para llevar a efecto un sistema de *conscripción* que obligue a los ciudadanos a abandonar sus casas y ocupaciones para tomar las *armas* bajo la pena de *traición,* para sostener unas doctrinas que el pueblo estaba seguro que no necesitaban del auxilio de la fuerza, y cuyo triunfo pudo y debió obtenerse por las vías constitucionales".

"Representando *solemnemente* como por la presente representa contra las referidas resoluciones el *partido de la unión,* no puede dejar de manifestar su firme determinación de mantener los mismos principios de conducta que le dirigieron hasta aquí, y mientras por una parte continuarán haciendo una enérgica oposición a la ley viciosa de aranceles; por la otra jamás se separarán de los goces de aquellos derechos inalienables que por herencia pertenecen a todo *ciudadano americano.* Desaprobando en consecuencia toda intención de violencia insurreccionaria y antilegal, *proclaman* por la presente, su resolución de proteger sus *derechos* por todos los medios constitucionales, y al hacerlo así quieren continuar manteniendo el carácter de pacíficos ciudadanos, a menos de que sean compelidos a levantarse *contra una opresión intolerable.—*Tomas Tayler, Presidente.—Henry Middleton.—David Johnson.—Richard I. Manning.—Starling Tuckec.— Vicepresidentes (siguen ciento ochenta firmas). Dado en Colombia el viernes 14 de diciembre de 1832, año cincuenta y cinco de la independencia de los Estados Unidos de América.—Autorizado.—Franklin J. Moses.—James Edward Henry.—Secretarios de la Convención".

Esta disputa que hizo temer resultados funestos a la causa de la libertad y de la república, se terminó por la prudente y moderada conducta del Presidente Jackson y de los agentes ilustrados y patriotas de que echó mano para una empresa tan delicada. Al Congreso general manifestó la conveniencia y aun necesidad que había en moderar los aranceles, lo que se verificó sobre las bases propuestas por el excelente M. MacLane y con la cooperación de MM. Livingston, Secretario de Relaciones, y Poinsett, diputado en la legislatura de la Carolina del Sur.

Los que conocen la distancia que hay entre el modo de tratar los negocios en los Estados Unidos del Norte de América, y los Estados Unidos Mexicanos, buscarán inútilmente las causas en la diferente organización de sus poderes. En las costumbres, en la enorme distancia que existe entre las capacidades materiales y mentales de ambos países; en sus hábitos, en sus intereses, en sus creencias mismas es en donde el legislador filósofo debe encontrar el origen de la dirección divergente que toman los negocios entre los descendientes de los ingleses y los descendientes de los españoles.

CAPÍTULO XII

Washington es una ciudad nueva en el Distrito de Columbia cedido al gobierno general por el Estado de Maryland. Su círculo es de dos leguas cuadradas como el de Mérico. La ciudad es de aspecto triste, aunque tiene vistas muy agradables. Pero las calles son demasiado anchas y hay una gran distancia de unas casas a otras. Se ha formado una población por grupos aislados de edificios, de manera que aún no presenta aquel conjunto de casas y población que hace dar un golpe de vista de una ciudad. Hay un pequeño teatro en Washington y varias posadas. La de Gadsby, que es en la que yo estuve y seguramente se reputa la mejor, es bastante cara y no ofrece las comodidades que las de Baltimore, Filadelfia y Boston.

La principal calle es la que llaman *Pennsylvania Avenue,* se extiende por el centro de la ciudad desde la casa del Presidente al Capitolio. Tiene más de milla y media. El Presidente, como he dicho, no tiene guardias, ni alabarderos ni otro aparato. Va a su iglesia presbiteriana los domingos como cualquier ciudadano, y toma su asiento entre los demás sin ninguna distinción. Cuando en los primeros meses del año de 1833, vimos en México al señor Pedraza, y después al señor Farías funcionando de Presidentes, presentarse con la misma sencillez en los lugares públicos, y vivir en lo privado del mismo modo, creímos que ya en la República Mexicana se introducía la simplicidad de nuestros vecinos en sus primeros magistrados, y que jamás veríamos otra vez el aspecto y fausto virreinal, ¡dulce pero vana ilusión! A una milla de Washington, está un pueblo llamado Georgetown, en donde está un convento de monjas bajo el nombre de Hermanas de la Visitación. Habrá, como sesenta cuyas principales ocupaciones son dar educación gratuita a las jóvenes que se confía a su cuidado. La escuela gratuita está bajo la enseñanza de las más jóvenes, que tienen más de cuatrocientas niñas aprendices. El más importante establecimiento consiste en una pensión que se encuentra en un estado bastante floreciente. Estos conventos no son como los de España, en donde son encerradas las víctimas de un voto inconsiderado y prematuro para toda su vida. Cuando sus inclinaciones han variado, o sus intereses lo exigen, la ley no las fuerza a permanecer encerradas, viviendo en un perpetuo tormento que la Divinidad no puede aceptar. Salen a mejorar su condición y a vivir en la sociedad como madres de familia o de otra manera decorosa. En este convento estaban dos hijas del general Iturbide, cuando visité a la señora viuda.

Anualmente celebra sus sesiones en Washington la célebre sociedad establecida hace cerca de treinta años, cuyo objeto filosófico es redimir esclavos y enviarlos a *Liveria,* nombre dado a una colonia establecida en la costa de Africa para recibir estos seres desgraciados. En la memoria presentada por M. Clay en diciembre de 1829 se dice "que uno de los primeros actos de la sociedad, fue despachar un agente a explorar la costa de Africa, y buscar un lugar a propósito para la colonia. La elección recayó en una persona capaz de desempeñar tan pesado encargo. Se realizó la compra de un terreno fértil en 1822, que se ha aumentado posteriormente. El país comprado a las autoridades se extiende hasta cerca de doscientas millas de costa, en puntos ventajosos para el comercio, y en clima análogo a la complexión de los negros. La sociedad fundó esta colonia bajo la denominación de Liveria; estableció pueblos, labró las tierras, y elevó fortalezas para defenderse de los naturales. Cada año o antes, si las circunstancias pecuniarias de la sociedad lo permitían, se enviaban buques de los Estados Unidos cargados de esclavos emigrantes con los utensilios de agricultura, o de algunos oficios para sus trabajos, así como de lo necesario para su establecimiento. Jamás ha habido dificultad en transportar colonos cuando lo han permitido los fondos de la sociedad. Más bien han faltado fondos para verificarlo con todos los que lo solicitan con ansia. Los gastos del transporte eran mayores en los primeros años, en el día sólo son veinte pesos por persona, y es probable que serán todavía menores.

En el primer período de su existencia los colonos tuvieron que luchar con las tribus de los naturales, hasta llegar a declarar una guerra abierta. Tuvo una terminación feliz, tan luego como se convencieron de la mayor capacidad, valor y disciplina de los colonos.

Los colonos tienen un gobierno adecuado para proteger sus derechos, sus personas y propiedades, así como para mantener el buen orden. El agente de la sociedad es gobernador, comandante general y supremo jefe judicial. Los colonos participan del gobierno por la elección que hacen de varios oficios y empleos subalternos. Eligen anualmente las comisiones de los trabajos públicos, de agricultura, de sanidad, las que se encargan de la superintendencia de objetos importantes. La colonia ha establecido escuelas para la instrucción de la juventud, y levantado templos para el culto público que se practica con toda regularidad; por último tienen una librería pública con más de doce mil volúmenes, y su imprenta en que se publica la gaceta periódica. Los colonos se ejercitan en el comercio, agricultura o artes mecánicas según sus conocimientos e inclinaciones. Las tierras producen arroz, maíz, yuca, café, papas y todo género de vegetales: en poco tiempo dará azúcar, añil y otras producciones tropicales. El comercio se hace ventajosamente cambiando sus efectos con los nativos del país que dan marfil, gomas, plantas de tinte, drogas medicales y otros artículos que hacen subir a la suma de sesenta mil pesos que se aumentan anualmente".

Esta sociedad tiene ramos en muchos de los Estados de la Unión americana, en donde hay un verdadero y filosófico entusiasmo, por extinguir gradualmente la esclavitud y levantar una nación de negros civilizados en las costas de Africa. "Es imposible mantener por más tiempo el abuso de la esclavitud en algunos de nuestros Estados, decía M. Nort, presidente del Colegio de la Unión de Nueva York. No es necesario una insurrección doméstica, ni una intervención extranjera para echar abajo una institución tan repugnante a nuestros sentimientos y tan opuesta a todas nuestras instituciones. La opinión pública se ha pronunciado ya sobre esto; y la energía moral de la nación efectuará tarde o temprano su abolición. Pero la cuestión que se ofrece luego, es la de que ¿en qué estado quedará esta clase restituida a la libertad? En las otras naciones las razas se han confundido mezclándose las unas con las otras y haciendo una masa general. Aquí no estamos en el mismo caso. Nuestros esclavos manumitidos permanecerían en la tercera, cuarta, milésima generación lo mismo que hoy día son: esto es una clase distinta, degradada e infeliz. De consiguiente cuando se hayan roto sus cadenas, y esto sucederá evidentemente, de una vez, o por grados, es claro que este país se encontrará cubierto con una población tan inútil como miserable; una población que con su aumento disminuirá nuestras fuerzas, y su número sólo traerá crímenes y pobreza. Esclava o libre siempre será para nosotros una calamidad. ¿Por qué pues, hemos de dudar un momento en estimular su salida del país? Es prudente y laudable restituir a Africa como ciudadanos, los hijos de aquella comarca, que como esclavos y cargados de cadenas hemos traído, con agravio de la humanidad de ella".

Tal es el espíritu general de los habitantes de los Estados Unidos sobre esta clase tan diferente en color, como en cualidades morales de las otras. No es cierto que mezcladas las castas jamás desaparecerían sus estigmas naturales. Las cuarteronas en la Luisiana y Carolina desmienten esta aserción. ¿Pero cuántos siglos se necesitarían para que esto se verificase? Y entre tanto los inconvenientes de la permanencia de la casta negra en los Estados Unidos son de mucha consideración, para que un pueblo previsor y que calcula admirablemente sus intereses deje de tomar providencias que le libren de los males o que al menos los disminuyan. Los últimos sucesos de Nueva York y Filadelfia entre las clases blanca y negra, son anuncios de lo que puede temer aquella nación en lo porvenir.

Regresé a Nueva York por el mismo camino por donde había ido a Washington. Antes de mi llegada a los Estados Unidos se había comenzado a difundir una sociedad bajo la denominación de *Sociedad de la Templanza*. Todo establecimiento que tiene por objeto hacer profesión de un principio, de alguna virtud particular, o de alguna doctrina, viene siempre a terminar en el extremo y muchas veces en la extravagancia y el ridículo. Pocas veces deja de apoderarse el entusiasmo de sus miembros y profesores, y las conscuencias son algunas veces perjudiciales. ¿Qué cosa al parecer más racional y útil que el establecimiento de sociedades, cuyo objeto sea el predicar y dar ejemplos de sobriedad y templanza? Sin embargo, los primeros profesaban renunciar a todos los licores espirituosos: los segundos ya añadieron el vino, cerveza, sidra y demás fermentados: los terceros proscribieron el uso del café, del té, chocolate y todo género de estimulantes. Dios sabe hasta dónde conducirá esta nueva secta que felizmente hasta hoy no está asociada a ningunos misterios ni dogmas religiosos. En uno de los sermones que ha publicado el Dr. Beecher de Boston sobre esta nueva doctrina, se leen los notables consejos siguientes: "Yo sé que muchos defienden el uso moderado de los espirituosos; pero esto es lo mismo que hablar del uso prudente que se puede hacer de la peste. Otros han recomendado la cerveza como un cordial que puede suplir a los acostumbrados a tomar espirituosos; pero aunque la cerveza no críe hábitos de intemperancia tan rápidamente, no tiene el poder de desterrarlos: al fin produce los mismos efectos con esta sola diferencia que no disminuye los órganos vitales con la acrimonia y celeridad que el aguardiente, y sólo conduce a sus víctimas al sepulcro con más lentitud haciéndolos gradualmente idiotas y estúpidos, sin los arrebatos frenéticos de la locura causada por el primero. Algunos propusieron el vino como una cosa inocente para distraer los hábitos de intemperancia y mantener la salud; pero los hábitos no pueden ser sacados de sus quicios, así como un voraz apetito no es satisfecho con una sobria y templada mesa. ¡Inútiles precauciones que tienen suceso una vez entre mil! Son los esfuerzos de un niño contra un gigante: los esfuerzos de un perro de falda contra un león".

Evidentemente se han disminuido los hábitos de intemperancia en los Estados Unidos, de una manera visible. Pero han resultado muchos perjuicios de ese absoluto abandono de los espirituosos y licores fermentados.

Muy frecuentes son las muertes repentinas de las personas que en los calores del estío, después de algún curso, beben el agua fría pura sacada de las bombas, y todos los médicos convienen en que mezcladas con un poco de aguardiente no causan tan funestos efectos. ¿Qué dirían los de estas sociedades si viesen nuestras pulquerías los días de fiesta, y todavía más a los indios de Yucatán caídos aquí y allá en los caminos públicos, en las calles y en las plazas? Semejantes espectáculos no se presentan nunca en los Estados Unidos, ni en las ciudades cultas de Europa.

En muchas circunstancias de mi viaje, me encuentro con descripciones de viajeros sobre los mismos lugares, y de personas que he visitado. Tal es la de que ahora voy a ocuparme, y es el paseo que hice en compañía de mi amigo M. Poinsett a *Hyde Park,* posesión del Dr. Hosack sobre el río Hudson. Esta es una casa de campo formada sobre las colinas elevadas al lado izquierdo del hermoso río, y desde donde se descubren puntos de vista todos pintorescos. El Dr. Hosack es un americano instruido educado en Escocia, y casado con una muy rica propietaria del Estado de Nueva York. Ha embellecido aquel sitio, con bosques artificiales, jardines y plantaciones de árboles y frutos exóticos. Debo hacer mención de la amabilidad, del trato de toda la familia del Dr. Hosack. Allí conocí la hija del célebre Fulton, joven de dieciocho años entonces: llena de gracias, y una de las bellas jóvenes del Estado de Nueva York.

Poco tiempo después salí con el mismo M. Poinsett para la Nueva Inglaterra, habiendo tomado la ruta por el río del Norte *Hudson River.* Hablaré después de varios puntos de este río que merecen particular mención, cuando refiera mi viaje a *West Point* con el señor Salgado.

Albany, a la orilla derecha del río, está ciento cuarenta y ocho millas de Nueva York, y se hace el viaje en diez horas, en buques de vapor. Se pagan dos pesos, aunque esto varía hasta cuatro. Paramos en *Cinttendew Hotel;* uno de los más concurridos de la ciudad por las gentes empleadas y grandes comerciantes. Está situado en una de las colinas más elevadas de la ciudad, y domina una gran parte de ella. M. Poinsett me presentó a M. Cambreleng, diputado al Congreso general, uno de los más instruidos y elocuentes. Entonces estaba ocupado en extender el proyecto de dictamen sobre los aranceles; proyecto que después fue adoptado en la ruidosa cuestión de los *nulificantes.*

La casa del Estado, en donde se reúnen las Cámaras, es un edificio nuevamente construido, y tiene dos salas para las dos asambleas de senadores y diputados con sus correspondientes oficinas, todo muy bien distribuido y arreglado. La vista desde la cúpula de este edificio, es pintoresca. Domina el río toda la ciudad, y se ven a lo lejos las elevadas montañas de Catts Hill, de que he hablado otra vez.

La Constitución del Estado de Nueva York fue formada en 1821. El Poder Ejecutivo reside en el gobernador, que es nombrado por el pueblo cada dos años: al mismo tiempo que el vicegobernador que preside el Senado y que ejerce las funciones del primero en caso de muerte, o separación por algún motivo. El Poder Legislativo lo ejercen las dos Cámaras del Senado que se compone de treinta y dos miembros elegidos cada cuatro años, y la asamblea de veintiocho diputados que se reúnen anualmente. Los miembros de este cuerpo son nombrados por partidos que llaman condados, en número proporcionado a su población. Para la elección de senadores el Estado está dividido en ocho distritos, cada uno de los cuales nombra cuatro senadores, de los que se renueva uno cada año. La elección de gobernador, teniente-gobernador, senadores y miembros de la asamblea se verifica el primer lunes del mes de noviembre, y continúa por tres días. La legislatura puede variar estos días por disposiciones legales. El año político da principio con el año nuevo, y la legislatura se reúne anualmente el primer martes de enero. La Constitución concede el derecho de sufragio para los destinos públicos, a todos los ciudadanos varones de la clase blanca desde veintiún años de edad, que hayan residido un año antes en el Estado y seis meses en el condado en que se hace la elección. Los ciudadanos de la casta africana necesitan poseer bienes raíces de un valor al menos de doscientos cincuenta pesos libres de todo gravamen para tener el derecho de votar. El gobernador nombra el canciller y jueces con aprobación del Senado. Los jueces y el canciller permanecen en sus destinos durante el tiempo de su buen comportamiento; pero sólo hasta la edad de sesenta años. Los demás jueces de los partidos duran cinco años.

Ya he hablado otra vez del famoso canal que desde esta ciudad comienza, y por el espacio de más de ciento veinte leguas va a parar al lago Erie de donde toma sus aguas, así como de varios otros arroyos que encuentra. Es digno de notarse que en esta parte del Estado de Nueva York se encuentran los nombres de las antiguas ciudades griegas o romanas, como Roma, que es una pequeña población sobre el canal. Troya, un pueblo cerca de Albany. Utica. Hay una porción de cataratas en este camino. La de Genesee, tiene de elevación cerca de ciento sesenta pies, la da Trenton, la de Mohawk, o de Little Fans, y otras. En la primera murió hace poco, un maniático llamado Sam Pateh, que se entretenía en saltar cataratas. Ya había otra ocasión hecho este salto de Leucade con facilidad. En la segunda vez cayó, y no se volvió a saber de él. Me acuerdo haber oído de un tal Rodríguez, igualmente maniático de Mérida de Yucatán, que andaba continuamente en las torres de las iglesias y en los más elevados edificios, saltando con admirable agilidad, y que murió en una de sus empresas.

Albany está poblada en su mayor parte, por descendientes de holandeses. Uno de los más notables personajes de esta ciudad, es el general Van Rensselaer, conocido bajo el nombre de Patron de Albany. Tuve conocimiento con él y su familia por conducto de M. Poinsett. Su hija, de edad de diecisiete años (en 1830) hablaba perfectamente el español, el francés, el italiano y su idioma. El general Rensselaer es sumamente rico, y su fortuna consiste principalmente en bienes raíces heredados de su abuelo, a quien la legislatura del Estado permitió el pleno dominio de las tierras que el Rey de Inglaterra le había concedido para colonizar. Ha hecho muchos beneficios al Estado, y hay un pueblo que lleva el nombre de la familia. De las cercanías de este pueblo, es el lugar del nacimiento de mi actual esposa.

Salimos de Albany, cruzando el río en la diligencia que entró en un buque llamado *Ferry Boat,* nombre genérico de esas barcas destinadas a pasar de un lado al otro los ríos de los Estados Unidos, que unas veces son movidas por vapor y otras por caballos. Nuestra dirección era para Lebanon, pueblo del mismo Estado, distante de Albany veinticinco millas, y en el que hay aguas y baños minerales: de consiguiente lugar concurrido en el estío, como en Europa los baños de Ems, Viesbadem, etc. En el camino no hay de notable más que un terreno llamado *Greenbuch,* en el que el Congreso de la Unión ha decretado se cultiven moreras para la cría de gusanos de seda, lo que se ha comenzado a hacer con éxito.

Llegamos a Lebanon en el mismo día, y nos alojamos en una de las grandes posadas de aquella pequeña población. Lebanon está colocado entre una barranca, rodeado de cerros y bosques que le hacen de aspecto sombrío, y además su población corta y pobre no ha embellecido. Las posadas son todas de madera y de grande extensión. Sus aguas termales no son buenas para beber, y el calor constante de ellas es de setenta y cinco del termómetro de Fahrenheit. El pueblo domina un pequeño valle, lo que le da una vista agradable hacia aquel punto. A una legua de Lebanon hay un convento de *Tembladores* o Shakers, secta extravagante de que voy a dar una breve descripción.

Tuvo su origen esta nueva religión en Manchester de Inglaterra, en 1747. Una mujer, llamada Anna Lee, se hizo recibir como madre de la sociedad en Cristo, como profetisa, como la maestra y directora de ella, y de consiguiente recibía revelaciones del espíritu de Cristo, de quien era una segunda representación, y conversaba con ellos a menudo, como otros tantos de que están llenas nuestras leyendas. En consecuencia de las persecuciones de las autoridades y de las otras sectas, Anna Lee emigró a los Estados Unidos con sus discípulos en 1774, hace sesenta años, en donde se le reunieron otros de Nueva York y Nueva Inglaterra. Compraron unas tierras para vivir en comunidad, y allí fundaron su primer establecimiento. Anna

Lee murió diez años después dando testimonios hasta su última hora, de la firmeza de su fe y santidad de su doctrina.

La sociedad llamada de Milenarios: sus principios religiosos son: Unidad de Dios. Jesucristo, según ellos, no era hijo de Dios, ni coeterno a la Divinidad, sino una emanación de ella en el tiempo por la operación del poder divino. Dicen que la religión consiste más bien en la práctica de la virtud que en la fe, o en doctrinas especulativas; que el hombre fue creado inocente, aunque libre para elegir entre lo bueno y lo malo; pero que habiendo perdido su rectitud original, ninguno pudo salvarse hasta la venida de Cristo: que Cristo tomó a su cargo elevar la naturaleza humana caída, y sobreponerse al poder de la muerte, lo que en efecto hizo. Pero que la iglesia se apartó del verdadero espíritu de Cristo, mezclándose en los intereses de este mundo, y entonces el antecristo se puso a su cabeza; que la manifestación de la segunda aparición de Cristo comenzaba otra vez en la persona de Anna Lee, y por ella se anunciaba al mundo el mismo espíritu divino que habitó en Cristo. La confesión de los pecados es uno de los principales artículos de su fe, conforme al texto evangélico que dice: "aquél que oculta sus pecados no prosperará; pero el que los confiesa y abandona tendrá misericordia". Sus principales mandamientos son: "1° Deberes para con Dios. Amarás al Señor con todo tu corazón, conságrale todas tus facultades. 2° Deberes para con el hombre. Amarás a tu prójimo como a ti mismo. En esta regla se comprenden todas las obligaciones del hombre para con sus semejantes. 3° Separación del mundo. Mi reino no es de este mundo. De aquí la obligación de abstenerse de toda intervención en la política y renuncia de todo encargo de honor y vanidades mundanas. 4° Paz. Cristo es el príncipe de la paz: por consiguiente sus discípulos deben mantener este espíritu. Si mi reino fuere de este mundo, entonces mis siervos deberán pelear. 5° Simplicidad de palabra. 'Guarda tu lengua del mal y tus labios del fraude'. Todo género de lenguaje profano; conversación inútil y falsedad, se debe evitar: todo título de honor o distinción, se debe huir. No os llaméis Rabbi (Doctor). 6° Uso legítimo de la propiedad. Cristo pidió que sus discípulos fuesen una misma cosa con él. Esta unidad debe entenderse en las cosas temporales y espirituales. La iglesia primitiva se estableció sobre estos principios: los apóstoles vivieron en común. 7° Vida virginal. Invocan el ejemplo de nuestro Salvador. 'Los casados cuidan de las cosas del mundo, y el modo como han de agradar a sus maridos y a sus mujeres; pero el no casado cuida de las cosas del Señor, y el modo en que puede ser santo en el cuerpo y en el alma'. Los hijos de este mundo se casan y son dados en matrimonio; pero los que son contados dignos del otro mundo y de la resurrección de entre los muertos, ni se casan, ni son dados en matrimonio". Los *shakers* o tembladores consideran el matrimonio como una institución puramente civil, con la que los verdaderos cristianos nada tienen que ver.

Creen también que la libertad de conciencia es el derecho más sagrado que Dios ha dado a los hombres. Recomiendan a todos vivir conforme al dictamen de su conciencia, como único medio de hacerse agradable ante los ojos de Dios. Su culto es muy singular, y debe parecer extravagante a los que sólo juzgan por lo que han visto en su país. Yo concurrí un domingo 15 de agosto de 1830 a su iglesia que es un edificio cuadrado sin ningún género de ornamento, ni altar ni púlpito, y sólo en forma de sala, con un número de bancas para los extranjeros o espectadores. Dio principio su culto con una ligera alocución que hizo uno de sus ministros a los espectadores, reducida a suplicarles guardasen toda la compostura y decoro debidos a la asamblea de un pueblo religioso que adoraba al Ser supremo conforme creía que debía serle más grato. "La razón y la sagrada escritura apoyan nuestra manera de alabar a Dios, decía el sacerdote milenario. Los israelitas bailaron después de pasar el mar Rojo: David bailó y lo mismo el pueblo de Israel delante del arca santa: y Jeremías dice que *las vírgenes se regocijan en la danza; y que los jóvenes y los viejos bailarán juntos*. Jesucristo en la parábola del hijo pródigo dice: a su regreso a la casa paterna hubo *músicas y bailes*. Luego tenemos en nuestro favor las Escrituras. La razón dicta igualmente que el cuerpo así como el alma se ejerciten en actos de devoción hacia el Creador; y que habiendo Dios creado todos los poderes activos del hombre para su honor y gloria, no sea sólo la lengua la que le tribute homenaje. Las manos y los pies que son útiles al hombre en su propia utilidad y servicio, deben igualmente ofrecer su culto a la Divinidad. En los demás ritos y cultos se canta: otros han empleado el baile, nosotros usamos de uno y otro".

Después de este discurso, comenzó la función. Separados en dos lados diferentes hombres y mujeres, formados en línea, dieron principio a un baile reducido a algunas simples y fáciles evoluciones, cantando al mismo tiempo en un todo igual y en una música nada agradable. Movían al mismo tiempo las manos como en ademán de llamar a alguno, y estuvieron así danzando y cantando por el espacio de hora y media. Siguió el sermón reducido a intentar probar la verdad y divinidad de la secta y de sus dogmas.

El vestido de los *shakers* es en las mujeres una túnica de lana fina, ceñida con una cintura de cuero, medias de lana o algodón, una capucha, o bien una gorra, todo muy bien puesto y sumamente aseado. Yo vi a estas gentes comer juntos, los labradores bajo los árboles; los artesanos en sus talleres, y las encargadas de los almacenes en sus grandes refectorios o comedores. Tienen como quinientos acres de tierra que cultivan y sacan semillas, que venden por todos los Estados Unidos. Yo compré algunas, y se remitieron a Veracruz a don Alejandro Troncoso, de aquel comercio, para entregar al actual Presidente Santa Anna en 1830. Venden, además, cepillas, canastas, abanicos de plumas, escobas, retículos o bolsas, y una porción de utensilios domésticos. Los sobrantes de sus fondos los depositan en los bancos de los Estados Unidos, y tienen ya más de medio millón. Viven separados los hombres de las mujeres, y guardan la castidad más severa. Evidentemente mayor que nuestros frailes. Generalmente, son pálidos y no representan una salud muy lozana. Parece que así debe ser contrariando la más fuerte inclinación de la naturaleza humana. Las autoridades no se mezclan en sus cosas, ni ellos usan de los derechos políticos de votar ni ser elegidos. Viven bajo sus reglas sin más policía ni autoridad. Después veremos un pueblo manufacturero que sin seguir una secta religiosa y sólo bajo los reglamentos de compañías manufactureras vive casi del mismo modo; aunque más naturalmente. La agricultura y horticultura son las principales ocupaciones de estos sectarios. La cabeza visible de su iglesia, es un ministerio compuesto de dos sacerdotes y dos sacerdotisas elegidos entre ellos.

CAPÍTULO XIII

Salida de Nueva Lebanon.—Northampton.—Montana Holyoke.—Llegada a Boston.—Origen del estado de Massachussets.—Ciudad de Boston.—Penitenciaría de Charleston.—Anécdota de un prisionero.—Arsenal.—Visita a M. Adams.—Casa de M. Perkins.—Manufacturas de Lowell.

De Nuevo Lebanon continuamos M. Poinsett y yo por un camino montuoso aunque bastante bueno. Después de doce horas llegamos a Northampton a las ocho de la noche. Esta es una población del Estado de Massachussets en la Nueva Inglaterra sobre el río Connecticut, en la que hay algunas manufacturas de algodón, y se recogen excelentes cosechas de trigo, cebada, papas, habas y otras semillas útiles. A una milla de distancia, sobre una colina llamada Round Hill, está el establecimiento literario de M. Codswell en donde puse a mi hijo, y fue enviado al mismo tiempo otro yucateco llamado don Juan Cano, cuyo talento, aplicación y conducta le harán dentro de algunos años uno de los primeros hombres entre los mexicanos. El río Connecticut comienza a ser navegable por buques de vapor en este punto, y van hasta Hartfort, puerto del Estado del mismo nombre y su capital.

Por la mañana visitamos la montaña Holyoke, situada sobre el nivel del río y al lado opuesto, de unos mil pies a lo menos de elevación sobre su nivel. Sus vistas se extienden a los límites de los Estados de Conneticut, New Hampshire, y Nueva York. Hermosos valles, ríos y fuentes, prados, pueblos recién levantados de entre las florestas, todo forma un espectáculo sorprendente.

Desde el momento en que se entra en la Nueva Inglaterra se advierte una mejora en los caminos, posadas, agricultura, belleza de casas y jardines, en fin en todo lo que rodea el viajero y ha podido adquirir perfección con la ayuda de la industria. Todos estos pequeños pueblos, Northampton, Worcester, Ware, Belchertoon y demás hasta la entrada en Boston, parecen casas de campo formadas expresamente para diversión y placer. Tanta es la limpieza, la hermosura, y tan grande la belleza de esas pequeñas poblaciones. Los caminos son en su mayor parte formados por el método de Makadam.

Boston, hoy capital del Estado de Massachussetts, lo era antes de la independencia de la Nueva Inglaterra, compuesta de los Estados de New Hampshire, Vermont, Maine, Rhode Island, Connecticut y Massachussetts. Las diversas sectas de Inglaterra y la intolerancia de las dominantes, obligaron a una porción de ingleses, en 1620, a pasar a poblar esta parte de la América del Norte en busca de libertad. Esta causa y no el espíritu de comercio ni de ventajas materiales, impelieron a aquellos primeros pobladores a abandonar su patria, y buscar asilo en las florestas inhospitalarias del nuevo continente. Sus grandes padecimientos, los innumerables trabajos que sufrieron en un clima áspero, en un país sin recursos, hostilizados por los indios salvajes, y obligados a vivir los primeros días en sus buques mientras construían sus primeras habitaciones, les hizo dar el nombre de peregrinos. Pocos años después el memorable Cromwell intentó venir a esta colonia con todos sus sectarios los puritanos; pero Carlos I se opuso a aquella emigración por ser muy numerosa, reteniendo de este modo, sin imaginarlo, el mismo hombre que algunos años posteriormente le haría descender del trono y conducir al cadalso.

La ciudad de Boston está situada en una península en la gran bahía de Massachussetts. Tiene dos barrios que son Charleston y South Boston. En Charleston a donde se va por un puente de madera de cerca de media milla, hay una gran manufactura de vidrios que compite con las mejores de Inglaterra, aunque es más caro el valor de los efectos, que sólo pueden entrar en concurrencia con los de Europa, por los derechos impuestos de importación. También está en Charleston la penitenciaría, en donde había cuando estuve trecientos presos, y sólo catorce carceleros sin que se haya oído ejemplar alguno de escape ni intento de hacerlo, aunque como es de presumir, la mayor parte son gentes de audacia y de hábitos poco morigerados. Pero la rigurosa disciplina y la vigilancia continua de sus guardianes, es suficiente a mantenerlos quietos y dóciles en espera del término de sus condenas. En el día se ocupan en sus respectivos oficios, pasando a las horas de tomar sus alimentos por la cocina en filas, y van tomando sus platos para ir a comer en su cuarto cada uno. Dos veces al día rezan u oyen una exhortación religioso-moral, y por la noche son encerrados en sus pequeñas celdas. Un ejemplo melancólico para la humanidad, es la anécdota siguiente sacada de la obra de M. Hamilton, a quien se la refirió el alcaide de esta prisión.

Hace muchos años, antes del establecimiento de la actual prisión del Estado, o penitenciaría, un hombre con respetables relaciones pero de carácter terco, de costumbres perdidas y abandonadas, fue convencido de delito de robos nocturnos, y sentenciado a prisión perpetua en la cárcel de Charleston, en este Estado de Massachussetts. No se abatió su orgullo con la desgracia y el castigo: su conducta era altanera e insubordinada con sus carceleros, de tal manera que fue necesario separarle de los otros presos y sujetarle a una rigurosa disciplina. El primer año se mantuvo silencioso y ceñudo; y el eclesiástico que se presentaba, le encontró indócil e incrédulo. Pero en los meses siguientes fue cambiando gradualmente de maneras y de ideas. Su trato ya era más afable: se le encontraba por lo regular leyendo las escrituras: y el capellán y el carcelero se congratulaban de este cambio tan saludable en el prisionero. Ya hablaba de su vida pasada, y de las terribles ofensas que había cometido contra Dios y los hombres, lleno de dolor y arrepentimiento; y daba gracias al Creador de haberle conservado la vida para tener tiempo de implorar su misericordia. Ya la conducta del prisionero era edificante, y su conversación evangélica: cuantos le veían se interesaban en la suerte de tan buen cristiano, de manera que una porción de gentes de respeto intercedían cerca del gobernador del Estado para que le indultase, y este magistrado se inclinaba ya a verificarlo, cuando un día en que estaban con la mayor confianza, el carcelero y otras personas conversando con el preso, se echó encima del primero, le dio muchas heridas e intentó la fuga, aunque infructuosamente.

Fue conducido a un separo cargado de grillos, en donde permaneció por algunos años sin la menor esperanza de salir. Por último un hermano político suyo, persona de influencia y de fortuna en la Carolina del Sur, pasó a Boston, y salió responsable de la conducta del prisionero si se le daba indulto. Se accedió a su demanda, y para quitarle toda tentación de cometer los mismos delitos, le proveyó de todo lo necesario en la ciudad de Charleston de la Carolina.

El prisionero salió después de veinte años de su encierro, durante los cuales no había respirado el aire puro y libre del cielo, ni visto el sol en todo su esplendor. En este período Boston que era un pequeño pueblo cuando su encierro, se había convertido en una ciudad rica y hermosa. En cada paso que daba, tenía que admirar alguna cosa nueva. El aspecto físico y moral, los usos, los vestidos, los pensamientos, las preocupaciones y opiniones de la generación que veía, eran muy diversos de los de la generación que conoció. Las casas de madera que había visto aisladas y sin adorno, habían sido reemplazadas por edificios magníficos de mármol, piedra granito o de ladrillo; veía plazas y paseos en los lugares que dejó boscosos y silvestres: en suma parecía el habitante de otro planeta, venido a un mundo desconocido. A la vista de cosas tan nuevas, de un espectáculo tan vivo e interesante; rodeado de tantos objetos desconocidos y extraños, este hombre se deshizo en lágrimas, creyéndose transportado en una tierra desconocida.

Llegó a Charleston de la Carolina, en donde su cuñado le procuró un buen alojamiento y las comodidades de la vida. El primer año tuvo una conducta irreprensible, pero la hora del mal le indujo a visitar Nueva York. Allí encontró gentes de mala conducta, se asoció a ellos, volvió a robar de noche, y fue condenado a encierro perpetuo a Singsing, penitenciaría del Estado de Nueva York, de donde saldrá su cadáver. ¿Será la naturaleza humana tan incorregible como se manifiesta por este triste ejemplo? ¿Hay en la organización física del hombre propensiones irresistibles? Estas son cuestiones que agitan los phrenologistas y sus adversarios. No hay duda en que la organización material determina mucha parte de nuestro carácter moral.

El comodoro Morris, amigo antiguo de M. Poinsett, nos hizo el favor de acompañarnos al arsenal, en donde se estaba construyendo un dique de granito, destinado a construir y componer los buques de guerra. Su longitud es de trecientos pies, y su profundidad de veinticinco con cincuenta de latitud. El agua entra y sale a discreción, según la necesidad, y la forma es elíptica. El costo de la obra está calculado a quinientos mil pesos.

Al día siguiente pasamos a visitar a M. Adams, en su casa de Quincy. Este ilustre americano es hijo del presidente sucesor de Washington, y presidente que fue él mismo en el cuatrienio de 1824 hasta 1828. Había sido Secretario de Estado en la administración de M. Monroe, y ministro cerca del gobierno inglés. Jamás vi hombre de carácter tan frío y circunspecto. En la visita que duró más de media hora, apenas hablaríamos lo que en otras circunstancias se conversa en cinco minutos. ¿Qué hay de México? me preguntó. Después de algún silencio, le manifesté muy brevemente la serie de revoluciones que habían ocurrido. "Ustedes, me dijo, no estarán tranquilos por algunos años, hasta que no adopten instituciones análogas a sus circunstancias. Estas circunstancias se tienen que crear también". Nos despedimos y dejamos a este hombre raro en su casa solitaria, distante siete millas de Boston. Pasamos a ver a M. Perkins, uno de los más ricos habitantes de la Nueva Inglaterra, propietario de las ricas canteras de granito que suministran esta preciosa piedra para los edificios, muelles, empedrados, columnas, etc., de los pueblos comarcanos. Tomamos el té en su famosa casa de campo, enriquecida con un gran número de plantas exóticas y árboles frutales, flores y vegetales. M. Perkins tiene gusto particular en comer piñas de su jardín, peras y duraznos en el invierno, por medio de conservatorios de diversas temperaturas.

Como uno de los más ricos empresarios de las manufacturas de Lowell, nos convidó M. Perkins a pasar en su compañía a ver aquel pueblo prodigioso, levantado de entre bosques en el corto espacio de siete años. En ninguna parte el poder de la industria y de la libertad hace sentir tan palpablemente sus beneficios efectivos que en los Estados Unidos de América. Voy a dar una descripción de este admirable progreso, prestando el auxilio de la pluma diestra de un joven, llamado M. Chevalier, que al visitar este pueblo se sintió como inspirado a la vista del orden, prosperidad y buenas costumbres de los obreros de Lowell.

No es la guerra, esta *ultima ratio regum,* la que puede elevar un pueblo o una nación a la prosperidad. Un campo de batalla excitará el horror, o el entusiasmo febril, o la piedad y el asombro. La fuerza del hombre aplicada a producir, es más majestuosa que la fuerza humana aplicada a matar. Las pirámides y los templos de dimensiones colosales de Tebas; el coliseo o la iglesia de San Pedro de Roma, descubren más grandeza que un campo de batalla cubierto de muertos y de escombros, aun cuando hubiese trecientos mil cadáveres tendidos, como en esas grandes batallas en que Napoleón llenaba de espanto al Universo y cubría de gloria a la Francia. El poder del hombre es así como el de Dios, visible en las cosas pequeñas como en las grandes. Nada hay en el orden material de que nuestra especie tenga más derecho de gloriarse que de las invenciones mecánicas por medio de las cuales el hombre doma el vigor desordenado de la Naturaleza o desenvuelve su energía oculta. A la ayuda de la mecánica el hombre, en apariencia ser débil y miserable, extendiendo la mano sobre la inmensidad del mundo, toma posesión de sus torrentes, de sus vientos desencadenados, del flujo y reflujo del mar, de los metales y de los combustibles esparcidos en la superficie de la Tierra, u ocultos en su seno; de los líquidos que convertidos en vapor son el más poderoso agente en manos del hombre. ¿Hay en efecto cosa que inspire una idea más alta del poder del hombre que las máquinas de vapor bajo las formas que se le han dado para aplicarla al transporte, ya en los buques sobre el mar o los ríos, ya en los coches sobre la superficie de la tierra? Es más bien un ser viviente que una máquina. Marcha sola, corre como un caballo: algo más respira. En efecto el vapor que sale periódicamente de los cilindros y que se condensa en humo blanco, parece verdaderamente el aliento, la violenta respiración de un caballo en su carrera.

El que viese en medio de estos bosques, hace poco habitados por algunas naciones nómades, y hoy poblados aquí y allá por algunas casas recién levantadas, el que sin tener conocimiento de estas prodigiosas máquinas viese en una noche marchar un cuerpo despidiendo millones de chispas, respirando fuerte y frecuentemente, y correr con una rapidez desconocida sin un caballo ni otro animal que le de movimiento, creería sin duda ver uno de esos dragones o monstruos fabulosos que despiden llamas por la boca, y amenazan devorar al mortal desgraciado que encuentren en el camino. Hace pocos años que los brahamanes, viendo un buque de vapor luchar y vencer las corrientes de su sagrado Ganges, creyeron de buena fe esos padres de la ciencia antigua, que aquél era un animal desconocido recientemente descubierto por los ingleses sobre una tierra lejana.

En las sociedades modernas, los progresos de la mecánica han producido las manufacturas que prometen ser para el género humano, una fuente inagotable de prosperidad y bienestar. Las manufacturas inglesas producen en el día anualmente cerca de ochocientos millones de varas de tejidos de algodón, que equivale a una vara para cada individuo de los que pueblan la Tierra. Si todos los hombres vivientes se pusiesen a trabajar estas mantas con el solo auxilio de los dedos, es probable que al año no harían lo que sólo una parte de la Gran Bretaña produce. De manera que los trabajos del género humano serían absorbidos por un trabajo que, gracias a la mecánica y a las manufacturas, emplea cuando más millón y medio de hombres en aquella nación. Debemos inferir de esto que cuando el régimen manufacturero esté desenvuelto y arreglado, bastará el trabajo moderado de una porción de la especie humana, para procurar a todos las dulzuras de la vida material. Parece indudable que llegará este día; pero hasta hoy no ha podido establecerse este bello orden de cosas, y aún pasará algún tiempo para que se establezca. El sistema manufacturero es un descubrimiento nuevo; se desenvuelve cada día más, y desenvolviéndose se mejora. Vaya un ejemplo. El algodón importado en Inglaterra para las manufacturas, era en 1785 la cantidad de once millones de libras inglesas de peso. En 1816 ya subió a noventa millones, y en 1831 a doscientos cuarenta y cinco millones. Estos tres números están en estas relaciones: 1–9½–22¼. Sin embargo, este progreso es lento, y en los países en que las artes aun comienzan, debe serlo mucho más.

En esta América del Norte, es no obstante asombroso el desenvolvimiento del sistema manufacturero. ¿Quién no se maravillará a la vista del pueblo de Lowell, lugar silvestre hace diez años, y hoy una población de siete mil almas, con establecimientos manufactureros que compiten con los de Europa? "Apenas había vuelto en mí del aturdimiento que me causó el aspecto de esta ciudad improvisada, dice M. Chevalier; apenas había yo visto y tocado para asegurarme que no era una ciudad de cartón, como las que Potenkin había hecho construir sobre el paje de Catarina, con el fin de averiguar hasta qué punto la creación de las manufacturas en este lugar había suscitado, con respecto al bienestar y moralidad de la clase obrera, relativamente a la seguridad de los ricos y a la del orden público, los peligros que se habían experimentado en Europa: y gracias a las atenciones de los agentes superiores de las dos principales compañías *(Merrimack corporation, y Lawrence corporation)* he podido satisfacer mi curiosidad".

"Las fábricas de algodones solas, tienen empleadas seis mil personas en Lowell. De este número, cerca de cinco mil son jóvenes solteras de diecisiete a veinticuatro años, hijas de arrendatarios de los diversos Estados de la Nueva Inglaterra, particularmente de Massachussetts, Nueva Hampshire y Vermont. Allí están lejos de sus familias confiadas a sí mismas. Al verlas por la mañana y por la tarde en las calles vestidas con aseo y limpieza, salir de sus talleres y coger de las perchas que tienen cubiertas de flores, sus sombreros, sus gorras, sus chales y sus pañoletas, me dije a mí mismo, esto no es como en Manchester. Cuando se me ha manifestado el estado de los salarios, me he confirmado decididamente de que esto no era como en Manchester. Ved aquí los medios generales de los salarios tales como han sido pagados en el mes de mayo último por semana: es decir, por seis días de trabajo".

Operaciones preparatorias.	3 pesos.
Esto es desmontar y limpiar.	3 pesos 1 real.
	2 pesos 4 reales.
Hilar.	3 pesos 2 reales.
Tejidos de diversas cualidades.	3 pesos 2 reales.
	3 pesos 6 reales.
Tinturas y encolados.	
	4 pesos.
Medida y embalado.	3 pesos 2 reales.

"Los salarios de los obreros hábiles son notablemente más elevados, y suben hasta 6 pesos por semana".

Compárese ahora la situación de estos jornaleros con los de Europa, y se advertirá una diferencia enorme en favor de los de los Estados Unidos del Norte. Pocas mujeres hay en Europa de esa clase que ganen más de un real y medio por día, o doce reales por semana. Téngase presente, además, que los artículos de primera necesidad, pan, carne, azúcar, café, arroz, etcétera, son mucho más baratos en los Estados Unidos. De esta manera un gran número de obreras de Lowell, pueden economizar hasta un peso y medio por semana. Al cabo de cuatro años tendrán trecientos pesos, y es la dote con que salen a establecerse casándose con un joven que tenga otro tanto, y se aplican al ejercicio de una profesión.

En Francia y mucho menos en México, no podrá formarse idea de la posición de unas muchachas bonitas la mayor parte, desde veinte hasta treinta leguas de distancia de las casas de sus padres, entregadas a su sola virtud. A pesar de esto, no se advierten efectos deplorables en Lowell, a excepción de muy corto número de casos que no destruyen la regla general. La raza inglesa tiene costumbres muy diferentes que la española y francesa. Otros hábitos, otras ideas. La educación protestante traza alrededor de cada individuo un círculo más difícil de penetrar que el que forma la educación católica. Por una parte hay, es verdad, más frialdad, menos comunicación en las relaciones sociales, una ausencia más o menos absoluta de efusión y de confianza; pero por la otra se encuentra más respeto, más consideraciones por la personalidad de los otros. Lo que entre nosotros sería considerado como una pura travesura; una aventura insignificante, se reprobaría severamente en Inglaterra y los Estados Unidos del Norte. Así pues, ninguno se admire de ver en este país las hijas de los propietarios cultivadores del campo, aunsentarse de sus padres e irse solas a grandes distancias a establecerse en una ciudad en donde no conocen a nadie, y allí tres o cuatro años en su trabajo, hasta hacer una pequeña fortuna. Se hallan bajo la salvaguardia de la fe pública. Esto supone en las costumbres una reserva extremada, y en la opinión pública un rigorismo vigilante e inexorable. Es verdad que este rigorismo y esta reserva dan a la sociedad un colorido de tristeza y de tediosa montonía que cansa a los que no están acostumbrados a ella, pero cuando se reflexiona sobre los peligros a que el sistema contrario expone a las jóvenes incautas que se precipitan a los placeres; cuando se cuentan las víctimas que ha hecho esa facilidad de comunicación y ese abandono en otros países, es difícil no convenir que la frialdad e incomunicabilidad angloamericana, vale bien y mucho más que la amable y dulce sociabilidad francesa y mexicana.

Las compañías manufactureras velan sobre las costumbres de estas jóvenes obreras. Cada compañía ha construido un edificio que contiene número de piezas suficientes para alojarlas en sus pensiones que llaman *boarding houses*. Allí están bajo la protección y patrocinio de las matronas, que cuidan de la pensión, por la que pagan cada semana para su manutención sólo un peso o diez reales. Las matronas responden a la compañía de las costumbres de las jóvenes confiadas a su cuidado, y se manejan por reglamentos que les dan al efecto. Ved aquí un extracto de estos reglamentos.

1° Todas las personas empleadas por la compañía, deben ocuparse con asiduidad en sus labores las horas del trabajo. Deben también ser capaces de llenar el empleo de que están encargadas, o hacer esfuerzos al efecto. En todas las ocasiones y circunstancias sea por discursos, sea por su conducta, manifestarse penetradas de amor a la templanza y a todas las virtudes, y animadas del sentimiento de sus obligaciones morales y sociales. El agente de la compañía se esforzará a dar a todos buenos ejemplos. Cualquiera persona que sea notoriamente perezosa, disoluta o intemperante: o que tenga el hábito de ausentarse del servicio divino, que viole el reposo del domingo, o que sea dada al juego, será echada de la compañía. 2° No es permitido ningún licor espirituoso en el territorio de la compañía, a menos que sea por ordenanza del médico. Tampoco es permitido ningún juego de azar ni de naipes. El artículo 13 establece que todos los obreros deben habitar en estas pensiones.

Como Lowell es una población de obreros que todos están sujetos a estos reglamentos de la compañía, se concibe bien que es como un vasto monasterio, en donde poco tiene que hacer la autoridad civil. Son como grandes familias o colegios bajo sus constituciones particulares, cuyo objeto tiende a estimular el trabajo y mantener las buenas costumbres base de todo establecimiento social: y así como al cabo de diez o doce años, salen los jóvenes de los institutos literarios con el caudal de conocimientos y de saber, así las jornaleras y jornaleros dejan estos talleres, después de algunos años, con el capital que han hecho en numerario, fruto de sus economías, y además con los hábitos de amor al trabajo, respeto a la virtud, y horror al vicio. El domingo, que entre nosotros es un día de placer y de fiesta, en estos lugares se dedica a la oración, al recogimiento y al descanso. Este es uno de los muchos aspectos en que difiere el pueblo angloamericano del mexicano. Bajo el aspecto moral y religioso, entre los sudamericanos hay un abandono y menosprecio que está en contradicción palpable con nuestras profesiones religiosas, y el celo hipócrita que manifestamos por sostener un culto exclusivo. Esta reflexión conduce a una consecuencia muy melancólica para las nuevas repúblicas, pero que no deja de ser una verdad, y es que el principio de autoridad política entre nosotros, no pudiendo encontrarse como debía en una república, en esa reserva severa de las costumbres norteamericanas, en la inelasticidad de los hábitos de la vida, y en la rigidez religiosa del pueblo, al lado de la multiplicidad de sectas, nos hemos visto obligados a colocarlo en la fuerza material, en el terror sobre las mismas bases que estaba antes de la independencia, en lucha abierta con las instituciones y abiertamente incompatibles con los principios republicanos. Tan cierto es que la necesidad del orden y la de la libertad son esenciales a la naturaleza humana, y que es imposible fundar una sociedad con sólo uno de estos elementos. Si abandonáis una porción de las instituciones sociales a la libertad exclusivamente, estad ciertos de que el principio de orden se hará una parte no menos exclusiva sobre otro punto. Por desgracia aún no se establecen entre nosotros las leyes de equilibrio entre el orden y la libertad.

Los reglamentos de las compañías se observan religiosamente en Lowell. En las fábricas, que son edificios de una grande extensión, hay campanarios para llamar las gentes al trabajo, de manera que parecen conventos de una de nuestras ciudades. Pero en Lowell no hay demandantes con santos, no hay limosneros, no hay andrajosos y gentes miserables: en vez de ocuparse estas monjas del siglo diecinueve en hacer relicarios, escapularios y sudarios, se emplean en hilar algodón y hacer tejidos de todas calidades. En Lowell no hay pasatiempos ni diversiones; pero es un pueblo pacífico, habitado por gentes vestidas con gracia, aseo y decencia.

CAPÍTULO XIV

Batalla de Lexington.—Monumento.—Tremont House.—Constitución del estado. —Ilustración de sus habitantes.—Revista.—Observaciones de este periódico. —Escuelas.—Estado de la enseñanza en Nueva Inglaterra.—Comparación con los estados de México.—Ventajas de la educación popular.—Colegio de Cambridge. —Sociedad de Boston.—Isla de Nahan.—Rhode Island.—Nueva Providencia.—Su constitución.—Carácter de los yanquis.—Igual distribución de riquezas.—Estado de Connecticut, y su gobierno.—New Haven.—Convención de Hartfort.

En el camino de Boston a Lowell pasamos por Lexington, pueblo en que se dio la primera acción entre americanos e ingleses en la guerra de independencia. El general Gate había enviado ochocientos hombres para ocupar los almacenes de guerra que la asamblea de Massachussetts había mandado formar, y al pasar las tropas británicas por Lexington atacaron algunas tropas cívicas que allí había, matándoles ocho hombres. Continuaron su marcha pero a su regreso encontraron una reunión numerosa de milicianos, y se empeñó una acción reñida en que murieron doscientos setenta y tres ingleses, y ochenta y ocho norteamericanos. Primera sangre derramada entre las dos naciones. En la plaza de aquel pueblecillo hay un monumento erigido en 1799, en piedra granito, con la siguiente inscripción.

"Dedicado a la libertad y derechos del género humano. La libertad y la independencia de América sellada y defendida con la sangre de sus hijos. Este monumento es erigido por los habitantes de Lexington bajo el patrocinio y a expensas del Estado de Massachussetts, a la memoria de sus conciudadanos Enrrig Roberto Munroe, Mes. Jonas Parker, Samuel Hadley, Jonathan Harrington junior, Isaac Murrey, Caleb Harrington, Juan Brown de Lexington y Asaael Porter de Woburn, que cayeron en este campo las primeras víctimas bajo la espada de la tiranía británica, en la mañana eternamente memorable del 19 de abril de 1775. Se echó el guante; la sangre de estos mártires en la causa de Dios y de su patria fue el cimiento de estos Estados, colonias de aquéllos, y dio origen al espíritu, firmeza y resolución de sus conciudadanos. Todos ellos se levantaron como un solo hombre a vengar la sangre de sus hermanos, y a defender con la punta de sus espadas sus santos derechos. Osaron noblemente declararse libres: la lucha fue larga, sangrienta y lastimosa. El justo cielo aprobó este solemne llamamiento. La victoria coronó sus armas, y la paz, la libertad y la independencia de los Estados Unidos de la América, fueron su gloriosa recompensa". No es ciertamente muy elegante la inscripción; pero semejantes monumentos siempre inspiran un respeto religioso al que los contempla. Aún no hemos visto uno solo erigido en Calderón, las Cruces, y otros lugares célebres en la República Mexicana por los combates que en ellos se libraron en defensa de la misma causa. Yo propuse erigir uno sencillo en las Cruces; pero no se resolvió.

Después del combate de Lexington, el general inglés fortificó a Boston, y ambas partes se prepararon a la guerra. Los americanos ocuparon desde luego las alturas de las cercanías de la ciudad en donde se fortificaron. Los ingleses los desalojaron después de un combate obstinado, en que perdieron una tercera parte de sus tropas. El teatro de esta acción fue una colina llamada de Bunker, o Bunkers Hill, célebre en estos países desde entonces. Sobre esta colina hay un obelisco erigido en 1825, de doscientos veinte pies de altura.

La posada en que estuve en Boston, es la mayor que hay en los Estados Unidos. Se llama *Tremont house,* frente al teatro. El edificio es de ese hermoso granito-mica que abunda tanto en los Estados del Norte, especialmente en la Nueva Inglaterra. Pueden alojarse en este *hotel* cuatrocientas personas, y cuando estuve había a lo menos trescientas de ambos sexos. Se come en la mesa común, o bien la asistencia particular si uno quiere pagar un poco más. El servicio es exacto; los alimentos son muy bien sazonados; las camas cómodas y decentes; el alumbrado de aquella gran casa es de gas, y en todos los corredores se encuentra luz suficiente para andar. La paga es de trece pesos por semana fuera del vino.

Las calles de Boston son generalmente torcidas, y la mayor parte bastante estrechas: algunas están empedradas, otras con el piso hermoso y cómodo por el método de Makadan. Hay edificios muy notables de mármol blanco y de granito. La casa del Estado, edificada en una pequeña colina, se eleva a una altura que domina desde la cúpula todas las partes de la ciudad y de la bahía. Allí se reúnen las dos Cámaras que componen el cuerpo legislativo.

La Constitución de este Estado fue hecha en 1780 y reformada en 1821. El Poder Legislativo reside en el Senado y Cámara de Representantes, y ambos se llaman *Corte general de Massachussetts.* Los miembros de la Cámara de Representantes son elegidos cada año el segundo lunes de noviembre. Todo pueblo que tenga ciento cincuenta votantes alistados nombra un diputado: de allí en adelante otro más por cada doscientos veinticinco de aumento. El Senado tiene cuarenta miembros elegidos por los distritos anualmente el segundo lunes de noviembre. El gobernador es también elegido anualmente por el pueblo el segundo lunes de noviembre, y lo mismo el vicegobernador. Hay un consejo de gobierno compuesto de nueve miembros sacados de entre los senadores, por escrutinio de ambas Cámaras. El cuerpo legislativo se junta en Boston el primer miércoles de enero de cada año.

Todos los ciudadanos que tienen de veintiún años adelante pueden votar, con tal que hayan residido un año en el Estado, y seis meses precedentes al tiempo de las elecciones: y que haya pagado contribuciones al Estado dos años, a menos que la ley le exceptúe.

El Poder Judicial reside en jueces nombrados por el gobernador de acuerdo con el Consejo. La duración de sus destinos es *ad vitam aut culpam.*

Boston es una de las ciudades más ilustradas de los Estados Unidos, y el Estado de Massachussetts de los que han producido un gran número de personas sabias, oradores elocuentes, abogados instruidos y hombres de Estado célebres. Los Adams, los Franklins, los Hancoks, los Tiecnors, los Quincy, los Everetts y otros nombres semejantes ocupan lugar distinguido en los anales literarios y políticos de aquel país. El último de éstos es el principal editor de una Revista trimestre bajo la denominación de *Nort American Review,* comparable con las más clásicas revistas de Europa. A mi llegada a los Estados Unidos, en 1830, encontré en esta revista presentados los sucesos de México de diciembre de 1828, en que desgraciadamente tuve parte bajo los coloridos que les había pintado la pluma apasionada de M. Ward en su suplemento a su viaje a México. El mismo asunto, aunque bajo muy diferente aspecto, había sido tratado por la hábil mano de M. Walsh en *su Quarterly Review.*

Los editores de estos periódicos imitan las revistas inglesas, y prefieren los artículos más extendidos y los análisis discutidos a un mayor número de noticias superficiales o simples indicaciones. En uno de los números de esta revista, analizando la obra del P. Gnasi sobre los Estados Unidos, hay, dice, un colegio de jesuitas en George Town, cerca de Washington, y una institución literaria de los mismos en Nueva York: un colegio de sacerdotes de San Sulpicio en Baltimore, y una casa de educación en Emitsbourg. En el Kentucky y los dominicos ingleses tienen una escuela y una iglesia bajo la invocación de Santa Rosa de Lima. En los Estados del Oeste hay misioneros de San Francisco de Paula, y un convento de religiosas Carmelitas de Santa Teresa. En George Town, otro de hermanas Visitandinas. El abate *Dubois* fundó otro convento en Emitsbourg, para dar educación a las jóvenes, y él mismo formó otro en Filadelfia, en el que tiene el doble objeto de la educación y asistencia de enfermos. Este establecimiento no está solamente sostenido por la caridad de los católicos, sino aun de los protestantes. El abate Nerina ha fundado en Kentucky un convento de religiosas tituladas las *hermanas de María al pie de la Cruz,* y últimamente un ministro protestante convertido al culto católico, ha traído a Boston, su país natal, las Ursulinas, y les ha dejado fondos suficientes para su establecimiento. Aunque este progreso del catolicismo causó algunas alarmas a los amigos de la independencia religiosa, el redactor de la revista expone las suyas con la expresión de una tolerancia sincera tan religiosa como filosófica. En un país en donde no viene la fuerza de las leyes en apoyo de una religión exclusiva no hay nada que temer.

En Boston hay sesenta y ocho escuelas gratuitas fuera de veintitrés dominicales. Es cierto que en este Estado y el de Connecticut, es en donde la educación está más adelantada. Según el cálculo hecho por las relaciones oficiales venidas a la capital en 1830, entre sesenta mil personas, sólo había cuatrocientas que no sabían leer ni escribir, y de ciento treinta y un pueblos que presentaron sus estados de educación, ascendía a doce mil trescientos noventa y tres el número de niños de ambos sexos, que aprendían a leer, escribir, aritmética y álgebra, principios de geografía, historia, dibujo y religión, y sólo había cincuenta y ocho que no sabían leer y escribir, entre todos los niños desde catorce a veinte años. La suma anual destinada en la ciudad de Boston de los fondos públicos para este sagrado objeto, es desde cincuenta hasta setenta mil pesos.

El método de arreglar estos establecimientos en los Estados Unidos merece la atención de los mexicanos. Cada año se reúnen los representantes de los respectivos barrios y nombran diez o doce comisionados que llaman *trustees,* las cuales se encargan de la colectación de los fondos, de su distribución, del examen del estado de las escuelas, conducta de los maestros, número de niños, instrumentos, libros, etc. Estos recogen los productos de los legados, donaciones, concesiones de las legislaturas y demás productos destinados a la educación. Cuando han concluido su año, publican una relación en que se da cuenta al público de todo lo que han observado, las mejoras que juzgan deben hacerse, de los gastos, número de niños, etc. Ahora que escribo esto tengo a la vista la vigesimacuarta relación anual de los *trustees* de la sociedad pública de Nueva York, *Twenty fourth annual report of the public school society of New York.*

Se puede asegurar, sobre cálculos muy aproximados, que una tercera parte de los habitantes de los Estados de Massachussetts y Connecticut concurren a las escuelas, y que a excepción de dos mil personas, en una población de dos millones que tienen estos Estados, todos saben leer y escribir a lo menos. Compárese esta situación moral del pueblo de los Estados Unidos con uno o dos de nuestros Estados, y se conocerá cuál es la verdadera razón porque es imposible por ahora nivelar nuestras instituciones a las de nuestros vecinos, *particularmente en algunos Estados*. Los de México, por ejemplo, y Yucatán, de que tengo mayor conocimiento, se puede afirmar que, entre un millón doscientos mil habitantes que tiene el primero, y setecientos mil que tiene el segundo, habrá, cuando mucho, la proporción de uno entre veinte. Algo más: entre los cinco milésimos que saben leer y escribir dos quintos no conocen la aritmética, tres quintos ignoran hasta el significado de la voz geografía, historia, astronomía, etc. Cuatro quintos no saben lo que es la *Biblia, y los* nombres de Génesis, Paralipomenon, Evangelio, Apocalipsis son enteramente desconocidos. Añádase a esto que en Yucatán hay a lo menos un tercio de los habitantes que no hablan el castellano, y en el Estado de México un quinto. Los que cuentan por nada el grado de civilización de las masas para dar *instituciones a los pueblos, o son sumamente ignorantes, o son extremadamente perversos*.

Este estado de educación pública en los Estados Unidos puede muy bien justificar el llamamiento hecho a todas las clases de ciudadanos para tomar parte en las elecciones y demás funciones gobernativas. Yo tengo presente haber leído que uno de los grandes argumentos que se hacían para extender el censo electoral en Francia y en Inglaterra era la ignorancia de mucha parte del pueblo en algunas provincias. En el condado de Gales, por ejemplo, uno entre veinte sabe leer y escribir: en Escocia uno entre diez. En los departamentos meridionales de Francia se encuentran algunos en donde uno entre veinticinco sabe leer y escribir. Pero en estos lugares se encuentran muchas personas que compensan de algún modo la rudeza o ignorancia de las masas con su instrucción, experiencia y conocimientos generales.

M. Ortiz estaba de corregidor cuando fui a Boston. Tuve el honor de ser invitado a su mesa, a donde concurrieron varios personajes notables por su saber y largos servicios. M. Ortiz ha hecho sacrificios a la causa de la libertad, aunque no perteneció al partido democrático. Sus conexiones con los Adams, Webster, Everett y demás hombres de la antigua liga federal, le hacen colocar entre sus líneas.

El colegio de Cambridge es uno de los más célebres de los Estados Unidos. En la visita que hice a este establecimiento, puesto bajo la dirección de M. Quincy, tuve motivos para quedar satisfecho de las luces del rector, de la belleza del sitio, elegancia del edificio, riqueza literaria de su biblioteca y conservatorio de antigüedades. En el colegio de Cambridge se enseñan humanidades, ciencias físicas y matemáticas, historia, lenguas griega, latina, francesa, española y alemana; ideología y economía política. En el mismo pueblo visité a M. Gros, hombre que ha hecho una gran fortuna con el comercio de tenería; y emplea una parte considerable de ella en adquirir bellos cuadros y pinturas originales, o copias buenas de los mejores artistas. El Ateneo de Boston es un establecimiento que llama la atención del viajero ilustrado, por la gran cantidad de libros escogidos y monumentos curiosos. el señor Everett, junior, me hizo el honor de introducirme en esta sociedad.

En Boston hay una bella estatua de mármol del general Washington, hecha por M. Chantry, y en un cementerio cerca del paseo público está el sepulcro de Franklin y su familia. El paseo es una hermosa arboleda en un plano frente a la casa del Estado, cuyo único adorno, si tal puede llamarse es un estanque de ciento y veinte pies de largo, y mitad de ancho. Nada de estatuas, ni de fuentes, ni de pabellones, etc. En los Estados Unidos se busca lo necesario y lo útil. Aún no hay establecimientos de agrado y lujo.

La sociedad de Boston es generalmente ilustrada y se puede decir de buen tono. En el invierno hay bailes y partidas de té en donde se reúnen las gentes de los diferentes rangos de la sociedad, según sus diversos gustos, inclinaciones y profesiones.

A ocho millas de Boston hay una isla en la boca misma de la bahía, llamada Nahant, muy frecuentada en el estío para tomar baños de mar. Sus vistas son magníficas sobre el mar, las costas, pequeñas poblaciones y torres de Boston. Hay en la isla, que tendrá una milla de extensión, dos o tres buenas posadas, baños y casas de placer.

De Boston salí para el Estado de Rhode Island, tomando asiento en la diligencia. Como el Estado de Massachussetts es de los menos navegables por falta de ríos, es también en el que hay más carruajes proporcionalmente, y en el que los caminos se cuidan más, y las líneas de fierro se emprenden con más ardor. Los caminos generalmente son mucho mejores que en los demás Estados de la Unión. De Boston a Providencia hay cuarenta y cinco millas; comimos en Dedham, y llegamos a Providencia, capital del Estado de Rhode Island, sobre el río Providencia. Esta ciudad es manufacturera como todas las de Nueva Inglaterra, tiene de quince a dieciséis mil habitantes; un colegio en donde se enseña física, geometría, historia, lengua griega y latina, ideología y escritura.

El gobierno de este Estado está fundado sobre las bases de la Carta de concesión de Carlos II, cuando el establecimiento de la colonia, en 1663, y este es el solo Estado de la Unión que no tiene constitución escrita. El Poder Legislativo le ejerce la *Asamblea general* que consiste en un Senado y una Cámara de representantes. Esta se compone de setenta y dos miembros sacados seis de New Port; cuatro de cada una de las ciudades Providencia, Portsmouth y Warewich, y dos de cada uno de los pueblos del Estado. Son nombrados cada seis meses, en abril y agosto. El Senado se compone de diez miembros nombrados en abril anualmente.

Hay un gobernador, nombrado popularmente cada año, en abril, y un vicegobernador, elegido al mismo tiempo, que suple las veces de aquél. La asamblea se reúne cuatro veces por año: en *New Port,* el primer miércoles de mayo, que es el principio del año civil, es la primera sesión; hasta el primer miércoles de junio: el primer miércoles de octubre en *Providencia,* hasta el primer miércoles de noviembre: el de enero y el de marzo en los pueblos de *South Kingston, East Greenwich y Binsol.*

De Nueva Providencia a Nueva York hay ciento ochenta millas por el canal marítimo del *Sund.* La primera colonización de Providencia recuerda uno de aquellos melancólicos efectos de la intolerancia de las sectas religiosas que quieren el dominio exclusivo de sus dogmas. Los *puritanos,* perseguidos en Inglaterra bajo el gobierno de Carlos I, dejando su patrio suelo bajo la denominación de *Padres peregrinos,* vinieron a buscar en el Nuevo Mundo la libertad que no encontraban en el Antiguo. Pero apenas se habían establecido en la Nueva Inglaterra estas víctimas de la persecución, que contradiciendo no sólo sus principios anteriores, sino aun los de la moral universal, y especialmente la evangélica, que es la más tolerante, vinieron a ser *perseguidores* a su turno. Los socinianos y los cuáqueros en una palabra, todos los que no eran de sus opiniones o creencias religiosas, fueron arrojados violentamente y con ultraje de sus posesiones. Entre ellos se hallaba Rogerio Williams, clérigo puritano, que se aventuró a exponer lo que él consideraba evidencia de la apostasía, en las iglesias de Massachussetts. El clero al principio se propuso combatirle por argumentos teológicos y demostraciones. No habiendo podido conseguir desvanecer ni a él ni a los otros, ocurrió a la autoridad civil para que por la coacción arrojase de entre los *verdaderos creyentes,* un tan hábil como instruido enemigo. Rogerio William fue desterrado, y seguido por sus sectarios, continuó vagando en aquellos desiertos hasta que llegó a un lugar llamado por los indios mooshausic, en donde plantó su establecimiento llamando el pueblo Providencia.

Al formar la naturaleza a los habitantes de la Nueva Inglaterra, dice M. Hamilton, parece haberles querido dar doble *cantidad de cerebro y medio corazón.* En efecto este pueblo es quizá el más inteligente y astuto que se conoce. Cuando se dice *yanqui,* que es la denominación que se les da vulgarmente, ya se entiende que se quiere decir, hombre que entiende su negocio; que entre ser engañado o engañar hay diecinueve probabilidades contra una de que sucederá lo segundo. El carácter de estos habitantes, dice el mismo escritor, no es amable, ni inspira simpatías; pero dista mucho de ser tampoco menospreciable. Tienen un grado de energía, de fuerza y de independencia que no permite verlos con desprecio.

Las riquezas están más bien distribuidas en Nueva Inglaterra que en ninguna nación del globo. Aunque hay grandes capitalistas, no son extraordinarias las fortunas. No hay pobres, y es muy raro encontrar familias en la miseria. Regularmente al lado de los grandes palacios se ve gemir al desgraciado que pide pan para sus hijos. Aunque hay algunos mendicantes, son siempre de los extranjeros, especialmente irlandeses recientemente desembarcados mientras encuentran acomodo.

El Estado de Connecticut tiene trecientos mil habitantes, y está entre el canal marítimo, llamado *Sund,* y los Estados de Rhode Island, Massachussetts y Nueva York. Su capital es Hartfort, ciudad de cerca de nueve mil habitantes, sobre el río Connecticut, y puerto bastante frecuentado. La Constitución de Connecticut fue concedida por Carlos II en 1662, y reformada en 1818 por su *Asamblea general*. Hay Senado y Cámara de representantes. Esta se compone de doscientos ocho miembros que no tienen dietas ningunas. Los senadores son treinta y cuatro, y unos y otros son elegidos anualmente. El gobernador es elegido por el pueblo anualmente. Tiene trecientos pesos anuales. La asamblea se reúne un año en Hartfort y otro en Nueva Haven. El voto es universal en las clases blancas, entre los ciudadanos desde veintiún años de edad para arriba.

Nueva Haven es una de las bellas ciudades de los Estados Unidos, por su posición y la elegancia de sus edificios. Su población es de nueve mil almas, está construida en un banco extenso, y tiene cerca de dos millas de norte a sur, y tres de oeste a este. La academia de niños dirigida por M. Dwight, es notable por su magnitud, y sorprendería al que no supiese que en aquel pequeño Estado toda la atención de los habitantes se dirige a la educación de la juventud. El *Yale college* es otro establecimiento de educación que compite con la universidad de Cambridge, del Estado de Massachussetts. El número de estudiantes asciende a quinientos. El cementerio de esta ciudad es el mejor de los Estados Unidos, por su extensión, simetría, belleza de monumentos, arboleda y situación.

Antes de salir del Estado de Connecticut insertaré un documento interesante, que es el manifiesto de la famosa convención de Hartfort, tenida en 1814, siendo Presidente de los Estados Unidos M. Madisson, y en los momentos críticos de la guerra segunda con Inglaterra, cuando los Estados sufrieron inmensos quebrantos por la interrupción de su comercio, y el Congreso general expidió algunas leyes que no fueron de la aprobación de muchos de ellos. Los delegados de la convención eran de las legislaturas de Massachussetts, Connecticut y Rhode Island, de los condados de Grafton y Cheshire, en el Estado de Nueva Hampshire, del condado de Windham, en el Estado de Vermont. El número total era de veinticinco. Ved aquí el dictamen.

"La convención está profundamente penetrada de la grandeza y dificultad de las materias que debe tomar en consideración, pues que tienen por objeto nada menos que solicitar los medios de defensa contra los peligros; y de recursos contra la opresión, que emanan de los actos de su mismo gobierno, debiendo hacerlo sin violar los principios constitucionales por una parte, ni dejar ilusorias y vanas las esperanzas de un pueblo oprimido. El prescribir el sufrimiento y firmeza a aquellos que ya están cansados de su miseria, es algunas veces conducirlos a la desesperación; y el progreso a las reformas por las vías regulares es un medio fastidioso para aquellas gentes cuya imaginación les presenta, y cuyos sentimientos les facilitan vías más cortas. Pero cuando los abusos han sido reducidos a sistema y acumulados por muchos años, han invadido todos los ramos del gobierno y esparcido la corrupción en todos los departamentos del Estado: cuando se les han investido con el aparato y fórmulas legales, y recibido la fuerza de un Poder Ejecutivo de donde tomaron origen, entonces no pueden encontrarse otros remedios que los de la resistencia abierta y directa. Este triste recurso, aun cuando es justificable, no puede menos que ser penoso al buen ciudadano; y el *buen suceso de los esfuerzos no presta nunca seguridad contra los peligros del ejemplo*. Los antecedentes de la resistencia a una mala administración, son ansiosamente iniciados por aquellos que son naturalmente hostiles a la mejora. La necesidad pues, sólo la necesidad puede sancionar esta medida, y jamás debería extenderse en grado ni en duración más allá de lo que exige la misma necesidad, hasta que el pueblo, no en el fervor de un movimiento apasionado, sino en la calma y después de una madura deliberación, no resuelva cambiar su constitución.

"Es una verdad que no se oculta a ninguno, que existe una opinión que condena al gobierno de haber interpretado la Constitución de manera que ha dado lugar a varios abusos bajo el colorido de aquella ley, y que ya es llegado el tiempo de variarla. Los que así piensan miran los males públicos como inherentes a la Constitución. Ceden a la persuasión de que ningún cambio ni trastorno puede empeorar la situación del país. Esta opinión necesita probar su certidumbre; pero como la evidencia sobre que descansa no parece todavía concluyente, y como las medidas que pudiesen tomarse en consecuencia de su certidumbre, serían irrecusables, se han sometido algunas consideraciones generales, con la esperanza de poder reconciliar la moderación con la firmeza, lo cual puede salvar a aquéllos del remordimiento de una decisión inmatura, con la de apartar el mal o a lo menos asegurar la conciencia de la buena conducta, y al mismo tiempo un resultado feliz en último resorte.

"La Constitución de los Estados Unidos, bajo los auspicios de una sabia y virtuosa administración, ha probado corresponder ella sola a todos los objetos de la prosperidad nacional, bajo el punto de vista que se propusieron sus autores. No se puede citar un ejemplo en la historia de las naciones, de una transición tan rápida como la de los Estados Unidos desde el estado de abatimiento en que se hallaban, hasta el de prosperidad en que están hoy día; desde el de estados débiles y desunidos, hasta el de nación grande, poderosa y fuerte.

"Aunque este elevado estado de felicidad pública ha experimentado reveses desgraciados y aflictivos por el imperio de una política débil y desastrosa, los males públicos de que nos lamentamos no son peculiares a una forma de gobierno cualquiera. Los desórdenes y caprichos del poder, la corrupción de sus clientes, la opresión de la parte débil de la comunidad por los más fuertes intereses, las contribuciones pesadas, los gastos enormes, las guerras injustas y ruinosas son naturalmente los efectos de una mala adminitración en todas las edades y naciones. Sería de desear que los directores de estos Estados no diesen pasos que los comprometiesen desde su infancia en los embarazos de las antiguas y corrompidas instituciones. Pero supongamos que los han dado, y que su conducta llama enérgicamente al pueblo a deponerlos y a mudar de constitución. Pues aun en este caso, para atacar los abusos del poder y mudar la Constitución, tendríamos que perpetuar los males de la revolución.

"Además, la experiencia hecha hasta ahora de la Constitución para poder mantenerse en vigor, y para que el pueblo pueda reconocer sus ilusiones, ha encontrado los graves inconvenientes y obstáculos nacidos del estado del mundo político. Las feroces pasiones que han puesto en convulsión las naciones de Europa, han pasado el Océano y penetrado hasta el seno de nuestros conciudadanos, han facilitado a la administración los medios de pervertir la opinión pública con respecto a nuestras relaciones exteriores, hasta el grado de adquirir su apoyo en el desahogo de sus animosidades, y el aumento de sus partidarios. Además, una reforma de la opinión pública, como el resultado de una muy cara experiencia, en los Estados atlánticos del Sur no debe considerarse como desesperada. Ellos habían sentido que los Estados del Este no pueden continuar siendo exclusivamente las víctimas de una política caprichosa y apasionada. Habían visto igualmente que los grandes y esenciales intereses del pueblo son comunes entre todos los Estados. Ellos quieren evitar los fatales errores de un sistema que busca su venganza en los perjuicios comerciales y agrava por inútiles guerras, de imponderable extensión, los males que hace profesión de evitar. Ellos apartarán la influencia de teóricos visionarios, y reconocerán los beneficios de una política práctica. Ya se han manifestado los indicios de esta revolución deseada en las ideas de nuestros hermanos de aquellos Estados. Mientras tengamos esperanzas de estas disposiciones anunciadas, no debemos retardar ni detener sus progresos, excitando temores que chocarán con estas tendencias favorables, y frustrar los esfuerzos de nuestros más sabios y virtuosos hombres de Estado para acelerar estos felices cambios.

"Por último, si ha llegado el período en que se disuelva la Unión por los abusos multiplicados de sus administraciones, esto debería ser, si fuese asequible, en tiempo de paz, y el resultado de deliberaciones maduras. Evidentemente debería, substituirse esta forma de gobierno federal entre estos Estados, manteniendo relaciones federativas. Los acontecimientos pueden probar que las causas de nuestras calamidades son profundas y permanentes. Podrá suceder que resulte que estas desgracias proceden no solamente de la ceguedad de las preocupaciones, del orgullo de la opinión, de la violencia del espíritu de partido o de la confusión de los tiempos; podrá provenir también de la implacable combinación de los individuos, o Estados, para monopolizar el poder y los empleos, que hollan sin remordimiento los derechos e intereses de las otras secciones comerciales de la Unión. Aunque parezca que estas causas son radicales y permanentes, una separación por convenios equitativos debe preferirse a una alianza forzada, entre amigos aparentes; pero en realidad enemigos inflamados de odios recíprocos y celos devoradores, invitando de esta manera a los enemigos exteriores a tentar agresiones en nuestra patria. Pero la separación de uno o más Estados de la Unión, especialmente en tiempo de guerra, sólo puede justificarla una absoluta necesidad. Estas son las principales objeciones contra una medida precipitada que tienda a desunir estos Estados, y al entrar en el examen de ella, no podemos jamás dejar de recordar los últimos consejos de despedida del Padre de este país, y estos solos bastan a retenernos.

"Sobre estas consideraciones la comisión ha producido a conferenciar y deliberar en orden al estado alarmante de los negocios públicos, con especialidad en los puntos bajo el aspecto que afectan los intereses del pueblo que la ha comisionado para este objeto, y naturalmente ha sido conducida a considerar en primer lugar los peligros y penalidades que amenazan una pronta e inmediata opresión, con el objeto de solicitar los medios de evitar estos males, en segundo lugar buscar en principios más extensos y en remedios más generales las bases de una seguridad futura.

"Entre los objetos de queja y temor que pueden comprenderse bajo la primera proposición, la comisión ha creído deber ocuparse de las pretensiones avanzadas de los poderes generales sobre la autoridad que pueden ejercer en la milicia nacional. Así como acerca de la privación de medios de defensa en que han dejado los Estados del Este; en el mismo tiempo que se han hecho grandes requisiciones de hombres y dinero para objetos nacionales.

"La autoridad del gobierno general sobre la milicia se deriva de aquellas cláusulas de la Constitución que da poder al Congreso 'de dar decretos para llamar la milicia a ejecutar las leyes de la Unión, suprimir las insurrecciones y repeler las invasiones' igualmente 'decretar la organización, armamento y disciplina de la milicia, y disponer de aquella parte que se haya de emplear en el servicio de los Estados Unidos, reservando a los Estados respectivos el nombramiento de sus oficiales y la autoridad de disciplinarla conforme los reglamentos del Congreso general'. Por último, 'el presidente será el comandante en jefe del ejército y marina de los Estados Unidos y de la milicia de los Estados, *cuando sea llamada al actual servicio de los Estadas Unidos'*. Luego sólo en estos casos especificados tiene el gobierno nacional algún poder sobre la milicia, y de consiguiente en todos los demás casos y circunstancias este poder pertenece a los Estados respectivos y sólo a ellos. La convención pues no sólo con sentimiento sino con admiración, ve que bajo el colorido de las facultades conferidas en los términos claros y precisos, con las limitaciones que se ha visto, el gobierno general se haya arrogado el poder, y el Congreso de la Unión ha permitido en muchos casos de dirigir y disponer de la milicia cívica; lo que si se concede la autoridad de los Estados es absolutamente nula y negatoria sobre esta clase de hombres, y con poner a disposición del gobierno general las vidas y servicios de la gran masa del pueblo, pone en sus manos el poder de destruir a su arbitrio sus libertades, y erigir un despotismo militar sobre sus ruinas.

"No entra en el plan de este informe el presentar un maduro examen de los principios que sirven de base a estas pretensiones extravagantes, ni de las consecuencias a donde conduciría, así como las objeciones insuperables que ofrecería su admisión. Pocas observaciones generales y la manifestación del carácter de estas pretensiones, así como la recomendación de una oposición vigorosa a ella, serán muy oportunas.

"No podrá disputarse que conforme los términos de que usa la Constitución, el poder del gobierno general de disponer de la milicia está limitado a los casos expuestos. Uno de ellos debe existir como condición precedente al ejercicio de aquel poder, esto es, a menos que haya oposición a la ley; exista una insurrección, o se presente invasión extranjera; fuera de estos casos el Congreso y de consiguiente el presidente como su órgano, no tendrá más poder sobre la milicia que sobre un ejército extranjero.

"Pero si la simple declaración del presidente fuese considerada como texto infalible de la existencia de estos casos, entonces este importante poder dependería no sobre la verdad del hecho, sino sobre la infalibilidad del ejecutivo; y la limitación del poder no sería en consecuencia otra cosa que una restricción nominal, que podría eludirse cuando conviniese al que manda. De aquí se sigue que la decisión del presidente en el particular, no debe considerarse como concluyente. Tan grande es la obligación de las autoridades de los Estados de velar sobre las derechos *reservados* como la de los Estados Unidos la de ejercer los poderes que se les han *delegado*.

"La disposición del gobierno de la Unión de mantener en los distritos militares una pequeña guarnición de las tropas permanentes bajo las órdenes de un jefe de alta graduación, con facultades de llamar la milicia cívica al servicio, conforme a juicio lo exijan las circunstancias, tomando el mando de ellas, no está concedida ni por la Constitución, ni por ley alguna de los Estados Unidos: y aunque no negamos que el Congreso general puede delegar al Presidente de los Estados Unidos el poder de levantar la milicia en los casos de que hemos hecho mención, jamás concederemos que tenga la autoridad de substituir prefectos militares en todos los ángulos de la Unión, para que se sirvan a discreción de tales o tales casos. El establecer un comandante militar en algunos distritos, sin tropas permanentes bajo su autoridad, correspondientes a su graduación, con el objeto de tomar el mando de las milicias cívicas, poniéndolas en servicio activo, es una manifiesta evasión de la ley constitucional, que expresamente reserva a los Estados el nombramiento de los oficiales de su milicia, y no puede concebirse que sea otro el objeto de destacar estos oficiales que el de suplantar sus agentes a los gobernadores de los Estados, o a los jefes natos de sus milicias nacionales.

"Tampoco puede el Congreso delegar el poder de dividir las mismas milicias en diversas clases, y el de obligar a estas clases a suministrar por suerte o contrato, hombres aptos para la defensa de las fronteras por uno o más años. Porque si se admitiese el derecho de sortear la milicia cívica por un año para tal objeto general, no se podría concebir qué límite tendría la facultad discrecional de extender este sorteo en manos de los legisladores. De esta manera el conceder este poder en el Congreso general para que se hagan sorteos o conscripciones, y al ejecutivo el de decidir definitivamente cuando las emergencias lo exigen, sería convertir en ejército permanente todas las milicias, a disposición del Presidente de los Estados Unidos.

"El poder de compeler la milicia y demás ciudadanos de los Estados Unidos, por un servicio forzoso o conscripción para servir en el ejército permanente, conforme ha propuesto en su última nota oficial el Secretario de la Guerra, no está tampoco concedido por la Constitución al Congreso; y el ejercicio de tal facultad sería no menos peligroso a nuestras libertades, que hostil a la soberanía de los Estados. Los esfuerzos que se hacen para deducir esta facultad del derecho de levantar tropas, concedido por la Constitución, tienden a una manifiesta perversión del sentido de la cláusula constitucional que confiere aquel derecho, y son incompatibles con otras resoluciones del mismo instrumento. Las tropas de los Estados Unidos siempre se han reclutado por contratas, y jamás por conscripción; y de nada más necesitaría un gobierno al que se concediese la facultad de que hablamos, para poder usurpar la entera dirección de la milicia cívica en desprecio de la facultad de los Estados, pudiendo convertirla toda en ejército permanente.

"Debemos hacer aquí mención, como una circunstancia que anuncia la intención del ejecutivo, de establecer un absoluto dominio sobre los ciudadanos de todas clases, que el Secretario de la Marina ha dicho en su Memoria oficial terminantemente que el gobierno tiene el derecho de hacer levas de marineros para el servicio de la armada. De esta manera, una práctica que en una nación extraña ha sido mirada por el pueblo con horror, encuentra abogados entre aquéllos que han sido sus más vehementes acusadores.

"La ley que autoriza el alistamiento de los menores y aprendices para el ejército de los Estados Unidos, sin el consentimiento de sus padres o curadores, es igualmente repugnante al espíritu de la Constitución. Según la interpretación que los actuales agentes del poder dan a la facultad de levantar tropas, no solamente son sorteadas las personas de mayor edad, sino aun las que tienen capacidad legal para hacer contratas son habilitadas para anular los hechos en su beneficio por sus curadores. Semejante intervención en las leyes municipales y derechos de los Estados, nunca pudo ocurrir a los autores de la Constitución. Ella debilita el saludable dominio del padre sobre su hijo, del amo sobre su criado, del tutor sobre su pupilo, y es destruir las más importantes relaciones sociales, de manera que por la conscripción del padre y la seducción del hijo, el Poder Ejecutivo ejerce un dominio completo sobre toda la población masculina de los Estados Unidos.

"Tales son algunas de las odiosas formas del nuevo sistema propuesto por los directores de un país libre, bajo poderes limitados que emanan de la Constitución. Cuáles serán los proyectos que recibirán la sanción legislativa, no es fácil determinarlo. Pero es muy alarmante el percibir que estos proyectos emanan de la más alta autoridad; y no debe olvidarse que por el plan del Secretario de la Guerra la clasificación de la milicia abraza el principio de la contribución directa entre la población blanca exclusivamente; y que la Cámara de representantes ha hecho y sostenido con vigor una moción para sacar la milicia cívica de entre la población blanca, lo que hubiera sido en esta operación una tasa directa.

"En toda esta serie de medidas y proyectos para levantar hombres, esta convención nota un total desprecio de la Constitución y disposiciones a violar sus preceptos, y pide de cada uno de los Estados una firme y decidida oposición. El más férreo despotismo no puede imponer carga más pesada sobre un ciudadano, que obligarle a dejar su casa y ocupaciones para correr a guerras ofensivas emprendidas por el orgullo o pasiones de su señor. El ejemplo de la Francia ha recientemente manifestado que una cábala de individuos, usurpando el nombre del pueblo, puede transformar el gran cuerpo de ciudadanos en soldados, y entregarlos a las manos de un tirano. Ninguna guerra, a menos que sea tenida en justo horror por el pueblo, necesita de estos estratagemas para reclutar el ejército. Si las tropas levantadas y sacrificadas en las fronteras del Canadá hubiesen sido empleadas en la defensa de la patria, y si los millones que han sido disipados con vergonzosa profusión se hubiesen destinado a su pago, a la protección de las costas, al servicio de la marina, no veríamos ahora estos recursos anticonstitucionales. Aun todavía en este momento, si el gobierno deja a la Nueva Inglaterra el remanente de sus recursos, ella está dispuesta y tiene capacidad para defender su territorio, y a abandonar las glorias y ventajas de la guerra fronteriza a aquéllos que persisten en su continuación.

"Es innegable que esos actos del Congreso que violan la Constitución, son absolutamente nulos. Es, sin embargo, repugnante a las consideraciones y respetos que los Estados confederados deben al gobierno general comenzar con una visión abierta en cada infracción que adviertan de la Constitución. El modo y la energía de la oposición, debe ser siempre conforme a la naturaleza de la violación, a la intención de sus autores, a la extensión de la injuria inferida, a la determinación manifiesta de persistir en el error y al peligro de la dilación. *Pero en los casos de infracciones deliberadas, peligrosas y palpables de la Constitución,* infracciones que afecten la soberanía de un Estado y las libertades del pueblo, entonces no es sólo el derecho, sino el deber de aquel Estado interponer su autoridad para su protección, en la manera que mejor calcule para el feliz éxito. Cuando los acontecimientos que ocurren están fuera del alcance de los tribunales, o la dilación de las fórmulas puede perjudicar la causa pública, los Estados que no tienen un árbitro común deben ser sus mismos jueces, y hacer ejecutar sus mismas decisiones. Así será conveniente que los Estados esperen la última resolución acerca de las medidas propuestas por el Secretario de la Guerra pendientes ante el Congreso, y usar con oportunidad de su poder conforme al carácter que aquellas medidas tomen finalmente, de modo que puedan proteger su soberanía y los derechos y libertades de sus ciudadanos.

"Otro objeto que ha ocupado la atención de la convención, son los medios de defensa contra el enemigo común. Esta cuestión conduce naturalmente a investigar ¿si se han tomado las medidas convenientes, o hay motivo racional de creer que las tomará el gobierno para la defensa de los Estados del Este? 2º ¿Si los Estados pueden de sus propios recursos proveer a su misma defensa, y cumplir de esta manera con su cargo de contribuir a la tesorería nacional? 3° ¿Qué conducta debe adoptarse en lo general por los Estados en relación al grande objeto de la defensa?

"Sin detenernos por ahora en reflexionar sobre las causas de la guerra, debe asentarse como una verdad oficialmente anunciada, que el objeto de la administración actual es ocupar el territorio del Canadá y mantenerle como una prenda de la paz. Esta empresa, principiada en un período en que el gobierno poseía la ventaja de escoger el tiempo y la oportunidad de hacer un repentino descenso sobre las tierras de un enemigo poco preparado, hoy se ha desvanecido después de tres años de guerra. En este período se han hecho esfuerzos con sucesos varios y algunas veces brillantes, pero sin un sólido resultado. Las tropas inglesas se componen de veteranos regimentados; su armada ocupa el lago Ontario. Las filas americanas se han disminuido por las consecuencias de la guerra. Los reclutas están desalentados por el carácter impopular de la contienda y por la inseguridad de sus pagas.

"En la continuación de esta guerra favorita, el gobierno ha dejado los puntos más expuestos y vulnerables del país destituidos de todos los medios efectivos de defensa. El cuerpo de operaciones del ejército permanente, ha marchado a la frontera; los buques de la marina nacional han sido despojados de sus marineros para el servicio de los lagos, y el enemigo entre tanto devasta nuestras costas, bloquea nuestros puertos, entra en nuestros ríos y bahías, hace descensos en varias y distantes plazas, toma algunas por fuerza y amenaza todo lo que está a su alcance con la espada y el fuego. Las costas marítimas de cuatro Estados de la Nueva Inglaterra tienen de extensión cerca de setecientas millas, ocupadas generalmente por una población compacta, y expuestas a las devastaciones del enemigo. Esta costa en toda su extensión ha estado expuesta a frecuentes ataques, graves requisiciones y constantes alarmas. Los destacamentos de tropas permanentes que hay en algunos puntos sólo han sido pretextos del gobierno para colocar jefes de alta graduación en ellos. Su corto número los hace además inútiles e insignificantes.

"Estos Estados pues, han sido abandonados a sí mismos y obligados a tomar su propia defensa. La milicia cívica ha estado en continua alarma causada por las faenas de guarnición y otras fatigas, mientras que los gastos que se erogan en su manutención y que el gobierno general se niega a reembolsar, amenazan absorber los recursos de los Estados. El Presidente de los Estados Unidos ha rehusado considerar los gastos de la milicia cívica en servicio por la autoridad del Estado, para la defensa indispensable de su territorio, como una deuda de la Unión, bajo el pretexto de que los gobernadores se han resistido a poner estas milicias bajo las órdenes de los oficiales del ejército permanente. Los cuerpos de la milicia cívica puestos a disposición del gobierno, han sido disueltos, unos sin pagárseles, otros pagados en papel moneda de bajo precio. El aspecto de la siguiente campaña no promete ninguna esperanza de alivio a estos males. Por documentos auténticos, sacados por necesidad de manos de aquéllos cuyo interés es ocultar los embarazos del ejecutivo, aparece que la tesorería está en estado de bancarrota y que su crédito se halla por los suelos. Tan deplorable es el estado de nuestra hacienda que los que conservan sentimientos del honor y libertad de su patria, desearían ocultar este espectáculo melancólico, si aquéllos cuyo infatuamiento ha producido este estado de miseria fiscal, no se encontrarán ellos mismos obligados a levantar el velo delante el público.

"Si la guerra continúa no hay motivo alguno para descansar sobre los medios de defensa que empleará el gobierno general para salvar estos Estados de la desolación y de la ruina. Tampoco es posible que estos cinco Estados cumplan con este deber sagrado a sus expensas, si continúan soportando el peso de las contribuciones de la Unión. Después de los esfuerzos infructuosos de la administración para paralizar las empresas comerciales, su fatal perseverancia en este objeto ha conseguido su fin durante el período de esta funesta guerra. El comercio principal, fuente de riqueza en la Nueva Inglaterra, ha sido aniquilado. Restricciones, comisos, embargos, y la rapacidad más escandalosa de los oficiales de rentas, han completado su destrucción. Han desaparecido los diferentes objetos que se empleaban en trabajos productivos. La pesca ha participado de estas desgracias. Las manufacturas que el gobierno había manifestado apreciar y favorecer, han sido sentenciadas a luchar en su infancia con las contribuciones y obstáculos que no pueden menos que perjudicar su vuelo. El numerario ha desaparecido de la circulación. El interés territorial último que sentirá estas cargas, vendrá a ser luego su único sostén, y entonces se acabará. En tales circunstancias se imponen cargas a los Estados, cargas que no se habían jamás intentado, y que serán más pesadas en los que estén situados hacia la parte oriental del Potomac. El importe de estas contribuciones para el año que sigue, puede regularse a lo menos, de cinco millones de pesos sobre la Nueva Inglaterra, mientras que los gastos hechos en el año pasado, sólo en el Estado de Massachussetts, ascienden a un millón de pesos.

"Parece inútil establecer la inevitable circunstancia de que estos Estados no están en posibilidad de sufragar los gastos de que tienen necesidad para su propia defensa, teniendo que atender a los del gobierno nacional.

"La última cuestión acerca de la conducta que debe adoptarse por los Estados ofendidos, es de la más alta importancia. Cuando un pueblo grande y valiente se ve abandonado por su mismo gobierno, y reducido a la alternativa de someterse a un enemigo extranjero, o de apropiarse aquellos medios de defensa que son indispensables para su propia conservación, no puede permanecer pasivo expectador de una próxima ruina, que puede evitar, ni resignarse tranquilamente a que se disipen los restos de la fortuna pública, producto de su industria en la permanencia de medidas destructoras de sus mejores intereses.

"Esta Convención no se fía en sus mismas luces para expresar la convicción que tiene de la catástrofe a la que este estado de cosas tiende inevitablemente. Con la conciencia de su alta responsabilidad para con Dios y para con su país, solícita de continuar la Unión, así como la soberanía de los Estados; no queriendo oponer obstáculos a la paz; resuelta a jamás someterse al enemigo extranjero, y confiando en los cuidados y amparo de la Divina Providencia, quiere y protesta apartar los males que amenazan, hasta haber agotado todos sus recursos y esperanzas. Con estas intenciones y bajo estos principios propone un arreglo que puede conciliarse con el honor y los intereses del gobierno general y la seguridad de estos Estados. Semejante arreglo es fácil de hacerse si el gobierno nacional está dispuesto a ello. Está reducido a que estos Estados queden autorizados a defenderse por sí mismos con su propia milicia o con tropas que levanten. Deberán conceder una parte proporcionada de las mismas contribuciones que paga cada Estado, y debiéndose emplear exclusivamente en su defensa, cargarlas a la tesorería general. No tenemos duda que con tal arreglo podrá esta parte del país ser defendida con gran suceso y de una manera más económica y conveniente que por el camino seguido hasta aquí.

"Si esta petición hecha al Congreso general por las legislaturas de los Estados tuviese efecto, en el caso de que no sea asequible una paz honrosa con los enemigos, todo el pueblo de los Estados Unidos se pondrá en defensa, y entre tanto vendrá el período de un cambio en la administración, o quizá de las disposiciones hostiles del enemigo, para poder arreglar nuestros asuntos, bajo mejores auspicios. Muy grande sería el embarazo de esta convención si desconfiase del éxito feliz de estas medidas, en cuyo evento tendría que recomendar procedimientos ulteriores. Esto no sería materia a que alcanzan sus poderes. En un estado de cosas tan solemne y en la gran lucha que debía seguirse, las legislaturas de los Estados, o una convención en todo el pueblo, por medio de sus delegados expresamente nombrados a deliberar y resolver sobre graves emergencias, podría únicamente encontrarse el remedio.

"Pero esta convención no creería haber llenado los deberes que se le han impuesto si no presentase una reseña general de aquellas medidas que juzga esenciales para evitar a la nación una recaída en los peligros en que se encuentra, si por la bondad de la Divina Providencia sale libre de su actual crisis. Una mirada rápida sobre la historia de nuestra patria bajo la sabia administración de que sacó grandes ventajas, y el contraste que presenta aquella época feliz con el abismo en que la ha hundido una política errónea y desconcertada sobre teorías inciertas, será suficiente para conducirnos al fin propuesto. Sentado esto, recordaremos que la inmediata influencia de la Constitución federal, después de su primera adopción, y en el período de los doce años siguientes, sobre la prosperidad y beneficios nacionales, parecía prometer tanta solidez que se creía generalmente que tendría una trascendencia universal sobre todas las instituciones de las otras naciones. Nuestra patria participaba de todas las bendiciones con que la Providencia había favorecido los otros pueblos; y además una Constitución libre administrada por hombres de Estado grandes e incorruptibles, realizaba las más fundadas esperanzas de libertad e independencia. Los progresos de la agricultura eran estimulados por la certidumbre de una cosecha rica y abundante; el comercio, después de haber atravesado todos los mares, venía a deponer sobre nuestras costas las producciones de todos los climas. Las rentas públicas, aseguradas por la conciencia del honor, colectadas sin opresión y pagadas sin murmuración, eran destinadas a amortizar la deuda pública, y los vales nacionales se elevaron en proporción de su disminución. Las guerras y conmociones de las naciones europeas y la interrupción de sus relaciones comerciales, trajeron a ésta que no había tomado parte en sus querellas, pero que hubiera deseado aliviar las calamidades que las siguen, la áurea oportunidad de extender sus relaciones comerciales y de enriquecerse ella misma llevando sus producciones indígenas, y aunque se ofrecían algunas vejaciones al comercio, nacidas de las circunstancias inevitables y de las colisiones furiosas de las potencias beligerantes, los grandes y buenos hombres de aquella época, acomodándose a la fuerza de los acontecimientos que no podían dirigir, preservaban su país de las tempestades que agitaban el antiguo mundo, y atraían los restos de sus fortunas a estas playas. Los enemigos de las instituciones republicanas no podrán decir nada de nuestra república, respetada por fuera, próspera en el interior, con sabias leyes hechas por sus legisladores respetables, obedecidas por un pueblo satisfecho y feliz. Florecían las artes, se cultivaban las ciencias, las comodidades y conveniencias de la vida estaban distribuidas entre todos; y a las administraciones subsecuentes sólo quedaba el trabajo de recoger las ventajas y conservar los recursos que manaban de la política de sus predecesores.

"Mas apenas se había establecido una nueva administración en las manos de un partido opuesto a la política de Washington, se notó una determinación fija y confesada de variar el sistema que hasta entonces había producido tan sustanciales beneficios. No fueron con todo bastantes las consecuencias de este cambio, por los primeros años, a detener el prodigioso impulso dado hacia la prosperidad de la nación. Pero una tenaz perseverancia en los nuevos planes de la administración, desenvolvieron a la larga su deformidad; aunque no hasta un punto capaz de desengañar a la mayoría del pueblo, lisonjeado y entusiasmado por los falsos sistemas. Bajo la estéril influencia de este nuevo orden la decadencia de la nación ha sido uniforme y rápida. Las más ricas ventajas para asegurar los grandes objetos de la Constitución han sido repulsados con descaro, y la Europa, al respirar en la paz actual de la sangrienta lucha que ha sacudido sus antiguas instituciones, mira, atónita, este país remoto, feliz y envidiado en otro tiempo, envuelto en una guerra ruinosa e imposibilitado de hacer comercio con las otras naciones".

La Convención termina su largo informe con algunas proposiciones que los sucesos posteriores y la prosperidad ascendiente de aquella feliz nación han demostrado no haber sido conformes al espíritu de sus sabias instituciones; y este ruidoso acontecimiento no tuvo otras consecuencias, habiéndose conseguido un mes después la victoria brillante de la Luisiana, que cambió el aspecto político y mercantil de los Estadas Unidos del Norte, trayendo una paz ventajosa con la Gran Bretaña.

CAPÍTULO XV

Como mi regreso a Nueva York, después de mi viaje a Nueva Inglaterra, fue seguido del que hice a Europa, en la relación que continuaré dando de los Estados Unidos, no seguiré el orden de fechas; pues hablaré de Nueva York, igualmente visitado por mí en 1832, a mi vuelta de Europa. En este período conocí al célebre coronel Burr, abogado de muchos conocimientos en su profesión, hombre emprendedor y notable en los Estados Unidos en los primeros años que siguieron a su independencia.

El coronel Burr me fue presentado por el doctor John, que había estado algún tiempo en el Estado de Tabasco. Un día vi entrar a mi sala al referido doctor con un hombre pequeño, de edad de setenta años, de una fisonomía sumamente espiritual, y en el que, a pesar de estar medio paralítico, se descubre una fuerza mental y un carácter vigoroso. El coronel Burr habla medianamente francés, y tiene placer en usar de este idioma en la conversación. Fue Vicepresidente de los Estados Unidos en la presidencia de M. Adams padre, y en la elección de M. Jefferson para la presidencia fue empatada la votación en la Cámara por veintitrés veces. Aaron Burr se perdió en la opinión de sus conciudadanos por el desafío ruidoso con el virtuoso general Hamilton, del que resultó la muerte del segundo. Después de aquel tiempo M. Burr pasó a Europa a hacer olvidar con el tiempo a sus conciudadanos la sangrienta catástrofe. El gobierno inglés no le consintió permanecer mucho tiempo en Inglaterra, porque hizo liga estrecha con los *radicales, y mantenía* una comunicación íntima con los franceses revolucionarios. Posteriormente intentó apoderarse de la provincia de Texas, en donde *algunos dicen* que tuvo ánimo de hacerse proclamar emperador. Lo cierto es que hubo un escandaloso proceso; y aunque fue absuelto por dos jurados sucesivos, la opinión pública no le ha considerado justificado. En el día vive ejerciendo su facultad de abogado, y su talento forense le daría bastante para vivir si además no tuviese una fortuna adquirida, a la que se ha añadido su enlace últimamente hecho con una señora rica de Nueva York. En este mismo tiempo se hallaba en Nueva York el general don Francisco de Paula Santander, actual Presidente de la Nueva Granada. Había salido desterrado de Colombia, bajo la dictadura de Bolívar, quien le había hecho sentenciar a pena capital por una conspiración, en la que se suponía haber tomado parte, contra la vida del Dictador. Bolívar, como por gracia, le conmutó la pena capital en destierro de seis años. Del proceso, del que me dio una copia el general Santander, resultaba únicamente que alguno le había hecho confidencialmente una revelación del secreto de la conspiración tramada contra el usurpador. Sobre un cargo semejante Santander fue condenado a la pena capital, por no haber denunciado el complot. Este general fue obsequiado por los principales habitantes de Nueva York, y tengo presente que se le dio una comida pública a lo menos de ciento cincuenta cubiertos. Tuve ocasión de tratarle íntimamente en Francia, durante la navegación y en los Estados Unidos. En su posada, en Filadelfia, encontré al general don Manuel G. Pedroza, a quien no se había permitido desembarcar en las costas de México, por razones de Estado. El general Santander es un hombre honrado, amante de la libertad y capaz de discernir el verdadero camino de la felicidad de sus conciudadanos. Quizá es poco adicto a sus juicios más de lo conveniente. Pero su moderación y su tacto de negocios corrigen esta falta.

En este mismo tiempo se agitaba la elección de Presidente de los Estados Unidos. El general Jackson había sido electo en 1828, en concurrencia de M. Adams, en cuya reelección estaba empeñado el antiguo partido federativo, en contraposición del partido democrático. Muy dignos de atención son dos documentos publicados en aquella fecha entre otros mil, porque dan una idea del carácter de los partidos en los Estados Unidos. El primero es el que sostenía la elección del general Jackson, y el segundo el de M. Adams. Debe tenerse presente lo que he dicho ya en esta obra, de que cualquiera anuncia por los periódicos que se va a reunir una *Convención* o una junta para tal o cual objeto, cuando la opinión pública está dividida.

Junta Republicana de Edimburgo
(Estado de Nueva York)

"En una numerosa y respetable junta de republicanos del pueblo de Edimburgo, tenida en la fonda del corregidor Weeks Copeland, en dicho pueblo, en 13 de septiembre de 1828, para nombrar los delegados que deben ir a la Convención de este condado, con el objeto de tratar acerca del nombramiento de presidente para el año siguiente. John Rhodes fue llamado a presidir la junta, y Martin Buttler nombrado secretario. La comisión nombrada al efecto informó que se debían tomar las siguientes resoluciones, las que en efecto se aprobaron por unanimidad.

"Resolvimos: que no sólo es un derecho, sino un deber de los republicanos investigar la conducta de aquéllos que están puestos a la cabeza del gobierno; descubrir y detener sus arbitrariedades, y reprimir los ejemplos de corrupción y desorden. La junta opina que en la presente crisis está llamada enérgicamente a hacer esta investigación. *Resolvimos:* que no podemos sostener la conducta de la actual administración con nuestros próximos sufragios, por su desarreglo en el manejo de los negocios; su menosprecio de muchos de nuestros más distinguidos ciudadanos; su profusión en las recompensas prodigadas a sus favoritos; el abandono de sus obligaciones por ocuparse en las elecciones; los medios poco decorosos que ha empleado para sostener su existencia en el poder, y asegurar la reelección. *Resolvimos:* que estamos persuadidos de que el general Andres Jackson es el hombre que ha cubierto su país de gloria, y que sus servicios a la nación le hacen acreedor a las más altas recompensas: que por sus sólidos principios, su ardiente amor a su patria, manifestado en los días de mayor peligro, su devoción a la democracia, su vida sencilla y distante de todo fausto, sus servicios incomparables a la nación es un ciudadano a propósito para refrenar los progresos de la prodigalidad, detener la marcha de la corrupción y reinstalar el gobierno en la pureza de sus antiguos principios. *Resolvimos:* que por éstas y otras consideraciones, aprobamos el nombramiento de Andres Jackson para la presidencia, y que emplearemos nuestros esfuerzos para que se logre su elección. *Resolvimos:* que esta confianza se aumenta porque creemos que él desea ascender a este puesto elevado por la voz del pueblo, sin ayuda de los fondos públicos, de los influjos del gabinete, ni por intrigas, ruegos ni amenazas. *Resolvimos:* que aprobamos el nombramiento de John C. Calhoun para el oficio de vicepresidente; persuadidos de que durante el curso de su vida pública se ha conducido de una manera que le hace acreedor a nuestros sufragios. *Resolvimos:* que no debemos dar gracias a ninguno de nuestros diputados ni senadores por haber abusado bastardamente de su privilegio de francatura, para enviar por todos los Estados innumerables folletos y papeles impresos que contienen manifiestos absurdos para sostener una elección que reprueban los hombres civilizados y más los republicanos ilustrados. *Resolvimos:* que no estamos de acuerdo con la opinión manifestada en Utica, que sostiene el partido de la actual administración, proponiendo para gobernador y vicegobernador personas adictas a ella. *Resolvimos:* que esta acta sea firmada por el presidente y secretario, y publicada en la *Gaceta de Saratoga*.

"John Rhodes, presidente.
"M. H. Buttler, secretario"

EL SISTEMA AMERICANO
Convención de la administración republicana

"En esta Convención de delegados adictos a la administración del actual gobierno nacional, venidos de todos los pueblos del condado de Saratoga, tenida en la sala de ayuntamiento, en el pueblo de Ballston Spa, el miércoles 22 de octubre de 1828, el general John Prior fue llamado a la silla, y John House y James M. Crea fueron nombrados secretarios. Se *resolvió:* que la ilustrada y patriótica administración actual de nuestro gobierno nacional es digna de nuestros más ardientes votos, y que usaremos de todos los medios honrosos para procurar la reelección de John Quincy Adams en la presidencia, y elección de Ricardo Rush para el oficio de vicepresidente. *Resolvió:* que aprueba muy cordialmente el nombramiento de Smith Thompson para el cargo de gobernador de este Estado, y el de Francis Granger para vicegobernador, y estamos dispuestos a sostener sus nombramientos por nuestros sufragios. *Resolvió:* que tenemos entera confianza en los talentos e integridad de John M. Lean, junior, de Washington, y cordialmente unidos con la convención republicana de este distrito, le recomendamos para senador. *Resolvió:* que los delegados de cada pueblo nombren uno entre ellos para componer una comisión escogida, con instrucciones para informar a la Convención acerca de las personas que deben ser los candidatos para los oficios del condado.

"Habiéndose retirado la dicha comisión y vuelto a la sala de la Convención, informaron que habían convenido por unanimidad en recomendar los siguientes candidatos. Para elector a John Child, para diputado a John Taylor, para sheriff a John Dunming, para escribano del condado a Thomas Palmer, para miembros de la legislatura a Guilbert Waring, Josue Mandeville y Calvino Wheeler, para corono a Herman Rockwell, Dirck L. Palmer, Hugh Alejandro y Nathan D. Sherwood. Después de lo cual, habiéndose leído y aprobado cada recomendación individualmente y por unanimidad, se resolvió que Salmon Child, Sanmuel Treeman, Eduardo Watrous, James M. Crea, Amon Brown, Increase W. Child y Moises Williams sean los que compongan la comisión central para el año venidero: y que los delegados elegidos por los pueblos a esta Convención sean los que compongan una comisión de vigilancia en sus respectivos lugares, para llevar a efecto las elecciones arriba referidas: por último, se *resolvió* que esta acta sea firmada por el presidente y secretarios".

La proclama es como sigue: "Ciudadanos: en un gobierno como el nuestro en que cada uno de los ciudadanos tiene en sus manos una porción del soberano poder, es de toda importancia que haga uso de la autoridad con que está investido con juicio esclarecido. La próxima elección de presidente es de la más vital importancia para la felicidad y adelantos de los Estados Unidos, y de consiguiente ella determinará si ha de pertenecer o ser desechada una administración virtuosa e ilustrada, y si medidas que afectan profundamente los intereses de esta vasta mayoría de nuestros conciudadanos, han de ser promovidas o abandonadas. La administración actual del gobierno general, está a la cabeza de un gran sistema político que promete llevar a efecto empresas que extiendan los recursos, aumenten la riqueza y promuevan todos los principios que aseguren la independencia del país. Hace muchos años que la Gran Bretaña rehusa recibir en sus puertos los efectos que producen los Estados del Norte y Mediodía, mientras este país recibe anualmente de aquella nación el valor de muchos millones de sus manufacturas; y de aquí ha resultado que todo nuestro oro y plata ha tomado aquel camino para pagar sus mercancías. De aquí ha resultado que nuestros labradores no han encontrado mercado para el sobrante de sus productos, y todas las clases de la sociedad se han visto en graves embarazos por este entorpecimiento de la circulación. Nuestro gobierno ha provisto al remedio de estos males, prosiguiendo la industria americana en la competencia que ofrece la extranjera, por una ley del país sobre la máxima de comprar de aquéllos sólo lo equivalente a lo que ellos compran de nosotros, llevando a efecto la doctrina de Jefferson, de plantar el manufacturero y el labrador uno enfrente del otro, y creando así un mercado doméstico para el sobrante de nuestros puertos. Por la adopción de este sistema económico, tan conveniente a nuestra situación, tan inseparable de nuestra prosperidad y tan honroso a nuestro carácter, es por lo que la actual administración ha sido atacada. Nuestros conciudadanos del Sur se han abandonado a facciosas y antilegales amenazas de disolver la Unión en el caso de que M. Adams sea reelecto. Nosotros confiamos que nuestros conciudadanos no están dispuestos a abandonar sus intereses, abandonando al actual gobierno para complacer una facción malhadada. Si estáis, pues, preparados a asegurar vuestros propios derechos contra la violenta facción del Sur, unid vuestros sufragios en las próximas elecciones, y sostened la causa de los principios de vuestra patria. Los candidatos que os hemos presentado para ser elegidos, han sido bien conocidos de vosotros. Son los amigos decididos de la administración, y ninguno duda de sus cualidades y capacidad para el desempeño de los respectivos oficios a que les destinamos.

"JOHN PRIOR, presidente.

"JOHN HOUES; JAMES M. CREA, secretarios"

La última parte de esta proclama hace alusión a la cuestión ruidosa de aranceles de que ya he instruido suficientemente a mis lectores, insertando los documentos en su lugar. De esta manera tratan las elecciones en los Estados Unidos; pero el principio salvador del país, es que cuando se ha hecho la elección por la mayoría, ya todos callan delante de la ley. Mucho contribuye para esto el que la elección de presidente emane directamente del pueblo, y de consiguiente no esté sujeta a las intrigas y maniobras a que da lugar un nombramiento hecho por las legislaturas en un país en donde las elecciones son indirectas. De esta manera el presidente dista mucho de su legítimo origen, que debe ser la voluntad de la mayoría de los ciudadanos.

En este mismo tiempo estaba en Nueva York don José T. Salgado, desterrado de México por asuntos políticos. En su compañía hice un viaje a West Point, uno de los puntos más pintorescos del mundo.

West Point es el punto en que está la escuela militar, colocada sobre una vasta plataforma que pertenece a una rama de los Alleghanis, y a sus pies corre el majestuoso Hudson. La meseta está elevada más de trecientos pies sobre el nivel del río, y de consiguiente el aire es sano, los estudiantes gozan de buena salud. El estado mismo de aislamiento de este instituto, les pone al abrigo de la corrupción de las ciudades, al mismo tiempo que les obliga a entregarse a sus estudios sin distracciones. La instrucción y las costumbres ganan al mismo tiempo. El número de estudiantes es de doscientos veinte: son recibidos gratuitamente, luego que el Secretario de la Guerra de los Estados Unidos comunica la orden del Presidente. Las condiciones que deben tener los jóvenes, son de quince a dieciocho años de edad; buena letra, conocimiento perfecto de la lengua inglesa y poseer los primeros elementos de aritmética. El curso de estudios es de cuatro años, en cuyo período aprenden las matemáticas, astronomía, física experimental, ciencias militares, historia natural, geografía, lengua francesa, historia, dibujo, filosofía moral y las leyes de la Unión. Se les enseña al mismo tiempo el manejo de armas, el ejercicio de campaña y la práctica del arte militar en general. Con este objeto se destinan dos meses del año a hacer en las comarcas cercanas excursiones, en donde los estudiantes levantan planos, toman posiciones y se acostumbran a las fatigas de la campaña.

Las ciencias matemáticas son las en que se ocupan más activamente. Se exigen de los colegiales conocimientos de mucha extensión y superiores a los que en Europa se requieren generalmente para hacer un buen oficial de infantería o caballería. Se da mucha importancia a las matemáticas en los Estados Unidos, seguramente porque hay todavía y habrá por mucho tiempo una grande cantidad de territorios que explorar y fecundar, a cuyo efecto los conocimientos matemáticos son sumamente útiles.

El Estado Mayor de la escuela se compone de un jefe comandante de la institución, que debe tener un oficial de artillería o de ingenieros, de un profesor de historia natural y de física, con un ayudante: de un profesor de matemáticas con un segundo: de un profesor de ingenieros con un segundo; de un eclesiástico profesor de elocuencia y literatura; de un maestro de dibujo; de un profesor de lengua francesa; de un maestro de esgrima, y de un médico.

La biblioteca es bien escogida. Se compone de obras de estadística, historia natural, historia civil y militar. Entre estas últimas se encuentran todas las cartas de las campañas francesas, enriquecidas de estampas muy ricas. Igualmente están las campañas de Federico el Grande y los tratados de fortificación de Vauban. La colección de cartas que es preciosa, contiene entre otros los puertos del Báltico y mar del Norte por Beautemps, Beaupré.

West Point fue durante la guerra de la revolución un punto importante, del que intentaron apoderarse varias veces los ingleses. Aún se ven los escombros de algunas fortificaciones de aquella época. Allí ven los viajeros el lugar de las tiendas de Washington, los jardines de Kosciuzko cultivados por sus propias manos, y el cenotafio de este ilustre guerrero polaco. Era difícil elegir un lugar más rico en recuerdos, más propio para hacer nacer en el corazón de los jóvenes el amor de las virtudes patrióticas, y un ardor noble por estudios que contribuyen a mantener la gloria y la independencia nacional. Las vistas sobre el río Hudson son románticas, llenas de bellezas naturales y capaces de animar la imaginación.

En todo el establecimiento reina el orden y la decencia, y la instrucción es bastante avanzada. Hace pocos años que un joven indio de la tribu de los crecks, llamado Moniac, ocupaba un lugar distinguido entre los estudiantes. Yo he oído elogios acerca de sus conocimientos matemáticos, de personas que le vieron resolver diversas cuestiones de geometría y análisis con gran facilidad. Este rasgo y muchos que podría citar de indios mexicanos que hacen honor a su patria, desmienten la aserción de Buffon y Reynal de que los indígenas de las Américas no pueden llegar al grado de inteligencia que los habitantes del antiguo mundo.

Los estudiantes de este instituto están divididos en compañías, y hacen el servicio militar bajo las órdenes y dirección de un oficial del ejército, que les da lecciones de táctica. Cada uno obtiene un grado según su mérito y sus adelantos en sus estudios, conforme a las reglas particulares de cada clase. Los cadetes están acampados durante dos meses cada año, en cuyo período sólo se ocupan de ejercicios militares. Entonces reciben dos raciones por día y dieciséis pesos mensuales, lo que hace poco más de veintiocho pesos. A la salida de la escuela cada estudiante recibe una comisión o empleo en uno de los cuerpos militares, según su capacidad y mérito. Algunos salen a continuar sus estudios y recibir más amplias instrucciones en los grandes colegios de Europa, con su mismo sueldo.

Es una gran parte de la alta política de los gobiernos favorecer una dirección literaria, científica e industrial que conviene imprimir al movimiento natural del espíritu humano. La actividad, la agitación misma de los espíritus en nuestras nuevas repúblicas, favorecen los progresos de la civilización, y esa abundancia de vida que produce largos y violentos sacudimientos políticos y militares, que han conmovido el edificio social en los nuevos Estados, ha tenido, bajo algunos aspectos, efectos saludables, como las inundaciones del Nilo reparten la fecundidad sobre las tierras que han cubierto con sus aguas. Esta actividad que no puede parecer peligrosa, sino a los que tienen proyectos de tiranía y de opresión, que quisieran extinguir a los hombres superiores, de carácter firme y capaces de concebir pensamientos y planes de un interés general, vendrá a ser útil y provechosa cuando reciba una buena dirección, y sus efectos serán benéficos a la moral pública, al libre desenvolvimiento de las facultades intelectuales, a la estabilidad de instituciones filantrópicas, haciendo la gloria de los directores.

En Nueva York hay una casa de refugio para los jóvenes delincuentes de ambos sexos en donde se les enseñan oficios análogos a sus disposiciones, y no están expuestos a corromperse por los malos ejemplos de los criminales de las otras cárceles. Hay igualmente un hospicio de sordomundos, y un asilo de locos. En todos estos establecimientos hay el mejor orden, y nada falta a los desgraciados a quienes la suerte ha condenado a sufrir. El interés que toman los encargados de velar de la dirección de estas instituciones y la perfecta cooperación que encuentran en todos sus agentes, son verdaderamente laudables y dignos de ser propuestos como modelos. Los que comparen este establecimiento con nuestro San Hipólito de México, notarán en el hospicio mexicano magnificencia de edificio, dotaciones grandes de empleados y administradores, un templo espacioso, muchos reglamentos y rentas cuantiosas, al lado de la falta de limpieza, de la poca asistencia a los dementes; mientras que en el norteamericano el edificio es proporcionado a la necesidad, hay una capilla, el cuidado y esmero para con los lunáticos es admirable, el aseo y limpieza de camas y ropas no deja que desear, y los sueldos son sumamente moderados.

En el Estado de Nueva York hay dos grandes prisiones sobre el modelo poco más o menos de la de los Estados de Massachussetts y Pensilvania de que ya he hablado. Estas son Singsing, sobre el río Hudson, y Auburn sobre el Oswego. Esta última tiene quinientos cincuenta cuartos, en cada uno de los cuales hay un preso. Su encierro no es como el de los de la Penitenciaría de Filadelfia, para permanecer solitarios por todo el tiempo de su condena. Habiendo considerado la legislatura del Estado que el ejercicio corporal es de necesidad para conservar la salud, se les destina al trabajo durante el día, bajo las más estrictas reglas. Luego que entra el sentenciado, se le da la ropa de la prisión, se le lee el reglamento y se le instruye de sus obligaciones. Estas se reducen a obedecer las órdenes y trabajar con actividad y en silencio; a hablar siempre con respeto a los custodios de los prisioneros; a no hablar sin necesidad ni aun a los mismos guardianes; no cantar ni bailar ni hacer ruido alguno; no separarse del local en que están destinados sin permiso; no distraerse de su trabajo ni descansar un momento. Tampoco les es permitido recibir cartas, ni tener especie alguna de comunicación de afuera. Todas las que tengan de este género, deben ser por conducto de sus custodios. Cada preso tiene una biblia a costa del Estado. Por las infracciones que cometen del reglamento o de las advertencias verbales son inmediatamente castigados con la pena de azotes con un látigo de cuero. Los castigos son tan prontos y tan inmediatos a las faltas, que hay muy raros ejemplos de que se cometan éstas. Por la mañana temprano se toca la campana y los carceleros abren las celdas de los presos. Estos salen a un patio común en verano, o en gran salón en invierno, se lavan las caras y las manos en vasijas destinadas al efecto, y a continuación pasan en línea, como soldados, a sus respectivos trabajos. Los nuevos presos, si tienen oficio, trabajan en él, si no se les enseña el que escojan. Trabajan regularmente doce horas. Comen en refectorio y siempre de espaldas los unos de los otros en el mayor silencio. Cuando necesitan los criados, levantan las manos y se les sirve lo que quieren. El tiempo de cada comida es regularmente de media hora. Al retirarse por la noche se lavan otra vez las manos y la cara. Se les mantiene siempre la ropa aseada.

Los domingos, después de lavarse, en lugar de trabajar van a la capilla, en donde el capellán hace el servicio divino. Los que saben leer y escribir, que son raros, van a la escuela dominical, en donde reciben la instrucción conveniente.

Las raciones de cada preso por día son diez onzas de carne de cerdo, o dieciséis de vaca; diez onzas de harina de trigo, doce de harina de maíz cocida; papas calientes y medio cuartillo de centeno hecho en forma de café, endulzado con melaza; en la comida se les da sopa hecha de caldo de vaca, espesada con harina de maíz; pan, papas y agua fría. Para cenar una especie de polenta de maíz que llaman *musk* y agua fría. Esta cantidad de alimento se ha considerado la necesaria para mantener a los presos en perfecta salud.

La ganancia media de cada preso se calcula en el día de dos a tres reales. De este fondo salen los gastos de prisión, la que es tan aseada y limpia que no puede apetecerse más. Los presos antes de salir en libertad están obligados a contar su vida, y decir que género de profesión han ejercido y van a ejercer. Esto hará una colección curiosa de anécdotas, de que podrán sacarse útiles observaciones acerca del carácter nacional, y aun de la naturaleza humana. De ciento sesenta que habían salido, ciento doce se enmedaron completamente, y veintiséis continuaron malos; el resto indiferentes. Los presos dicen que su mayor pena es el no poder conversar, ni tener noticias de lo que pasa afuera. Es necesario confesar que estas precauciones son necesarias, y llorar sobre la suerte del hombre condenado a sufrir tan grandes privaciones. Aquí no puede decirse con el Dante:

Qui vive la pietá quand'è ben mona.

CONCLUSIÓN

Los Estados Unidos, dice muy bien M. Hamilton, son el pueblo quizá menos expuesto a revoluciones en el día. Pero su estabilidad consiste, añade, en la única circunstancia de que la *gran mayoría de los habitantes son propietarios*. No hay duda en que ésta es una, pero no la única causa de la tranquilidad inalterable de aquel dichoso pueblo. En los sistemas sociales no puede resolverse una cuestión por la explicación de una sola circunstancia. La España, por ejemplo, se mantuvo tranquila hasta el año de 1808, bajo el yugo tiránico de la monarquía, inquisición y gobierno militar; y esta paz sepulcral no podía explicarse solamente por una sola causa, a saber, el *terror que inspiraba* la forma establecida. Había además la ignorancia, la superstición, el inmenso influjo de los frailes y clérigos, apoyo de los grandes, en suma, un orden de cosas establecido, y coordinado de modo que unas sostenían a las otras. Estableced en esa misma España o en México la ley *agraria,* distribuid con igualdad las propiedades, y los resultados serán poner en confusión todas las clases, envilecer los valores, alimentar y dar estímulo a la holgazanería y multiplicar los desórdenes.

Verdad es que una de las principales causas de la estabilidad de las instituciones de los Estados Unidos de la América del Norte es la situación feliz de la inmensa mayoría de los habitantes. Pero al lado de estos goces materiales el pueblo coloca el santo derecho de intervenir en todas las transacciones que tienen por objeto organizar los poderes públicos; las garantías individuales que les asegura sus leyes, la libertad de escribir y publicar sus opiniones; la que tienen de adorar a Dios conforme les dicte su conciencia; y la convicción profunda e indestructible en que están todos sus ciudadanos de que la ley es igual para todos, y que no hay instituciones formadas para favorecer una clase, ni una jerarquía de privilegiados.

Al echar una ojeada rápida sobre esa nación gigantesca, que nació ayer y que hoy extiende sus brazos desde el Atlántico hasta el Pacífico y mar de la China; el observador quedó absorto y naturalmente se hace la cuestión, de cuál será el término de su grandeza y prosperidad. No es el poder de las conquistas ni la fuerza de las armas; tampoco el prestigio ni las ilusiones de un culto que reúne a las reglas de la moral los misterios del dogma, es un orden social nuevo, brillante, positivo; un sistema político que ha excluido todos los privilegios, todas las distinciones consagradas por los siglos anteriores, el que ha hecho esa prodigiosa creación. A la vista de este fenómeno político, los hombres de Estado de todos los países, los filósofos, los economistas se han detenido a contemplar la marcha rápida de este portentoso pueblo, y conviniendo unánimes en la nunca vista prosperidad de sus habitantes al lado de la sobriedad; del amor al trabajo, de la libertad más indefinida, de las virtudes domésticas, de una actividad creadora y de una religiosidad casi fanática, se han esforzado a explicar las causas de estos grandes resultados.

¿Qué han sido las repúblicas antiguas, ni las anarquías de la edad media, ni las confederaciones europeas, en comparación de esta nación extraordinaria? Atenas es una democracia tumultuosa, de cuatro leguas de extensión, dominada por oradores hábiles que saben explotarla a su beneficio. Esparta, una vasta comunidad sujeta a reglas más bien que a leyes; una familia más bien que una sociedad, sin independencia individual; sin estímulo para las artes, las ciencias ni las virtudes; un orden religioso semejante al de los templarios, que no puede servir de modelo a ningún pueblo moderno. ¡Roma! ¿En qué época esa orgullosa república hizo jamás la felicidad de las masas? El pueblo romano fue un pueblo opresor de los otros, y oprimido él mismo por sus patricios, aun en sus días de mayor libertad. Tribunos turbulentos, víctimas muchas veces de sus furores demagógicos y de los odios del patriciado, mantienen en fermentación una plebe que se contenta con una diminución de sus deudas, con distribuciones ocasionales de trigos, o con un apólogo contado con sagacidad. ¡Ensayos mezquinos, aunque lecciones útiles para llegar un día al establecimiento del sistema americano!

En efecto, la escuela política de los Estados Unidos es un sistema completo; obra clásica, única: un descubrimiento semejante al de la imprenta, al de la brújula, al del vapor; pero un descubrimiento que aplica la fuerza moral de las inteligencias individuales a mover la gran máquina social hasta hoy arrastrada, más bien que dirigida, tirada por resortes facticios, compuesta de combinaciones heterogéneas, mosaico monstruoso de trozos unidos de feudalismo, superstición, privilegios de castas, legitimidades, santidades y otros elementos contranaturales; y escombros de ese diluvio de tinieblas que inundó al género humano durante doce centurias.

Muy bien pueden los publicistas europeos librarse a interpretaciones, vaticinios, conjeturas y comentarios siniestros sobre las constituciones, porvenir, estabilidad y leyes de los Estados Unidos. Lo que no pueden negar, es, que no hay ni hubo jamás un pueblo en que los derechos del ciudadano fuesen más respetados, en que los individuos tuviesen más participación en el gobierno, en que las masas estuviesen más perfectamente niveladas en todos los goces sociales. ¿Qué género de argumento es contra sus instituciones el anunciar a una nación un porvenir desgraciado, catástrofes melancólicas, cuando al presente está llena de vida, de felicidad y de ventura? Los que no pueden resistir a la convicción de los hechos palpables, de una experiencia diaria, recurren a vaticinios funestos y predicen ya la disolución de la gran república. Nosotros les contestaremos que vale más el bien presente, que esperanzas nunca realizadas: que no habrá un hombre ni pueblo que prefiera vivir en la opresión o en la miseria, a la existencia feliz e independiente de aquella república; sólo porque algunos malhumorados políticos le dicen que aquella situación próspera no durará doscientos años. No, jamás se debilitará la fuerza de ese ejemplo vivo y perseverante de utopía social, con semejantes argumentos. Espiad enhorabuena sus pequeñas y efímeras asonadas; exagerad el calor de sus debates públicos; los tumultos de sus elecciones; sus rarísimas aberraciones de fanatismo presbiteriano; su aversión a la casta negra, sus dificultades por su sistema de esclavitud, sus cuestiones de aranceles, embarazo momentáneos de sus bancos; comentad de la manera más desfavorable estas crisis políticas y económicas; una solución positiva, una peripecia feliz y pronta viene a contestar todos vuestros argumentos. Aquel pueblo, lleno de vida y movimiento, continúa su curso á un fin, y desde las fronteras de la Nueva Escocia, hasta las de Nuevo México, el norteamericano sólo obra sobre estos principios: *trabajo y derechos del ciudadano.* Su código es conciso, pero claro, neto, perceptible. En las cuestiones combinadas, en que no pueden decidir por no estar al alcance de las clases menos ilustradas, se refieren enteramente a aquella parte que les ha parecido haber merecido mejor su confianza, por una serie de acciones y decisiones rectas y de resultados benéficos.

Todos los que intentan hacer mejoras sociales en los pueblos que marchan al progreso, echan la vista sobre la Gran Bretaña, o sobre los Estados Unidos del Norte; tipos verdaderos y originales de organizaciones sociales, sólidas y progresivas. Pero la primera, nación grande, señora del Océano, depósito de inmensas riquezas, fecunda en hombres eminentes y profundos, aún tiene que dar muchos pasos hacia un orden más liberal, más económico, en suma más independiente de las antiguas trabas feudales; y sus *wighs y sus radicales,* después de sus triunfos de la emancipación católica, de su *bill* de reforma parlamentaria, de la organización ministerial, reclaman nuevas mejoras para ponerse en algún modo al nivel de la segunda. Aún están pendientes cuestiones de un alto interés político, resueltas en los Estados Unidos desde su nacimiento. Los diezmos, los privilegios de los grandes, la absoluta separación del culto y de las funciones administrativas, los mayorazgos y otras menos esenciales, consecuencias de aquéllas, son puntos que se agitaron por mucho tiempo en los periódicos, en las tribunas, en los clubes y en el gabinete. ¡Qué sacudimiento no tendrá que experimentar la colosal Albión antes de ver definitivamente terminadas estas materias! Sus grandes publicistas, sus ministros lo han anunciado últimamente. "Mucho se ha hecho, decía hace poco, uno de ellos a sus conciudadanos que le obsequiaban; pero aún nos resta mucho más que hacer". Palabras llenas de sentido y de grandes esperanzas.

Después de que en la lucha emprendida en los Estados Unidos del Norte, pocos años después de su emancipación, entre el partido aristocrático y democrático, éste quedó victorioso, hasta el punto de haber enteramente desaparecido aquél, lo que es otro fenómeno en la historia de los pueblos, todas las cuestiones que se han agitado en las tribunas, periódicos y juntas populares han sido puramente económicas. La Convención de Hartfort, que en 1814 intentó suscitar los antiguos principios federalistas, no encontró apoyo en ninguna parte, y desde entonces no hay un solo hombre de Estado que ose presentarse a defender el sistema de Hamilton y Adams. El poder popular en toda su plenitud, gobernando una nación rica, poderosa y de una inmensa extensión, dirigiéndola con sabiduría, con moderación, con tino, y viendo desenvolverse bajo su administración los elementos de una grande prosperidad territorial, industrial y mercantil, es quizá el argumento más poderoso que puede ponerse contra las eternas declamaciones de los absolutistas y aristócratas.

En tal estado de cosas doscientos mil europeos emigran anualmente a los Estados Unidos a buscar un asilo en su miseria, y el precio de su trabajo y sus fatigas; libres de las rebajas a que les sujetan las contribuciones en el antiguo mundo, y de las trabas que ponen sus sistemas más o menos arbitrarios, con brazos activos y robustos encuentran luego ocupación, y dentro de pocos meses propietarios de un terreno que fecundan sus sudores, forman poblaciones en lugares poco antes habitados solamente por los lobos, osos y otros animales selváticos. Ciudades populosas improvisadas, buques de vapor que remontan ríos y lagos a miles de leguas del Océano, en tierras apenas descubiertas y desconocidas al mundo civilizado; manufacturas transportadas por artesanos hábiles de la Europa, imprentas volantes que multiplican los pensamientos y las ideas, difundiendo la ilustración; misioneros de todos los cultos que de Italia, Alemania, Francia, Inglaterra y otros puntos van a predicar los dogmas del evangelio, cada uno conforme lo entiende o le profesa; y que en los principios de moral convienen enteramente. El amor de Dios y del prójimo es la base de todas las religiones. Emigrados de Irlanda, de Francia, de México, de Colombia, de España, de Italia, de uno y otro hemisferio, que en las agitaciones políticas de sus países, obligados a dejar la dulce patria, van a informarse en qué consiste la envidiable tranquilidad de aquel pueblo. Ved aquí el espectáculo que presentan los Estados Unidos del Norte. Añadid sus ciudades marítimas; esa Nueva York, tercer puerto del Universo, recibiendo en su bahía tres mil buques anuales, que vienen cargados de las producciones de las cuatro partes del mundo; esa Nueva Orleans, depósito de cien ciudades que envían a ella sus frutos por el inconmensurable Misisipí, y por cuyo conducto se proveen mil poblaciones de los artículos extranjeros. Esa Filadelfia, ciudad de paz, de hermandad y de monotonía, rodeada de casas de campo, bellas como sus hijas, fundada sobre el agradable Delaware y el delicioso Schuylkill, ocupa un lugar distinguido en la escala mercantil. Baltimore, Charleston, Boston, ciudades notables por la ilustración de sus habitantes, la actividad de su comercio, la situación ventajosa de sus puertos, la hospitalidad de sus vecinos, en suma esa franqueza, esa seguridad, esa libertad de que gozan todos los hombres, sin trabas de pasaportes, sin aparatos de soldados, sin embarazos de policía, son circunstancias que no pueden dejar de conducir a la prosperidad y al aumento progresivo de todos los ramos.

Los que acusan al pueblo americano del Norte de rudo e insociable, no reflexionan en los elementos que han entrado en la formación de aquella nación singular. Familias perseguidas que venían a buscar la libertad y la subsistencia en los helados e incultos bosques de la América septentrional, debieron entregarse a trabajos ásperos y difíciles, sufrir privaciones dolorosas, y acostumbrarse a una sobriedad de alimentos, de palabras y de comunicación, a que les condenaba la necesidad de sus tareas continuas. Ved aquí los padres de los norteamericanos. A éstos se han agregado los agricultores y artistas que han pasado posteriormente de Holanda, de Alemania e Irlanda, gentes generalmente laboriosas, económas, taciturnas, exclusivamente dedicadas a sus empresas, y pensad luego cómo han podido venir los Washington, los Jefferson, los Franklin, los Adams, los Clinton, los Madisson, los Clay, los Webster, los Livingston, los Hamilton, los Monroe, los Jackson, los Vanburen, los Dwight y otros muchos hombres de Estado, escritores célebres, sabios profundos, literatos distinguidos, economistas e ilustres generales que han elevado el país a su alto grado de prosperidad y de gloria.

El pueblo de los Estados Unidos es sagaz, económico y amante de acumular capital para lo porvenir. Así debe ser naturalmente. Porque además de su origen del que hereda estas cualidades, en un clima como aquél, en donde el hombre se ve obligado a trabajar dos cuartas partes del año para una estación severa que le reduce a su habitación y a la chimenea, no puede abandonarse al acaso, confiado en la fertilidad del terreno y en la benignidad de las estaciones. Los pueblos del mediodía de la Europa y del Asia fueron siempre los *menos laboriosos,* y en España se advierte que los gallegos, los catalanes y vascos son más agricultores que los pueblos de las Andalucías y Castillas; y tienen además un carácter más serio, menos comunicativo y flexible. Los progresos de la educación primaria, a que ponen el mayor interés los americanos, y la facilidad de sus comunicaciones, harán con el tiempo las costumbres de aquel pueblo más dulces y sociales.

Antes de terminar este libro, no debo desentenderme de las relaciones políticas que deberán progresivamente aumentarse entre los Estados Unidos del Norte y los Estados Unidos Mexicanos, y la influencia que los primeros ejercen sobre los segundos indudablemente. No hay un ejemplo más seductor para una nación que no disfruta de libertad completa, que el de una vecindad en donde se presentan en todos los actos públicos, en todos los escritos, lecciones y prácticas de una libertad indefinida, y en la que en vez de los desastrosos cataclysmos que han inundado algunos pueblos en sus revoluciones anárquicas, o en sus sangrientos sistemas despóticos, se ofrece el espectáculo de los tranquilos goces de una numerosa parte del género humano, elevada por la energía simultánea de sus inteligencias populares a un rango social eminentemente libre y feliz. ¿Podían los legisladores de la nación mexicana resistir a una seducción tan fuerte cuando tuvieron en sus manos arreglar los destinos de sus comitentes? El modelo era sublime; pero inimitable. Los que se aplican a copiar un cuadro de Rafael o Miguel Angel, aciertan a veces a imitar algunas sombras, algunos rasgos que les acercan más o menos al original. Jamás, sin embargo, se llegan a igualar aquellas sublimes concepciones. Los artistas originales no copian ni imitan a los otros; inventan, crean sobre los modelos de la Naturaleza y estudian sus secretos y misterios divinos.

Una de las plagas políticas que han causado muchos males a algunos pueblos, ha sido la falsa persuasión de sus legisladores de que tal organización o tales leyes tendrían su efecto, y serían puestas en práctica, sólo porque la mayoría de sus representantes las sancionaban. Semejante error estaba combatido por las doctrinas de todos los grandes escritores y por la experiencia de todos los siglos. Pero el ejemplo de trece repúblicas dadas a luz a fines del siglo pasado, en el Nuevo Continente, que no solamente se han mantenido sino que aumentándose progresivamente han llegado a ser veinticuatro, formando una gran federación, produjo una sensación tan grande y tan universal en los espíritus, que desde luego se consideraron destruidas las antiguas doctrinas con tal suceso. El raciocinio parecía concluyente. Colonia inglesa de que por entonces se ocupaba poco el mundo político y comercial, que con la sola denominación de colonias se suponían envilecidas, ignorantes y esclavizadas, elevadas súbitamente al rango de naciones libres; en consecuencia de una declaración bien redactada de derechos del hombre y de los pueblos, ¿por qué no haremos otro tanto, dijeron muchos escritores, políticos y filósofos del antiguo mundo, nosotros depositarios de las ciencias, maestros del género humano, dueños del comercio de las naciones, herederos de la gloria de los griegos y de los romanos, padres de esos pueblos emancipados? Los grandes acontecimientos sobrevenidos después en ambos hemisferios han probado suficientemente el impulso irresistible que dio al movimiento social la aparición de aquel astro en la esfera de las naciones.

¿Cuáles deberán pues ser las consecuencias del ejemplo constante y próximo que presentan los Estados Unidos del Norte a la nación mexicana, joven, sin experiencia, llena de vida y deseosa de sacudir los restos de sus antiguas cadenas? En el círculo estrecho de la Europa continental, existe un derecho público implícito en parte, y en parte explícito, un código tradicional, redactado por trozos y convenido en otros; convenido en algunos puntos por todos los gobiernos y en el todo por muchos de ellos; este derecho público europeo es el de la conservación de ciertos principios monárquicos, base de toda la actual política europea. Sobre este código, bosquejado por primera vez en Pilnitz hace cuarenta años, modificado varias veces según los diversos intereses de las altas partes contratantes, se modelan y toman los diferentes cambios de los gobiernos europeos. En América es otra cosa. Sin estar proscrito el principio monárquico, es evidente que la opinión tal cual puede aplicarse en las repúblicas nacientes, es casi exclusivamente democrática. Allí no hay intervenciones ni alianzas, ni maniobras diplomáticas, ni bolsas, ni elemento algunos bastante influente para determinar la forma monárquica. El único que existe en algunos puntos, es el poder eclesiástico cuya debilidad está demostrada con la experiencia de sus esfuerzos infructuosos hasta aquí.

De consiguiente la influencia de los Estados Unidos sobre México, será con el tiempo un poder de opinión, de enseñanza de magisterio, tanto más fuerte cuanto que será puramente moral; fundado sobre sus doctrinas y lecciones. Pero hay más. Diez mil ciudadanos de los Estados Unidos se establecen anualmente en el territorio de la República Mexicana, especialmente en los Estados de Chihuahua, Coahuila y Texas, Tamaulipas, Nuevo León, San Luis Potosí, Durango, Zacatecas, Sonora, Sinaloa y Territorios de Nuevo México y Californias. Estos colonos y negociantes llevan con su industria los hábitos de libertad, de economía, de trabajo; sus costumbres austeras y religiosas, su independencia individual y su republicanismo. ¿Qué cambio no deberán hacer en la existencia moral y material de los antiguos habitantes estos huéspedes emprendedores? Cartagena fue un pueblo cartaginés, Cádiz un pueblo fenicio, Marsella un pueblo griego por muchos siglos, porque sus colonos fueron de aquellas naciones. La República Mexicana vendrá pues dentro de algunos años a ser amoldada sobre un régimen cómbinado del sistema americano con las costumbres y tradiciones españolas.

Pero es necesario distinguir en la nación mexicana aquella parte poblada, disciplinada, fundada por decirlo así, en los moldes de su antigua metrópoli, de la parte desnuda de habitantes, y de consiguiente susceptible de una nueva población, diversa enteramente de la otra. En la primera existirá por muchos años todavía la lucha de principios opuestos que se han plantado en sus instituciones y será inevitable la guerra civil, mientras que en la segunda los colonos americanos, alemanes, irlandeses e ingleses forman pueblos enteramente libres, que prosperarán pacíficamente bajo la influencia de sus instituciones democráticas, y más que todo de sus hábitos al trabajo, de sus ideas y convicciones acerca de la dignidad del hombre y del respeto que se debe a las leyes. Así pues, mientras que los Estados de Puebla, Chiapas, Oaxaca, México, Querétaro, Michoacán, Guanajuato continúan entregados al brazo militar y eclesiástico en pena de sus preocupaciones, de su ignorancia y de su superstición; mientras que en el seno de estos Estados algunos patriotas generosos e ilustrados harán esfuerzos para elevar a sus conciudadanos al nivel de las instituciones adoptadas, y procurarán darles lecciones de libertad y de tolerancia; mientras estos elementos opuestos encienden el combate entre una juventud ardiente, amante del progreso y de la civilización, y un clero ignorante, apegado fuertemente a sus privilegios y rentas; sostenido por algunos generales y oficiales reliquias del antiguo ejército español, sin fe, sin honor, sin patriotismo, poseídos de una sórdida avaricia y entregados a vicios degradantes, mientras esto pasa en estos Estados, los otros se poblarán, se enriquecerán, procurando evitar ser contaminados por los desastrosos acontecimientos de sus hermanos del mediodía.

El término, sin embargo, será, el triunfo de la libertad en estos Estados; y sobre los escombros góticos y de privilegios insostenibles, se levantará una generación gloriosa e ilustrada, que poniendo en movimiento todos los elementos de riqueza de que abundan, asociará al fin esa clase indígena degradada y envilecida hasta hoy, a la familia civilizada, enseñándola a pensar y a estimar su dignidad elevando sus pensamientos. ¿Qué barrera podrá oponerse a este torrente que ha nacido hace veinticuatro años en un pequeño pueblo del Bajío, oscuro en su origen, sin dirección ni cauce, devastando cuanto encontraba, hoy un río majestuoso que recibe aguas puras y cristalinas de otros países, y que fecundará todo el territorio mexicano? Inútiles esfuerzos opondrá una generación envilecida, heredera de las tradiciones y creencias castellanas, y defensoras sin grandes resultados de sus antisociales doctrinas. El sistema americano obtendrá una victoria completa aunque sangrienta.